COMPARATIVE POLITICS 96/97

Fourteenth Edition

139701

W9-CHN-048

Editor

Christian Søe
California State University, Long Beach

Christian Søe was born in Denmark, studied in Canada and the United States, and received his doctoral degree in political science from the Free University in Berlin. He is a political science professor at California State University, Long Beach. Dr. Søe teaches a wide range of courses in comparative politics and contemporary political theory, and actively participates in professional symposiums in the United States and abroad. His research deals primarily with developments in contemporary German politics, and he has been a regular observer of party politics in that country, most recently during the campaign leading up to the 1994 election of a new Bundestag. At present Dr. Søe is observing the shifts in the balance of power within the German party system, with particular attention to its implications for the formation of new government coalitions and changes in policy directions. Three of his most recent publications are a biographical essay on Hans-Dietrich Genscher, Germany's foreign minister from 1974 to 1992, in *Political Leaders of Contemporary Western Europe;* a chapter on the Free Democratic Party in *Germany's New Politics;* and another chapter on the Danish-German relationship in *The Germans and Their Neighbors.* Dr. Søe is also coeditor of the latter two books. He has been editor of *Annual Editions: Comparative Politics* since its beginning in 1983.

Annual Editions
A Library of Information from the Public Press

Cover illustration by Mike Eagle

**Dushkin Publishing Group/
Brown & Benchmark Publishers**
Sluice Dock, Guilford, Connecticut 06437

This map has been developed to give you a graphic picture of where the countries of the world are located, the relationship they have with their region and neighbors, and their positions relative to the superpowers and power blocs. We have focused on certain areas to more clearly illustrate these crowded regions.

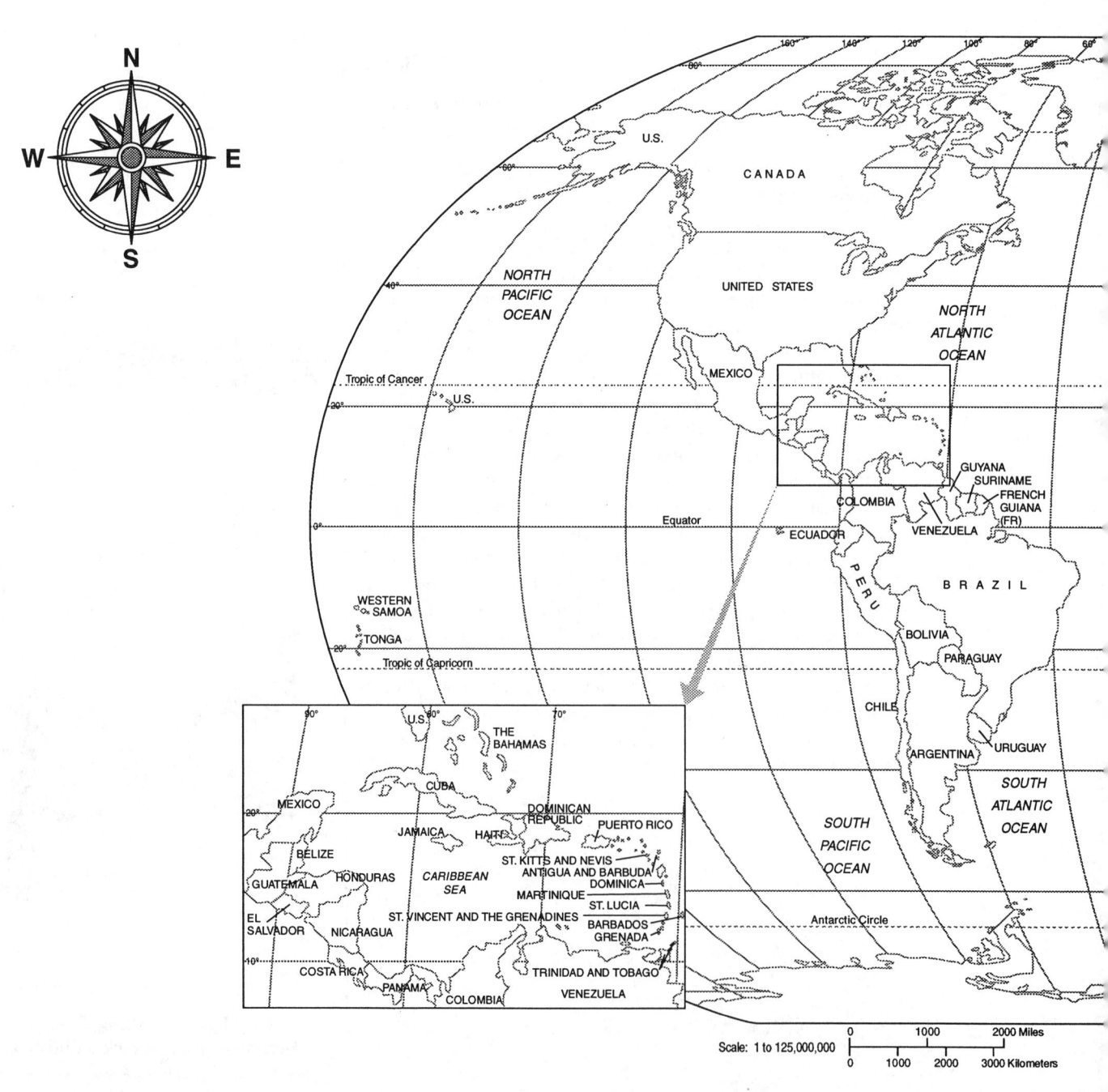

Scale: 1 to 125,000,000

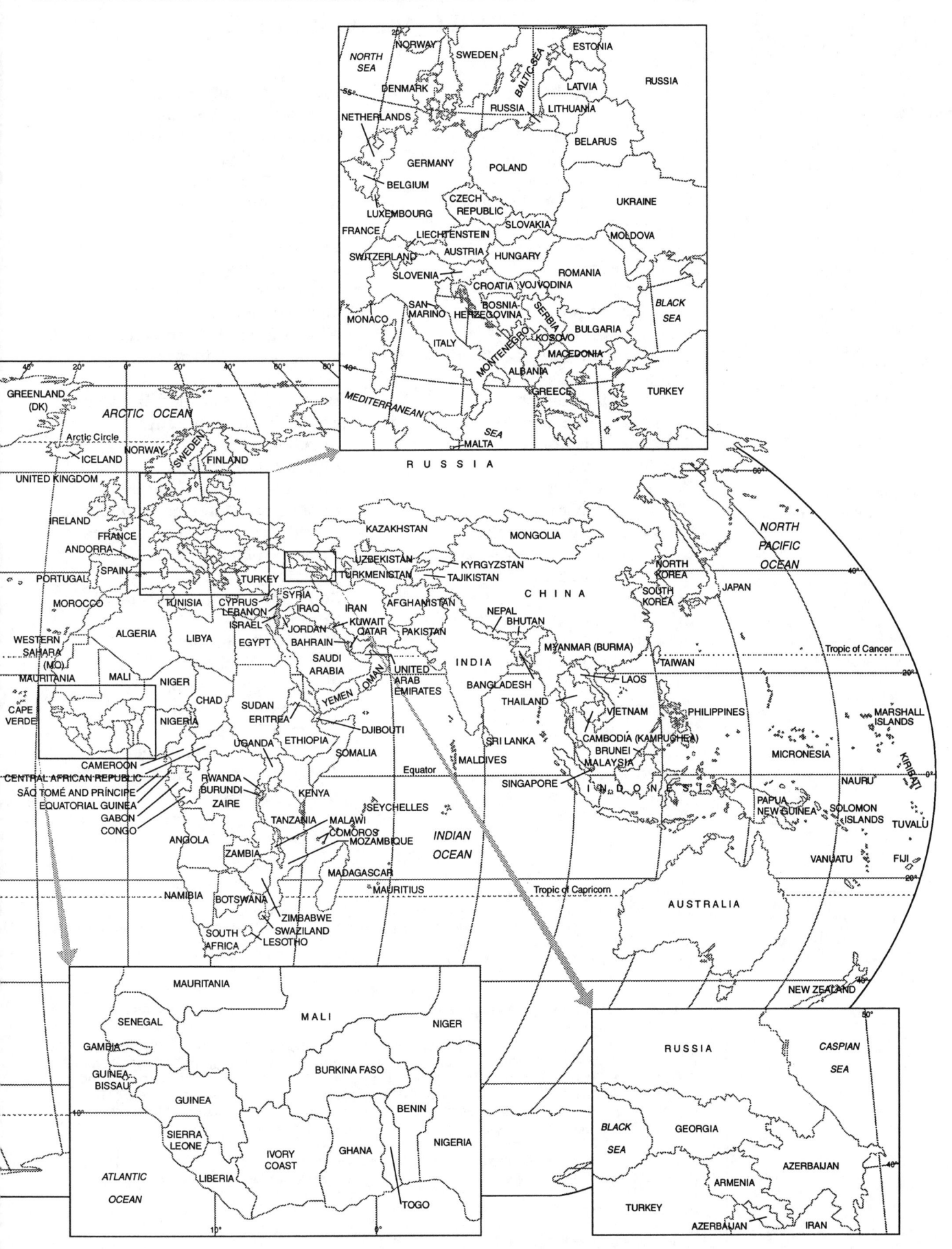

The Annual Editions Series

Annual Editions is a series of over 65 volumes designed to provide the reader with convenient, low-cost access to a wide range of current, carefully selected articles from some of the most important magazines, newspapers, and journals published today. Annual Editions are updated on an annual basis through a continuous monitoring of over 300 periodical sources. All Annual Editions have a number of features designed to make them particularly useful, including topic guides, annotated tables of contents, unit overviews, and indexes. For the teacher using Annual Editions in the classroom, an Instructor's Resource Guide with test questions is available for each volume.

VOLUMES AVAILABLE

Abnormal Psychology
Africa
Aging
American Foreign Policy
American Government
American History, Pre-Civil War
American History, Post-Civil War
American Public Policy
Anthropology
Archaeology
Biopsychology
Business Ethics
Child Growth and Development
China
Comparative Politics
Computers in Education
Computers in Society
Criminal Justice
Developing World
Deviant Behavior
Drugs, Society, and Behavior
Dying, Death, and Bereavement
Early Childhood Education
Economics
Educating Exceptional Children
Education
Educational Psychology
Environment
Geography
Global Issues
Health
Human Development
Human Resources
Human Sexuality

India and South Asia
International Business
Japan and the Pacific Rim
Latin America
Life Management
Macroeconomics
Management
Marketing
Marriage and Family
Mass Media
Microeconomics
Middle East and the Islamic World
Multicultural Education
Nutrition
Personal Growth and Behavior
Physical Anthropology
Psychology
Public Administration
Race and Ethnic Relations
Russia, the Eurasian Republics, and Central/Eastern Europe
Social Problems
Sociology
State and Local Government
Urban Society
Western Civilization, Pre-Reformation
Western Civilization, Post-Reformation
Western Europe
World History, Pre-Modern
World History, Modern
World Politics

Cataloging in Publication Data
Main entry under title: Annual Editions: Comparative Politics. 1996/97.
   1. World politics—Periodicals. 2. Politics, Practical—Periodicals. I. Søe, Christian, comp. II. Title: Comparative Politics.
ISBN 0–697–31687–4   909′.05   83–647654

Fourteenth Edition

Printed in the United States of America

Editors/ Advisory Board

EDITOR

Christian Søe
California State University
Long Beach

ADVISORY BOARD

Louis J. Cantori
University of Maryland
Baltimore

Leonard Cardenas
Southwest Texas State University

Parris Chang
Pennsylvania State University
University Park

Maureen A. Covell
Simon Fraser University

Jane Curry
Santa Clara University

Robert L. Delorme
California State University
Long Beach

John Echeverri-Gent
University of Virginia

Richard S. Flickinger
Wittenberg University

E. Gene Frankland
Ball State University

Ronald Inglehart
University of Michigan

Karl H. Kahrs
California State University
Fullerton

Aline M. Kuntz
University of New Hampshire

Frank A. Kunz
McGill University

Gregory S. Mahler
University of Mississippi

Anthony M. Messina
Tufts University

Joyce Marie Mushaben
University of Missouri
St. Louis

Helen E. Purkitt
United States Naval Academy

Martin Slann
Clemson University

Frederick R. Swan
Livingstone College

Joel D. Wolfe
University of Cincinnati

Rodger Yeager
West Virginia University

Eleanor E. Zeff
Drake University

Charles E. Ziegler
University of Louisville

Members of the Advisory Board are instrumental in the final selection of articles for each edition of Annual Editions. Their review of articles for content, level, currentness, and appropriateness provides critical direction to the editor and staff. We think you'll find their careful consideration well reflected in this volume.

STAFF

Ian A. Nielsen, Publisher
Brenda S. Filley, Production Manager
Roberta Monaco, Editor
Addie Raucci, Administrative Editor
Cheryl Greenleaf, Permissions Editor
Deanna Herrschaft, Permissions Assistant
Diane Barker, Proofreader
Lisa Holmes-Doebrick, Program Coordinator
Charles Vitelli, Designer
Shawn Callahan, Graphics
Lara M. Johnson, Graphics
Laura Levine, Graphics
Mike Campbell, Graphics
Libra A. Cusack, Typesetting Supervisor
Juliana Arbo, Typesetter
Jane Jaegersen, Typesetter
Marie Lazauskas, Word Processor

To the Reader

In publishing ANNUAL EDITIONS we recognize the enormous role played by the magazines, newspapers, and journals of the *public press* in providing current, first-rate educational information in a broad spectrum of interest areas. Within the articles, the best scientists, practitioners, researchers, and commentators draw issues into new perspective as accepted theories and viewpoints are called into account by new events, recent discoveries change old facts, and fresh debate breaks out over important controversies. Many of the articles resulting from this enormous editorial effort are appropriate for students, researchers, and professionals seeking accurate, current material to help bridge the gap between principles and theories and the real world. These articles, however, become more useful for study when those of lasting value are carefully *collected, organized, indexed,* and *reproduced* in a *low-cost format,* which provides easy and permanent access when the material is needed. That is the role played by ANNUAL EDITIONS. Under the direction of each volume's *Editor,* who is an expert in the subject area, and with the guidance of an *Advisory Board,* we seek each year to provide in each ANNUAL EDITION a current, well-balanced, carefully selected collection of the best of the public press for your study and enjoyment. We think you'll find this volume useful, and we hope you'll take a moment to let us know what you think.

This collection of readings brings together current articles that will help you understand the governments and politics of foreign countries from a comparative perspective. Such a study not only opens up a fascinating world beyond our borders; it will also lead to greater insights into the American political process.

The articles in unit one cover the United Kingdom, Germany, France, Italy, and Japan in a serial manner. Each of these modern societies has developed its own political framework and agenda, and each has sought to find its own appropriate dynamic balance of continuity and change. Nevertheless, as the readings of unit two show, it is possible to point to some common denominators and make useful cross-national comparisons among these and other representative democracies. Unit three goes one step further by discussing the impact of two major changes that are rapidly transforming the political map of Europe. One of them is the irregular, sometimes halting, but nevertheless impressive growth of the European Union (EU), which until November 1993 was called the European Community (EC). The other is the political and economic reconstruction of Central and Eastern Europe after the collapse of this region's communist regimes.

Unit four looks at developments in some of the developing countries, with articles on Mexico, sub-Saharan Africa and the Union of South Africa, China, and India. A careful reader will come away with a better understanding of the diversity of social and political conditions in these countries. Additional readings cover the newly industrialized countries of Eastern and Southern Asia—the "tigers" and "dragons" of this region's socioeconomy, which have managed to generate a self-sustaining process of industrial modernization.

Unit five considers three major trends in contemporary politics from a comparative perspective. Although the "third wave" of democratization may have already crested, it is nevertheless a still-vital force of change in the politics of many countries. The widespread shift toward a greater reliance on markets to perform the task of economic allocation, in place of centralized planning and heavy governmental regulation, is also of great significance in our study. This move is frequently toward a mixed economy, and it should not be misunderstood as being a victory of doctrinaire laissez-faire. Finally, the surge of what has been called "identity politics," with particular emphasis on exclusive cultural or ethnic group assertions, is a development that bears careful watching.

There has rarely been so interesting and important a time for the study of comparative politics as now. We can already see that the political earthquakes of 1989–1991 have altered the landscape with consequences that will be felt for many years to come. The aftershocks continue to remind us that we are unlikely to ever experience a condition of political equilibrium.

This is the fourteenth edition of *Annual Editions: Comparative Politics*. It is a sobering reminder that the first edition appeared just as the Brezhnev era had come to a close in what was then the Soviet Union. Over the years, each new edition has tried to reflect the developments that eventually brought about the post–cold war world of today. In a similar way, this present edition tries to present information and analyses that will be useful in understanding today's political world and its role in setting the parameters for tomorrow's developments.

A special word of thanks goes to my own past and present students at Long Beach State University. Susan B. Mason, Deborah Lancaster, Linda Wohlman, Jon Nakagawa, Mike Petri, Rich Sherman, and Ali Taghavi. They are all wonderfully inquisitive and help keep me posted on the concerns and needs that this anthology must try to address. It is a great joy to work with all these present and former students, whose enthusiasm for the project is contagious.

I am very grateful to members of the advisory board and the Dushkin Publishing Group/Brown and Benchmark Publishers as well as to the many readers who have made useful comments on past selections and have suggested new ones. I ask you all to help me improve future editions by keeping me informed of your reactions and suggestions for change: Please remember to complete and return the postage-paid article rating form in the back of this book.

Christian Søe
Editor

Unit
1

Pluralist Democracies: Country Studies

Twenty-two selections examine the current state of politics in Western Europe, the United Kingdom, Germany, France, Italy, and Japan.

The concepts in bold italics are developed in the article. For further expansion please refer to the Topic Guide and the Index.

Unit 2

Modern Pluralist Democracies: Factors in the Political Process

Thirteen selections examine the functioning of Western European democracies with regard to political ideas and participation, ethnic politics, the role of women in politics, and the institutional framework of representative government.

The concepts in bold italics are developed in the article. For further expansion please refer to the Topic Guide and the Index.

Unit

3

Europe—West, Center, and East: The Politics of Integration, Transformation, and Disintegration

Fourteen selections examine the European continent: the European Union, Western European society, post-communist Central and Eastern Europe, and Russia and the other post-Soviet Republics.

Unit 4

Political Diversity in the Developing World

Eleven selections review the developing world's economic and political development in Latin America, Africa, China, India, and newly industrialized countries.

Unit 5

Comparative Politics: Some Major Trends, Issues, and Prospects

Nine selections discuss the rise of democracy, how capitalism impacts on political development, and the political assertion of group identity in contemporary politics.

The concepts in bold italics are developed in the article. For further expansion please refer to the Topic Guide and the Index.

Topic Guide

This topic guide suggests how the selections in this book relate to topics of traditional concern to students and professionals involved with the study of comparative politics. It is useful for locating articles that relate to each other for reading and research. The guide is arranged alphabetically according to topic. Articles may, of course, treat topics that do not appear in the topic guide. In turn, entries in the topic guide do not necessarily constitute a comprehensive listing of all the contents of each selection.

TOPIC AREA	TREATED IN	TOPIC AREA	TREATED IN
Africa's Politics	54. Africa: Falling off the Map? 55. Why Is Africa Eating Asia's Dust? 56. Post-Mandela South Africa	Elections and Parties	1. Next Prime Minister 3. British Third Party Bids 7. Outstripping Adenauer 8. New Leader for the Social Democrats 12. Fifth President of the Fifth Republic 17. Italy's Dirty Linen 18. Unhappy italy 21. Japan's New Prime Minister 24. Guide to the West European Left 25. Europe's Far Right 28. Women, Power, and Politics 31. What Democracy Is . . . and Is Not 33. Campaign and Party Finance 34. Electoral Reform 43. Ex-Coms 47. Splintering of Russia's Reformers 48. Post-Soviet Politics 52. Common Sense over Charisma 53. Mexico: The Long Haul 62. Dangers and Dilemmas of Democracy 63. Democracy and Growth
Britain's Government and Politics	1. Next Prime Minister 2. Newts Across the Pond 3. British Third Party Bids 4. Revamping Britain's Constitution 5. What Is Scotland's Future 6. After the Talking Stopped 23. Left's New Start 24. Guide to the West European Left 32. Parliament and Congress 33. Campaign and Party Finance 34. Electoral Reform 35. Presidents and Prime Ministers 36. Citizens Immune to Euro-Fever 38. Challenge to EMU 40. Diagnosis: Healthier in Europe 41. Europe and the Underclass 42. Inequalities in Europe		
Central and Eastern Europe	26. Migration Challenge 27. Europeans Redefine What Makes a Citizen 43. Ex-Coms 44. Return of the Habsburgs *and* Rich Man, Poor Man 61. New Era in Democracy 62. Dangers and Dilemmas of Democracy 64. Capitalism and Democracy 65. Preserving Prosperity 67. Communal Conflicts and Global Security 68. Debate on Cultural Conflicts	Ethnicity and Politics	5. What Is Scotland's Future? 6. After the Talking Stopped 10. Eastern Germany: The Eagle's Embrace 25. Europe's Far Right 26. Migration Challenge 27. Europeans Redefine What Makes a Citizen 36. Citizens Immune to Euro-Fever 42. Inequalities in Europe 44. Return of the Habsburgs 48. Post-Soviet Politics 54. Africa: Falling off the Map? 56. Post-Mandela South Africa 67. Communal Conflicts and Global Security 68. Debate on Cultural Conflicts 69. Jihad vs. McWorld
China's Government and Politics	57. China—The End of an Era 61. New Era in Democracy 63. Democracy and Growth 64. Capitalism and Democracy		
Conservatives and Conservative Parties	1. Next Prime Minister 2. Newts Across the Pond 7. Outstripping Adenauer 12. Fifth President of the Fifth Republic 17. Italy's Dirty Linen 21. Japan's New Prime Minister 34. Electoral Reform	European Union	1. Next Prime Minister 2. Newts Across the Atlantic 4. Revamping Britain's Constitution 7. Outstripping Adenauer 8. New Leader for the Social Democrats 11. Germany's Reckoning 13. Will the Real France Stand Up? 14. Political Strikes and Demonstrations 26. Migration Challenge 27. Europeans Redefine What Makes a Citizen 36. Citizens Immune to Euro-Fever 37. Europe's Parliament on the Move 38. Challenge to EMU 40. Diagnosis: Healthier in Europe 41. Europe and the Underclass 42. Inequalities in Europe
Developing Countries	50. Let's Abolish the Third World 51. 'Third World' Is Dead, but Spirits Linger 52. Common Sense over Charisma 53. Mexico: The Long Haul 54. Africa: Falling off the Map? 55. Why Is Africa Eating Asia's Dust? 56. Post-Mandela South Africa 57. China—the End of an Era 58. India's Juggernaut of Change 59. Miracles beyond the Free Market 60. Confucius Says: Go East, Young Man 61. New Era in Democracy 67. Communal Conflicts and Global Security 68. Debate on Cultural Conflicts 69. Jihad vs. McWorld	Federal and Unitary Systems	4. Revamping Britain's Constitution 5. What Is Scotland's Future? 6. After the Talking Stopped 10. Eastern Germany: The Eagle's Embrace 16. Tocqueville in Italy 18. Unhappy Italy 36. Citizens Immune to Euro-Fever 44. Return of the Habsburgs *and* Rich Man, Poor Man 46. Reform of Russia 56. Post-Mandela South Africa 66. Cyberspace 69. Jihad vs. McWorld

Pluralist Democracies: Country Studies

- **The United Kingdom (Articles 1–6)**
- **Germany (Articles 7–11)**
- **France (Articles 12–15)**
- **Italy (Articles 16–19)**
- **Japan (Articles 20–22)**

The United Kingdom, Germany, France, and Italy rank among the most prominent industrialized societies in Western Europe. Although their modern political histories vary considerably, they have all developed into pluralist democracies with diversified and active citizenries, well organized and competitive party systems and interest groups, and representative forms of governments. Japan appears to be less pluralist as a society, but it occupies a similar position of primacy among the few representative democracies in Asia.

The articles in the first unit cover the political systems of the United Kingdom, Germany, France, Italy, and Japan. Each of these modern societies has developed its own set of governmental institutions, defined its own political agenda, and found its own dynamic balance of continuity and change. Nevertheless, as later readings will show more fully, it is possible to find some common denominators and make useful cross-national comparisons among these and other representative democracies. Moreover, the Western European countries all show the impact of three major developments that are transforming the political map of the continent: (1) the growth of the European Union, or EU, as the European Community (EC) has been officially known since November 1993; (2) the rise of new or intensified challenges to the established political order after the end of the cold war, often reflected in a weakening of the traditional party system; and (3) the spillover effects from the reconstruction efforts in the countries of Central and Eastern Europe after their recent exit from communist rule.

The continuing political importance of Europe has been underscored by these developments. The integration of the European Community, which led to the European Union, has been a process spanning several decades. However, it accelerated markedly in the last half of the 1980s as a result of the passage and procedural implementation of the Single European Act, which set as a goal the completion of a free market among the 12 EC-member countries by the end of 1992. Then the Maastricht Treaty, which was signed in 1991 and ratified in 1993, outlined a further advance toward supranational integration by setting up the goal of achieving a common European monetary system and foreign policy toward the end of the decade.

By contrast, there was little advance notice or planning connected with the upheaval that ended many decades of communist rule in Central and Eastern Europe between 1989 and 1991. In the center of the continent, the reunification of Germany in 1990 epitomizes the tremendous upheaval that swept away much of the political order created by the cold war. Each of the former communist-ruled countries has embarked on a cumbersome path of reconstruction that involves the transition from a party-and-police state with a centrally planned economy to a pluralist democracy with a market-oriented economy. By now it is clear that this process will take longer, involve more setbacks, and produce more painful dislocations than anyone had imagined a few years ago.

The **United Kingdom** provides our first focus on comparative politics, with articles on Great Britain, Scotland, and Ire-land. *Great Britain* has long been regarded as a model of parliamentary government and majoritarian party politics. In the 1960s and 1970s, however, the country became better known for its chronic governing problems. Sociopolitical observers spoke about the spread of a British sickness—"Englanditis"—a condition characterized by such problems as economic stagnation, social malaise, political polarization, and a general incapacity of the elected government to deal effectively with such a situation of relative deterioration.

As if to defy such pessimistic analyses, if only temporarily, Britain by the mid-1980s began to pull far ahead of other Western European countries in its annual economic growth. This apparent economic turnabout could be linked in part to the policies of Prime Minister Margaret Thatcher, who had come to power in May 1979 and introduced a drastic change in economic and social direction for her country. She portrayed herself as a conviction politician, determined to introduce a strong dose of economic discipline by encouraging private enterprise and reducing the role of government, in marked contrast to what she dismissed as the consensus politics of her Labour and Conservative predecessors. Her radical rhetoric and somewhat less drastic policy changes spawned yet another debate about what came to be called the Thatcher Revolution and its social and political consequences.

For the mass electorate, however, nothing seems to have been so upsetting as the introduction of the community charge, a tax on each adult resident that would replace the local property tax as a means of financing local public services. Although this so-called poll tax was very unpopular, Thatcher resisted all pressure to abandon the project before its full national implementation in early 1990.

The politically disastrous result was that, as a revenue measure, the poll tax was anything but neutral in its impact. It created an unexpectedly large proportion of immediate losers, that is, people who had to pay considerably more in local taxes than previously, while the immediate winners were people who had previously paid high property taxes. Not surprisingly, the national and local governments disagreed about who was responsible for the high poll tax bills, but the voters seemed to have little difficulty in assigning blame to Margaret Thatcher and the Conservative Party as originators of this unpopular reform. Many voters were up in arms, and some observers correctly anticipated that a tax rebellion would undermine Thatcher's position in her own party and become her political Waterloo.

John Major, who was chosen by his fellow Conservative members of Parliament to be Thatcher's successor as prime minister and leader of the Conservative Party, had long been regarded as one of her closest cabinet supporters. He was thought to support her tough economic strategy, which she often described as "dry," but to prefer a more compassionate, or "wet," social policy without indulging in the Tory tradition of welfare paternalism, against which Margaret Thatcher had also railed. Not surprisingly, he abandoned the hated poll tax. His undramatic governing style was far less confrontational than that of his predecessor, and some nostalgic critics were quick to call him dull. In the Persian Gulf War of 1991, Major continued Thatcher's policy of giving strong British support for firm and ultimately military measures against the government of Iraq, which had invaded and occupied oil-rich Kuwait. Unlike his predecessor after the Falkland Battle almost a decade earlier, however, he did not follow up on this quick and popular military victory by calling for general elections.

By the time of Thatcher's resignation, Labour appeared to be in a relatively good position to capitalize on the growing disenchantment with the Conservative government. The big political question had become whether or not Prime Minister Major could recapture some lost ground. Under its leader, Neil Kinnock, Labour had begun to move back toward its traditional center-Left position, presenting itself as a politically moderate and socially caring reform party. Labour had a leading position in some opinion polls, and it won some impressive victories in by-elections to the House of Commons. In the shadow of the Persian Gulf War, Labour was overtaken by the Conservatives in the polls, but its position improved again a few months later.

As the main opposition party, however, Labour was now troubled by a new version of the Social Democratic and Liberal alternatives that had fragmented the non-Conservative camp in the elections of 1983 and 1987. The two smaller parties, which had operated as an electoral coalition, or "Alliance," in those years, had drawn the conclusion that their organizational separation was a hindrance to the political breakthrough they hoped for. After the defeat of 1987, they joined together as the Social and Liberal Democrats (SLD) but soon became known simply as Liberal Democrats. Under the leadership of Paddy Ashdown, they have attempted to overcome the electoral system's bias against third parties by promoting themselves as a reasonable centrist alternative to the Conservatives on the Right and the Labour Party on the Left. Their strategic goal was to win the balance of power in a tightly fought election and then, as parliamentary majority makers, enter a government coalition with one of the two big parties. One of their main demands would then be that the existing winner-takes-all electoral system, based on single-member districts, be replaced by some form of proportional representation (PR) in multimember districts. Such a system, which is used widely in Western Europe, would almost surely guarantee the Liberal Democrats not only a relatively solid base in the House of Commons but also a pivotal role in a future process of coalition politics in Britain. Given their considerable electoral support, the Liberal Democrats would then enjoy a position comparable to or even better than that of their counterparts in Germany, the Free Democrats (FDP), which has been a junior member of governments in Bonn for decades.

The rise of this centrist "third force" in British electoral politics during the 1980s had been made possible by a temporary leftward trend of Labour and the rightward movement of the Conservatives a few years earlier. The challenge from the middle had the predictable result: The two main parties eventually sought to recenter themselves, as became evident in the general election called by Prime Minister Major for April 9, 1992. The timing seemed highly unattractive for the Conservatives as governing party, for Britain was still suffering from its worst recession in years. Normally, a British government chooses not to stay in office for a full five-year term. Instead it prefers to dissolve the House of Commons at an earlier and politically more convenient time. It will procrastinate, however, when the electoral outlook appears to be dismal. By the spring of 1992, there was hardly any time left for further delay, since an election had to come before the end of June, according to Britain's five-year limit ruling. At the time, many observers expected either a slim Labour victory or, more likely, a "hung" Parliament, in which no party would end up with a working majority. The latter result would have led either to a minority government, which could be expected to solve the impasse by calling an early new election, or a coalition government including the Liberal Democrats as the majority-making junior partner.

The outcome of the 1992 general election confounded all those who had expected a change in government by giving the Conservatives an unprecedented fourth consecutive term of office. Despite the recession, they garnered the same overall percentage of the vote (about 43 percent) as in 1987, while Labour increased its total share only slightly, from 32 to 35 percent. The Liberal Democrats received only 18 percent, about 6 percent less than the share that the Alliance had won in its two unsuccessful attempts to break the mold of the party system in 1983 and 1987. In the House of Commons, the electoral system's bias in favor of the front-runners showed up once again. The Conservatives lost 36 seats but ended up with 336 of the 651 members—a small but sufficient working majority, that is, unless a major issue should fragment the party. Labour increased its number of seats from 229 to 271—a net gain of 42 but far short of an opportunity to threaten the majority party. The Liberal Democrats ended up with 20 seats, down from 22. A few seats went to representatives of the small regional parties from Northern Ireland, Scotland, and Wales.

Since the 1992 election, John Major has run into considerable difficulties with a wing of his own party that follows Thatcher in opposing his European policy. It was only by threatening to dissolve Parliament and call a new election that Major brought the dissidents into line during a crucial vote on the Maastricht Treaty in the summer of 1993.

The Labour Party, with its newest leader, Tony Blair, has made some tremendous advances in the regular opinion polls. The opposition party would probably win a general election today, but it is hampered by its own factional disputes. The major ideological and strategic cleavage runs between traditional socialists and more pragmatic modernizers, who wish to continue the centrist reform policies of Tony Blair. But the issue of Europe would also trouble the Labour Party if it were to take over the government. Only the Liberal Democrats seem to be united in their commitment to a more fully integrated Europe.

One of the most interesting issues in contemporary British politics is the demand for constitutional change. In the late 1980s, an ad hoc reform coalition launched Charter 88, which called for a written constitution with a bill of rights, proportional representation, and a redefinition and codification of other basic "rules of the game" in British politics. The chartists chose the tricentennial of Britain's Glorious Revolution of 1688 to launch their effort, which has kindled a broad discussion of citizenship rights in the country.

One of the recurrent reform suggestions is to set up a special regional assembly for Scotland within the United Kingdom. This is an issue for which the Conservatives have shown much less concern than Labour or the Liberal Democrats. The failure of the Scottish Nationalist Party to make a major electoral breakthrough in 1992 has reinforced the present government's conviction that there is far less support for "devolution" or outright separation in Scotland than is often claimed. The regional problems associated with Northern Ireland are far more divisive, but they now appear headed for a resolution acceptable to all sides.

Germany was united in 1990, when the eastern German Democratic Republic (GDR) was merged into the western Federal Republic of Germany. The two German states had been established in 1949, four years after the total defeat of the German Reich in the Second World War. During the next 40 years, their rival elites subscribed to the conflicting ideologies and interests of East and West in the cold war. East Germany comprised the territory of the former Soviet Occupation Zone of Germany, where the communists exercised a power monopoly and established an economy based on central planning. In contrast, West Germany, which emerged from the former American, British, and French zones of postwar occupation, developed a pluralist democracy and a flourishing market economy. When the two states were getting ready to celebrate their fortieth anniversaries in 1989, no leading politician was on record as having foreseen that the German division would come to an end the following year.

Mass demonstrations in several East German cities and the westward flight of thousands of its citizens forced the GDR government to make an increasing number of concessions in late 1989 and early 1990. The Berlin Wall ceased to be a hermetical seal after November 9, 1989, when East Germans began to stream over it into West Berlin. Collectors and entrepreneurs were breaking pieces from the Wall to keep or sell as souvenirs before public workers could even begin to set about removing the rest of this symbol of the cold war and Germany's division. Under new leadership, the ruling communists of East Germany introduced a form of power sharing with noncommunist groups and parties. It was agreed to seek democratic legitimation through a free election in March 1990, which, it was hoped, would reduce the westward flight of thousands of East Germans and its devastating effect on the economy.

Although the East German communists initially conceded only to abandon their claim to an exclusive control of power and positions, by the time of the March 1990 election, it was clear even to them that the pressure for national unification could not be stemmed. The issue was no longer whether the two German states would be joined together, but *how* and *when*. These questions were settled when an alliance of Christian Democrats, largely identified with and supported by Chancellor Helmut Kohl's party in West Germany, won a surprisingly decisive victory, with 48 percent of the vote throughout East Germany. It advocated a short, quick route to unification, beginning with an early monetary union in the summer and a political union by the fall of 1990. This also meant that the new noncommunist government in East Germany, headed by Lothar de Maizière (CDU) followed a shortcut route to merger with the Federal Republic under Article 23 of the West German Basic Law. The Social Democrats won only 22 percent of the East German vote in March 1990. That amounted to a defeat for its alternative strategy for unification, which would have involved the protracted negotiation of a new German constitution, as envisaged by Article 146 of the Basic Law.

During the summer and fall of 1990, the governments of the two German states and the four former occupying powers completed their so-called two-plus-four negotiations and obtained mutual agreement on the German unification process. A monetary union in July was followed by a political merger in October 1990. In advance of unification, Bonn was able to negotiate an agreement with Moscow in which the latter accepted the gradual withdrawal of Soviet troops from East Germany and gave the nod for membership of the larger, united Germany in NATO, in return for considerable German economic support for the Soviet Union. The result was a major shift in both the domestic and international balance of power.

The election results of 1990 suggested that national unification could eventually modify the German party system significantly. By the time of the next national election, in October 1994, it became evident that a new east-west divide had emerged in German politics. This time, the far-Left PDS was able to nearly double its support and attract 20 percent of the vote in the east, where only one-fifth of Germany's total population lives. At the same time, the PDS won slightly less than 1 percent of the vote in the more populous west and thus fell below the famous "5 percent hurdle." The PDS was nevertheless able to gain parliamentary entry because it met an almost forgotten alternative requirement of winning at least three single-member districts. Thus the political descendants of the former ruling communists are now represented in the Bundestag by 30 deputies, who prefer to present themselves as democratically sensitive far-Left socialists.

Despite a widespread unification malaise in Germany, Kohl's conservative-liberal government won reelection in 1994. His Christian Democrats, benefiting from a widely discussed and perceived improvement in the German economy after the spring, garnered 41.5 percent of the vote; his Free Democratic ally barely scraped through with 6.9 percent. Together the two parties had a very slim majority of 10 seats more than the combined total of the three opposition parties—the SPD (36.4

percent), the Greens (7.3 percent), and the PDS (4.4 percent). In the upper house, or Bundesrat, the SPD had a huge majority of the seats, based on their control of many state governments.

France must also cope with major political challenges within a rapidly changing Europe. The bicentennial of the French Revolution was duly celebrated in 1989. It served as an occasion for public ceremonies and a revival of historical-political debates about the costs and benefits of that great exercise in the radical transformation of a society. Ironically, however, by this time there was mounting evidence that the sharp ideological cleavages that marked French politics for so much of the past two centuries were losing significance. Instead there was emerging a more pragmatic, pluralist form of accommodation in French public life.

This deradicalization and depolarization of political discourse are by no means complete in France. If the communists have become weakened and ideologically confused, Jean-Marie Le Pen's National Front on the extreme Right can arouse populist support with its xenophobic rhetoric directed primarily against the country's many residents of Arab origin. The apparent electoral appeal of such invectiveness has led some leaders of the establishment parties of the more moderate Right to voice carefully formulated reservations about the presence of so many immigrants. An entirely new and different political phenomenon for France is the appearance of two small Green parties, one more conservative and the other more socialist in orientation.

As widely expected, the Socialists suffered a major setback in these parliamentary elections of 1993. After the second round of voting, held a week after the first, it was clear that the conservative alliance of the center-Right Giscardists (the Union pour la Démocratie Française, or UDF) and the neo-Gaullists (the Rassemblement pour la République, or RPR) had garnered about 40 percent of the popular vote. However, that gave them an overwhelming majority of nearly 80 percent of the seats in the 577-seat National Assembly.

The Socialists and their close allies were among the losers in this largest electoral landslide in French democratic history. Receiving less than 20 percent of the popular vote, or about one-half as much as five years earlier, they plummeted from their previous share of 282 seats in 1988 to only 70 seats. The communists, with about half as many votes, were able to win 23 seats because much of their electoral support is concentrated in a few urban districts. With a similar share of the vote, the ultra-Right National Front won no seats at all. The environmental alliance was doubly disappointed, winning a smaller share of the vote than expected and capturing no seats either.

François Mitterrand's seven-year presidential term lasted until May 1995. After the parliamentary rout of the Socialists in March 1993, he had been faced with the question of whether to resign early from the presidency or, as under similar political circumstances in 1986, to begin another period of "cohabitation" with a conservative prime minister. Mitterrand opted for the latter solution, but he made sure to appoint a moderate Gaullist, Édouard Balladur, as the new prime minister. Balladur in turn appointed a new, compact government that included members from all main factions of the conservative alliance. For a time, Balladur enjoyed considerable popularity, and he decided to enter the presidential race in 1995 instead of leaving Jacques Chirac, a former prime minister, to be the only Gaullist candidate. The presidential race in France tends to become highly individualized, and eventually the tough and outspoken Chirac pulled ahead of his more consensual and lackluster party colleague. In the first round of the presidential election, however, a plurality of the vote went to the main socialist candidate, Lionel Jospin, a former education minister and party leader. In the runoff election, two weeks later, Chirac defeated Jospin and thus ended

14 years of socialist control of the presidency. He appointed another Gaullist, Alain Juppé, prime minister.

The articles in this section include evaluations of Jacques Chirac's political leadership as well as other articles that give a perspective on what some observers insist on calling "the new France." In fact, contemporary French politics and society combine traits that reflect continuity with the past with others that suggest considerable innovation. In the last months of 1995, for example, French politics suddenly took on a dramatic form and immediacy when workers and students resorted to massive strikes and street demonstrations against a new austerity program introduced by the conservative government. The proposed cutbacks in social entitlements such as pension rights appeared to be sudden and drastic. They were difficult to explain to the public at large, and many observers saw the political confrontation in France as a major test for the welfare state and its concurrent social market economy, which are now being squeezed in the name of international competitiveness throughout Western Europe.

The loss of great ideological alternatives may help account for the mood of political malaise that many observers claim to discover in contemporary France. But the French search for political direction and identity in a changing Europe has another major origin as well. The sudden emergence of a larger and potentially more powerful Germany next door cannot but have a disquieting effect upon France, even though opinion polls in 1990 showed a strong support for the right of the Germans to choose national unification. French elites now face the troubling question of redefining their country's role in a post–cold war world, in which the Soviet Union has lost its power and influence while Germany has gained in both.

Italy is roughly comparable to France and Great Britain in population and economic output, but it has a different political tradition that includes a long period of fascist rule and a far more persistent element of north-south regionalism. The country became a republic after World War II and, using a system of proportional representation, developed a multiparty system in which the center-Right Christian Democrats played a primary role as the major coalition party. The Communists, as second major party, were persistently excluded from government at the national level. They played a considerable role in local politics, however, and embarked relatively early on a nonrevolutionary path of seeking social reforms in a pluralist society. Under their recently adopted new name, the Democratic Party of the Left (PDS), the former Communists essentially adopted social democratic reform positions. In 1993 and 1994, they experienced a political revival that was fueled as Italian voters abruptly turned away from the Christian Democrats and other corrupt establishment parties.

In late March 1994, Italy finally held what was at the time regarded as the most important parliamentary elections in over four decades. Once again Italian voters demonstrated their disgust with the old government parties, but the end result provided at least as much confusion as previous contests. Using a new electoral system in which three-quarters of the members of parliament are elected on a winner-takes-all basis and the rest by proportional representation, they decimated the centrist alliance, which included the former Christian Democrats. On the Left, an alliance led by the PDS won 213 of the 630 seats in the Chamber of Deputies, compared to the 46 seats for the main centrist group. But it was the Freedom Alliance of the Right that triumphed by winning 366 seats. It consisted of an incongruous coalition of three main groups, of which the strongest was the *Forza Italia* (Go Italy) movement, led by the media magnate Silvio Berlusconi. The others were the fascist-descended National Alliance (formerly MSI), led by Gianfranco Fini, and the federalist Northern League, led by Umberto Bossi. Berlusconi, who had campaigned against both corruption (the centrists)

and communism (the PDS), had catapulted himself and his party to the front by a skillful use of the electronic media. He faced the difficult task of creating a government based on a fractious coalition in which the leader of the regionalist Northern League showed contempt for the centralist ideology of the neofascists. Berlusconi's government lost its parliamentary majority when Bossi's Northern League finally pulled out of the coalition. A new caretaker government of technocrats headed by the banker Lamberto Dini took over the reins in January 1995. Dini surprised observers by managing to generate sufficient parliamentary toleration to hold on for a full year. In April 1996, however, Italy went to the polls in an attempt to find a stable parliamentary base for a new government. The prospects were clouded, not least because the country would again use the hybrid electoral system that had resulted in such confusion two years earlier.

Japan, the fifth country in this study of representative governments of industrial societies, has long fascinated students of comparative politics and society. After World War II, a representative democracy was installed in Japan under American supervision. This political system soon acquired indigenous Japanese characteristics that set it off from the other major democracies examined here.

For almost four decades, the Japanese parliamentary system was dominated by the Liberal Democratic Party, which, as the saying goes, is "neither liberal, nor democratic, nor a party." It is essentially a conservative political force comprising several delicately balanced factions. These are often personal followerships identified and beaded by political bosses who stake out factional claims to benefits of office. At periodic intervals, the LDP's parliamentary hegemony has been threatened, but it was always able to recover and retain power until 1993. In that year, it lost several important politicians who objected to the LDP's reluctance to introduce political reforms. As a result of these defections, the government lost its parliamentary majority. A vote of no-confidence was followed by early elections in July 1993 in which the LDP failed to recover its parliamentary majority for the first time in almost four decades. By December 1995, the LDP had recaptured the prime ministership as the result of winning a parliamentary majority for its candidate, Ryutaro Hashimoto. He became the country's eighth prime minister in seven years and appointed a cabinet that seemed to be dominated by the old guard of Liberal Democrats. Observers differed about the significance of this political change in Japan.

Looking Ahead: Challenge Questions

How has Tony Blair taken major steps to reform the image and program of his Labour Party? Why are the main issues that seem to divide the Conservatives in the House of Commons?

How has Chancellor Helmut Kohl managed to stay in power so long? What are some of the political problems facing the Social Democrats?

What are the signs that French politics have become more centrist or middle-of-the-road for the main political parties?

Explain the recent shake-up in the Italian party system. Compare the outcomes of the 1994 and the 1996 parliamentary elections.

Explain the political outcome and significance of the 1993 parliamentary elections in Japan.

THE NEXT PRIME MINISTER

Tony Blair, Britain's youngest-ever Labour leader, has managed to renew the Party in an unprecedented manner, but can he do the same to the nation?

SIDNEY BLUMENTHAL

ON April 9, 1992, when the Labour Party lost its fourth successive election to the Conservatives, people began to speak of Britain as a permanent one-party nation. Before the election, it seemed inconceivable that the Conservatives could win. After the election, it seemed inconceivable that they could ever lose. There was no opposition that could beat them. The Labour Party had struggled for ten years to alter its image—from that of a reckless, union-run party of nationalizing socialists to that of a modern, forward-looking party able to govern. But the voters remained wary. Although the polls had shown Neil Kinnock and his party ahead of John Major until Election Day, people finally fell back upon what they had come to regard as the natural ruling party.

Replacing the Labour leader after a traumatic defeat had become an anthropological ceremony akin to killing the king: the Party would symbolically cut off its head and get a new one. Neil Kinnock, the Welsh "windbag," ardent, emotional, and given to poetic flights of rhetoric, was succeeded by John Smith, who was Kinnock's opposite in manner. Smith wasn't charismatic, daring, or new, and all those negatives recommended him: he made Labour seem safe. A stolid Scotsman who was a barrister by trade, he was respected on all sides for his civility, integrity, and steadiness. Over the next two years, Smith fostered enough of a sense of security to put Labour twenty points ahead in the polls. Then, on May 12, 1994, the fifty-five-year-old Smith died from a heart attack. For the next week, poli-

tics stood still. Even Conservative politicians wept in public.

Tony Blair, then the forty-one-year-old shadow Home Secretary, had admired Smith. One of Blair's first political acts had been to write a policy paper for Smith when Smith was a minister in the last Labour Government, in the seventies. Later, the two men travelled together to Party meetings. Now, in a period of national mourning, Blair saw the greatest opportunity of his political career. Under Smith's benign tutelage, Blair, the Party's most fervent modernizer, had been frustrated by the slow pace of change, fearing that it would once again produce defeat. Within hours of learning of Smith's death, Blair decided to make a bid for the Labour leadership, and immediately organized his campaign with an efficiency undeterred by grief. "The moment that John died, everyone was distraught by his death," Philip Gould, Labour's chief strategic consultant, recalls. "At the same time, everyone realized that the moment was now. Out of that great sadness came this new figure, an entirely new Labour leader. Either event would have been powerful. Both events occurring together were really powerful. They reframed attitudes toward Labour."

Since Margaret Thatcher became Prime Minister, in May of 1979, the Conservative Party's victories can be attributed partly to its formidable strength in the art of political war. The Conservatives were the first in Britain to run a political campaign in the American style, using slick, negative advertising created by the firm of Saatchi & Saatchi. (The image of Labour's inepti-

tude was crystallized in a stark Saatchi-designed 1979 poster depicting an unemployment line with the slogan "Labour Isn't Working.") In 1992, the Conservatives discovered that the formula still worked; they seemed endlessly able to exploit the image of Labour as a decrepit captive of narrow-minded trade unions, as a party incapable of governing. Campaigns became repetitive affairs.

When Blair won the leadership contest, in July of 1994, the Tory marketing machine instantly began whirring again, ready to stamp a denigrative image upon its new victim. "Bambi" was the label it gave him, signifying that he was a wide-eyed innocent, wobbly on his legs. The tag also reflected the Conservatives' complacent belief that Labour leaders aren't really about the getting of power: Blair was a fawn sent to the slaughter. In the months that followed, the Tories introduced "Islington Man." Blair favors un-Labourlike pin-striped suits and has a large Victorian house in Islington, a gentrified borough of North London. The new tag was intended to classify him as nothing but an ambitious yuppie.

Neither label stuck, so a year later the Tories tried again, with "Stalin," which, not surprisingly, also failed to catch on with the public. In "Bambi," the Tories had misread the near-constant smile spread across Blair's face, mistaking geniality for softness. In "Stalin," they misread his single-mindedness as that of an old-style party boss. But Blair's unique quality, and the underlying reason he has aroused anxiety in a proportion almost equal to his popularity, is that he rejects all the accepted distinctions of class. In a country where an accent is as important as lineage, Blair's impeccable Oxford diction lacks both the cadences of the industrial north and the haughtier tones of the Home Counties. It's the accent of a well-spoken professional who projects confidence and charm. The Tories have always believed that the country is theirs to command. Blair's classlessness contains an assumption to rule that they have never encountered before. He personifies the new leadership class; he is what Britain may become.

Early last October, in Brighton, Blair appeared before the assembled Party for his second conference as the leader of what he has christened New Labour. Such annual conferences are crucibles of a party's policies and image. "I know that, for some of you, New Labour has been painful," he said. "There is no greater pain to be endured in politics than the birth of a new idea. . . . We have transformed our party. Our constitution rewritten. Our relations with the trade unions changed . . . But, I didn't come into politics to change the Labour Party. I came into politics to change the country. And I honestly believe that if we had not changed, if we had not returned our party to its values, freed from the weight of outdated ideology, we could not change the country. We could not win, and, even if we did, we would not have governed in the way Britain needs." On a personal note, he continued, "It has been hard, I know. Hard for me sometimes. Last year Bambi, this year Stalin. From Disneyland to dictatorship in twelve short months. I am not sure which one I prefer." He paused. "O.K., I prefer Bambi. Honestly." The Labour delegates laughed appreciatively, giving a kind of voice vote of acquiescence to the unreserved will to power which stood before them.

For the first time, the Tories began to feel a dread in facing Labour. In late October, a poll in the *Sunday Times* revealed that Labour had decisively seized the center ground: fifty per cent of those polled now called the Party moderate. Labour's gains were directly at the Tories' expense: only thirty-four per cent termed the Conservative Party moderate, and thirty-nine per cent labelled it right-wing. In November, a Gallup survey showed Labour thirty-

nine and a half points ahead of the Tories. The *Sunday Times*, a Conservative thunderer, whined in an editorial, "This is not the way it is supposed to be. Electorates are meant to see the incumbent party as the safe choice and the opposition as a risk. Mr. Blair has managed to run Labour, in the eyes of voters, into a safety-first party."

With the dawning of 1996, John Major awoke to discover that deaths and defections had reduced his majority in the House of Commons to five seats. Major is not required to call an election until May of 1997, but he will have to do so sooner if his majority collapses. Of a chance to contest the Prime Ministership, Blair says, "I think we are ready, and I think they literally have nothing left. I mean everything that is now done—the budget, the legislative program—is simply about trying to wrong-foot the Labour Party, and, you know, the country could really do without eighteen months of this nonsense."

Not since 1964, when Labour won (by a bare four-seat majority) on the allure of Harold Wilson's "White Heat of Technology" vision, which was considered at the time the British equivalent of John F. Kennedy's New Frontier, has Labour been perceived as future-oriented. But Wilson, a leader of the old Labour right, did not remake his party; indeed, he backtracked from the mild reform efforts of his predecessor, Hugh Gaitskell. James Callaghan, who governed as Labour's last Prime Minister, from 1976 to 1979, inherited a relic of a party, its constituency limited and its ideas exhausted. Blair has managed to give Labour a broad popular support such as it hasn't truly had since Clement Attlee succeeded Winston Churchill, in 1945. In one year, Blair has increased dues-paying Party membership by a third, bringing in a hundred and fifteen thousand new members, most of them from the middle class.

B LAIR, stripped momentarily of his pin-striped suit jacket, is hovering over the kettle in the kitchen of his Islington house. "Would you like a cup of fruit tea? Sugar with that? Lemon?" His wife, Cherie Booth, who is a Queen's Counsel (or Q.C., the senior-barrister

title held by Rumpole of the Bailey), appears, adjusts her shoes, straightens her black suit, and, with a quick "Bye, dear," races out the door on the way to her law office. The front hallway is full of sports equipment and toys belonging to the Blairs' three young children, and an acoustic guitar, which is Blair's. He carries the tea tray into a living room furnished with floral-patterned chairs and sofa, and bookcases containing bound volumes of the *Weekly Law Review*.

Blair enjoys few things more than holding forth on the ills of contemporary society. He described for me, at some length, his view of the two central problems facing Western countries: how to insure economic security in a time of global technological change, and how to revive a sense of moral purpose amid widespread social fragmentation. "I think those are challenges to which the right really doesn't have an answer," he says. "The right's response is, in effect, to say, 'We want to re-create the world of fifty or sixty years ago, where the woman stayed at home, the man worked, gays were kept in the closet.' We are not going to re-create those days. I also reject, however, what I would call sixties student liberalism. In the end, there was an anarchic feel to that, and a belief that it didn't much matter what you did—you did your own thing. It was a sort of social libertarianism that is the mirror image of the economic libertarianism of some of the new right."

Blair sees himself in the same predicament as other politicians who are grappling with the problems of a transitional politics. "What is fascinating is the degree to which these problems are the same everywhere," he says. "There is great danger that we will get caught in the wedge between the new right and what I call here the old left, who simply accuse us of selling out the principles of the Labour Party or the Democrats. This is where, curiously, the critics from left and right come together."

Blair's critics have interpreted his skepticism about the old Labourism as evidence that he lacks political convictions. The Conservative right and the Labour left have united in their portrayal of him as a practitioner of "designer politics"—a chronic waffler taking his direction from pollsters and media spin-masters. From the left, he has earned two new sobriquets: Tory Blair and Tony Blur. The Conservative line on him has become a spiral of contradictory propositions: He is weak; he is tyrannical. He has duped the voters with his charm tactics; they will not be fooled, because those supporting him are really showing a preference for true conservatism. He has manipulated the Labour Party into serving his own ambition; Labour is completely unchanged and will swamp him in its misery in the end.

Biparty skepticism of Blair crystallized last November, when *The Spectator*, the high-Tory weekly, honored Roy Hattersley at its Parliamentarian of the Year luncheon. Hattersley, a leader of the Labour right for decades, has lately taken to defending the old ideals against the new pragmatism. (He wistfully inscribed his recently published memoir to an old friend with a reference to the Labour Party victory of half a century ago: "From one man of '45 to another.") The seemingly odd pairing of conservative host and socialist guest suited both, for the object of their scorn was the dreaded Blairism. At the luncheon, Hattersley decried the state of his party at length. It had been turned, he claimed, into "less of a moral crusade and more of a marketing exercise."

A year earlier, David Hare had presented "The Absence of War," his play about the Labour Party's identity crisis. (He had been allowed to roam freely inside the 1992 campaign.) Hare depicted a party held captive to a psychology of self-defeat, in which confidence was undermined by the feeling that ideals were being sacrificed to political strategy and that any move forward registered as disloyalty to the hallowed past. In the final scene, to the fading strains of Elgar's "Enigma" Variations, the losing Labour leader speaks of the strangled death of hope:

My own mother died. She died in an air-raid. In South London, during the blitz. It's almost my very first memory, my aunts weeping as they gave me the news. And since then . . . fifty years' honest endeavor. Fifty years doing my best. Being told everything I love and value no longer meets the needs of the day.

Reaction to the play from Labour Party leaders ranged, according to Hare, from public hostility to private approval. Kinnock himself attended a performance. "Neil was incredibly gracious," Hare said. "He said it was a horrendous experience for him to sit through."

Modernization by definition demanded a leader who advanced without feeling that he was leaving behind his true self.

The Right Honourable Anthony Charles Lynton Blair was born in Edinburgh in 1953, the second son of Leo Blair, a barrister, and Hazel McLay, a housewife. Blair's middle names are a combination of the given and the stage names of Leo's biological father. Until the press began investigating Blair's personal background last year, he says he did not know that Leo had been born illegitimate and was raised by foster parents, or that Leo's real parents were music-hall entertainers. Leo Blair was brought up by a Glasgow shipyard worker and his wife, and as a young man he belonged to the Young Communist League. In the mid-fifties, Leo moved with his wife and sons to Adelaide, Australia, where he taught law for three years. Then the family moved to the industrial city of Durham, in northern England, where Leo became a successful lawyer and transformed himself into a Tory activist. In 1963, the self-made man sought a parliamentary seat as a Conservative, but he was hit by a stroke during the campaign and was left unable to speak for three years. Leo's illness devastated the family emotionally and financially.

At the age of thirteen, Tony was sent to Fettes, a traditionally Spartan boarding school in Edinburgh, where he rebelled against the authorities and grew his hair long. At St. John's College, Oxford, in the seventies, he was the lead singer in a rock band called Ugly Rumours, and gained distinction for his rendition of the Rolling Stones' "Live with Me." At Oxford, Blair was very social, but also earnest and studious. His thinking was heavily influenced by Peter Thomson, a graduate student in theology from Australia who was also an ordained Anglican priest. Blair joined Thomson's circle of post-Marxist, New Left searchers, and they introduced him to the works of the prewar Scottish theologian John Macmurray. In a country that is largely indifferent to religion, Blair is a practicing Anglican who has also embraced the communitarianism of the Christian-socialist tradition. Apart from attending two demonstrations against the neo-Fascist National Front, Blair was not politically active on campus, and he did not join the Labour party. "That would have been regarded as terribly right-wing," he says. Membership was unfashionable, dull, the mark of a hack. It is rare, though, for someone to emerge later in life in the Labour leadership who did not begin the climb early.

In 1975, Blair graduated and moved to London. There a Labour elder prevailed upon him to join the Party's Chelsea ward. He was restless (his mother had died that year), and kicked around Paris for a few months, getting work as a barman and as an insurance clerk. Later that year, he decided to become a barrister—a career that requires acceptance into an apprenticeship, called a pupillage. In 1976, he presented an unimpressive résumé at the law chambers of Alexander Irvine, Q.C., whose best friend, since his days at Glasgow University, was John Smith, then the youngest minister in the Callaghan Cabinet.

"My first impression was of colossal enthusiasm, determination, and charm," Irvine says of Blair, but Irvine had already accepted a top graduate from the London School of Economics—a Labourite from Liverpool named Cherie Booth. "I had a firm view that I wasn't to take two pupils," Irvine says. "I hadn't done so before. He succeeded in persuading me he wanted to be my pupil—an important element in any sales pitch. One of his principal skills was absorbing enormously complicated material. Make your best points on the issues—he was very good at that." In 1980, Irvine's two pupils, now barristers, married. Cherie Booth came from a family of Catholic working-class Party activists (her father, Tony Booth, played a militant left-winger in the landmark television comedy "Till Death Us Do Part," which was exported to America as "All in the Family"), and she was professionally and politically ambitious. "They are a political household," Irvine says about the Blairs. "He will confide in her. It is undoubted. It's one of these marriages where they will almost naturally think as one."

THE sequence of Labour's political march of folly had begun long before the dismal, strike-filled winter of 1978-79, which resulted in Margaret Thatcher's election as Prime Minister. Industrial disorder had been a major factor in bringing down the previous Conservative Government, of Edward Heath, in 1974, and Labour was defined more than ever by its relationship to the assertive unions, whose willingness to press their demands to the point of paralyzing Britain seemed contemptuous not only of public order but of the economic condition of a nation facing an inflationary surge. Callaghan was the quintessential Labour leader, born into the working class and bred in the Party incubator—a "keeper of the cloth cap." He was of the Labour right, but his policy was to play left against right to sustain himself in the middle. He could not control the union leadership, however. The more the unions acted out, the more impotent Callaghan appeared and the more the Labour Party itself was rejected as inimical to governing. Callaghan's defeat was a statement about the pathology of a party that allowed Margaret Thatcher to rule for eleven years without ever winning a popular majority.

The Conservatives won with 43.9 per cent to Labour's thirty-seven; they had a forty-three-vote majority in the six-hundred-and-thirty-five-member House of Commons. Since it was the Labour right that had lost power, the Labour left argued that it should be allowed to implement its mandate. Much of the leadership of the right split off with great fanfare to launch a new political party, the Social Democrats, and for a while it was the most popular party in the country. (It splintered in several directions, though, and by 1989 it had vanished.) Tony and Cherie Blair, who did not abandon Labour, found themselves in a hive of factional conflict in which they opposed the far left.

Within the Party, the trade unions could no longer muster their former support, and a vacuum was filled by contentious left-wing groups. "When the old blocs of Labour declined," Blair says, "they were supplanted by interest groups, and the result of that was that a committee would set itself up calling itself the race committee and decide your race policy, or a women's committee would decide your women's policy, and an environment committee would decide your environment policy, and before you know it what you have is a conglomeration of policies that do not appeal to the broad mass of the country at all."

In 1979, Blair told Alexander Irvine, who was well connected in the Party, that he wanted to stand for Parliament. Irvine introduced him to Smith, and Blair wrote a brief for him against the Conservatives' privatization schemes. In 1982, Blair ran his first race, in a by-election in Beaconsfield, which was a Conservative stronghold in Buckinghamshire. (He was selected, as every candidate is, by a local Party committee. Residence in the constituency is not required, and candidates shop around for favorable sites.) He gained publicity as a fresh face for Labour, but the election took place just weeks after Thatcher led Britain into the Falklands War. Blair finished third, gaining only ten per cent of the vote. The following year, he and Cherie made plans to run for separate seats. He did not have a good district, and he felt his hopes ebbing. "I could see everything disappearing," he told a BBC interviewer. Irvine advised him to wait for the right opportunity, and Blair reluctantly followed his advice. At his thirtieth-birthday party, he felt that his political career had ended before it began. But a week later a newly redrawn seat opened up in the safe Labour constituency of Sedgefield, in northeast England. "I remember Tony ringing up from the hall after he had been selected, with cheers ringing in the background," Irvine says.

Blair was elected handily, but Cherie was defeated in her bid. Over all, the election of 1983 was a shattering loss for Labour, and especially for the left wing. The Party had run on a program of unilateral nuclear disarmament and extensive nationalizations—the longest suicide note in political history, it was

widely called. Labour received 27.6 per cent of the vote; the Tories, who won with 42.4 per cent, now had a hundred-and-forty-four-seat majority. (The Liberals and the Social Democrats, in an alliance, won 25.4 per cent.)

The shock of 1983 eradicated the left-right schism within the Party but did not fill the vacuum. The Labour right had ushered the tormenting Thatcher into office and had done nothing to reform the Party internally, and now its leaders were either fretting or defecting. The left had accelerated Labour's fracturing. Anthony Wedgwood Benn, the hard left's great romantic, who had given up his peerage to become Tony Benn, M.P., went down to glorious, exemplary defeat in his constituency. The socialist intellectual Michael Foot, who had been ill cast as Party leader, resigned. Neil Kinnock succeeded him.

MODERNIZATION could not consist of the triumph of one discredited side or the other; rather, it required the recasting of the Party as a whole. Essentially, this amounted to a generational shift in leadership. In the House of Commons, Blair shared a small office with another young new member, Gordon Brown. A former chairman of the Scottish Labour Party, Brown had a brilliant mind and was, like Blair, thinking through the problem of remaking the Party. They had been mobilized by the 1983 debacle, and soon they became the advance guard of the "Kinnocracy"—spokesmen for the commitment to reform. They hatched what they sometimes describe as the Project: an effort to strip first the Labour Party, and then Britain, of nostalgia.

There was another figure who entered into the Project at this juncture, and he has since become perhaps the most influential politico within the Labour Party. In 1985, in anticipation of an election two years hence, and in an effort to counter the devastating campaigns devised by the Saatchis, Kinnock appointed Peter Mandelson, a former producer at London Weekend Television, as the Party's communications director. Mandelson is of the same generation as Blair and Brown, and is close to both of them. He was at Oxford at the time Blair was, and he had always been interested in politics. His grandfather was Herbert Morrison, who served as president of the London County Council and as Clement Attlee's Deputy Prime Minister. Mandelson believes that his grandfather was denied the Prime Ministership through internal Party wrangling, and admits that he is seeking in some way to vindicate his memory. Mandelson, who knows everybody in the media and in politics, is sinuous and sophisticated. He has become the focus of scorn for those opposed to the Project—the evil genie behind it all.

Mandelson orchestrated frequent media appearances for Blair and Brown to attack Tory policies. He hired Hugh Hudson, the director of "Chariots of Fire," to produce a soaring biographical spot about Kinnock. And he replaced the Party's traditional symbol, the red flag, with a red rose, a symbol borrowed from European Social Democratic parties. That act won him the nickname Red Rose Pete. In 1987, Labour lost again, gaining only 30.8 per cent of the vote. Yet Blair believes that a turn was made in that election: "Peter masterminded the Labour Party's 1987 campaign, which we lost, but were it not for him and Neil Kinnock waging a brilliant campaign we would have ended up going out of business."

In the following years, Blair, who was shuttling between shadow Cabinet posts, openly admired Thatcher for her political fortitude and clarity. "The key to Mrs. Thatcher's political success has been in destroying and re-creating contours of electoral support," he wrote in *The New Statesman*. Privately, he came to believe that Kinnock was not pressing modernization fast enough and that, despite Labour's initial lead in the polls at the beginning of the 1992 race, the Party was likely to lose. "It was winnable, but it was only winnable if the Labour Party was perceived to be a transformed political party," Blair says. "And it wasn't. . . . I was angry in the '92 election because people didn't trust Labour. The Conservatives now think that they won it by their strategy, but I think we lost it." The Conservatives won with 41.9 per cent to Labour's 34.2; the

Tory majority was twenty-one seats. In the purging ritual, Neil Kinnock resigned, and John Smith was elected leader. While some columnists wondered if Labour should have skipped a generation and made Blair leader, he had hesitated to become Smith's deputy in the race, and that prize went to a dour Party traditionalist, Margaret Beckett. Blair regretted his own passivity, and determined not to make the same mistake again.

T HOUGH Kinnock had lost, Bill Clinton had won. For Blair and the modernizers, this was a sign that they, too, might be redeemed. In January, 1993, Blair and Gordon Brown travelled to Washington to meet with members of the new Administration and learn how they had won. They returned to rumblings from the Labour traditionalists, who accused them of seeking to perpetrate "Clintonization" on the Party. Blair was now shadow Home Secretary, assigned the task of neutralizing the Tories' tough position on crime. He had to defend Labour from the charge of softness without echoing the Conservatives' draconian policy. Blair honed his position into a quotable phrase: "Tough on crime, tough on the causes of crime." He travelled to Washington again, this time to learn how the Clinton Administration had overcome the once prohibitive political advantage the Republicans had on the crime issue. He expected to be fencing for years with the Tories on volatile social issues and then, at last, if John Smith should win, to become Home Secretary.

Smith's patience seemed an asset, an antidote to Kinnock's chippiness. When Major's popularity began to plummet, Smith adopted the attitude of King Log, simply waiting for events to occur. An aide called it "the long game," but it was less a strategy than a reflection of Smith's temperament. Under pressure from Blair and his allies at the 1993 Party conference, Smith pushed for and won what was called "one member, one vote," or OMOV: a reduction of the percentage of the bloc vote granted to the trade unions in determining the Party's leadership, and an increase in the constituency members' influence. But Smith

rejected use of the phrase new Labour and any alteration of the Party's written charter, and he banished Peter Mandelson, openly disdaining "the black art of public relations." Blair worried that Smith would not press for any further reforms.

By the afternoon of the day of Smith's death, May 12, 1994, Blair had decided he would run for leader, even though it meant challenging his friend Gordon Brown, whose ambition had always been to lead the Party. The race between Blair and Brown was a phony campaign, a contest between political brothers which didn't involve fratricide. Brown assembled his team, delivered one public speech, and quickly concluded he could not win. Blair, for his part, pressed forward, and thereby gained strength. So, after a dinner at a fashionable Islington restaurant with Blair, Brown ended his bid before ever announcing it. "There was no struggle," Brown told me tersely. Brown, not admitting that he was wounded, appeared statesmanlike; Blair appeared impregnable. Blair faced two traditionalists, Margaret Beckett and the Scotsman John Prescott, and won easily.

"I would hesitate to say Tony was lucky because my friend Smith died, but in the brutal political sense he was lucky," Alexander Irvine, Blair's mentor, says. "To be clinical about it, despite the fact that Gordon has a major intellect, and projects it as such, the overriding image would have been Another Worthy Scotsman. That might have forced attention on the predominance of Scots in the Labour Party and the extent to which Labour had become marginalized to its strongest point. That was the negative case for Gordon. The positive case for Tony is that he's fantastically good news at the box office."

Upon his election as leader, Blair told Philip Gould, Labour's top political consultant, that he was "not going to fudge any decisions in relation to the Party," explaining that the concept was "to produce New Labour." Three months later, in October of 1994, in Blackpool, Blair appeared at his first Party conference as leader, against a backdrop of a new banner, which read, "New Labour, New Britain." In a speech he said, "Let us say what we mean and mean what we say." Then he announced a sweeping and historically resonant act: Labour's charter would be rewritten. He was proposing nothing less than stripping the temple of its holy of holies—expunging its Clause IV. This clause was not mere words but a religious credo, engraved on the back of membership cards: "To secure for the workers by hand or by brain the full fruits of their industry and the most equitable distribution thereof that may be possible upon the basis of the common ownership of the means of production, distribution and exchange, and the best obtainable system of popular administration and control of each industry or service." Clause IV was a summons to the socialist Jerusalem.

Credited to the Fabian socialist Sidney Webb, Clause IV had been adopted in 1918, as a right-revisionist response to the Bolshevik Revolution. But it had become a sacred text for the left. For decades—ever since Hugh Gaitskell briefly entertained the notion of changing it, in 1959—Labour leaders, including Kinnock and Smith, had veered away from the trouble that change might cause. "It was an ancient shibboleth, and people used to say, 'O.K., let's not touch it,'" Blair says. "And my argument against that was if we're going to prove to people that the Labour Party is changed and is genuinely a value-based party, not a party that still has within its constitution a quasi-Marxist figment of ideology, then we should have the courage to just go out and change it. If in truth we can't change it, then there is something pretty fundamentally wrong with the way we are." At the Party conference, a vote was taken on whether to affirm Clause IV. It passed by 50.9 per cent to 49.1: the largest trade unions opposed a change. For six months, Blair stumped Party halls around the country for a spring vote, and as a result he won this one resoundingly. "Now, that was a bit like breaking a spell," he says.

"Few politicians are good at taking the high ground and throwing themselves off it," observed Mandelson, who had tried a decade earlier to deal with Clause IV by stealth—by simply neglecting to have it printed on the back of the membership cards. "Tony does it, and takes enormous care to bring everyone else behind him. He manages the process of risk taking with great application to detail."

BLAIR has gathered around him a fairly close-knit if eclectic circle of aides and advisers, all devoted to him and the Project as one cause. His oldest friend in the group is Anji Hunter, whom he met when they were both teen-age school rebels. As his "personal political adviser," she runs the office, serves as a liaison to other Members of Parliament and leaders of the Party, and speaks to Blair perhaps dozens of times a day. Jonathan Powell, the chief of staff, was drawn not from the ranks of the Party but from the Foreign Service. He was First Secretary at the British Embassy in Washington—the link between it and the Clinton Administration. His brother, Sir Charles Powell, was the foreign-policy and defense adviser to Thatcher, and was often referred to as the Deputy Prime Minister. Alastair Campbell, a personal friend, with whom the Blair family sometimes vacations, was the aggressive political editor of the tabloid *Daily Mirror* until last year, and is now Blair's press secretary. Peter Mandelson, who had become an M.P. for Hartlepool, was promoted to the front bench in the Commons, a place that publicly acknowledges his influence. Alexander Irvine is relied upon for his judgment, and if Blair wins he will almost certainly become the Lord Chancellor, overseeing the nation's judicial system. Philip Gould, who analyzes the polling and develops themes, spent the fall of 1992 in the Clinton campaign's war room in Little Rock. Meanwhile, Gordon Brown has made his peace with Blair, and has become the most important member of the shadow Cabinet, in charge of economic strategy.

The rise of Blair's kitchen Cabinet has stirred some resentment among the traditionalists, but Blair has muted these feelings by choosing as his deputy his onetime rival John Prescott. Prescott is a classic Labour leader, a former ship's steward who rose through the ranks. He is bluff, candid, and fearless, and is now a Blair loyalist.

THE Project is, of course, as much a reaction to the long legacy of Conservative rule as it is to Labour's fecklessness. If Thatcher is the stepmother to Major, she is also the midwife to Blair. By creating conditions that forced changes in the Labour party, she helped bring him forward as its leader. But it is what she has done to the Conservative Party that has made it possible for Blair to become Prime Minister.

The Tory political tradition was patrician, imperial, and designed to conserve the existing social order. Since Benjamin Disraeli warned against turning Britain into a battlefield of opposing classes in "Sybil, or The Two Nations," the novel he wrote in 1845, his fusion of patriotism and paternalism has defined one-nation Toryism. Disraeli's vision, rooted in feudalism, was of an organic society of which the Conservative Party was the political expression. Its aim was to balance the classes and preserve established institutions. He justified reforms to improve the conditions of the working class as essential to social cohesion. The hero of Disraeli's novel delivers a parliamentary speech (echoing one that Disraeli actually gave) addressed to the aristocracy: "If you wished for time to retain your political power, you could only effect your purpose by securing for the people greater social felicity."

Conservatism, of course, never reconciled the classes or the regional disparities in the United Kingdom. Margaret Thatcher's reaction to this problem was to adopt a radical right-wing philosophical position against the very idea of one nation. Thatcher's mesmerizing strength as a "conviction politician" battered down the old Toryism. Her brand of postimperial nostalgia consisted of exalting the imperial individual as if "society" were another word for Soviet socialism. There was considerable to-do when she said that "there is no such thing as society," only individuals and families. She disdained those who invoked the injustices of class as whiners lacking the grit to go into business. She heaped scorn on one-nation Toryism as the blithering of yesterday's men: the "feeble" and "timid" public-school weaklings and appeasers of statism, as she put it in her memoir. With an intense belief in her own righteousness, she split the Conservative Party and orphaned the paternalistic one-nation idea that had been the ideological fundament of the Party for more than a century.

Will Hutton, the economics editor of the pro-Labour newspaper the *Guardian*, offered a sharp critique of the consequences of Thatcherism last year in his book "The State We're In." Hutton described a society increasingly riven by class, socially less cohesive, and politically more centralized. "Indeed," he concluded, "the crisis of Conservatism is more deep-seated and threatening to its internal cohesion than is commonly recognized."

ONLY three Prime Ministers in this century have served longer than John Major: H. H. Asquith, Harold Macmillan, and Margaret Thatcher. Yet his impact has been nearly invisible. Major's unpopularity is of a strange variety, born of a lack of strong feelings. He is neither loved nor hated. When he became the Prime Minister, he promised, in the wake of Thatcher's Sturm und Drang, a nation "at ease with itself." But his ineffectuality has only rarely allowed him to strike the pose of a man at ease.

In September, 1992, five months after Major's surprise election victory, the pound sterling crashed out of the European exchange-rate mechanism. Black Wednesday, as it was called, severely challenged the assumption that the Conservatives were the most competent economic stewards. (Black Wednesday also triggered revolts within the Party over joining Europe.) Since then, Major has been swamped by endless factional battles, botched initiatives, and private scandals throughout the ranks of his party, but in July of last year he proved his political will to survive by forcing a vote on his leadership. He was opposed only by John Redwood, a right-wing backbencher, whose slogan was "No Change, No Chance," and whose program included halting the decommissioning of the royal yacht, Britannia. Major won easily, insuring his position as Prime Minister until the next election. But he had drained the Tories of possibility: he was all that was left.

With great alacrity, Blair captured the center ground the Conservatives had lost by redefining the idea of one nation. Thatcherism has given him his opportunity to prove the relevance of his Christian socialism and to make the case that social cohesion can be gained by means other than an aristocratic paternalism or an unfettered market. His one-nation politics also enables him to lift the taint from Labour as a sectarian, class-bound movement.

In a series of speeches beginning last October at Labour's party conference in Brighton, Blair openly developed his one-nation concept. "One nation," as he defines it, means restoring a sense of community, and can be achieved only by overcoming class. "I want us to be a young country again," he said, adding a new spin on jingoism. "Not resting on past glories. Not fighting old battles . . . Not saying, 'This was a great country.' But 'Britain can and will be a great country again.'" In a foreign-policy speech on November 30th, Blair accused the Tory right of being "the Little Englander party, content to be on the margins of Europe and often, as over Bosnia . . . isolationist." Britain, he said, can only be "strong in the world because we are cohesive at home, and strong in Europe. . . . Britain as one nation."

After spending Christmas in Australia, Blair went to Singapore, where, on January 8th, he delivered a speech to the business community, declaring his commitment to "one-nation politics" and proposing to make everyone "stakeholders." The welfare system would be reformed to serve as a program to enable people to enter the labor force as skilled workers. The "sharing of the possibility of power, wealth, and opportunity" would not rest on "the tax and benefit regime." But dealing with a global economy requires an active government that engages the market by spurring savings and making public investments, especially in education. Citizens, he went on, are not simply widgets but stakeholders where they work. The modern corporation, he argued, should be seen not as "a mere vehicle for the capital market" but as "a community or partnership." Rights and responsibilities extend

throughout the society, from top to bottom. That speech (inspired in part by Will Hutton's book) has provoked an intense debate over the new ideological fault lines he has drawn.

A political token of the redefinition of "one-nation politics" came in October with the unprecedented defection of Alan Howarth, the former Tory Minister of Education, from the Conservative to the Labour side. "I'm a one-nation man, not a class warrior," Howarth told me. "Tony's values in politics are very much mine. Each move in the Conservative Party is more to the right. The world outside recognized that the best Thatcher did is shared wisdom—goodbye to the big central state. But the world also recognizes unrestrained market forms will destroy all relationships. You need to sustain the cohesion of society. The Tory Party hasn't adjusted. Major's sole aim is to keep the Tory Party in office. It's not obvious what he wants to do except survive. Major is increasingly a prisoner of the right wing of his party."

THE Conservative Party's internal divisions have so far made it impossible for it to develop a coherent strategy against Blair, or even to gauge the seriousness of the threat he poses. Two mutually exclusive strategies reflect the split within the Party. The right's approach is called "clear blue water." It means that the Conservatives ought to be creating sharp differences between themselves and Labour by moving farther right. The other approach, that of the remnant of one-nation Tories, is called simply "Coke." It means that the Conservatives ought to emphasize that they, not the deceptively positioned Labour, are at the true center of the country, that they are "the real thing." Some on the right see their best chance for power not in a Major victory and a prolongation of his regime but in his defeat, followed by a Blair Government they believe they could discredit, after which the field would be cleared for them. This strategy might be called "Gingrich." John Redwood, Major's challenger from the right, travelled to Washington in September and again last month to discuss this third way with Newt Gingrich himself and his pollster, Frank Luntz, who devised the Contract with America. "Gingrich would say, paradoxically, [that the Republicans'] losing the Presidency made it easier for him—to that extent he benefitted from the Bush defeat," Redwood told me. "Our party is still in power. My argument is that we can avoid defeat, stick to our principles."

Still others in the Conservative camp believe that Blair has yet to face real tests. "Don't forget, Tony Blair is just in a honeymoon," says Shaun Woodward, who was the communications director for the Conservative Party in its last campaign. "He has to manage the Labour Party. Management is not an easy game. And nobody should underestimate Major. His critics say he can't clear the hurdle, but he does. He wins. Underestimate this man at your peril." Charles Moore, of the *Daily Telegraph*, noted, "The Tories are ruthless in elections. That ought to be enough. If I were a Tory propagandist, I'd repeat—you have to repeat—'Tony Blair is the leader of the Labour Party, a bad vehicle for running the country.' The press is terribly important. If the jackals of the right-wing press go after Blair, the fear thing will really get going. Terror will be struck in the hearts of middle England."

The question for Blair is not whether the mostly Conservative press will support him but whether it will rabidly oppose him. Much speculation centers on Rupert Murdoch, who owns the *Times*, the *Sunday Times, News of the World*, the *Sun* (the largest tabloid), and Sky-TV. In the past, his media were powerful instruments in the Tory cause. But, Moore says, "Murdoch might play a double game. Murdoch's a total cynic. Maybe Blair will prevent the onslaught."

Last July, Murdoch invited Blair to address executives at his NewsCorp Leadership Conference on Hayman Island, off the Great Barrier Reef, in Australia. Blair has met with Murdoch several times since. It is not so much sympathy for the devil as a tactic to blunt or forestall him. "The press has certainly become far more even in its handling of us," Blair says. "They went after Neil Kinnock ferociously, ferociously. Really, they got to the stage

where it was really pretty grotesque propaganda. At the moment, anyway, that has not reëmerged."

Operationally, Labour is attaining parity. The Party is currently spending two million pounds to acquire two floors of a building near the House of Commons, for an up-to-date media center. But the glimmering of success is unfamiliar to Labour, and Blair's progress still arouses disquiet. "There's tremendous admiration, tremendous enthusiasm, but not much trust," one leader of the Labour left in Parliament told me. "So long as the show is rolling along in a successful way, he's got no problem. But the cost of his failure could be very high."

Blair's modernization of the Labour Party is a test run for the larger, harder part of the Project: modernizing Britain. England is not Greece to America's Rome, as Harold Macmillan suggested it would become. England has become England to America's Rome, an outlying country of often amusing people best appreciated for their dramatic art of self-presentation. "The real challenge to Britons is to succeed in the modern global economy—the proper relation of markets and public action," Gordon Brown says. "Tony has proved how Labour is capable of transforming the Party. Now we must have a modern view of Britain's place in the world. The battle is one to establish the agenda."

Thatcher's task in presenting her view of Britannia Restored was simplified by the Cold War and Labour's antinuclear pacifism. Britain, under her reign, was holding the line of containment, and was, ipso facto, strong. The crushing of the Argentines in the Falklands War gave an adrenaline rush to the idea that Britain was a muscular power. Thatcher's real fear was Europe. In time, she split the Tories over it, and the Party remains heavily weighted toward the "Euroskeptics," who include Major. And there is, among the public, a pervasive anxiety that Britain, the foremost great power at the beginning of the century, is now weak and backward compared with Europe. (According to Gordon Brown's own new figures, the

country has now fallen behind Italy in per-capita income.) But Blair believes that the policy of muddling through, without full engagement in Europe, must lead to further decline and might even fray the Anglo-American special relationship.

O N November 29th, Air Force One landed in London. Clinton's relations with John Major had begun on a badly strained note. In the fall of 1992, operatives from the Tory central office had parachuted into Washington like commandos in a desperate, doomed attempt to rescue the campaign of George Bush; meanwhile, the Home Office searched for material that would prove that Clinton had engaged in unpatriotic acts while protesting the Vietnam War as a Rhodes Scholar at Oxford. But now, in Westminster, standing before the entire Parliament, the President praised John Major, who, silently but visibly, mouthed the words "Thank you."

Then Clinton went to see Blair. They tested themes on each other that they would later use in key speeches: Blair's "stakeholder society" address and Clinton's State of the Union. The main problem was social insecurity, and there was only so much change people could take at one time. Clinton said that he had focussed his energies on legislative achievements to the neglect of communicating with the public. Blair replied that Thatcher and Reagan had been able to get out their messages more successfully. He said that left-of-center parties faced particular problems in this respect, partly because commentators often failed to understand what they were about. In the absence of an intellectual movement, the vacuum was being filled by cynicism and disillusion. Clinton said that it was not possible to win voters in favor of big government anymore, an idea he finally expressed in public in his State of the Union address. He said that the larger themes should be liberty, progress, and unity. Blair observed that the age of overarching initiatives like Britain's Beveridge Plan, which had inaugurated the welfare state in 1945, was over. Implicit in this exploratory discussion was the intention of both sides to set the Anglo-American special relationship on a new basis: the Transatlantic Project.

Blair and his circle believe that Clinton's reëlection is a crucial factor for them. "Clinton win? Not important," a deadpan Peter Mandelson told me. "Nothing. No effect." Then he started biting all his nails at once and shaking. A Clinton defeat would be seen in Britain as an augury for Blair. A Clinton victory would make Major appear hopelessly retrograde and give Blair a sense of inevitability.

Blair believes that the difficulties Clinton has encountered are far less personal than political in character, and that, therefore, the American experience might foreshadow the resistance he will meet. Any change from a long-established regime is bound to stir up a fervent opposition. Blair's polling has already detected in the electorate a reactionary populist nationalism simmering beneath the surface, which might

find a focus for its rage in an incumbent Labour Government. But, whatever their similarities, Clinton and Blair operate in very different political systems. Blair in power would not be checked and balanced; with a certain majority, he could propose and dispose. The experiment that Clinton proposed at the beginning of his Administration, but which was frustrated, therefore might be tested first in Blair's Britain. Then Blair would face the true crisis of transition: coping with a politics of raised expectations while instituting programs that would not immediately lift living standards. "Probably the most important thing is that I don't think any project such as this becomes clear to the public until you are in government and you're doing things," he told me.

Blair had expected that Britain's election would be held in 1997, after America's. But in December one Conservative Member of Parliament died

and another defected to the Liberal-Democrat Party. Pro-European Tories claimed that there might be more defections if the Party didn't steer away from the right. The leader of the Party's right, Defense Minister Michael Portillo, a Thatcher protégé, dared them to leave. A group of old-line Tories announced that they were going to write their own one-nation manifesto. Margaret Thatcher weighed in with a blast at them as "no-nation conservatives" and at Major for being insufficiently right-wing. Studying actuarial charts and the Party's widening schisms, Major privately ordered the central office to prepare battle plans for a potential campaign within six months. But Major has embraced no strategy. He seems to be planning on winning a mandate for entropy.

Tony Blair, sitting in a green-leather armchair in the Office of the Opposition Leader in the House of Commons, is at ease yet impatient. "If not now, when?" he asks.

Newts Across the Pond Rework the British Right

Ready, aim, think: Britain's parties fire up intellectual agendas for the next election

Alexander MacLeod

Special to The Christian Science Monitor

LONDON

Call it a slugfest of the mind. Britain's political parties are arming their intellectual torpedoes in anticipation of coming general elections, due in less than 18 months.

Think tanks across the political spectrum are scrambling to generate the one "big idea" that could make or break the campaign.

Not surprisingly, Newt Gingrich's Contract With America, which had such an impact on American voters in 1994, figures high in the Conservatives' mental gymnastics. Much of the policy production is being generated by the right wing of Prime Minister John Major's party.

Some of it is even coming from Margaret Thatcher, his influential predecessor. Her Thatcher Foundation is largely dedicated to opposing close European integration, and until now she has rarely commented on domestic policies.

IRON LADY CHIPS IN

But in a televised speech Jan. 11, Mrs. Thatcher urged fellow Conservatives to stick to cutting back big government and encouraging private enterprise. Her speech was widely interpreted as a sharp attack on Mr. Major and his failure to hold to a Thatcherite line since he took over from the Iron Lady.

Major himself clearly is feeling the need for a stronger intellectual underpinning before he faces a rejuvenated Labour Party, led by the youthful Tony Blair, though it may be doubted whether he entirely welcomed comments from Thatcher.

As well as strengthening his own policy unit at 10 Downing Street, the prime minister has begun to seek ideas from Politeia. This think tank is setting out to take the Thatcherite domestic agenda several steps further. Warwick Lightfoot, one of its leading members, has just sent Major a paper arguing for getting rid of laws dating back to the 1960s that safeguard workers against unfair dismissal and downsizing.

This spate of idea-mongering among Conservatives has been triggered by a concerted campaign on the left, aimed at ending the Labour Party's 16 years in the political wilderness.

Lined up behind party leader Blair are a host of think tanks to help him convince voters and leaders of big business that his party at last has a coherent and appealing set of policies.

During a recent visit to Singapore, Blair gave a test run to what a senior adviser says is Labour's "big idea" for the coming election campaign. Drawing on advice from the leftist Policy Studies Institute, Blair pledged that a Labour government would create a "stakeholder economy" giving every citizen a stake in the creation of wealth.

Labour, he said, would "work with the grain of global change" and foster "a national team spirit." It also would ensure that the benefits of economic growth are fairly distributed and that "all our citizens are part of one nation and get the chance to succeed."

MIFFED MODERATES

Blair's use of the term "one nation" angered Deputy Prime Minister Michael Heseltine, who dismissed the Labour leader's speech as "a series of sound bites."

For many decades moderate Conservatives such as Mr. Heseltine have claimed to be committed to the "one nation" concept, meaning that their party aims to unite people, regardless of class and income.

The cut and thrust of ideas across the Conservative-Labour divide is heating up as Blair attempts to give his party's candidates a credible "song sheet" for the election campaign.

But as Conservatives eye the 30-point lead Labour has notched in opinion polls under Blair's leadership, there is at least as much competitive thinking going on within their party, especially over European policy.

Even as Conservatives like Thatcher and John Redwood—who unsuccessfully challenged Major for the party leadership last summer—push the Conservatives for a more right-wing stance against European integration, some 50 members of Parliament have taken the opposite view, and are producing a pamphlet arguing the case for a single currency and a united Europe.

CALL TO ORDER

Clearly upset by the trend toward ideological dissension in the governing party, Major warned his followers against so much public squabbling.

"If the Conservative Party does not realize the opportunities that lie ahead and throws it away by disputes within itself, then it will lose the election," he declared in a televised interview.

Major's call for an end to party infighting was supported by David Willetts, a member of Parliament. His book "Modern Conservatism" argues that Conservatives must "marry the disciplines of the market and the rigors of competition with a social cohesion that is necessary to enable people to live better lives."

A similar attempt to sail between political extremes marks the ideas of Peter Mandelson, who is also a member of Parliament and one of Blair's most influential advisers.

In a book soon to be published, Mr. Mandelson will argue that "New Labour," as Blair increasingly calls his party, already has jettisoned old socialist shibboleths, such as opposition to the free market, and occupies the middle ground of politics.

"There is nothing wrong with capitalism with a social conscience or a human face," Mr. Mandelson says.

British Third Party Bids For Role as Kingmaker

Liberal Democrats Woo Labour for Alliance

Alexander MacLeod

Special to The Christian Science Monitor

LONDON

Three's a crowd in American politics. But Britain's third party could help shape the course of the government well into the next century.

The nation's main opposition party, Labour, may join an alliance with the Liberal Democrats, the nation's third-largest party, to keep the ruling Conservatives out of power for at least 10 years.

If put into effect, the concept of "partnership politics" at the core of the plan would transform voting patterns in Britain.

Senior Labour and Liberal Democrat (Lib Dem) figures were reported to have already begun informal talks about a post-election parliamentary partnership between their two parties.

The Conservative Party is widely expected to lose general elections due by next spring, but the partnership would help keep the Conservatives out of power in the next elections five years later as well.

Tony Blair, the Labour leader, has given a cautious welcome to a partnership initiative launched Jan. 22 by Paddy Ashdown, his Liberal Democrat counterpart.

Mr. Ashdown's centrist party currently holds 25 House of Commons seats. It has usually tried to distance itself from both Labour and the Conservatives. But Ashdown made it clear in a widely reported speech that he is seeking a deal with Mr.

Blair to cooperate on legislation to modernize Britain.

But he made his offer conditional on Labour accepting electoral reform, including a new voting system to be put to the people in a referendum.

Labour Party officials say privately that Blair wants to explore Ashdown's partnership plan in greater detail and is attracted by a deal that would promise the two parties a working parliamentary majority over the Conservatives for at least a decade.

In the last two or three years, the Liberal Democrats have won a string a by-election victories in constituencies that normally vote Conservative, and the party's electoral appeal will be a powerful bargaining chip in Ashdown's dealings with Blair.

Opinion polls have shown that in several areas of Britain, voters fed up with the Conservatives would rather vote Lib Dem than support Labour. The defection to the Lib Dems from government ranks earlier in January of Emma Nicholson, a Conservative Member of Parliament, underlined the attractions Ashdown's party has for dissatisfied Conservatives.

Ashdown's partnership politics agenda does not call for a formal coalition with Labour—he admits publicly that some sections of his party would think that would be going too far.

Instead, he is proposing cooperation on key sectors of policy. He pinpointed education, welfare and health reform, the environment, and policy toward Europe

as areas where Labour and the Lib Dems could work together.

If Blair and Ashdown reach agreement on a post-election deal, Labour will be able to count on Lib Dem strength in key areas of the country, such as southwest England, preventing the Conservatives from winning seats.

But the price Ashdown will ask for Blair's agreement to a deal may not be to the taste of many Labour activists. He wants the Labour leader to accept the need for proportional representation (PR) in the allocation of House of Commons seats.

PR systems vary from country to country, but the general aim is to avoid a "first past the post" outcome in elections.

At present, if there are several candidates for one seat, and the vote is split among them, it is possible for a candidate to win with as little as one-third of the vote. All the other candidates lose.

Under PR, seats in Parliament would be distributed according to the proportion of votes gained by each party in each constituency and nationwide. This would almost certainly greatly increase the number of Lib Dem MPs in the House of Commons.

The Conservatives lean against PR, although it operates in many conservatively led European countries such as Germany.

In terms of his own personality, Ashdown's backing could help a Labour government. He is a charismatic campaigner with a flair for oratory.

Revamping Britain's Constitution

The case for reform

**The British think something has gone wrong with their system of government.
This article, the first in a series, explains what may have to be done**

THE constitution is antiquated and anti-democratic. Britain's government is overcentralised and insufficiently accountable. Its citizens' basic freedoms are sorely in need of protection. So say many Britons. Others reply that Britain remains one of the world's most stable democracies, its ancient institutions widely admired and copied. Its unwritten constitution, a monument to pragmatism, is flexible enough to meet the demands of a changing society.

Britain is not the only country in which such an argument is taking place. One of the chief ironies of the end of the 20th century is that, as democracy takes new root in many parts of the ex-communist world and elsewhere, a growing number of ordinary voters in the older democracies of Europe and North America seem to be increasingly disenchanted with the way their political systems work. In the United States, Italy, France and Japan, to name but a few, there is deep disrespect for both politicians as a class and the current processes of politics.

It is particularly awkward for constitutional reformers in Britain that almost all of the changes they would like to make in the British system are already in place in one or other of these countries, without having saved them from their share of the general malaise. Nevertheless, the need for reform may be even greater in Britain than elsewhere, because Britain's constitutional arrangements are among the oldest and therefore, arguably, the most rusty of them all.

The Labour Party has promised a radical programme of constitutional reform, embracing a bill of rights, elected assemblies for Scotland and Wales, devolution of power to England's regions, more freedom for local government, reform of the House of Lords and a referendum on changing Britain's electoral system. The Conservatives have set their face against all of these changes as unnecessary, dangerous and a threat to the continued existence of the United Kingdom. Either Britain is poised on the brink of root-and-branch constitutional reform or, as so often in the past, it is about to embark on years of political dispute and learned verbiage which will, in the end, lead to little or nothing.

That may sound cynical. Campaigning groups such as Charter 88 (with over 60,000 signatories) have demonstrated a growing interest in changes to the way Britain is governed. A MORI opinion poll for the Joseph Rowntree Reform Trust, published in May, found 79% of respondents in favour of a written constitution, 79% wanting a bill of rights, 81% for a freedom-of-information act and 77% supporting the more frequent use of referendums. Innumerable polls have shown that nearly four in five Scottish voters want their own elected parliament in Edinburgh. The demotion of local government under the Tories, and the appointment of thousands of quangos to run bits of the public sector, appear to be widely resented. People hold members of Parliament in low esteem and regard many of the country's institutions with less and less respect; or so they tell the pollsters.

Yet translating such disaffection into actual reforms will be difficult. Past attempts to change overtly the way Britain is governed have failed miserably. In 1969 Labour's last attempt to reform the House of Lords, though supported by the Tory front bench, ran aground after an alliance of backbenchers from both sides of the House of Commons vehemently opposed it. In the 1970s the Labour government spent years, and enormous amounts of political capital, pushing devolution bills through the Commons, only to see their proposals fail in subsequent referendums to gain the required support of 40% of the Scottish and Welsh electorates. Indeed, the Welsh rejected the plan by a margin of four to one.

Why bother?

One obstacle to reform is the fact that most of the proposed changes are meant to reduce the power of central government, but can be pursued only by the party in power—which, naturally, finds the idea less than appealing. In this century constitutional reform has been, typically, far more attractive to oppositions than to governing parties. The Tories flirted with reform in the 1970s while out of power, when Lord Hailsham famously complained that Britain's constitutional arrangements were moving it towards an "elective dictatorship". A few years later, as Margaret Thatcher's first Lord Chancellor, he—and most other Tories—had lost their interest in radical reform.

If Labour wins the next general election, after nearly two decades in opposition, it may undergo a similar transformation, despite its current commitment to an ambitious agenda of constitutional change. Reducing its newly won power through reforms—which themselves are bound to be complicated and contentious—could soon seem less urgent than wielding that power to pursue its own policies on education, health, the economy and foreign affairs.

It is also far from clear whether the public's low regard for British institutions shows an appetite for real change or simply dislike of an unpopular Tory government that has been in office for too long. A set of fresh faces at the top may be enough to cheer up most voters. If it does, the demand for constitutional change may fade away.

The biggest obstacle to constitutional reform may indeed be the ingrained conservatism that runs through both main parties and the wider electorate. Most Britons seem wary of rapid change, suspicious of grand schemes of improvement and reluctant to abandon the tried and true for the uncertainties of the new. The case for constitutional reform is a powerful one. But all too often its advocates assume that the need for reform is obvious, and opposition to it merely self-interested. In fact, reformers confront, and need to refute, a "traditionalist" view which has always exercised a powerful grip on the popular imagination.

An intelligent traditionalist will point out that politicians and political institutions currently seem to be unpopular with voters throughout the industrialised world, not just in Britain. Despite the anomalies and inconsistencies in Britain's constitution, he would argue, the country is not obviously governed any worse than most other rich countries. Nor does it seem at all likely to tip into despotism.

Particular policies and governments may prove unpopular from time to time. But Britain's parliamentary system of government has weathered vast social changes without the upheavals seen in many countries that have written constitutions. Most other nations have been forced to adopt these after military defeat, revolution or political collapse. Britain is facing no such crisis. Small adjustments may have to be made occasionally, as in the past. But why overhaul a system which has taken more than 300 years to evolve, and whose accumulated wisdom has been admired and imitated throughout the world?

The trouble with this view is that it relies

on a misreading of Britain's own constitutional history. The key concepts pioneered by Britain which have so much influenced the growth of democracy elsewhere—the separation of the executive, legislative and judicial branches of government to provide institutional checks and balances, and the guarantee of fundamental rights protected from the encroachments of an overmighty government—were born of Parliament's battle to restrain the monarch in the 17th and 18th centuries; but they were never firmly established in Britain itself.

In 1765 Sir William Blackstone, the leading English legal authority at the time, wrote that the total union of the executive and legislative branches of government "would be productive of tyranny". Over the next century such a union is precisely what Britain achieved. The cabinet in effect assumed the executive role of the monarch. With the extension of the voting franchise to the middle and working classes and the rise of mass parties, the cabinet (and more particularly the prime minister) could stay in office only by exerting an iron discipline on its party supporters in the Commons, further concentrating power in its hands. By 1867 Walter Bagehot was praising the cabinet's control of nearly all government affairs, its "near complete fusion of the executive and legislative powers", as the "efficient secret" of the constitution.

When in 1885 Albert Venn Dicey came to write "The Law of the Constitution", the book that has most shaped debate on the subject, the British system of government not only bore little resemblance to the written democratic constitutions being adopted elsewhere; it barely made intellectual sense. In Dicey's view the British constitution was based on two fundamental principles: the absolute sovereignty of Parliament and the rule of law. There is an inherent contradiction in this description. A truly sovereign parliament would be unconstrained even by the law, which it would be free to change at any time. And this is precisely what British governments have done on many occasions when the law—even the common law built up over centuries by the courts—has stood in their way.

Use and abuse

Curiously, parliamentary sovereignty seemed too extreme a proposition even for Dicey, its greatest champion. A committed unionist, he was appalled at Gladstone's policy of Irish home rule and complained, quite correctly, that it was a fundamental constitutional change. But his doctrine of parliamentary sovereignty left no fundamental distinction between the handling of constitutional changes and of trivial changes to the highway code (there is still no such distinction today). So Dicey, remarkably, became the first to advocate the referendum in Britain as "the one available check on the recklessness of party leaders."

Since Dicey's day the doctrine of parliamentary sovereignty has bequeathed Britain a system of government which looks distinctly odd compared with those of other established democracies. After the powers of the House of Lords were drastically curtailed in 1911, parliamentary sovereignty came to rest solely with the Commons. And party discipline in the Commons has meant that, most of the time, real sovereignty has rested, in effect, with the cabinet.

In other words, the British people are invited every four or five years to choose one of two small committees of mostly professional politicians to run the government as they see fit, constrained only by what they think is politically possible, with almost no legal or institutional checks on what they can do. Voters are not directly consulted on any of the issues which come up in the intervening years, be they declarations of war or the regulation of dogs that bite too often. And then, at the next general election, they are again offered the choice between two small committees of politicians.

No party since 1935 has won more than 50% of the votes cast. And yet their minority victories have not stopped both Tory and Labour governments from claiming the right to steer the country abruptly in new directions. The Labour government of 1945 launched a massive nationalisation programme and created the welfare state after winning 48% of the votes cast. In the 1951 election the Labour government lost power to the Tories, a defeat widely seen as a decision by the voters to call a halt to further socialist measures, even though Labour's share of the votes cast actually rose from 46% in 1950 to 49% (exceeding that of the victorious Tories by a percentage point). And Mrs (now Lady) Thatcher launched her free-market counter-revolution after winning 44% of the vote in 1979 and only 42% and 43% in her two subsequent elections.

Such governments were, as the current system's proponents argue, strong ones. But strength and effectiveness are not the same thing. One result of "strong" governments may be to set policies swinging like a pendulum, as a new government indignantly reverses many of the old one's decisions. And the electoral system has recently been brutal to third parties, in effect disenfranchising millions of voters. In the 1983 and 1987 elections the Liberal-Social Democrat alliance received 25% and 23% of the votes respectively, but only 4% of seats in the Commons. In 1992 the Liberal Democrats received 18% of the votes, more than half of those cast for Labour, but only 3% of Commons seats, compared with Labour's 42% of seats.

In this system cabinet ministers, and the vast official bureaucracy over which they preside, have been the exclusive arbiters of what the public should know. British governments run by both main parties have been among the most secretive of all the western democracies, refusing to grant the

public, from whom they are supposed to derive their legitimacy, any legal right to information about, or held by, their government. Often the voters discover what the government has really been up to only when ministers leak information to discredit each other, or when some scandal or blunder forces it to divulge information to limit the damage to its own political prospects.

With no bill of rights to constrain them, both Labour and Tory governments have extended police powers, restricted press freedom, and sometimes suspended the ordinary workings of the criminal law. These moves, touching the basic freedoms of all citizens, have been impossible to challenge in British courts.

Last year the government severely restricted the right to silence in criminal trials—allowing judges and juries to draw adverse inferences from a defendant's refusal to testify—after little debate in the Commons. The measure is contained in a mere four sections of a giant 169-section law. Whatever the merits or demerits of this action it did, at a stroke, eliminate a right which had for centuries been thought a pillar of Britain's judicial system. This might have deserved a bit more debate, and some reference to the citizens whose rights were being so curtailed.

Down the Eurohole

Explicit constitutional reform to rein in the powers of government may have proved difficult in the past, but the lack of a codified constitution has allowed governments to innovate in ways which, in most other democratic countries, would be deemed to involve constitutional changes, and so subject to special procedures to win the consent of the electorate. Since 1979, for example, the Tories have drastically reduced the powers of local authorities.

And, when it comes to Europe, the enormous discretion in the hands of British governments has led to what can best be described as a giant constitutional cock-up. The Tory government which led Britain into the European Community in 1973 explicitly promised in a 1971 white paper that membership presented "no question of any erosion of essential national sovereignty" and that "our courts will continue to operate as they do at present". Any constitutional implications were also played down during Labour's referendum in 1975, and were brushed aside by the Thatcher and Major governments when they signed the Single European Act and the Maastricht treaty.

In fact, EU membership has blown a hole through the middle of Dicey's doctrine of parliamentary sovereignty. The Maastricht rebels are right about this. European Union law now takes precedence over laws passed at Westminster. After some hesitation, Britain's judges have concluded that, when an act of Parliament directly clashes with an EU directive or treaty, it is the EU law which must prevail, unless Parliament's law explicitly repudiates or violates the Treaty of Rome—which would probably lead to Britain's withdrawal from the EU.

Even an avid pro-European should feel uncomfortable that so momentous a change to the foundations of Britain's system of government was made without informing or consulting the British electorate. France and Germany, and other EU countries, made changes to their written constitutions to endorse the transfer of powers to the EU. Britain seems to have sleepwalked to the same destination. The electorate was never given any real choice in the matter. Even Tory ministers seem befuddled by the issue, continually complaining about the meddling of Brussels even though it is their governments that transferred powers to the EU.

Today government in Britain seems remote and unresponsive. Many services once managed locally—housing, hospitals and education—are now controlled from Westminster and administered by bureaucrats and political appointees. As centralisation has accelerated, the frustration of ordinary citizens has grown, expressed in open cynicism about the motives and behaviour of politicians and an increasingly visible indifference to politics itself.

Even the ministers running this overcentralised system often seem more like its prisoners than its beneficiaries. The Tories since 1979, like their predecessors, have first accumulated power at the centre to push through specific changes, and then found that, to operate the immense government machine they have helped to expand, they needed to delegate some authority. But, without explicit constitutional guidelines, these efforts have foundered.

The creation of quangos and independent government agencies, instead of devolving managerial power as intended, has merely stuffed the public administration with political appointees, and has so tangled the lines of accountability that it is now almost impossible to pin the responsibility on anyone when something goes wrong. Too often ministers blame civil servants for implementing policies poorly even while civil servants blame ministers for thinking up bad policies in the first place.

The fiasco of the poll tax in 1990 can also, some say, be viewed as a constitutional failure. Intended to restore accountability, and taxation powers, to local government, the poll tax was widely seen as just the opposite: an attempt by an overmighty government to jam an unpopular change down the throats of the populace. This provoked a mass protest of delayed or non-payment by millions of normally law-abiding citizens. Though legally enacted, the poll tax was widely viewed as illegitimate.

More participators, fewer spectators

All the changes now proposed by reform-ers—a written constitution, a bill of rights, devolved assemblies, proportional representation, an elected second chamber—are directed at a single goal: dispersing power through Britain's political system. Traditionalists are right to argue that Britain is not facing war, revolution or political collapse. But they are wrong to assume that it is only some wrenching crisis which justifies or makes possible constitutional change. Although few democratic nations have faced the kind of top-to-bottom changes now advocated by British reformers, many other countries (New Zealand is one example) have made significant constitutional changes without facing such a crisis.

Building a new British constitution will take years. Each addition or change will have to be debated and agreed upon. The eventual outcome will require more than the support of a single political party. And it may be that even these changes will not suffice; remember that many countries which already enjoy them are today angrily rebellious about the state of their politics.

The result, if this great effort does in the end succeed, will be a noisier, more rambunctious Britain. Getting new things done may then be more difficult than it has been in the past. But this does not defeat the case for reform. Indeed, it is the case for reform. The smooth exercise of silent power is the ideal of the autocrat, not the democrat.

Why Britain needs a bill of rights

Basic human and political rights in Britain enjoy no special legal protection, as they do in most other democratic countries. In our second article on constitutional reform, we argue that this should be changed

BRITAIN invented both the phrase "a bill of rights" and the concept of one. Yet today Britain is the only country in Western Europe which either has not incorporated the European Convention on Human Rights into its domestic laws or does not already have, like Ireland, a bill of rights which provides similar legally enforceable protections for the individual. Britain granted a bill of rights to Hong Kong in 1991 and the government has promised one for Northern Ireland as part of a new overall political settlement there. Opinion polls by MORI this year and in 1991 for the Joseph Rowntree Reform Trust found that 79% of respondents were in favour of a bill of rights for all of Britain. Labour and the Liberal Democrats now also back the idea.

Given such widespread public support, and Britain's anomalous position among democracies in not having a bill of rights, the argument for introducing one would seem to be an open-and-shut case. Yet it is not, and considerable opposition remains. John Major's government, like its Conserva-tive and Labour predecessors, is hostile to the idea, as are many—on both the right and the left—who see it as a threat to the sovereignty of Parliament (founded on the 1689 Bill of Rights, which enumerated the rights of Parliament, not those of individuals).

An effective bill of rights would, indeed, be an infringement of parliamentary sovereignty; but this would be its principal attraction, not an argument against it. Bills of rights are designed to protect fundamental rights from the actions of transient majorities in the legislature in the longer-term interests of the citizenry as a whole. In most countries, none of the rights thus protected is exempt from revision or abolition by the electorate. But, because they are deemed fundamental, revision is made far more difficult than changes to an ordinary law, through special procedures that require more than simple majorities.

Individual liberties enjoy no such protection in Britain. Governments can eliminate a right, no matter how basic or how long-standing, in a single vote in the House of Commons and have, on some occasions, used their extraordinary powers to do just that.

Traditionalists argue that, in practice, this matters not at all. British liberties, they say, have been better protected by Parliament and the common law built up over centuries by the courts than they would have been by any abstract listing of rights. They often accompany this argument with grandiose proclamations about Britain being a beacon of liberty in a turbulent and uncertain world.

Sadly, this is no longer true, if it ever was. One revealing test is Britain's record before the European Court of Human Rights in Strasbourg. The court has decided 37 cases against the United Kingdom, giving it one of the worst records of any of the 35 signatories to the European Convention. This means that actions in a wide range of areas which British courts, Parliament and successive governments had accepted as perfectly proper were rejected by the Strasbourg court as violations of basic rights.

This is a serious indictment of the state of civil liberties in Britain. The court is not staffed with starry-eyed idealists. In fact, the court's judges have tried to interpret the convention as narrowly as possible to avoid overruling elected governments. Nevertheless even this cautious court has found against the British government on issues that include telephone tapping, birching, discriminatory immigration rules, homosexuality, the law of contempt of court, the rights of prisoners and those accused of a crime, the rights of the mentally ill, press freedom, and sexual equality, among other issues—culminating in the celebrated ruling in September that the killing of three IRA terrorists on Gibraltar was unlawful. Often such findings have forced a revision of British laws.

Britain may not be about to lapse into despotism or tyranny, but that is not the immediate danger facing any established democracy. What British governments have repeatedly failed to do is to meet minimal standards of conduct when it comes to respecting the rights of individuals. It might be argued that the Strasbourg court is sufficient redress against such wrongs. But it is slow and costly. A British bill of rights would make redress easier and cheaper, and thus restore at least some popular respect for Britain's own system of justice.

A stronger objection to a bill of rights is that it is, in many ways, anti-democratic because it transfers power from elected representatives to unelected judges. It does do this, but such a transfer of power is not necessarily anti-democratic. Democracy itself, in all its myriad forms, derives its legitimacy from the consent of the governed, and that consent can only be given freely when certain basic rights—for example, freedom of speech, assembly and the press or the protection from arbitrary arrest—are respected.

British citizens have never had any positive, enforceable legal rights and still do not, except those awarded to them by specific statutes. Instead, liberty in Britain has been essentially negative: citizens have been traditionally free to do anything not specifically prohibited by law.

This may have seemed a reasonable proposition in the 19th century, when governments were tiny and there were far fewer laws. But since then the trickle of legislation has become a flood. The growth of the modern state in Britain, as elsewhere, has meant that government now intrudes into every nook and cranny of life, regulating everything from medical care to buildings to the terms on which employees can be hired or sacked. The purely private sphere has diminished greatly.

Trampling liberty for convenience

Today the view of liberty as merely the residue of activity not directly controlled or prohibited by governments is too weak a concept to protect individuals from the gradual erosion of rights and freedoms. Such rights are rarely assaulted directly by governments (though the British government's restrictions last year of an accused person's right to silence is one sorry example). Basic liberties are more commonly brushed aside or trampled by governments in a hurry to solve specific problems, or merely to do what is politically convenient.

When people complain (as thousands have, in the past few years) about over-zealous bureaucrats, especially those implementing European laws, their complaints often reflect this imbalance between official power and the individual's recourse against it. Meddling social workers, bullying police officers, autocratic planning officials and the like, even when they seem to act unreasonably, are often acting within the law, which frequently gives them wide discretion. Few people think "the government" is hostile to their liberties. And yet, at some time or other, almost everyone thinks "those little dictators" at the town hall, the Ministry of Agriculture or in Brussels commit outrages against both common sense and liberties—though few realise that such complaints make one of the strongest arguments for a bill of rights.

This is why even countries that, like Britain, have indisputably democratic governments have chosen belatedly to introduce a bill of rights. Canada enacted a new one in 1982. New Zealand adopted one in 1990.

It is undeniable that a bill of rights can hand a great deal of power to judges. Bills of rights, by their very nature, have to be written in broad terms. This leaves enormous scope for judicial interpretation. Not everyone concerned to enhance civil liberties in Britain is happy with that prospect.

One group of critics argues that Britain's judiciary—in the case of England and Wales selected by the Lord Chancellor, a member of the cabinet, from a small circle of top lawyers—has proven too biased towards the interests of governments, and too illiberal, to protect the rights of all citizens. Court rulings upholding police restrictions on the right of movement during the 1984-85 miners' strike; backing the broadcasting ban on Sinn Fein, the political wing of the IRA; and failing to lift the injunction against newspaper publication of the book "Spycatcher", have left a bitter taste for many.

Judges, argue such critics, may not always be better guarantors of rights than a democratically elected legislature. They point to the history of the American Supreme Court which, at various times, denied that freed slaves could become citizens and ruled that racial segregation was legal. And a bill of rights is no panacea against rights violations. Today Japan has an extensive bill of rights, which its citizens and courts largely ignore.

And yet, in the case of Britain, this seems unduly pessimistic. British judges have been constrained by the fact that they have no written constitution, or bill of rights, to guide them. In their absence, they have also had no explicit authority to strike down a law or action of government solely because it breached a basic human right. Indeed, the tradition has been that they should not do so. Given such a power, British judges would undoubtedly use it.

Handing more power over to judges would not necessarily guarantee more protections for the individual against the encroachments of government. A conservative judiciary might restrict freedoms, which is one reason why a more open selection procedure for British judges would be desirable if a bill of rights were established. And yet it seems likelier that even the current crop of judges would, like most of their modern counterparts abroad, produce a more liberal, rather than a more illiberal, interpretation of the law once given the chance to do so. Even within their current confines—deciding whether the government or public bodies have acted within the existing law—British judges have over the past 30 years created, for the first time, a useful body of administrative law to hold the exercise of government power in check.

Other critics, most within Westminster or Whitehall, argue just the opposite: that British judges would be all too keen to use their new powers. Once empowered to knock down laws, they say, judges cannot restrain themselves from acting as unelected legislators. They point, once again, to America's Supreme Court, which has created an immense body of case law far exceeding anything envisaged by the authors of the American constitution.

Even some advocates of a British bill of rights feel uncomfortable with the degree of power wielded by America's Supreme Court. Liberty, Britain's leading civil-liberties lobby group, favours an approach similar to that of Canada, which allows Canada's national parliament or provincial assemblies to bypass the courts by enacting laws that explicitly state that they are overriding the country's Charter of Rights.

In fact, any British bill of rights is likely to contain such a formal opt-out because, without a completely new written constitution defining the roles of Parliament and the courts, judges will have no independent legal authority to strike down acts of Parliament in any case. Bills seeking to incorporate the European Convention on Human Rights into British law recognise this fact by saying that judges will interpret the convention as prevailing over any act of Parliament—as they do now with European Union law—unless the act explicitly states that it intends to override the convention. The latest such bill, sponsored by Lord Lester, a Liberal Democrat peer, has passed the Lords, but is likely to be killed by the government in the Commons.

Such opt-outs should assuage fears that unrestrained judges would frustrate the concerted will of a large majority of the population. In practice, though, opt-outs are unlikely to be used very often. Passing a law which openly declares that it breaches the bill of rights is likely to prove unpalatable for most governments. The Canadian parliament has never passed a law overriding Canada's Charter of Rights, though two provincial assemblies have passed three such laws, one of which was knocked down by Canada's Supreme Court as too sweeping.

What's in, what's out?

Which specific rights should a bill of rights contain? There is, predictably, much debate on this subject even among those who favour the general idea. A minimum seems to be the rights enumerated in the European Convention, which the British government, after all, agreed to respect as long ago as 1951, when it ratified the document.

Incorporating the convention into British law, which Labour and the Liberal Democrats have promised to do, would be a big step. Though British citizens have had the right to pursue their cases under the convention at Strasbourg since 1966, doing so costs thousands of pounds in lawyers' fees, and cases are not heard for years. For most citizens it provides no realistic remedy against government abuse.

Incorporation would, in effect, give British citizens a bill of rights for the first time whose protections could be claimed in British courts. Judges might, of course, ignore its provisions, but this is unlikely. The Law Lords, Britain's most senior judges, united behind Lord Lester's bill for incorporating the convention into British law. In fact, incorporation could revolutionise British jurisprudence, not only empowering the Law Lords to overturn law that breach basic rights—unless they contain explicit provisions overriding the convention—but also obliging judges and juries to keep basic civil rights in mind when trying cases in the lower courts, and providing further grounds for appeal when they are breached.

But many supporters of a bill of rights want to go further. For one thing, the convention itself contains broad exceptions (not contained in the brief summary in our box). Some of these are sensible. Rights clash, and any list of rights will have to be interpreted by judges in the light of national security or threats to society. Even the cherished freedom of speech provision in America's bill of rights has not been interpreted as banning all obscenity laws or the prosecu-

tion of someone who stands up in a crowded cinema and shouts "fire".

But the repetition throughout the convention of phrases such as "subject only to such limitations as are prescribed by law and are necessary in a democratic society in the interests of public safety", sometimes followed by lists of more specific restrictions, seems to invite judges to focus on the exceptions, rather than the rights to be protected, and could be used to nullify the entire convention. Pruning the convention of such exceptions after incorporating it into British law would probably improve it.

Far more controversial is the idea of adding social and economic rights—such as a right to a job, education, medical care, welfare or protection of the environment—to the mostly civil and political rights contained in the convention. Labour wants, eventually, to do something like this, as do many others who are keen on the idea of a bill of rights. Such a move might be popular. Rowntree's most recent poll found that the favourite item suggested for a British bill of rights was the "right to hospital treatment on the National Health Service within a reasonable time", which was backed by 88% of those asked, giving it even more support than the right to a fair trial before a jury, backed by 82%.

Besides mere popularity, there is also a respectable argument for considering the inclusion of economic and social rights. It is difficult to enjoy your political and civil rights, or participate in a democracy, if you cannot feed or clothe yourself, obtain an education, or avoid dying from disease. And the line dividing the two types of rights can be fuzzy. For example, the right to equality, contained in both the 14th amendment to the American constitution and most other country's bills of rights, has been interpreted by judges in Europe as including equal pay for equal work for women, but having nothing to do with equal pay by American judges.

Moreover, rights can, over time, seem to shift between the two categories. When the right to bear arms was inserted into America's bill of rights in 1791, with the memories of the revolution against Britain still fresh, it seemed necessary for the maintenance of a free society, and so qualified as a political right. Today it seems more of a threat to such a society, and an obstacle to sensible gun control. No country drawing up a bill of rights today would consider such a provision a basic political right.

Nevertheless, some attempt to draw a line between the two categories of rights

should be made, and America's experience with the right to bear arms argues for confining a bill of rights to a minimal list of the political and civil rights essential to the functioning of a liberal democracy, such as those contained in the European Convention. Interpreting even these basic rights is problematic enough, and they can often clash, as they seem to do in the case of abortion (the right to life against the right to privacy) creating "hard" cases which will always leave some dissatisfied.

Remedies to economic and social deprivation should be sought elsewhere, through either political action or the courts using normal laws. Few people in Britain are so deprived of necessities that they cannot vote or participate, if they wish, in the democratic process. In a developed country like Britain, trying to turn access to economic resources into a matter of fundamental rights, giving them a higher status than the ordinary law, seems doomed. Such decisions usually have to be made as the result of a bargaining process between groups. Generally, this should be the stuff of everyday politics, not a subject for the courts.

In fact, the likeliest result of making a bill of rights too extensive, and including economic obligations on governments which courts cannot enforce, would be to undermine the entire concept of the bill of rights, and so weaken obstacles to breaches of the basic rights which it was originally designed to protect.

It is impossible to avoid the conclusion that any bill of rights, even if it contains only a minimal list of basic rights, will force Britain's judges to wade into the political arena. But the different objections to this that are hurled from both ends of the political spectrum—that judges are liable to usurp the role of legislators or to be too swayed by public opinion—miss the point, which is to place restraints in the path of governments. Interpreting how rights should be applied in the complex circumstances of a modern state, where the basic rights of different groups can sometimes clash, is bound to be controversial and rarely clear-cut. Reasonable men are bound to differ on such interpretations. And judges would be truly strange characters if they shared none of the views held by most of their fellow citizens.

A bill of rights cannot elevate contentious, political issues to an abstract plane beyond the reach of the rest of society. What it can do is to nurture a culture of liberty in a society which already recognises its value, and to create a judiciary which sees the protection of liberty as one of its primary tasks.

What is Scotland's future?

Anthony King

Foreigners seldom know what to call the country. "England" will clearly not do. It excludes Scotland and denies the separate identity of Wales. "Great Britain" (first used following the 1707 Act of Union between England and Scotland) is better but excludes Northern Ireland. The proper name (since the Irish republic seceded in 1921) has been "the United Kingdom of Great Britain and Northern Ireland". But who wants to say that?

There is just a chance that the name may have to change again. The Scots have long been a nation. Some of them now want to form a state—and almost all favour a degree of domestic self-rule that could lead to statehood. The British Conservatives in 1996 will set their faces against any move that could have that result.

The reality of Scottish nationhood is not questioned. The Scots have their own national football side, their own national dress, their own banknotes, their own newspapers, their own national drink (more Scotch is consumed per head in Scotland than anywhere else) and even their own national dish (though there is no export market for haggis). Above all, the Scots are a nation because they think they are. Surveys invariably find that most Scots feel themselves to be Scottish first and British second.

Nor can the claim to statehood be dismissed as absurd. With a population of 5.1m, Scotland has more people than Finland, Norway or Ireland. It attracts substantial inward investment and has a per capita GDP not substantially lower than England's. Outside the United Kingdom but inside the EU, Scotland could undoubtedly go it alone.

But should it? The Scottish National Party (SNP) says yes. It points to Scotland's pre-1707 history of independence, to Scots' undoubted sense of national identity and to the fact that since 1970 Scotland has been governed for 19 out of 25 years by a predominantly English political party enjoying the support of fewer than 40% (and latterly fewer than 30%) of Scottish electors. "Independence in Europe" is the SNP's current slogan.

But all the British parties say no to statehood. They draw attention to nearly 300 years of intimate English-Scottish association, to the comradeship of the two world wars (Scottish regiments still figure largely in the British army) and to the fact that separation would diminish the international standing of both countries. Not least, they point, like Quebec's federalists, to the job losses and loss of central government subsidies that would inevitably follow independence. "Scotland free", they say, "would be Scotland poor".

At this point, however, the British parties part company. The Conservatives, nowadays little reliant on Scottish votes, oppose any form of home rule. They insist that a Scottish government and administration would only create an expensive additional layer of bureaucracy. They also maintain that home rule would lead to statehood and independence.

Labour and the Liberal Democrats disagree. They insist that the Scots, being a nation, have a right to home rule and also that, granted home rule, the Scots would be more, rather than less, likely to want to remain within the United Kingdom.

All sides have now staked out their positions. Most Scots want home rule but shy away from complete independence. They will back Labour and the Liberal Democrats (and in some cases, *pour encourager les autres,* the SNP). But the real battle in 1996 will be for English hearts and minds. In the run-up to the next election, can the Tories persuade enough Englishmen that Scottish devolution means Scottish independence (and that that would be a bad thing)?

After the Talking Stopped

An IRA bomb in London underscores the dangers of a peace initiative

Fred Barbash
Washington Post Foreign Service

LONDON

There was no game plan for Northern Ireland, no secret deal, no honest broker and no shuttle diplomacy. The peace process that began 18 months ago—amid deeply conflicting emotions of hope and doubt—was grounded fundamentally on a blind faith that as long as the parties could be kept talking, violence might cease.

As it turned out, there was merit to this simple approach. For longer than anyone had envisaged, this reed-thin technique seemed to work. But there was a danger in it as well, the obverse side: What would happen when the conversation stopped, which is effectively what happened a few weeks ago?

The answer came Feb. 9 when the Irish Republican Army bombed London's largest office and residential development, killing two people and injuring dozens. The blast also dealt a potentially lethal blow to attempts to resolve Northern Ireland's generation of "troubles." On his visit here in December, President Clinton had hailed the peace process as an example to the world.

How did this symbol of hope so suddenly become, once again, a symbol of horror?

While blame for the bomb rests squarely with the IRA, responsibility for the lack of progress in the talks belongs to politicians on all sides both here and in Northern Ireland. The talking stopped because they placed hurdles in its way; the music died because the tune became "conditions" rather than concessions.

And that happened, most likely, because between the IRA cease-fire declaration on Aug. 31, 1994, and now, political conditions have changed. For different reasons, officials crucial to the talks have grown politically weaker rather than stronger. They reacted by becoming more rather than less intransigent. By the end, they backed themselves into corners from which they were unwilling or unable to escape.

Ingredients that have sustained other negotiations in other conflicts were absent: There was no outside third-party broker, who by virtue of trust or fear could "knock heads together." There was no equivalent of Serbian President Slobodan Milosevic, who could step in for his own reasons and call the shots for one party or the other. While many observe the tragic conflict in Northern Ireland, it presents no threat to global or regional stability and attracts only intermittent interest from the rest of the world. There is no oil in Ireland—north or south.

The troubles of Northern Ireland are rooted deep in history. Britain controlled Ireland for some 300 years, suppressing Catholicism and Irish nationalism by force. After years of conflict, it withdrew from the predominantly Catholic southern 26 counties in the 1920s but retained control of the majority Protestant six counties in the north of the island, now known as Northern Ireland.

◼

THE PARTITION PRODUCED two opposing movements: Irish nationalism, or republicanism, which favors reunification with the republic to the south, and "unionism," or "loy-alism," which seeks to keep the region as part of the United Kingdom. The former is composed largely of Catholics, who regard themselves as the victims of British and Protestant oppression; the latter is made up primarily of Protestants.

Both communities harbor violent paramilitary organizations that have wreaked havoc in the province for the past 25 years with reprisal attacks. Both also maintain above-board political parties.

The peace process that began 18 months ago was initiated largely by the British and Irish governments, with considerable help from John Hume, leader of Northern Ireland's nationalist Social Democratic and Labor Party, and Gerry Adams, president of Sinn Fein, the legal political wing of the IRA. Adams in particular managed to persuade the IRA to declare the cease-fire after convincing it that the nationalist movement had gotten nowhere using violence and other means might prove more productive.

Initially, there appeared to be some flexibility on all sides. Negotiating positions seemed to be just that—positions subject to negotiation.

British Prime Minister John Major put aside early demands that the IRA and Sinn Fein declare the cease-fire permanent as a precondition to the start of formal, high-level contacts between the British government and Sinn Fein. Major also put his name to a framework document with the government of Ireland that proposed some ideas once considered unthinkable in London, such as allowing the government in Dublin to have a formal, if limited, voice in the governance of Northern Ireland.

Unionist parties, while loathing that notion, seemed willing to talk about the document, which also contained a promise that the future of Northern Ireland would be determined by the consent of the majority. Sinn Fein, while opposing that idea, also appeared ready to proceed.

The process started to get bogged down about seven months ago, with Major's demand that before formal talks could start, the IRA had to begin decommissioning its arsenal of weapons and explosives. Sinn Fein refused, saying it had proved its commitment to the peace process and that decommissioning should be a subject for talks, not a precondition. Decommissioning, it said, was "surrender."

Months passed with no change on either side. The political situation did change, however. Major's Conservative Party saw its parliamentary majority dwindle to the point where it became more and more dependent on the support of the nine Northern Ireland unionists to keep control of Parliament.

The traditional leaders of Ulster unionism confronted two challenges: competition from fringe Protestant organizations in Northern Ireland capturing increasing television exposure by adopting more conciliatory positions on the peace process; and the resignation of James Molyneaux

as longtime leader of the main unionist organization, the Ulster Unionist Party.

In his place, party members in September elected a more outspoken and younger member of Parliament, David Trimble, who ran on a platform urging less rather than more compromise in the peace process. The new leader also came forward with the party's own proposal to get the talks going: hold an election in Northern Ireland to let voters choose up sides.

No one budged, and talk of a crisis in the peace process replaced talk about the talks themselves. In November, Major and Irish Prime Minister John Bruton tried to restore momentum by appointing an international commission, headed by former U.S. Senate majority leader George Mitchell, to make recommendations on decommissioning so that negotiations on substantive political matters could begin independently of the weapons issue by the end of February.

Mitchell's panel recommended on Jan. 24 that Major drop his demand for weapons disposal as a precondition to talks, provided Sinn Fein and all other parties promised to use only peaceful means to advance their cause.

Major endorsed the report and

said he would indeed drop that demand, but he then substituted a different condition: the proposal for an election in Northern Ireland originally proposed by Trimble.

Officials in Dublin were stunned. The nationalists were bound to reject the election idea, they said, because of the outnumbered Catholics' past disappointments at the polls in Northern Ireland.

The Dublin-London relationship reached a new low. Predictably, both Sinn Fein and the moderate Social Democratic and Labor Party, which has always opposed violence, angrily rejected Major's condition.

Most analysts say that was the watershed moment, a signal the talking could go no further. Officials in Dublin and London were holding emergency cabinet meetings, trying to find a way to keep the peace process alive. Bruton went on television Feb. 11 to advance his proposal for an effort similar to the U.S.-brokered Bosnian peace talks near Dayton, Ohio, in which Northern Ireland's political leaders would lock themselves in a building until they agree on something.

Ulster unionist spokesmen immediately rejected the idea.

Security forces here and in Belfast and Dublin have prepared themselves for the possibility of more violence.

Outstripping Adenauer

Jonathan Carr

Jonathan Carr: freelance journalist and author living in Germany.

Undaunted by sceptics at home and abroad, Helmut Kohl aims to crown his career as German chancellor by giving Europe a decisive push in 1996 towards economic and political unity. A tall order—even for Europe's elder statesman or, as he ironically calls himself now that François Mitterrand of France has left office, "the last of the dinosaurs".

Mr Kohl has said time after time (often to jeers of disbelief) that his main ambition is to root a united Germany in a united Europe. After five years of economic and social upheaval, the two former German states are now growing steadily together, rather to their surprise. There is still far to go but with German unity rattling along Mr Kohl has turned his main attention to Europe.

To the vexed question whether the European Union (EU) should take on more members or seek closer integration ("widen or deepen" in Euro-speak), the chancellor has a simple—to his critics impractical—answer. It must do both. He reckons that if the Union pursues one course without the other it will face either growing unrest among the East European states already clamouring for entry, or the disintegration of much that it has already achieved, including the (still imperfect) single market.

Wouldn't a weaker Europe actually benefit Germany, letting it use its economic and political clout all the better to play a dominant role? Mr Kohl, who is strong on history, regards that idea as dangerous nonsense. But he cannot be

sure that his possible successors, whatever their current pro-Europe credentials, will seek to bind Germany into a united continent with the same zeal.

Hence Mr Kohl's ambitious timetable. He wants to see at least Poland, Hungary and the Czech Republic join the EU as soon as 2000, albeit with longish transitional periods to bring their economies up to scratch. By then he believes the EU will have overhauled its institutions and procedures and gone far to forge a common foreign and security policy. Last but not least, member states willing and able should have begun to implement the third stage of economic and monetary union (EMU), with a European central bank and a common currency.

Most of that presupposes a breakthrough in 1996 at "Maastricht-2", the follow-up inter-governmental conference on the Union's future. With Britain foot-dragging and Franco-German ties looking less cosy since the abrasive Jacques Chirac replaced Mr Mitterrand as president of France, Mr Kohl's chances look slim. Still, the undiminished French yearning to see the Deutsche Bundesbank and its currency Europeanised away is regarded as a trump card by the government in Bonn (though naturally not by the Bundesbankers in Frankfurt). In return for a go-ahead on EMU, Mr Kohl's men think political concessions can and must be wrung from the French, including greater powers for the European Parliament and more majority decision-taking by the council of ministers.

Quite apart from squaring his partners abroad, Mr Kohl has plenty of convincing to do at home. The *Länder*, the regional states, groan that over the years they have lost too much power to the federal government in Bonn. They will fight against losing even more now to Brussels. Moreover, since Maastricht-1 in

1991, Germans have grown still more fearful that their buoyant D-mark will be sacrificed to a shaky Euro-substitute. To help quell the angst, Mr Kohl will insist on strict adherence to the "convergence criteria" by all those states entering the EMU club. He was not always as tough on this issue.

Germany itself faces another severe economic and financial squeeze in 1996. Economic growth may slow to around only 2% (after inflation) and the jobless total will stay stubbornly high. So will state debt. The costs of unity are partly to blame but so is the Kohl government's pre-unity failure to deregulate more firmly, chop state subsidies and revamp the bloated social-security system. Now all these tasks need facing at once. With most taxes and deductions at record levels, Germans are in no mood for a floppy EMU which would also bring them higher inflation by the back door.

Mr Kohl is taking on the critics and doubters from a weak parliamentary base. The centre-right coalition between his Christian Democratic Union, the Bavarian Christian Social Union and the liberal Free Democrats has a majority of only ten in the Bundestag. The opposition Social Democrats hold sway in the Bundesrat, the second chamber where the *Länder* are represented and which can veto some legislation. Can the chancellor get his way all the same?

Probably. In 1996 Mr Kohl will become federal Germany's longest-serving government leader, surpassing the 14-year record set right back in 1949-63 by Konrad Adenauer. He has his own party wholly under his thumb and dominates what is admittedly one of post-war Germany's most forgettable cabinets. Policy tends to get made outside cabinet and parliament in that near-invisible process of wheeling and dealing in which Mr

Kohl has always excelled. For better or worse (and it is hardly what the constitution's founding fathers foresaw), Mr Kohl's all-pervasive role looks more like a French president's than a federal chancellor's.

In theory, Mr Kohl's coalition might be brought down by its jittery union partner, the Free Democrats. This, however, is unlikely. The liberals only scraped back to the Bundestag in the 1994 federal election; they have been all but obliterated in the provinces. The Social Democrats, again rent by leadership squabbles since losing the 1994 election, do not look like credible partners at the moment. The next federal election is not until 1998. There will be three *Länder* polls in 1996 (Baden-Württemberg, Rhineland-Palatinate and Schleswig-Holstein) but they will have little impact on the power balance in Bonn.

Nothing, it seems, will shift Mr Kohl unless he shifts himself. Before the 1994 election he said he would not run again in 1998, but he has conspicuously failed to repeat that pledge since. The best guess is that if he gets most of his way on European policy at Maastricht-2 he will feel he has achieved his main ambitions and will make way for a successor. If not, he will stay on to fight over Europe and probably to win another term.

A New Leader for the Social Democrats. A New Orientation as Well?

German Opposition Leader Ousted

SPD moves to left as Scharping loses ballot gamble to Lafontaine

Peter Norman

Peter Norman in Mannheim

Germany's opposition Social Democratic party took a sudden turn to the left yesterday when Mr Rudolf Scharping invited Mr Oskar Lafontaine to challenge him for the leadership—and lost.

The dramatic change at the top of Germany's largest party followed Mr Scharping's failure to inspire an SPD congress with a lacklustre keynote speech. It failed to quell delegates' frustration and anger at the quarrelling that had brought the party so low.

But his defeat sent a charge through the delegates, who were surprised to be presented with a choice. Mr Lafontaine, prime minister of the state of Saarland, had not emerged as a challenger for the post of party chairman until early yesterday.

On Wednesday, Mr Lafontaine had brought the congress cheering to its feet with an impassioned address that emphasised the party's duty to fight for peace abroad and against unemployment at home. His task now is to unite the party and defeat the centre-right coalition government of Chancellor Helmut Kohl at the next German election, scheduled for 1998.

The euphoria that greeted Mr Lafontaine's rhetorical tour de force was in marked contrast to the respectful applause Mr Scharping earned for his introspective address that focused on the recent problems of the party and his own inadequacies.

Speculation that Mr Lafontaine would stand for the post of chairman mounted through the night after his speech, as his supporters mobilised backing for him among delegates.

But it was 47-year-old Mr Scharping who set in motion the vote that has almost certainly dashed his hopes of standing as the SPD's candidate for the chancellorship in the next general election.

He told delegates the party needed "clarity on personnel issues" and he had asked Mr Lafontaine if he wanted to be a candidate for the chairmanship. Mr Lafontaine took up the challenge, turning what would have been a walk-over for Mr Scharping into a two-horse race.

Mr Lafontaine gained 321 votes against 190 for Mr Scharping. There were two abstentions among the 513 valid votes cast at the congress in Mannheim, in central Germany.

Immediately after the vote, Mr Lafontaine appealed for the support of all in the party. He received instant backing from Mr Scharping, who called on all party members to give their "unlimited" support to the new chairman.

Ironically, Mr Scharping was then given a rousing standing ovation as Mr Lafontaine expressed his appreciation for his work as party chairman. The congress then voted to make the defeated leader one of the SPD's five deputy chairpersons with the overwhelming support of 482 of 517 votes cast.

Mr Lafontaine later praised Mr Scharping's decision to let him stand as "a great human gesture and a signal for co-operation".

Mr Lafontaine is 52 and was the SPD's unsuccessful candidate for the chancellorship in 1990. He comes from the left of the party, but, yesterday, in a demonstration of his wish to unite the SPD, he called on delegates to vote Mr Gerhard Schröder, the right-of-centre prime minister of Lower Saxony, into the party's 45-strong managing board. However, Mr Schröder failed to win sufficient votes in the first round of polling.

●━━●━━●━━●━━●━━●━━●

Triumph of the Little Man

Germany's SPD will take a less predictable line on economic and monetary union under its new leader, says Quentin Peel

They always said Oskar Lafontaine was irrepressible, and now he has proved it. He has survived an assassination attempt, a devastating election defeat by Chancellor Helmut Kohl, a scandal over his pension rights, and media mockery over his "champagne socialism" lifestyle. Now the little man from the Saarland is back in charge of Germany's Social Democratic party.

His coup at the SPD congress in Mannheim this week was masterly, as his brilliant oratory won over a big majority of delegates to dump their dull leader, Mr Rudolf Scharping.

In doing so, he comprehensively outmanoeuvred the third man in the triumvirate which dominates the SPD, the nakedly ambitious Mr Gerhard Schröder, prime minister of Lower Saxony, who had made no secret of his desire to replace Mr Scharping.

The SPD has decided to live dangerously in opting once again for Mr Lafontaine, the impish, impulsive, vain and brilliant prime minister of the Saarland, the depressed former coal and steel area on the Franco-German border.

Mr Scharping represented the solid mainstream of the party, seeking to shift it back to the middle ground disciplining the wilder pacifists, environmentalists, and fundamentalists on its left wing. His leaden style and lack of inspiration, far from reassuring the conservative German electorate, simply alienated them.

Oskar, as they all call him, is the opposite. He is by far the best public speaker in the party, he thinks fast on his feet and he flirts with the ideas of the party fringes—while always keeping a very canny eye on the safe centre ground. Sometimes, he can be too clever by half and gets carried away with the intelligence of his own ideas. Often, he can be irreverent when he should be serious, but at least he is never predictable.

He was the man they say was favoured by Mr Willy Brandt, the father-figure of the SPD over the past three decades, who promoted ambitious young "grandchildren" to take over the leadership. Oskar got there first, ahead of Mr Scharping and Mr Schröder, when he was nominated as candidate for chancellor against Helmut Kohl in the unification election of 1990. But he blew it by being altogether too honest.

To this day, Mr Lafontaine cannot forgive or forget the circumstances of that defeat. He warned the people of Germany, east and west, that unification would be painful and costly. He insisted that they would have to pay higher taxes. And he sounded as if he was against the whole process of unification as a result.

Indeed, at one level, he probably was. He used to argue that German unification was irrelevant in the modern world. "It must remain our goal to overcome the nation state in a united Europe," he said then. "The

---

The Thoughts of Oskar Lafontaine

On German monetary union:

"If the D-Mark is introduced in [East Germany] too fast and without preparation, it will be unbelievably expensive for the ordinary man, and the [East German] economy will be destroyed."

(August 1990)

On European economic and monetary union:

"There should be no European currency unless it is absolutely certain that it will be just as stable as the German mark."

(October 1994)

On Emu and electioneering:

"We cannot simply ignore what three-quarters of the people of Germany are thinking. . . . Monetary union concerns me particularly because I had already warned that inner-German monetary union would lead to job losses, tax increases, and long-term transfer payments to the east.
"I want to make sure that monetary union is not carried out in the same way, without people being perfectly clear what it will mean to them."

(November 3, 1995)

---

transfer of national sovereignty to supranational institutions does not mean we will lose power, but that we will gain freedom."

Yet while those sentiments make him a passionate pro-European in the mainstream of the German political tradition, his doubts over the whole manner of German monetary union have made him a deep sceptic over European economic and monetary union (Emu). Although a large majority of the SPD remains in favour of Emu, the party's line will be much less predictable under the guidance of Mr Lafontaine.

In the last election campaign he called for the renegotiation of the Maastricht treaty, and on the eve of this week's party conference in Mannheim, he refused to rule out making Emu a major election issue at the next national polls, in 1998.

He was bitterly opposed to the manner of monetary union between east and west Germany because of the havoc he knew it would wreak with uncompetitive east German state industries. They simply collapsed in

the face of a flood of western imports, and the demands for rapidly rising D-Mark wages from their workers.

But Chancellor Kohl was much shrewder. He exploited the wave of national emotion over unification, and instinctively knew that the immediate effects of monetary union would be popular: east Germans went on a spending spree with their D-Marks, buying up western cars and consumer goods, little dreaming that their own inefficient factories would pay the price.

As he campaigned through the liberated zones of the GDR, Mr Lafontaine was never able to disguise his obviously greater empathy with his French neighbours in the Saarland than with the stolid ex-communist citizens of the east. And he failed to gain much sympathy from a knife attack six months before the election, speaking out from his hospital bed against the whole process of monetary union.

In 1990 he won a majority of the youth vote. But he failed to win the east, and he failed to win the grey

vote, and they are much more reliable voters in the end.

Mr Lafontaine retired to his fortress in the Saarland to lick his wounds, and at one stage his political career looked at an end. He was accused of self-enrichment by claiming a full state pension as the former mayor of Saarbrücken, on top of his generous salary as a state premier. But he survived a vote of no confidence in his local parliament, shrugging off the accusations as a "dirty smear campaign".

He did the same when Spiegel magazine portrayed him on its front cover as a would-be Louis XIV, living a luxury lifestyle in his humble homeland, and lavishing state funds on smart offices in Paris. Somehow, the dirt failed to stick.

In the end, he has proved that his party cannot do without him. It is far too early to predict if the change of leadership will be successful in unseating the seemingly immovable Chancellor Kohl and his Christian Democrats at the 1998 elections. But it will make political life in Germany far more exciting over the next three years.

●━●━●━●━●

Lesson of a 'Truly Shocking' Meeting in Bonn

Judy Dempsey reports on the fears raised by the talks between the leaders of the SPD and the former communist PDS

Hours after Mr Oskar Lafontaine, leader of Germany's opposition Social Democratic party (SPD), met Mr Gregor Gysi, parliamentary head of the Party of Democratic Socialism (PDS) in Bonn on Tuesday evening, Chancellor Helmut Kohl's governing coalition went on the offensive.

Mr Peter Hintze, general secretary of Mr Kohl's Christian Democratic Union (CDU), said the PDS, suc-

cessors to east Germany's former communists, wanted to ennoble itself with democratic credentials with help from the SPD.

Mr Edmund Stoiber, the conservative Christian Social Union premier of Bavaria, described the meeting as "truly shocking".

The response illustrates the governing coalition's fear that the SPD, under its new leader, may be able to

forge a left-wing majority with the Greens and backed by the PDS after the 1998 election. It also signals the dangers the SPD would face if it adopted this course.

"The SPD could lose some support from the centre if it moves to the left to win over the PDS," said Mr Gert-Joachim Glässner, professor of political science at Berlin's Humboldt University.

But Mr Andre Brié, the PDS's chief strategist, said the SPD had to do something about the PDS if it wanted to gain any political presence in eastern Germany.

The PDS poses a dilemma for the other parties because of its power base in eastern Germany. There, it is the third largest party, enjoying about 20 per cent support, compared with the SPD's 25 per cent and the CDU's 38 per cent.

Because the left vote is split in eastern Germany, the CDU is able to govern in four of the six states. Three of those states, Mecklenburg-Vorpommern, Thuringia and Berlin, are made up of so-called grand (but fragile) coalitions, with the SPD playing junior partner to the CDU. It is only in Brandenburg where the SPD enjoys an absolute majority.

The one state which has proved a kind of litmus test for the SPD, and the PDS, is Saxony-Anhalt. Since June of last year a minority government of the SPD and Greens has depended on the support of the PDS, the price the SPD paid for preventing the CDU, the largest party, from being returned to power.

Since then, the PDS has continued to make ground.

In the federal elections last year it increased its seats in the Bundestag, the parliamentary lower house, by 14 to 30. In the Berlin city elections this October it won 14 per cent of the overall vote—ahead of the Greens—and 36 per cent in the eastern part of the city.

With the support of the PDS, the SPD and the Greens could form the next Berlin government.

But Mr Brie believes the SPD is not yet ready to make such an ideological leap because of the past, and fear of losing the centre ground.

These are the fears which haunt the SPD. Some of its members, most notably Mr Wolfgang Thierse, a deputy leader of the party and an east German, have bitter memories of how the PDS's communist predecessors forced the merger of the Social Democrats with the communists after 1949.

Another concern of the SPD is the democratic credentials of the PDS. Although Mr Gysi, and Ms Petra Pau, the 32-year-old head of the PDS in Berlin, insist the PDS is a modern socialist party, it is in fact an ideological hybrid. More than 90 per cent of its 125,000 membership are former Communist party members. Some 60 per cent are aged 60 and over. As such, it is a home to the elderly and disciplined cadres who are crucial for the grassroots of the party.

But increasingly, because the SPD is weak and as yet has no clear political strategy in eastern Germany, the PDS has attracted two new strands of voters: the youth and a section of east Germany's new entrepreneurs.

More than 35 per cent of those aged between 18 and 25 voted for the PDS in the Berlin elections. That age group now makes up 10 per cent, and rising, of the membership. Many self-employed and members of professions, including academics, teachers, managers and civil servants, also vote for the PDS in eastern Germany.

"The west German politicians are mistaken if they think the PDS is a protest party or a party of the losers of German unification," said Mr Glässner. "It is getting a stable membership which wants a left-wing party. Much will depend on how the SPD organises itself in the east or works with the PDS," he added.

The PDS has attracted such a strong and stable following for several reasons. Since the SPD is weak in the region and federally, this has allowed the PDS to retain the left vote. Also, Ms Pau believes that the more the CDU depicts the PDS as a renegade party of communists and the more the CDU tells the east Germans the past 40 years have been worthless, the more voters will support the PDS out of a feeling of "east German" solidarity.

Man Who Put Cheer Back in German Greens

Joschka Fischer's mainstream strategy has damaged the Social Democrats, writes Michael Lindemann.

Just days after elections for the Berlin city parliament, Mr Joschka Fischer, Germany's most talked about Green politician, must be asking whether his revamped Green party may have been too successful. The Greens won 13.2 per cent of the votes cast, up from 9.2 per cent in 1990 and the second biggest gains after the Party of Democratic Socialism, the former east German Communist party.

More important, the party emerged as one of the few that is about equally represented in both west and east Berlin.

In the process, however, the Greens have in part contributed to the collapse of the Social Democrats—from whom they are estimated to have won 35,000 voters. The SPD is now so weak in Berlin that it is unlikely to opt for a so-called red-green coalition along the lines of those that govern several of Germany's states.

In Berlin the Greens appear to have benefited from an array of urban issues, ranging from environmental problems to kindergarten places, which they have proved adept at tackling. But the result is also believed to reflect the influence of the former Frankfurt taxi driver who now runs the Greens and is doing all he can to make it ready for government—not just in Berlin but also, he

hopes, in Bonn after the next federal elections in 1998.

While he claims to be as radical as ever, Mr Fischer is also trying to teach his fellow party members a little pragmatism.

Just a few years ago he was demanding an overhaul of the tax system to take account of environmental factors, regardless of cost. Mr Fischer now accepts that this can only be achieved if it can be funded from savings elsewhere in the budget.

Talking to his voters at home in Frankfurt has convinced him, he says, that the German taxpayer will not accept any more charges after the costs resulting from German unification. "They have reached the absolute limit of what they will accept," he says. The message seems to be getting across and not just in the big cities. A recent opinion poll gave the Greens 12.2 per cent of the national vote, much of it at the expense of the SPD and the ailing Free Democratic party.

The Greens are also a younger party than the SPD and not heavily dependent on unionised, working class voters, a shrinking political species.

Meanwhile, the Green leader is turning his mind to the future of the European Union, which is to be dis-

cussed at the intergovernmental conference next year.

Germany's Social Democrats (SPD) are continuing to lose ground to the Greens in western Germany and to the Party of Democratic Socialism (PDS), successor to the former Communist party, in east Germany, according to an opinion poll published yesterday by the Allensbach institute, writes **Judy Dempsey in Bonn.**

In west Germany, where the Christian Democrats (CDU) remain the largest party, the SPD's share of the vote has slipped from 36.4 per cent to 30.1 per cent. Support for the Greens has surged from 7.3 to 13 per cent. In east Germany, support for the SPD has fallen from 31.5 to 22.4 per cent, while the Greens' vote is 9.4 per cent against 4.3 per cent.

He is convinced that in the 21st century European countries will have to work more closely with one another to compete with the Americas and Asia.

That means, Mr Fischer says, that there has to be monetary union and for this to be workable it must be accompanied by a political union.

He also wants to see a European constitution that could in some way bring together the divergent views represented by the Union's 15 member states.

Mr Fischer's solution is to maintain national parliaments largely as they are, but to create a "first chamber" made up of the leaders of the national parliaments across the EU. That would be supplemented by an executive council of ministers based on the Swiss model, he says.

"It wouldn't then be a European union the way one sometimes imagines it," he said. "But things somehow have to move in that direction because I don't think Europe has a future as an economic community [only]."

The fact that Mr Fischer is ruminating about the future of Europe is a measure of how far he has come.

But before he or his party can have any real say about the future of the continent they will need to retain their attractiveness to the electorate, keep their distance from the Bonn

political establishment and hope that the SPD can keep up with them. While the SPD surveys the ruins, Mr Fischer is doing what he can to ready his party for government. In the middle of August he sprang a special report on party members, urging them to drop a full-blooded commitment to pacifism, another central tenet of party policy.

The fall of the safe areas in Bosnia demanded, Mr Fischer argued, that the Greens should be readier to condone the use of force in cases where that might save lives.

EASTERN GERMANY

The eagle's embrace

BERLIN

In the five years after unification, the campaign to make East Germany much like the West has made remarkable progress. That has brought curses as well as blessings

A LITTLE while after beginning its journey, the train from Halle to Naumburg stops at a decrepit shack. Starting again, it passes through an eerie landscape of smokestacks and industrial tubing; after travelling through three kilometres of this monumental plumbing, it stops again: another shack. This is Leuna Werke, one part of the smoggy trinity that once made up most of East Germany's chemical industry.

The sight and smell of the monstrous factory will appal any western Germans on the train; they are used to factories tamed and prettified. The impact is like the shock of seeing a long-absent sibling sick and unrecognisable beneath a skein of medical gadgetry—unwholesome gadgetry for which you are paying the bill.

Caring for the sick has been a national preoccupation since eastern Germany's

16m citizens joined the federal republic on October 3rd 1990. By many measures, it has been done remarkably well. Eastern Germans now consume two-thirds as much as their western brothers per head, far more than the citizens of other post-communist countries. By 2000 Germany's new *Länder* in the east will have an infrastructure nearly as good as the west's. Capital stock per employable head will, in telecoms, be 96% of western levels, predicts DIW, a Berlin-based think-tank; in roads, energy and water the level will be 94%.

The cost to western Germany has been immense, dwarfing the Marshall Plan aid for that territory's own earlier reconstruction. This year's expected net transfer of DM155 billion ($108 billion) will be equivalent to about 40% of eastern Germany's GDP; Marshall Plan aid, by contrast, averaged less than 2% of West Germany's annual output in the late 1940s. Eastward transfers from western Germany since 1991 have totalled some DM750 billion. Since the new *Länder* produce just 60% of what they consume and invest, those transfers will persist. But Germany has absorbed this enormous blow to its finances with its currency stronger than ever, its budget deficit headed lower and its merchandise trade surplus intact; by almost any standards, that is a spectacular achievement.

Germans would not be Germans if at this point they repaired to trattorias to uncork self-congratulatory bottles of chianti. On both sides of the wall that was they dwell gloomily on the "wall in the mind" that still is. *Die Zeit*, a weekly newspaper, calls its series on unification "United, but not together". Gregor Gysi, a leader of the Party of Democratic Socialism (PDS), which inherited the membership if not

the ideology of East Germany's communist party, says that while he may see a few redeeming features in unification, most west Germans ("Wessis") do not.

Mr Gysi has a point. High taxes, topped up by a 7.5% "solidarity surcharge" on income tax, stir resentment. Liberal-minded western Germans seem almost embarrassed by their eastern brothers ("Ossis"), fearing that their benighted ways will somehow taint Germany as a whole. One young journalist likens unification to "sharing a bathroom with a stranger".

From the other side, western Germans are seen as the people who took over institutions, destroyed industries and jobs through swift privatisation, stole markets from local producers of beer and soap powder, reclaimed property they had not seen in decades and, in a few cases, plundered public coffers. They joke bitterly that the difference between *Wessis* and Russians is that they could get rid of the Russians.

The dashed expectation that Germany would knit itself together quickly and seamlessly is itself characteristically German. Lombards do not brood about Sicily's failure to catch up with northern Italy after more than a century of political unity—rather, some of them look for ways of getting rid of it. But in Germany "solidarity" is an obsession. The constitution itself calls for "unity of living standards in the federal territory". In four decades the pursuit of solidarity has not eliminated economic differences among regions, but it has smoothed them out, and it has also given Germany a relatively even distribution of income among classes.

This solidarity is the means to a yet more precious end: "security" (*Sicherheit*), Germany's national goal. Where differences in outlook or living standards are stark, security can be threatened. Unification posed such a threat. West Germany's answer was to remake the new *Länder* in its own image as rapidly as possible. Eastern Germany's half decade of achievement and failure flows from that high-handed generosity.

East German unemployment rate, August 1995, %

9.6	Male
18.6	Female

Source: National statistics

MECKLENBURG WEST POMERANIA
10.8
19.8

BRANDENBURG
9.0
18.2

EAST BERLIN
10.7
12.9

SAXONY-ANHALT
11.3
20.2

THURINGIA
8.9
18.8

SAXONY
8.3
18.9

Former boundary between East and West Germany

1. PLURALIST DEMOCRACIES: Germany

The shock of the new

It could have been different. Some intellectuals, mainly on the left, pleaded for a more-deliberate unification based on rethinking the constitution. They called for a third way between capitalism and communism. Eastern Germans roundly rejected that idea in their first free elections in 1990. The course they chose instead brought to the new *Länder* all the apparatus of the federal republic; not just the west's constitution, but also its laws, bureaucracy, teaching methods, banks and countless other institutions.

In that package there were many blessings, as any East European trying to write laws and build institutions from scratch will tell you. But their effect was two-edged. The principle of *Gleichbehandlung*—equal treatment of citizens petitioning the state, one underpinning of solidarity—required the wholesale import of the west's bureaucratic procedures, and of bureaucrats who knew how to manipulate them. It felt like colonisation. The feeling was exacerbated when *Wessis* snuffed out *Ossi* practices that they might have copied—such as starting foreign-language lessons early in school.

Solidarity's most urgent and most costly demand, though, was for a surge in incomes—a demand that destroyed the means for producing them. The conversion of Ostmarks to D-marks at a rate of one for one for wages and most savings, when their purchasing power was a fraction of the D-mark's, boosted eastern German wages and forestalled massive westward migration. At the same time it destroyed what little value remained in eastern factories.

The contrast with West Germany's postwar economic miracle could not be greater. The West Germans brought forth their *Wirtschaftswunder* against a background of low wages and expectations. East Germans expected to catch up almost immediately. West Germans were sheltered by an undervalued currency and a local market not yet fully integrated into the world economy; East Germans had to adjust to one of the world's strongest currencies and full-blooded international competition.

Output plunged. Employment dropped from 9.8m in 1990 to a low of 6.2m in 1993. The current unemployment rate of 13.9% is six points above western Germany's. If workers in subsidised training schemes and early-retirement programmes were counted as unemployed, the rate would be close to 25%. Women of working age, four-fifths of whom had jobs in East Germany, suffered disproportionately. Their unemployment rate of 18.6% is double that for men.

During the radical and painful surgery—which included more than 15,000 privatisations—money was pumped in to shore up incomes and spur investment, creating a boom of sorts. GDP in the new states jumped 9.2% in real terms last year, making this Europe's fastest growing region. A re-

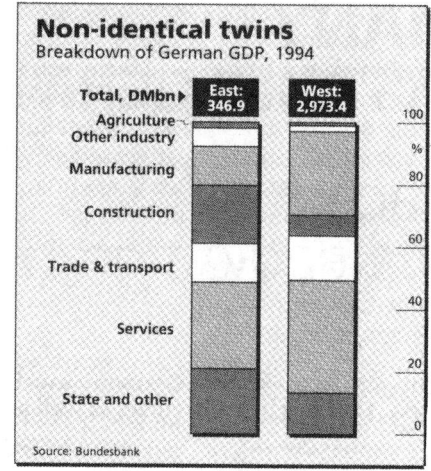

Non-identical twins
Breakdown of German GDP, 1994

Total, DMbn ▶ East: 346.9 — West: 2,973.4
- Agriculture
- Other industry
- Manufacturing
- Construction
- Trade & transport
- Services
- State and other

Source: Bundesbank

peat performance is expected in 1995. But the growth is lop-sided.

Goods and services—including government services—that have to be produced close to their consumers are thriving. Brands forced off the shelves by carpet-bagging western retailers are fighting their way back. *Ossis* are now smoking the f6 brand of cigarettes and drinking Club cola from choice rather than necessity. Local food producers have boosted their share of the home market from 30% in 1991 to 40% now.

The problem is a dearth of exports, and so of manufacturing jobs. Eastern Germany sold a scant DM30 billion of goods and services to western Germany last year, according to an estimate by three economic institutes. Its share of total German exports is just one-tenth its share of the population. That performance is bound to improve with investment; it started to rise last year. But there is a long way to go. Last year just 3% of manufacturers' output consisted of easily tradable goods.

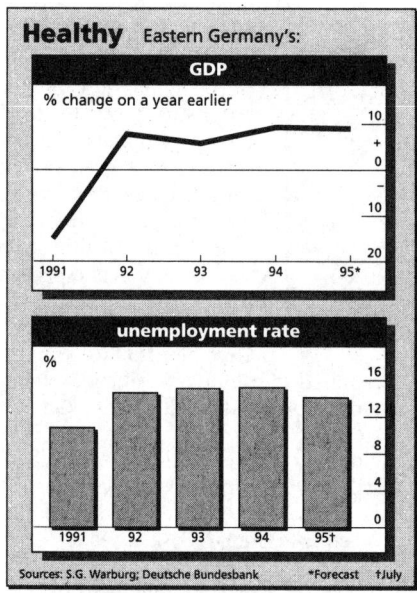

Healthy Eastern Germany's:

GDP
% change on a year earlier
1991 92 93 94 95*

unemployment rate
%
1991 92 93 94 95†

Sources: S.G. Warburg; Deutsche Bundesbank *Forecast †July

Germany's bear-hug made life especially difficult for manufacturers. Productivity has soared since 1990, thanks largely to massive redundancies, but it was still just half of western Germany's last year, while unit labour costs were 30% higher. The break-up of East Germany's conglomerates destroyed supplier networks, leaving a shoal of small firms either tightly bound to western owners or floundering around without a clear idea of what to do and gasping for capital. Less than half the east's firms are profitable.

Hoping to heal

It is broke; it does need fixing. Attempts to do so are going on all over the place. Where once the dreary *Kombinate* held sway there are now state-of-the-art transplanted factories. Where communism left industrial monocultures, state governments are nurturing networks of related industries. These are ambitious, expensive plans.

Thuringia wants to be eastern Germany's high-tech mecca. Jena, its third-biggest city, has a mix of universities and small technology-oriented firms that it hopes are reminiscent of what you might find in Palo Alto. The city's economy is dominated by Jenoptik, a successor to the giant Carl Zeiss glass and optical conglomerate which once employed a third of its people. Jenoptik is now owned by the state of Thuringia, which uses it as a tool of industrial policy. The company has stakes in some two dozen local firms. Its builders have supplied the firms with modern working quarters; its foreign subsidiaries provide missing supply and marketing networks; its profits from commercial-property projects, which dominate Jena's centre, cover the firms' losses.

Every self-proclaimed "science city" indulges in hype. Jena is no exception. Ulrich Hilpert, a professor at Jena's Friedrich Schiller University, surveyed 200 "research-oriented" Thuringian firms and found that a quarter did no in-house research and development work. Furthermore, they tended to prefer isolation to collaboration. But Mr Hilpert is probably over-harsh. Thuringia in general, and Jena in particular, have lost fewer jobs than most regions, at least partly due to their concentration of technological know-how.

The neighbouring state of Saxony-Anhalt has nothing similar to boast about. It is home to the infamous chemical triangle, the machine-tool industry and the copper mines at Mansfeld, all among eastern Germany's hardest-hit industries. It is pouring public money into the rescue of the chemical industry. One corner of the triangle, called Buna, is to be transformed by America's Dow Chemical into a modern producer of plastics and basic chemicals. The price of this transformation is state aid of up to DM10 billion to cover the cost of environmental cleaning as well as new investment. Since Dow plans to keep only 3,000 of the

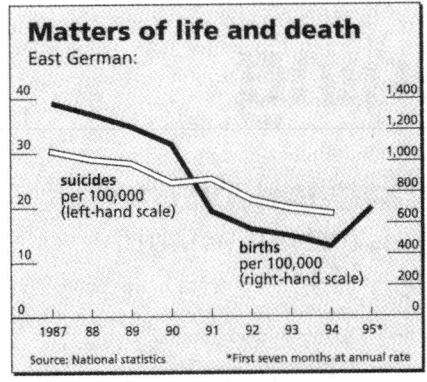

Matters of life and death

East German:

suicides per 100,000 (left-hand scale)

births per 100,000 (right-hand scale)

Source: National statistics   *First seven months at annual rate

30,000 workers originally employed at Buna and the smaller sites it is taking over, the subsidy could work out at more than DM3m per job.

That still leaves Saxony-Anhalt with 200,000 workers on the dole. The state economics minister, Klaus Schucht, plans to guarantee at least DM200m in bank loans to the state's 13,500 small enterprises as a way of producing more jobs. Still, what to do about the blighted area around Mansfeld, where the closure of the copper mine pushed effective unemployment to more than 30%, nearly stumps him. His idea: to "open the area for worldwide pilgrimage" to Luther's birthplace nearby.

In one way or another, though, there seems to be enough money to buy the new Länder viable economies. At current rates of investment, eastern Germany's capital stock and productivity should match western Germany's within a decade—assuming westerners' patience with subsidies does not run out before then. The sight of empty office buildings and over-sized sewage plants built with western taxpayers' money has prompted some western politicians to call for big cuts in aid to the east, forgetting that western industries have profited mightily from them.

When the state begins subsidising the renovation of restaurant toilets, as Brandenburg has started to do, things may be going too far. And some subsidies, though helpful to industry, do not have the desired social effects. Subsidies for capital investment are giving investors every incentive to buy robots rather than hire workers. That makes eastern Germany's new factories among the world's most productive, but it does not create many jobs. The OECD warns that unemployment "could remain very high even after catch-up [in investment] is achieved."

Some might say that not many more jobs are possible. The east already has almost as many jobs per head (if you count government-financed work schemes) as the west: 40% for the new states' population against 44% for the old, according to DIW. But that ignores perhaps the most important of the many cultural differences between the two Germanies. Eastern women expect to work; Regine Hildebrandt, an easterner who is Brandenburg's minister of employment, rejects the notion that they should be content with Kinder and Küche, as many of their western sisters are. They are used to factories and offices as the centres of culture, sport and social life. "Work was a part of every person," she says.

United up to a point

This difference is typical of that which the eastern states have lost—not just work, but Weltanschauung too. To most easterners the new institutions and values remain alien. The nearly universal improvement in living standards is not scorned; in August 63% still welcomed unification, according to a poll by Allensbach. Yet the same pollster found that only 34% had a good opinion of Germany's social-market economy; a year ago just 38% thought democracy was the best form of government.

Heinz Sahner of Halle's Martin Luther University argues that, while laws and institutions have been transferred successfully, the western outlook has not. The selfishness and inequality that capitalism needs have not replaced the group spirit of socialism—a spirit more appealing in the absence of the socialism from which it sprung. He is surely right; but Germany's capitalism is constrained, and that should make the rift less hard to bridge. Imagine the clash of values had America, with its skimpy social safety-net and its extremes of wealth and poverty, taken on an East Germany.

It is still a big change for eastern Germany—the area's fifth new political system this century. Conspicuous allegiance to any one of them has met with punishment by the next—which has made Ossis wary of public life. Fewer Ossis than Wessis vote; fewer join political parties, churches, charities or the other institutions that mediate between individuals and governments in Germany. Though communist elites are still active in the rest of Eastern Europe, and even win elections, they have been all but wiped out in Germany. Ossis may be pardoned the cynical reflection that Germany had more use for ex-Nazis than for ex-communists.

Peter Massing, an educator at the centre of Germany's effort to teach democratic esprit to the east, trains teachers for the civics and politics course that has replaced Staatsbürgerkunde (state citizenship) as a subject in eastern schools. At present less than 30% of those teaching the course have any training in the subject, which Mr Massing regards as "catastrophic for democracy". Almost no history teachers have been retrained. Germany's sense of its past and its present, so endlessly discussed in the old Länder, is apparently being allowed to fester in the new.

The east will change more; but the west may change too, and for the better, as it comes to terms with its new Länder. Workers and managers, for example, may sometimes work together better in the east. Günter Reissmann, head of the workers' council at Jenoptik, says workers want to have a commitment to their company. They want to help shape strategy; they are flexible and work overtime without pay, when need be. These post-communist worker-entrepreneurs, Mr Reissmann says, scorn the "dogma" of IG Metall, the union to which they (and he) belong. At FAM, a company in Magdeburg that makes equipment for moving minerals and packages, the marketing manager says he does not know whether he makes more money than his colleagues on the factory floor.

Luckily, capitalism and democracy have ways of winning adherents without propaganda or even education. The birthrate climbed between October 1994 and April 1995 for the first time since unification, one sign that the shock is beginning to wear off. Another sign of normality can be found late on Friday nights in the Ost Rock disco at the Culture Brewery in Berlin's Prenzlauer Berg. Here the playlist features bands like Puhdys, Karat and City, Ossi groups given to a surprisingly melodic brand of rock. Unlike the "Ostalgie" clubs that have sprouted up lately, the disco does not flaunt Ossi kitsch. Steffen Menzel, who checks wrist-stamps at the door, says most of the patrons are Wessis looking for a friendly atmosphere.

They may be looking for something else, too. The Ost Rock disco is one of the few in Berlin that plays music exclusively sung in German. Near-wordless techno is the city's staple. Perhaps Wessis are indulging in cultural patriotism through the backdoor of Ossi music. That is how tomorrow's solidarity may be forged.

Germany's Reckoning

Hard questions are being raised about whether the Continent's premier economic power can retain its position in a global economy without sacrificing its high wages and social safety net.

Mary Williams Walsh

Times Staff Writer

OBERPFAFFENHOFEN, GERMANY

Guenter Pfeiffer has traveled the corporate-restructuring route before, and he knows its bumpy road.

Pfeiffer recalls when four years ago, at the trough of the last German recession, strategic planners at Daimler-Benz, the parent company of the Dornier airplane factory where he works, "came for the first time with their big scythe." They cut 1,000 of his colleagues from the payroll.

There was pain then but also some hope: Electronics technician Pfeiffer recalls that he and his remaining co-workers were told that if they concentrated on their core product, the Dornier 328 twin-turboprop regional transport, all would be well.

It hasn't turned out that way. The German economy is faltering again, and the mass layoffs and cutbacks have resumed. Dornier is now trying to cut another 700 jobs from its remaining payroll of 2,500. "Not a very nice way of motivating employees," Pfeiffer said glumly.

Even more unsettling, some observers say the predicament of Dornier and other German companies signals something much bigger: the demise of this country's postwar socioeconomic compact, a much-admired agreement that gave workers a significant voice in the running of their plants, ensured generous wages and job security for all, and helped this country avoid much of the labor unrest that plagues nearby Italy and France.

Hard questions are now being raised about whether, in the end, Germany can hold on to its competitive position in a global economy without sacrificing its sterling labor standards and tightly woven social safety net.

"The laws of the world economy are brutal," said Hans-Peter Froehlich, an economist at the Institute for the German

Germany's vaunted post–World War II socioeconomic covenant, with its generous wages, guaranteed voice for workers and rigid workplace rules, has all but priced its industrial economy out of the world market. Now the country's corporations are shipping jobs overseas by the tens of thousands to countries—including the United States—where they can make products for far less. A comparison of Germany and other industrialized nations:

Total manufacturing labor costs, dollars per hour (including wages and mandatory nonwage contributions, 1994 figures)

W. Germany	$30.32
Switzerland	28.60
Belgium	25.76
Norway	25.06
Japan	24.83
Austria	24.27
Netherlands	24.05
Denmark	23.73
Sweden	21.38
France	19.94
United States	19.29
Italy	18.76
E. Germany	18.29
Canada	18.22
Ireland	15.28
Britain	15.21
Spain	13.96
Greece	8.41
Portugal	6.32

Economy, a conservative think tank in Cologne. "We will have to make changes. Sometimes, when I am putting my children to bed at night, these thoughts come into my mind, and I think that they may not be able to enjoy the same standard of living that I enjoy. We will have to work a lot harder, a lot more flexibly, and

maybe for lower wages, to earn our living in today's environment."

For many Germans, Froehlich adds, even thinking such thoughts is still taboo.

The current questions about German competitiveness have far-reaching implications. Germany has the most powerful economy in Europe, and when it lags, the whole continent suffers.

Already, 4.1 million work-age people are officially jobless in Germany, more than 10% of the work force. The real number is certainly much higher—perhaps as high as 6 million—because the official jobless rate doesn't include people in make-work and training programs, or those who have given up looking for jobs altogether.

And only a minority of the official jobless are believed to be the victims of a temporary, cyclical downswing; most appear to have no long-term place in the work force at all. The costs of this situation are daunting, not only in terms of human unhappiness, but also for the government, which must provide unemployment compensation, welfare and make-work programs for these burgeoning millions.

The ballooning cost of these state outlays has been named as one of the culprits behind Germany's current inability to meet budget-deficit targets for Europe's planned currency unification—a central goal of the German government. The budget deficit here was 3.6% of domestic output last year, higher than the 3% allowed by The Maastricht Treaty on European Unification.

Bonn recently announced a 50-point reform package aimed at stimulating the economy, creating jobs and bringing the budget deficit into line. But what has yet to be calculated are the long-term social costs of making the German economy attractive enough to lure the new investment needed to create jobs for this country's unemployed millions.

The root of the problem, say Germany's managers, is that the costs of German labor and social benefits have simply made this country an unacceptably expensive place to do business. Until these costs are reduced, they say, Germany's vast, structural unemployment will remain.

"We have a cost crisis that built up slowly and gradually ever since the 1970s," said Froehlich, whose institute is supported by German business. "It became much more apparent in the past five years as new markets have opened up in Asia and Eastern Europe. All of a sudden, new countries, new continents have appeared on the scene, competing on the basis of much lower labor costs and much higher working hours."

Consider labor costs in the manufacturing sector in western Germany. Approaching $30 an hour, they are the highest in the world, according to figures prepared by the institute. (Manufacturing labor costs in eastern Germany appear lower at first glance, but when the figures are adjusted for productivity, the former East gets the dubious distinction of world labor-cost champ.)

German managers also blame what they refer to as labor "inflexibility"—the laws, contracts and customs that, in this country, govern everything from how workers may be fired (with six months' notice) to who can work on Sundays (cake-shop clerks and gas-station attendants; nearly every one else must take the official "pause").

Thanks to western German union agreements, manufacturing employees work fewer hours a week—36.6, on average—and have more vacation days than their counterparts in any of the 18 industrialized countries in which the institute keeps track.

The amount of time that factory machines may actually run in Germany, by law, is the shortest of any industrialized nation. The Sunday pause is so strict that even gardening is *verboten*.

And the overall tax burden in western Germany is the highest of any of the countries measured by the institute. Eastern Germany comes in third.

All this must sound extremely inhospitable to an American manager, accustomed as he or she is to such great German no-nos as hiring and firing at will,

paying lower wages to the young and inexperienced, and keeping the plant operating on weekends.

And Froehlich says foreign investment statistics for Germany bear out this impression. Though American companies are traditionally well represented here, these days Germany is getting less new foreign investment than all but two of the 11 countries the institute tracks. Much smaller European countries, such as Sweden and the Netherlands, now look more attractive to foreign business planners than mighty Germany.

German managers, ever mindful of this country's bad historic experience with economic depression and labor unrest, say that although they need to make Germany a competitive place to do business again, they still want a system that gives Joe Lunchpail a fair shake.

"We certainly will not, and don't want, as an industry, to introduce this hire-and-fire system that you have in America," said Christian Poppe, senior vice president at Daimler-Benz Aerospace, the Daimler division that includes Dornier. "We are proud of our social network."

But two blows struck the Germany economy last year, reducing companies' willingness to accept their heavy social obligations indefinitely. One was a national manufacturing wage agreement that was well above the inflation rate. The other was the sudden rise of the mark against the U.S. dollar, which suddenly made German products too expensive to export, no matter how lean and mean a manufacturer was.

The Dornier aircraft factory in Oberpfaffenhofen is a showcase of the foreign-exchange cost squeeze, for all international airplane sales are booked in dollars but many of Dornier's costs are incurred in marks. As the mark rose against the dollar last year, so did Dornier's costs, while its revenues fell—irrespective of those painful cost-cutting measures that parent company Daimler has implemented in 1992.

Daimler is far from alone in redoubling its quest for competitiveness now. The recent release of uniformly bad government economic data for 1995—particularly in the area of unemployment—has elicited an array of proposals on how to revamp the country's "social market economy" without wrecking it.

Germany's unions argue that tens of thousands of jobs could be created if factories would just stop giving their current staffs overtime and instead hired

Average number of hours worked per week, per worker (manufacturing sector, 1994)	
Portugal	42
Switzerland	40.5
Japan	40
Greece	40
Italy	40
Luxembourg	40
Spain	40
Sweden	40
United States	40
France	40
Ireland	39
Netherlands	38.8
Britain	38.6
Eastern Germany	38.6
Austria	38.6
Belgium	37.8
Norway	37.5
Denmark	37
Western Germany	36.6

Average number of hours worked per year, per worker (manufacturing sector, 1994)	
United States	1,896
Portugal	1,882
Japan	1,880
Switzerland	1,838
Greece	1,832
Sweden	1,824
Ireland	1,794
Luxembourg	1,784
Spain	1,772
France	1,755
Britain	1,752
Italy	1,744
Norway	1,740
Eastern Germany	1,737
Belgium	1,729
Austria	1,722
Netherlands	1,714
Denmark	1,687
Western Germany	1,620

Source: Institute for the German Economy

new employees. Union leaders have promised to demand no real wage increase next year, if only industry will pledge to create vast numbers of new jobs in this way.

But managers hoot at this idea: They want to lay workers off, not hire tens of thousands more of them. They are pushing for new flexibility in the workplace—making it easier for individual plants to opt out of national collective bargaining agreements, for instance.

1. PLURALIST DEMOCRACIES: Germany

Meanwhile, the German government is offering its own 50-point reform program, which includes sell-offs of state-owned companies, reductions in various state benefits and changes to the tax system.

Also on Bonn's to-do list are supplements for the microscopic amount of venture capital now available in Germany, incentives for people to open new businesses, pumped-up investment in construction and other pro-business measures.

The government's package has been widely hailed as a logical and humane approach to Germany's competitiveness crisis. Although it envisions some reductions in social benefits, officials argue there is room for cutting these without shredding the whole social compact that has kept Germany peaceful for the last 50 years.

For instance, the state-led early retirement and unemployment compensation schemes are notoriously easy to cheat, so the government is proposing to tighten these up. Also up for discussion are reductions in the government provided health-insurance program, which is unbelievably lavish by American standards. For example, a German who feels a bit ill can head off to a spa and charge much of the cost of his treatment to the state.

Norbert Walker, chief economist for Deutsche Bank, Germany's largest, speaks for many when he says Germans should be willing to part with such "archaic structures," in the name of restoring the overall health of their national economy.

It remains unclear when and whether the government will be able to push all of its measures through. Some have been floated unsuccessfully before. And with elections scheduled in three states in March, Bonn will certainly be reluctant to do anything too bold until the voters are safely out of the polls.

Also unclear is whether such reforms will be enough, given the scope of Germany's current problems. Unions, managements and the government are all talking about cutting unemployment in half by 2000. But even if all of Bonn's proposals go through, non-wage costs to German industry will remain relatively high: Employers will still be paying into federal kitties for health care, pensions and unemployment compensation at the rate of 40% of wages, barely less than the current 41%.

In America, by comparison, employers must pay just 29% of wages into such state benefits funds.

Still, Germany's current search for solutions holds out the intriguing possibility that an economy doesn't have to undergo brutal, American-style mass layoffs and dislocations to be successful. Perhaps with the milder mixture of reforms that government, unions and industry are talking about, this country can resume its competitive position without letting its high pay and benefits standards be dragged down by global competition.

Optimists say it can be done.

"I think [Germany's social safety net] can be financed," Daimler-Benz's Poppe said. "You don't have to be discouraged. It's just very hard to find the starting point."

The Fifth President of the Fifth Republic

The judgment of Paris

Though the French right now controls all the levers of power, Jacques Chirac's victory was narrow, his programme vague and his promises hard to fulfil

PARIS

ON MAY 7th Jacques Chirac, founder of the Gaullists' Rally for the Republic (RPR), became the fifth president of France's Fifth Republic, winning 52.6% of the vote. It was third time lucky for the man defeated in 1981 and 1988. His victory marks the end of François Mitterrand's 14 years of Socialist rule, the longest reign of any modern French president.

Mr Chirac based his campaign on a promise of "profound change" and a "break with the past", which most voters said they wanted. But he failed to explain what he meant by that. France's course over the next seven years—the normal presidential term of office—remains hazy.

This is not because of any checks and balances in the political system. In addition to the presidency, Mr Chirac and the right control over 80% of the seats in the National Assembly, two-thirds of the Senate, 20 of the 22 regional councils, four-fifths of the departmental councils, and most of the big towns. Never before has there been such a concentration of power under the Fifth Republic. Yet the first round of the election a fortnight earlier, in which a record 37% of the vote went to fringe candidates, suggests that French politics is deeply divided.

So, for all his control over the levers of power, Mr Chirac lacks a convincing mandate. Only 20.8% voted for him in the first round—the lowest score for any president since elections under the present system began in 1965. In the second round, a record 6% of blank ballot papers meant that Mr Chirac in fact won only 49.5% of votes cast, making him the first president ever to be elected with less than half the total poll. More than two in five of those who voted for him in the second round did so, according to exit polls, largely to stop the Socialists. The fear of "another seven years of socialism" was his trump card.

Despite Mr Chirac's attempt during the campaign to present himself as a candidate above the party-political divide (his campaign slogan was "*La France pour tous*"), most of the traditional left-right voting patterns re-emerged in the second round. The right-wing candidate did best among farmers, businessmen, shopkeepers, artisans, the liberal professions (doctors, lawyers, and so on), and the retired. The Socialist candidate, on the other hand, attracted most of his support among the middle- and lower-income groups, especially in the public sector.

Despite the earlier bitter fighting between the two Gaullist rivals, 85% of supporters of the prime minister, Edouard Balladur, switched their vote to Mr Chirac. So did most of the supporters of the far-

right, anti-Maastricht candidate, Philippe de Villiers. Only the 15% of voters who had plumped first time round for Jean-Marie Le Pen's extreme-right National Front proved recalcitrant. After Mr Le Pen's scornful dismissal of Mr Chirac as being "like Jospin [the Socialist candidate], only worse", nearly half of his backers abstained or cast a blank ballot; 40% voted for Mr Chirac.

Mr Chirac nevertheless succeeded in broadening the right's traditional electoral base to include for the first time a majority of the under-35s, as well as over 40% of blue-collar workers and those describing themselves as under-privileged. He has promised to make the fight against what he calls the the twin scourges of unemployment and poverty his top priority.

Although defeated, the Socialists have

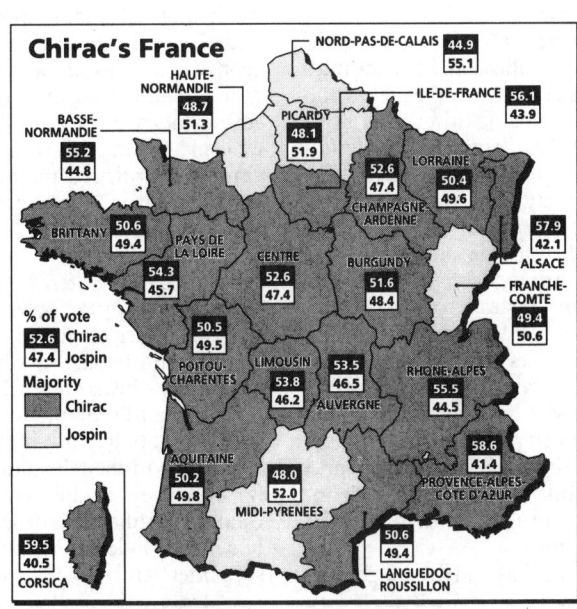

Chirac's France

NORD-PAS-DE-CALAIS 44.9 / 55.1
HAUTE-NORMANDIE 48.7 / 51.3
ILE-DE-FRANCE 56.1 / 43.9
BASSE-NORMANDIE 55.2 / 44.8
PICARDY 48.1 / 51.9
LORRAINE 50.4 / 49.6
CHAMPAGNE-ARDENNE 52.6 / 47.4
BRITTANY 50.6 / 49.4
PAYS DE LA LOIRE 54.3 / 45.7
CENTRE 52.6 / 47.4
BURGUNDY 51.6 / 48.4
ALSACE 57.9 / 42.1
FRANCHE-COMTE 49.4 / 50.6
POITOU-CHARENTES 50.5 / 49.5
LIMOUSIN 53.8 / 46.2
AUVERGNE 53.5 / 46.5
RHONE-ALPES 55.5 / 44.5
PROVENCE-ALPES-COTE D'AZUR 58.6 / 41.4
AQUITAINE 50.2 / 49.8
MIDI-PYRENEES 48.0 / 52.0
LANGUEDOC-ROUSSILLON 50.6 / 49.4
CORSICA 59.5 / 40.5

% of vote
52.6 Chirac
47.4 Jospin

Majority
Chirac
Jospin

good reason to be pleased with their 47.4% of the vote. Four months ago, they were being written off as moribund after a series of disastrous election results culminating in the abysmal 14.5% obtained in last year's European elections. Michel Rocard, the former Socialist prime minister and one-time presidential hopeful, described his party as "a field of ruins". Jacques Delors, ex-president of the European Commission, decided not to run for the presidency. Lionel Jospin, an erstwhile party leader and one-time education minister, but otherwise virtually unknown, stepped into the breach—and astonished everyone by leading the contest in the first round (with 23.3% of the vote) and remaining untrounced in the second.

In doing so, he has given back hope to the left and may have created a momentum which, his friends hope, can lead to a broad new social-democratic movement. "Even if it is not an electoral victory, it is a political success," said Mr Jospin. Although he has

turned down suggestions that he should take over the leadership of the Socialist Party, his future as a prominent figure on the left seems assured. The right can expect to face a punchier opposition, which has been lacking over the past two years of right-wing government.

Mr Mitterrand is expected to hand over power officially some time toward the end of next week. The new government will be formed soon after that, probably with Alain Juppé, the present foreign minister at its head (see box). Mr Juppé burbles that the new administration, which in the name of right-wing unity will almost certainly include a sprinkling of Mr Balladur's supporters, will go straight to work on a programme of "profound change, but in a calm and determined manner". Among the first reforms it will introduce, according to Mr Juppé, will be a reduction of employers' social-security contributions and special financial measures to create jobs for the 1.2m people who have been unemployed for more than a

year. These measures are likely to be financed by spending cuts and a "temporary" rise in taxes, despite Mr Chirac's campaign promise to lower the nation's tax burden which, at 44% of GDP, is the highest of any of the G7 countries.

In his victory speech Mr Chirac acknowledged the "difficulty of the task which awaits us". Just as well. During his campaign, he made a number of incompatible promises. He said he would raise public-sector wages, boost pensions, encourage job-creation, increase spending, give more help to farmers and provide more teachers—while simultaneously cutting the budget deficit (6% of GDP last year) and taxes. He cannot do all these things. But by promising them, he has inflamed expectations. The trade unions have already planned a series of public-sector strikes for the end of this month. "Good luck, Mr Chirac!" said Mr Jospin, conceding defeat. The new president will need it.

Which sort of Gaullist will he choose?

JACQUES CHIRAC is a Gaullist—but of what kind? Clues will be found in what happens to the two main pillars of his campaign, Philippe Séguin, the president of the National Assembly, and Alain Juppé, acting president of the Gaullist party and outgoing foreign minister.

Each stands for distinct and largely opposing kinds of Gaullism. Both were influential in the presidential campaign, which is why candidate Chirac often seemed to be contradicting himself. Both want their loyalty to the president-elect rewarded (and both have presidential ambitions of their own). How can the incoming president Chirac reconcile them—and their views?

The dark and brooding Mr Séguin represents the Gaullist left. From the mid-1980s, he was denouncing the party's "ultra-liberal", right-wing drift (under none other than Mr Chirac) and urging a return to the social and popular roots of "true Gaullism". Over the past two years, he has repeatedly condemned the policies of Edouard Balladur, the outgoing prime minister, describing them as "a veritable social Munich". Instead, he has called for the introduction of "une autre politique" (alternative policies), breaking from what he sees as the paralysing economic orthodoxy of the past decade, which, in his view, exaggerated the importance of low inflation, budget-deficit reduction and monetary stability—at the cost of high unemployment. All that, he says, must be turned on its head.

In the past, he has said that the govern-

ment should scrap the franc fort and cut interest rates to boost growth (though he has been quiet about that of late). He wants more vigorous government action to stimulate job-creation, even at the expense of widening a budget deficit already close to a record 6% of GDP.

Although Mr Séguin served as minister for health and social security in Mr Chirac's second government (1986-88), he really hogged the headlines only when, together with Charles Pasqua, the outgoing interior minister, he led the campaign for a rejection of the Maastricht treaty in the French referendum on it three years ago. He proved a formidable orator, as he has again in Mr Chirac's presidential campaign. In 1992, he railed against the "total economic and historic absurdity of Maastricht", denounced the loss of national sovereignty to advancing "European federalism" and faceless European technocrats, and criticised the drift towards a single currency. For good measure, he attacked the GATT, which, he said, should be abolished. Against all expectations, barely 51% of the French voters gave the Maastricht treaty their blessing.

The dapper Mr Juppé, who served as budget minister in Mr Chirac's second government, beats quite a different drum. A confirmed Europhile who helped persuade a wobbly Mr Chirac to vote for Maastricht in the referendum, he stands for a more moderate, centrist strand of Gaullism. Although not an ultra-liberal like Alain Madelin, another close Chirac supporter (and possible finance minis-

ter), Mr Juppé believes the state should not intervene too much. He belongs to the orthodox mainstream of economic thinking of Mr Balladur's government; he supports the franc fort.

In recent interviews, Mr Juppé has said that the "only response" to France's present difficulties is the single European currency and that this should be introduced "as soon as possible". He would have liked it by 1997, but reckons that France's big budget deficit makes 1999 more likely. Mr Chirac, too, now says he prefers that date—hence, he says, it is essential to start cutting the deficit now. But, as Mr Séguin has pointed out, "one of the central problems of the new government will be to ensure compatibility between a policy which makes the fight against unemployment an absolute priority and the move towards a single currency."

Both Mr Séguin and Mr Juppé have been tipped as possible prime ministers in the new government. Choosing Mr Séguin would imply that Mr Chirac is serious about "breaking with the past". But the signs point to Mr Juppé, and to continuity. If he is chosen, Gaullism's moderate strand will, for the moment, be in the ascendant. But the powerful and vocal Mr Séguin has many admirers across the country, whom the new president will ignore at his peril. Mr Séguin, who has said he will never serve in a government headed by Mr Juppé, is a past master at shooting poisonous darts at rivals while quietly biding his time.

Left-right divide begins to blur

Voting patterns point to shifts in France's political sub-strata

John Ridding in Paris

At a cursory glance, the voting patterns suggest it was business as usual in Sunday's French presidential showdown.

The vote was split relatively evenly between left and right, with Mr Jacques Chirac's winning score of just under 53 per cent of the ballot placing him in the middle of the five presidents of France's fifth republic. Traditional geographical strongholds, such as the south-west for the Socialists, remained strong.

But beneath the broader trends lay some significant shifts in the substrata of French politics. The way French regions, age groups and social classes cast their ballots suggests that the traditional left-right distinction,

though still present, has become more volatile and may be altering its composition.

According to preliminary data from exit polls and voter samples, the Gaullist president-elect retained his party's dominance among pensioners and independent workers from the agricultural, commercial and industrial sectors. He also performed more strongly than usual with the under 35s, winning a majority of support from this age group for the first time in his three presidential campaigns.

Part of the explanation lies in Mr Chirac's more dynamic and populist image compared with that of Mr Lionel Jospin, his Socialist rival, and his message that he would take tough

action to create jobs. This same message helped the Gaullist mayor of Paris increase his appeal to the working class.

Comparing the Chirac electorate of 1995 with that of 1988 shows that the proportion of the working class backing rose from about 30 per cent to almost 45 per cent.

Mr Chirac, however, faced a more difficult struggle in garnering the votes of the fractured French right. This is broadly apparent from the fact that the rightwing vote fell from about 60 per cent of the first round total to Mr Chirac's eventual score of 52.64 per cent.

The explanation lies partly in the stance of the extreme-right National

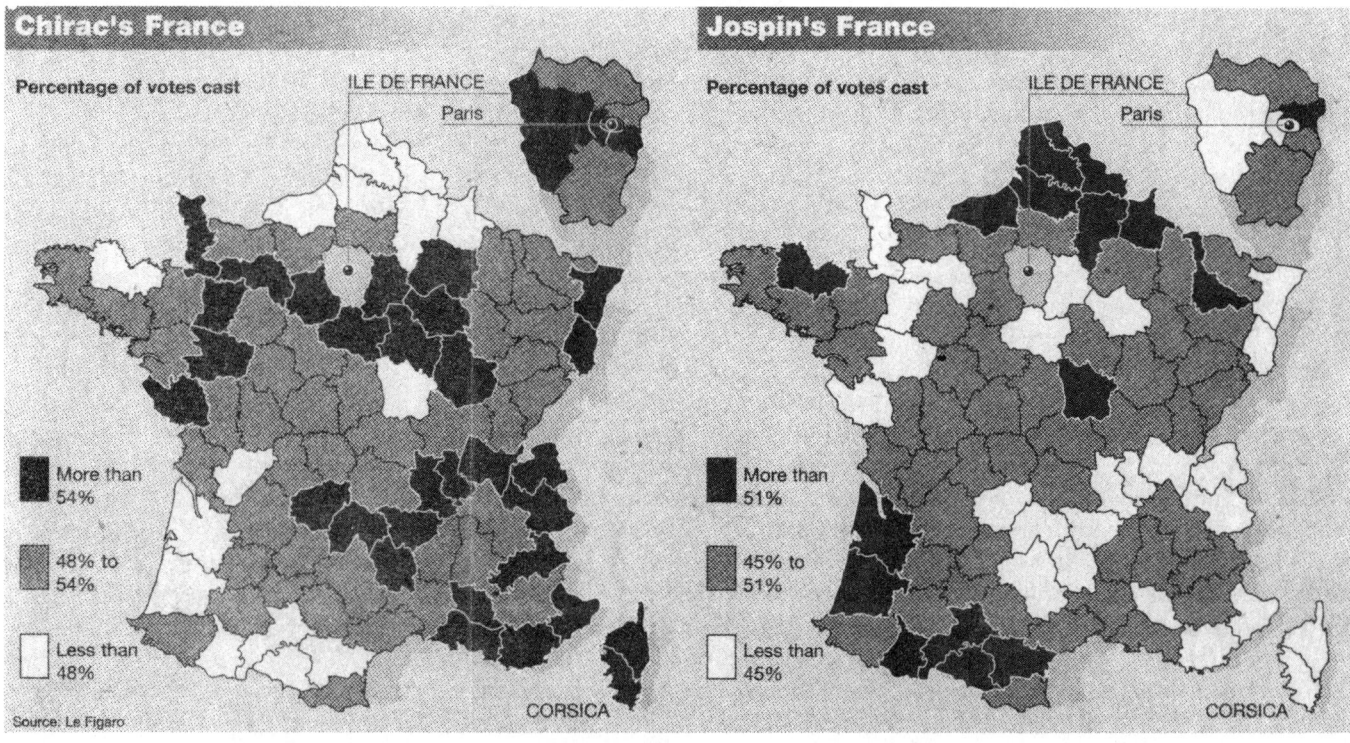

Front, which scored a record 15 per cent of the vote in the first round of the election on April 23 and which demonstrated most clearly the splintering of support across the political spectrum.

Mr Jean-Marie Le Pen, the National Front leader and a fierce critic of Mr Chirac, refused to endorse the Gaullist mayor and announced he would cast a blank ballot. In the event, so did many of his supporters.

Estimates based on exit polls indicate that about 55 per cent of Mr Le Pen's 4.6m supporters backed Mr Chirac in the second round, compared with about 65 per cent in the run-off vote of the 1988 election against François Mitterrand.

Mr Chirac fared better among the supporters of Mr Edouard Balladur, the Gaullist prime minister and erstwhile favourite for the Elysée, with only about 10 per cent casting their vote for the left. A further 10 per cent, however, appear to have abstained.

On the left, unity was greater. "The transfer of Communist votes was impeccable," said Mr Robert Hue, the party leader, referring to estimates that less than 5 per cent of Communist voters had failed to fall in line with Mr Lionel Jospin, the Socialist candidate. The failure rate was higher, however, with supporters of Ms Arlette Laguiller, the leader of the Trotskyist Workers Struggle party.

If the voting patterns suggest Mr Chirac will face some problems in guaranteeing the unity of the right, they also provide encouraging geographical shifts, particularly with the approach of next month's municipal elections. The right strengthened its grip in the Rhône Alps region, the engine room of the French economy and home to Lyons, France's second biggest city. Not surprisingly, his Paris power-base voted solidly behind him, while gains were achieved in several cities of the left, notably Marseilles.

For the Socialists there were few regional gains.

But traditional bastions, in the south-west, in several Brittany cities, and in the north-east remained firm. Buoyed by Mr Jospin's surprisingly strong showing, the Socialists will now redeploy their forces to make inroads in the municipal polls.

●━●━●━●━●━●

The right's last piece in the jigsaw

Despite support in the assembly, the new French president will find it hard to meet expectations, says David Buchan

The chorus of *"On a gagné"* ("We've won") went on until dawn yesterday in the Place de la Concorde, as Parisians celebrated the fact that their mayor had effectively become the mayor of France. It was a personal achievement for Mr Jacques Chirac to have persevered and, against what looked like long odds only three months ago, to have become president at his third attempt.

But his margin of victory over Mr Lionel Jospin, the Socialist candidate who three months ago was barely known outside his party, was far from sweeping. Mr Chirac won a 52.6 per cent share of the vote, and his score in last month's first round was, at 20.8 per cent, the lowest of anyone who has gone on to win the presidency of the Fifth Republic.

Mr Chirac has done more than most successful presidential candidates to fuel the expectations surrounding his victory. He has promised radical change not only from 14 years of Mr Mitterrand's socialism but also from the way his own Gaullists and the other forces of the centre-right have governed France over the past two years.

"I realise the difficulty of the task that awaits us," he warned in his speech to cheering supporters in the Paris Hotel de Ville, the city hall. But, given the centre-right's hold on the country's political institutions, he has fewer excuses than any of his predecessors if he fails to put his programme into practice.

Mr Chirac's victory comes on top of big conservative gains in regional and parliamentary elections in 1992–93. The result is that the Gaullist Rassemblement pour la République (RPR) and its coalition partner, the centre-right Union pour la Démocratie Française (UDF), now hold the Elysée presidential palace, 480 out of the National Assembly's 577 seats, a majority in the Senate, 21 of the country's 22 regions, and three-quarters of its 95 mainland departments.

In the 230 French towns with a population of more than 30,000, the RPR-UDF now has 110 mayors, but might gain more at next month's municipal elections on the coat-tails of Mr Chirac's presidential victory. Almost the only part of France's political structure on which there is a nominal leftwing majority is the Constitutional Council. But precisely because the right faces so few checks and balances, president-elect Chirac will want to be seen to use his institutional power carefully.

He has promised to be a more modest president than his predecessors, having denounced "the monarchical deviation" of recent Elysée incumbents. He claims, unconvincingly, that by giving France a more parliamentary style of government he would be returning to the founder of the Fifth Republic's original intention. This is patently not so; President de Gaulle disliked parties and parliaments.

What is certainly true is that, in contrast to Mr Edouard Balladur, who has adored being prime minister for two years, Mr Chirac hated his two stints (1974–76 under President Valéry Giscard d'Estaing and 1986–88 under President Mitterrand) in the Matignon. His dislike of prime ministerial duties makes it likely that he will give plenty of scope to his prime minister—to be appointed some time after he himself is formally installed as president, probably early next week.

The favourite for the job is Mr Alain Juppé, the foreign minister. He showed his considerable diplomatic skills by remaining in the Balladur cabinet without ever concealing his loyalty to Mr Chirac. An opinion poll on Sunday night showed that Mr. Juppé would be the most popular choice as prime minister, with 30 per cent backing him for the Matignon, ahead of 23 per cent favouring Mr Philippe Séguin, the National Assembly president.

Mr Séguin is not only a heavyweight within the RPR, but has also inspired the "social Gaullist" streak in Mr Chirac's presidential campaign. He was an early opponent of Mr Balladur, whom he accused of a "social Munich" surrender to high unemployment. It was Mr. Séguin who has most strongly urged Mr Chirac to stake everything on reducing unemployment, even if this entails letting budget discipline and the timetable for European monetary union slip. If there were any doubt of his influence over Mr Chirac, it was removed on Sunday when the president-elect singled out "the fight against unemployment" as "our principal battle" to come.

Mr Chirac's platform includes elements from both Mr Juppé and Mr Séguin. Mr Juppé is a straightforward pro-European and believes that cutting deficits is the best way to bring down interest rates and so gain job-creating growth. Mr Séguin publicly says he accepts the Maastricht treaty against which he campaigned at the time of the 1992 referendum, but privately rails against the way that Maastricht reduces governments' room for manoeuvre in fiscal and monetary policy.

But there is a third person—Mr Alain Madelin, an economic liberal in the Balladur government—who makes up the policy triangle around Mr Chirac. Mr Madelin is not rated a likely prime minister, because he comes from the UDF, only fragments of which originally sided with the mayor of Paris. His importance is rather that he offers Mr Chirac a philosophic way of reconciling the Juppé-Séguin positions. The state can spend more to create jobs and at the same time reduce its budget deficit, argues Mr Madelin, because cutting income and inheritance taxes as well as bureaucratic red tape will so stimulate the economy that tax receipts will increase.

However hands-off a president Mr Chirac wants to be, he now has to decide how he wants the Juppé-Séguin-Madelin trio to play. It is clear that all three will have some part in the Chirac orchestra. Mr Chirac can, of course, always chop and change later on. Indeed French presidents always do; they have in the past never kept the same prime minister for their seven-year term.

One advantage of picking Mr Juppé for the Matignon would be to assure some continuity in foreign policy, where Mr Chirac faces some tricky early choices, particularly on Europe. The president-elect has said his foreign priority is early talks with Chancellor Helmut Kohl to ensure a common Franco-German diplomatic front both at next month's European Union summit in Cannes and in next year's EU constitutional conference.

The latter task will not be easy. Mr Chirac's desire to boost the role of the EU Council of Ministers at the expense of the Brussels Commission and the Strasbourg parliament is more akin to the aims of Britain's Conservatives than of Germany's. But Mr Chirac seems hopeful. Talking in an interview last week of the importance of maintaining France's prime relationship with Germany without excluding others like Britain, he said France's "vocation" in next year's conference would be "to synthesise the different points of view".

Europe and employment will undoubtedly dominate Mr Chirac's first 100 days in the Elysée. He will probably have little trouble in using the existing big RPR-UDF majority to vote through his early measures. He has no need to discipline former Balladur supporters, virtually all of whom have swung behind him.

However, Mr Jospin's stout performance has already put fresh heart into the opposition Socialist party. Mr Jospin and those young, former Socialist ministers such as Mrs Martine Aubry and Mr Dominique Strass-Kahn, who played a big part in his successful campaign, have promised to "rebuild the left". Their first test will be next month's municipal elections. A decent showing there would put the Socialist party on the road to regaining some of its much-depleted parliamentary strength at the next National Assembly elections.

The assembly has a five-year term and the elections must be held by March 1998. By not dissolving the Assembly on his election—as Mr Mitterrand did in 1981 and 1988—Mr Chirac will assure himself relatively smooth sailing in parliament with the centre-right majority over the next three years.

The eventual price, however, could be a resurgent left winning back its parliamentary majority. If that were to happen, President Chirac would have to live with a left-wing government for the last four years of his term. But at least Mr Chirac, unlike most other elected leaders, is about to embark on a term of office long enough to carry him into the next century.

Will the Real France Stand Up?

Jean-Marie Colombani

Jean-Marie Colombani: editor of *Le Monde*.

Anyone returning to France after a gap of 14 years, the period of time separating the start of the presidencies of the socialist François Mitterrand and that of his Gaullist successor, Jacques Chirac, would have real problems understanding the nation. France appears full of complaints, misery, defeatism and talk of catastrophe. It is almost as if the country had collapsed during this period. However, a quick glance at national economic figures, the key ones used by bankers, shows a different picture. France is a country which has been powerfully strengthened in industrial, financial and commercial might. Its external trade is in considerable and sustained surplus and its GDP per head is among the highest in Europe. This is combined with an inflation level of 2% or lower, with a rise to 3% forecast for 1996.

It is indeed hard to believe that such contrary opinions are held about the same country. One has to wonder about this national mania for self-denigration which leaves the French and the rest of the world, including the financial markets, believing that the country is seriously sick despite apparent proof to the contrary. This schizophrenia will become more pronounced in 1996.

In this warp of economic perception, the role of the politician has been central. Each and every election campaign has been conducted under the banner of economic reform. Whichever party is in power is accused by would-be successors of nothing less than responsibility for the decline of France. The recent presiden-tial campaign saw the winner vigorously denounce the weakening of the country. But once in power, another question starts to pop up: "Is change really needed after all?"

Mr Chirac has talked much of reform. But his ideas remain quite unformed and hazy. He starts out on seven years in office with little by way of an agenda. If one has to define his strategy, the first tactic which comes to mind is that of opportunism. This is already being directed at the March 1998 legislative elections. Mr Chirac has chosen to bring in radical measures early, especially changes in the funding of social security, at the risk of short-term unpopularity. But he reckons that by 1998 he will have redressed the political balance, and will be able to offer a more politically acceptable face, handing back some tax breaks to the electorate.

From the beginning, President Chirac and his present prime minister, Alain Juppé, have confirmed their commitment to economic and monetary union with Germany, planned for 1999. This requires France to conform to the norms set by the Maastricht treaty, and to bring down its budget deficit to 3% of GNP. In a broad sense, these are measures that were being taken in the autumn of 1995. They are, of course, at odds with the president's promises to promote consumer spending, so freely made earlier in the year.

Mr Chirac had dwelt at length during his campaign on what he called "the social fracture". This exists. Alongside a level of wealth never reached before, there has appeared real poverty and so-cial division, In inner-city suburbs, there is a concentration of immigrants who have problems feeling at home in France. This is territory for the electoral progress of the extreme right at the expense of traditional parties. The underlying problems are of a scale and nature that cannot be solved in a few months. Mr Mitterand, after two terms as president, had to concede that he had been unable to reduce these inequalities. After 14 years, they have, in fact, grown significantly. Public opinion expects strings to be pulled in 1996 to speed the pick-up of the economy, a measure described by Mr Chirac as the real cure for unemployment. This would be the only way to reduce social-security deficits on a permanent basis. If the commitment to a single currency prevents this, the public will feel even grumpier.

On the European front, Mr Chirac must make 1996 the year in which to make his mark. The calm of his first spell of office has been somewhat ruffled by the resumption of French nuclear tests in the Pacific. The French claim that the tests are for the benefit of Europe and that the nuclear capability of France is available for European defence as a whole is seen as less convincing than it actually is.

Mr Chirac has done much to improve relations with Britain in 1995. In 1996 his attention will be elsewhere. After all, a president of France has one overriding priority in foreign policy—to lead Europe on terms of equal footing with the chancellor of Germany. It is in this area that the French president still has to prove himself.

Political Strikes and Demonstrations: Two Views

— — — — — —

More than a French Labor Dispute, but No New System in Sight

Flora Lewis

PARIS—Three weeks into the paralyzing strike of transport workers and other public sector employees, French tempers are fraying. But what has been remarkable so far is the tolerance, indeed the signs of solidarity that the general public has shown for stoppages that are ruining many small businesses in the Christmas season and making life miserable for practically everybody.

That is conclusive evidence that this is much more than a labor dispute.

It is a social and economic challenge with deep roots, even if they are not fully articulated. And while it is taking a special form in France, because of specific French conditions and history, it reflects a crisis creeping up on most industrial societies as the profound transformations of recent years work their effect.

When the trouble started last month, there were first student demonstrations demanding much more funding for a university system that has expanded from 300,000 students when France was brought to a halt in 1968 to 2.2 million today. But 1968 was about the need for change. In 1995 the fight is to resist proposed, and necessary, change.

The government announced a plan to reform social security, the financing of the state-owned railways and some pension rights this November. Then the railway workers went out, along with municipal transport. For the first few days, the protests were specific. But they quickly changed to a demand that the government's whole reform program be canceled. By the time Prime Minister Alain Juppé agreed to the railway workers' most immediate demands, it was not enough at all. The issue had become government's role in the economy and its relations with the public.

On one level, the widespread anger had to do with the abrupt reversal of policies promised during the presidential election campaign only six months ago. Jacques Chirac ran on a pledge to fight unemployment, heal the "social fracture" between comfortable France and its losers, and ease tax burdens.

Of course he couldn't do it. When Finance Minister Alain Madelin publicly advocated an austerity program to tackle the huge public debt and budget deficit, he was summarily fired. Mr. Juppé reorganized the cabinet and ordered practically the same program a few weeks later. People felt that the government had not only misled them but was taking them for helpless fools.

There was no serious attempt to explain and debate the situation, no effort to consult and listen to the people's fears and priorities. With unemployment stubbornly at a distressing 12 percent, it was public sector workers who have job security who took to the streets. Significantly, a major demand of the railroad workers was cancellation of the restructuring plan and the threat of some privatization, which they foresaw would lead to lay-offs.

But private sector workers were sympathetic, because they felt that the strikers were also defending their interests in preserving the "acquis social," the welfare and entitlements system built up over nearly a century of struggle between once unregulated capital and labor.

There is a deeper level of friction, however, and, along with the need for democracies to do a much better job of explaining their economic management, it can serve as a warning to other countries facing the same problems of change made necessary by the globalized economy and the technological revolution of the late 20th century.

These problems have been the subject of academic seminars and studies for well over a decade. But now, with high unemployment, lower growth, the mountains of debt piled up over long years of government spending unrequited by revenue, they are no longer abstract. They are hitting more and more everyday lives, darkening hopes for the future.

Unfortunately, here and in some other European countries the blame for the crunch is often shifted to the European Union and the plan for a single currency. True, the Maastricht treaty set the timing and the specific scenario. But in fact the social and economic urgencies would press and have to be accommodated even if the Union didn't exist. Now at last the government is saying that, but without convincing because there is still no acknowledgment of underlying realities.

The social critic Alain Touraine succinctly makes the point that the 20th century model for regulating society, so hard fought, has run out of capacity, overtaken by new economic relations that cannot be arranged by the state and require a new premise. But no new system has been proposed, except unbuffered exposure to a savage, impersonal market.

So, fearful of what painful reform will bring people are defending the status quo without regard for ever more costly and painful consequences. There will be some kind of compromise, and it will hurt an economy already severely penalized by the strikes. But there will be no winners.

Global markets and high technology have changed the playing ground. The old formulas won't restore it. Mr. Touraine calls for inventing "a new kind of social democracy." France's agony is not unique.

●—●—●—●—●—●

U.S.–British Capitalism or Europe's Model of 'Social' Capitalism?

William Pfaff

PARIS—Newsweek has written that the strikes which currently disrupt France's society and economy are a futile attempt to deny the reality that the Europeans' "easy life" is over. The implacable evolution of the global economy means no more free universal health care in Europe, the magazine says.

And no more free universities. No more generous unemployment benefits. No more subsidized orchestras and opera and ballet companies. From now on Europeans will have to live pinched and mean lives—just like modern Americans, the magazine seems to be announcing, with grim satisfaction.

Newsweek is correct to the extent that what is going on in France, in the guise of a defense of various established privileges, or abuses, is an inarticulate refusal (which enjoys the sympathy of a majority of the French) to accept the version of capitalism now practiced in the United States and Britain.

This is not the capitalism of Adam Smith. It is the new economic ideology which has emerged in American and British universities and editorial rooms during the past 15 years.

I am not speaking of monetarism, which is an innovative and useful interpretation of economic forces, although certainly not a comprehensive or infallible one. I am talking about two arguments currently made in the United States and Britain, which have become extremely influential elsewhere, including in Brussels, the European Union's headquarters.

The first argument maintains that totally unfettered trade among societies at all levels of economic, social, and political development is an unqualified good and will eventually produce a better life for all who take part in this trading system.

There is no reliable evidence that this is true. The argument relies on the experience of the advanced industrial countries' trade with one another since the end of World War II. This has been trade among societies at roughly the same level of industrial sophistication.

Japan, industrially backward in 1945, subsequently prospered through a policy of domestic protectionism and exploitation of open markets in the United States and Europe, and thereby joined the ranks of the advanced industrial economies. But Japan still resists the open trade policy demanded by Washington.

The argument expresses a theory about the future which rests upon observations made by David Ricardo (1772-1823) on the trade relationships of his day, which bear little resemblance to those of the contemporary global economy. The current empirical evidence concerning globalized trade's effect on living standards in the advanced industrial countries is negative. American living standards have fallen since 1980.

The second argument says that the sole appropriate criterion for corporate decisions is return on invested capital, and that any other consideration, including concern for the well-being of the workforce and of the community in which the corporation functions, distorts economic rationality. The concept of a "social return" on investment, or of a corporate social responsibility, is peremptorily and arbitrarily ruled out by this theory.

This, too, is sheer ideology, and a pernicious one

because it tends to destroy the well-being of living people for the sake of a utopian future.

The most bizarre feature of today's politico-economic scene is that capitalism, in the form currently taught in American and European schools of management, and practiced by international corporations, is behaving as Leninism and Stalinism did in the first half of this century. It is destroying the prosperity or livelihoods of millions for the sake of the promised well-being of generations to come. This is not only intellectually disreputable, it is immoral.

This economic ideology has turned American capitalism from the machine for creating wealth and improving human lives that it was from 1940 to 1980, into a machine for impoverishing society and destroying employment—to the benefit, chiefly, of a narrow class of corporate managers and a somewhat larger class of corporate investors.

The American worker without a college education made $11.23 an hour in 1979, on average. In 1993 he made $9.92, in inflation-adjusted dollars. The university-educated employee made $15.52 in 1979 and in 1993 was up to $15.71, a 19-cent gain. The average chief executive officer of a large American company made some 40 times the wage of an average worker two decades ago, and now makes 190 times a worker's salary, according to a sampling of executive compensation in 424 very large companies, cited recently in The New Yorker.

Americans have accepted a lowering of their living standards during the last decade and a half with strange docility. The French are not a docile people.

The convulsion now gripping France is not a considered affair. It is inspired by many selfish and corporatist interests among the strikers. But it also defends that European version of capitalism which is called social capitalism or "Rhineland capitalism" (because it has been most successful in Germany).

The European model has held that social return, or social responsibility, is as important as investment return to the enterprise, and is essential to the society in which the corporation functions. This model is under intellectual and economic attack from the ideology now uncritically promulgated by Democratic as well as Republican administrations in the United States, and by Britain's Conservatives.

The battle continues, in part because the Anglo-American trade ideology is rejected by Japan and the Asian "tiger" economies, all of them protectionist in fact if not in name. The new ideology has made substantial gains in Europe, which is why this upheaval in France is so interesting.

Without intending to be so, it has become a campaign in the struggle over the social and economic future of Europe—and perhaps of America as well.

The Bulldozer Hits a Roadblock

President Jacques Chirac of France isn't afraid to take a stand, but critics are beginning to wonder if there is a method to his manliness.

Craig R. Whitney

Craig R. Whitney is the Paris bureau chief of The Times. His last article for the Magazine was on the Bundesbank.

May 7, 1995, 11 P.M.: Jacques Chirac has just won a seven-year term as President of France, and Paris, where he has been Mayor for 18 years, is holding a street party. Young people tooting horns and waving banners with Chirac's apple-tree campaign symbol pour into the Place de la Concorde for a celebratory rock concert. Chirac, a conservative neo-Gaullist promising "fundamental change" to a country profoundly unsettled by years of high unemployment and economic uncertainty, is sprayed with Champagne as he thanks supporters for helping him win nearly 53 percent of the vote. Then he gets into a gray Citroën sedan and heads back to the Hôtel de Ville, pursued by television cameramen on motorcycles. Noisy celebrations continue through the warm spring night.

Six months later, reality returns with a chill. On a cold, gray afternoon, Chirac is perched on an uncomfortable green-blue settee in his gilded second-floor office of the Élysée Palace. As the light fades in the garden out back, 20,000 students are thronging the streets, this time in bitter protest against campus austerity policies and budget cuts. In a few days, the biggest wave of social unrest in a decade will break, with hundreds of thousands of transport workers closing down the rail network, the Paris Metro and mass transit in most other cities for three weeks. Those strikes will paralyze the country and cost the economy as much as $1.5 billion.

Chirac, dressed in a dark blue jacket, charcoal slacks and black loafers, looks younger than his 63 years. The Spanish Prime Minister is coming later in the afternoon, but Chirac seems to have nothing but time. A half-hour chat stretches to an hour, uninterrupted by a single buzz or telephone call.

"Change is difficult," he says in his velvety deep baritone, as if he had foreseen the turmoil all along. "I was elected to restore and reinforce social cohesion in a country in crisis. I have seven years to do that. I'm a leader, not a follower. I never look at the polls, and I'm not changing one iota."

But over the next few weeks, with his popularity rating slipping into the single digits, he has to change. He orders his handpicked Prime Minister, Alain Juppé, to back off a sweeping plan to reform pensions for railroad workers and other public-sector employees and to trim the deficit-ridden rail network of unprofitable branch lines. The state-run comprehensive health insurance system, though, is heading for bankruptcy, and Chirac vows to hold firm on his plans to avoid that debacle. But he urges Juppé to sit down with the unions and do a better job of convincing them this time of the need for reform.

Abrupt shifts in strategy are nothing new for Chirac. While the "Bulldozer" can be bullheaded, he also zigs and zags and has a reputation for being unpredictable and impetuous—a latter-day Gaullist without de Gaulle's mystical vision. As de Gaulle would have done, Chirac waved aside jeers and insults from around the world and went ahead with French underground nuclear weapons tests in the South Pacific because he felt they were needed to preserve French military independence. But as de Gaulle would never have done, Chirac went on "Larry King Live" last October to explain, in English, that there would be fewer than the eight tests originally planned and that these would be the last such tests ever. Eventually, he would halt the program after six blasts, while calling for a worldwide ban on further nuclear tests.

Like de Gaulle, Chirac is a proud man who cannot abide humiliation, and he was enraged when United Nations peacekeepers were taken hostage in Bosnia early last summer to forestall NATO air raids. But the similarities end there. He pressed the United States to become militarily involved in Bosnia, accepted the Dayton peace accords, placed French forces in the NATO peacekeeping force under an American general and ordered France to rejoin most of the NATO military structure, 30 years after de Gaulle pulled out in a huff over American domination.

Chirac likes America and Americans, and he sought in his recent visit to Washington and Chicago to cement good relations between the

United States and France. But, he adds, "I also want Americans to learn that Europe really exists." He also does not shy from reminding American officials, including President Clinton on one occasion, that "you can't continue to want to be in charge of everything but pay for nothing."

WHILE CHIRAC IS PROUD OF HIS CATalytic role in resolving the Bosnian wars, his reputation rides on what he does at home. The early signs have not been encouraging. On taking office, Chirac promised "fundamental change" to solve the enormous social and economic problems France has to deal with if it is to play a leading role in 21st-century Europe. He would attack the nation's almost 12 percent unemployment rate and growing homelessness, he said, by lowering taxes, raising the minimum wage and encouraging businesses to give jobs, and hope, to the young and the long-term unemployed. "Jobs are the priority of priorities," he swore.

Under the French constitutional system, the President issues general policy guidelines, but it is up to the Prime Minister and the Government to carry them out. Even though Chirac's neo-Gaullist party, Rally for the Republic, and its allies had an overwhelming majority in both houses of the French Parliament, Juppé was stymied by the contradictions at the heart of the President's program. In essence, Chirac was asking him to square the circle — cut budget deficits and create jobs, cut deficits and cut taxes at the same time.

By October, unemployment was still at about 11.5 percent and the public mood was turning sullen. Chirac saw the shift himself — "You'd have to be blind not to see it" — and, characteristically, reversed himself. Jobs were still his priority, he declared in a long television interview on Oct. 26, but before the economy could begin generating jobs, the $60 billion deficit would have to be drastically cut.

In the short term, of course, deficit cutting tends to increase unemployment, raising the possibility that Chirac had something else on his mind when he made budget deficits his highest priority. Indeed, like many European leaders, he finds himself in the politically dangerous position of needing to reduce the French deficit to qualify for membership in the European monetary union scheduled for the end of the decade. Germany wrote the rules, which include stern provisions barring membership for any country with an annual budget deficit higher than 3 percent of gross domestic product at the end of 1997. The French deficit is now about 5 percent, but Chirac wants to avoid the political poison of appearing to bow to outside pressure.

"My objective, when I fight against deficits and make them the absolute priority, is not the single-currency objective, the European objective," he insisted in the October television interview. "It's

the struggle against unemployment, which is itself the cause of additional expenditures and social strains." But in France, as subsequent events demonstrated, it is political suicide to attack the root cause of unemployment — expensive, state-mandated job benefits and minimum wages that discourage the hiring of workers, particularly at the lower levels.

Instead, Chirac outlined an unemployment strategy based on the tenuous connection between deficits and interest rates. It would take about two years, he said, to reduce the budget deficit enough to bring down interest rates to the point where economic growth would then start creating jobs and bringing down unemployment. That's a long stretch to wait for results, but Chirac insisted, "I have time."

Juppé, with a clear and manageable mandate to go after deficits first, attacked with all the rigor, logic, intellectual arrogance and contempt for political horse-trading for which graduates of the National School of Administration are famous. First he dismissed nearly all the women in his Cabinet to get down to fighting trim, and then he unveiled a technocratic masterpiece.

It was a complicated, comprehensive, ambitious plan to attack the major sources of the deficits all at once: the public employee pension system that, to cite one example, allowed railroad engineers to retire at age 50 at three-quarters pay; the deficit-ridden 20,275-mile rail system itself and the $50 billion shortfall in the state-run health insurance and pension system, which covers nearly every citizen in France. The package included a new 0.5 percent income tax that would hit nearly all taxpayers, increases in health insurance premiums paid by retired people and a provision that would allow the Government to make changes in the system by decree. Juppé chose to spring the plan as a surprise on the powerful French public-sector labor unions, which have had a statutory role in administering the system since 1945.

But Chirac had campaigned on tax cuts, not increases. So when angry transport workers shut down the rail system and public transport in protest against plans to reform their pension system and reduce rail service, millions of French workers in private industry quietly sympathized.

By the beginning of December, with France virtually paralyzed, Juppé and Chirac still acted as though the traditional, Gaullist authoritarian style were still working and the trouble would blow over. As Chirac departed on a long-planned trip to Africa, the most important labor leader in the struggle, Marc Blondel of an anti-Communist union, Workers' Force, was beginning to call for Juppé's resignation as the price of sending his troops back to work. Demonstration after demonstration mobilized more than the two million people Juppé had once joked it would take to get him to quit.

Returning to the Élysée, Chirac decided — what else? — that it was time to change course. Show yourself, he urged Juppé. Make your case. Don't expect them to take your word for it.

Not until Dec. 5 did Juppé do so, before Parliament and then in a televised speech promising dialogue that only further infuriated the unions. Slowly, he began backing off. After a huge demonstration filled the streets of the capital on Dec. 12, he abandoned the pension reform and, with Chirac's backing, froze the plan to reorganize the railroads. By mid-December, the Government was promising to open dialogue and negotiations with the unions, and with the approach of the holidays the strikers began going back to work.

Juppé kept his job, but the strikes were a disaster for Chirac. He and his Government have now begun courting the unions to try to build consensus on changes needed to insure the fiscal stability of the health insurance and pension systems. There is considerable doubt that soothing words alone will calm the workers, who early this month greeted a revised plan with renewed threats of demonstrations.

Still, the dialogue was long overdue, a touch of humility aimed at staving off the humiliation of defeat. And for a man twice defeated for the Presidency, who twice served as Prime Minister under presidents who detested him, the avoidance of humiliation is something of an obsession.

CHIRAC IS HIMSELF A GRADUATE OF THE ELITE National School of Administration, which has been grinding out brilliant technocrats for 50 years. But Chirac also has a common touch. He prefers a cold Mexican beer to a glass of wine, and a genuine American meal like a hot turkey sandwich with gravy to a pseudo-Escoffier meal. While he strongly supports the law that requires French television stations to show mainly French films, to sustain Europe's most important film industry, friends say he would rather watch a Gary Cooper western than a mannered French romance. During the campaign, he obviously enjoyed working the crowds, signing autographs for everybody within reach.

Chirac's complicated relationship with the United States began in the summer of 1953, when he and two companions from Sciences-Po, the prestigious Institute of Political Studies in Paris, scraped together enough money to make the trip. Chirac's father, a bank employee, let his son attend summer courses at Harvard College. To support himself, the 20-year-old took a job in a Howard Johnson's restaurant, one that long ago disappeared from Harvard Square.

Chirac loves to tell the story. "My first job was as a soda jerk," he says, using the English words. He began washing dishes in the basement kitchen, but management soon rewarded him with a promotion upstairs, where he learned to make banana splits and developed his taste for hot turkey sandwiches.

"Howard Johnson himself lived in Boston in those days, and when he heard that a French student was working for him, he asked to see me and told me to come back before I returned to France," Chirac says. "I did, and he gave me a letter of reference." Chirac still has the note.

Has he kept in touch with a young woman from South Carolina, Florence Herlihy? He whoops. "My fiancée!" She had a white Cadillac convertible and a delicious Southern accent that reduced him to quivering jelly when she called him "honey chile." He says he once tried to track her down. But not even his friend George Bush, with all the resources of the White House switchboard, could find her.

Chirac père made him call off that "engagement," and Chirac returned to marry a fellow student at Sciences-Po, Bernadette Chodron de Courcel, in 1956. Chirac's own family, from the hardscrabble Corrèze region of south-central France, came from peasant origins. As a student, he had sold the Communist daily l'Humanité on the Left Bank, and he still prefers tête de veau, a peasant dish, to veal cordon bleu. It was Bernadette who introduced him to the tweedy elegance of the 16th arrondissement and the Gaullist haute bourgeoisie.

Out of school, he landed a job as a junior aide in the office of de Gaulle's Prime Minister, Georges Pompidou. A few years later, at Pompidou's urging, he returned to Corrèze to start his own political career by running for a seat in the National Assembly. "It's a dour, rocky area where people tend to be taciturn, but Chirac hit it off with them," says Denis Tillinac, a publisher friend of Chirac who comes from the area. "He wasn't a typical technocrat at all. He paid court to every woman in sight, chain-smoked Winston cigarettes and made people feel that he really cared about them."

Chirac swept to victory in 1967 and, five years later, was named Minister of Agriculture by Pompidou, who had become President. Chirac pushed French farmers' interests on the rest of Europe more vigorously than any minister before or since. "I know them and I like them," Chirac boasted.

By 1974, after Pompidou's death, Chirac became Prime Minister under Valéry Giscard d'Estaing, a man of unmatched arrogance who kept Chirac on a tight leash and regularly humiliated him at Cabinet meetings. In 1976 Chirac, fed up, resigned and started his neo-Gaullist party, and a year later, he had bulldozed his way into the Hôtel de Ville, Paris's City Hall.

But he lost his first bid for the Presidency in 1981, dividing the conservative camp and allowing the Socialist François Mitterrand to get in, many critics thought; his second try, against Mitterrand in 1988, at the end of Chirac's second stint as Prime Minister, also ended in failure.

Mitterrand's contempt for Chirac was boundless — "easily carried away, no personal convictions, always listens to the last person who talks to him," Mitterrand once said; "it would be dangerous to put France in his hands." Chirac once said he had no idea Mitterrand detested him so much, but when Mitterrand died of prostate cancer on Jan. 8, Chirac immediately went to the former President's office to pay his respects and saluted him as "a great figure."

After her husband's defeat at Mitterrand's hands in 1988, Bernadette Chirac lamented, "Maybe the problem is that the French just don't like my husband." His victory last May came only after a series of betrayals by men of his own party. Édouard Balladur, a fellow conservative who was Prime Minister from 1993 to 1995, was supposed to leave the Presidency to Chirac, or so Chirac thought, but ran against him, supported by other former friends of Chirac like the tough former Interior Minister, Charles Pasqua.

"Poor Jacques, he's so often disappointed by the men in his life," says Line Renaud, a French actress and singer who is among Chirac's many friends in show business. Today, the presidential adviser closest to Chirac is his 33-year-old daughter, Claude, yet there is no doubt that the family has suffered from his obsession with his political career.

When Claude and her older sister, Laurence, were growing up, Chirac was mostly in the office or out on the hustings, not at home. Laurence studied medicine and became a doctor, but suffered from depression and developed severe anorexia. In 1990 she tried suicide by jumping from an apartment window. While she survived, she has never fully recovered.

Two years later, Claude, a political consultant in a public relations agency, married Philippe Habert, an admirer of Chirac who worked at Le Figaro, the center-right daily paper. Within months, Habert committed suicide.

Chirac never discusses these things in public. Even his closest aides say they do not ask, for example, how Laurence is faring. Claude Chirac does not give interviews. But it was she who advised her father — famous for jiggling his feet and looking clenched and nervous on television — on how to loosen up. Today she has an office in the presidential annex across the street from the Élysée.

"She takes care of communications, but not the press, and organizes my trips," her father says. "She played a very important role in my campaign, but she is never visible."

She was briefly visible, though, at the signing of the Bosnia peace treaty — a poignant blond figure, much resembling her mother, sitting on a chair near one of the French windows in the Élysée ballroom, her eyes on her father. She was wearing an open sweater over a smock that confirmed what the French gossip magazines had been writing: that she had decided to become a single mother.

While the family continues to play down Claude's role, her hand was clearly visible in the careful staging of Chirac's New Year's Eve message, taped in his office with a close focus on the President and a ticking mantel clock in the background. Contrition was written all over his face when Chirac said that one thing he had learned was that profound changes cannot be imposed by fiat.

"You can't change France without the French," he admitted. "Every one of us thirsts for respect, for explanations. All of us, together, will have to find paths of dialogue."

His address to the nation the evening of Mitterrand's death was also widely praised for sounding a penitential and statesmanlike note, and after he and Juppé backed off nearly every controversial element of the deficit-cutting plan, Chirac's popularity began slowly recovering after the beginning of the year. But with the country in a mistrustful mood and the labor unions newly militant, supporters and critics alike agree that Chirac's troubles have only just begun.

Tocqueville in Italy

DAVID L. KIRP

MAKING DEMOCRACY WORK: Civic Traditions in Modern Italy. *By Robert Putnam. Princeton. 258 pp. $24.95.*

What makes a government responsive to the just wishes of its citizens? *Making Democracy Work* offers provocative and persuasive new ways to think about this ancient and pivotal political question. Political scientist Robert Putnam pays close attention to evidence—from historical accounts, personal narratives and survey data collected during a twenty-year experiment with local government—about how ordinary people's lives intersect with the power of the state. *Making Democracy Work* makes the past—a millennium's worth of the past—entirely relevant to today's headline stories. It takes up the classic chicken-and-egg puzzle of public life—does economic prosperity make *civitas* possible or is it the other way around?—and reaches conclusions that should prompt students of politics and economics alike to rethink their assumptions.

Seminal, epochal, path-breaking: All those overworked words apply to a book that, to make the point brazenly, is a *Democracy in America* for our times. But while Tocqueville drew his insights from a new nation famously experimenting

David L. Kirp is professor of public policy at the University of California, Irvine.

with representative government, Putnam has voyaged to Italy, perhaps the most unlikely place among Western nations to look for instruction in matters democratic. For nearly half a century in that country, coalition governments dominated by the Christian Democrats came and went with breathtaking speed, even as the very same politicians stayed on. And on—Amintore Fanfani, several times a prime minister and holder of innumerable Cabinet jobs into the 1980s, was a contemporary of Harry Truman. While the Christian Democrats were loved only by their families, they nonetheless regularly found their way back to Rome through the expedient of Communist-bashing. When the Socialists became a politically credible force, they too styled themselves as an alternative to the evils for which Communism stood. Always the Communists were in opposition.

In the aftershock of the end of the cold war, these arrangements started to collapse; keeping the Communists out of the government was no longer a rationale for ruling. Early in 1992, some brave Italian magistrates began poking around in the dustbins of national political life. While the investigations initially concentrated on petty misdeeds in Milan, the sweep of the corruption unearthed by Operation Clean Hands was stunning: Boatloads of politicians, Christian Democrats and Socialists alike, turned out to be on the payrolls of the biggest private and state companies, as well as the Mafia. This has proved too much to stomach, even in a

country where, as Sicilian novelist Giuseppe Tomasi di Lampedusa observed, everything must change so that nothing will change. Now there is a new government led by a banker with no discrediting political ties, a new electoral law and a new emphasis on regional rather than national authority.

It is in Italy's twenty regional governments, not in the Roman corridors of power, that Putnam and his colleagues have been nosing about for more than two decades (forever in the world of social science research, usually impatient for quick results). In 1970, barely a century after the country was first unified, the regions were granted new power to manage their affairs; and this taste of authority led, not surprisingly, to demands for more. Now these regions control as much as a third of the national budget, and their responsibilities include managing hospitals and health care, public safety, economic development, agriculture and housing.

Across Italy, the regional governments get more respect from the citizenry than do the overseers in Rome. Far more striking are the differences from one region to the next. In some places, public services are efficiently managed, with innovations ranging from family health clinics to environmental standards; officials are responsive and citizens are genuinely pleased. By contrast, other regional governments are cesspools, corrupt and exploitative, where personal connections rather than public priorities count for everything and the populace is grudging and resentful. What explains why the same form of government functions so well in some places, so badly in others? What makes democracy work?

None of the obvious explanations suffice. The formal administrative structures are almost identical from one region to another. Party politics or ideology isn't critical either, since Communists, Socialists and Christian Democrats can all handle or bungle the job. Social stability doesn't account for the performance of government, nor does the eucational level of the populace. Most surprising, economic modernization isn't the key either. Some "have not" regions actually do a better job of managing their public business than their economically better-off counterparts.

What's crucial, it turns out, is the "civic-ness" of regional life—voter turnout (not homages to patronage), newspaper readership and membership in associations ranging from sports clubs to Lions Clubs, unions to choral societies—any kind of participation that "seems to depend less on *who* you are than on *where* you are." Where people perceive a public world framed by exploitation, corruption, individual powerlessness, citizenship is stunted. In such places, civic life only confirms the wisdom of cynicism—everyone is expected to violate the rules and to do otherwise is foolish. Once again, Tocqueville was right. "The most

democratic country in the world now," he wrote in *Democracy in America*, "is that in which men have in our time carried to the highest perfection the art of pursuing in common the objects of common desires and have applied this new technique to the greatest number of purposes."

Writing a quarter of a century ago, in *The Moral Basis of a Backward Society*, political scientist Edward Banfield argued that "amoral familism"—"maximize the material, short-run advantage of the nuclear family; assume that all others will do likewise"—explained the failure of civic life in some regions of Italy. Putnam puts the community and its "stocks of social capital" first. The supply of mutual trust, civic involvement and reciprocity naturally grows, as "virtuous circles" take on a life of their own. By contrast, someone trapped in a world of distrust and exploitation is unlikely to survive by promoting collaboration, for "the strategy of 'never cooperate' is a stable equilibrium."

That conclusion leads Putnam to search for the historic roots of the civic community, an inquiry that takes him all the way back to the twelfth century, when radically different political regimes first appeared in different regions of Italy. Autocratic rule, imposed in the South by Norman conquerers, became the regional norm, while unprecedented forms of self-government emerged in the very parts of the North where civic engagement and

successful government presently prevail.

These successful communities, says Putnam, did not become civic because they were rich. On the contrary: The historical record strongly suggests that, over the past 150 years at least, they became rich because they were civic, even as feudal, fragmented regions have slipped deeper into backwardness. The mutual aid societies and choral groups of our times can be traced back to the guilds, religious fraternities and tower societies in the medieval communes of Northern Italy, while in parts of the South, as a nineteenth-century writer observed, "One feels too much the 'I' and too little the 'we.'"

This is an account of Italy, but its implications are global—and sobering. There are no quick fixes, no mass inoculations of social capital that will turn Bosnia into Bologna, no ready way to imprint P.T.A.s or AIDS services organizations (or, more pertinently, their underlying values) in the Slovak Republic or the old East Germany. Nor, closer to home, is it an easy matter to nurture the practice of civic life that Tocqueville praised but that seems imperiled in the daily news accounts—the chronicles of our own amoral familism—whether about the highways of Miami or the hopelessly homeless on the streets of Anytown, U.S.A. In this respect, *Making Democracy Work* is one of the saddest stories a social scientist has ever told.

Italy's Dirty Linen

Denis Mack Smith

Getting the Boot:
Italy's Unfinished Revolution
by Matt Frei.
Times Books, 273 pp., $23.00

The Crisis of the Italian State:
From the Origins of the Cold War to
the Fall of Berlusconi
by Patrick McCarthy.
St. Martin's, 230 pp., $39.95

1.

Fifty years ago the collapse of Mussolini's authoritarian regime left his country in chaos, out of which emerged a new parliamentary republic. The achievements of this republic have since then been widely discussed, most recently by two of the more perceptive foreign observers now living in Italy. Matt Frei is an always well-informed journalist who reports for the BBC, and his new book contains a wealth of fascinating comments. Patrick McCarthy writes as a professor of European Studies at the Johns Hopkins University Bologna Center and treats the subject more analytically than Frei, with an even greater accumulation of detailed and persuasive evidence. From quite different perspectives they reach broadly similar conclusions. Both describe the enormous changes for the better that have taken place in Italy since the dark days of military defeat in 1945 and show how, after casting off the incubus

of fascism, Italy moved with impressive speed from being predominantly agricultural to becoming one of the major industrial nations in the world, with a great increase of individual prosperity. In fifty years its people have also made notable contributions in virtually every field of Western culture.

Yet the main theme of both authors is not these undoubted successes. It is rather the more difficult story of how Italy's political practices have been corrupt, self-destructive, and often more hindrance than help to social or economic development. Although the main Italian parties have all produced a few politicians of stature and integrity, in general "the political class"—the active politicians and civic leaders—has not measured up to the sophistication or to the enterprise and intelligence of ordinary citizens.

Admittedly the historical setting was not propitious. Fascism had its origin and classic manifestation in Italy after 1922: the word "fascism," like "mafia" and "vendetta," has come into universal currency from the Italian language, and the Fascist heritage has lingered beneath the surface of political life. Another divisive impediment has been communism, which as a consequence of Mussolini's ham-fisted politics, found far more support in Italy than in other Western countries. Further back in history, many centuries of foreign occupation and authoritarian rule en-

couraged qualities of rebelliousness and individualism which, however admirable at the time, attenuated any sense of allegiance to the state or the community.

Such ingrained habits are not quickly changed. Italy has been a unified state for not much more than a century, and loyalties even today are sometimes as much regional as national. Some Italians continue to blame the Risorgimento for having created an artificial union of disparate peoples that allowed prosperous northern Italians to exploit an impoverished south. Others have put some blame on the Vatican which, after many years of refusal to recognize the existence of an Italian nation, was subsequently, Frei writes, "responsible for some of the worst aspects of modern Italy"; McCarthy claims that it was "the prime cause of the new state's weakness." Pius IX and Pius X both issued anathemas against liberalism and democracy. Pius XI tried to persuade the Christian Democrats to ally themselves with fascism after 1922; so did Pius XII favor an alliance with the neo-fascists in 1952, though such an arrangement would have forfeited Italy's liberal credentials in Europe and handed victory to the extreme left in the perilously balanced elections of 1953.

Unlike other West European countries, the left in Italy has never won a national election, with the result that the Christian Democrats dominated fifty successive governments after 1945. This lack of any rotation in power was an anomaly and obviously unhealthy for any democracy; but it was supported by voters out of fear that a change from Christian-Democratic dominance would mean a victory for communism. What justified this fear was that the Italian Communists received subsidies from Soviet Russia until the 1980s and continued to talk favorably of revolution and proletarian dictatorship. Moreover, Palmiro Togliatti, their first leader, had been associated with some of Stalin's worst crimes. McCarthy, however, argues that Togliatti was no longer a genuine revolutionary after 1945 but merely feigned toughness in order to disarm the Leninist faction inside his party. Frei, while not going quite so far, writes that where the Communists held power in local government, as in the city of Bologna, they set an unmatched example of good administration, aiming to create "not so much a socialist workers' paradise" as "a monument to bourgeois good living and civic values."

This suggests an awkward comparison with the national administration, since the permanent occupation of central government by the Christian Democrats led to corrupt practices on so huge a scale that they eventually destroyed their party and greatly damaged the republic. One possible judgment in retrospect is that anticommunism, however expedient at first, persisted too long, both as an excuse to please the Americans and a convenient pretext to keep corrupt Italian politicians in power. Many foreign observers have forgotten that Togliatti's party, after playing a useful part in drafting the republican constitution, gave indispensable help to conservative governments in the daily business of legislation and supported the conservatives in crushing left-wing terrorism. One level-headed Christian-Democrat prime minister, Aldo Moro, defied American advice when he tried in the 1970s to bring the Communists into his coalition; in doing so he made what McCarthy calls "the postwar order's only serious attempt to reform itself." But this caused Moro to be unpopular with powerful interests at home as well as abroad, and after his tragic assassination by left-wing terrorists of the Red Brigades in 1978, the politicians of the

old order made sure that the experiment was not repeated.

The background to these events remains partly mysterious, and some of Italy's dirty secrets have been uncovered only by the much greater freedom of information in the United States—for example, American information about bribes of Italian officials by the Lockheed company led in 1978 to the ignominious resignation of an Italian head of state. The Communists were revealed to have accepted Soviet money, for which they were attacked as unpatriotic; but Washington turns out to have paid considerable sums to anti-Communist parties, including the neo-fascists. In 1990, Italian ministers and members of parliament were astonished to learn not only that for forty years a secret paramilitary force in their country had been trained and supplied by NATO and the United States in order to resist a possible Communist coup, but that some of the extracurricular activities of this undercover force seem to have had more dubious objectives, including personal profit, and were a grave threat to liberal government. The parliament has had difficulty in discovering whether the Italian secret services ever performed a useful and acceptable function: they are now known to have maintained disreputable links with both the mafia and right-wing terrorists, and their deviant behavior in repeatedly frustrating judicial investigation of terrorist crimes was a disgrace.

Another Italian anomaly was the preponderant size of the state sector in the economy, an imbalance inherited from Mussolini but further extended after 1945, when additional increases in state-controlled industries became an invaluable source of political patronage as well as of payoffs to politicians. Private industries such as Fiat, Pirelli, Olivetti, Benetton, Gucci, and Armani were admired and envied abroad for their success, whereas Italian state industries became a byword for inefficiency, featherbedding, and profligacy. All the major banks were inside the state sector, and they were often managed by party hacks who had absolutely no experience of banking.

McCarthy, in his best but most complex chapter, describes how Eugenio Cefis, a talented but dangerously power-seeking industrialist, used political intrigue and financial juggling with state-owned resources to fuse

ENI, the energy conglomerate, with the Edison electricity firm and the giant Montecatini chemical combine. In doing so he damaged three major industries; his successors, seeking to recoup some of the huge losses he incurred, then spent a hundred million dollars bribing politicians to use vast amounts of taxpayers' money to dissolve the partnership.

Political bribery can be found in every country, but in Italy it was allowed to proliferate almost unhindered, in part because the electoral system worked to prevent any alternation among the parties in power. According to Frei, no contracts for public works were signed with private or public companies unless a substantial bribe, or *tangente*, had been paid to the politicians involved; the naive assumption was that the lucky recipients would at once turn over the whole amount to their party. Even the Communists, though they denounced such illegal payments, yielded occasionally to temptation by accepting them when local administration was in their hands.

"The bribe was not only used as a lubricant for business," Frei writes, "it was often its sole purpose." The result was that the Italian landscape became littered with unfinished motorways, unused canals, abandoned hospitals, and building sites whose completion had sometimes never been intended. This systematic extortion of funds through public contracts was as harmful as the extorted "protection money" that supported the mafia. Both led to increased prices for consumers and losses to the government. Yet without these bribes the parties and politicians would have had to reduce lavish styles of life they had come to take for granted; McCarthy suggests that as a result the whole political system might have collapsed.

At the same time, social services were in effect taken over by politicians, who freely and corruptly distributed state-paid disability pensions in return for electoral support. Frei explains that in a country of fifty-eight million people there were four million disability pensioners, "about whom the most invalid thing was their ailment"; he might have added that in 1993 they included 150 members of parliament, one of them because of his "obesity." As many as a quarter of the population enjoyed some kind of index-linked pension because many people became legally qualified for retirement before the age of forty. Such retirement payments accounted for a quarter of the national budget. Any amateur economist might have foreseen that such extravagance could not continue without disaster, but ambitious politicians continued to outbid each other in the competition to buy votes. The public debt rose from 55 percent of gross domestic product in 1981 to 92 percent in 1987, and to over 120 percent in 1994—far beyond what Italy promised to maintain under the Maastricht treaty. Worse still, the example of their elected representatives reinforced the belief of taxpayers that politics had no connection with moral obligation or civic duty, a lesson that encouraged people to react in kind. In fact, without the wholesale evasion of taxes, the astronomical national debt would have been contained. Half of the value-added tax seems not to have been paid, and in some regions the figure rose to almost 90 percent. An investigation by the leading financial newspaper, *Il Sole 24 Ore*, found that

> the worst tax dodgers are economists and statisticians, followed closely by furriers, accountants, and stockbrokers. Those who dodged least...were doctors, who failed to declare, on average, only 20.5 percent of their annual income.

2.

In most governments after 1963 the Socialist Party was a junior partner inside Christian-Democrat coalitions and readily adapted to the prevailing practices of clientelism and *tangenti*. The Socialists won only between 9 and 14 percent of the popular vote after 1948, as compared with the Christian Democrats, who had 33 to 40 percent, and the Communists, who won between 22 and 34 percent. Despite this numerical discrepancy the Socialist Bettino Craxi became prime minister in 1983, since his support was needed to provide the dominant party with a safe anti-Communist majority. In the late 1980s Craxi indignantly told Frei that he had never committed a single illegal act. A few years later he was convicted and given an eight-year prison sentence for some of the many crimes charged against him, and he then escaped to Tunisia pending an appeal. One of Craxi's friends told the judges about stacking billions of illegally contributed lire in bundles at Socialist Party headquarters. Another friend confessed to having paid Craxi $16 million for favors, and the courts soon learned that this was only a small fraction of the illegal money that he or his party received.

Cabinet ministers from the Socialist Party, by demanding bribes before they took action, delayed rescue operations to save Venice from destructive flooding; they also siphoned off millions of dollars from the relief funds allocated to Bangladesh, Somalia, and Senegal. A Christian-Democrat minister of health was sent to prison for taking a regular cut from the money allotted for medicines, hospitals, and other help for patients with AIDS. One of this minister's senior officials had such a stranglehold over the drug companies that he and his wife accumulated fourteen Swiss bank accounts and kept one hundred million US dollars in cash at his various apartments and houses, along with a hundred gold ingots. When arrested he said this represented "forty years of personal savings," but unlike others he at least admitted to having "bent the rules a little."

Such details could not be revealed before 1992 because, by a private agreement between the parties, hundreds of deputies and senators used parliamentary immunity as a means of avoiding investigation, exposure, and possible prosecution. But rumors of vast corruption and of lawless official behavior became more and more current. Possibly no other Western country has so many major mysteries of state, so many unsolved crimes that were one way or another linked to high officials. As Frei and McCarthy observe, the truth has still not been established about military coups that were allegedly threatened in 1964 and 1970. Nor do we have the full story of the misappropriation of relief funds on a huge scale after horrific earthquakes; or about the murderous bombing in Milan in 1969 and a subsequent bombing in Bologna that together killed over a hundred people. In each case the evidence was deliberately falsified by the authorities, presumably to protect those responsible. We know something, but hardly enough, about the ways that the P-2 Masonic lodge acted outside the law during the 1970s to bribe politicians and engage in other corrupt financial and political dealings. Its members included cabinet ministers, top military officers, judges, and leading industrialists. .

Among the "illustrious deaths" of Italian public figures, the details of many are still vague—for example, details of the murder of Aldo Moro in 1978. The killing of the famous Sicilian bandit Salvatore Giuliano in 1950 became clear only after a newspaper discovered that the official account was a cover-up by the police to conceal their complicity with the mafia. The circumstances surrounding the plane crash in which the highly controversial oil baron and public official Enrico Mattei died in 1962 remain unclear; so do many questions about the deaths of the iniquitous "Vatican bankers" Roberto Calvi and Michele Sindona in the early 1980s. The Christian-Democrat leaders who refused to negotiate with left-wing terrorists to save the life of Aldo Moro were nevertheless willing to save a minor kidnapped party official from the same terrorists, with whom, Frei tells us, they persuaded the infamous Neapolitan Camorra to intervene, and whom they then paid what seems to have been an enormous ransom.

These are only a few of a long series of mysteries in which the public has been inclined to suspect the worst since the authorities have concealed the truth. Fortunately, however, there has in recent years been much more openness after an unexpected shift in the balance of political forces. A necessary catalyst was the end of the cold war and the fall of the Berlin wall; many voters now felt they no longer had to support parties that for more than forty years, by magnifying and exploiting the fear of communism, had maintained an increasingly unmerited dominance over Italian politics.

Another momentous change came when the Italian Communist party dissolved itself in 1990, permitting its more moderate members to form a quite different Democratic Party of the Left, which the die-hards refused to join. In Sicily the Catholic mayor of Palermo, Leoluca Orlando, broke ranks with the discredited Christian Democrats to form an anti-mafia and anti-government group. Another Christian Democrat, Mario Segni, led a similarly divisive movement inside his party, hoping to displace the older generation of politicians by modifying the practice of proportional representation. Equally important in changing the political balance was the formation of Umberto Bossi's Lombard League which, along with other regional groups in the north, achieved a remarkable electoral success as a populist party of protest against corruption and over-centralized government.

These new political groups, though they had little hope of winning a majority in parliament, and though their members often disagreed with each other, opened the way to new and quite different political alliances which reflected a growing popular frustration with the political establishment. Among Sicilians who, either from fear or insular pride, had frequently made excuses for the mafia, there was an increased awareness that this murderous organization was damaging their prosperity as well as their reputation in the outside world.

Government officials, too, after failing for decades to arrest convicted murderers who lived undisturbed in the center of Palermo, began to understand that the mafia connection, instead of winning votes as usual, might now do the opposite. It was too late for leading politicians to deny their own past by heading a movement for reform. But they were forced onto the defensive by a clause in the constitution that permitted the abrogation of existing laws by means of a popular referendum. Two such votes in 1991 and 1993 led to changes in electoral practices that allowed new parties more scope and left the Christian-Democratic and Socialist parties floundering. Distrust of the parties and of the government they installed was increased by their extravagant mismanagement of the economy. Lower profit margins forced some businessmen to resist demands for *tangenti*, a fact that not only reduced the amount of money available to politicians but at last encouraged aggrieved industrialists both to name the politicians who had been bleeding them and to seek protection from the courts.

Additional pressure on the Christian-Democrat politicians to accept changes in the system must have come, at least in private, from the Church; and much more publicly it came from the rest of Europe, where Italy's mounting budget deficit diminished the country's standing and credit-worthiness. Italians had enthusiastically joined the European common market but they caused offense by their reluctance to carry out many European Community decisions

that they disliked. There was irritation in Brussels when EU funds allocated for the relief of poverty vanished into the pockets of politicians in Rome or were sometimes sent to southern farmers who turned out not to exist.

As the main parties lost face and lost respect, the courts were at last able to step into the vacuum of power and act effectively, with results that were immediate and dramatic. Politicians had for many years hindered the judiciary in its dealings with the mafia, but a group of courageous judges and policemen, notably Giovanni Falcone and Paolo Borsellino in Palermo, took the initiative and scored important successes against the *malavita*. In places where witnesses had been too frightened to speak out, hundreds of senior and junior mafiosi, realizing that the usual political protection was no longer reliable, turned state's evidence, while hundreds of others were imprisoned.*

In Milan, where the main problem was political corruption, Antonio Di Pietro and Francesco Saverio Borrelli led another group of investigating magistrates who brought to court a cross-section of the political and industrial elite, producing a mountain of incriminating evidence. Di Pietro quickly became the most popular man in the country, more popular than pop stars or soccer players and far more popular than any minister or prime minister. The very suddenness and completeness of this change was telling: it suggested that a small group of politicians had been allowed to flourish at the expense of the community.

The most prominent representatives of this political class were the Socialist Craxi and the Christian Democrat Giulio Andreotti. The latter had been a minister in thirty governments since 1947 and was seven times prime minister, twice during the years between 1989 and 1992. As late as February 1992, Andreotti and Craxi expected to form a new government that would halt further investigations into political crime and perpetuate their joint condominium. Either was a possible candidate for the presidency of the republic; but in May 1992 their plans went awry when the brutal murder of Falcone by the mafia on a road near Palermo shocked the electoral college

---

*See Adrian Lyttelton's review of Alexander Stille's *Excellent Cadavers*, *The New York Review*, October 5, 1995.

into choosing someone outside the main party machines. After fifteen inconclusive votes the choice fell on Oscar Luigi Scalfaro, a Christian Democrat with a reputation for probity and good judgment, qualities that were constantly required during the next three years. The sense of panic was intensified when Borsellino, too, was murdered by the mafia in Sicily, and when several former ministers were arrested in Milan. Parliament once more voted to protect Craxi from indictment but then changed its mind as a result of public indignation. The judicial officials announced that three other former prime ministers were under police investigation. Andreotti, the most powerful man in the country, finally volunteered to waive his own parliamentary immunity from prosecution. (His trial on charges of collaborating with the mafia has only just begun and may go on for years.)

With the political parties in such disarray, four emergency governments between 1992 and 1995 tried to restore confidence and repair the damage. The first was led by Giuliano Amato, a Socialist with a reputation for honesty who made a valiant attempt to contain the budget deficit both by reducing pensions and tax evasion and by starting to privatize state-owned enterprises. His successor in 1993, Carlo Azeglio Ciampi, was a much respected governor of the Bank of Italy who had never been in parliament and was free from party affiliations. Ciampi's government of unelected academics and technical experts had the great advantage of not needing to buy votes; its honesty in confronting the crisis won it more admiration than any other government since the days of De Gasperi in the early 1950s.

Its chief task was to change the existing procedure for parliamentary elections, something that the dominant parties had not been able to do without risking political suicide. Proportional representation had created a large number of parties in parliament, leading to coalition governments that were unable to act decisively, could not agree on necessary reforms, and were held together mainly by a corrupt involvement in patronage. Ciampi and his advisers suggested a majoritarian method of voting that might produce a more homogeneous parliamentary majority and a more coherent opposition. Hitherto the opposition parties, with no expectation of ever winning power, had lacked the incentive for constructive criticism and accepted that their best hope of influencing policy lay in some kind of half-hearted cooperation with the government.

Unfortunately Ciampi's new law was watered down by parliament and the election of March 1994 produced ten different parties, so making another heterogeneous coalition inevitable. It was led by Silvio Berlusconi, one of the half a dozen richest people in Italy, a television, publishing, and real-estate mogul who had been a close ally of Craxi on the left, but now surprisingly allied himself with neo-fascists on the extreme right. Berlusconi's new party, Forza Italia, organized only two months before the election, nevertheless won 21 percent of the vote, a brilliant success that was helped by his ownership of all the main commercial television stations (and of a leading soccer team in a country that is passionate about football). His promise to create a million new jobs gave him further popularity, although Frei points out that unemployment actually increased during his seven months in office. He also promised not to raise taxes; but the budget was already so far out of control that this was merely populist electioneering.

Berlusconi's chief political weakness was that his two main coalition allies had entirely different aims: Umberto Bossi of the Northern League favored local autonomy and a federal division of Italy, while Gianfranco Fini, formerly an ardent fascist, inherited Mussolini's belief in strong centralized government. Bossi was violently anti-fascist, while Fini called Mussolini the greatest politician of the century. But Fini was a skillful political strategist and in January 1994, realizing that identification with fascism had no future, he persuaded his neo-fascists to dissolve their party and change into what he now called the National Alliance. He announced that it was democratic, anti-totalitarian, and anti-racist; but it was also nationalistic, with some mild overtones of anti-Americanism.

Such an ill-assorted coalition was bound to be ineffective and its members were soon quarreling. It was also weakened in the eyes of public opinion by apparent conflicts of interest that Berlusconi took no serious step to correct. As well as controlling most of commercial television, he now used his position to appoint new managers of the state television network in order to curb criticism of his government. As prime minister he also controlled the public-sector banks to which his commercial enterprises were heavily in debt; it was suspicious that he refused many requests to create a blind trust and put his own enormous business empire in escrow. He also proposed an amnesty for indictments of tax evasion and illegal real-estate development, which was not reassuring when he himself came under judicial investigation for these same offenses. He attempted to hinder the judiciary in its prosecutions over *tangenti* and even arranged the release of some of the worst offenders, until public indignation forced him to back down. McCarthy concludes that Berlusconi was so busy looking after his personal interests that he had no time to consider serious political reforms. Frei finds his government an almost complete failure. The collapse of the stock exchange and in the value of the lira showed how wide the loss of public confidence had become at the end of his time in office. Forza Italia lost much of its previous share of the vote in the local elections of November 1994. (Berlusconi himself was recently indicted for bribery and faces a trial in January 1996.)

Both books under review take the story down to January 1995, when President Scalfaro appointed Lamberto Dini as prime minister for what was Italy's fifty-fourth government in fifty years. Like Ciampi, Dini came from the much respected Bank of Italy and once again chose his ministers from outside parliament. During the following months he was remarkably successful in restoring confidence at home and in the international finan-

cial markets. But Italy's deeper political problems will be solved only when another election shows whether a discredited political elite can be replaced. Since 1945 the country has not lacked admirable politicians—the Christian Democrats Alcide De Gasperi and Oscar Luigi Scalfaro, the Communists Giorgio Amendola and Enrico Berlinguer, the Socialists Norberto Bobbio and Giuliano Amato, the Republicans Ugo La Malfa and Giovanni Spadolini, not to mention economic experts such as Luigi Einaudi, Carlo Ciampi, Dini, and Romano Prodi, the University of Bologna economist and former state administrator who is now trying to put together a center-left coalition.

Writing in January, McCarthy concluded that, until either the left or a center-left coalition comes to power, the reform of the Italian state will be impossible. Since then, Dini's stabilizing policy and Prodi's partial success may justify at least some degree of optimism. Nor is it entirely out of the question that Fini or some other conservative may create a genuinely democratic party of the right. Frei adds that renovation will also require a collective change in mentality, a keener sense of political morality, and a greater trust in the state. Italy might then become what, with pardonable exaggeration, he calls a paradise on earth.

Unfortunately, Italian-style politics still seem an almost insuperable obstacle to good government. Not only does the present administration lack a safe parliamentary majority, but the two most prominent politicians in the country—Andreotti and Berlusconi—are being prosecuted for bribery and corruption. Not only has the autumn budget not yet been passed, but the public debt continues to spiral out of control while the value of the lira has been falling dramatically. Another election cannot be avoided in the next few months and will hardly produce a credible result if Dini is unable before then to curb Berlusconi's virtual monopoly of commercial television. In other words, we may be watching the most critical test since 1945 of the Italian political system.

Unhappy Italy

Beppe Severgnini

Beppe Severgnini: writes for *Corriere della Sera*; author of "Inglesi" (Rizzoli, 1990; Hodder & Stoughton, 1991) and "Un Italiano in America" (Rizzoli, 1995).

In Italy, 1996 will be an election year. And this general election will deliver a government that will take the country to the end of the century. Everybody—an anxious president, the squabbling political parties, a confused electorate—seems to be holding their breath: hence Italy's present calm.

Italy, in other words, will have a chance to do right in 1996 what it did wrong in 1994. After two years of scandals and political upheaval, the general election of that year delivered a winner (Silvio Berlusconi), a winning coalition (the centre-right) and a programme of a kind. But it all turned sour in a matter of months. Mr Berlusconi showed that he was not ready to relinquish control of his media interests, and Umberto Bossi's Northern League started to fight with the other parties of the government coalition. When Mr Berlusconi eventually quit, Lamberto Dini and his "technocrats" took over and put through an overdue reform of the pension system.

Although a small political masterpiece—Machiavelli would have been proud to have had Mr Dini as a grandchild—the present precarious balance cannot last much beyond the spring. If it does, it will be to spare the embarrassment of not having a government while holding the presidency of the European Union. The general election will be close. The two coalitions have similar strengths, and show similar weaknesses. The centre-left, led by Romano Prodi and built around the PDS (Democratic Party of the Left), needs to decide what to do with the unrepentant communists and the Northern League (Mr Bossi's threats and calls to arms have become something of a national joke). On the right, the main question-mark hovers over Mr Berlusconi himself. If he leads the coalition he helped to found, many moderates will not vote for it; if he steps back, the coalition will have to find another charismatic leader, in a country where political charisma is at a premium.

To whom might the two coalitions turn? In both cases, Mr Dini, strange as it may seem. The prime minister represents the mythical "centre", able to deliver those crucial votes needed for victory. If he is indeed wooed by both sides, the following will become apparent: first, that the two coalitions have similar programmes (or none); second, that "amateur time" in Italian politics is over. Mr Dini's attractiveness, to many Italians, is that he is an old hand and a skilled operator (as his handling of the 'no confidence' motion in October made clear). His time in Washington (at the World Bank) and then with Banca d'Italia gives him credibility at home and abroad.

1996's election will complete the sweeping changes in Italy's political leadership that started in 1994. Two former prime ministers, Giulio Andreotti and Bettino Craxi, will meet their judicial destiny; leaders such as Mr Bossi and Mario Segni—the stars of the early 1990s—are going to fade away. Former magistrate Antonio Di Pietro, the popular hero of the *Mani Pulite* (Clean Hands) investigation, might consider establishing his own centre party, under the fatherly-eye of Oscar Luigi Scalfaro, the President of the Republic and Irene Pivetti, chair of the lower house of parliament.

The establishment inherited from the so-called "First Republic", though, will show resilience. Entrenched in public jobs, they will wait to know the winners' names, before rushing to their side. A scandal named *Affittopoli* (or *Casa nostra*, Our Home, a cruel reference to *Cosa nostra*, the Mafia) has revealed this group to be vast, and shameless: big flats, in the historic centres of cities such as Rome and Milan, are given out to trade unionists, top civil servants and party apparatchiks for token rents. It is likely that similar scandals will erupt in 1996. For instance, who owns the thousands of cellular telephones whose bills are paid for with public money?

No matter who wins the general election—the centre-right, which is closer to Mr Dini's convictions and to the country's mood, might have the edge—1996 will signal something of a revolution. Italians now seem ready to accept that one side will win, and the other will lose. This may seem obvious. It is not. Digesting the majority system has taken the nation almost three years.

Another revolution—launched in 1992 when magistrates in Milan started to uncover an extraordinary web of political corruption—will come to an end. Italy is tired of emergencies; the country has not lost its appetite for justice, but it has exhausted its capacity for indignation. This will help to bring about a "political solution" to the *Mani Pulite* investigation, allowing restitution of assets and plea bargaining.

More good news will be around in 1996. Wasting money—in the south, in frauds, in ill-conceived public projects—will decrease; not because of the new leadership's wisdom or of enhanced public morality, but because there is less money to be wasted. Slowly and painfully, transport, telecommunications and the fiscal system in Italy will catch up with the modern world. When domestic resistance is strong (take air transport), European pressure will prove to be decisive. Do not expect bold, American-style deregulation: Italy will get there, but in its own slow time, and in its own convoluted way.

Although inflation, at around 6%, will outstrip GDP growth of 2.7%, Italy is keen to rejoin the ERM; but the country has little chance of participating fully in monetary union while its public debt remains high. The first six months of 1996, when Italy will hold the presidency of the European Union, will see a flurry of diplomatic activity. Well-meaning, but hardly decisive. As the events in the former Yugoslavia have shown, to the weaknesses of the UN, NATO and the EU, Italy adds a dimension of its own.

Italy

Mess continues

THAT Italian ritual, the search for a new government, was on again this week as President Oscar Luigi Scalfaro tried to find a successor to Lamberto Dini, who resigned as prime minister on January 11th. Mr Dini's quiet exit, on realising that he no longer had a majority in parliament, hardly made a ripple in Italy's often choppy financial markets. But, beyond the ritual, a debate which could yet change the nature of Italian politics is under way.

Even Italians have been puzzled by the labyrinthine goings-on: Mr Scalfaro arranged meetings this week with no fewer than 26 delegations, representing as many political parties and parliamentary groups.

For most of his compatriots it was further proof, if it were needed, that electoral reform has failed. First-past-the-post voting rules for three-quarters of the seats in parliament were adopted before the 1994 election, but the new system has failed to clarify political choices for the voters.

When the first government elected under the new rules (led by the media tycoon Silvio Berlusconi) collapsed a year ago after just seven months, Mr Dini was appointed to head a government of non-elected technicians. His brief was to carry out a set of limited if needed reforms. Since then, things have hardly become clearer. At the latest count there were 13 distinct groups in parliament, plus a batch of mavericks and motley breakaways from the two loose coalitions which, when they fought the 1994 election, gave voters the illusion that Italy had adopted a bipolar system.

Now the political leaders have run out of reasons to keep Mr Dini's government afloat. They must either go for a snap election or agree among themselves both on an agenda of political reform and on a cabinet to carry them out. Some say Mr Scalfaro favours reform. He has argued before that, if an election were held today under the same rules, with a quarter of the seats dished out by the old system of pure proportional representation, the vote could produce the same stalemate. That is why electoral reform is back at the top of the agenda.

An array of proposals is now in the offing. Umberto Bossi, the federalist Northern League leader who did well in the last elections but is expected to fare worse this time, is most radical. He wants a specially elected assembly to rewrite the constitution under the auspices of the current parliament—a process that could take two years. Mr Berlusconi is now also urging electoral reform. In a startling U-turn just before Christmas, he proposed himself as prime negotiator. He suggested, among other things, that a cabinet of representatives from the two main coalitions, his own centre-right lot and the centre-left, should be entrusted with governing for more than a year.

Mr Berlusconi's change of heart may owe a lot to his problems with the law. This week he, his brother Paolo and nine others went on trial in Milan for alleged corruption. In court, Mr Berlusconi was all smiles for the cameras. But with the trial under way it would be hard for him to stand as coalition leader. Even if he did, and won, it would be nigh-impossible for Mr Scalfaro to put him forward as prime minister.

Not that Mr Berlusconi has forgotten how to talk tough. This week he lambasted Antonio Di Pietro, the Milanese prosecutor who four years ago launched the "clean hands" inquiry that took the lid off political corruption and, by the by, brought Mr Berlusconi and various managers of his Fininvest media-to-retail group to trial on charges of bribing tax inspectors to wink at phoney audits. Mr Berlusconi accuses Mr Di Pietro of running his inquiry to further his own political ambition. The prosecutor, who unexpectedly left the judiciary in December 1994, has indeed toyed with the idea of using his huge popularity to stand for office.

At the end of last year, both men were put under investigation in Brescia, near Milan. A local prosecutor asked for Mr Berlusconi to be charged with trying to blackmail Mr Di Pietro into giving up his job in Milan. The same magistrate also asked for Mr Di Pietro to be charged with abuse of office, for allegedly accepting a soft loan from a crooked businessman before the "clean hands" era began. The Brescia courts may decide later this month whether the charges should be formally laid.

This latest episode is a depressing distraction from the urgent business of political and electoral reform, whose future now seems to hinge on a compromise between the centre-right's proposal for prime ministers to be directly elected and the centre-left's suggestion of French-style two-round run-offs in national elections. If Mr Scalfaro fails to engineer a compromise, he would rather keep Mr Dini a few weeks longer in power than risk a government void just when Italy is presiding over the presidency of the European Union.

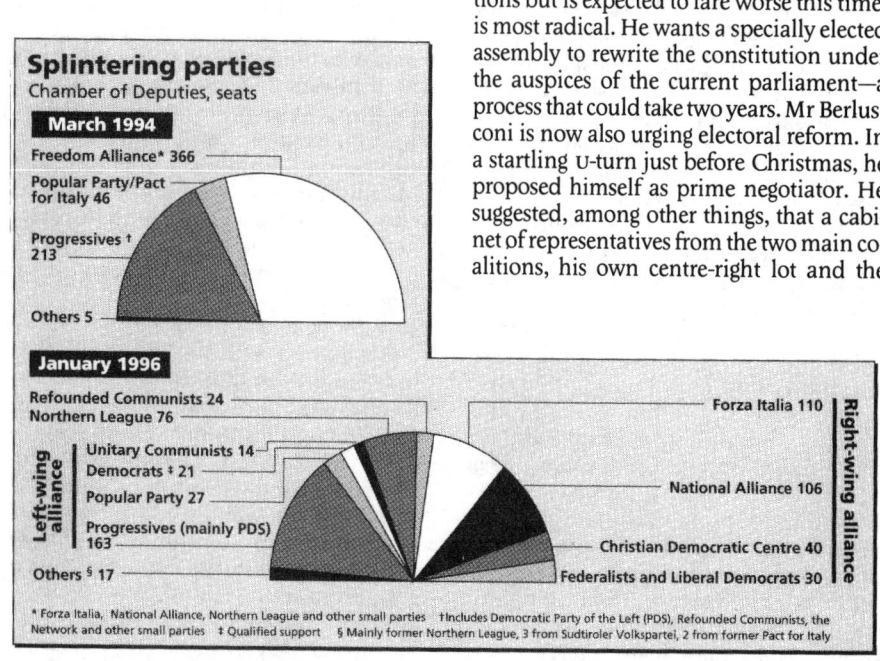

Splintering parties
Chamber of Deputies, seats

March 1994

Freedom Alliance* 366
Popular Party/Pact for Italy 46
Progressives † 213
Others 5

January 1996

Refounded Communists 24
Northern League 76
Unitary Communists 14
Democrats ‡ 21
Popular Party 27
Progressives (mainly PDS) 163
Others § 17

Left-wing alliance

Forza Italia 110
National Alliance 106
Christian Democratic Centre 40
Federalists and Liberal Democrats 30

Right-wing alliance

* Forza Italia, National Alliance, Northern League and other small parties   † Includes Democratic Party of the Left (PDS), Refounded Communists, the Network and other small parties   ‡ Qualified support   § Mainly former Northern League, 3 from Sudtiroler Volkspartei, 2 from former Pact for Italy

Reforming Japan

The Third Opening

Ichiro Ozawa believes that Japan, for the third time in little over a century, needs radical reform. In this article, he explains why he finds the prospect exhilarating

NATIONS are nurtured by myths. Japan is no exception. If I mention the "third opening of Japan", most Japanese will immediately know what I mean, just as if I were citing the need for a new Magna Carta. Unless outsiders place what is happening in Japan today in the context of our history and our myths, they will find it difficult to understand the particular turning-point we are facing in our long evolution as a nation.

Our myths arise from the fact that we are a group of narrow islands off the coast of Asia, coming only sporadically into contact with our continental neighbours down through the years. We take comfort in our homogeneity, in our capacity to absorb influences from the mainland at our own pace, in timespans measured by centuries rather than decades. For us, much more than for Britain, "the jungle begins at Calais"—in our case, the Korea Strait. In essence, we see ourselves as a cosy village society where consensus is the norm and where we all live by unspoken rules to make life tolerable in a green but crowded land with few natural resources.

The first great challenge to these myths came in 1853, when Commodore Matthew Perry and his heavily armed "black ships" dropped anchor in Tokyo (then known as Edo) Bay, and sent a message from President Millard Fillmore demanding that Japan open its doors to trade with the world. Until then, the Tokugawa Shoguns who had ruled Japan since 1603 had imposed a near-total ban on travel into or out of the country, the single exception being the port of Nagasaki, in southern Japan, where Dutch and Chinese merchants were allowed to bring in their wares.

Ichiro Ozawa is the president of the New Frontier Party and leader of the Japanese opposition. A former secretary-general of the Liberal Democratic Party, Mr Ozawa left the LDP in 1993, precipitating the end of 38 years of conservative rule. He was the architect of the coalition that ruled Japan in 1993-94.

BY INVITATION

The Shogunate officials knew that their antiquated shore batteries were no match for Perry's cannons. They had no recourse but to give way, choosing to do so as little as they could. In so doing, they set in motion a nationwide debate between advocates of continued isolation and reformers who wanted to open up the country. The debate lasted 15 years—a period of great turmoil, ending only with the collapse of the Shogunate, the abolition of feudalism, and the establishment of a reform-minded central government under the direct rule of the Emperor Meiji. This series of events is known today as the first opening of Japan.

The Meiji era, which lasted for nearly half a century, was a heady time for Japan. The young reformers gathered around the emperor knew that for Japan's survival, they had to make drastic changes in the political, economic and social institutions of their country. One of the five pledges with which Meiji inaugurated his reign was to "seek knowledge throughout the world". His reformers created a modern army and navy, introduced capitalism, universal education, and a limited form of constitutional democracy, including the concept of equality under the law.

But the grafting of Western institutions and values on to traditional patterns of Japanese thought and behaviour was not achieved without great strain. The Meiji reformers were mostly bureaucrats and administrators, and, although they saw the need for elected parliaments, they preferred Bismarck to Gladstone—that is, they limited both the powers of parliament and the numbers of those able to vote for it. It was not until the early 1920s that Takashi Hara, the first commoner to become prime minister, introduced universal adult male suffrage. His reward was assassination. From the late 1920s, Japan became increasingly militaristic and authoritarian, embarking on adventures in China which led to confrontation with the United States and Britain and ended in disastrous defeat in the second world war.

Japan's surrender in 1945 and the sweeping reforms brought about during a six-year occupation by American forces under the command of General Douglas MacArthur constitute what many of us call the second opening of Japan. The second opening, like the first, began as a result of conflict with foreigners but continued differently because most of the changes took place under foreign duress. Yet the main planks of the occupation reforms embodied ideas and programmes begun in the Meiji period and were genuinely popular with voters: land reform, dissolution of the *zaibatsu* (giant financial and industrial trusts), freedom of speech and assembly, free trade unions and women's suffrage. A new constitution was drafted, including the famous article nine renouncing the right to go to war and banning the use of armed force. At least in form, Japan became a fully-fledged parliamentary democracy, with political power in the hands of the people's elected representatives.

Under the impetus of these reforms, and helped by the cold war which kept Japan firmly within America's orbit and under the protection of the US-Japan security treaty, our people concentrated single-mindedly on economic recovery and growth. With no natural resources to speak of beyond the education and talents of our citizens, we imported raw materials from all over the world and exported manufactured goods to all the world. By the late 1960s we had outstripped West Germany as the non-communist world's second largest economy, surpassed in size only by the United States.

Our political progress, however, did not keep pace with the explosive growth of our economy. Conservative political forces quickly came together to form the Liberal Democratic Party (LDP). But the opposition Socialists remained ideologically stuck in the rhetoric of the cold war, advocating the dissolution of the alliance with the United States and an unarmed neutrality that could only benefit the Soviet Union. Voters used the Socialists and other opposition parties to express dissatisfaction with the government of the day, but never in such numbers as to deprive the LDP of power. While we remained a parliamentary democracy in form, in practice the LDP was continuously in office, except for a brief period in 1947-48.

That long hold on power bred corruption, enhanced by the cosy village nature of Japanese society. Meanwhile, from outside Japan, and particularly from America and Europe, we began to hear increasingly shrill demands to open up our markets; outsiders also urged us to assume a diplomatic role in the international community commensurate with the size of our economy and its weight in the world.

The new frontier

To my mind, what these pressures building up inside and outside our country amount to is nothing less than a demand for the third opening of Japan—for changes as drastic and far-reaching as the ones brought about by the Meiji reformers and by the American occupation after 1945. That, indeed, is what my party, the New Frontier Party, stands for. If our programme succeeds, we will have brought about a revolution that will complete the work begun by the Meiji reformers more than 100 years ago. It will embody the most far-reaching changes that our country has ever known, and enable us to join the ranks of what I call the world's normal democratic states.

We have in Japan today the institutional forms of parliamentary government, but with a content rather different from what is regarded as normal in American or European democracies. Ours still reflects consensus politics and an isolationist mentality that excludes outsiders. The goal of the New Frontier Party is to break this mould and to bring about alternation in government between two political parties that will compete with each other on the basis of policy, not of factions or of personalities.

The Liberal Democrats' post-war monopoly of power was broken in July 1993, when Tsutomu Hata and I led a group of reform-minded colleagues to rebel against the party leadership and to establish a new party, the Japan Renewal Party. Together with other opposition parties, we won the general election that month and formed the Hosokawa coalition government. The following year, the Liberal Democrats made a deal with their sworn enemies, the Socialists, and returned to power. In reaction to this unholy alliance, all the main opposition parties except the Communists came together in December 1994 to establish the New Frontier Party.

Today, at least in form, we have the beginnings of a two-party system. On one side stands the government—a coalition of the LDP, the Socialists and the *Sakigake* or Harbingers, a minor party. The coalition was headed first by a Socialist, Tomiichi Murayama, and now by a Liberal Democrat, Ryutaro Hashimoto. Despite their differences in ideological outlook, the LDP and the Socialists are essentially status quo parties. They mouth the slogans of reform, but in fact they want to keep their vested interests.

The new agenda

By contrast, our party is dedicated to the cause of reform. We call for thoroughgoing changes in politics, in the economy, in education and in society. In politics, we have been partially successful in that, during our brief year in power, we changed the election system from one of multi-seat districts to one which has 300 single-seat constituencies and 200 seats to be voted for on a proportional-representation list. It is somewhat like the German system. Each voter will have two votes and can cast his ballot both for his local candidate and for the party of his choice.

The world has not yet recognised the revolutionary nature of this change because the first election under the new system has yet to be held. At the latest, however, the next general election must be held in July 1997. It could come much sooner—possibly this summer or autumn. It may not immediately bring about a permanent two-party system but, as voters become used to the system, minor parties will fade away. The Socialist Party, recently renamed the Social Democratic Party, will be the top candidate for extinction.

In each of the 300 single-seat constituencies, voters will have two clear points of view to choose between—that of the ruling coalition and that of the New Frontier Party. Many legislators, even those belonging to our party, are uncomfortable with this prospect. They want to build coalitions based on interests and personalities, as they have been doing till now, and are not sure that voters will respond to policy-based appeals. I am convinced, however, that the New Frontier Party must make this sort of appeal to the voters.

Lessons from Iwate

My own constituency in Iwate is largely rural but I have insisted that farmers, like other citizens, must face the fact of international competition and not simply hide behind protective barriers. My recipe for change brings pain to my constituents but so far I have managed to be re-elected with substantial majorities. I feel certain that, nationwide, voters will respond to political leadership if that leadership can provide a clear, compelling vision of the future and realistic steps to achieve it.

For us, there is no alternative to the third opening of Japan—to opening our markets wide to the international community, to chopping down the thicket of rules and regulations which are choking initiative, creativity and economic growth. I have no illusions about the difficulty of our task. Japan has been a regulated society for more than 1,000 years. We have a lot of people, little land, and few natural resources. For everyone to share in an economy of scarcity, there have to be regulations, and on the whole people have accepted these regulations. In modern times, the concept of fairness, of equality, has taken precedence over the concept of individual freedom. We are a society without vast gaps between rich and poor, management and workers. We would like to keep it so, but not at the cost of stifling personal freedom and individual initiative.

Despite my experience with voters in Iwate, I know that most Japanese still feel uncomfortable and disoriented by the prospect of living in a society with few regulations and where each person will have to be more self-reliant and take greater responsibility for his or her own actions. Nevertheless there is no other way for Japan to move into the 21st century and survive. What we are embarked upon is a revolutionary process, and it will not be completed in a day.

We want lean government at the centre, and more power devolved to local entities. At the moment, Japan has a highly centralised system with no clear division between the central and local governments. Ultimately we will have about 300 local authorities nationwide—small enough to be close to the voters, large enough to carry out effective government—to replace the present hodgepodge of prefectures, cities, towns and villages.

Educational reform may be the most important of the reforms we propose. Universal education was one of the great achievements of the Meiji reformers. Japan today is one of the world's most literate nations. But our education system remains stuck in the 19th century, emphasising rote learning and stuffing students with all sorts of relevant and irrelevant information. We need education that will foster self-reliance and creativity. Group values like fairness and equality are important, but the primary emphasis must be on allowing the individual to develop. Education is an area in which we may not see results for ten years or more. But we must begin now, for we are already far behind the leaders in this field.

Japan and the world

Internationally, I have long advocated a much more active and participatory stance in world affairs, with the proviso that we remain in close partnership with the United States.

Some Japanese argue that, with the cold war over and with America no longer as overwhelming a military and economic superpower as it used to be, we should form closer ties with Asia, perhaps even play the role of honest broker between China and the United States. I disagree. I hope that China, as its economy grows and its people prosper, will successfully make the transition from authoritarianism to democratic government. I also hope that China and Taiwan will settle their differences peacefully on the basis of their common recognition that Taiwan is part of China. But these are not yet foregone conclusions. North Korea is an even more troubling neighbour than China. Asia needs the American security presence, and the US-Japan security treaty provides the means for America not only to protect Japan but to remain involved with Asia. Furthermore, Japan's own past record in Asia is not forgotten. We will be accepted and considered nonthreatening by our Asian neighbours only to the extent that we retain a strong security relationship and economic partnership with the United States.

This does not mean that we will agree with America in all respects nor that we will fail to advance our own point of view. We may have as many disagreements with America as do Britain, France or Germany. But like them, our disagreements should always take place within the context of our basic alliance. Alliance with America is as essential for Japan as it is for Europe—perhaps more so, because in Asia we have nothing like NATO or the European Union.

We want a permanent seat on the United Nations Security Council, and pledge to play a leading role in the affairs of that body. The United Nations is far from perfect, but it is the only international forum we have, and we want to make it better. How can we do so unless we participate in all its activities, including peacekeeping? I have proposed that Japan establish a stand-by force, separate from the present Self Defence Force, that will be available for UN peacekeeping duties whenever called upon by the Security Council and the secretary general.

Our constitution forbids going to war as a sovereign right of the Japanese government, but I submit that it by no means forbids Japan from placing its forces under UN command for peacekeeping duties. In fact, the preamble of the constitution talks of preserving "our security and existence, trusting in the justice and faith of the peace-loving peoples of the world." How can we do so, how can we "occupy an honoured place in an international society striving for the preservation of peace, and the banishment of tyranny and slavery, oppression and intolerance," if we do not participate fully in UN peacekeeping?

Ultimately, the idea that underlies the third opening of Japan is the need to change society. We have to move from decisions by consensus, so called, into the essence of democracy, decision-making by the majority, with the minority accepting those decisions in the belief that today's minority will become tomorrow's majority. Our new election system is one means to this end, but I am under no illusions that we can reach our goal without repeated setbacks. Still, the 21st century is less than four years away, and it is urgent not only to get the process started but to make sure that it becomes irreversible.

Japan's New Prime Minister

Vote Puts Japan's Former Ruling Party Back at Helm

Teresa Watanabe

Times Staff Writer

TOKYO—After more than two years in the political shadows, Japan's conservative Liberal Democratic Party roared back to prominence Thursday as prickly trade minister Ryutaro Hashimoto was sworn in as prime minister and named a Cabinet anchored by the party's Old Guard.

Hashimoto, the LDP's president, became Japan's eighth premier in seven years, succeeding outgoing Socialist Prime Minister Tomiichi Murayama, by capturing 288 of 489 votes cast in a special parliamentary poll. Hashimoto betrayed no emotion as he bowed deeply upon announcement of his victory—the culmination of a 32-year political career in which he has distinguished himself as one of Japan's most seasoned leaders and sharpest policy minds.

"I feel a great amount of responsibility," Hashimoto said. "I'd like to run a government that is not only reformist but also creative."

Hashimoto's ascension had been hailed as a blow for firm leadership in a nation adrift, but he baffled many analysts by appointing a Cabinet conspicuously lacking in political heavyweights and public appeal.

Delicately balanced among the coalition's three partners, the lineup appears short on political chieftains or policy wizards able to push through solutions to such pressing problems as Japan's lingering recession, financial scandals, tax reform and demands to relocate some of the U.S. military basis from Okinawa, analysts said.

In two notable choices, Hashimoto named as chief Cabinet secretary Seiroku Kajiyama, an ace at back-room power politics whose staunch opposition to political reform triggered the LDP's demise in 1993. Although Kajiyama told reporters that the Cabinet's motto would be "let's create something new," he represents a throwback to the days of factional struggles and money politics championed by the late LDP godfather, Kakuei Tanaka.

If Kajiyama lacks fresh appeal, however, he is endowed with the parliamentary skills and brute political muscle Hashimoto will need to take on formidable opposition leader Ichiro Ozawa, analysts said. The three men all mastered the rough-and-tumble politics of their common mentor, Tanaka, promising a dramatic clash of long-time blood feuds between Japan's most powerful political figures.

Hashimoto entrusted the financial portfolio—in a nation now battered by money scandals and spiraling bad debts—to a man with little knowledge or experience in the field, veteran Socialist legislator Wataru Kubo.

With 16 of 20 ministers being first-time Cabinet members, analysts said Hashimoto's lineup appeared less designed for serious statecraft than for gearing up for general elections expected sometime this year.

"This is not a Cabinet that will do something," said Gerald Curtis, a Columbia University political science professor who spoke by phone from New York. "It is a weak Cabinet with the Old Guard LDP in the co-pilot's chair. Powerful people don't want to be in a Cabinet that won't last long and who want to prepare for elections instead."

But Yukio Okamoto, a political consultant and former Foreign Ministry official, said the lackluster Cabinet means the formidable team of Hashimoto and Kajiyama could dominate policy and this would lead to quick resolution of problems.

"In a sense, Mr. Hashimoto has no stumbling blocks in front of him," Okamoto said.

Fukashi Horiye, a Keio University political analyst and law professor, said the Cabinet was skillfully crafted to dodge opposition attacks and minimize conflict among the Liberal Democrats, Socialists and New Party Harbinger. The appointment of a Socialist finance minister may neutralize opposition to a consumption tax hike, scheduled for debate this fall, and deflect attacks on the coalition's proposed $6.2-billion bailout of housing-loan firms. That is because the Socialists were removed from the center of power that created the financial mess in the late 1980s, while Hashimoto, as finance minister at the time, represented it.

The LDP's stronger sway in the new Cabinet could hasten resolution of the Okinawa problem; Murayama was sympathetic to the simmering resentment there against U.S. military bases and showed reluctance to ram through orders to accept them. But the appointment of relatively junior politicians to the posts of foreign and trade minister indicated that no major U.S.-Japan initiatives would be proposed.

New Foreign Minister Yukohiko Ikeda, 58, has served as Japan Defense Agency chief but is best known for his more illustrious father-in-law, the late Prime Minister Hayato Ikeda. The new trade minister, Shupei Tsukahara, 48, is a nondescript lower house member delicately described by the Yomiuri Shimbun as needing to "explore his political capabilities further."

Hashimoto named one woman and political outsider, health bureaucrat Ritsuko Nagao, as justice minister. He parceled out 11 posts to the LDP, six to the Socialists and two to the New Party Harbinger.

Around Tokyo, expectations of the new government appeared low, and some criticized it for passing around the prime ministership without seeking a mandate from voters, as Ozawa is demanding.

"Now I'm lost because you can't distinguish one party from the other," said Chie

Fujimaki, a homemaker in her 50s. "Whichever party takes leadership, there won't be much difference. I've given up."

"This Cabinet was born of politics, and the public had nothing to do with it, so the public has lost expectations of political reform," said Akira Fujita, 37, a patent lawyer. "Unless everything is destroyed, Japan won't change."

Chiaki Kitada and Mengumi Shimizu of The Times' Tokyo Bureau contributed to this report.

─◆─◆─◆─◆─◆─◆─

Political Survival Is the Name of the New Game

Norman D. Levin

Norman D. Levin, a senior analyst at RAND, was on the policy-planning staff at the State Department from 1984–87.

Beneath the surprise resignation of Japanese Prime Minister Tomiichi Murayama and his replacement by Ryutaro Hashimoto, coupled with the election of Ichiro Ozawa as head of Japan's main opposition party, is a country in the throes of a political transition. For those eager for rapid and radical change, this transition can be frustrating. So gradual are the changes that one may fairly conclude there really is no change. But the trends are unmistakable.

The sudden changes at the political top have spawned two contrasting interpretations. According to one, Hashimoto's rise heralds the advent of a new era, with strong leadership in Tokyo and major policy changes ahead. Japan is portrayed as having reached a fork in the political road: A "titanic" battle between "reformers" and the "old guard" over Japan's future course is coming.

The second interpretation stresses not change but continuity. Indeed, some observers worry that the changes in political leadership may even end the reforms begun by previous governments and reverse progress toward a more open and responsive nation.

After nearly four decades of one-party rule, two failed "reformist" governments and a year and a half of feeble Socialist Party leadership, Japan certainly appears ripe for new departures. Economic growth remains anemic. The banking

system is in disarray. And other problems—such as a budget deficit that could reach nearly $240 billion this year and growing strains in Japan's relationship with the United States—reinforce the impression that change is inevitable. "New vision" books by both Hashimoto and Ozawa have fed this premonition of impending change.

But in the short term, any expectations for dramatic change are likely to be disappointed. Whatever Japanese leaders may say about "new visions," the name of the game in Japan is not policy but political survival. This preoccupation is spurred by Japan's new electoral system, which replaces multiple-seat constituencies (three or four candidates could make it into the Diet on only a fraction of the vote) with single-seat districts (the victor will be the top vote-getter).

In addition to these structural changes, the unity required to institute major new departures is present in neither of the dominant political groupings. This is certainly true in the coalition led by Hashimoto: Fundamental philosophical differences among the ruling parties preclude agreement on any but the lowest common denominator. But the main opposition grouping is similarly constrained. Here, political rivalries and intramural differences raise broader questions about how long Ozawa will be able to hold his followers together. Indeed, the substantive

policy differences within each of the coalitions make those between Hashimoto and Ozawa pale by comparison.

Finally, no consensus—or, by all appearances, desire—exists for radical policy change among the Japanese public. There are, to be sure, many signs of public dissatisfaction with, and even cynicism about, Japanese politics. These include sharply declining voting rates, rising numbers of people identifying themselves as supporters of no political party and a new willingness to elect non-traditional candidates to prominent political offices. Many Japanese would welcome stronger leadership. But the general mood is more one of apathy than agitation, which does not readily translate into demands for new policies.

Predictors of a continuation of the status quo find support in these same developments. If nothing else, the "sudden" resignation of a Japanese prime minister (which virtually everyone in Japan believed was long overdue), prompting the back-room selection of another prime minister from a different party (which most Japanese commentators deplored), based on a "policy platform" cobbled together almost overnight (which not even coalition leaders themselves disguised as anything but a hodge-podge of past compromises) hardly augurs a "new" Japan.

But worries about a reversion to past practices are also exaggerated. Leaving

From the *Los Angeles Times*, January 14, 1996, pp. M1, M6. © 1996 by The Los Angeles Times. Reprinted by permission.

aside the fact that "reform" did not make much headway even under "reformist" governments, the underlying political transition continues. This evolution is now being driven as much by the new electoral system as by any individual Japanese leader. At least one or two elections under the new system will probably be necessary before the future can be discerned. But three trends suggest its general direction:

• *An evolutionary move to a new party system.* The era of one-party dominance is over. Of course, a future "conservative-conservative" merger or coalition is not inconceivable, particularly if the contentious Ozawa exits the political stage. But for now, the trend is toward some form of two-party structure. This is reflected in the results of last July's upper-house election, which decimated the Socialists, nearly obliterated the Sakigake Party and other minor parties and left the Liberal Democratic Party and the New Frontier Party as the two overwhelmingly dominant forces.

Weaker candidates in need of improving their chances at the polls will gravitate toward one or the other of the major parties. As a result, the momentum for change will likely accelerate once elections for the more powerful lower house are held under the new electoral system. Such a development, were it to occur, would create a responsible alternative to LDP rule. It also would be an important step in the development of a more "mature" democracy.

• *A gradual weakening of the importance of traditional power brokers and the rise of new younger leaders.* This trend dates to the LDP's breakup and fall from power in 1993, when factional bosses lost both their ability to guarantee cabinet and high party posts for their members and their role as principal provider of funds for their members' political activities. While the factions continue to exist informally, their importance is waning. Skillful and ambitious younger leaders are gradually filling the vacuum. This is likely to continue under the new electoral system as each party searches for "fresh" faces to strengthen its popularity.

This search appears to have already begun: As of last November, more than one-fourth of the single-seat candidates designated by the LDP for the next election were non-incumbents; the ratio was greater than one-third for the Socialists and almost one half for the Sakigake. Each of the major political parties has a long way to go in opening up its recruitment and decision-making practices. But this trend has the potential to infuse new blood into tired political organizations, while encouraging increased participation in politics.

• *An increasing voice for Japanese voters.* It is sobering but worth recalling that, until 1993, the Liberal Democratic Party was essentially the only game in town. No other party was perceived as capable of governing. With the split of the LDP and the adoption of the new electoral system, however, politicians have begun dispersing to the two major parties, which are both regarded as capable of running things. Even if the two parties pursue relatively similar policies, Japanese voters will have the power to punish the incumbent party for not living up to its promises. Indeed, the incentive to do so will be great because there would be no negative consequences. This will not only magnify the importance of responsive leadership, but the public will also have a louder say in national policies.

For Japan, the strengthening of these trends means life as a more "normal" country. At home, both domestic and foreign-policy issues are more likely to be buffeted by internal politics. Abroad, Japan is more likely to speak with a clearer, more focused voice. Changes are likely to remain evolutionary in nature and be carried out incrementally. Absent an external crisis, it's the way things generally happen in Japan.

Intellectual Warfare

The reviews of James Fallows's latest book are emblematic of our complacency about the nature and implications of Japan's economic strength

Chalmers Johnson

Chalmers Johnson is the president of the Japan Policy Research Institute, in Los Angeles, California. He is the author of many books on East Asian politics, including Japan: Who Governs?

**LOOKING AT THE SUN:
The Rise of the
New East Asian Economic
and Political System**

*by James Fallows.
Pantheon, 517 pages,
$25.00.*

THE Cold War has now been over for five years, but there's been no real change in America's military pretensions. Less than three years remains before Hong Kong, the world's third largest financial center (after New York and London), is turned over to China. The English-language business press proclaims that the U.S. economy is strong and the Japanese economy weak, even though the Japanese save just under a fifth of their national income and the Americans save next to nothing. Japan's 1993 per capita income was $36,615, as compared with the United States' $24,075; Japan's 1993 current-account surplus was $131.1 billion, while the current account deficit of the United States was $105.7 billion; and Japan's economy is starting to revive as the headquarters for the East Asian manufacturing megalopolis, while the U.S. economy still depends primarily on domestic overconsumption. It will not be long before Americans will have to start paying premium interest rates to attract foreign savings to finance their self-indulgence. And there seems not to be a single American leader devoting one iota of attention to this situation.

Kenneth Courtis, the chief strategist for the Deutsche Bank in East Asia, in a recent essay called "Before the Storm," warned that this inattention to the trend of events is highly dangerous. I believe that it is caused by the grip of vested interests perpetuating the Cold War system—a resistance to reality rivaling that of Brezhnev's Russia in its complacency and hostility to new information. There are many indications that we are artificially becalmed, trapped in the horse latitudes, and waiting for some incident to make the intrinsic situation extrinsic. Such an incident would reveal how the global balance of power has changed and how hollow our claims of being the unipolar superpower actually are.

The current drift of events suggests an extended version of France's *drôle de guerre*, which lasted from the declaration of war in September of 1939 until the actual arrival of the German armies in May of 1940. As was the case then, we are today in an eerie time, stranded in the inertia of Cold War relationships while we wait for the real contours of the new world order to emerge from the fog. Some people are preparing for the approaching storm; others do not want to think about it; a great many are trying to kill the meteorologists who are predicting it.

ONE example of the current intellectual warfare being waged is the reception given to James Fallows's *Looking at the Sun*, which was published last year. According to strict publishing standards, I should not be discussing Fallows's book and *The Atlantic* should not be publishing my remarks. Fallows is the Washington editor of this magazine, which published several excerpts from his book, the manuscript of which I read and vetted. I am indelibly linked with Fallows because we are both what the Japan lobby calls "revisionists"—that is, people who have had the temerity to "revise" orthodox theoretical pronouncements: either that since Japan is rich, it must have learned how to operate its economy from the Econ 101 courses taught in American universities, or that since Japanese economics do not fit the gospel according to Saint Adam Smith, Japan's economy is doomed to collapse any day now.

But the issue here is not the conventions of the publishing world but the biggest and most misunderstood event of the end of the twentieth century: the shift of the global economic center of gravity to the Western Pacific. The end of the Cold War has finally exposed to view something that the Cold War itself both fostered and camouflaged: the enrichment of Asia. How that happened and what it means for the future are the keys to the new world order.

JIM Fallows, a journalist with an Oxford degree in economics, is the author of *National Defense*, which won the National Book Award in 1981. Having heard about the enrichment of Asia, and being curious about the people who produced it, he took himself and his family to live there for four years. Fallows divided his time between Japan, the superpower of the region, and Malaysia, the richest of the platforms for Japanese manufacturing in Southeast Asia. His book does not deal with China or take Korea or Indonesia as seriously as it might have. But Fallows studied and wrote unerringly on the likely next entries into the category of miracle economies—Vietnam and perhaps Burma—and every American should read his chapter on the Philippines, since that country is the only part of Asia whose legacy is unambiguously ours. I know of no better contemporary guide than Fallows to the role of the ethnic Chinese in Southeast Asia, the historical underpinnings of Japan's state-guided capitalism, or the differences between the Thai and Malay outlooks on the world. But none of these aspects of his book has surfaced in any of the savage attention it has received.

Instead Fallows has been excoriated for a "visceral hostility" to Japan (the *Los Angeles Times*), for being a "MITI lover" (*The Wall Street Journal*; the reference is to Japan's Ministry of International Trade and Industry, an economic-strategy agency that has guided Japan's postwar growth and is similar to the American Joint Chiefs of Staff), and for writing "a defective guide to what economics teaches about national development strategies and the functioning of modern industries" (*The New York Times*). The last reviewer acknowledges that he is "an infrequent Asian traveler" and that "laissez-faire theories fit the Asian experience badly," but he nevertheless cites an American economist from the 1880s—a time when the United States was one of the most heavily protected economies on earth—to the effect that Asia has nothing to teach us about economic growth. Writing in *The New Republic,* Ian Buruma declares Fallows to be a "neo-Orientalist," of the never-the-twain-shall-meet persuasion (Buruma actually quotes Kipling's bromide), and faults him for failing to understand that the Japanese machine politician Ichiro Ozawa really admires "British parliamentary democracy."

Buruma is an interesting case. A British-accented author of books about Japanese sexual fantasies, travel in Asia, cricket, and how the Germans have wept enough for their wartime deeds but the Japanese have not, Buruma really is innocent of the structure and properties of

the Japanese economy. Nonetheless, *de haut en bas*, Buruma takes Fallows up on the subject of economics.

Even if we assume, for the sake of argument, that Fallows is absolutely right, that there is such a thing as a specifically Asian system, combining mercantilism with authoritarian politics, does this disprove the main case for classical economics? Ricardo and Smith said that nations benefit from keeping their markets open for trade, even if other nations keep their markets closed. Consumers benefit from cheaper products, and competition keeps producers efficient and quality-conscious. Fallows does not believe this. He thinks it is a dogma that blinds the Anglo-Saxon world to the reality of the East. This is why he thinks the United States should devise an industrial strategy if it is not to follow Britain's giggling slide into the sea.

With the statement "Fallows does not believe this," Buruma begins to reveal that reviews of Fallows's book are not really book reviews at all but acts of faith —what the Inquisition called *autos-da-fé*—and are intended to warn the unsuspecting of possible heresy. This kind of warning disguised as criticism is becoming a regular, if subliminal, feature of discussions about Asian capitalism. Fallows is certainly not the first writer about the challenge of Asia to be savaged by reviewers and yet still be widely read. Michael Crichton was called politically incorrect, a Japan-basher, and a racist for writing his novel *Rising Sun*, about how a Japanese company seeking a share of the American microelectronics market bribed and blackmailed a U.S. senator—a fictional treatment of the daily occurrences Pat Choate detailed in *Agents of Influence*. It now looks as if Jeff Shear's excellent and revealing *The Keys to the Kingdom: The FS-X Deal and the Selling of America's Future to Japan* is to be accorded similar treatment. *The Wall Street Journal* has recently declared Shear to be a "New Mercantilist" who favors supporting high-tech industries in the United States. Shear's reviewer says this viewpoint is silly, because "countries don't compete in most business, businesses do" and "no trade [in the Pacific] is going to occur except win-win transactions."

The issue raised by Fallows is the possibility that the Japanese have put together the institutions of capitalism in a more effective way than is taught in English and American academies. He has also remembered what Adam Smith had to say about the functions of the state in market economies. Even the functions that Smith considered basic—appropriate education of the labor force, construction of the infrastructure on which manufacturing depends, the "night watchman" functions of guaranteeing public safety—our state fails to fulfill in a competitive manner. And Smith was interested in the minimalist state. The Japanese have shown the world that there are many things the state can do in a market economy in order to make it work well—things that never crossed Smith's mind or that would not have mattered in his eighteenth-century setting. These include the management of technology (the great variable that cancels "comparative advantage"), the management of the change of industrial structure (for example, from capital-intensive to knowledge-intensive industries), and the management of competition to ensure the availability of high-value-added jobs (for example, the making of computer chips instead of potato chips) for one's own citizens. When Fallows's critics intone that he fails "to recognize that the enemy was really us" (*New York Times*) and that "the Japanese people aren't so different from us after all" (*Wall Street Journal*), they are deliberately deflecting scrutiny from what Fallows actually says. His book is the most straightforward kind of call to action: the challenge of Asia, like the Cold War itself, requires acknowledgment of the challenge and policies to match it, not just incessant knocking on wood by vested interests fearful of change.

ECONOMICS has become the Marxism-Leninism of our society—the official ideological expression of how the United States works and why it "won" the Cold War. Its adepts, the professional economists of our society, have the same interest in preserving their usually tenured (in violation of market forces) positions as did the masters of ML at Moscow State University until August of 1991. The greatest single threat to their continued dominance is the prowess of the Japanese economy and the emulation of that economy by everybody else in Asia, from China to Kazakhstan. It is not the wealth of Asia that is threatening but how the Asians obtained it. Conventional U.S. economic theory says that the state cannot be effective in the economy. We believe this because of our own history of struggles against the state and because the ideology of the Cold War maintains that laissez-faire vanquished socialism. We also have practical evidence that our nonmilitary bureaucrats are often more expensive than they are effective. But the evidence from East Asia is overwhelming. Nonadversarial relations between the public and private sectors can produce safe, sane societies with astonishingly high levels of evenly distributed income. Our theorists must either dismiss this evidence or start thinking about the only choices left to them—retooling in the Japanese language (very hard to do after age thirty-five) or early retirement.

Fallows knows this, and should not be too surprised by the treatment he has received. It is a good sign that he scored. But readers should ignore the reviews and read the book, because it is also an excellent guide to the struggles that will almost certainly dominate our politics within a very short period of time. China and Japan are the only two foreign countries today that could threaten the national security of the United States if we had relations of conflict with them. One is the world's biggest society, the other among the world's richest in terms of per capita income. Just as the century changes, the world is witnessing a basic change in Asia from enrichment to empowerment. The nineteenth century was the time of the victimization of Asia. In China it took the form of imperialist enclaves, of which Hong Kong is one of the last remaining. In the rest of Asia (except for the buffer state of Thailand) it took the form of European, American, and Japanese colonialism. The twentieth century has been the time of revolt against this imperialism, including the Chinese Revolution (the biggest revolution among all the cases), revolts by subject peoples during interimperialist wars, and wars of national liberation in Indonesia, Indochina, and Malaya.

These wars are now over, and only a few embers from them still smolder. Rich Americans are starting to take luxury cruises to Vietnam, disembarking at Danang for a quickie bus tour to Hue. Vestiges of the old victimization and its consequences still linger in the soon-to-change status of Hong Kong, the not-soon-to-change status of Taiwan, the partition of Korea, and the influence of the U.S. Seventh Fleet. The enrichment of Asia occurred during the Cold War and depended to one degree or another on the opportunities made available by the conditions that prevailed. Today enrichment is a self-sustaining process, still benefiting from the openness of the American market but no longer dependent upon it. During 1993, using Japan's definitions and accounting methods, Japan had a trade surplus of $53.6 billion with the rest of Asia, as against a surplus of $50.2 billion with the United States. The shift from mere enrichment to empowerment is clearly on the agenda. It has started to show up in Asians' growing irritation with the American tendency to deliver sermons on human rights, free trade, multilateral diplomacy, democracy, and virtually anything else, regardless of the United States' own rather tacky record in many of these areas. (Singaporeans, when we lectured them on the evils of flogging, commented on how we dealt with some of our dissidents at Waco, Texas.)

THE empowerment of Asia is going to come as a shock to a lot of Americans. They have not been "looking at the sun," as Jim Fallows puts it, but have been following the advice of the *Los Angeles Times*: "America, take off your sunglasses." Nor are our universities doing a good job of preparing people for the Pacific century. Professors these days are totally devoted to what they call theory—nineteenth-century English economic theory, rational-choice theory, French literary theory, and gender theory—to the exclusion of all forms of empiricism, language study, and awareness of differences in national character. In contrast to the days when universities provided expertise on Russia and China, today people seeking such knowledge must turn to think tanks.

This is one of the reasons I retired early from the University of California and am involved in creating a research institute devoted to policy issues in the Asia-Pacific region. The government itself has access to less genuine expertise on Asia—that is, the expertise of people who have studied and lived in Asia and who read and speak an Asian language—than it has had at any other time since the 1940s.

When Americans wake up to the shift in the balance of power to Asia, they are likely to feel betrayed and angry. They will wonder why they were not warned. Jim Fallows is one of the few issuing a warning. He is also responding seriously to Japan's emergence as a major economic power—one whose economy is three fifths the size of the United States, the first economy in history to produce a $100 billion trade surplus, and the economic equivalent of two Germanys in the Pacific. History teaches us that inattention, drift, and appeasement are not the proper ways to deal with such a nation. In the past comparable policies have led to war. Copying Japan is also not the way to go, and Fallows explicitly warns against it. We must use our own national heritage and resources to match Japan, not copy it, just as we matched but did not copy the former USSR. We would be crazy to imitate, for example, Japan's persistent waste of female talent because of the influence of its rigid gender-based division of labor. We are decades ahead of Japan in terms of integrating women and minorities into all levels of our labor force. This is not a time for complacency, however. Shortly the widespread American belief that Japan is finished will be exposed as an idiotic conceit. We will then have the choice of either matching Japan or adjusting to its ascendancy.

Fallows and the few others like him are not anti-Japanese. They may well be the only true friends Japan has in the West. The issue for the next century, as it has been for the one now ending, is how, short of war, to adjust to the rise of new sources of power and the decline of old ones. Complex factual knowledge of the sort contained in *Looking at the Sun* is the first requirement.

Modern Pluralist Democracies: Factors in the Political Process

- **Political Ideas, Movements, and Parties (Articles 23–25)**
- **The Ethnic Factor in West European Politics (Articles 26 and 27)**
- **Women and Politics (Articles 28–30)**
- **The Institutional Framework of Representative Government (Articles 31–35)**

Observers of Western industrialized societies frequently refer to the emergence of a new politics in these countries. They are not always very clear or in agreement about what is supposedly novel in the political process or why it is significant. Although no one would dispute that some major changes have taken place in these societies during the past couple of decades, affecting both political attitudes and behavior, it is very difficult to establish clear and comparable patterns of transformation or to gauge their endurance and impact. Yet making sense of continuities and changes in political values and behavior must be one of the central tasks of a comparative study of government.

Since the early 1970s, political scientists have followed Ronald Inglehart and other careful observers who first noted a marked increase in what they called postmaterial values, especially among younger and more highly educated people in the skilled service and administrative occupations in Western Europe. Such voters showed less concern for the traditional material values of economic well-being and security and instead stressed participatory and environmental concerns in politics as a way of improving democracy and the general quality of life. Studies of postmaterialism form a very important addition to our ongoing attempt to interpret and explain not only the so-called youth revolt but also some more lasting shifts in lifestyles and political priorities. It makes intuitive sense that such changes appear to be especially marked among those who grew up in the relative prosperity of Western Europe after the austere period of reconstruction that followed World War II. In more recent years, however, there appears to have been a revival of material concerns among younger people, and economic prosperity and security seem less certain. There are also some indications that political reform activities evoke less interest and commitment than earlier.

None of this should be mistaken for a return to the political patterns of the past. Instead, we may be witnessing the emergence of a new, still somewhat incongruent mixture of material and postmaterial orientations, along with both old and new forms of political self-expression by the citizenry. Established political parties appear to be in somewhat of a quandary about how to redefine their positions, at a time when the traditional bonding of many voters to one or another party seems to have become weaker. Many observers speak about a widespread condition of political malaise in industrialized countries, suggesting that it shows up not only in opinion polls but also in a marked decline in voter participation and, on occasion, a propensity for voter revolt against the establishment parties and candidates. Without suggesting a simple cause-effect relationship, the British observer Martin Jacques has pointed to parallels between electoral malaise/dealignment and the vague rhetoric offered by many political activists and opinion leaders. He believes that the end of the cold war and the collapse of communism in Europe have created a situation that demands a reformulation of political and ideological alternatives. In that sense, he finds some paradigmatic significance in the great political shake-up of the Italian party system.

At this point, at least, it seems unlikely that Italy will set an example for many other democracies. Most established parties seem to have developed an ability to adjust to change, even as the balance of power within each party system shifts over time and occasional newcomers are admitted to the club. Each country's party system remains shaped by its unique political history, but there do seem to be some very general patterns of development. One frequently observed trend is toward a narrowing of the ideological distance between the moderate Left and Right in many European countries. It now often makes more sense to speak of the center-Left and center-Right.

Despite such convergence, there are still some important ideological and practical differences between these two orientations. The Right is usually far more ready to accept as inevitable the existence of social and economic inequalities as well as the hierarchies they produce. It normally favors lower taxes and the promotion of market forces—with some very important exceptions intended to protect the nation as a whole (national defense) as well as certain favorite groups and values within it. In general, the Right sees the state as an instrument that should provide security, order, and protection of an established way of life. The Left, by contrast, emphasizes that government has an important task in promoting opportunities, delivering services, and reducing social inequities. On issues such as higher and more progressive taxation, high rates of unemployment, and inflation, there continue to be considerable differences between moderates of the Left and Right.

Even as the ideological distance between Left and Right narrows, there are also signs of political differentiation within each camp. On the center-Right side of the party spectrum in European politics, economic neoliberals (who speak for business and industry) can be distinguished from the social conservatives (who are more likely to advocate traditional values and authorities). European liberalism has its roots in a tradition that favors civil liberties and tolerance but that also values individual achievement and laissez-faire economics. For such European neoliberals, the state has an important but very limited role to play in providing an institutional framework within which individuals and social groups pursue their interests. Traditional conservatives, by contrast, emphasize the importance of social stability and continuity and point to the social danger of disruptive change. They often value the strong state as an instrument of order, but many of them also show a paternalistic appreciation for welfare state programs that will help keep "the social net" from tearing apart.

In British politics, Margaret Thatcher promoted elements from each of these traditions in what could be called her own brand of "business conservatism." The result is the peculiar tension between "drys" and "wets" within her own Conservative Party, even after she ceased to be its leader. In France, on the other hand, the division between neoliberals and conservatives runs more clearly between the two major center-Right parties, the Giscardist UDF, and the neo-Gaullist RPR. In Germany, the Free Democrats would most clearly represent the traditional liberal position, while some conservative elements can be found among the Christian Democrats.

There is something of a split identity also among the Christian Democrats, who until recently were one of the most successful political movements in Europe after World War II. Here the idealists, who subscribe to the socially compassionate teachings of the Church, have found themselves losing influence to more efficiency-oriented technocrats and political managers. The latter seem to reflect little of the original ideals of personalism, solidarity, and subsidiarity that originally set the Christian Democrats off from both neoliberals and conservatives in post–war Europe. It remains to be seen whether political setbacks for the Christian Democrats in Italy will lead to more than a mere face-lift. Their new name of Popular Party seems unintentionally self-ironic and has done little to stem their recent electoral losses. In Germany, however, the Christian Democrats have managed to remain chancellor party despite some slippage in their electoral appeal.

On the Left, democratic socialists and ecologists stress that the sorry political, economic, and environmental record of communist-ruled states in no way diminishes the validity of their own commitment to social justice and environmental protection in industrial societies. For them, capitalism will continue to produce its own social problems and dissatisfactions. No matter how efficient capitalism may be, they argue, it will continue to result in inequities that require politically directed redress. Many on the Left, however, show a pragmatic acceptance of the modified market economy as an arena within which to promote their reformist goals. Social Democrats in Scandinavia and Germany have long been known for taking such positions. In recent years, their colleagues in Great Britain and France have followed suit by abandoning some traditional symbols and goals, such as major programs of nationalization. The Socialists in Spain, who governed that new democracy after 1982, went furthest of all in adopting business-friendly policies before their loss of power in early 1996.

Some other Western European parties further to the Left have also moved in the centrist direction in recent years. Two striking examples of this shift can be found among the Greens in Germany and the former Communist Party of Italy. The Greens are by no means an establishment party, but they have served as a pragmatic coalition partner with the Social Democrats in several state governments and have gained respect for their mixture of practical competence and idealism. Their so-called realist faction (Realos) has clearly outmaneuvered its more radical rivals in the party's fundamentalist (Fundi) wing. The Italian communists have come even further toward a center-Left position. Years before they adopted the new name of Democratic Party of the Left (PDS), they had abandoned the Leninist revolutionary tradition and adopted reformist politics similar to those of social democratic parties elsewhere in Western Europe. Not every Italian communist went along, and a fundamentalist core broke away to set up a new party of Refounded Communists.

Both center-Left and center-Right moderates face a dual challenge from the populists on the Right—who often seek lower taxes, drastic cuts in the social budget, and a curtailment of immigration—and the neofascists on the ultra-Right. These two orientations have distinguishing elements, such as in Italy, where the populist Northern League and the partly neofascist National Alliance represent positions that are polar opposites on such key issues as government decentralization (favored by the former, opposed by the latter). In part, the electoral revival of the right-wing parties can be linked to anxieties and tensions that affect some socially and economically insecure groups in the lower middle class and some sectors of the working class. Ultra-Right nationalist politicians and their parties typically eschew a complex explanation of the structural and cyclical problems that beset the European economies. Instead they simply blame external scapegoats, namely the many immigrants and refugees from Eastern Europe as well as developing countries in northern Africa and elsewhere. The presence of the far-Right parties inevitably has an effect on both the balance of power and the political agendas that occupy the more centrist parties. Almost everywhere, for example, some of the established parties and politicians have been making symbolic concessions on the refugee issue to prevent it from becoming monopolized by extremists. In this unit, several articles address this issue specifically.

Women and politics is the concern of the third section in this unit. There continues to be a strong pattern of underrepresentation of women in positions of political and economic leadership practically everywhere. Yet there are some notable differences from country to country as well as from party to party. Generally speaking, the parties of the Left have been readier to place women in positions of authority, although there are some remarkable exceptions, as the center-Right cases of Margaret Thatcher in Great Britain and Simone Weil in France illustrate.

On the whole, the system of proportional representation gives parties both a tool and an added incentive to place female candidates in positions where they will be elected. But here too there can be exceptions, as in the case of France in 1986, when women did not benefit from the use of proportional representation in the parliamentary elections. Clearly it is not enough to have a relatively simple means, such as proportional representation, for promoting women in politics; there must also be an organized will among decision makers to use all available tools for the exact purpose of such a clearly defined reform.

This is where the policy of affirmative action may be a strategy. The Scandinavian countries illustrate best how breakthroughs can occur. There is a markedly higher representation of women in the parliaments of Denmark, Finland, Iceland, Norway, and Sweden, where the political center of gravity is somewhat to the Left and proportional representation ensures party lists that are more representative of the population as a whole. Iceland has a special women's party with parliamentary representation. Women are found in leading positions within most

of the parties of this and the other Scandinavian countries. Under these circumstances, it usually does not take long for the more centrist and moderately conservative parties to adopt the new concern of gender equality. It may even move to the forefront; women have held the leadership of three of the main parties in Norway (the Social Democrats, the Center Party, and the Conservatives), which together normally receive roughly two-thirds of the total popular vote. It is worth pointing out that in contrast to Margaret Thatcher, who included no women in her cabinet between 1979 and 1990, Norway's first female prime minister, Gro Harlem Brundtland, used that position to increase the number of women in ministerial positions (8 of 18 cabinet posts). The present Swedish government of Social Democrats, which took power in 1994, has an equal number of women and men in the cabinet.

In another widely reported sign of change, the relatively conservative Republic of Ireland has chosen Mary Robinson as its first female president. It is a largely ceremonial post, but it has a symbolic potential that Mary Robinson, an outspoken advocate of liberal reform in her country, is willing to use on behalf of social change. Perhaps most remarkable of all, the advancement of women into high political ranks has now also touched Switzerland, where they did not get the right to vote until 1971.

Altogether, there is undoubtedly a growing awareness of gender discrimination in most Western countries. It seems likely that there will be further significant improvement in this situation over the next decade if the pressure for reform is maintained. Such changes have already occurred in areas where there once were significant political differences between men and women. At one time, for example, there was a considerably lower voter turnout among women, but this gender gap has been practically eliminated in recent decades. Similarly the tendency for women to be somewhat more conservative in party and candidate preferences has given way to a more liberal disposition among younger women in foreign and social policy preferences than among men. These are aggregate differences, of course, and it is important to remember that women, like men, do not represent one unified, monolithic bloc in political attitudes and behaviors but are themselves divided by various interests and priorities. One generalization does seem to hold, however, namely that there is much less inclination among women to support parties and candidates that have a decidedly radical image. The vote for extreme right-wing parties in contemporary Europe tends to be considerably higher among male voters.

There are also some very important policy questions that affect women more directly than men. Any statistical study of women in the paid labor force of Europe could supply conclusive evidence to support three widely shared impressions: (1) there has been a considerable increase in the number and proportion of women who hold paid jobs, (2) these jobs are more often unskilled and/or part-time than in the case of men's employment, and (3) women generally receive less pay and less social protection than men in comparative positions. Such a study would also show that there are considerable differences among Western European countries in the relative position of their female workers, thereby offering support for the argument that political intervention in the form of appropriate legislation *can* do something to improve the employment status of women—not only by training them better for advancement in the labor market but also by changing the conditions of the workplace to eliminate both obvious and hidden disadvantages for women.

The socioeconomic status of women in other parts of the world is often far worse. According to the 1995 report of the UN Development Program, although there have been some rapid advances for women in the fields of education and health care provision, the doors to economic opportunities are only barely ajar. In the field of political leadership, the picture is more varied, as the UN report indicates, but women generally hold few positions of importance in national politics. To be sure, there have been some remarkable breakthroughs; for example, in South Africa women won 100 of the 400 seats in the first postapartheid parliament in 1994.

The framework of government is the subject of the fourth section of this unit. Here the articles examine and compare a number of institutional arrangements: essential characteristics and elements of a pluralist democracy, major systems of representative government, various rules governing campaign and party finance, different electoral systems, and the presidential and prime ministerial forms of executive.

The topic of pluralist democracy is a complex one, but Phillipe Schmitter and Terry Lynn Karl manage to present a very comprehensive yet concise discussion of the subject. Next, Gregory Mahler focuses on the legislative-executive relationship of parliamentary and congressional systems, drawing mainly upon the British, Canadian, and American examples, and he avoids the trap of idealizing any one way of organizing the functions of representative government. In the next essay, Arthur Gunlicks approaches the issue of campaign and party finance from an interesting angle: he asks what Americans might learn from the manner in which this problem is resolved in several other democracies. The article "Electoral Reform: Good Government? Fairness? Or Vice Versa. Or Both" examines the advantages and disadvantages of different electoral systems and shows that proportional representation need not result in political instability or paralysis. Richard Rose compares the political executive in the United States, Great Britain, and France and finds that each system has unique constraints upon arbitrary rule that can easily become obstacles to prompt, decisive action.

Looking Ahead: Challenge Questions

How do you explain the recent shifts toward the political center made by parties of the moderate Left and moderate Right? How do Social Democrats present themselves as reformers of capitalism? What are the main sources of electoral support for the far-Right political parties?

Why are women so poorly represented in parliaments and other positions of political leadership? How do institutional arrangements, such as election systems, both help and hinder improvement in this situation? Which parties and countries tend to have a better record of female representation?

Would you agree with the inventory of democratic essentials as discussed by Schmitter and Karl? What do you regard as most and least important in their inventory? What are some major traits of a good constitution?

What are the major arguments made in favor of the parliamentary system of government and the main arguments for and against proportional representation? What do you think the United States could learn from the manner in which other democracies handle campaign and party finance? What are some main differences among the executive structures in Great Britain, France, and the United States; how important are they in shaping the governmental style and direction of each country?

The left's new start

A future for socialism

IN MUCH of Europe, left-wing politics is enjoying a revival. Scandinavian voters, who not long ago seemed to have abandoned their tradition of social democratic government, are putting left-of-centre parties into office again. Last month Hungary ditched its reformist pro-business government in favour of a "socialist" party made up of former communists; Social Democrats will do well in Germany's elections in October, opinion polls say; in Britain, the Labour Party trounced the Tories in recent local elections and stands a good chance of forming the next government; across the European Union, socialists expect to do well in elections to the European Parliament on June 9th and 12th. The revival is by no means universal—socialist parties are in trouble in Spain, France and Italy, to name just three—but it is nonetheless striking.

Just as striking is the fact that traditional ideas cannot claim the credit for the left's popularity. Today's socialist parties have all but abandoned many of their old policies. By the end of the 1980s most of Europe's left-of-centre parties already advocated (albeit grudgingly) slimmer government, lower taxes and privatisation—measures to which they were once bitterly opposed. Where parties called "socialist" are doing better, it is partly because they no longer espouse socialism.

This is a good thing. The left's traditional policies of widespread public ownership and punitive taxation only ever promised equality of disappointment. However, the realignment of the left is not as good a thing as it could be. Traditional socialists who ask why the left should seek power at all, if it is only to implement a soft-focus version of conservatism, ask a good question. For the sake of intelligent debate about public policy (ie, for the sake of good government) the left needs to do more than ditch the discredited policies of its past. It needs to develop a new programme that is not just economically literate, welcome though that would be, but distinctive as well.

Same means, different ends

In a variety of countries, attempts to do this are under way (see pages 17-19). Few of these efforts are promising, for a reason that is both revealing and dispiriting: most socialist modernisers remain instinctively hostile to market economics.

Some "market socialists" say, for instance, that capitalism would be all right as long as firms worked in a different way. They propose batteries of regulation to increase worker participation in management, to oblige firms to take a longer-term view, to make them more sensitive to the needs of their "stakeholders" (as opposed to the people who merely own them), and what not. Other modernisers see environmental questions as the niche for a new socialism. Still others emphasise the role of trade and industrial policies in maintaining some supposedly desirable mix of activities. The list goes on—each such policy justified by an elaborate appeal to the concept of "market failure". This idea remains the hallmark even of modernised socialism, central both to its substance and its presentation. The market alone cannot do this, cannot do that. State intervention—cleverer than before, but broadly based and, in its way, hardly less ambitious—remains the offered remedy.

Such thinking is profoundly misguided. In a sense market failure is pervasive. Competition is "imperfect", production and exchange involve externalities, the future is uncertain; for all these reasons, markets fail to allocate resources precisely as they would in the textbook world of basic economics. By the same test, there is much to be said for central planning. But this century's most important economic lesson is that, except in textbooks, government failure is broader, more damaging in economic terms and much more threatening to individual liberty than market failure.

The question is whether socialists can accept that truth whole-heartedly; rather than, as at present, half-heartedly, with

10,000 qualifications, or not at all. The answer may well be No. For many, "socialism" by definition cannot accept the market as the right framework for organising society. After all, socialism has a history. Its roots lie in an analysis of society that denies not merely the efficiency but also the moral content of free interaction among economic agents. If that analysis is bankrupt (and it is), what is there left for "socialism" to say?

Plenty, as it happens—with or without that label. The aims of socialism as a programme of social and economic reform, as opposed to the analysis of socialism as an intellectual discipline, have always been the source of its popular support. Goals such as reducing poverty, promoting equality of opportunity, and improving the quality of public services for all remain enormously appealing. In these aims, not in the arcane theories of economic planning, lies the reason why so many people for years invested in socialism their hopes for a happier and healthier society.

If those goals, as opposed to the ideological apparatus in which they were once couched, matter most to today's socialists, there is no reason why the left cannot be as vigorous in its enthusiasm for market economics as the right. If leftist parties could bring themselves to believe that the market is wonderful (not merely useful if kept in its place), that it has delivered the vast majority (not a privileged minority) of people in the West to material well-being which they would never have attained otherwise, that it must be trusted to co-ordinate the great bulk of society's activities, then they could be far more effective in pursuing their aims as social reformers.

These aims constitute an agenda that is not only distinctive but which also attacks the right at its weakest spot. In many countries (notably Britain), conservative governments have failed to reform welfare systems in such a way as to prevent, let alone reverse, increasing poverty. They have failed to invest adequately in the forms of education (notably nursery education, and basic training in literacy and numeracy) that do most to interrupt the transmission of failure from one generation to the next. They have failed to maintain the supply of some public services (such as public transport) to those who have no choice but to rely on them.

Left-of-centre parties account for this partly by saying that conservative governments, unlike them, are not chiefly concerned about the people who suffer as a result. By and large, this is true. But the policies that are needed in response do not call for a searching critique of the market economy. In the aggregate, the market provides the resources for effective action; case by case, moreover, it is often the only effective way to deliver help to the people who need it. The goals of defeating poverty, expanding economic opportunities for the less well-off, and improving the quality of public services will only in fact be achieved by people who can say the words "market" and "capitalism" without sneering.

Exploiting the market

In framing market-friendly policies with aims such as these in view, left-of-centre parties actually have two decisive advantages over their conservative counterparts. First, they can more readily attack certain sorts of privilege. In many countries in Europe and elsewhere, the fiercest opponents of change are those who have traditionally benefited from the restrictive practices established over the years by the middle-class professions: doctors, accountants, lawyers and so forth. The left may be—and certainly ought to be—less willing than the right to defer to such interests. Second, the left's motives in reform are less in doubt. As a result, as "socialist" governments in Australia and New Zealand have shown, leftist reformers can often be more radical than right-of-centre governments in pursuit of efficiency, as well as in pursuit of equity.

This is especially true in management of the public sector. By getting better value for taxpayers' money, and by pruning subsidies to the better off, socialists can deliver more and better services to the people who need them.

Consider Britain's reforms of the National Health Service. By the end of the 1970s, the NHS had become a startlingly wasteful bureaucracy. The best that could be said for it was that it was comparatively cheap: Britain spent massively on health care, but less so than most other rich industrial countries. The service worked badly. Access to medicine and treatment was controlled by rationing; the system was slow and growing slower; standards of treatment and hospital accommodation compared poorly with those abroad.

The reforms undertaken by successive Conservative administrations—the attempt to introduce an "internal market", to ensure that resources were allocated according to the needs of users rather than the convenience of producers—made good sense. In principle, the changes were entirely consistent with the preservation of taxpayer-financed health care for all. In principle, they were capable of putting whatever resources the government devoted to the NHS to better use—meaning faster, better care, including for the least well-off. Voters remained intensely suspicious, however, not least because the government presented its plans as though saving money counted for more than improving the quality of the service. And the Labour Party vilified the reforms from the start, arguing that market economics has no place in the provision of health care.

If Labour wins power, it should think again. However much it plans to spend on health care, the intelligent use of market forces within the system would be its greatest ally in helping those who rely upon it. And because Labour would be trusted by the electorate to keep the NHS intact and free at the point of use, it could actually go further and faster than the Tories in improving the system.

The same goes for socialist parties in other countries, and for other forms of public investment. Adopt road-use pricing, for instance, and use the proceeds from that market-friendly policy to increase investment in railways and other forms of public transport. Introduce competition and market forces into education, by extending the freedom of parents to choose their children's schools, thus encouraging popular schools to grow and unpopular ones to shrink. In these and other areas, left-of-centre governments might still choose to spend more on public investment than conservative ones. That could make sense—but only if a framework (the market) was in place to ensure that the resources were well used.

Respect for market forces and incentives, together with a determination to help the unfortunate, can be expensive. A policy to equip the unemployed for work costs a lot: more, often, than it costs to keep failing industries afloat. However, measures that improve training opportunities for the unemployed make better sense than measures to defend a dying firm. They speed the creation of jobs in the right industries, promoting growth across the economy as a whole. Welfare reform is even more difficult than labour-market reform. It is costly and complicated to help the poor without worsening the poverty trap that is caused by the interaction of benefits and taxation. The remedy involves benefits that are better-targeted, but withdrawn more gradually as income rises, and minimal taxation at the bottom of the income scale. This costs money.

A left-of-centre party should nonetheless be ambitious in both these areas—making it all the more important to pare public spending of the kind that helps people who do not need to be helped. Here too, a left-of-centre government could be more daring than a conservative one. Acting as always in the name of equity and efficiency, it could make benefits to the elderly poor more generous, but reduce or eliminate benefits to the elderly not-poor; it could recover more of the costs of university education from the beneficiaries; it could narrow tax breaks and subsidies for the well-off; it could launch a vigorous assault on support (in the form of inflated prices and other sub-sidies) for farmers, thereby raising revenue for other purposes while cutting the cost of food.

A question of priorities

Much of this may seem unthinkable for Europe's socialists— like support for privatisation ten years ago. If so, it is because the character of the left, though altered and improved, needs to change further. Socialism must continue to define itself less in terms of means (we will manage the economy and civilise the market) and more in terms of priorities (we will help society's losers). The left should do this not merely to strengthen its elect-ability further, though that would be one result. It should do it mainly because, once in power, it would then be far more likely to change society, as it wants to, for the better.

Guide to the west European left

The left in western Europe is going through a difficult spell. If the Spanish Socialists are beaten this year, not one large country will have a left-of-centre government. **Paul Anderson** looks at what has gone wrong

O f course, as Tony Blair always reminds us, the next election in Britain is by no means in the bag for Labour. However desperate the plight of the ruling Conservatives might look today, it could be very different when the country goes to the polls.

All the same, it does look as if Labour is going to win the next election—its first general election success since October 1974. Elsewhere in western Europe, left parties are in a less happy position. The centre-left is in government in only one of the five biggest west European countries, Spain, and it is likely that Felipe González's Socialist government will be ousted on 3 March 1996. In Germany, the Social Democrats are way behind the centre-right government in the opinion polls—and the French Socialists are only just recovering from their defeat in the 1993 general election. Apart from Britain, Italy is the only country of the "big five" where the centre-left has a good chance of winning a general election in the near future.

In the smaller countries, the picture is brighter: indeed, at present every one has Socialists in government, whether as sole ruling party (Greece, Portugal, Sweden, Norway) or as part of a coalition (Netherlands, Belgium, Austria, Switzerland, Finland, Denmark, Ireland, Luxembourg). Each governing left party is different—but they also have much in common. Nearly all of them, particularly those in EU governments that are attempting to meet the Maastricht treaty criteria on economic and monetary union, have had to introduce tough (and unpopular) austerity budgets despite persistently high unemployment; and in

many cases the result has been the defection of Social Democrat and Socialist voters to parties of the far left and far right.

Will the same happen in Britain under a Blair Labour government? It is certainly likely to have to introduce unpopular measures of economic policy—but it is unclear whether disillusioned Labour voters will turn to the political extremes. The British electoral system has so far mitigated against the emergence of credible electoral parties of far left or far right. But if the electoral system is changed after Labour's promised referendum, our politics could take on a more continental hue.

Germany

If the German left sneezes, the rest of the west European left catches pneumonia. And the past 13 years have been less than glorious for the German Social Democratic Party (*Sozialdemokratische Partei Deutschlands*—SPD), the biggest of all Europe's social democratic parties.

After the liberal Free Democratic Party (*Freie Demokratische Partei*—FDP) abandoned SPD chancellor Helmut Schmidt's centre-left West German coalition government in 1982, the SPD went into opposition at federal level. It has remained there ever since, losing general elections to chancellor Helmut Kohl's centre-right ruling coalition in West Germany in 1983 and 1987 and in Germany as a whole in 1990 and 1994.

The SPD has been consistently outpolled in elections to the *Bundestag* (federal lower chamber) by the centre-right

Christian Democratic Union (*Christlich Demokratische Union*—CDU) and its Bavarian sister party, the Christian Social Union (*Christlich Soziale Union*—CSU). It has been unable to prise the FDP away from the CDU/CSU. Worse, it has been unable to stop the emergence and survival of the Greens (*Die Grünen*), who bounced back from a disastrous showing in the 1990 unification election to take 7.1 per cent in 1994 and are currently riding high in the opinion polls. Perhaps unsurprisingly, the SPD has spent much of the past decade engulfed by a crisis of confidence unprecedented since 1945.

It's not quite that the SPD thinks of itself as a natural party of government: before 1966, when it entered a "grand coalition" with the CDU/CSU, it had been excluded from federal government since the foundation of the *Bundesrepublik* in 1949. But the SPD was dominant in federal politics throughout the late 1960s and 1970s, and its regional power-base in the *Länder* (states) was formidable. (It remains so: a majority of *Länder* today have SPD-dominated governments, which gives the party a majority in the *Bundesrat*, the federal upper chamber.) It took the SPD several years to recuperate from the defection of the FDP and the emergence of the Greens as a serious electoral force in 1982-83—and the recovery was still incomplete when the party was subject to the even greater shock of unification.

The problem goes back to the last years of the Schmidt administration, which managed to alienate working-class voters with its austerity programme and the left with its enthusiasm for the stationing of new Nato intermediate-range nuclear

From *New Statesman & Society*, January 5, 1996, pp. 24-28. © 1996 by *New Statesman & Society*, a publication of Guardian News Service, Ltd. Reprinted by permission.

missiles in Germany. After the FDP jumped ship in 1982, the SPD spent several years desperately attempting to regain the support of both the working class and the largely middle-class protest movement against the missiles. It failed on both counts and lost ground to both the Greens and the ruling coalition in 1983 and again in 1987.

In the late 1980s, the SPD's fortunes improved, largely because of the thaw in the cold war. In the 1989 Euro-elections the SPD came within a whisker of overtaking the CDU/CSU share of the vote, and, with the charismatic radical Saarland premier, Oskar Lafontaine, as candidate for the chancellorship, the SPD seemed well placed to win the 1990 federal election. Then, however, the Berlin wall came down, and the party made the disastrous mistake of refusing to back immediate German unification—largely for economic reasons. In 1990, the party's vote was 33.5 per cent, its worst showing since the 1950s. In former East Germany it did particularly badly as the Party of Democratic Socialism (*Partei des Demokratischen Sozialismus*—PDS), the successor to the ruling East German communist party, split what there was of a left vote.

The SPD has still not recovered. After of the 1990 defeat, Lafontaine dropped out of the leadership, to be replaced by Schleswig-Holstein premier Björn Engholm; and after Engholm resigned in 1993 in the wake of a bizarre scandal, the post fell to Rhineland-Palatinate premier Rudolf Scharping. Scharping adopted a cautious strategy of wooing the centre and big business while shunning the idea of coalition with either the Greens or the PDS—and it didn't work. In the 1994 Euro-elections, the SPD took just 32.2 per cent of the vote, and later in the year it managed only 36.4 per cent in the federal election.

Remarkably, Scharping survived as leader after the defeat but, after a series of disastrous local and regional election results, he came under increasing criticism from within the SPD. At the time, it seemed that the main threat to his leadership came from Gerhard Schröder, the Lower Saxony premier. In fact, it was Lafontaine who dealt Scharping the fatal blow, at the November 1995 SPD conference in Mannheim. Lafontaine unexpectedly forced a vote on the party leadership, and won. The SPD, languishing in the opinion polls, immediately gained 5 per cent support.

Whether Lafontaine can keep up the momentum remains to be seen. His openness to dealing with the Greens and, more controversially, the PDS, which took 19.8 per cent of the east German

vote in the 1994 general election, could easily backfire with voters hostile to the old East Germany. If it doesn't, he is likely to be chosen as SPD candidate for the chancellorship in the 1998 general election. The first indication of his fortunes will be a set of *Land* elections in March 1996.

While the SPD has been in the doldrums, the Greens—now firmly in the hands of pragmatists—have been doing better than ever, taking more than 10 per cent of the vote in regional and local elections. Many observers reckon that they will replace the FDP as the party that either the SPD or the CDU/CSU must woo to form a federal government.

France

The 1980s saw the Socialist Party (*Parti Socialiste*—PS) dominate French politics as never before. After François Mitterrand won the presidency (at his third attempt) in April 1981, the PS, backed by the French Communist Party (*Parti Communiste Française*—PCF), won a landslide victory in elections for the National Assembly. Mitterrand, who appointed PCF ministers to his first government, tried to implement a radical Keynesian economic programme. He was forced to abandon it in 1982-83; the PCF quit the government in disgust at the ensuing austerity; and the right won the next legislative elections in March 1986—but the period of *cohabitation* between Mitterrand and the centre-right government of Jacques Chirac lasted only two years. In 1988, Mitterrand was returned for a second term, and the PS won the subsequent National Assembly election.

Today, all that seems ancient history. In 1993, the PS, led by former prime minister Michel Rocard, suffered a humiliating legislative election defeat, taking only 54 National Assembly seats to the right's 460. In 1994, it fared even worse in the Euro-elections—partly because of the intervention of the charismatic (but subsequently disgraced) Marseilles millionaire Bernard Tapie, whose centre-left *Energie Radicale* alliance took 12 per cent of the vote to the PS' 14.5 per cent. Last year, the PS candidate for the presidency, Lionel Jospin, a man chosen only because former European Commission president Jacques Delors refused to stand, was beaten by Chirac. Even though Jospin did better than expected, taking 23 per cent of the vote in the first round (more than any other candidate) and a creditable 47.4 per cent in the second, his defeat forced even PS loyalists to recognise that their party's hegemony had come to an end.

What went wrong? Both Mitterrand

and the PS became embroiled in a series of scandals in the early 1990s, and Mitterrand's manoeuvring to block Rocard's chances of succeeding him as president did major damage—most notably after he replaced Rocard as prime minister in 1991 with the incompetent Edith Cresson. But by far the most important factor behind the decline of the PS was Europe.

After it abandoned "Keynesianism in one country", the Mitterrand administration increasingly saw European integration as its flagship project. Along with former PS finance minister Delors, who took over the Commission in 1984, Mitterrand was one of the key figures behind the creation of the single European market; and the deal struck in Maastricht in 1991 on European economic and political union was essentially a Franco-German affair, with the French getting commitments to a single currency in return for concessions to the Germans on political union and independence for the European central bank. In preparation for the creation of a single currency, the value of the franc was tied to the Deutschmark in the exchange rate mechanism.

The problem was that Mitterrand had not foreseen German unification—or rather the hike in interest rates with which the Bundesbank decided to pay for it, which forced up French interest rates and unemployment. The popularity of the government slipped steadily through the early 1990s. In September 1992's referendum on Maastricht, called by Mitterrand after Denmark voted "no" to the treaty, the French voted "yes" by the narrowest of margins. Six months later came the National Assembly election debacle.

Not all the French left was tainted by Maastricht. The Eurosceptic PCF played a large part in the "no" referendum campaign. But it was in no position to benefit. Under the leadership of Georges Marchais, it had retreated into the hard-left ghetto after quitting government in 1984, and its slow but steady decline since the 1940s had turned into a collapse. The PCF had shunned the new social movements, closing off the possibility of renewal through an influx of middle-class environmentalists and feminists (which meant that, once the French Greens tired of the PS' attentions, they became resolutely hostile to the left), and its bone-headed Stalinism had destroyed its credibility among the intelligentsia. Meanwhile, disaffected working-class voters in its heartlands had turned increasingly to the far right. Even in defeat in 1993, the PS polled twice as many votes as the PCF.

So where does the French left go now? The PS has been thrashing about since 1993, first shifting left and then backing the centrist Jospin—now its leader and dominant figure—but there has been a partial recovery in its fortunes in recent months as the right-wing government's popularity has slumped. As for the PCF, Marchais' successor as general secretary, Robert Hue, seems to have at least slowed his party's decline. But it is unlikely that the left will benefit greatly from the wave of strikes and protests that swept France before Christmas (the PS has no real union link these days, and the PCF's union connections have been weakened). The PS and PCF are bereft of ideas and—Jospin apart—credible leaders. It looks as if it will be some time before the left returns to power.

Italy

Not for the first time, the left in Italy faces the possibility of making a breakthrough into government in the next few months—and the fear that it will be left out in the cold yet again.

The Party of the Democratic Left (*Partito Democratica della Sinistra*—PDS) and its centre-left allies are doing well in the opinion polls. If they manage to postpone a general election long enough to expand the centre-left alliance (and to legislate to ensure that former prime minister Silvio Berlusconi does not again use his television stations for political propaganda), there's a good chance of a centre-left coalition taking power in Italy later this year. If Berlusconi manages to force an election sooner rather than later, however, the centre-left is more likely to be disappointed yet again.

Many observers have a sense of *deja vu*. Two years ago, in the run-up to the March 1994 general election, there seemed to be a real prospect of a centre-left victory. The PDS, alone of the major parties, had survived more-or-less unscathed from the scandals that had wrecked Italy's political class in the early 1990s, and it looked well positioned to take advantage. Instead, the election resulted in a victory for Berlusconi's Forza Italia in alliance with the ex-fascist National Alliance (*Alleanza Nazionale*—AN) and the regionalist Northern League (*Lega Nord*).

The PDS took just 21 per cent of the vote in 1994 and failed to pick up support from among former voters for the disgraced Italian Socialist Party (*Partito Socialista Italiano*—PSI) as it had hoped. An even worse performance in the Euro-election in June led to the resignation of PDS leader Achille Ochetto and the appointment of his deputy, Massimo D'Alema, as his replacement. D'Alema was the choice of the party leadership but not the ordinary members (who were

merely "consulted" about the decision), and he has been unable effectively to stamp his authority on the PDS. It was no surprise when, early last year, the PDS reluctantly accepted that Romano Prodi, a Catholic economist backed by the small centrist Popular Party (*Partito Popular Italiana*—PPI, the left wing of the former Christian Democrats) would lead the centre-left into the next election.

One effect of the PDS decision to back Prodi, however, was to sharpen divisions between the PDS and the hard-left *Rifondazione Comunista* grouping, founded in 1991 by those communists who objected to the creation of the PDS. Rifondazione took 6 per cent in the 1994 general election and has since performed well in local elections. It has opposed the austerity programme of the technocratic government of prime minister Lamberto Dini, appointed after the fall of Berlusconi a year ago and backed by the PDS, and it has recently capitalised on left-wing voters' disgust at the PDS' attempt to attract the Northern League to the centre-left alliance by backing League-sponsored anti-immigrant legislation.

How all this pans out in the next few months is impossible to predict with any certainty. Much depends on what Dini and Antonio Di Pietro, the magistrate who symbolises the anti-corruption drive of the early 1990s, do next. Di Pietro, who leans to the right, has declared his intention of going into politics—and is popular enough to sway large numbers of voters, even though he has himself been charged with corruption. Dini leans to the left. If both opt to back the centre-left, the PDS will be ecstatic; if only Dini does life will be sweet; but if the two join together to try to create a new centre-right bloc in competition with the centre-left, the PDS will be miserable.

Spain

Is the writing on the wall for Felipe González and his Spanish Socialist Workers' Party (*Partido Socialista Obrero Español*—PSOE)? Certainly their position has looked more and more precarious since they won the 1993 general election, their fourth win in a row since 1982. The PSOE, which relied from 1993 until late last year on the backing of Catalan nationalists, fared miserably in the 1994 Euro-elections, losing votes both to the right-wing Popular Party (*Partido Popular*—PP) and the communist-led United Left (*Izquierda Unida*—IU), and ever since has looked incapable of bouncing back in this year's general election, now fixed for 3 March.

One problem for the PSOE and

González has been a string of corruption scandals, the most damaging of which is the long-running saga of GAL, a government-sponsored death-squad that murdered several Basque separatists in the mid-1980s. Another bugbear has been unemployment, which has increased to 24 per cent from 16 per cent in 1990. Yet another is the decreasing utility of the PSOE's accusations that the right is tainted with fascism—a ploy that made a crucial difference even in 1993. It is now more than 20 years since the death of Franco, and younger voters are uninterested in the right's antecedents. The PP is favourite to form the next government, possibly with Catalan nationalist support.

Of course, there are many who would question whether the PSOE is genuinely a party of the left: it has from the start of its period in office adopted a market-oriented economic philosophy closer to that of Margaret Thatcher than to the ideas of northern European social democratic parties.

This is one major reason for the survival (and recent success) of IU, which emerged out of the "no" campaign for the 1986 referendum on Nato membership, which was dominated by the Eurocommunist Spanish Communist Party (*Partido Comunista de España*—PCE). At the time, most commentators reckoned that nothing could stop the decline of PCE membership and support, but IU, led since 1988 by the popular PCE general secretary Julio Anguita, has proved the sceptics wrong. Its 13.5 per cent in the 1994 Euro-elections was better than the PCE got in its late-1970s heyday.

FURTHER READING

There is a vast literature on the left in western Europe. Some of the best recent titles are the following:

Stephen Padgett and William E Paterson: *A History of Social Democracy in Postwar Europe* (Longman, 1991)

Perry Anderson and Patrick Camiller (eds): *Mapping the West European Left* (Verso, 1994)

Richard Gillespie and William E. Paterson: *Rethinking Social Democracy in Western Europe* (Cass, 1993)

Dick Richardson and Chris Rootes (eds): *The Green Challenge* (Routledge, 1994)

Research by Paul Anderson, Andy Brown and Patrick Fitzgerald

Europe's far right

Something nasty in the woodshed

Millions of Europeans are voting for far-right parties. Is democracy under threat? Or is the far right becoming less far out?

BY CHRISTMAS, a militantly anti-immigrant party with Nazi echoes could be part of an Austrian government. Mussolini's successors might be back in an Italian coalition some time next year. In Russia, xenophobic nationalists could be riding high in parliament—and aiming for the presidency. Even in civilised France, a xenophobic populist won 15% of the vote in the first round of the presidential election and has seen the mayoralties of some famous cities drop into the hands of his *confrères*. Does this mean that the far right as we have known it is back?

The answer is a firm but uncomplacent No. First point: what the far right stands for has changed. Even if far-right parties in Austria and Italy do well, they are less frightening than most people recently thought, and far less so than their ancestors in the 1930s. Most would now accept that multi-party systems are the best form of democracy, that power should be won and held only by the ballot box, and that nobody is above the law. Some east Europeans (especially in Russia) may not pass that test of respectability. But fascism in its old west European clothing is dead. The main parties on the Italian, French and Austrian far-right have even junked most of the old state corporatism that characterised the 1930s.

A second qualification is that nowhere is there much chance of an extreme right-winger winning power untrammelled. Jörg Haider's Freedom Party, Austria, or Gianfranco Fini's National Alliance, in Italy, could win power only as junior partners in a coalition. Russia's Vladimir Zhirinovsky has been sliding down the polls (see chart). France's Jean-Marie Le Pen has virtually no chance even of sharing power nationally.

And consider the countries where the far right did once hold sway. In Germany, the Nazi-shadowing Republican Party has shrivelled to about 3% of the national vote. The Iberian far right has virtually vanished. In the smaller countries of western Europe, latest opinion polls and elections at various levels usually give the far right less than 10%.

Right fists forward
Elections and polls, % of votes

Russia
Liberal Democratic Party

Austria
Freedom Party

France
National Front

Italy
National Alliance

Germany
Republican Party

1986 87 88 89 90 91 92 93 94 95 Latest

That is a far cry from the dark days of the 1930s. Despite the continuing existence of parties that are more or less fascist, the movement may have peaked. It is more worrying in eastern Europe than it is in the west. But even there, in a number of countries where leaders have handed out doses of unpleasant but necessary economic medicine, the threat is already diminishing or is likely to do so in the next few years. The appeal of the whackier sort of populist that burst forth from nowhere in the flush of post-communism to win big votes (Poland's Stanislaw Tyminski, for example, and Russia's Mr Zhirinovsky), is already fading as electorates become more sophisticated.

That is not to say the new ultra-rightwingers are unworrying. The latest one with a hope of power is Austria's Mr

Haider, whose Freedom Party may, according to some opinion polls, get nearly a third of the vote in a general election in December. The son of a high-ranking Nazi official, he has praised aspects of Hitler's rule. Once he thinks (often mistakenly) that he is out of earshot of the Viennese media, he tends to bash racial minorities, homosexuals and foreigners.

But he is able, sharp-witted and has learned not to rant, especially on television. Like Mr Fini in Italy, he has junked the old fascist corporatism in favour of the free market and recently chucked the pan-Germanism of old Austrian fascism. His hostility to the European Union goes down well in a country that is imposing austerity policies in an effort to meet the Maastricht criteria for economic and monetary union. Above all, he scores palpable hits against the corrupt, stagnant duopoly of the centre-left Social Democrats and centre-right People's Party, which have governed Austria as a shared fief virtually since 1945, dishing out jobs, contracts and even housing to its hitherto pliant constituents. Many Austrians think these parties deserve to lose.

That does not mean that Mr Haider deserves to win. The December election will be a three-way tussle, with the two long-ruling parties (which fell out over next year's budget) and Mr Haider's party all unlikely to win an outright majority. The question is whether Wolfgang Schüssel, the newish leader of the centre right could stomach teaming up with Mr Haider. So far, he has been studiously non-committal.

Look east, and tremble

In Italy, prospects are even muddier. Nobody knows when an election might happen or which parties will club together. A year ago, an opinion poll had Mr Fini as the country's most popular politician. The latest ones put his National Alliance in third place, with about a fifth of the vote, while the Democratic Party of the Left would get around a quarter and Silvio Berlusconi's Forza Italia something in-between. But, with Mr. Berlusconi due to stand trial on bribery charges, Mr Fini could press a claim to lead a right-wing coalition. And if the right does do well in Italy's next general election (anything could happen) then Mr Fini, like Mr Haider, would have a chance of power—even of becoming prime minister.

It is in the former Soviet block, where democracy has shallower roots, that the far right is more troubling. Ethnic turmoil, poverty, and the cynicism and corruption of voters and politicians, provide fertile ground for extremists of all kinds. In Slovakia, a populist prime minister, Vladimir Meciar, rails against gypsies and Hungarians, and retains power by allowing an even nastier far-right party to hold the defence and agriculture portfolios in his coalition. In Latvia, where Russians account for a

third of the population, a German-Latvian populist, who is appealing against a conviction in Germany for inciting racial hatred there, astonished pundits by nearly winning a recent general election. In Hungary, a more jocular populist, Jozsef Torgyan of the Independent Smallholders' Party, currently tops the opinion polls, by vilifying both the old communists and the new capitalists, stirring nationalist resentments, and praising God and "family values"—a rich recipe that goes down well across the whole of the old Soviet empire.

Even here, though, there are reasons for hope. Especially in ethnically homogeneous countries such as the Czech Republic and Poland, where the economy is improving, the far right is fading. Except for Latvia, the nationalist far right has shrunk in the rest of the Baltic area, and has dwindled in Belarus and Ukraine. If Hungary's so-far-sensible Socialists are tough enough on the economy, the appeal of Mr Torgyan's populist protest may well fizzle out by the time the next elections come round in 1998.

The biggest worry has been Russia, where the acrid Mr Zhirinovsky's 22% was the biggest vote for any party in the general election two years ago. But now that most Russian parties make nationalist noises, Mr Zhirinovsky seems to have faded too. The most popular party in Russia is the Communist Party and the biggest threat to democracy there comes from the left, not the right.

The trouble, though, is that the rhetoric of right and left is hard to distinguish. Nor, at either end of the spectrum, do parties comfortably pass the respectability test: their loyalty to democracy cannot be taken for granted. All the same, more moderate nationalists such as General Alexander Lebed—who is the most popular of Russian politicians—are less frightening than Mr Zhirinovsky. And there is still a good chance that politicians at the extremes will be outvoted by those nearer the centre. Give Russia another four years of moderation and even there the extremists should start to crumble.

The Migration Challenge
Europe's Crisis in Historical Perspective

James F. Hollifield

James F. Hollifield is Assistant Professor of Political Science at Auburn University.

Few issues have had a greater impact on the politics and society of contemporary Western Europe than immigration. The variety of national responses to the migration crisis would seem to indicate that each state is designing its own policy, and that there is little to link one national experience with another. Moreover, a majority of West European governments and elites have rejected any comparisons with the American experience, arguing that the United States is a nation of immigrants, with much greater territory and a political culture that is more tolerant of ethnic and cultural differences. In recent years, the American "model" of a multicultural and immigrant society has been deemed by many political and intellectual elites in Western Europe a bad model, which can only lead to greater social and political conflict—such critics point to the 1992 riots in Los Angeles. Yet the problems of immigration control (and ultimately the assimilation of foreign populations) in Europe are much the same as in the United States, for two reasons.

First, the global economic dynamic which underlies the migration crisis is similar in the two regions. The great postwar migrations to Western Europe and the United States began, for the most part, in response to the demand for cheap labor and the pull of high-growth economies, which in the 1950s and 1960s literally sucked labor from poorer countries of the periphery, especially Mexico, the Caribbean, southern Europe, North Africa and Turkey. These labor migrations (and *demand-pull* forces) were subsequently legitimized by the receiving states through what came to be known as guestworker and bracero policies. This economically beneficial movement of labor was consistent with the liberal spirit of the emerging global economy.

But what started as an efficient transfer of labor from poor countries of the South to the North, rapidly became a social and political liability in the 1970s, when growth rates in the OECD countries slowed in the aftermath of the first big postwar recession of 1973-74. The recession led to major policy shifts in Western Europe to stop immigration or, at least, to stop the recruitment of foreign workers. At the same time, however, demand-pull forces were rapidly giving way to *supply-push* forces, as the populations of poorer, peripheral countries began to grow at a rapid pace and their economies weakened. Informational and kinship networks had been established between immigrants and their home countries (via families and villages). These networks helped to spur immigration, despite the increasingly desperate attempts by receiving states in Western Europe to stop all forms of immigration.

Global economic (push-pull) forces provide the necessary conditions for international migration, especially the continuation of immigration in Western Europe after the implementation of restrictionist policies in the 1970s. But to understand fully the crisis of immigration control in the 1980s and 1990s, we must look beyond economics to liberal political developments in the major receiving states. The struggle to win civil and social *rights* for marginal groups, including ethnic minorities and foreigners, and the institutionalization of these rights in the jurisprudence of liberal states provide the sufficient conditions for continued immigration. Therefore, to get a complete picture of the migration crisis we must look at the degree of institutionalization of rights-based politics in the countries of Western Europe and at the struggle to redefine citizenship and nationhood in states such as France, Britain and Germany.

The migration tides of the 1950s and 1960s created new and reluctant lands of immigration in Western Europe

From *Harvard International Review*, Summer 1994, pp. 26-29, 67-69. © 1994 by the Harvard International Relations Council. Reprinted by permission.

and brought to the fore questions of citizenship, the rights of minorities and multiculturalism. The migration crisis also led to the rise of anti-immigrant, right-wing parties opposed to the extension of rights to non-citizens, ethnic minorities and asylum seekers. These right-wing political and social movements amounted to a populist/nativist backlash tinged with neofascism and opposed to rights-based, liberal politics. But the migration crisis also demonstrated the extent to which new civil and social rights for foreign and ethnic minorities had become embedded in the jurisprudence, institutions and political processes of the West European states since 1945. A new sensitivity to the rights of minorities and refugees grew out of the experiences of the Second World War and the Cold War, making it difficult for states simply to expel or deport unwanted migrants, as was done in earlier periods.

Origins of the Migration Crisis

The origins of the migration crisis in Western Europe can be traced to three historical developments, each of which contributed to the political-economic dynamic described above. First is the crisis of *decolonization* which led to an unsettled period of mass migrations from roughly 1945 to 1962-63. The political and economic significance of these movements of populations early in the postwar period should not be underestimated, for it was the aftermath of war and decolonization that created new ethnic cleavages and a new ethnic consciousness in these societies and, thereby, laid the groundwork for the rise of extremist, populist and nativist movements such as the *Front National* in France and the *Republikaner* in Germany.

The second and perhaps most important wellspring of the migration crisis in Western Europe is the set of public policies known as guestworker (*Gastarbeiter*) or rotation policies. These policies for recruiting ostensibly temporary foreign workers began as early as 1945 in Switzerland, whose policy came to be viewed as the model for guestworker programs in other West European countries. The central feature of these policies was the concept of rotation, whereby foreign unmarried male workers could be brought into the labor market for a specified, contractual period and sent back at the end of this period. They could be replaced by new workers as needed. This was a rather neat macroeconomic formula for solving what was shaping up to be one of the principal obstacles to continued high rates of non-inflationary growth in the 1950s and 1960s. In fact, it seemed to be working so well in the Swiss case that the newly reorganized Organization for Economic Cooperation and Development (OECD) recommended the policy to European states that were experiencing manpower shortages. The Bonn government forged a consensus in 1959-60 among business and labor groups to opt for a policy of importing labor rather than taking industry, capital and jobs offshore in search of lower labor costs, as was being done in the United States. This was the beginning of the largest guestworker program in Western Europe, which would eventually bring millions of Turks, Yugoslavs and Greeks to work in German industry.

Two fateful turning points in the history of the German guestworker program are of interest. The first came in 1967-68, following the shallow recession of 1966. It was at this point that the Grand Coalition government (1966-69) successfully stopped Turks and other guestworkers from entering the labor market, and sent many of them home. This operation was so successful that there was little resistance to bringing the guestworkers back in 1969-70, when the West European economies were heating up again. The second fateful turning point in the history of the *Gastarbeiter* program in Germany came in 1973 when the attempt was made to stop all recruitment of foreign workers, to repatriate them and to prevent family reunification. It was at this point that the relatively new liberal features of the German state came fully to the fore to prevent the government and administrative authorities from stopping immigration (especially family reunification) and deporting unwanted migrants.

France is often mentioned as a European country that pursued guestworker-type policies, a somewhat misleading conception. The Provisional or Tripartite Government under General Charles de Gaulle (1945-46), as well as the first governments of the Fourth Republic, did put in place policies for recruiting foreign labor. But the new workers were defined from the outset as *travailleurs immigrés* (immigrant workers). Policies of Fourth Republic governments encouraged foreign workers to settle permanently because immigration was part and parcel of population policy, which was itself a reflection of pronatalist sentiments among the political elites.

As the French economy boomed in the 1960s, authorities rapidly lost all control over immigration. But instead of sucking more labor from culturally compatible neighboring countries, such as Italy and Spain (which were beginning to develop in their own right), the French economy was supplied principally by the newly independent states of North Africa (Algeria, Morocco and Tunisia). By the end of the 1960s, Algerians were rapidly becoming the most numerous immigrant group. Their special post-colonial status gave them virtual freedom of movement into and out of the former *metropole* of France. The principal "mode of immigration" during this period was immigration "from within," whereby foreigners would enter the country (often having been recruited by business), take a job and then have a request be made on their behalf by the firm for an adjustment of status.

By the early 1970s, the rapid increase in North African immigration convinced the Pompidou government that something had to be done to regain control of immigration. The deep recession of 1973-74, which brought an abrupt end to the postwar boom, simply confirmed this judgment. The new government under Valery Giscard d'Estaing took fairly dramatic steps to close the immigration valve, using heavy-handed statist and administrative measures to try to stop immigration, repatriate immigrants and deny "rights" of family reunification. Thus, the French followed much the same logic as the Germans in attempting to use foreign workers, on one hand, as a kind of industrial reserve army and, on the other, as shock absorbers to solve social and economic problems associated with recession—especially unemployment. Other labor-importing states in Western Europe followed the same guestworker logic in changing from policies of recruitment to suspension.

2. PLURALIST DEMOCRACIES: The Ethnic Factor in West European Politics

The migration crisis in Western Europe in the 1980s and 1990s cannot be fully understood apart from the history of the guestworker programs. These programs created the illusion of temporary migration, leading some states (especially Germany) to avoid or postpone a national debate over immigration and assimilation policy. This problem was compounded by the statist attempts in 1973-74 to stop immigration and repatriate foreigners, which furthered the "myth of return" and heightened public expectations that governments could simply reverse the migratory process. Also, taking such a strong, statist stance against further immigration made it virtually impossible for French and German governments in the 1980s and 1990s even to discuss an "American-style," legal immigration policy. Instead, immigration became a highly charged partisan issue, leading to soul-searching debates about national identity and citizenship. The more practical questions—which an American policymaker or politician might ask—of "how many, from where, and in what status," simply could not be asked. The result of trying to slam shut the "front door" of legal immigration led to the opening of side doors and windows (for family members and seasonal workers). Most importantly, the "back door" was left wide open (especially in Germany) for refugees and asylum-seekers. Not surprisingly, many would-be legal and illegal immigrants (as well as legitimate asylum-seekers and others) flooded through the back door in the 1980s and 1990s.

At present, it would appear that the politics of xenophobia, nativism and restrictionism prevail and that each state is defining immigration and refugee policies in idiosyncratic and nationalistic terms.

The third historical development in the migration crisis is the influx of *refugees* and *asylum-seekers*, which is causally related to colonialism and to the failed guestworker policies. Large-scale refugee migrations began in Europe in the aftermath of the Second World War and with the advent of the Cold War. In practice, flight from a communist regime was sufficient grounds for the extension of political asylum in most of the countries of Western Europe. The famous Article 16 of the West German Basic Law, which granted an almost unconditional right to asylum for any individual fleeing persecution, was written with refugees from the East in mind, especially ethnic German refugees.

Refugee and asylum policies in Western Europe functioned rather well for almost three decades from roughly 1950 to 1980 (during most of the Cold War), but with the closing of front-door immigration policies in the 1970s, political asylum became an increasingly attractive mode of entry for unwanted migrants who would come to be labeled "economic refugees." As governments across Western Europe struggled to redefine their immigration and refugee policies in the wake of severe economic recessions and rising unemployment, the pace of refugee migrations increased. The first efforts to address this new movement of populations came at the level of the European Community, where it was thought that national governments could simultaneously reassert control over refugee movements and avoid the painful moral and political dilemmas involved in limiting the right to asylum. The Single European Act of 1985 set in motion a new round of European economic integration, which included the goal of "free movement of goods, persons, services and capital"—in effect, the establishment of a border-free Europe. It quickly became clear, however, that achieving this goal would require European states to agree upon common visa and asylum policies.

Toward this end, five states (France, Germany, and the Benelux countries) met in the Dutch town of Schengen, and in 1985 unveiled the Schengen Agreement as a prototype for a border-free Europe. The Agreement called for the elimination of internal borders, the harmonization of visa and asylum policies and the coordinated policing of external borders, leading to the construction of a symbolic "ring fence" around the common territory. Schengen, which was enlarged to include Italy, Spain and Portugal, was followed in 1990 by the Dublin Agreement, which established the principle that refugees must apply for asylum in the first EC member state in which they arrive. But no sooner had the states of Western Europe begun to focus on a common policy for dealing with the refugee and asylum issue, than had the entire international system in Europe changed with the collapse of communist regimes in East-Central Europe and, finally, the collapse of the Soviet Union itself.

The euphoria associated with the "triumph of liberalism" over communism did contribute, at least briefly, to a surge of refugee migration. That surge lasted for about four years, from 1989 to 1993. Governments were forced to reconsider and rewrite sweeping constitutional provisions, which guaranteed the right to asylum, at the same time that new irredentist movements swept the Balkans, Transcaucasia, and other formerly communist territories, leading to civil wars and new refugee migrations.

How have the states of Western Europe and the EC responded to the migration crisis? The responses can be identified at three levels. The first is political, in the sense that politicians, especially on the right, have exploited the migration crisis for political gain. The second is a policy-level response, which has lurched from one extreme to another. Liberal and assimilationist policies of amnesty (for illegals) have been followed by harsh crackdowns on asylum-seekers and attempts to make naturalization more difficult. Finally, emerging from this cauldron of political and policy debates is a search for national "models" of immigration, which range from tempered pluralism in Britain to stringent assimilation in France.

The Search for a National Model

France was the first state in Western Europe to feel the full political force of the migration crisis, in part because of the stunning victory of the left in the presidential and parliamentary elections of 1981. The socialists won the elections partly on a liberal platform, which promised to improve civil rights for immigrants by giving them a more firm legal standing. To carry out these promises, the first socialist government of Pierre Mauroy enacted a conditional amnesty, which led to the legalization of well over 100,000 undocumented immigrants. Other measures also were taken to limit the arbitrary powers of the police to carry out identity checks, to grant long-term (10-year) resident permits to foreigners and to guarantee the rights of association for immigrant groups. These liberal policies, carried out in the wake of the left's electoral breakthrough and with the right in a state of temporary disarray, provided an opening for a little-known populist and neo-fascist candidate, Jean-Marie Le Pen, and the *Front National* (FN). The early 1980s was also a period of recession, rising unemployment and general insecurity, especially among workers. Le Pen and his group seized the moment and won what seemed to be a small victory (16.7 percent of the vote) in the town of Dreux, near Paris. But this was the beginning of an intense period of immigration politics, as the right struggled to regain power and Le Pen, under the banner of *La France aux français*, garnered more support from an extremely volatile electorate.

The traditional parties of the right, *Rassemblement pour la République* (RPR) and *Union pour la Démocratie Française* (UDF), under the leadership of Jacques Chirac, Mayor of Paris, began to attack the socialists' handling of the immigration issue. The socialists responded by defending liberal and republican principles of naturalization and assimilation, holding out the prospect of voting rights for resident aliens in local elections, while promising to enforce labor laws (employer sanctions) in order to crack down on illegal immigration. In the parliamentary elections of 1985, which were fought under new rules of proportional representation, the right won a narrow victory. The FN won over 30 seats in the new parliament, giving Le Pen a forum in which to pursue his anti-immigrant, populist, nativist agenda. The Minister of the Interior in the government of *cohabitation* (headed by Chirac), Charles Pasqua, launched a series of initiatives and bills, which came to be known as *la loi Pasqua*. They intended to give greater power to the police to arrest and deport undocumented migrants, and to deny entry to asylum-seekers, who would not be allowed to appeal their cases to the office for protection of refugees (OFPRA).

Immigrant rights groups, such as *SOS-racisme*, *France Plus*, MRAP and the GISTI, organized protests and legal appeals to stop the reform. Thousands marched in the streets under banners that read *ne touche pas mon pote* (don't touch my buddy) and the French Council of State was called upon to review the legality (and constitutionality) of the government's immigration policy. In the end, the government made a decision to appoint a special commission composed of leading intellectual and political figures. The commission held public hearings and wrote a long report, concluding that French republican principles of universalism and the right of foreigners born in France to naturalize (*jus soli*) should be upheld. At the same time, the commission stressed the importance of maintaining the assimilationist, republican principles, inherent in French immigration law and practice. The right lost the presidential

and parliamentary elections of 1988, essentially failing to capitalize on the immigration issue, while Jean-Marie Le Pen succeeded in gaining 14.5 percent of the vote on the first ballot of the presidential elections. But the FN received only one seat in the new parliament, which was elected according to the old two-round, single member district rules used throughout the history of the Fifth Republic until 1985. Le Pen cried foul, arguing that the voices of a significant proportion of the French electorate were not being heard, and opinion polls, which showed that over a third of the voters supported the positions of the FN, seemed to bear him out.

The socialist government of François Mitterrand and Michel Rocard continued to defend rights of foreigners, but also launched a campaign for tougher enforcement of labor laws and set up a new council for integration (*Haut Conseil à l'Intégration*) to study ways of bringing immigrants into the mainstream of French social, economic and political life.

French Immigration Policy in the 1990s

Immigration in France continued during this period of the 1980s at a rate of about 100,000 annually, and refugee migrations picked up to about 25,000 annually. As the country slipped slowly into recession in 1991-92, the left began to lose its nearly decade-long grip on power. The parliamentary elections of 1993 were fought in part over the issue of immigration control, with the right feeling little compulsion to restrain anti-immigrant, populist and nativist sentiments among the public. In fact, the decision was made to try to steal the thunder of Le Pen and the FN by proposing harsh measures for dealing with illegal immigration and asylum seekers. The badly divided socialist party suffered a crushing defeat in March 1993, and the reinvigorated right (RPR-UDF), under the new leadership of Edouard Balladur, wasted little time in implementing draconian measures (by French standards) to stop immigration. Once again, Pasqua was named to head the Interior Ministry, and with the right controlling nearly 80 percent of the seats in the National Assembly, he proposed a series of bills to reform immigration, naturalization and refugee law (*la loi Pasqua II*). These measures amounted to a broadside attack on the civil and social rights of foreigners. They sought to undermine key aspects of the republican model, as spelled out in the *Ordonnances* of 1945, especially residency requirements for naturalization, the principle of *jus soli* and the guarantee of due process for asylum-seekers.

La loi Pasqua II also included a bill designed to prevent illegal immigrants from benefiting from French social security, particularly health care. This legislation immediately opened a rift in the new French cabinet between the hardline Minister of Interior and Regional Development, Pasqua, and the more liberal-republican Minister of Social, Health and Urban Affairs, Simone Veil, who argued successfully that emergency medical care should not be denied to foreigners. *Pasqua II* also sought to limit the civil rights of immigrants and asylum-seekers, by increasing the powers of the police and the administration to detain and deport unwanted migrants. Under the new policy, the police are given sweeping powers to check the identity of "suspicious persons." Race is not supposed to be sufficient grounds for stopping an individual, but any immigrant (legal or otherwise) who threatens "public order" can be arrested and deported.

Immigrant workers and students are obliged to wait two years, rather than one, before being allowed to bring their families to join them in France, and illegal immigrants cannot be legalized simply by marrying a French citizen. Finally, *Pasqua II* resurrected the Chirac government's proposal to reform French nationality law (1986), which requires the children of foreigners born in France to file a formal request for naturalization between the ages of 16 and 21, rather than automatically attributing French citizenship to them at age 18.

These repressive measures, which were designed specifically to roll back the rights of foreigners, immigrants and asylum seekers, immediately drew fire from those institutions of the liberal and republican state that were created to protect the rights of individuals. The Council of State, as it had done several times before, warned the government that it was on shaky legal ground, especially with respect to the "rights" of family reunification and political asylum. But the rulings of the Council of State are advisory; no matter how much moral, political and legal weight they may carry, the government can choose to ignore them. The rulings, however, can presage binding decisions of the Constitutional Council, which has limited powers of judicial review. This is precisely what happened in August 1993, as the Constitutional Council found several provisions of the new policy (*Pasqua II*) to be unconstitutional.

All this political and legal maneuvering in 1993 has led inexorably to a full constitutional debate over immigration and refugee policy in France. French President François Mitterrand, who has considerable constitutional responsibilities and political and moral authority, has stayed for the most part on the sidelines. The Minister of the Interior, Pasqua, has continued doggedly to pursue more restrictionist immigration and naturalization policies, at the levels of both symbolic and electoral politics. Any political victories on this front would seem to come at the expense of the principal rivals of the RPR-UDF, namely the FN on the right and the Socialist Party on the left.

These policy and political responses to the migration crisis in France constitute a tacit recognition that there is only so much any state can do to alter push-pull forces, and that a "roll back" of civil and social rights is the most effective way to control or stop immigration. But in France, as in the US and Germany, administrative and executive authorities are confronted with a range of constitutional obstacles associated with the liberal and republican state. The republican model, with its universalistic and egalitarian principles, remains essentially intact, despite repeated assaults from the French right. France still has the most expansive naturalization policies of any state in Western Europe and it has preserved the principles of *jus soli*, as well as due process, equality before the law and the right to asylum. Whether the republican model will survive the current assault and whether it can serve as a broader European model remains to be seen.

The German Response

Until recently, debates over immigration and refugee policy in Germany were confined to policy and administrative elites or academic and intellectual circles. But in the late 1980s, and especially since unification, politicians have seized on the immigration and refugee issue. A full-blown national debate has erupted, with politicians vying for mass support and various social movements on the left and the right seeking to influence policymaking. Unlike France, Germany does not have an established "national model" around which to organize this debate. Debates over immigration, naturalization and refugee law are not, however, devoid of ethnonationalist or ethno-cultural arguments. The current German nationality law dates from 1913; there are clear historical and national overtones in the debate. But the experience of the Holocaust and the defeat suffered in World War II make it difficult for German authorities to appeal to the past as a way of coping with immigration. Until 1989, a consensus existed among political and policy elites simply to avoid debates over immigration, naturalization and citizenship issues. Foreigners were granted social and civil rights, but barriers to naturalization remained high and the politically explosive issue of reforming the nationality code was avoided.

This ostrich-like approach to immigration policy and the elite's consensus not to raise the issue simply fell apart under the pressure of events in the 1980s. Decades of repressed nationalism have come bubbling to the surface in contemporary party politics. Polls, which showed rising opposition to immigration, encouraged politicians to take up the issue. When Helmut Kohl was chosen to head the new government of the right in 1982, he introduced a new *Ausländerpolitik*, but in the election campaign of 1982-83, the issue simply disappeared from the national agenda. In effect, policy and political elites decided to return to the earlier consensus of silence. Also strong was an appeal to the founding (economic) myth of the Federal Republic, or *Wirtschaftswunder*, that seemingly intractable social, economic and even political problems could be solved by another German economic miracle. But this economic solution proved insufficient to solve the problems of immigration control and assimilation, especially with rising unemployment rates and severe housing shortages. By the mid- to late-1980s, foreigners were increasingly being blamed for taking jobs, housing and public services away from German citizens.

In the Bavarian *Landtag* elections of 1986, the CSU raised the issue of immigration control, in part to counter the break-away of a small faction of the party, under the leadership of a former talk show host, Franz Schonhuber. This faction became the *Republikaner* party and gained 3 percent of the vote. In the following years the *Republikaner* continued to make inroads at the level of state and local politics. With the collapse of the German Democratic Republic and the unification of Germany in 1989-90, it appeared that the *Republikaner* had lost its appeal. It received only 2.1 percent of the vote in the first all-German, federal election in 1990. But its fortunes were to improve in the early 1990s. Clearly, with the collapse of Communism and the end of the Cold War, some of the restraints on overt expressions of German nationalism were removed and the immigration issue was no longer taboo. A new anti-foreigner slogan, *Ausländer raus*, became the rallying cry of far-right, skinhead and neo-Nazi groups. The massive influx of asylum seekers from 1989-93 contributed to the atmosphere of crisis, placing more pressure on the government to act, and making it easier for politicians (of the right) to use the immigration and asylum issue to get votes.

In 1990, the newly reelected government of Kohl faced two problems: how to facilitate the integration and naturalization of the large foreign population, without alienating more of the right-wing electorate, and how to build a consensus for changing Article 16 of the German Constitution to stem the rising tide of asylum seekers, while keeping the front door open to ethnic German refugees from the East. The first task was at least partially accomplished by rushing a bill through parliament to facilitate naturalization of second-generation immigrants, thereby solidifying the rights of resident aliens, and removing some of the legal ambiguities concerning residency, work permits and family reunification. This was done quietly in the midst of the social and political euphoria following unification.

The sufficient conditions for immigration...are likely to persist, even if they are weakened by attacks from the extreme right and lack of popular support.

Reform of immigration and refugee policy was given a new urgency in 1992 and 1993 by a series of much-publicized racist attacks against foreigners, including a firebombing by skinheads in the town of Solingen resulting in the death of five Turks who were permanent residents of the Federal Republic. More racist attacks occurred, however, just weeks after the Christian-Liberal government and the Social Democrats agreed in May 1993 to amend Article 16 of the Constitution. Although the language of the new asylum law, which states that "those politically persecuted enjoy the right to asylum," is consistent with the Geneva Convention, in practice the new law allows the German government to turn back asylum-seekers who arrive through a safe country. Since about 80 percent of refugees enter through Poland and the Czech Republic, an agreement had to be reached with these states to allow for the *refoulement* of asylum-seekers. Since the new policy was instituted, the number of migrants apprehended trying to enter the country illegally has skyrocketed.

Despite a great deal of rhetoric following racial violence and fatal attacks on foreigners in 1993 and 1994, the Kohl government was unable to change German nationality law, which dates from 1913 and rests on the principle of *jus sanguinis* (blood, rather than soil or place of birth). The German law also does not allow dual citizenship. Hence, millions of foreign residents have been granted some civil and social rights, but without naturalization. They remain outsiders without full political rights, even though in many cases they have been born, reared and educated in Germany.

The Immigration Issue in Southern Europe

The countries of southern Europe—Italy, Spain, Greece and Portugal—are still far from developing national models for immigration control and assimilation. As the traditional receiving states in northern Europe tried to close their borders to new immigration in the 1970s and 1980s, more unwanted migrants (especially from Africa) began to enter the EC via the soft underbelly of Italy, Spain and Greece. Political change (democratization in Greece, Spain and Portugal) together with high levels of economic growth contributed to the influx of unwanted migrants. Policy responses have lurched from one extreme to another, in the face of a growing political backlash against foreigners, especially in northern Italy where the anti-immigrant Northern League has been capturing about one fifth of the vote in recent elections. Amnesty was extended to illegal immigrants in Spain (1985) and Italy (1987) in the hopes of bringing marginal groups and ethnic minorities into the mainstream of society by offering protections under the rubric of social welfare. But the push to establish a border-free Europe, as a result of the Single European Act, the Schengen Agreement and, finally, the Maastricht Treaty (which holds out the prospect of a kind of European citizenship in the next century), has forced the states of southern Europe to reformulate their immigration and refugee policies. To be a part of a border-free Europe, they must demonstrate a capacity for controlling their borders and stopping illegal immigration.

The perceived failure of national policies and the lack of a dominant national model for dealing with the migration crisis have led many governments in Western Europe to look for a Europe-wide solution to the problem of immigration control. The hope here is that the states of the European Union will be able to accomplish together what they have been unable to accomplish alone: stop immigration.

A European Solution to a Global Problem?

From the Treaty of Rome (1957) to the Maastricht Treaty, the logic of European integration has driven the states of Western Europe to cooperate on border control issues. The logic is one of both inclusion (free movement of goods, services, capital and *people*) and exclusion (a common tariff policy, an economic and monetary union and common visa and asylum policies). But common visa and asylum policies have proved illusive. The prospect of a truly border-free Europe places enormous pressure on member states to cooperate in the policing of external borders.

Control over population and territory are key aspects of national sovereignty that strike at the heart of notions of citizenship and national identity. Since ceding this aspect of sovereignty to a supranational organization such as the EU is a potentially explosive political issue, member states, as well as the European Council and the Commission, have proceeded with great caution. In Dublin in 1990, the European Council established the principle that refugees can apply for political asylum in only one member state. Shortly thereafter, the Schengen Group, which had been enlarged from the original five (France, Germany and Benelux) to include Italy, Spain and Portugal, met to sign the Convention that set in motion a process for lifting all border controls among these states. Britain, as an island-nation, steadfastly refused to get involved in the Schengen process for fear of losing its natural advantage in border control. Still, the inclusionary and exclusionary logic of Schengen seems to be taking hold in post-cold war Europe, as other states and regions have scrambled to join the border-free club. Only Switzerland and Denmark have been reluctant to jump on this bandwagon.

How will "Europe" respond to the global migration crisis? We can learn some things by looking at the recent past, especially the liberal dynamic of *markets* (demand-pull and supply-push) and *rights* (civil, social and political) described above. We must also compare the European and American experiences, because the EU and the United States will be the pacesetters in searching for an international solution to the global migration crisis. Will there be separate American and European models for coping with migration, or will the two models converge? The liberal dynamic and the recent past point to convergence. With the end of the Cold War, all OECD states have experienced an upsurge in migration because (happily) people are freer to move, and because (sadly) ethnic and nationalist forces have been unleashed, causing a wave of refugee migration. The liberal logic of interdependence and economic integration has reinforced the propensity of people to move, in search of higher wages and a better way of life. Supply-push remains strong, but demand-pull is weak. Most of the OECD states are in (or just emerging from) recession. Nevertheless, with slower population growth (especially in Western Europe and Japan) and higher levels of economic growth, demand for immigrant labor is likely to increase as we move closer to the turn of the century. The necessary economic conditions for immigration are present and likely to strengthen, hence all OECD states will be forced to deal with this reality. But what will political conditions, which are the sufficient conditions for immigration, be like in the receiving states?

At present, it would appear that the politics of xenophobia, nativism and restrictionism prevail and that each state is defining immigration and refugee policies in idiosyncratic and nationalistic terms. The rights of immigrants and refugees have been restricted and infringed in Europe and the United States, as governments (freed from the bipolar constraints of the Cold War) have sought to roll back some of the liberal political developments (especially in the area of civil rights) of the past forty years. But liberal-republican institutions and laws are quite resilient. It seems unlikely that what have come to be defined as basic human or civil rights will simply be suspended for non-citizens. Therefore, the sufficient conditions for immigration, which are closely linked to the institutions and laws of the liberal-republican state, are likely to persist, even if they are weakened by attacks from the extreme right and lack of popular support. It is also unlikely that liberal-republicanism will be abandoned or overridden by supranational institutions, such as the EU. The same institutional and legal checks found at the level of the nation-state are evident at the European level.

Since immigration is likely to continue, pressure will mount for states to cooperate in controlling and managing the flow. The states of Western Europe already have taken several steps in this direction at the level of the European Union. But no national or regional model for integration of the large and growing foreign populations has emerged. Policies for controlling the doors of entry (front, side and back) will emerge, barring some unforeseen international catastrophe. Redefining citizenship and nationhood in the older states of Western Europe, however, will be a much longer and more painful process. It remains to be seen which states are best equipped, politically and culturally, to face this challenge.

Europeans Redefine What Makes a Citizen

Craig R. Whitney

PARIS

Children born on French soil to foreign parents used to acquire French citizenship automatically, but since 1993 they have had to apply for it before their 18th birthdays. Like the rest of Western Europe, France has tightened citizenship rules to discourage immigration. Nearly three million people in France, immigrant and native alike, are unemployed, and extreme-right political movements have persuaded 15 to 20 percent of the electorate that unemployment would vanish if the immigrants went home.

In Germany, it can be easier for a child whose family lived in Russia for 200 years to become a German citizen than it is for an American or for the German-born child of a Turkish "guest worker," even if that child speaks no Turkish and has been educated in German schools. Germany defines citizenship by bloodline. So Russian descendants of the ethnic Germans whom Catherine the Great brought over to farm the Volga River Valley can come back to Germany as citizens under the country's law of return. But most others wanting to acquire German citizenship might find it easier to pass through the eye of a needle.

Britain, which admitted millions of people from its former African and Asian colonies until the 1970's, long ago raised the barriers. A proposal in the late 1980's to try to settle nerves in Hong Kong, which reverts to China next year, by giving full British passports to thousands of the colony's most dynamic business leaders and investors met with howls of protest from British politicians afraid of a backlash from their constituents. A recent attempt by Chris Patten, the colony's Governor-General, to revive the proposal fell on deaf ears.

While the creation of European Union points to a continent drawing closer together, with many countries issuing European rather than national passports, the efforts to limit immigration seem to be resulting in more rigid definitions of citizenship rather than more relaxed ones.

STILL GUARDING THE BORDERS

The anti-immigrant mood is widespread in Europe these days, and it's one of the reasons why the 15-nation Union has not yet made good on a promise made five years ago to do away with internal border controls and create a true common market that could eventually stimulate the economic growth needed to bring down chronic high unemployment.

Nine of the 15 nations eventually agreed to try to do away with inspection of passports and identity cards at crossing points along their borders by Jan. 1, 1993, but that was postponed by more than a year. Belgium, Germany and Spain don't guard their frontiers with France anymore but France, despite its claim to be at the core of the new Europe, unilaterally delayed the elimination of border controls by six more months at the turn of the year.

The French are worried about drug smuggling as well as illegal immigrants, and basically they aren't yet confident that their neighbors will do the job of barring the door for them as well as they can do it themselves.

For centuries, most of Europe has defined nationhood by ethnicity, even if citizenship follows different rules. Liberty, equality and fraternity means French citizenship today for 1.8 million people whose ancestors weren't Gauls, most of them from its former North African colonies.

But in Germany, a country where 6.9 million foreigners live, barely a trickle ever become citizens. Of the nearly 2 million Turks living there, only 19,000 acquired German citizenship in 1994. Many who might qualify (by having lived in Germany for 15 years without a criminal record and by being self-supporting) don't apply because they would have to give up Turkish citizenship and the right to own or inherit property in Turkey, if they ever got it.

Citizenship, immigration and asylum are all connected issues. After the unification of Germany in 1990, refugees began pouring into the country, and in 1992, 438,191 people from the Balkans, central Europe and elsewhere claimed political asylum there. What most of them really wanted was a better life, but until 1993, German asylum law entitled anybody who set foot on German soil to make a claim and to make years of appeals if the claim was denied.

The seemingly uncontrollable influx led to fire-bombings and anti-foreigner violence by neo-Nazi and other extremist groups and to a more general public clamor to cut back the flow of asylum-seekers.

In 1993, the German Parliament changed the asylum law to make it possible for German authorities to repel unqualified applicants at the point of entry. Asylum applications plummeted, and last year they had dropped to about 127,000.

More than half of these people were fleeing countries where xenophobia exploded into war. With the disintegration of Yugoslavia, hundreds of thousands of people who had lived as "Yugoslavs" in a multi-ethnic state were driven out of their homes, raped and murdered simply because they happened to be Muslim, Croat or Serb.

CAN SLOVAKS BE CZECHS?

While Bosnia may be an extreme example, the results of intolerance can be seen elsewhere. Even in the Czech Republic, widely viewed as the most tolerant and democratic of all the formerly communist states of central Europe, a Czech human rights group estimates that about 20,000 Gypsies have been denied citizen-

ship since 1993. No citizenship means no health benefits or pension rights, and Gypsies are not the only ones who have problems because of the Czech Republic's law, which grants citizenship most easily to ethnic Czechs. Slovaks, no matter how long they had lived in the Czech part of the country, became foreigners the instant the country split up, and had to apply for Czech citizenship if they wanted it. Many did not qualify. International organizations have urged Czech officials to change the law, but so far they have made no move to do so.

Problems like these exist on a larger scale throughout much of the former Soviet Union, causing political insecurity in central and eastern Europe. Disenfranchised Russian minorities in Belarus, Ukraine and the Baltics look to Russia for protection that Russian nationalists like Vladimir Zhirinovsky would be only too happy to give them.

Chaos produces political backlash, which is why the nationalist, Communist and Agrarian opposition to President Boris N. Yeltsin will have about 250 of the 450 seats in the Parliament that was elected last month.

Here in France, where double-digit unemployment may be the undoing of the welfare state, the right-wing National Front leader Jean-Marie Le Pen wins votes by saying that the 3 million unemployed French workers would find jobs if 3 million immigrants would go back where they came from.

But demographic experts say he's wrong. Low birth rates in France, and in Germany and Britain too, mean that workers from outside will be needed to pay the pensions of the baby-boomers who will start retiring after the turn of the century.

Maintaining their high standard of living is definitely something that appeals to the hearts of well-off Europeans, who might eventually be driven by economic self-interest into simplifying citizenship rules.

Women, Power and Politics:
The Norwegian Experience

Irene Garland

Irene Garland, a Norwegian social scientist, lives in London.

Three Scandinavian countries all have more than one third of women representatives in their national assemblies. In Norway the Prime Minister is a woman as are 9 out of 19 cabinet ministers as well as the leaders of 2 of the other political parties.

Commentators trying to explain this phenomenon have looked back through history and pointed to the independence of Norwegian women as far back as the Viking era, when they kept the homefires burning while their menfolk were away plundering. Others have referred to more recent times. Outstanding women, however, are to be found in most countries at some time or another. The reason for Norwegian women being so successful in gaining political power must therefore be found somewhere else. My belief is that the explanation is of a practical nature and is to be found in the post-war era.

Common to the three Scandinavian countries is a structure of progressive social democracy and election systems based on proportional representation. If one compares the number of women in parliaments across the world, one finds that proportional representation is the single most important element for women to gain entry into politics. However, it was the ability to use this system to their advantage, and the fact that a group of women managed to agree on a common course across party lines, that made it possible to break the mold of the male dominated political scene in Norway.

A SPECTACULAR BEGINNING

The year was 1967 and Brigit Wiik—editor, author, mother and leader of the Oslo Feminist Movement—recalls in her book a chance meeting between herself and Einar Gerhardsen on the street in Oslo. Einar Gerhardsen was a leader of the Labor Party and had been Prime Minister almost continuously since the war. He was, at the time, in opposition, having lost the previous election. With the local elections coming up he agreed to a quota for women on the Labor party lists. In doing so he saw an opportunity to activate a new group of voters for his party, and when his agreement was presented to the party in power, they felt compelled to do the same. With the two largest parties both agreeing to give a quota to women, representatives from The National Advisory Council for Women, The Working Women's Association and the Oslo Feminist Movement, formed a group to lead the campaign to get women into politics by harnessing the female vote. They used a professional PR firm to lead the campaign—a first in Norway. The result surprised everyone; there was a national increase in women representatives of 50%, and whereas there had been 179 local communities without women's representation prior to the election, afterwards the number was reduced to 79. Subsequent campaigns further increased the number of women in local government by 50%—except for 1975.

From *Scandinavian Review*, Winter 1991, pp. 18-25. © 1991 by the American-Scandinavian Foundation. Reprinted by permission.

2. PLURALIST DEMOCRACIES: Women and Politics

WOMEN IN THE NATIONAL ASSEMBLY— THE STORTING

Though there was no campaign to elect women to the national assembly, there seems to have been a spill-over effect. Political parties were quick to recognize the advantage in gaining the female vote and soon extended the quota system to parliamentary elections.

Women's representation in parliament increased steadily from the 1969 election in parallel with what happened in the local elections.

WOMEN START WINNING THE ARGUMENTS

After the 1967 election the Central Bureau of Statistics started to separate voters by gender for the first time, and the 1970s saw an upsurge in research into the history of women's lives and living conditions. Young female researchers were for the first time given the opportunity and the funding to look into their own past, a hitherto ignored area of academic research, and much empirical data was collated during this decade. The history of women's lives ran to 18 volumes and a history of women writers to 3 volumes.

Once they gained entry into the corridors of power, women were increasingly taking up issues of importance to themselves and to the family. Such issues gained in importance by producing results at the ballot box. They could, therefore, not be ignored in party politics and as a result, became part of the overall political agenda.

Enabling policies such as the right to maternity leave and the ability to return to work after giving birth were important for women who wanted to have the choice between having a career and becoming a full-time housewife. With the increased number of women investing in higher education, going back to work was not only seen as a means of personal fulfillment, but became an economic necessity for those who needed to pay back their student loans. The availability of choice was also seen as central to the equality debate— why should men be able to have both a family and a career while women were forced to make a choice? The idea that there was such a thing as a "natural" place for a woman in the home despite qualifications or inclinations was rejected. If women were designed for domesticity by nature itself, then how could one explain the fact that women, given a chance, did very well in the outside world? The patriarchs were at a loss for an answer.

LAWS ARE CHANGED

The 1970s saw a number of typical feminist arguments being brought forward and legislation or common practices changed as a result. One such issue was the one over Miss and Mrs. Throughout the 1960s feminists had opposed the use of these titles and the alternative Ms. had not won approval. During the 1960s ardent feminists would reply to anyone asking if

THE INCREASE IN WOMEN'S REPRESENTATION

Local govern-ment elections	pre-1967	1967	1971	1975	1979
Women as a % of total	6.3	9.5	15	15	22.8
Parliamentary elections	1945–53	1969	1973	1977	1981
Women as a % of total	4.7	9.3	15	23.9	25.8

Maternity leave	2 weeks prior to confinement 30 weeks after confinement with full pay
Leave from work & the right to return	mothers have the right to a further year off work without pay
Paternity leave	fathers have the right to 2 weeks off work with pay, dependent on trade union agreement (applies to all civil servants)
Breast-feeding	mothers have their hours of work cut to accommodate breast-feeding
Children's illness	both parents have a right to 10 days off work with pay when a child under 12 is ill

	Born	Married	Children	Education
Gro H. Brundt-land Prime Minister (Labor)	1939	1960	4	Degree in medicine; MA (Harvard)
Ase Kleveland Minister of Cultural Affairs (Labor)	1949	Co-habits	None	Part law degree; Studied music
Anne E. Lahn-stein Leader, Centre Party	1949	1975	3	Social worker
Kaci K. Five Leader, Conser-vative Party	1951	1972	2	Political Science degree

they were Miss or Mrs. that it was none of their business whether they were married or not. These days no one would ask and such titles are not in general use.

Another issue was that of surnames upon marriage. Women regarded giving up their own names as losing their identities. The law on surnames has now changed so that couples can choose which name to use. Some prefer to keep their maiden name. Some couples take on her name after marriage instead of his, but many women prefer to attach their husbands' name to their own. The latter is the case with the three female party leaders. Children are no longer automatically given their fathers' surname—again it is subject to parental choice.

The debate on surnames formed part of a wider debate about the right to a separate identity for women after marriage. The argument was for women to be able to carry on with their own careers and not to take on the role of supporting player to that of their husbands. Marriage should not become synonymous with taking on the cooking, cleaning and entertaining in addition to their own jobs. Entertaining could equally well be done in a restaurant anyway. Men would have to grow up and stop relying on their wives taking over where their mothers had left off. Cooking and darning became part of every boy's curriculum at school—the emphasis was on enabling men to become self-sufficient.

This also extended to quotas being set for men in certain professions, such as nursing, which until then had been dominated by women.

WOMEN IN POWER TODAY

The quota system helped the Prime Minister, **Gro Harlem Brundtland,** on her way to power. When she became Prime Minister in 1981 for the first time, it was she who introduced the idea of 50/50 gender representation in the cabinet. Having formed her third government at the most recent election, she has taken with her a team of young and capable women. Mrs. Brundtland followed in her father's footsteps—he was a doctor and a cabinet minister—and has been involved in politics from an early age. She is known for her enormous capacity for work, and certainly her record of achievements bears witness to just this. In addition to working full time she has managed to raise a family of four children. Her first job was as a medical officer on the Oslo Board of Public Health. The first ministerial position came in 1974 when she was appointed Minister for the Environment. She was appointed leader of the Labor Party in 1981, the same year that she became Prime Minister at the age of 42, the youngest ever to hold this office.

Internationally she has served on The Palme Commission which published its report on "Common Security" in 1982. This was followed by her chairing the World Commission on Environment and Development whose report, "Our Common Future," was published in 1987. She has published many scientific papers and received numerous prizes in acknowledgement of her work in different fields.

The new leader of the Conservative Party, **Kaci Kullman Five,** also started in politics quite young. Her mother, an elegant looking lady in her 60s, is still active in the local conservative party in Baerum where Mrs. Five first started out. After serving as deputy leader locally, she joined the national party, and was elected

to parliament in 1981. Her first major office was as Deputy Secretary of State for commercial affairs in the Foreign Office in 1989. Having a degree in political science, she has served on the standing committees for foreign policy and constitutional affairs and on the finance committee. She has also published a book.

The third female party leader is **Anne Enger Lahnstein** of the rural Centre Party, who comes from a farming background. She headed the national action against free abortion in 1978–79, and was a member of the Nordic Council from 1979 on, but she did not enter parliament until 1985. She was head of the Oslo Centre Party from 1980–83. From 1983 on, she served as the deputy leader of the national party until she took over as its leader this year.

Ase Kleveland, the new Minister of Culture, differs from the others in that she has not gone through the rank and file of a party. She studied classical guitar and music theory for a number of years and during the '60s and '70s was one of Norway's best known popular singers. Ms. Kleveland won the Norwegian finals of the Eurovision Song Contest and later hosted the TV program for this contest the year it was held in Norway. She headed the Norwegian Musician's Union for a period and her most recent job was as a manager of the first amusement park in Norway. She was due to take over as Cultural Director for the Olympics to be held in Lillehammer in 1994 on the very day she was offered her cabinet post.

COMBINING CAREER AND FAMILY

Combining career with family commitments is no easy task, though office hours in Norway are short—9 to 4—giving more time for both parents to spend with their children. The smaller towns and communities constitute less danger to children which also makes it easier on working parents. Often though, it would seem that having a husband with flexible working arrangements such as a researcher or a journalist helps, and there is no doubt that joint efforts are necessary when both parents work. Fathers do take a much greater part in the up-bringing of their children and in the running of homes, than previously. This "new" role for fathers has now become the norm.

The Prime Minister's children are all grown up now and she is in fact a grandmother, but her husband's job as a researcher and writer no doubt being able to work from home when the need arose, must have been a help. Anne Lahnstein's children are in their teens, only Kaci Five has a young child (8 years old), and she said in an interview that she had to work very hard in order to make time for the family—something she viewed as important. Her husband is an editor and doubtless has to take his turn in looking after the children.

SOUR GRAPES?

It is perhaps inevitable that dissenting voices be heard when so many women reach such high positions in society. Recently a study has been published suggesting that men are leaving politics in Norway because, since it has become dominated by women, it is also becoming a low-paid occupation. Men, it is claimed, are opting for the better paid, higher status jobs in the private sector.

With increased internationalization, they argue, there are many constraints on national assemblies, and important decisions are being made elsewhere; Parliament is no longer the power house it used to be.

Research by Ms. Hege Skjeie from the Institute for Social Studies, disagrees with these conclusions. It is quite true that politicians whose wages are part of the civil service wage scale are lower than those received for the top jobs in the private sector and also that many professions dominated by women are badly paid. However, wages in the state sector have always been considered low relative to private industry, and this was the case before women started to take an interest in a career in politics. Ms. Skjeie's studies found that the men leaving politics did so because of age—they had all served for quite some time. Others had in fact lost their seats or been ousted from positions of leadership within their parties—some by women. There was certainly no difficulty in recruiting young men into

politics, and as regards the power and status associated with politics one could point to Ase Kleveland, Minister of Culture, who had the choice between politics and the Olympic Committee, and chose politics in spite of its uncertainties.

"I'M ON QUOTA—AND I LOVE IT!"

There can be no doubt that it was the quota system that made it possible for Norwegian women to enter politics in such a big way. The power that comes from parliament cannot be underestimated—it has given weight to arguments that had been previously ignored and as such has changed social attitudes of both sexes to the roles and rights of men and women alike. This change could not have taken place without political backing and without such backing, it would not have received such broad social acceptance. However, it is clear that when women work together across party lines, as was the case in Norway during the early days, that is when they achieve the most. Campaigning is also necessary as the experience of 1975 showed—no campaign, no increase in women's representation. The clock cannot be turned back, but even in Norway many women feel that there is no ground for complacency.

Political power is only half the battle

Norwegian women still lag in the workplace

Norway is the only country where children ask their parents if a boy can grow up to be prime minister and get told that at present, the answer is "no way."

Nowhere else in the world do women have more political clout. In last fall's national election, Prime Minister Gro Harlem Brundtland and the leaders of the nation's two main opposition political parties were women. Helped by a quota system that recommends women make up at least 40 percent of every political party's list of candidates for Parliament, women hold almost half the seats in the cabinet and in Parliament. Norway has even changed its Constitution to allow the first-born daughter—rather than just the eldest son—to succeed to the throne upon the death of the monarch. "Norway is a leading country in the field of equal rights," says Brundtland, a physician, a mother of four and the daughter of a doctor and former cabinet minister.

One of a continuing series on the status of women around the world

---

She is only half right. Despite their political gains, Norwegian women remain second-class citizens in the job market. They are hired last, fired first, denied equal pay for the same work as men and held back from promotions to top executive jobs. New laws pushed through by women politicians were supposed to end all that. But Norway's experience suggests that reforming the law is not enough to guarantee women a fair shake.

Anne Soyland, spokesperson for the Norwegian Women's Front, a feminist lobby, blames the women politicians for the disparity between women's political gains and their lowly status in the workplace. "They are not real women," she says. "Once they get elected, they join the elite and stop working as hard as they should for feminist causes."

Where men still rule. Others think the real reason is that legislation can only do so much. New laws have not changed the realities of private industry, where men still rule—and do the hiring and promoting. "Put crudely," says sociologist Oystein Holter, "that means men inject male values into personnel decisions. Perhaps a man gets the job because his military service is regarded as a better qualification than a woman rival's child-care experience. No sexual discrimination is involved, just a value judgment, and you cannot legislate against that. Instead, you have to change attitudes."

A Norwegian woman's place has traditionally been in the home, as in Henrik Ibsen's classic play *A Doll's House*. Wives stayed away from business; husbands never put the teakettle on. Inflation and economic necessity have now pushed wives into the work force but largely in lower-paying positions, such as nurses or secretaries.

Catching up. That is changing, but slowly. Women now outnumber men in Norway's law and medical schools but trail significantly in business schools. Meanwhile, Norway's legislative reforms have produced some surprising results. Women now get 52 weeks of paid maternity leave, but only if the husband takes off the first month, too. If he doesn't, the wife's paid leave is cut in half. The idea is to encourage fathers to help with a baby from the beginning, in the belief that once they start, they will stay engaged in child rearing. But the policy has led to unexpected results: In many divorce cases, Norwegian fathers are now fighting for child custody.

Women politicians wind up in some seemingly no-win situations. Greta Berget, then a very pregnant minister of family affairs, announced last year that she would take only a two-month maternity leave, rather than the full year, because she was too busy in her government job. Feminists denounced her as a traitor for not taking the full entitlement. Male chauvinists said a government minister had no business getting pregnant and taking any time off.

For all the advances in women's rights, Norwegians are not sure that they ultimately will be more successful than other nations in creating a society in which women can be equally fulfilled as wives, mothers and professionals. For now, they are counting on improvements in child care and job rights to allow women to put families first at some stages of their lives, and to focus on their careers at others.

For all that has changed in Norway, much remains the same. "There is nothing more feminine than being pregnant," insists government minister Berget. Nor do men consider themselves emasculated by the rising political power of women. "Sexual attraction is alive and well in Norway," confirms sociologist Holter.

BY FRED COLEMAN IN NORWAY

Despite Global Gains, Women's Status Still Suffers

Robin Wright

Times Staff Writer

WASHINGTON—In India, a postmark pronounces that "a daughter is as good as a son." Israel's Supreme Court decrees that a woman's right to equal treatment supersedes millennia-old religious law. To curtail female infanticide, a Chinese regional authority outlaws prenatal tests to determine sex.

The women's movement, once the preserve of wealthy Western countries, is spreading to the rest of the world.

"What is so impressive is that most of these women have had to fight against far greater odds in societies where they were totally marginalized, and even the idea of a [women's] movement was not accepted," said Myra Bovinic, president of the International Center for Research on Women in Washington. "The way it has mushroomed caught even me by surprise."

Yet on the eve of the International Conference on Women in Beijing next month, women everywhere fare worse than men by just about all measures, concludes the 1995 U.N. Development Program report.

"Women and men still live in an unequal world," said the report, which was released last week. " . . . While the doors to education and health opportunities have opened rapidly for women, the doors to economic and political opportunities are barely ajar."

GAINS AND LOSSES

Two decades after the United Nations' first women's conference, in Mexico City, urged change, economic progress is particularly elusive.

On one hand, women's financial institutions have grown, and with them economic clout. Bangladesh's Grameen Bank, which grants small loans to help destitute women set up microenterprises, has 3 million clients in 37,000 villages and has inspired imitations in 30 countries. Nearly half of the women who have received Grameen loans are no longer living in poverty, according to the U.S. Agency for International Development.

Likewise, one of the world's largest unions, with 30 million members, is the Self-Employed Women's Assn. in India. As Asia's first mass women's network, it provides petty vendors, casual laborers, service-sector workers and others with education, a credit union, welfare services, child care and instruction on everything from reproductive rights to widows' benefits.

Yet at the same time, women's salaries lag behind men's in all countries but one—Paraguay—according to the U.S. Commerce Department. Globally, women are growing poorer.

"Poverty has a woman's face," said the U.N. Development Program report. "Of 1.3 billion people in poverty, 70% are women."

Among rural women particularly, the number in poverty exceeds 600 million and is growing by 15 million a year, according to estimates of the International Fund for Agricultural Development in Rome.

The International Center for Research on Women calls it the "feminization of rural poverty." A report from the center places the blame on worldwide economic crises, civil conflicts and natural calamities, in addition to cultural changes that have eroded the extended family system and sparked an increase in single motherhood.

Botswana is widely heralded as Africa's democratic success story, yet the country's laws do not always reflect this. For example, Botswanan law stipulates that husbands collect refunds on income taxes deducted from their wives' paychecks.

And the government denies citizenship to children of Botswanan women who marry foreign men, even if the family lives in Botswana. In contrast, citizenship is automatic to the offspring of Botswanan men married to foreign women, even if they live abroad.

"If women in developed societies still have to fight battles, then women in poor countries have to fight real wars, sometimes over the most basic issues everyone else takes for granted," said Selim Jahan, co-author of the U.N. Development Program report.

WORKING WOMEN

The employment picture for women is also mixed.

The worldwide female work force has skyrocketed, breaking barriers even in the strictest patriarchal societies.

In Saudi Arabia, females must have written permission from men to travel and are forbidden to drive or show their faces in public. Yet the number of businesswomen registered with the Chamber of Commerce in Riyadh has increased fivefold in five years to 2,000, reports the International Labor Organization. Most of them are in retail or real estate.

Among other Muslim societies, Bangladesh imposed a female quota of at least 10% for high civil-service jobs, while Pakistan reserves 5% of all government jobs for women.

In China, where Mao Tse-tung once pronounced, "Women hold up half the sky," the first law passed by the Communist government that took over in the 1940s banned the holding of concubines and empowered women to own property, choose their husbands, sue for divorce and use their own names. China's constitution is among the few that openly pledges, "Women enjoy equal rights with men in all spheres of life."

As a result, the number of Chinese women now working in government, finance, education, culture, public health and the media is growing faster than the number of men, an official study says.

Women in China dominate the profitable livestock industries and account for half of farm output. Budding village enterprises employ 40 million women. Thanks to economic reforms, women now contribute 40% of a family's income, up from 25% two decades ago.

Yet women workers worldwide are vastly undervalued. The Old Testament book of Leviticus declared a woman's value to be three-fifths of a man's—a rule of thumb that seems to prevail thousands of years later.

As a worldwide average, women are paid 30% to 40% less than their male counterparts for the same work, the U.N. Development Program said. And women's economic contributions are undervalued or not valued to the tune of $11 trillion a year, it said.

"In virtually every country of the world, women work longer hours than men yet share less in the economic rewards," said Mahbub ul-Haq, the Development Program report's principal author. "If women's work were accurately reflected in statistics, it would shatter the myth that men are the main breadwinners of the world."

Globally, only 20% of managers and fewer than 6% of senior managers are female. Women fare poorly even at the United Nations; only six of the more than 180 ambassadors to the United Nations are women, while women head only four of 32 U.N. agencies.

VICTIMS OF CHANGE

Women are often the primary victims of economic change.

As China streamlines its economy by privatizing some government-owned enterprises, many businesses are laying workers off to save money. Women, according to the U.S. State Department's 1995 human rights survey, account for 60% of those dismissed, mainly because enterprises seek to shed their maternity and child-care costs.

Altogether, women are closing the gap with men. But at the current rate, according to another U.N. study, it will take 500 years for women globally to gain equal standing with men in jobs and positions of power.

On the political front, women have made monumental inroads even in Africa, the poorest and least developed region, since the last U.N. women's conference, in Kenya, in 1985.

In South Africa's 1994 elections for a post-apartheid Parliament, women won 100 of the 400 seats—far more representation than women have in most older democracies and a reflection of the movement's expanding goals.

In East Africa, Uganda now has a female vice president. Burundi has a female foreign minister. Tanzania's National Assembly is about 15% female. Rwanda's first female prime minister was killed in the 1994 massacres.

"In many cases, women in developing countries have become more active and made more progress than their Western counterparts in the political sphere," said Charlotte Bunch, director of Rutgers University's Center for Women's Global Leadership.

Worldwide, seven of the 10 elected female heads of state or government are from poor countries: Bangladesh, Dominica, Nicaragua, Pakistan, Turkey and Sri Lanka (where both the president and prime minister are women). In all of modern history, only 11 other women have been elected to similar jobs.

Politics can be a dangerous pursuit for women. Police broke up a joint meeting of the Kenyan League of Women Voters and the International Federation of Women Lawyers last year, assaulting many of the participants with batons and truncheons.

Opportunities have actually diminished for females in many of the formerly socialist countries that are embracing democracy and free markets.

East European governments have far fewer women than their Communist predecessors. And China admits that women hold limited positions of influence in the government and Communist Party—and none in the Politburo.

LEADERSHIP SHARE

Worldwide, the percentage of seats in Parliament held by women in 1993 actually dropped to 10% from 12% in 1989. And some females are just getting the vote. In June, a Kuwaiti parliamentary committee approved a plan for female suffrage—a century after New Zealand's women became the first to win the vote.

"Women are still far from sharing equally in decision-making. In fact, they are all but excluded," according to the U.N. Development Program report.

And where women do gain a foothold, they hold leadership roles largely at the local level in most developed and developing societies, including the United States, Bunch said.

"When you move into the larger policy issues at the regional or national level, women's representation drops dramatically," she said. "Women are allowed in the arena of politics that is most close to home—and therefore the more mundane."

"Women in poor countries are waging tough battles to win equality with their male counterparts," said U.N. expert Mary Chamie. "But gaining any kind of equality with women in developed societies is a virtually unwinnable war, at least in their lifetimes."

WHAT DEMOCRACY IS . . . AND IS NOT

Philippe C. Schmitter & Terry Lynn Karl

Philippe C. Schmitter is professor of political science and director of the Center for European Studies at Stanford University. Terry Lynn Karl is associate professor of political science and director of the Center for Latin American Studies at the same institution. The original, longer version of this essay was written at the request of the United States Agency for International Development, which is not responsible for its content.

For some time, the word democracy has been circulating as a debased currency in the political marketplace. Politicians with a wide range of convictions and practices strove to appropriate the label and attach it to their actions. Scholars, conversely, hesitated to use it—without adding qualifying adjectives—because of the ambiguity that surrounds it. The distinguished American political theorist Robert Dahl even tried to introduce a new term, "polyarchy," in its stead in the (vain) hope of gaining a greater measure of conceptual precision. But for better or worse, we are "stuck" with democracy as the catchword of contemporary political discourse. It is the word that resonates in people's minds and springs from their lips as they struggle for freedom and a better way of life; it is the word whose meaning we must discern if it is to be of any use in guiding political analysis and practice.

The wave of transitions away from autocratic rule that began with Portugal's "Revolution of the Carnations" in 1974 and seems to have crested with the collapse of communist regimes across Eastern Europe in 1989 has produced a welcome convergence toward [a] common definition of democracy.[1] Everywhere there has been a silent abandonment of dubious adjectives like "popular," "guided," "bourgeois," and "formal" to modify "democracy." At the same time, a remarkable consensus has emerged concerning the minimal conditions that polities must meet in order to merit the prestigious appellation of "democratic." Moreover, a number of international organizations now monitor how well these standards are met; indeed, some countries even consider them when formulating foreign policy.[2]

WHAT DEMOCRACY IS

Let us begin by broadly defining democracy and the generic *concepts* that distinguish it as a unique system for organizing relations between rulers and the ruled. We will then briefly review *procedures*, the rules and arrangements that are needed if democracy is to endure. Finally, we will discuss two operative *principles* that make democracy work. They are not expressly included among the generic concepts or formal procedures, but the prospect for democracy is grim if their underlying conditioning effects are not present.

One of the major themes of this essay is that democracy does not consist of a single unique set of institutions. There are many types of democracy, and their diverse practices produce a similarly varied set of effects. The specific form democracy takes is contingent upon a country's socioeconomic conditions as well as its entrenched state structures and policy practices.

Modern political democracy is a system of governance in which rulers are held accountable for their actions in the public realm by citizens, acting indirectly through the competition and cooperation of their elected representatives.[3]

A *regime or system of governance* is an ensemble of patterns that determines the methods of access to the principal public offices; the characteristics of the actors admitted to or excluded from such access; the strategies that actors may use to gain access; and the rules that are followed in the making of publicly binding decisions. To work properly, the ensemble must be institutionalized—that is to say, the various patterns must be habitually known, practiced, and accepted by most, if not all, actors. Increasingly, the preferred mechanism of institutionalization is a written body of laws undergirded by a written constitution, though many enduring political norms can have an informal, prudential, or traditional basis.[4]

For the sake of economy and comparison, these forms, characteristics, and rules are usually bundled together and given a generic label. Democratic is one; others are autocratic, authoritarian, despotic, dictatorial, tyrannical, totalitarian, absolutist, traditional, monarchic, oligarchic, plutocratic, aristocratic, and sultanistic.[5] Each of these regime forms may in turn be broken down into subtypes.

Like all regimes, democracies depend upon the presence of *rulers*, persons who occupy specialized authority roles and can give legitimate commands to others. What distinguishes democratic rulers from nondemocratic ones are the norms that condition how the former come to power and the practices that hold them accountable for their actions.

The *public realm* encompasses the making of collective norms and choices that are binding on the society and backed by state coercion. Its content can vary a great deal across democracies, depending upon preexisting distinctions between the public and the private, state and society, legitimate coercion and voluntary exchange, and collective needs and individual preferences. The liberal conception of democracy advocates circumscribing the public realm as narrowly as possible, while the socialist or social-democratic approach would extend that realm through regulation, subsidization, and, in some cases, collective ownership of property. Neither is intrinsically more democratic than the other—just *differently* democratic. This implies that measures aimed at "developing the private sector" are no more democratic than those aimed at "developing the public sector." Both, if carried to extremes, could undermine the practice of democracy, the former by destroying the basis for satisfying collective needs and exercising legitimate authority; the latter by destroying the basis for satisfying individual preferences and controlling illegitimate government actions. Differences of opinion over the optimal mix of the two provide much of the substantive content of political conflict within established democracies.

"However central to democracy, elections occur intermittently and only allow citizens to choose between the highly aggregated alternatives offered by political parties . . ."

Citizens are the most distinctive element in democracies. All regimes have rulers and a public realm, but only to the extent that they are democratic do they have citizens. Historically, severe restrictions on citizenship were imposed in most emerging or partial democracies according to criteria of age, gender, class, race, literacy, property ownership, tax-paying status, and so on. Only a small part of the total population was eligible to vote or run for office. Only restricted social categories were allowed to form, join, or support political associations. After protracted struggle—in some cases involving violent domestic upheaval or international war—most of these restrictions were lifted. Today, the criteria for inclusion are fairly standard. All native-born adults are eligible, although somewhat higher age limits may still be imposed upon candidates for certain offices. Unlike the early American and European democracies of the nineteenth century, none of the recent democracies in south-

ern Europe, Latin America, Asia, or Eastern Europe has even attempted to impose formal restrictions on the franchise or eligibility to office. When it comes to informal restrictions on the effective exercise of citizenship rights, however, the story can be quite different. This explains the central importance (discussed below) of procedures.

Competition has not always been considered an essential defining condition of democracy. "Classic" democracies presumed decision making based on direct participation leading to consensus. The assembled citizenry was expected to agree on a common course of action after listening to the alternatives and weighing their respective merits and demerits. A tradition of hostility to "faction," and "particular interests" persists in democratic thought, but at least since *The Federalist Papers* it has become widely accepted that competition among factions is a necessary evil in democracies that operate on a more-than-local scale. Since, as James Madison argued, "the latent causes of faction are sown into the nature of man," and the possible remedies for "the mischief of faction" are worse than the disease, the best course is to recognize them and to attempt to control their effects.[6] Yet while democrats may agree on the inevitability of factions, they tend to disagree about the best forms and rules for governing factional competition. Indeed, differences over the preferred modes and boundaries of competition contribute most to distinguishing one subtype of democracy from another.

The most popular definition of democracy equates it with regular *elections*, fairly conducted and honestly counted. Some even consider the mere fact of elections—even ones from which specific parties or candidates are excluded, or in which substantial portions of the population cannot freely participate—as a sufficient condition for the existence of democracy. This fallacy has been called "electoralism" or "the faith that merely holding elections will channel political action into peaceful contests among elites and accord public legitimacy to the winners"—no matter how they are conducted or what else constrains those who win them.[7] However central to democracy, elections occur intermittently and only allow citizens to choose between the highly aggregated alternatives offered by political parties, which can, especially in the early stages of a democratic transition, proliferate in a bewildering variety. During the intervals between elections, citizens can seek to influence public policy through a wide variety of other intermediaries: interest associations, social movements, locality groupings, clientelistic arrangements, and so forth. *Modern democracy, in other words, offers a variety of competitive processes and channels for the expression of interests and values—associational as well as partisan, functional as well as territorial, collective as well as individual. All are integral to its practice.*

Another commonly accepted image of democracy identifies it with *majority rule*. Any governing body that makes decisions by combining the votes of more than half of those eligible and present is said to be democratic, whether that majority emerges within an electorate, a parliament, a committee, a city council, or a party caucus. For exceptional purposes (e.g., amending the constitution or expelling a member), "qualified majorities" of more than 50 percent may be required, but few would deny that democracy must involve some means of aggregating the equal preferences of individuals.

A problem arises, however, when *numbers* meet *intensities*. What happens when a properly assembled majority (especially a stable, self-perpetuating one) regularly makes decisions that harm some minority (especially a threatened cultural or ethnic group)? In these circumstances, successful democracies tend to qualify the central principle of majority rule in order to protect minority rights. Such qualifications can take the form of constitutional provisions that place certain matters beyond the reach of majorities (bills of rights); requirements for concurrent majorities in several different constituencies (confederalism); guarantees securing the autonomy of local or regional governments against the demands of the central authority (federalism); grand coalition governments that incorporate all parties (consociationalism); or the negotiation of social pacts between major social groups like business and labor (neocorporatism). The most common and effective way of protecting minorities, however, lies in the everyday operation of interest associations and social movements. These reflect (some would say, amplify) the different intensities of preference that exist in the population and bring them to bear on democratically elected decision makers. Another way of putting this intrinsic tension between numbers and intensities would be to say that "in modern democracies, votes may be counted, but influences alone are weighted."

Cooperation has always been a central feature of democracy. Actors must voluntarily make collective decisions binding on the polity as a whole. They must cooperate in order to compete. They must be capable of acting collectively through parties, associations, and movements in order to select candidates, articulate preferences, petition authorities, and influence policies.

But democracy's freedoms should also encourage citizens to deliberate among themselves, to discover their common needs, and to resolve their differences without relying on some supreme central authority. Classical democracy emphasized these qualities, and they are by no means extinct, despite repeated efforts by contemporary theorists to stress the analogy with behavior in the economic marketplace and to reduce all of democracy's operations to competitive interest maximization. Alexis de Tocqueville best described the importance of independent groups for democracy in his *Democracy in America*, a work which remains a major source of inspiration for all those who persist in viewing democracy as something more than a struggle for election and re-election among competing candidates.[8]

In contemporary political discourse, this phenomenon of cooperation and deliberation via autonomous group activity goes under the rubric of "civil society." The diverse units of social identity and interest, by remaining independent of the state (and perhaps even of parties), not only can restrain the arbitrary actions of rulers, but can also contribute to forming better citizens who are more aware of the preferences of others, more self-confident in their actions, and more civic-minded in their willingness to sacrifice for the common good. At its best, civil society provides an intermediate layer of governance between the individual and the state that is capable of resolving conflicts and controlling the behavior of members without public coercion. Rather than overloading decision makers with increased demands and making the system ungovernable,[9] a viable civil society can mitigate conflicts and improve the quality of citizenship—without relying exclusively on the privatism of the marketplace.

Representatives—whether directly or indirectly elected—do most of the real work in modern democracies. Most are professional politicians who orient their careers around the desire to fill key offices. It is doubtful that any democracy could survive without such people. The central question, therefore, is not whether or not there will be a political elite or even a professional political class, but how these representatives are chosen and then held accountable for their actions.

As noted above, there are many channels of representation in modern democracy. The electoral one, based on territorial constituencies, is the most visible and public. It culminates in a parliament or a presidency that is periodically accountable to the citizenry as a whole. Yet the sheer growth of government (in large part as a byproduct of popular demand) has increased the number, variety, and power of agencies charged with making public decisions and not subject to elections. Around these agencies there has developed a vast apparatus of specialized representation based largely on functional interests, not territorial constituencies. These interest associations, and not political parties, have become the primary expression of civil society in most stable democracies, supplemented by the more sporadic interventions of social movements.

The new and fragile democracies that have sprung up since 1974 must live in "compressed time." They will not resemble the European democracies of the nineteenth and early twentieth centuries, and they cannot expect to acquire the multiple channels of representation in gradual historical progression as did most of their predecessors. A bewildering array of parties, interests, and movements will all simultaneously seek political influence in them, creating challenges to the polity that did not exist in earlier processes of democratization.

PROCEDURES THAT MAKE DEMOCRACY POSSIBLE

The defining components of democracy are necessarily abstract, and may give rise to a considerable variety of institutions and subtypes of democracy. For democracy to thrive, however, specific procedural norms must be followed and civic rights must be respected. Any polity that fails to impose such restrictions upon itself, that fails to follow the "rule of law" with regard to its own procedures, should not be considered democratic. These procedures alone do not define democracy, but their presence is indispensable to its persistence. In essence, they are necessary but not sufficient conditions for its existence.

Robert Dahl has offered the most generally accepted listing of what he terms the "procedural minimal" conditions that must be present for modern political democracy (or as he puts it, "polyarchy") to exist:

1. Control over government decisions about policy is constitutionally vested in elected officials.
2. Elected officials are chosen in frequent and fairly conducted elections in which coercion is comparatively uncommon.
3. Practically all adults have the right to vote in the election of officials.
4. Practically all adults have the right to run for elective offices in the government. . . .
5. Citizens have a right to express themselves without the danger of severe punishment on political matters broadly defined. . . .
6. Citizens have a right to seek out alternative sources of information. Moreover, alternative sources of information exist and are protected by law.
7. . . . Citizens also have the right to form relatively independent associations or organizations, including independent political parties and interest groups.[10]

These seven conditions seem to capture the essence of procedural democracy for many theorists, but we propose to add two others. The first might be thought of as a further refinement of item (1), while the second might be called an implicit prior condition to all seven of the above.

8. Popularly elected officials must be able to exercise their constitutional powers without being subjected to overriding (albeit informal) opposition from unelected officials. Democracy is in jeopardy if military officers, entrenched civil servants, or state managers retain the capacity to act independently of elected civilians or even veto decisions made by the people's representatives. Without this additional caveat, the militarized polities of contemporary Central America, where civilian control over the military does not exist, might be classified by many scholars as democracies, just as they have been (with the exception of Sandinista Nicaragua) by U.S. policy makers. The caveat thus guards against what we earlier called "electoralism"—the tendency to focus on the holding of elections while ignoring other political realities.
9. The polity must be self-governing; it must be able to act independently of constraints imposed by some other overarching political system. Dahl and other contemporary democratic theorists probably took this condition for granted since they referred to formally sovereign nation-states. However, with the development of blocs, alliances, spheres of influence, and a variety of "neocolonial" arrangements, the question of autonomy has been a salient one. Is a system really democratic if its elected officials are unable to make binding decisions without the approval of actors outside their territorial domain? This is significant even if the outsiders are relatively free to alter or even end the encompassing arrangement (as in Puerto Rico), but it becomes especially critical if neither condition obtains (as in the Baltic states).

PRINCIPLES THAT MAKE DEMOCRACY FEASIBLE

Lists of component processes and procedural norms help us to specify what democracy is, but they do not tell us much about how it actually functions. The simplest answer is "by the consent of the people"; the more complex one is "by the contingent consent of politicians acting under conditions of bounded uncertainty."

In a democracy, representatives must at least informally agree that those who win greater electoral support or influence over policy will not use their temporary superiority to bar the losers from taking office or exerting influence in the future, and that in exchange for this opportunity to keep competing for power and place, momentary losers will respect the winners' right to make binding decisions. Citizens are expected to obey the decisions ensuing from such a process of competition, provided its outcome remains contingent upon their collective preferences as expressed through fair and regular elections or open and repeated negotiations.

The challenge is not so much to find a set of goals that command widespread consensus as to find a set of rules that embody contingent consent. The precise shape of this "democratic bargain," to use Dahl's expression,[11] can vary a good deal from society to society. It depends on social cleavages and such subjective factors as mutual trust, the standard of fairness, and the willingness to compromise. It may even be compatible with a great deal of dissensus on substantive policy issues.

All democracies involve a degree of uncertainty about who will be elected and what policies they will pursue. Even in those polities where one party persists in winning elections or one policy is consistently implemented, the possibility of change through independent collective action still exists, as in Italy, Japan, and the Scandinavian social democracies. If it does not, the system is not democratic, as in Mexico, Senegal, or Indonesia.

But the uncertainty embedded in the core of all democracies is bounded. Not just any actor can get into the competition and raise any issue he or she pleases—there are previously established rules that must be respected. Not just any policy can be adopted—there are conditions that must be met. Democracy institutionalizes "normal," limited political uncertainty. These boundaries vary from country to country. Constitutional guarantees of property, privacy, expression, and other rights are a part of this, but the most effective boundaries are generated by competition among interest groups and cooperation within civil society. Whatever the rhetoric (and some polities appear to offer their citizens more dramatic alternatives than others), once the rules of contingent consent have been agreed upon, the actual variation is likely to stay within a predictable and generally accepted range.

This emphasis on operative guidelines contrasts with a highly persistent, but misleading theme in recent literature on democracy—namely, the emphasis upon "civic culture." The principles we have suggested here rest on rules of prudence, not on deeply ingrained habits of tolerance, moderation, mutual respect, fair play, readiness to compromise, or trust in public authorities. Waiting for such habits to sink deep and lasting roots implies a very slow process of regime consolidation—one that takes generations—and it would probably condemn most contemporary experiences *ex hypothesi* to failure. Our assertion is that contingent consent and bounded uncertainty can emerge from the interaction between antagonistic and mutually suspicious actors and that the far more benevolent and ingrained norms of a civic culture are better thought of as a *product* and not a producer of democracy.

HOW DEMOCRACIES DIFFER

Several concepts have been deliberately excluded from our generic definition of democracy, despite the fact that they have been frequently associated with it in both everyday practice and scholarly work. They are, nevertheless, especially important when it comes to distinguishing subtypes of democracy. Since no single set of actual institutions, practices, or values embodies democracy, polities moving away from authoritarian rule can mix different components to produce different democracies. It is important to recognize that these do not define points along a single continuum of improving performance, but a matrix of potential combinations that are *differently* democratic.

1. *Consensus:* All citizens may not agree on the substantive goals of political action or on the role of the state (although if they did, it would certainly make governing democracies much easier).
2. *Participation:* All citizens may not take an active and equal part in politics, although it must be legally possible for them to do so.
3. *Access:* Rulers may not weigh equally the preferences of all who come before them, although citizenship implies that individuals and groups should have an equal opportunity to express their preferences if they choose to do so.
4. *Responsiveness:* Rulers may not always follow the course of action preferred by the citizenry. But when they deviate from such a policy, say on grounds of "reason of state" or "overriding national interest," they must ultimately be held accountable for their actions through regular and fair processes.
5. *Majority rule:* Positions may not be allocated or rules may not be decided solely on the basis of assembling the most votes, although deviations from this principle usually must be explicitly defended and previously approved.
6. *Parliamentary sovereignty:* The legislature may not be the only body that can make rules or even the one with final authority in deciding which laws are binding, although where executive, judicial, or other public bodies make that ultimate choice, they too must be accountable for their actions.
7. *Party government:* Rulers may not be nominated, promoted, and disciplined in their activities by well-organized and programmatically coherent political parties, although where they are not, it may prove more difficult to form an effective government.
8. *Pluralism:* The political process may not be based on a multiplicity of overlapping, voluntaristic, and autonomous private groups. However, where there are monopolies of representation, hierarchies of association, and obligatory memberships, it is likely that the interests involved will be more closely linked to the state and the separation between the public and private spheres of action will be much less distinct.
9. *Federalism:* The territorial division of authority may not involve multiple levels and local autonomies, least of all ones enshrined in a constitutional document, although some dispersal of power across territorial and/or functional units is characteristic of all democracies.
10. *Presidentialism:* The chief executive officer may not be a single person and he or she may not be directly elected by the citizenry as a whole, although some concentration of authority is present in all democracies, even if it is exercised collectively and only held indirectly accountable to the electorate.
11. *Checks and Balances:* It is not necessary that the different branches of government be systematically pitted against one another, although governments by assembly, by executive concentrations, by judicial command, or even by dictatorial fiat (as in time of war) must be ultimately accountable to the citizenry as a whole.

While each of the above has been named as an essential component of democracy, they should instead be seen either as indicators of this or that type of democracy, or else as useful standards for evaluating the performance of particular regimes. To include them as part of the generic definition of democracy itself would be to mistake the American polity for the universal model of democratic governance. Indeed, the parliamentary, consociational, unitary, corporatist, and concentrated arrangements of continental Europe may have some unique virtues for guiding polities through the uncertain transition from autocratic to democratic rule.[12]

WHAT DEMOCRACY IS NOT

We have attempted to convey the general meaning of modern democracy without identifying it with some particular set of rules and institutions or restricting it to some specific culture or level of development. We have also argued that it cannot be reduced to the regular holding of elections or equated with a particular notion of the role of the state, but we have not said much more about what democracy is not or about what democracy may not be capable of producing.

There is an understandable temptation to load too many expectations on this concept and to imagine that by attaining democracy, a society will have resolved all of its political, social, economic, administrative, and cultural problems. Unfortunately, "all good things do not necessarily go together."

First, democracies are not necessarily more efficient economically than other forms of government. Their rates of aggregate growth, savings, and investment may be no better than those of nondemocracies. This is especially likely during the transition, when propertied groups and administrative elites may respond to real or imagined threats to the "rights" they enjoyed under authoritarian rule by initiating capital flight, disinvestment, or sabotage. In time, depending upon the type of democracy, benevolent long-term effects upon income distribution, aggregate demand, education, productivity, and creativity may eventually combine to improve economic and social performance, but it is certainly too much to expect that these improvements will occur immediately—much less that they will be defining characteristics of democratization.

Second, democracies are not necessarily more efficient administratively. Their capacity to make decisions may even be slower than that of the regimes they replace, if only because more actors must be consulted. The costs of getting things done may be higher, if only because "payoffs" have to be made to a wider and more resourceful set of clients (although one should never underestimate the degree of corruption to be found within autocracies). Popular satisfaction with the new democratic government's performance may not even seem greater, if only because necessary compromises often please no one completely, and because the losers are free to complain.

Third, democracies are not likely to appear more orderly, consensual, stable, or governable than the autocracies they replace. This is partly a byproduct of democratic freedom of expression, but it is also a reflection of the likelihood of continuing disagreement over new rules and institutions. These products of imposition or compromise are often initially quite ambiguous in nature and uncertain in effect until actors have learned how to use them. What is more, they come in the aftermath of serious struggles motivated by high ideals. Groups and individuals with recently acquired autonomy will test certain rules, protest against the actions of certain institutions, and insist on renegotiating their part of the bargain. Thus the presence of antisystem parties should be neither surprising nor seen as a failure of democratic consolidation. What counts is whether such parties are willing, however reluctantly, to play by the general rules of bounded uncertainty and contingent consent.

Governability is a challenge for all regimes, not just democratic ones. Given the political exhaustion and loss of legitimacy that have befallen autocracies from sultanistic Paraguay to totalitarian Albania, it may seem that only democracies can now be expected to govern effectively and legitimately. Experience has shown, however, that democracies too can lose the ability to govern. Mass publics can become disenchanted with their performance. Even more threatening is the temptation for leaders to fiddle with procedures and ultimately undermine the principles of contingent consent and bounded uncertainty. Perhaps the most critical moment comes once the politicians begin to settle into the more predictable roles and relations of a consolidated democracy. Many will find their expectations frustrated; some will discover that the new rules of competition put them at a disadvantage; a few may even feel that their vital interests are threatened by popular majorities.

" . . . democracies will have more open societies and polities than the autocracies they replace, but not necessarily more open economies."

Finally, democracies will have more open societies and polities than the autocracies they replace, but not necessarily more open economies. Many of today's most successful and well-established democracies have historically resorted to protectionism and closed borders, and have relied extensively upon public institutions to promote economic development. While the long-term compatibility between democracy and capitalism does not seem to be in doubt, despite their continuous tension, it is not clear whether the promotion of such liberal economic goals as the right of individuals to own property and retain profits, the clearing function of markets, the private settlement of disputes, the freedom to produce without government regulation, or the privatization of state-owned enterprises necessarily furthers the consolidation of democracy. After all, democracies do need to levy taxes and regulate certain transactions, especially where private monopolies and oligopolies exist. Citizens or their representatives may decide that it is desirable to protect the rights of collectivities from encroachment by individuals, especially propertied ones, and they may choose to set aside certain forms of property for public or cooperative ownership. In short, notions of economic liberty that are currently put forward in neoliberal economic models are not synonymous with political freedom—and may even impede it.

Democratization will not necessarily bring in its wake economic growth, social peace, administrative efficiency, political harmony, free markets, or "the end of ideology." Least of all will it bring about "the end of history." No doubt some of these qualities could make the consolidation of democracy easier, but they are neither prerequisites for it nor immediate products of it. Instead, what we should be hoping for is the emergence of political institutions that can peacefully compete to form governments and influence public policy, that can channel social and economic conflicts through regular procedures, and that have sufficient linkages to civil society to represent their constituencies and commit them to collective courses of action. Some types of democracies, especially in developing countries, have been unable to fulfill this promise, perhaps due to the circumstances of their transition from authoritarian rule.[13] The democratic wager is that such a regime, once established, will not only persist by reproducing itself within its initial confining conditions, but will eventually expand beyond them.[14] Unlike authoritarian regimes, democracies have the capacity to modify their rules and institutions consensually in response to changing circumstances. They may not immediately produce all the goods mentioned above, but they stand a better chance of eventually doing so than do autocracies.

NOTES

1. For a comparative analysis of the recent regime changes in southern Europe and Latin America, see Guillermo O'Donnell, Philippe C. Schmitter, and Laurence Whitehead, eds., *Transitions from Authoritarian Rule,* 4 vols. (Baltimore: Johns Hopkins University Press, 1986). For another compilation that adopts a more structural approach see Larry Diamond, Juan Linz, and Seymour Martin Lipset, eds., *Democracy in Developing Countries,* vols. 2, 3, and 4 (Boulder, Colo.: Lynne Rienner, 1989).

2. Numerous attempts have been made to codify and quantify the existence of democracy across political systems. The best known is probably Freedom House's *Freedom in the World: Political Rights and Civil Liberties,* published since 1973 by Greenwood Press and since 1988 by University Press of America. Also see Charles Humana, *World Human Rights Guide* (New York: Facts on File, 1986).

3. The definition most commonly used by American social scientists is that of Joseph Schumpeter: "that institutional arrangement for arriving at political decisions in which individuals acquire the power to decide by means of a competitive struggle for the people's vote." *Capitalism, Socialism, and Democracy* (London: George Allen and Unwin, 1943), 269. We accept certain aspects of the classical procedural approach to modern democracy, but differ primarily in our emphasis on the accountability of rulers to citizens and the relevance of mechanisms of competition other than elections.

4. Not only do some countries practice a stable form of democracy without a formal constitution (e.g., Great Britain and Israel), but even more countries have constitutions and legal codes that offer no guarantee of reliable practice. On paper, Stalin's 1936 constitution for the USSR was a virtual model of democratic rights and entitlements.

5. For the most valiant attempt to make some sense out of this thicket of distinctions, see Juan Linz, "Totalitarian and Authoritarian Regimes" in *Handbook of Political Science,* eds. Fred I. Greenstein and Nelson W. Polsby (Reading Mass.: Addison Wesley, 1975), 175–411.

6. "Publius" (Alexander Hamilton, John Jay, and James Madison), *The Federalist Papers* (New York: Anchor Books, 1961). The quote is from Number 10.

7. See Terry Karl, "Imposing Consent? Electoralism versus Democratization in El Salvador," in *Elections and Democratization in Latin America, 1980–1985,* eds. Paul Drake and Eduardo Silva (San Diego: Center for Iberian and Latin American Studies, Center for US/ Mexican Studies, University of California, San Diego, 1986), 9–36.

8. Alexis de Tocqueville, *Democracy in America,* 2 vols. (New York: Vintage Books, 1945).

9. This fear of overloaded government and the imminent collapse of democracy is well reflected in the work of Samuel P. Huntington during the 1970s. See especially Michel Crozier, Samuel P. Huntington, and Joji Watanuki, *The Crisis of Democracy* (New York: New York University Press, 1975). For Huntington's (revised) thoughts about the prospects for democracy, see his "Will More Countries Become Democratic?," *Political Science Quarterly* 99 (Summer 1984): 193–218.

10. Robert Dahl, *Dilemmas of Pluralist Democracy* (New Haven: Yale University Press, 1982), 11.

11. Robert Dahl, *After the Revolution: Authority in a Good Society* (New Haven: Yale University Press, 1970).

12. See Juan Linz, "The Perils of Presidentialism," *Journal of Democracy* 1 (Winter 1990): 51–69, and the ensuing discussion by Donald Horowitz, Seymour Martin Lipset, and Juan Linz in *Journal of Democracy* 1 (Fall 1990): 73–91.

13. Terry Lynn Karl, "Dilemmas of Democratization in Latin America," *Comparative Politics* 23 (October 1990): 1–23.

14. Otto Kirchheimer, "Confining Conditions and Revolutionary Breakthroughs," *American Political Science Review* 59 (1965): 964–974.

Parliament and Congress:

Is the Grass Greener on the other side?

Gregory S. Mahler

Gregory Mahler is chair of the Political Science Department at the University of Mississippi.

Aristotle long ago observed that man is a "political animal." He could have added that man, by his very nature, notes the political status of his neighbours and, very often, perceives their lot as being superior to his own. The old saying "the grass is greener on the other side of the fence" can be applied to politics and political structures as well as to other, more material, dimensions of the contemporary world.

Legislators are not immune from the very human tendency to see how others of their lot exist in their respective settings, and, sometimes, to look longingly at these other settings. When legislators do look around to see the conditions under which their peers operate in other countries, they occasionally decide they prefer the alternative legislative settings to their own.

Features which legislators admire or envy in the settings of their colleagues include such things as: the characteristics of political parties (their numbers, or degrees of party discipline), legislative committee systems, staff and services available to help legislators in their tasks, office facilities, libraries, and salaries. This essay will develop the "grass is greener" theme in relation to a dimension of the legislative world which is regularly a topic of conversation when legislators from a number of different jurisdictions meet: the ability or inability of legislatures to check and control the executive.

The Decline of Parliament

The theme of the "decline of parliament" has a long and well-studied history.[1] It generally refers to the gradual flow of true legislative power away from the legislative body in the direction of the executive. The executive does the real law-making — by actually drafting most legislation — and the legislature takes a more "passive" role by simply approving executive proposals.

Legislators are very concerned about their duties and powers and over the years have jealously guarded them when they have appeared to be threatened. In Canada (and indeed most parliamentary democracies in the world today), the majority of challenges to legislative power which develop no longer come from the ceremonial executive (the Crown), but from the political executive, the government of the day.

It can be argued that the ability to direct and influence public policy, is a "zero sum game" (i.e. there is only room for a limited amount of power and influence to be exercised in the political world and a growth in the relative power of the political executive must be at the expense of the power of the legislature). It follows, then, that if the legislature is concerned about maintaining its powers, concerned about protecting its powers from being diminished, it must be concerned about every attempt by the political executive to expand its powers.

Others contend that real "legislative power" cannot, and probably never did reside in the legislature. There was no "Golden Age" of Parliament. The true legislative role of parliament today is not (and in the past was not) to create legislation, but to scrutinize and ratify legislation introduced by the Government of the day. Although an occasional exception to this pattern of behavior may exist (with private members' bills, for example), the general rule is clear: the legislature today does not actively initiate legislation as its primary *raison d'être*.

Although parliamentarians may not be major initiators of legislation, studies have indicated a wide range of other functions.[2] Certainly one major role of the legislature is the "oversight" role, criticizing and checking the powers of the executive. The ultimate extension of this power is the ability of the legislature to terminate the term of office of the executive through a "no confidence" vote. Another role of the legislature involves communication and representation of constituency concerns. Yet another function involves the debating function, articulating the concerns of the public of the day.

Professor James Mallory has indicated the need to "be

From *Canadian Parliamentary Review*, Winter 1985/86, pp. 19-21. Reprinted by permission of the Committees and Parliamentary Associations Branch of the House of Commons in Ottawa, Ontario.

realistic about the role of Parliament in the Westminster system."[3] He cites Bernard Crick's classic work, *The Reform of Parliament*: "... the phrase 'Parliamentary control,' and talk about the 'decline of parliamentary control,' should not mislead anyone into asking for a situation in which governments can have their legislation changed or defeated, or their life terminated... Control means influence, not direct power; advice, not command; criticism, not obstruction; scrutiny, not initiation; and publicity, not secrecy."[4]

The fact that parliament may not be paramount in the creation and processing of legislation is no reason to condemn all aspects of parliamentary institutions. Nor should parliamentarians be convinced that legislative life is perfect in the presidential-congressional system. In fact, some American legislators look to their parliamentary brethren and sigh with envy at the attractiveness of certain aspects of parliamentary institutions.

Desirability of a Congressional Model for Canada?

Many Canadian parliamentarians and students of parliament look upon presidential-congressional institutions of the United States as possessing the answers to most of their problems. The grass is sometimes seen as being greener on the other side of the border. The concepts of fixed legislative terms, less party discipline, and a greater general emphasis on the role and importance of individual legislators (which implies more office space and staff for individual legislators, among other things) are seen as standards to which Canadian legislators should aspire.

A perceived strength of the American congressional system is that legislators do not automatically "rubber stamp" approve executive proposals. They consider the president's suggestions, but feel free to make substitutions or modifications to the proposal, or even to reject it completely. Party discipline is relatively weak; there are regularly Republican legislators opposing a Republican president (and Democratic legislators supporting him), and vice versa. Against the need for discipline congressmen argue that their first duty is to either (a) their constituency, or (b) what is "right", rather than simply to party leaders telling them how to behave in the legislature. For example, in 1976 Jimmy Carter was elected President with large majorities of Democrats in both houses of Congress. One of Carter's major concerns was energy policy. He introduced legislative proposals (that is, he had congressional supporters introduce legislation, since the American president cannot introduce legislation on his own) dealing with energy policy, calling his proposals "the moral equivalent of war." In his speeches and public appearances he did everything he could to muster support for "his" legislation. Two years later when "his" legislation finally emerged from the legislative process, it could hardly be recognized as the proposals submitted in such emotional terms two years earlier.

The experience of President Carter was certainly not unique. Any number of examples of such incidents of legislative-executive non-cooperation can be cited in recent American political history, ranging from President Wilson's unsuccessful efforts to get the United States to join the League of Nations, through Ronald Reagan's contemporary battles with Congress over the size of the federal budget. The Carter experience was somewhat unusual by virtue of the fact that the same political party controlled both the executive and legislative branches of government, and cooperation still was not forthcoming. There have been many more examples of non-cooperation when one party has controlled the White House and another party has controlled one or both houses of Congress.

This lack of party discipline ostensibly enables the individual legislators to be concerned about the special concerns of their constituencies. This, they say, is more important than simply having to follow the orders of the party whip in the legislature. It is not any more unusual to find a Republican legislator from a farm state voting against a specific agricultural proposal of President Reagan on the grounds that the legislation in question is not good for his/her constituency, than to find Democratic legislators from the southwestern states who voted against President Carter's water policy proposals on the grounds that the proposals were not good for their constituencies.

Congressional legislators know that they have fixed terms in office — the President is simply not able to bring about early elections — and they know that as long as they can keep their constituencies happy there is no need to be terribly concerned about opposing the President, even if he is the leader of their party. It may be nice to have the President on your side, but if you have a strong base of support "back home" you can survive without his help.

Are there any benefits to the public interest in the absence of party discipline? The major argument is that the legislature will independently consider the executive's proposals, rather than simply accepting the executive's ideas passively. This, it is claimed, allows for a multiplicity of interests, concerns, and perspectives to be represented in the legislature, and ostensibly results in "better" legislation.

In summary, American legislative institutions promote the role of the individual legislator. The fixed term gives legislators the security necessary for the performance of the functions they feel are important. The (relative) lack of party discipline enables legislators to act on the issues about which they are concerned. In terms of the various legislative functions mentioned above, congressmen appear to spend a great deal of their time in what has been termed the legislative aspect of the job: drafting legislation, debating, proposing amendments, and voting (on a more or less independent basis).

While many parliamentarians are impressed by the ability of individual American legislator to act on their own volition it is ironic that many congressional legislators look longingly at the legislative power relationships of their parliamentary bretheren. The grass, apparently, is greener on the *other* side of the border, too.

Desirability of a Parliamentary Model

The "decline of congressional power" is as popular a topic of conversation in Washington as "the decline of parliamentary power" in Ottawa or London. Over the last several decades American legislators have sensed that a great deal of legislative power has slipped from their collective grasp.[5] Many have decried this tendency and tried to stop, or reverse this flow of power away from the legislative branch and toward the executive.

One of the major themes in the writings of these congressional activists is an admiration for the parliamentary model's (perceived) power over the executive. Many American legislators see the president's veto power, combined with his fixed term in office, as a real flaw in the "balance of powers" of the system, leading to an inexorable increase in executive power at the expense of the legislature. They look at a number of parliamentary structures which they see as promoting democratic political behavior and increased executive responsibility to the legislature, including the ability to force the resignation of the executive through a non-confidence vote. The regular "question period" format which insures some degree of public executive accountability is also perceived as being very attractive .

Critics of the congressional system do not confine their criticism only to the growth of executive power. There are many who feel there is too much freedom in the congressional arena. To paraphrase the words of Bernard Crick cited earlier, advising has sometimes turned into issuing commands; and criticism has sometimes turned into obstruction. This is not to suggest that congressional legislators would support giving up their ability to initiate legislation, to amend executive proposals, or to vote in a manner which they (individually) deem proper. This does suggest, however, that even congressional legislators see that independence is a two-sided coin: one side involves individual legislative autonomy and input into the legislative process; the other side involves the incompatibility of complete independence with a British style of "Responsible Government".

In 1948 Hubert Humphrey, then mayor of Minneapolis, delivered an address at the nomination convention of the Democratic Party. In his comments he appealed for a "more responsible" two party system in the United States, a system with sufficient party discipline to have *meaningful* party labels, and to allow party platforms to become public policy.[6] Little progress has been made over the last thirty-seven years in this regard. In the abstract the concept of a *meaningful* two party system may be attractive; American legislators have not been as attracted to the necessary corollary of the concept: decreased legislative independence and increased party discipline.

While American Senators and Representatives are very jealous of executive encroachments upon their powers, there is some recognition that on occasion — usually depending upon individual legislators' views about the desirability of specific pieces of legislation — executive leadership, and perhaps party discipline, can serve a valuable function. Congressional legislators are, at times which correspond to their policy preferences, envious of parliamentary governnments' abilities to carry their programs into law because MPs elected under their party labels will act consistent with party whips' directions. They would be loath to give up their perceived high degrees of legislative freedom but many of them realize the cost of this freedom in this era of pressing social problems and complex legislation. Parliamentary style government is simply not possible without party discipline.

A Democratic Congressman supporting President Carter's energy policy proposals might have longed for an effective three-line whip to help to pass the energy policies in question. An opponent of those policy proposals would have argued, to the contrary, that the frustration of the president's proposals was a good illustration of the wisdom of the legislature tempering the error-ridden policy proposals of the president. Similarly, many conservative Republican supporters of President Reagan have condemned the ability of the Democratic House of Representatives to frustrate his economic policies. Opponents of those policies have argued, again, that the House of Representatives is

doing an important job of representing public opinion and is exercising a valuable and important check on the misguided policies of the executive.

Some Concluding Observations

The parliamentary model has its strengths as well as its weaknesses. The individual legislator in a parliamentary system does not have as active a role in the actual legislative process as does his American counterparts, but it is not at all hard to imagine instances in which the emphasis on individual autonomy in the congressional system can be counterproductive because it delays much-needed legislative programs.

The problem, ultimately, is one of balance. Is it possible to have a responsible party system in the context of parliamentary democracy which can deliver on its promises to the public, and also to have a high degree of individual legislative autonomy in the legislative arena?

It is hard to imagine how those two concepts could coexist. The congressional and parliamentary models of legislative behavior have placed their respective emphases on two different priorities. The parliamentary model, with its responsible party system and its corresponding party discipline in the legislature, emphasizes efficient policy delivery, and the ability of an elected government to deliver on its promises. The congressional model, with its lack of party discipline and its emphasis on individual legislative autonomy, placed more emphasis on what can be called "consensual politics": it may take much more time for executive proposals to find their way into law, but (the argument goes) there is greater likelihood that what does, ultimately, emerge as law will be acceptable to a greater number of people than if government proposals were "automatically" approved by a pre-existing majority in the legislature acting "under the whip".

We cannot say that one type of legislature is "more effective" than the other. Each maximizes effectiveness in different aspects of the legislative function. Legislators in the congressional system, because of their greater legislative autonomy and weaker party discipline, are more effective at actually legislating than they are at exercising ultimate control over the executive. Legislators in the parliamentary system, although they may play more of a "ratifying" role in regard to legislation, do get legislation passed promptly; they also have an ultimate power over the life of the government of the day.

The appropriateness of both models must also be evaluated in light of the different history, political culture and objectives of the societies in which they operate. Perhaps the grass is just as green on both sides of the fence.

Notes

[1]There is substantial literature devoted to the general topic of "the decline of legislatures." Among the many sources which could be referred to in this area would be included the work of Gerhard Loewenberg. *Modern Parliaments: Change or Decline?* Chicago: Atherton. 1971; Gerhard Loewenberg and Samuel Patterson,

Comparing Legislatures, Boston: Little, Brown, 1979; or Samuel Patterson and John Wahlke, eds., *Comparative Legislative Behavior: Frontiers of Research,* New York: John Wiley, 1972.

[2]A very common topic in studies of legislative behavior has to do with the various functions legislatures may be said to perform for the societies of which they are a part. For a discussion of the many functions attributed to legislatures in political science literature, see Gregory Mahler, *Comparative Politics: An Institutional and Cross-National Approach* (Cambridge, Ma.: Schenkman, 1983, pp. 56-61.

[3]J. R. Mallory, "Can Parliament Control the Regulatory Process?" *Canadian Parliamentary Review* Vol. 6 (no. 3, 1983) p. 6.

[4]Bernard Crick, *The Reform of Parliament,* London, 1968, p. 80.

[5]One very well written discussion of the decline of American congressional power in relation to the power of the president can be found in Ronald Moe, ed., *Congress and the President,* Pacific Palisades, Calif.: Goodyear Publishing Co., 1971.

[6]Subsequently a special report was published by the Committee on Political Parties of the American Political Science Association dealing with this problem. See "Toward a More Responsible Two-Party System," *American Political Science Review* Vol. 44 (no. 3, 1950), special supplement.

Campaign and Party Finance: What Americans Might Learn from Abroad

Arthur B.Gunlicks

University of Richmond

When the Clinton Administration took office in January 1993 with a Democratic-controlled Congress, many Americans were hoping that the long-standing "gridlock" between the Congress and President would finally be broken on a wide variety of issues, not the least of which was a reform of campaign finance laws and practices. Ross Perot had raised the issue during the presidential campaign, and Democratic-passed reform legislation which had been vetoed by President Bush now seemed to have a good chance of being revived, perhaps modified, passed, and signed by the new President.

It was not to be. Democratic House leaders gave President Clinton's campaign reform proposals of May 7, 1993, a lukewarm reaction, and Senator Robert Dole threatened to use the filibuster to block congressional action. Reform is a risky business for both parties, and what looks good from the perspective of political scientists or even the White House may not be very appealing to politicians in the trenches who worry that would-be challengers might actually have a fighting chance. In any case, the Democrats in the Senate and House could not agree on a compromise bill, and by the time they finally did in the fall of 1994 their efforts were defeated by the inability to end a Republican filibuster in the Senate.

After the Republican takeover of both the Senate and House following the 1994 midterm elections, any serious hope for political finance reform was dead. First, because the Republican "Contract with America" set entirely different priorities, and, second, because "gridlock" had returned and there was little hope that the Republican-dominated Congress and the Democratic President could agree on reform measures. Certainly any proposals calling for federal subsidies or tax expenditures would have no chance in a Republican Congress determined to reduce drastically federal expenditures and the federal deficit. Still, Ross Perot continued to talk about political finance reform, and House Speaker Newt Gingrich and President Clinton agreed informally in early summer 1995 to work together to promote campaign finance reform. In fact, not much has happened since then, although the issue refuses to go away.

It is easy and very tempting to argue that we should look at what other Western democracies do and adopt some of their practices. One of the difficulties we face, however, lies in the uniqueness of our political system, which raises questions about the relevance of foreign experiences. First, we have to focus on the party system. Our politics are candidate-oriented. In most democracies, they are more party-oriented. Many of us may regret this fact and even devote some energy and effort toward strengthening American parties, but the probability of a major change seems slight. The party orientation found elsewhere has an effect on political financing. Indeed, the concept of "political finance" is likely to mean candidate and campaign financing in the United States and party financing in other democracies. Therefore, it is not surprising that the administration backed away from the idea of funneling public funds to the parties.

Second, our institutions are different. Virtually all countries that we might look to for comparison are parliamentary democracies. France may have a semi-presidential system, but its parliamentary features still distinguish it from the United States. Most democracies are unitary states. Canada, Australia, Germany, Switzerland and Austria are federal states, but they differ in significant respects from the United States in their division of powers as well as in population and/or size of territory. They are also parliamentary democracies.

Third, we have a political culture which is not very conducive to government assistance to political parties. Anti-party and anti-government sentiments in the United States have deep roots, and reform proposals that might cost taxpayers money and bring about more government involvement must overcome serious obstacles. It may be that public financing is not very popular in other countries, either, but the fact remains that it is widespread abroad and not here.

It is clear that the kind of massive public funding of parties found, for example, in Germany, Austria, and Sweden has little prospect of being implemented in the United States. The generously funded party foundations which perform a number of useful tasks in Germany and Austria also are unlikely ever to

Original version of this revised article first appeared in *Party Line*, Spring/Summer 1993, pp. 7-8. © 1993 by Arthur B. Gunlicks. Reprinted by permission.

gain majority support in Congress. Public funding on this scale would he unacceptable for very practical budgetary reasons, let alone the different American party system and political culture.

What, then, are some foreign practices that might be deserving of some careful consideration in spite of the odds against their passage? It should be possible to convince the public—and then Congress—that television and radio stations must provide a certain amount of free media time, a common practice in almost every other democracy. The Clinton Administration's proposal to provide congressional candidates vouchers to pay for television, printing and postage if they agree to adhere to spending limits is a step in the right direction, but it differs significantly from other democracies where free time is provided to the parties rather than individual candidates. Free billboard and poster space for political advertisements might also be offered by local governments, as is common in Europe. There can be no question, however, that the focus on individual candidates in this country makes free television time and billboard space more complicated to administer. It would probably be very difficult to convince Americans to ban altogether the purchase of media time by individual candidates, as is done in Canada, Britain and the European Continent.

In order to reduce the influence of the widely disliked PACs, which are not found abroad, one can make a strong case for limiting the amounts they may give individual candidates. Thus it is not surprising that the Clinton Administration has moved at least modestly in this direction. But placing limits on PACs raises the question of where the necessary campaign money is to come from besides wealthy candidates, their supporters, and other private interests. Some European countries, e.g., Germany, provide generous tax deductions for donations to political parties. The very modest deductions that were available in the United States were eliminated in the 1986 tax reforms. Surely small donations of up to at least $250 should be encouraged through tax deductions and/or public matching funds for candidates who have demonstrated that they enjoy minimal political support. Contributions to political parties should be promoted, and parties should be encouraged to assume more responsibility for financing the campaigns of their candidates. Perhaps "soft money" *to the parties* could be better regulated rather than banned, as appears to be a goal of the Clinton proposals.

We do, of course, have a $3 federal tax check-off to pay for *presidential* campaigns and national political conventions, but only a small percentage (15–18 percent) of taxpayers actually check the appropriate boxes even though it costs them nothing. A few states also have tax check-offs for helping to finance certain candidates or parties, while another handful of states have tax add-ons, where the taxpayer actually increases his or her tax liability by giving up a small portion of the refund due. As a result, only about one percent of state taxpayers participate in tax add-on schemes. In other words, the amount of public political financing that exists in the United States, except for presidential races, is minimal.

To level the playing field even more, Congress could again try to impose limits on individual spending by candidates in the hope that the Supreme Court might reconsider its decision in *Buckley v. Valeo.* The British and Canadians have limited expenditures by individual candidates without, at last check, weakening freedom of speech in any notable way. The British also require candidate approval of what we call "independent expenditures," which has hardly led to a serious undermining of free speech.

Some reformers have argued that tightening the regulation of parties and candidates, such as improved disclosure and reporting procedures, would "clean up" problems of political finance. Aside from the suspicion that such proposals reflect the "puritan" streak in American political culture, it is difficult to see how these measures would deal effectively with the funding problems we face.

If large amounts of money are being spent by individual candidates, PACs and special interests in general, and there is understandable public dissatisfaction with this state of affairs, it seems apparent that alternate sources of financing must be found. Placing ceilings on expenditures is probably not a very effective solution. Tightening regulations will not produce more private donations. The dilemmas—and there are several—are that alternatives seem to be very expensive, and there is the problem of increasing dependency on the state. This dependency may lead to a separation of the party from the grassroots, as appears to be happening in Germany and several other countries, especially Italy, which voted *recently* in a referendum to end public subsidies for the parties.

American parties are a very long way from becoming dependent on the state for their finances. Indeed, by international comparison we rank low on the dependency scale, especially if one excludes the presidential campaigns. Were we to adopt free media time, free billboard space, tax deductions for small donations to parties and candidates, or modest public subsidies for legislative candidates, all of which are practices common in numerous other democracies, we would not solve all of our current problems. But it seems difficult to believe that the conditions of political financing in the United States would not benefit from the adoption of some of these measures.

Arthur B. Gunlicks is the editor of *Comparative Party and Campaign Finance in Europe and North America,* published by Westview Press.

ELECTORAL REFORM

Good government? Fairness? Or vice versa. Or both

Italians want to junk proportional representation. Others could usefully adopt it. Which electoral system is best? The arguments are many. So are the answers

BRITAIN elects its House of Commons by the simplest possible system: single-member constituencies in which the front-runner wins, even if he has under 50% of the votes. In 1983, 7.8m votes, a quarter of the total, went to the "third party", the Alliance. It got 23 seats. The Labour Party got 8.5m votes—and 209 seats. No wonder half of all Britons say they would like a fairer system.

Italy uses systems of proportional representation (PR) that are elaborately fair. It has also had 52 governments, mostly coalitions, since 1945, all dominated by the Christian Democrats. Italian government is famously inept, its parties—not only the Christian Democrats—infamously corrupt. No wonder Italians have just voted massively to adopt the British system for three-quarters of their Senate seats; the Chamber of Deputies will probably go much the same way.

These two countries exemplify—in parody—the arguments about electoral reform. Britain's "first past the post" system (FPTP) nearly always produces a single-party government with an overall, and solid, Commons majority. Unless that party itself is split—as now, over the Maastricht treaty—the government can override all opposition. The result, given a decisive prime minister, should always be decisive government.

In contrast, look at Italy, Israel or Poland. Their PR is as fair as it comes. Umpteen parties, even tiny ones with 1-2% of the national vote, can win seats. With 3% or 4%,

they can make or break policies and governments, as Israel's religious parties notoriously have done. It sounds like a recipe for feeble government, with the tail—as the enemies of PR put it—wagging the dog.

The choice looks clear: good government or fair representation? In fact, not so. British governments have often been feeble; Israel's often decisive, even fierce. Italy's governments are unstable and inept; not so Germany's, although the Bundestag they rest on is shaped by PR. True, it keeps out small parties. Yet most post-1949 German governments have had a "tail", the Free Democrats (FDP).

As for the corruption now disgusting Italy's voters, its cause, arguably, is too long tenure of office, not the electoral system. Japan has no formal PR, but its ever-ruling Liberal Democrats are hardly clean. True, PR at times prevents complete clear-outs of government; but the parties that stay in office, despite swings among voters, are usually small, as in Germany (Italy is a special case; its large Communist party was not acceptable as an alternative in government to the Christian Democrats).

Corruption anyway springs more from the climate of society—and state control of the economy—than from any parliamentary arrangements. Most government in India (an FPTP country) is corrupt within weeks of taking office. The African minister

who is not, by British standards, corrupt, is acting very oddly indeed by African ones (or indeed by British ones of the 18th century: not to help one's friends—and oneself—is, like elective democracy, a recent, North European curiosity of human behaviour).

So FPTP offers no monopoly, or even guarantee, of good government. But neither does PR of fairness. Americans fret about many aspects of their political system, but not its fairness between parties; and—given that no third party exists—its results are decently proportional. Still not fair, maybe. All Americans have one vote, but of wildly different values: Alaska's 400,000 voters elect two senators, as do California's 23m. Yet why is that so? Because the founding fathers chose so. And few Americans are bothered by this either.

That is a reminder that fairness has many faces. As much as a party, the voter may want a given person to speak for him. FPTP allows for this. He may want one kind of person. Women hold few seats: in the late 1980s, about 30% in the Nordic PR countries, 5-20% in many others whose parties, in filling the party lists used in PR, take little, if any, note of this; and 5-15% in FPTP countries. Even fewer members come from poor, ethnic minorities. A few constitutions (India's, eg) reserve seats for them. Some American electoral boundaries are drawn to help them. Mostly, they must rely on accidents of geography, notably inner-city concentration.

Nor is the voter picking only his representative. He votes for certain policies, and—save in presidential systems—for a government; a serious one, not a bunch of clowns. A PR system could be as fair as Snow White in reflecting party support, and yet, at times, frustrate all these hopes. Would the result fairly represent the electorate?

It depends who, where and for what

America offers another reminder: that neither fairness nor effectiveness exists *in vacuo*. They depend on their context.

An elected body may spring from long democratic tradition or little, from a multicultural society or a homogeneous one. It may be national or local. It may be part of a two-house set-up (America gets territorial fairness in its Senate, demographic from the House). It may provide a government, as do European parliaments, or just legislate and oversee one, as in America. It may be mainly a sounding-board, like the 12-nation parliament of the European Community. And what is "right" here, or for one function, may be wrong there, or for another.

Britain offers an example. Its local government cries out for PR, since the national demography to which parties adapt is not reproduced locally. Voting in 1991 left 15 of 36 English "metropolitan" districts with councils that were 80%-plus Labour (nine of them 90%-plus). Of 296 "non-met"—less urban—councils, 31 had no Labour members, 35 no Liberal Democrats. Point made? Yet it proves nothing about the Commons.

With so many ifs and buts, it is easy to say if it ain't broke don't even think of fixing it. Who would today invent Britain's House of Lords, a jumble of hereditary peers, bishops and judges, plus assorted notables (or party hacks) picked by successive prime ministers? Yet, in its way, it works. If it can survive—and reforming it is a barely an issue in Britain—maybe anything can, even should.

Should? A wise country leaves well, or even only moderately well, alone. After Holland's PR elections, it can take months even to form a government. Yet few Dutchmen worry, any more than Americans do about Alaska. But when a majority (Italy) or a large minority (Britain) feels grossly ill-served or ill-treated, it is time to think again.

Beside Italy, Poland has recently opted for change. Its infant post-Communist democracy chose extreme PR, and in its late-1991 elections paid the price. In all, 67 "parties" fought; the best-placed won only 13% of the vote, and the legislature now includes 29—often shifting—groups. A new electoral law, though it too is PR-based, will limit such follies.

New Zealand, now using FPTP, may go the other way. A referendum last September backed a switch to PR (mainly, as in Italy, to punish politicians). Even Britain's Labour Party is looking at PR, if less because of Liberal complaints than of its own fears that FPTP—which in the past served it well—may leave its Tory rivals for ever running solid one-party governments on 40% of the vote.

Britain's love of FPTP is criticised beyond its borders, because, except in Northern Ireland, it elects members to the European Parliament by this system. So the Tory-Labour balance swings wildly, while large Euro-constituencies crush other national parties. In 1984, the Alliance won 18.5% of the Euro-vote, but no seats; ditto the Greens in 1989, with 14.5%. The result distorts not just British representation but the make-up of the whole parliament.

France's recent elections aroused worries about its two-round voting. This was de Gaulle's substitute for the instabilities of PR, only briefly replaced by PR again in the mid-1980s. Its results can be fair enough. Not this year. Right-wing parties, with 39% of the vote, took 80% of the seats. The National Front, with 12½%, got none. Nasty as the Front is, many Frenchmen doubt that democracy should leave so many voters voiceless.

Pros and cons

Italians' dislike of PR far outruns French or British anxieties the other way. That is natural: they identify it with lousy government. And bad government both hits the whole nation and impinges visibly and constantly on daily life; the disfranchisement felt by third-party voters does neither. Yet worries about FPTP and related systems go deeper. It is representative democracy, not good government, that is the essence of "western" politics. *The Economist*, discussing these issues two years ago, wrote flatly that

> And since the perception of fairness is the acid test for democracy—the very basis of its legitimacy—the unfairness argument overrules all others.

There is a more pragmatic reason. Politicians can, and in Europe mostly do, provide decent government with PR. Unless, as in America, history has dumped third parties, FPTP cannot, except by chance, and normally does not provide fair representation. Human wit can get round the faults of PR; it cannot—except in drawing electoral boundaries—act on the crude mechanics of FPTP.

Yet any shift toward PR must, if possible, avoid its faults in advance. Its critics list many, not all as solid as they sound:

• **Too complicated.** Nonsense. What some think the best system, the single transferable vote, is indeed complex. But the Irish can work it, so why not others?

• **Too many small parties.** That depends how far fairness is pushed. A threshold can hold numbers down: Germany's fierce 5% one has usually kept the Bundestag to just four parties, rarely five. Is it acceptable to exclude 4.9% of opinion—or, as recently in Eastern Europe, several times 4.9%? FPTP too can let in many small parties, if (but only if) each has a regional base.

• **Too many weak coalitions.** Coalitions, yes. Weak, maybe. PR produces both.

• **Too much power for small "pivotal" parties.** Germany's FDP is often cited. In 1982 it quit a coalition with the SDP and joined the CDU. Undemocratic? Six months later the policy shift that the FDP had sought was endorsed by the voters. The "tail-and-dog" case too is weak. On minor issues dear to them, small parties may get their way (as in Israel). On big issues, in politics as in physics, small bodies can only influence large ones, not rule them. West German unification-seeking softness toward Russia in 1989 is cited. That began with the FDP foreign minister; but it was backed by Chancellor Kohl.

• **Policy decided in inter-party haggling after an election, not by voters during it.** Often true, shamefully so in Italy, though its smoke-shrouded deals were more about posts than policy. But the idea that it is "unfair" for those who backed the biggest party in a coalition to see its policy then diluted is bogus: in politics as in marriage, if you cannot win outright, you must compromise.

• **Too much power for party bosses.** In party-list systems, that is nearly always true. But STV lets voters choose among a party's candidates; so does Japan's simple system. Any coalition adds to the power of party machines in government—and (notoriously in Italy, notedly in Germany) in patronage and appointment to public bodies, not least state television. One can argue whether or not one-party patronage, as in Britain, is even worse. A better answer is open under any system: less patronage.

• **Weak links between a member and his constituents.** This is true of PR using large electoral districts, not in the ones of 3-5 members used in Ireland (and Japan). Members of the Irish Dail feel pressure, they say, to look after constituents, because their support may slip away not only to rival parties but to other members of their own. British critics fear such a member may care only for a section of his constituents. That may happen; PR supporters, in reply, praise the voter's freedom to choose which member he turns to. Districts of 5-7 members, as in most of Belgium, Spain or France in its PR days, allow both PR and acceptable member/voter links.

Many answers

For countries seeking less PR, the considerations, curiously, are much the same, since not even the angry Italians want the pure milk of FPTP. For them too the trick is to find a balance between proportionality and the faults voters feel in their form of PR. They too must remember the many faces of fairness, and ask, in each case, what function the elected body serves, what they want to achieve (punishing politicians, however deservedly, is an inappropriate answer) and is it worth the upheaval? Only zealots think one solution fits every case.

Presidents and Prime Ministers

Richard Rose

Richard Rose is professor of public policy at the University of Strathclyde in Glasgow, Scotland. An American, he has lived in Great Britain for many years and has been studying problems of political leadership in America and Europe for three decades. His books include Presidents and Prime Ministers; Managing Presidential Objectives; Understanding Big Government; *and* The Post-Modern Presidency: The World Closes in on the White House.

The need to give direction to government is universal and persisting. Every country, from Egypt of the pharoahs to contemporary democracies, must maintain political institutions that enable a small group of politicians to make authoritative decisions that are binding on the whole of society. Within every system, one office is of first importance, whether it is called president, prime minister, führer, or dux.

There are diverse ways of organizing the direction of government, not only between democracies and authoritarian regimes, but also among democracies. Switzerland stands at one extreme, with collective direction provided by a federal council whose president rotates from year to year. At the other extreme are countries that claim to centralize authority, under a British-style parliamentary system or in an American or French presidential system, in which one person is directly elected to the supreme office of state.

To what extent are the differences in the formal attributes of office a reflection of substantive differences in how authority is exercised? To what extent do the imperatives of office—the need for electoral support, dependence upon civil servants for advice, and vulnerability to events—impose common responses in practice? Comparing the different methods of giving direction to government in the United States (presidential), Great Britain (prime ministerial and Cabinet), and France (presidential and prime ministerial) can help us understand whether other countries do it—that is, choose a national leader—in a way that is better.

To make comparisons requires concepts that can identify the common elements in different offices. Three concepts organize the comparisons I make: the career that leads to the top; the institutions and powers of government; and the scope for variation within a country, whether arising from events or personalities.

Career Leading to the Top

By definition, a president or prime minister is unrepresentative by being the occupant of a unique office. The diversity of outlooks and skills that can be attributed to white, university-educated males is inadequate to predict how people with the same social characteristics—a Carter or an Eisenhower; a Wilson or a Heath—will perform in office. Nor is it helpful to consider the recruitment of national leaders deductively, as a management consultant or personnel officer would, first identifying the skills required for the job and then evaluating candidates on the basis of a priori requirements. National leaders are not recruited by examination; they are self-selected, individuals whose driving ambitions, personal attributes, and, not least, good fortune, combine to win the highest public office.

To understand what leaders can do in office we need to compare the skills acquired in getting to the top with the skills required once there. The tasks that a president or prime minister must undertake are few but central: sustaining popular support through responsiveness to the electorate, and being effective in government. Success in office encourages electoral popularity, and electoral popularity is an asset in wielding influence within government.

The previous careers of presidents and prime ministers are significant, insofar as experience affects what they do in office—and what they do well. A politician who had spent many years concentrating upon campaigning to win popularity may continue to cultivate popularity in office. By contrast, a politician experienced in dealing with the problems of government from within may be better at dealing effectively with international and domestic problems.

Two relevant criteria for comparing the careers of national leaders are: previous experience of government, and previous experience of party and mass electoral politics. American presidents are outstanding in their experience of campaigning for mass support, whereas French presidents are outstanding for their prior knowledge of government from the inside. British prime ministers usually combine experience in both fields.

Thirteen of the fourteen Americans who have been nominated for president of the United States by the Democratic or Republican parties since 1945 had prior experience in running for major office, whether at the congressional, gubernatorial or presidential level. Campaigning for office makes a politician conscious of his or her need for popular approval. It also cultivates skill in dealing with the mass media. No American will be elected president who has not learned how to campaign across the continent, effectively and incessantly. Since selection as a presidential candidate is dependent upon winning primaries, a president must run twice: first to win the party nomination and then to win the White House. The effort required is shown by the fact that in 1985, three years before the presidential election, one Republican hopeful campaigned in twenty-four states, and a Democratic hopeful in thirty. Immediately after the 1986 congressional elections ended, the media started featuring stories about the 1988 campaign.

Campaigning is different from governing. Forcing ambitious politicians to concentrate upon crossing and re-crossing America reduces the time available for learning about problems in Washington and the rest of the world. The typical postwar president has had no experience working within the executive branch. The way in which the federal government deals with foreign policy, or with problems of the economy is known, if at all, from the vantage point of a spectator. A president is likely to have had relatively brief experience in Congress. As John F. Kennedy's career illustrates, Congress is not treated as a

---

Looking presidential is not the same as acting like a president.

---

means of preparing to govern; it is a launching pad for a presidential campaign. The last three presidential elections have been won by individuals who could boast of having no experience in Washington. Jimmy Carter and Ronald Reagan were state governors, experienced at a job that gives no experience in foreign affairs or economic management.

A president who is experienced in campaigning can be expected to continue cultivating the media and seeking a high standing in the opinion polls. Ronald Reagan illustrates this approach. A president may even use campaigning as a substitute for coming to grips with government; Jimmy Carter abandoned Washington for the campaign trail when confronted with mid-term difficulties in 1978. But public relations expertise is only half the job; looking presidential is not the same as acting like a president.

A British prime minister, by contrast, enters office after decades in the House of Commons and years as a Cabinet minister. The average postwar prime minister had spent thirty-two years in Parliament before entering 10 Downing Street. Of that period, thirteen years had been spent as a Cabinet minister. Moreover, the prime minister has normally held the important policy posts of foreign secretary, chancellor of the exchequer or both. The average prime

minister has spent eight years in ministerial office, learning to handle foreign and/or economic problems. By contrast with the United States, no prime minister has had postwar experience in state or local government, and by contrast with France, none has been a civil servant since World War II.

The campaign experience of a British prime minister is very much affected by the centrality that politicians give Parliament. A politician seeks to make a mark in debate there. Even in an era of mass media, the elitist doctrine holds that success in the House of Commons produces positive evaluation by journalists and invitations to appear on television, where a politician can establish an image with the national electorate. Whereas an American presidential hopeful has a bottom-up strategy, concentrating upon winning votes in early primaries in Iowa and New Hampshire as a means of securing media attention, a British politician has a top-down approach, starting to campaign in Parliament.

Party is the surrogate for public opinion among British politicians, and with good reason. Success in the Commons is evaluated by a politician's party colleagues. Election to the party leadership is also determined by party colleagues. To become prime minister a politician does not need to win an election; he or she only needs to be elected party leader when the party has a parliamentary majority. Jim Callaghan and Sir Alec Douglas-Home each entered Downing Street this way and lost office in the first general election fought as prime minister.

The lesser importance of the mass electorate to British party leaders is illustrated by the fact that the average popularity rating of a prime minister is usually less than that of an American president. The monthly Gallup poll rating often shows the prime minister approved by less than half the electorate and trailing behind one or more leaders of the opposition.

In the Fifth French Republic, presidents and prime ministers have differed from American presidents, being very experienced in government, and relatively inexperienced in campaigning with the mass electorate. Only one president, François Mitterrand, has followed the British practice of making a political career based on Parliament. Since he was on the opposition side for the first two decades of the Fifth Republic, his experience of the problems of office was like that of a British opposition member of Parliament, and different from that of a minister. Giscard d'Estaing began as a high-flying civil servant and Charles de Gaulle, like Dwight Eisenhower, was schooled in bureaucratic infighting as a career soldier.

When nine different French prime ministers are examined, the significance of a civil service background becomes clear. Every prime minister except for Pierre Mauroy has been a civil servant first. It has been exceptional for a French prime minister to spend decades in Parliament before attaining that office. An Englishman would be surprised that a Raymond Barre or a Couve de Murville had not sat there before becoming prime minister. An American would be even more surprised by the experience that French leaders have had in the ministries as high civil servants, and particularly in dealing with foreign and economic affairs.

The traditional style of French campaigning is plebiscitary. One feature of this is that campaigning need not be incessant. Louis Napoleon is said to have compared elections with baptism: something it is necessary to do—but to do only once. The seven-year fixed term of the French president, about double the statutory life of many national leaders, is in the tradition of infrequent consultation with the electorate.

The French tradition of leadership is also ambivalent; a plebiscite is, after all, a mass mobilization. The weakness of parties, most notably on the Right, which has provided three of the four presidents of the Fifth Republic, encourages a personalistic style of campaigning. The use of the two-ballot method for the popular election of a president further encourages candidates to compete against each other as individuals, just as candidates for the presidential nomination compete against fellow-partisans in a primary. The persistence of divisions between Left and Right ensures any candidate successful in entering the second ballot a substantial bloc of votes, with or without a party endorsement.

On the two central criteria of political leadership, the relationship with the mass electorate, and knowledge of government, there are cross-national contrasts in the typical career. A British or French leader is likely to know far more about government than an American president, but an American politician is likely to be far more experienced in campaigning to win popular approval and elections.

Less for the President to Govern

Journalistic and historical accounts of government often focus on the person and office of the national leader. The American president is deemed to be very powerful because of the immense military force that he can command by comparison to a national leader in Great Britain or France. The power to drop a hydrogen bomb is frequently cited as a measure of the awesome power of an American president; but it is misleading, for no president has ever dropped a hydrogen bomb, and no president has used atomic weapons in more than forty years. Therefore, we must ask: What does an American president (and his European counterparts) do when not dropping a hydrogen bomb?

In an era of big government, a national leader is more a chief than an executive, for no individual can superintend, let alone carry out, the manifold tasks of government. A national leader does not need to make major choices about what government ought to do; he inherits a set of institutions that are committed—by law, by organization, by the professionalism of public employees, and by the expectations of voters—to appropriate a large amount of the country's resources in order to produce the program outputs of big government.

Whereas political leadership is readily personalized, government is intrinsically impersonal. It consists of collective actions by organizations that operate according to impersonal laws. Even when providing benefits to individuals, such as education, health care, or pensions, the scale of a ministry or a large regional or local government is such as to make the institution appear impersonal.

Contemporary Western political systems are first of all governed by the rule of law rather than personal will. When government did few things and actions could be derived from prerogative powers, such as a declaration of war, there was more scope for the initiative of leaders. Today, the characteristic activities of government, accounting for most public expenditure and personnel, are statutory entitlements to benefits of the welfare state. They cannot be overturned by wish or will, as their tacit acceptance by such "antigovernment" politicians as Margaret Thatcher and Ronald Reagan demonstrates. Instead of the leader dominating government, government determines much that is done in the leader's name.

In a very real sense, the so-called power of a national leader depends upon actions that his government takes, whether or not this is desired by the leader. Instead of comparing the constitutional powers of leaders, we should compare the resources that are mobilized by the government for which a national leader is nominally responsible. The conventional measure of the size of government is public expenditure as a proportion of the gross national product. By this criterion, French or British government is more powerful than American government. Organization for Economic Cooperation and Development (OECD) statistics show that in 1984 French public expenditure accounted for 49 percent of the national product, British for 45 percent, and American for 37 percent. When attention is directed at central government, as distinct from all levels of government, the contrast is further emphasized. British and French central government collect almost two-fifths of the national product in tax revenue, whereas the American federal government collects only one-fifth.

When a national leader leads, others are meant to follow. The legitimacy of authority means that public employees should do what elected officials direct. In an era of big government, there are far more public employees at hand than in an era when the glory of the state was symbolized by a small number of people clustering around a royal court. Statistics of public employment again show British and French government as much more powerful than American government. Public employment in France accounts for 33 percent of all persons who work, more than Britain, with 31 percent. In the United States, public employment is much less, 18 percent.

The capacity of a national leader to direct public employees is much affected by whether or not such officials are actually employed by central government. France is most centralized, having three times as many public employees working in ministries as in regional or local government. If public enterprises are also reckoned as part of central government, France is even more centralized. In the United States and Great Britain, by contrast, the actual delivery of public services such as education and health is usually shipped out to lower tiers of a federal government, or to a complex of local and functional authorities. Delivering the everyday services of government is deemed beneath the dignity of national leaders in Great Britain. In the United States, central government is deemed too remote to be trusted with such programs as education or police powers.

When size of government is the measure, an American president appears weaker than a French or British leader. By international standards, the United States has a not so big government, for its claim on the national product and the national labor force is below the OECD average. Ronald Reagan is an extreme example of a president who is "antigovernment," but he is not the only example. In the past two decades, the United States has not lagged behind Europe in developing and expanding welfare state institutions that make government big. It has chosen to follow a different route, diverging from the European model of a mixed economy welfare state. Today, the president has very few large-scale program responsibilities, albeit they remain significant: defense and diplomacy, social security, and funding the federal deficit.

By contrast, even an "antigovernment" prime minister such as Margaret Thatcher finds herself presiding over a government that claims more than two-fifths of the national product in public expenditure. Ministers must answer, collectively and individually in the House of Commons, for all that is done under the authority of an Act of Parliament. In France, the division between president and prime minister makes it easier for the president of the republic to avoid direct entanglement in low status issues of service delivery, but the centralization of government necessarily involves the prime minister and his colleagues.

When attention is turned to the politics of government as distinct from public policies, all leaders have one thing in common, they are engaged in political management, balancing the interplay of forces within government, major economic interests, and public opinion generally. It is no derogation of a national leader's position to say that it has an important symbolic dimension, imposing a unifying and persuasive theme upon what government does. The theme may be relatively clear-cut, as in much of Margaret Thatcher's rhetoric. Or it may be vague and symbolic, as in much of the rhetoric of Charles de Gaulle. The comparative success of Ronald Reagan, an expert in manipulating vague symbols, as against Jimmy Carter, whose technocratic biases were far stronger than his presentational skills, is a reminder of the importance of a national political leader being able to communicate successfully to the nation.

In the United States and France, the president is both head of government and head of state. The latter role makes him president of all the people, just as the former role limits his representative character to governing in the name of a majority (but normally, less than 60 percent) of the voters. A British prime minister does not have the symbolic obligation to represent the country as a whole; the queen does that.

The institutions of government affect how political management is undertaken. The separate election of the president and the legislature in the United States and France create a situation of nominal independence, and bargaining from separate electoral bases. By contrast, the British prime minister is chosen by virtue of being leader of the largest party in the House of Commons. Management of Parliament is thus made much easier by the fact that the British prime minister can normally be assured of a majority of votes there.

An American president has a far more difficult task in managing government than do British and French counterparts. Congress really does determine whether bills become laws, by contrast to the executive domination of law and decree-making in Europe. Congressional powers of appropriation provide a basis for a roving scrutiny of what the executive branch does. There is hardly any bureau that is free from congressional scrutiny, and in many congressional influence may be as strong as presidential influence. By contrast, a French president has significant decree powers and most of the budget can be promulgated. A British prime minister can also invoke the Official Secrets Act and the doctrine of collective responsibility to insulate the effective (that is, the executive) side of government from the representative (that is, Parliament).

Party politics and electoral outcomes, which cannot be prescribed in a democratic constitution, affect the extent to which political management must be invested in persuasion. If management is defined as making an organization serve one's purpose, then Harry Truman gave the classic definition of management as persuasion: "I sit here all day trying to persuade people to do the things they ought to have sense enough to do without my persuading them. That's all the powers of the President amount to." Because both Democratic and Republican parties are loose coalitions, any president will have to invest much effort in persuading fellow partisans, rather than whipping them into line. Given different electoral bases, congressmen may vote their district, rather than their party label. When president and Congress are of opposite parties, then strong party ties weaken the president.

In Great Britain, party competition and election outcomes are expected to produce an absolute majority in the House of Commons for a single party. Given that the prime minister, as party leader, stands and falls with members of Parliament in votes in Parliament and at a general election, a high degree of party discipline is attainable. Given that the Conservative and Labor parties are themselves coalitions of differing factions and tendencies, party management is no easy task. But it is far easier than interparty management, a necessary condition of coalition government, including Continental European governments.

The Fifth Republic demonstrates that important constitutional features are contingent upon election outcomes. Inherent in the constitution of the Fifth Republic is a certain ambiguity about the relationship between president and prime minister. Each president has desired to make his office preeminent. The first three presidents had no difficulty in doing that, for they could rely upon the support of a majority of members of the National Assembly. Cooperation could not be coerced, but it could be relied upon to keep the prime minister subordinate.

Since the election of François Mitterrand in 1981, party has become an independent variable. Because the president's election in 1981 was paralleled by the election of a Left majority in the assembly, Mitterrand could adopt what J.E.S. Hayward describes in *Governing France* as a "Gaulist conception of his office." But after the victory of the Right in the 1986 Assembly election resulted in a non-Socialist being imposed as premier, Jacques Chirac, the president has had to accept a change of position, symbolized by the ambivalent term *cohabitation.*

Whether the criterion is government's size or the authority of the national leader vis-à-vis other politicians, the conclusion is the same: the political leaders of Great Britain and France can exercise more power than the president of the United States. The American presidency is a relatively weak office. America's population, economy, and military are not good measures of the power of the White House. Imagine what one would say if American institutions were transplanted, more or less wholesale, to some small European democracy. We would not think that such a country had a strong leader.

While differing notably in the separate election of a French president as against a parliamentary election of a British prime minister, both offices centralize authority within a state that is itself a major institution of society. As long as a French president has a majority in the National Assembly, then this office can have most influence within government, for ministers are unambiguously subordinate to the president. The linkage of a British prime minister's position with a parliamentary majority means that as long as a single party has a majority, a British politician is protected against the risks of cohabitation à la française or à la americaine.

Variations within Nations

An office sets parameters within which politicians can act, but the more or less formal stipulation of the rules and resources of an office cannot determine exactly what is done. Within these limits, the individual performance of a president or prime minister can be important. Events too are significant; everyday crises tend to frustrate any attempt to plan ahead, and major crises—a war or domestic disaster—can shift the parameters, reducing a politician's scope for action (for example, Watergate) or expanding it (for example, the mass mobilization that Churchill could lead after Dunkirk).

In the abstract language of social science, we can say that the actions of a national leader reflect the interaction of the powers of office, of events, and of personality. But

in concrete situations, there is always an inclination to emphasize one or another of these terms. For purposes of exposition, I treat the significance of events and personality separately: each is but one variable in a multivariate outcome.

Social scientists and constitutional lawyers are inherently generalizers, whereas critical events are unique. For example, a study of the British prime ministership that ignored what could be done in wartime would omit an example of powers temporarily stretched to new limits. Similarly, a study of Winston Churchill's capacities must recognize that his personality prevented him from achieving the nation's highest office—until the debacle of 1940 thrust office upon him.

In the postwar era, the American presidency has been especially prone to shock events. Unpredictable and non-recurring events of importance include the outbreak of the Korean War in 1950, the assassination of President Kennedy in 1963, American involvement in the Vietnam War in the late 1960s, and the Watergate scandal, which led to President Nixon's resignation in 1974. One of the reasons for the positive popularity of Ronald Reagan has been that no disastrous event occurred in his presidency—at least until Irangate broke in November 1986.

The creation of the Fifth French Republic followed after events in Vietnam and in Algeria that undermined the authority and legitimacy of the government of the Fourth Republic. The events of May 1968 had a far greater impact in Paris than in any other European country. Whereas in 1958 events helped to create a republic with a president given substantial powers, in 1968 events were intended to reduce the authority of the state.

Great Britain has had relatively uneventful postwar government. Many causes of momentary excitement, such as the 1963 Profumo scandal that embarrassed

---

The French tradition of leadership is ambivalent.

Harold Macmillan, were trivial. The 1956 Suez war, which forced the resignation of Anthony Eden, did not lead to subsequent changes in the practice of the prime ministership, even though it was arguably a gross abuse of power vis-à-vis Cabinet colleagues and Parliament. The 1982 Falklands war called forth a mood of self-congratulation rather than a cry for institutional reform. The electoral boost it gave the prime minister was significant, but not eventful for the office.

The miner's strike, leading to a national three-day working week in the last days of the administration of Edward Heath in 1974, was perceived as a challenge to the authority of government. The prime minister called a general election seeking a popular mandate for his conduct of industrial relations. The mandate was withheld; so too was an endorsement of strikers. Characteristically, the events produced a reaction in favor of conciliation, for which Harold Wilson was particularly well suited at that stage of his career. Since 1979 the Thatcher administration has demonstrated that trade unions are not invincible. Hence, the 1974 crisis now appears as an aberration, rather than a critical conjuncture.

While personal factors are often extraneous to government, each individual incumbent has some scope for choice. Within a set of constraints imposed by office and events, a politician can choose what kind of a leader he or she would like to be. Such choices have political consequences. "Do what you can" is a prudential rule that is often overlooked in discussing what a president or prime minister does. The winnowing process by which one indi-

---

Campaigning for office makes a politician conscious of a need for popular approval.

---

vidual reaches the highest political office not only allows for variety, but sometimes invites it, for a challenger for office may win votes by being different from an incumbent.

A president has a multiplicity of roles and a multiplicity of obligations. Many—as commander in chief of the armed forces, delivering a State of the Union message to Congress, and presenting a budget—are requirements of the office; but the capacity to do well in particular roles varies with the individual. For example, Lyndon Johnson was a superb manager of congressional relations, but had little or no feel for foreign affairs. By contrast, John F. Kennedy was interested in foreign affairs and defense and initially had little interest in domestic problems. Ronald Reagan is good at talking to people, whereas Jimmy Carter and Richard Nixon preferred to deal with problems on paper. Dwight D. Eisenhower brought to the office a national reputation as a hero that he protected by making unclear public statements. By contrast, Gerald Ford's public relations skills, while acceptable in a congressman, were inadequate to the demands of the contemporary presidency.

In Great Britain, Margaret Thatcher is atypical in her desire to govern, as well as preside over government. She applies her energy and intelligence to problems of government—and to telling her colleagues what to do about them. The fact that she wants to be *the* decision-maker for British government excites resentment among civil servants and Cabinet colleagues. This is not only a reaction

to her forceful personality, but also an expression of surprise: other prime ministers did not want to be the chief decision-maker in government. In the case of an aging Winston Churchill from 1951-55, this could be explained on grounds of ill health. In the case of Anthony Eden, it could be explained by an ignorance of domestic politics.

The interesting prime ministers are those who chose not to be interventionists across a range of government activities. Both Harold Macmillan and Clement Attlee brought to Downing Street great experience of British government. But Attlee was ready to be simply a chairman of a Cabinet in which other ministers were capable and decisive. Macmillan chose to intervene very selectively on issues that he thought important and to leave others to get on with most matters. Labor leader Neil Kinnock, if he became prime minister, would adopt a noninterventionist role. This would be welcomed in reaction to Thatcher's dominating approach. It would be necesary because Kinnock knows very little about the problems and practice of British government. Unique among party leaders of the past half-century, he has never held office in government.

In France, the role of a president varies with personality. De Gaulle approached the presidency with a distinctive concept of the state as well as of politics. By contrast, Mitterrand draws upon his experience of many decades of being a parliamentarian and a republican. Pompidou was distinctive in playing two roles, first prime minister under de Gaulle, and subsequently president.

Differences between French prime ministers may in part reflect contrasting relationships with a president. As a member of a party different from the president, Chirac has partisan and personal incentives to be more assertive than does a prime minister of the same party. Premiers who enter office via the Assembly or local politics, like Chaban-Delmas and Mauroy, are likely to have different priorities than a premier who was first a technocrat, such as Raymond Barre.

Fluctuations in Leaders

The fluctuating effect upon leaders of multiple influences is shown by the monthly ratings of the popularity of presidents and prime ministers. If formal powers of office were all, then the popularity rating of each incumbent should be much the same. This is not the case. If the personal characteristics of a politician were all-important, then differences would occur between leaders, but each leader would receive a consistent rating during his or her term of office. In fact, the popularity of a national leader tends to go up and down during a term of office. Since personality is held constant, these fluctuations cannot be explained as a function of personal qualities. Since there is no consistent decline in popularity, the movement cannot be explained as a consequence of impossible expectations causing the public to turn against whoever initially wins its votes.

The most reasonable explanation of these fluctuations in popularity is that they are caused by events. They may be shock events, such as the threat of military action, or scandal in the leader's office. Alternatively, changes may reflect the accumulation of seemingly small events, most notably those that are reflected in the state of the economy, such as growth, unemployment, and inflation rates. A politician may not be responsible for such trends, but he or she expects to lose popularity when things appear to be going badly and to regain popularity when things are going well.

Through the decades, cyclical fluctuations can reflect an underlying long-term secular trend. In Europe a major secular trend is the declining national importance of international affairs. In the United States events in Iran or Central America remain of as much (or more) significance than events within the United States. In a multipolar world a president is involved in and more vulnerable to events in many places. By contrast, leaders of France and Great Britain have an influence limited to a continental scale, in a world in which international relations has become intercontinental. This shift is not necessarily a loss for heads of government in the European Community. In a world summit meeting, only one nation, the United States, has been first. Japan may seek to exercise political influence matching its growing economic power. The smaller scale of the European Community nations with narrower economic interests create conditions for frequent contact and useful meetings in the European arena which may bring them marginal advantages in world summit meetings too.

If the power of a national leader is measured, as Robert A. Dahl suggests in *Who Governs?*, by the capacity that such an individual has to influence events in the desired direction, then all national leaders are subject to seeing their power eroded as each nation becomes more dependent upon the joint product of the open international economy. This is as true of debtor nations such as the United States has become, as of nations with a positive trade balance. It is true of economies with a record of persisting growth, such as Germany, and of slow growth economies such as Great Britain.

A powerful national leader is very desirable only if one believes that the *Führerprinzip* is the most important principle in politics. The constitutions and politics of Western industrial nations reject this assumption. Each political system is full of constraints upon arbitrary rule, and sometimes of checks and balances that are obstacles to prompt, clear-cut decisions.

The balance between effective leadership and responsiveness varies among the United States, Great Britain, and France. A portion of that variation is organic, being prescribed in a national constitution. This is most evident in a comparison of the United States and Great Britain, but constitutions are variables, as the history of postwar France demonstrates. Many of the most important determinants of what a national leader does are a reflection of changing political circumstances, of trends and shock events, and of the aspirations and shortcomings of the individual in office.

Europe—West, Center, and East: The Politics of Integration, Transformation, and Disintegration

- The European Union: From EC to EU (Articles 36–38)
- Revamping the Welfare State (Articles 39 and 42)
- Post–Communist Central and Eastern Europe (Articles 43–45)
- Russia and the Other Post-Soviet Republics (Articles 46–49)

Most of the articles in this unit are in some way linked to either of two major developments that have fundamentally altered the political map of Europe in recent years. The first of these major changes is the long-term movement toward supranational integration of many Western European states within the institutional framework of the European Community (EC), which officially became the European Union (EU) on November 1, 1993. Here the development has primarily been one by which sovereign states forsake some of their traditional independence, especially in matters dealing with economic and monetary policies. Some important decisions once made by national governments in Paris, Rome, Bonn, and Copenhagen have become the province of the EU representatives in Brussels. To be sure, the trend toward integration is neither automatic nor irreversible, as recent events have underscored. Nevertheless, the process continues to be very important in shaping the politics of Western Europe.

One important indication of the EU's continuing attractiveness is that other countries seek to join. Austria and two more Scandinavian countries (Sweden and Finland) became the newest EU members in 1995, after entry had been approved in national referendums in each country. In the case of another Scandinavian country, Norway, the voters decided against membership for a second time in recent history. In Norway, there is a deep split between supporters and opponents, with an overwhelming resistance to membership coming from farmers and fishers as well as many women. A similar but weaker gender split is noticeable in the other Scandinavian countries, including Denmark, which has been a member since 1973. It appears that many Scandinavian women fear losing some of their social rights within such a European union in which gender equality has not yet reached the level enjoyed in their own countries.

A second major challenge to the established Western European state system is far more abruptly dislocating. It involves the disintegration brought about by the sudden collapse of communist rule in Central and Eastern Europe at the end of the 1980s. Here states, nations, and nationalities have broken away from an imposed system of central control and now assert their independence from the previous ruling group and its ideology. In their attempts to construct a new order for themselves, the post-Communist countries are encountering enormous difficulties. Their transition from one-party rule to pluralist democracy and from centrally planned state socialism to a market-based economy has turned out to be much rougher than had been anticipated. This resulting destabilization has had an enormous impact on Western Europe as well. There is already considerable evidence that many people have a nostalgia for the basic material security provided by the communist welfare states of the past. Communist-descended parties have responded by abandoning much of their Leninist political baggage and engaging in the competitive bidding for votes with promises of social fairness and security. In Poland and elsewhere, such parties have recently gained political leverage, but they must now operate in a pluralist political setting and have adopted different strategies and goals than in the past.

A closer look at the countries of Western Europe reveals that they have their own internal problems, even if in a far less acute form than their counterparts to the East. Their relative prosperity rests on a base built up during the prolonged postwar economic boom of the 1950s and 1960s. By political choice, a considerable portion of their affluence was channeled toward the public sector and used to develop generous systems of social services and social insurance. Between the early 1970s and the mid-1980s, however, Western industrialized societies were beset by economic disruptions that brought an end to the long period of rapidly growing prosperity. The last half of the 1980s marked some improvement in the economic situation throughout most of Western Europe, partly as a result of some favorably timed positive trade balances with the United States. In the early 1990s, however, economic recession took these countries in its grip once again. It is becoming clear that there are more fundamental reasons why these societies can no longer take increasing affluence for granted in a more competitive global economy. Today almost every one of them is beset by economic problems that economists deem to be structural in origin, rather than just cyclical and therefore passing. In other words, it will take much more than an upturn in the business cycle to galvanize these economies.

The earlier economic shock that first interrupted the prolonged postwar boom had come in the wake of sharp rises in the cost of energy, linked to successive hikes in the price of oil imposed by the Organization of Petroleum Exporting Countries (OPEC) after 1973. In the 1980s, OPEC lost its organizational bite as its members began to compete against one another by raising production and lowering prices rather than abiding by the opposite practices in the manner of a well-functioning cartel agreement. The West's exploitation of new oil and gas fields in the North Sea and elsewhere also helped alleviate the energy situation. The resulting improvement for the consumers of oil and gas helped the Western European economies recover, but as a whole they did not fully rebound to their earlier high growth rates. The short Persian Gulf War did not seriously hamper the flow of Middle East oil in 1991, but it once again underscored the vulnerability of Europe to external interruptions in its energy supply.

Because of their heavy dependence on international trade, Western European economies are especially vulnerable to the kind of global recessionary tendencies that we have encountered during the past few years. Another important challenge to these affluent countries is found in the stiff competition that they face from the newly industrialized countries (NICs) of East and South Asia, where productivity is higher and labor costs remain much lower. The emergent Asian factor probably contributed to the increased tempo of the European drive for economic integration in the late 1980s. Some observers have warned of the possibility that major trading blocs in Europe, North America, and Eastern Asia could replace the relatively free system of international trade established in the post-1945 period.

A related issue is how the increase in international trade within and outside the European Union will affect the established social market economies of continental Europe. The economic gains derived from international competition could have a positive consequence by providing a better base for consolidating and invigorating the social welfare systems, as described by Joel Havemann in his article "Diagnosis: Healthier in Europe." However, a different scenario seems to be starting in which there will be a drastic pruning and reduction in social services, carried out in the name of efficiency and international competitiveness. The social problems that have resulted in Europe's growing underclass are presented in the essay "Europe and the Underclass: The Slippery Slope." There are other demographic and economic challenges to the corporatist and welfare state arrangements that appear to have served these countries so well for so long. The debate about the best policy response to such problems will probably continue to agitate Western Europeans for years to come. It seems clear, however, that the famous "Swedish Model" will also have to be revamped.

In the mid-1980s, there was widespread talk of a malaise, a "Europessimism," that had beset these countries. Thereafter the mood appeared to become more upbeat, and for a while some observers even detected a swing toward what they labeled "Europhoria." Although political savvy would add some salt to such easy generalizations about public mood swings, there seems once again to be a more sober, even pessimistic, spirit abroad in Western Europe. Astute observers link this latest shift in mood to the economic and social problems associated with recessionary developments as well as with the dislocations that have accompanied the end of the cold war.

The demise of the Soviet bloc removed one major external challenge but replaced it with a set of others. The countries of Western Europe were simply unprepared for the chaotic conditions left behind by the former communist regimes to the East, all of which are now deeply affected by the fierce competition for scarce capital as they seek to attract investments that will build them new and modern economic infrastructures. At the same time, the daily poverty and disorder of life in Eastern Europe have encouraged a migration to the relatively affluent societies of the West.

Those who attempt the big move to the "Golden West" resemble in many ways the immigrants who have been attracted to the United States in the past and present. The major point of difference is that many Western Europeans are unwilling to accept what they regard as a flood of unwanted strangers. The newcomers are widely portrayed as well as perceived as outsiders, whose presence will drain the generous welfare systems and threaten not only to economic security but also the established way of life. Such anxieties are the stuff of sociocultural tensions and conflicts. One serious political consequence has been the emergence of anti-immigrant populism on the far Right. In response, the governments in several countries have changed their laws on citizenship, asylum, and immigration.

There can be no doubt that the issues of immigration and cultural tensions in Western Europe will occupy a central place on the political agenda in the coming years. Some of the established parties have already made symbolic and substantive accommodations to appease protesting voters, for fear of otherwise losing them to extremist ultra-Right movements. But it is important to remember that there are also groups that resist such compromises and instead oppose the xenophobic elements in their own societies. Some enlightened political leaders and commentators seek to promote the reasonable perspective that migrants could turn out to be an important asset rather than a major liability. This argument may concede that the foreign influx also involves some social cost in the short run, at least during a recessionary period, but it emphasizes that the newcomers can be a very important human resource that will

contribute to mid- and long-term economic prosperity. Quite apart from any such economic considerations, of course, the migrants and asylum-seekers have become an important test of liberal democratic tolerance on the continent.

Prudent observers had long warned about a premature celebration of "Europe 1992," which in appearance highlighted the abolition on restrictions in the flow of goods, capital, services, and labor by January 1, 1993, under the EC's Single Europe Act (SEA), adopted and ratified a few years earlier. They suspected that the slogan served to cover up some remaining problems and some newly emerging obstacles to the full integration of the European Community. These skeptics seemed at least partly vindicated by the setbacks that have followed the new and supposedly decisive "leap" forward taken in the summit meeting of EC leaders at the Dutch town of Maastricht in December 1991. The Maastricht Treaty surpassed the SEA in delineating additional steps toward supranational integration during the last half of the 1990s. It envisaged a common European monetary system and a federal European Reserve Bank as well as common policies on immigration, environmental protection, external security, and foreign affairs. In three of the twelve member countries—Denmark, Ireland, and France—ratification of the treaty was tied to the outcome of national referendums. In the first of these expressions of the popular will, Danish voters in June 1992 decided by a very slim majority of less than 2 percent to reject the treaty. A huge Irish majority in favor of the treaty was followed by a very slim French approval. The negative Danish vote seemed to have had the effect of legitimating and releasing many pent-up reservations in other member countries. But in May 1993, Danish voters approved a modified version of agreement, pruned down to meet Denmark's reservations. Some weeks later, British prime minister John Major was able to hammer together a fragile parliamentary majority for the treaty in the House of Commons. Here too, however, their agreement was a customized version of the treaty, tailored to provide some special opt-provisions designed to meet Britain's reservations. The last formal hurdle to the Maastricht Treaty was passed in Germany, where the Constitutional Court turned down a legal challenge based on its alleged violation of national sovereignty. But the difficult ratification process has revealed widespread political resistance that continues to hamper the course toward a federal union.

As several of the articles in this section point out, European Union has effectively reached a crossroads. The European nation-state has turned out to have more holding power than some federalists had expected, especially in a time of economic setbacks and perceived threats to the social order. The absence of a quick and coherent Western European response to the violent ethnic conflict in former Yugoslavia has added a further reason for doubt concerning the EU's imminent progression toward an elementary form of political federation. For these and other reasons, the present seems to be a time for new thought and debate about the EU's further goals and its route for reaching them.

While much academic and political ink has been spilled critiquing the problems of a transition from a market economy to state socialism, we have little theory or practice to guide Eastern Europeans moving in the opposite direction. A new and major theoretical issue that has important policy consequences thus concerns the best strategy for restructuring the economies of the former communist countries. Some academics believe that a quick transition to a market economy is a preferable course, indeed the only responsible one, even though it will be disruptive and painful in the short run. They argue that such a "shock" or "big bang" approach will release human energies and bring economic growth more quickly and efficiently; they

warn that halfway measures not only bring stagnation but could end up making the economic plight of these countries even worse than at present.

Others have come out in favor of a more gradual means for economic change. They argue that the strategy of the neoclassical economists, who would introduce a market economy by fiat, not only ignore its cultural and historical preconditions but also underestimate the social pain and turmoil that accompany a too-fast transition. In effect, these critics contend that the strategy of shock therapy has brought a lot of shock but very little therapy. Such gradualists therefore recommend pragmatic strategies of incremental change, accompanied by a rhetoric of lower expectations, as the politically more prudent course of action. It is likely that a mixture of these two approaches will be the practical policy outcome; we may have some better insights into the relative merits of each argument in a few years. Decision makers in these countries must often learn on the job and cannot afford to become inflexible and dogmatic in such matters in which the human stakes are so high.

The same debate has been carried out in the former Soviet Union during the past few years. In some ways, it could be argued that Mikhail Gorbachev, the last Soviet head of government (1985 to 1991), failed to opt clearly for a definitive approach to economic reform. He also seems to have been ambivalent not only about the means but about the ends of his perestroika, or restructuring, of the centrally planned economy. He remained far too socialist for some born-again marketers in his own country, while communist hard-liners never forgave him for dismantling a system in which they had enjoyed at least a modicum of security and privilege.

But the Achilles' heel of the now-defunct Soviet Union turned out to be its multiethnic character. Gorbachev was not alone in underestimating the potential centrifugal tendencies of a country that was based on an ideological and political redefinition of the old Russian Empire. Many of the non-Russian minorities were ethnic majorities within their own territories, and this made it possible for them to long for greater autonomy or even national independence in a way that the scattered ethnic groups of the United States do not.

Gorbachev appears to have regarded his own policies of glasnost, or openness, and democratization as essential accompaniments of perestroika in his modernization program. He seems to have understood (or become convinced) that a highly developed, industrialized economy needs a freer flow of information, along with a more decentralized system of decision making, if its component parts are to be efficient, flexible, and capable of self-correction. In that sense, a market economy has some integral feedback traits that make it incompatible with the traditional Soviet model of a centrally directed, authoritarian command economy.

But glasnost and democratization were clearly incompatible with a repressive political system of one-party rule as well. They served Gorbachev as instruments that weakened the grip of the communist hard-liners and at the same time rallied behind him some reform groups, including many intellectuals and journalists. Within a remarkably short time after he came to power in 1985, a vigorous new press emerged in the Soviet Union that was headed by journalists who were eager to ferret out governmental misdeeds and report on political reality as they observed it. A similar development took place in the history profession, where scholars used the new spirit of openness to report in grim detail about past atrocities of the Soviet system that had previously been covered up or dismissed as bourgeois lies. There was an inevitable irony to the new truthfulness. Even as it served to discredit much of the past, along with any reactionary attempts to restore "the good old days," it also brought into question the foundations of the Soviet system and the leading role of the Communist Party. Yet Gorbachev had clearly sought to modernize and reform the system, not to bring it down.

Most important of all, glasnost and democratization gave those ethnic minorities in the Soviet Union, which had a territorial identity, an opportunity to demand autonomy and even independence. The first national assertions came from the Baltic peoples in Estonia, Latvia, and Lithuania, which had been forced back under Russian rule in 1940, after some two decades of national independence. Very soon other nationalities, including the Georgians and Armenians, expressed similar demands through the political channels that had been opened to them. The death knell for the Soviet Union sounded in 1991, when the Ukrainians, who constituted the second largest national group in the Soviet Union after the Russians, made similar demands for independence.

In a very real sense, then, Gorbachev's political reforms ended up as a threat not only to the continued leadership role by the Communist Party but also to the continued existence of the Soviet Union itself. Gorbachev seems to have understood neither of these ultimately fatal consequences of his reform attempts until quite late in the day. This explains why he could set in motion forces that would ultimately destroy what he had hoped to make more attractive and productive. In August 1991, an attempted hard-liner coup against the reformer and his reforms came far too late and was too poorly organized to succeed. In fact, the would-be coup d'état became instead a coup de grace for the Soviet Communists and, in the end, the Soviet Union as well. The coup was defeated by a popular resistance, led by Russian president Boris Yeltsin, who had broken with communism earlier and, as it seemed, more decisively. Somewhat reluctantly, Gorbachev declared the party illegal soon after he returned to office.

After his formal restoration to power following the abortive coup, Gorbachev had become politically dependent on Yeltsin and was increasingly seen as a transitional figure. His days as Soviet president were numbered; the Soviet Union ceased to exist a week before the end of 1991. It was formally replaced by the Commonwealth of Independent States (CIS), a very loose union that presently lacks any viable institutional framework to hold it together. Almost from the outset, the CIS seemed destined to be a transitional device. It could serve a practical purpose for the former Soviet republics while they negotiate what to do with the economic, military, and other institutional leftovers of the old system and develop new and useful links to one another. Undoubtedly, some would like to find a way to restore a stronger union among these new states.

There is an undeniably gloomy, hangover atmosphere enveloping much of post-communist and post-Soviet Europe. It seems clear that much will get worse before it gets better in the economic and social life of these countries. The political consequences are very important, because social frustrations can now be freely articulated and represented in the political process. The transition from one-party rule to pluralist democratic forms has turned out to be neither easy nor automatic. A turn to some form of authoritarian nationalist populism cannot be ruled out in several countries, including Russia. Former communists with leadership skills are likely to play a major role in the process in such countries as Poland and the Ukraine. They sometimes cooperate with ultra-Right nationalists, with whom they share the dream of a strong state.

Specialists on the former Soviet Union disagree considerably in their assessments of the current situation and what brought it about. One of the hotly debated issues concerns President Yeltsin's decision in September 1993 to use a preemptive strike to break a deadlock between his government and a majority in the Russian parliament (Duma). When a majority of the legislators, who had been elected over two years earlier, persisted in blocking some of his major economic reforms, Yeltsin dissolved parliament and called for new elections to be held in December 1993.

The electoral result was a political boomerang for Yeltsin. It resulted in a major setback for the forces that backed rapid and thoroughgoing market reforms. The new parliament, based on a two-ballot system of elections, was highly fragmented, but nationalists and former communists occupied pivotal positions in the Duma. Henceforth President Yeltsin played a more subdued role, and the new government pursued far more cautious reform policies than previously. The military invasion of Chechnya, a breakaway Caucasian republic located within the Russian federation, has not given Yeltsin a quick and easy victory, which might have reversed his slide into political unpopularity among Russians. Nor has it stemmed the surge of Russian nationalist politics, which seems based on a demand for cracking down on crime and social disorder. But neither the ultra-Right nor the former communists, who resist far-reaching market reforms, seem eager to return to the tradition of a centrally planned economy. In that limited sense, at least, the extensive Soviet chapter of Russian history appears finally to have been closed, even though that experience will continue at times to disturb the pattern of the country's future development.

New parliamentary elections in December 1995 provided a further setback for the democratic reformers in Russia. It was far less their rivals" strength than their own disunity and rivalry both before and after the election, however, that weakened the parliamentary position of the reformers. Together the reformers received close to a quarter of the vote: slightly more than the communists, led by Gennady Zyuganov, and twice as much as the far-Right nationalists in Vladimir Zhirinovsky's Liberal Democratic Party. Under Russian electoral law, however, the communists received 35 percent of the seats in the new Duma. Observers of Russian politics differed in their assessments of this development, but all agreed that it left the cause of political and economic reform in considerable disarray. During the spring of 1996, Russian political leaders had their eyes fixed on the presidential elections of June, in which the incumbent Boris Yeltsin faced the toughest political challenge of his career. The outcome could be crucial for Russia's political direction into the new millennium.

Looking Ahead: Challenge Questions

What are the major obstacles to the emergence of a more unified Europe? What differentiates the optimists and the skeptics as they assess the outlook for greater integration? What are the major institutional characteristics of the European Union, and why is there a widespread call for reform?

What is the evidence that the economic problems of Western Europe are not just cyclical but also structural in origin? What has been the impact of economic stagnation on the social services provided by the welfare state?

What are the main problems facing the newly elected governments in Eastern and Central Europe? How well are they doing in coping with the transition to political pluralism and a market economy?

Was Mikhail Gorbachev mistaken in believing that the Soviet Union could be reformed without being dissolved? How have the 1993 and 1995 parliamentary elections set back the cause of political and economic reform in Russia? What explains the electoral support received by the communists and the nationalists?

Citizens Immune to Euro-Fever

On paper, the Continent is united. But in daily life, people show little interest in being part of one Europe.

Tyler Marshall

Times Staff Writer

BRUSSELS—The question seemed simple enough. "Can one be a citizen of Europe?" a visitor asked a class of German high school seniors.

The class flunked.

Not one of the 17- and 18-year-olds at the Friedrich Ebert High School in Bonn knew that they are legally citizens of the European Union.

Nor, did they know that as citizens, they enjoy the rights to move freely within the union's 15 member countries, to live anywhere they want and to vote in local elections whenever they live.

"We've never talked about the European Union, so I know nothing about Article 8," said Andreas Gotze, 17, referring to the provision in the 1991 Maastricht Treaty that defines EU citizenship.

Precious few Europeans do.

Indeed, 38 years after the union's six founding nations forged the European Economic Community and four years after a larger group of 12 West European countries committed themselves to the European Union's more ambitious goal of political and economic unity, there is remarkably little awareness among ordinary people that they now belong to a greater whole or that they share a common destiny.

This lack of awareness is a great irony of the "European movement"—an irony that diminishes its truly impressive accomplishments of binding together a continent that has often torn itself apart, an irony that could threaten its future.

On the one hand, barriers that divided member countries for centuries have been dismantled over four decades at a pace exceeding the dreams of even those most committed to the ideal of European unity.

The resulting single economic market has provided the region's 370 million citizens with unprecedented prosperity and freedom of movement.

Anyone wanting to make the 1,500-mile trip from Berlin to Lisbon can cross the Netherlands, Belgium, France and Spain and enter Portugal without once showing a passport or being stopped at a frontier.

Michel Coemelberghs, 56, a courier for a Brussels delivery firm, needs only one long day to cover the 800 miles to a vacation spot in southern Spain that it took his father three days to reach 40 years ago.

On the other hand, the enormousness of these achievements appears to have done little to bring the lives of individual Europeans closer together or give them a shared set of reference points.

Yes, there is a European anthem (Beethoven's "Ode to Joy") and a European flag (blue with a circle of gold stars), and EU citizens tend to carry the same maroon passport. But there appears to be little real attachment to any of them.

"You won't find any surge of emotion from the strains of 'Ode to Joy,' " said Terry Venables, director of the Euro-Citizen Action Service, a Brussels-based advisory bureau. "The idea of 'citizens' Europe' has tended to be a gadget activity."

The fathers of modern European unity, such as Jean Monnet, Robert Schuman and Paul-Henri Spaak, are hardly known outside a small circle of Euro-enthusiasts, while earlier would-be European unifiers—Charlemagne, Napoleon or Hitler—simply don't fit as heroes or role models for a group of democracies in the late 20th Century.

"It is one thing for elites in Brussels [site of EU headquarters], Strasbourg [French site of the European Parliament] and some European capitals to identify with and work for a united Europe [but] quite another to attribute such sentiments and beliefs to the great mass of the middle and working classes," said Anthony D. Smith, a sociologist at the London School of Economics and a specialist in the origins of nationalism and patriotism.

He argued that the absence of any underlying patriotic commitment to the European ideal, or any well-developed sense of a broader feeling of community among Europeans, means that even current achievements could easily unravel.

"Until this is there, the edifice of 'Europe' at the political level will remain shaky," he said.

Europeans continue to define themselves almost exclusively in terms of their own nationhood.

Nightly television news broadcasts, for example, still concentrate on national subjects, except for occasional major events. The deaths of 11 Belgian U.N. peacekeepers at the start of the massa-

---

BACKGROUND: The Maastricht Treaty

The Maastricht Treaty, named for the Dutch city where the document was approved in 1991, promotes the concept of a single European citizenship. Under the treaty, the European Union—expanded this year to include 15 nations after Austria, Sweden and Finland voted to join—must work toward common policies in foreign affairs, security and eventually defense. There is also a timetable for monetary union, including a single currency, by 1999. And citizens of any member state are given the absolute right to live and work anywhere in the EU.

cres in Rwanda a year ago stunned Belgium but went completely unreported on the main evening news in neighboring Germany.

Even a rare night when Europeans did share a common experience—June's elections for the European Parliament—television commentators in most countries largely ignored the results in other nations, focusing on the elections' domestic political ramifications.

In schools, it is the narrower national histories and politics that dominate curricula on the next generation of Europeans. Of five secondary schools visited by The Times in Belgium and Germany, only one—in Brussels—has students who displayed any real knowledge of the European Union.

A teacher at the Friedrich Ebert school in Bonn explained his students' lack of knowledge of the EU by saying there is no room for it in the teaching plan.

'There's no such thing as a "European way of life" as there is [an American way of life] in the United States. National identities are still too strong.'

Marc Fallon
Law professor at Belgium's Catholic University of Louvain

The ultimate determination of what goes into school curricula at all levels lies with national governments, a fact that inhibits broader teaching about the EU. There was an effort in Britain in the 1980s to require EU instruction, but it was beaten back.

A 1990 study, "Young Europeans," carried out by the EU Executive Commission, discovered that in no member country could more than 10% of respondents ages 15 to 24 list the 12 nations that were then EU members. In Italy and Britain, the figure was 2%, in France, 3%.

This lack of awareness has helped keep horizons narrow.

Marc Fallon, a law professor at Belgium's Catholic University of Louvain who specializes in the rights of European citizens, believes that despite their new treaty rights and resulting benefits, including mutual recognition of professional qualifications, only 1% to 2% of EU citizens live outside their home countries.

"There's almost no difference compared to the past," Fallon said. "All this was done to encourage people to move, but nobody has. The door is open, but no one is walking through it."

In one sense, the reason for this is obvious: Language, culture and the Europeans' strong attachment to "home" remain powerful barriers for most of those now legally free to start again somewhere else.

"There's no such thing as a 'European way of life' as there is [an American way of life] in the United States," Fallon noted. "National identities are still too strong."

In one small measure of this diversity, the bestseller lists for fiction in the EU's four most populous countries—France, Britain, Germany and Italy—contain only one book in common: "Sophie's World," Norwegian Jostein Gaarder's tale of a schoolgirl's correspondence with a philosophy teacher.

In fact, much to the dismay of many Europeans nearly four decades after the European Economic Community was founded, the lone cultural thread that runs through all European countries is American—from fast food to casual fashion to pop music. Seven recordings on MTV's mid-April Europe-wide list of Top 20 hits were by American artists, the most from any one country; all 20 selections, including those by German and Belgian groups, were sung in English. Although familiar to a broad cross-section of the Continent, such phenomena are hardly the stuff to foster a greater European identity.

But there are other factors that have blunted any sense of shared experience among Europeans, so necessary for a viable political entity. Among them:

• From its inception, European unity has been a top-down revolution. It was a movement launched not by the masses but by a small group of idealistic technocrats working in the aftermath of World War II. It has been pushed forward ever since with a conspicuous absence of public involvement.

• The impenetrable nature of the EU's key institutions, their remoteness and their penchant for secrecy mean that they provide almost no opportunity for ordinary citizens to feel involved.

Although the job of Executive Commission president is easily the most visible and most powerful in the EU structure, the choice of Jacques Santer of Luxembourg to succeed Frenchman Jacques Delors last year was brokered with all the openness of a 19th-Century smoke-filled room, then presented to Europeans as a *fait accompli.*

Similarly, last July, the EU's Council of Ministers, a body made up of one representative from each member country, refused to disclose details of its new policy aimed at creating greater openness. The issue was a secret.

"The information deficit has become part of the democracy deficit," said a former EU commissioner for information, Joao de Deus Pinheiro of Portugal.

• There have been no crucial defining moments in the EU's brief history to engage ordinary people. It has fought no wars, has no charismatic heroes and has defended no cherished set of values or ideas in a manner that inspires the kind of supranational patriotism or loyalty that can bind diverse peoples together.

Instead, its battles to impose a value-added tax on British birdseed, erase an age-old Dutch candle cartel or override a German beer purity law have brought more ridicule than admiration.

"There is no European analogue to Bastille [Day] or Armistice Day, no European ceremony to the fallen in battle, no European shire of kings or saints," sociologist Smith said. "When it comes to the ritual and ceremony of collective identification, there is no European equivalent to national or religious ceremony."

Some observers believe that the answer to that lack—rather than manufacturing artificial Euro-holidays—lies in building more substance into such concepts as European citizenship and in making sure that younger generations learn about them.

As EU leaders discuss the idea of a European defense capability, the prospect of service in a European army has also been raised.

"Guarantees to human rights, civil rights and freedom of information need to be built into European citizenship, but also some duties," said Venables, the Euro-Citizen Action Service director. "If it had more obligations, there would be a lot more information on it."

Times researchers Isabelle Maelcamp in Brussels and Reane Oppl In Bonn contributed to this article.

Europe's Parliament on the Move

Long seen as a gravy train for second-rate politicians, the European Union's assembly is newly powerful. But with its business base spread over three countries, scrambling delegates wish it would settle on one home.

Tyler Marshall

Times Staff Writer

STRASBOURG, France—David Hallam's new life isn't easy. Since June, the 46-year-old father of three has been commuting among four offices in three countries. He works amid a cacophony of 11 languages and juggles a bewildering array of subjects, ranging from nitrate-vulnerable zones in rural areas to Europe's relations with Israel.

He lives out of a suitcase and carries his work around in a foot locker. How he makes it home to the west of England at the end of the week occasionally depends on how fast he manages a sprint through the airport in Frankfurt, Germany.

"I'm not certain where I am sometimes," Hallam, a member of what is arguably the world's most unusual elected assembly: the European Parliament.

With the assembly's committees in Belgium, the majority of its support staff in Luxembourg and most of its plenary sessions in France, much of Europe also finds it hard to know exactly where the Parliament is at any given time.

For most of its 44-year existence, few even cared. Remote from voters and with little real power, it was dismissed as an irrelevant talk shop, an expensive traveling circus or an unabashed gravy train whose members' principal mission seemed to be to drink and dine well on taxpayer money.

But times are changing in Europe. To the delight of some and the horror of others, the European Parliament is becoming important. Strengthened by an influx of new, more serious members, headed by a strong president and armed since November with important new powers ema-

nating from the Maastricht Treaty on political and economic union, the Parliament suddenly enjoys new status.

It now can veto international treaties, block nations aspiring to join the European Union and reject en masse those individuals nominated to the EU's powerful Executive Commission. For the first time, it also has gained a real voice in shaping laws in important areas such as education, health and consumer affairs. And it could gain still more power out of a major reform of EU institutions scheduled for next year.

"There's been a shift of power in the direction of Parliament," said Karel van Miert, a veteran EU commissioner. "You can't continue work pretending that this hasn't happened."

Today, the Parliament is also increasingly seen as an important vehicle for rekindling flagging public enthusiasm for the dream of uniting Europe and as an antidote to a "democracy deficit" that has plagued the 15-nation European Union in recent years.

For the growing group of serious Parliament members, this new responsibility translates into grueling schedules and an unending struggle to stay in touch at home yet also keep up with their traveling assembly.

Hallam, for example, who ran a small British public relations firm before winning election in June as the Labor Party's member representing the English Midlands counties of Hertfordshire and Shropshire, works out of his home near Birmingham. He has a constituency office three-quarters of an hour away in the town of Telford. His commute to Brussels takes about three hours, while the one to Strasbourg runs five or more, including a switch from plane to bus in Frankfurt.

And that's just the start.

As a member of a committee that monitors EU-Israeli ties, Hallam went to Washington to represent the Parliament at a Feb. 2 congressional prayer breakfast; he will travel to Israel next week, and in March he will be in Barcelona, Spain, where his fellow socialist members of the European Parliament plan to meet on their own.

The issues he deals with are complex. He often can't converse with his colleagues except through an interpreter. And at the end of most days, it's back to a hotel room.

"The job is more demanding than I thought," he said. 'I never thought I'd groan at the idea of a winter week in Barcelona.''

With their children ages 4, 3 and 6 months, Hallam's time away from home places added burdens on his wife. He says the hardest thing about the job is sitting at the other end of a telephone hearing his 3-year-old crying for her daddy. "That's when I really want to go home," he said.

But the Parliament's hard work has begun to show. In January, its stock jumped sharply as television cameras captured members quizzing nominees to the Executive Commission in the assembly's first-ever committee hearings on confirmation. They then engaged in a lively debate before voting by a 4-1 margin to accept the nominees. "It's a sign the public image no longer fits the realities," says Klaus Haensch, a German and the body's president.

If true, it's a good thing. Created in 1951 as a part-time advisory assembly whose members were appointed by their national parliaments, the European Parliament became a haven for second-rate politicians or a neglected accouterment for the ambitious. One colleague, for example, noted that during a three-year period, the leading French Socialist Laurent Fabius showed up only twice.

For many years, the majority of those who did show up seemed more intent on living well than on working hard. Old-timers still recall the devastating effect of a 1981 CBS television documentary titled "The Gravy Train." It contrasted the Parliament's empty seats and boring debates with scenes of members stuffing themselves at expensive Strasbourg restaurants.

"It was awful," recalled Guido Naets, a Belgian and the Parliament's chief spokesman for 14 years. "It was mean, it was selective, but it was real."

Add to this generous income levels and the picture was complete. (Members of the EU assembly are paid the same as members of their national parliaments—monthly levels that today range from $10,500 for the Italians to $4,362.50 for Hallam and his British colleagues down to $2,525 for their Spanish counterparts.)

With little real power, the Parliament was also quickly distracted by esoteric issues. For example, during a single morning in October, 1993, the assembly busied itself with resolutions that supported democracy in Equatorial Guinea, called on authorities in western India to distribute aid to earthquake victims on the basis of need, demanded information on the fate of 24 political prisoners in China

and urged a boycott of British Airways because it segregated cabins by gender on flights into and out of Saudi Arabia.

It was against this backdrop that Haensch turned his inaugural address as president of the new Parliament in July into a stern lecture. "If we wish to exploit all the opportunities offered by Maastricht, we must change our own method of working," he warned. "Let's stop trying to produce resolutions from the latest reports in the morning papers. We must find time for discussions on the great issues of European politics."

In an interview, Haensch elaborated on this theme. "Until Maastricht, the European Parliament was largely an advisory body and had little real power, so bad habits developed that now have to be corrected," he said.

Haensch said he wants higher attendance, more streamlined procedures, but above all the full use of the Parliament's new powers. "Before we had the right to advise. Now we can have a voice in the decisions themselves," Haensch said. "For me, the task is to assure the full and effective use of these new powers. I want the European Parliament's public image to be that of the true representatives of the citizens of Europe, against whose wishes political decisions about Europe can't be made."

But many are convinced that the Parliament will find it hard to shake its old image until it finds a permanent home. Certainly, for outsiders, the present setup is hard to take seriously.

While the Parliament's 19 standing committees meet in Brussels, the Belgian capital, for two weeks each month, most of the 12 full, one-week sessions are held 300 miles south in Strasbourg, which forces members to have offices and lodgings in both cities.

To further complicate matters, roughly two-thirds of the parliamentary staff is based in Luxembourg—from which staffers either commute to Strasbourg or Brussels or work mainly by phone or computer.

This transient existence has generated some bizarre rituals.

In both Brussels and Strasbourg, for example, the halls of parliamentary office buildings are lined with metal foot lockers, packed faithfully every few Fridays with files and other paraphernalia, then unpacked the following Monday.

In the 1960s, when the EU had six member states and the Parliament had 143 members with a few hundred other people in support, moving around was somehow manageable. But with a 15-nation EU, a Parliament with 626 members and a staff of almost 4,000, each move is cumbersome—and costly. Travel and hotel bills alone this year are expected to eat up 15% to 20% of the Parliament's $930-million budget—much of which, like the EU's entire budget, comes from sales levies (actually, value-added taxes) on Europe's consumers. And that's just the visible costs.

Friday afternoons are often devoted to packing; crucial hours on Monday are wasted on travel. "The whole thing is a shame," Naets said. "Families are disrupted, it's expensive, the Parliament is perceived as a traveling circus, and it's inefficient. You pack your trunk and find you've forgotten something important when you get there. I'm fed up."

But since none of the three countries seems willing to give up its claim to a share of the Parliament, the nomadic life goes on.

Indeed, about the only thing more absurd than the current arrangement is the attempt to end it—by building separate parliaments, one in Brussels, one in Strasbourg, to lure the assembly to a single location. The $1.1-billion structure in Brussels is expected to be completed in 1997, while a $500-million Strasbourg building is scheduled to be finished in late 1998.

With the Executive Commission already based in Brussels, Belgium would seem to be the obvious location. But because logic doesn't always prevail in the effort to unite Europe, French President Francois Mitterrand squeezed a commitment from the EU heads of government two years ago to acknowledge Strasbourg as the Parliament's permanent home.

Few see any end soon to the travel.

And in one respect, the train journey between Brussels and Strasbourg serves as a reminder that a less-than-perfect Parliament is a vast improvement on Europe's history.

The trip passes first through the Ardennes Forest, where thousands of Americans died in World War II fighting, then along remnants of the Maginot Line built by France between the world wars in a farcical attempt to stop Germany's military might.

"The European Union is frequently criticized and this European Parliament held up to ridicule, often despised and misrepresented almost everywhere," Haensch told his fellow members in July. "One thing, however, is certain. What would our fathers, grandfathers and great-grandfathers have given, in their time, to have a European Parliament . . . to air their disagreements instead of sending their nations' young people to their deaths in the trenches?"

THE CHALLENGE TO EMU

Europe learns its alphabet

Is monetary union a necessary part of the European Union?

AT THE pretty Dutch town of Maastricht, way back in December 1991, it had seemed so obvious. In the quest for "an ever closer union among the peoples of Europe", there would be "a single and stable currency". This would complete the final stage of an economic and monetary union (EMU) that might lead—automatically, some hoped and others feared—to a political union. EMU, Europe's leaders solemnly declared, would be fulfilled by the end of 1997 or, at the latest, by the start of 1999.

The obvious was never likely to be easy; there are too many social and economic disparities between the European Union's member states. There are also deeper rifts; sceptical Britain and Denmark have both won the right to opt out from EMU.

Now the question is whether the difficult is becoming the impossible, and what consequences, good or ill, will follow. After all, the value of economic and monetary union has been an article of faith for France and Germany ever since President Valéry Giscard d'Estaing and Chancellor Helmut Schmidt met in Aachen (the seat of Charlemagne, an earlier Euro-enthusiast) in September 1978 to agree on a "European monetary system". Their successors, François Mitterrand and Helmut Kohl, were notably devout. Even Jacques Chirac, France's new president, who has little of Mr Mitterrand's closeness to Mr Kohl and not much instinctive zeal for *le projet Européen,* feels obliged to preach EMU's virtues.

No wonder: for both France and Germany hang great hopes on the project, even if these are not exactly the same. To France, such a union is a means to harness German economic might to European (especially French) purposes. To Germany, it is a way of confirming a return to the neighbourly fold, with the prospect of supranational institutions to keep a federalising Europe in German-style order. For both countries, enemies in three wars in a mere 100 years, it ensures a "European Germany".

The faith has been tested in the past, not least in speculative attacks—most spectacu-larly in September 1992 and then again in July 1993—against the exchange-rate mechanism, a currency grid which is supposed to prepare the way for a single currency and demands that central banks support each other when currencies come under pressure. Today, there are new tests, ones which cannot be blamed (*pace* Jacques Delors, former president of the European Commission) on "Anglo-Saxon speculators".

This time the pressures reflect wider doubts within the European heartland, among both politicians and the people they supposedly speak for. The 1997 target for EMU has already been abandoned. It demanded that a majority of the EU's 15 members meet strict criteria of economic convergence, and by now it is clear that not enough of them will. By contrast, the 1999 target requires no majority: the treaty instructs those who do meet the criteria (save opt-out Britain and Denmark) to move to EMU willy-nilly. On that date the conversion rates of their currencies "shall be irrevocably fixed": the single currency will then exist in banking computer programmes and, within at most three years, in people's pockets.

All this may have seemed clever to the bureaucrats who drafted Maastricht's tortuous prose. The trouble is, the closer the 1999 deadline gets, the tougher the problems. Indeed, the true deadline arrives up to a year earlier. If Europe's banks are to be ready, they must know roughly that far in advance which countries have met the criteria. Since one criterion is to have maintained a stable exchange rate for two years, the years 1996 and 1997 become a decisive test of fiscal and economic rectitude as defined at Maastricht. The test is especially nerve-stretching for the Franco-German alliance because in 1998 France will hold a parliamentary election and Germany will choose a new chancellor.

The diverging definitions

No wonder, then, that politicians in Bonn and Paris are so worried. Frightened, thanks to paranoid memories of the Weimar republic, that the loss of the D-mark will resurrect inflation and bring un-German sloppiness into the conduct of monetary policy, at least 60% of the Germans oppose the mark's replacement by some form of Eurocurrency (the actual name of which is meant to be chosen at next week's EU summit in Madrid). To reassure them, the president of the Bundesbank, Hans Tietmeyer, and the finance minister, Theo Waigel, are competing with each other to stress that the economic convergence criteria must be strictly adhered to before EMU can happen: there will be no nods and winks for Germany's friends.

Mr Waigel does not stop there. Last month he proposed a "stability pact" for those countries that do qualify for EMU. The essence is that, once the monetary union exists, its members will have to follow even tighter economic criteria, at the risk of punitive fines if they do not. Indeed, Mr Waigel's strictures are so severe that some suspect him of duplicity; his aim (and that of some people in the Bundesbank), they say, is not to achieve EMU, but to prevent it.

That may be a conspiracy theory too far. More plausibly, Mr Waigel is just ensuring that the opposition Social Democrats in Germany, now headed by the combative Oskar Lafontaine, cannot accuse the government of opening the door to a dangerously floppy Eurocurrency. Even so, one look at France is enough to see the pain that the Maastricht criteria already bring, even without Mr Waigel's planned tightening.

Crippling strikes by public-sector unions, ill-tempered student protests, plummeting poll ratings for President Chirac and his prime minister, Alain Juppé—all are seen as the result of France's need to reduce government borrowing to the level decreed at Maastricht. France would have had to cut its budget deficit anyway, even if Maastricht had never happened. But, in most people's eyes, it is Maastricht that has made the government start cutting now. And that will not help to make EMU popular among the French.

The emerging objections

Is the potential gain worth the present pain?

Reprinted with permission from *The Economist,* December 9, 1995, pp. 19-21. © 1995 by The Economist, Ltd. Distributed by The New York Times Special Features.

3. EUROPE: The European Union

Advocates of a single currency can reel off the advantages. For business, EMU would eliminate the cost (reckoned to be some $30 billion a year) of foreign-exchange transactions and exchange-rate hedging. For individual Eurocitizens, it would rid them of currency-exchange robbery (go round the Union changing money at each border and you will end up with half the amount you started with). For governments, it would help to stabilise the international currency markets. For the Union's single market, inaugurated at the end of 1992 to allow the free movement of people, capital, goods and services, it would mean added efficiency and an end, within the monetary union, to "competitive" devaluations.

Maybe so. But there are serious counter-arguments. One is that the effect of transaction costs is exaggerated; if you want greater prosperity, there are other things that will provide much more of it. The single market, on this view, could be better improved by liberalising Europe's energy and telecoms industries, and by ensuring open public-sector procurement policies.

Another objection, which awakens the deepest instincts of national identity, is that EMU would mean a loss of sovereignty. Monetary policy would be set by a supranational European central bank, and governments would lose the ability to devalue their way out of a crisis.

Eurosceptics fear that EMU would be the start of a "United States of Europe", with a European central bank acting as its Federal Reserve and with something like a European ministry of finance potentially emerging out of the consequences of a single currency. This, of course, is exactly what Euro-enthusiasts would like. There is also a school of thought which says that for a country to join EMU would mean not so much losing sovereignty as merely pooling it with others. Indeed, it is the opportunity to escape the Bundesbank's current dictatorship over other people's exchange rates that so attracts the *énarques* who run French policy and who are determined that Europe should be administered in France's interest.

More prosaically, in a monetary union uncompetitive workers could no longer be cushioned by a falling exchange rate. Instead, they would either lose their jobs or have to accept lower wages. This too causes pain, personal and political. Nor could the sufferers' governments expect much help from their EMU colleagues: Article 104b of the Maastricht treaty specifically rules out a financial rescue by one country of another.

In theory, of course, nobody should need any help. The Maastricht criteria were drawn up to prevent such disparities within EMU. Economies are to "converge" by attaining certain bench-marks: exchange rates must be stable within the exchange-rate mechanism for at least two years before the selection for EMU membership is made; long-term interest rates must be within two

A long way to Shiloh

Commission forecasts, % of GDP				Maastricht criteria: deficit should not exceed 3%, debt 60%			
General government net lending/borrowing				General government gross debt			
1994	1995	1996*	1997*	1994	1995	1996*	1997*
Austria	-4.4	-5.5	-5.0	-4.6	65.2	68.0	69.9	71.5
Belgium	-5.3	-4.5	-3.1	-3.5	135.0	134.4	132.3	130.0
Britain	-6.6	-5.1	-3.7	-2.8	50.1	52.5	53.3	53.2
Denmark	-3.8	-2.0	-1.3	-0.5	75.6	73.6	72.7	70.5
Finland	-5.8	-5.4	-1.5	nil	59.8	63.2	64.6	64.5
France	-6.0	-5.0	-3.9	-2.9	48.4	51.5	53.4	54.2
Germany	-2.6	-2.9	-2.8	-2.4	50.2	58.8	59.5	59.3
Greece	-11.4	-9.3	-8.3	-7.3	113.0	114.4	114.0	113.1
Holland	-3.2	-3.1	-2.7	-2.2	78.0	78.4	78.2	77.8
Ireland	-2.1	-2.7	-2.0	-1.3	91.1	85.9	81.3	76.9
Italy	-9.0	-7.4	-6.0	-5.2	125.4	124.9	123.9	122.3
Luxembourg	2.2	0.4	0.6	0.7	5.9	6.3	6.7	6.8
Portugal	-5.8	-5.4	-4.7	-4.1	69.4	70.5	71.0	70.9
Spain	-6.6	-5.9	-4.7	-3.6	63.0	64.8	65.8	65.4
Sweden	-10.4	-7.0	-4.5	-3.2	79.7	81.4	80.8	79.8
EU average	-5.5	-4.7	-3.8	-3.1	68.1	71.0	71.6	71.3

Source: European Commission   *Assuming unchanged economic policies

percentage points and inflation within 1.5 percentage points of "the three best-performing member states in terms of price stability"; public deficits must be no more than 3% of GDP; and gross government debt must be no more than 60% of GDP.

It is these last two that are causing most of the trouble. A habit of welfare-state generosity, plus the recession of the late 1980s and early 1990s and the high interest rates that followed Germany's unification, has stretched most government balance-sheets well beyond the Maastricht norms.

It's not just France

The theory which Mr Juppé and others now chant like a mantra is that meeting the criteria will start a virtuous circle. Lower deficits will mean lower interest rates, which will mean more investment, more jobs and more tax revenue to lower the deficit once again and pay off the accumulated debt.

The paradox, of course, is that lower deficits will come only by raising taxes or reducing public spending—and neither of those things will in the short run produce more jobs. They will mean fewer jobs, and will therefore produce more of the sort of street protests now being endured by Mr Juppé as he belatedly begins to reform the social-benefits system that France, with or without Maastricht, can no longer afford.

One look at the appraisals just produced by the European Commission (see table) shows that Mr Juppé is not the only prime minister with problems. At the moment only Germany and tiny Luxembourg meet the Maastricht criteria in full. Ireland is allowed to join this dismally short list, despite a government debt of 85.9%, only because this figure is, in a loophole provided by the Maastricht-drafters, "approaching the reference value at a satisfactory pace".

How long will the list grow by decision-time, a bit over two years from now? Yves-Thibault de Silguy, the Frenchman who is the EU's commissioner for monetary affairs, reckons that if they stick to their present policies Finland, France and Holland will all qualify, along with the two potential spoil-sports, Britain and Denmark. With a bit more effort, Austria, Spain, Portugal and Sweden could get there, too. So could Belgium, if you make a hugely generous interpretation of that Maastricht loophole for its predicted debt level of some 130% of GDP.

Mr de Silguy's optimism may be right—but only (a) if governments are willing to tough it out and (b) if, as the commissioner hopes, some happy economic fundamentals "spur renewed healthy growth".

The first "if" is particularly tricky, since it means further austerity at a time of already appallingly high unemployment. Across the EU, a tenth of the workforce is without jobs. In France, the jobless rate is almost 12%, in Finland 17%, and in Spain nearly 23%. In such circumstances is it sensible, many wonder (including Philippe Séguin, the speaker of France's National Assembly and a potential prime minister should Mr Juppé stumble), to cut budget deficits and maintain currency parities for the sake of Maastricht's EMU timetable?

Such heretics have a point. The convergence criteria have the appearance of good economic housekeeping, but they are nonetheless arbitrary. Belgium manages to have a strong currency and low inflation despite its steepling debt ratio, the highest in the OECD. Most advanced economies, including Germany's, accommodate budget deficits well beyond Maastricht's 3%-of-GDP limit at some time in the economic cycle. In short, the convergence criteria are a strait-jacket unadjusted to the patient's size.

This is why Mr Waigel's stability plan is open to more than one interpretation. Once EMU happens, it is clearly sensible that its members should co-ordinate their economic policies, lest their economies diverge and split the whole venture apart. That is why disobedient members can be required under the Maastricht treaty to place non-interest-bearing deposits "of an appropriate size" into the communal coffers, and even pay fines "of an appropriate size". In the same fashion, those who do not at first qualify for EMU will still have to be well behaved (there are punishments if they run "excessive deficits"), lest they threaten those within EMU by self-serving devaluations.

But Mr Waigel's definition of obedience, and of the penalties for disobedience, is very tough. He says that, over the course of the whole economic cycle, EMU countries should have to keep their budget deficits limited to an average of 1% of GDP. Moreover, for every single percentage point that a country strays beyond the Maastricht limit of 3%, it should lodge a non-interest-bearing deposit equal to 0.25% of its GDP. Stay beyond the limit for two years and the deposit becomes non-returnable: in short, the offending country pays a fine.

This is strong stuff. If it had applied in 1991, Britain (which then met the entry criteria) would by now have handed over some 3% of its GDP, of which two-thirds would have become fines, and France 2.25% of its GDP, with half becoming a fine. Here, clearly, are the beginnings of supranational control over a country's economy.

It could also be self-defeating. Why worsen a budget deficit by fining the country that commits it? That will only make it harder for the country to accept EMU's disciplines. No wonder France's finance minister, Jean Arthuis, and his counterparts from other EU countries were careful in Brussels on November 27th to praise only the principle of Mr Waigel's proposal, not its details.

If getting to EMU will be difficult, so too,

it seems, will be staying there. For some, that is another reason, if not to abandon the goal of a single currency, at least to postpone it. They are worried about the discrimination inherent in a timetable which assumes that only some of the EU's members will at first be fit to join.

Spain and Portugal, in the Union only since 1986, fear they will be lost in the mist on Europe's periphery if, as seems likely, they cannot meet the 1999 deadline. Italy, a founder-member of the EU, feels insulted that Germany, a fellow founder-member, now openly states the obvious: Italy will not meet the deadline even if the lira re-enters the exchange-rate mechanism. Publicly, the Latin trio will question neither Maastricht's timetable nor its criteria. Privately, they are poised to press the case for "flexibility".

Will they succeed? They do not want a Europe in which some, mainly north Europeans, are more equal than others. But, in preparing for EMU, Europeans have already accepted the idea of a multi-speed process. In allowing opt-outs to Britain on EMU and social policy, and to Denmark on EMU, defence and European citizenship, they have also allowed different classes of membership. The amount of such "variable geometry" will doubtless increase if and when the EU expands eastwards. One way or another, whatever the verbal camouflage, some countries will almost certainly end up in a hard core that omits other countries.

That is too tricky an issue to be dealt with by an overburdened Madrid summit. So are the questions raised last month by Britain's prime minister, John Major: "How would Europe's institutions serve the interests of those countries which adopted the single currency and those who didn't? What would it mean for the Community budget? What would it mean for the single market?" Mr Major was making a fair point: countries outside EMU might respond to their weaknesses by allowing their currencies to depreciate against the single currency, to the detriment of the single market.

But Mr Major and his fellow leaders will give answers only for the EMU "scenario", as it is called: the date on which the qualifi-

ers will be selected (France wants the selection well ahead of its March 1998 election; Germany wants it delayed long enough into 1998 to have accurate economic data for 1997); the types and amounts of public debt and banking transactions to be denominated in the non-cash single currency; the date for minting coins and notes; the date on which existing currencies will cease to be legal tender; and, for the sake of a bemused public, the name of the single currency.

More haste . . .

Will their work be in vain? The answer will come not from Madrid, but from Bonn and Paris. Before EMU can happen, it has to be approved by the German parliament—and so, indirectly, by a still profoundly sceptical German people. That is why Germany's politicians are so determined to be strict about Maastricht.

But the same politicians know that EMU will be nothing without France. Over then to Messrs Chirac and Juppé: can they muster the will to outlast the worst social unrest since 1968, and bring the budget deficit within the Maastricht limit by 1997?

The longer the answer remains in the balance, the more tempting it will be to change either the criteria or the timetable. The first option would never be accepted by German opinion. That is why, in October, Germany's economy minister, Günter Rexrodt, held out hope of the second, endorsing a possible delay of "a year or two". The next day, he backed off: "A moratorium increases the danger that economic and monetary union will be talked away."

Maybe. But delay may be better than clinging stubbornly to a timetable set by people who had not thought through the difficulties of the project, and who have not persuaded their voters of the need for it. In any event, EMU is not necessarily the only way of moving towards that "ever closer union". The building of Europe requires a rock-steady foundation. Does this pass the test? It is not just the stability of France that is now being decided on France's streets.

Sweden: A Model Crisis

After World War II Sweden appeared to be the very model of a successful welfare state. In recent years, however, the country has suffered from acute social, economic and political problems. A prominent foreign observer of Sweden attempts to place the crisis of the Swedish Model in historical perspective.

Joseph B. Board

Joseph B. Board, Ph.D. in Political Science, is Robert Porter Patterson Professor of Government at Union College, Schenectady, New York. He has written on Sweden and been a visiting professor at Lund and Umeå Universities.

Crisis. Formerly an unfamiliar word in the Swedish political lexicon, it is far more commonly encountered nowadays. The Swedish public sector, a national success story in the 1950's and 60's, has fallen into a persistent state of crisis, which smoulders on even if it does not burst into flame, and from which no immediate escape is readily apparent. Unemployment, at 13%, is extremely high by Swedish standards. The national debt is close to 100% of GDP, and the annual budget deficit is running at 11% of GDP (the average for major industrial countries is 4%). There are strong political differences between the formerly inseparable trade unions and Social Democrats; the combined strength of two old parade horses like the Liberals and the Center party barely equals that of a surging Left Party (formerly the Communists). The refractory problems of public finance and declining political consensus are exacerbated by

ethnic tensions at home, a hesitant and ambivalent decision to join the European Union, and contentious debate over the meaning of Swedish neutrality. A divided government and society have not yet come to grips with the real questions, which are not peculiar to Sweden, and which are essentially more political than economic: how large should government be, and what is its proper role in society?

The rise of the Swedish Model

In 1870, Sweden was a poor, backward, inward-looking, socially and politically undemocratic country on the outer rim of Europe. One hundred years later, by 1970, Sweden was as affluent, per capita, and as democratic as any nation in the world. A socially laggard Sweden modernized itself more quickly and thoroughly than any nation in the world, with the possible exception of Japan.

By the 1950's, this developmental spurt had culminated in the so-called Swedish Model, a term never subject to precise definition. Sweden became world-renowned as the prime example of a prosperous, democratic welfare state, its wealth created by a vigorous private sector, but distributed in accordance with an egalitarian vision of social justice. Beatified by apologists for the Welfare State, demonized by its enemies, the Model was widely touted as a superior alternative to autocratic socialism or to socially deficient liberalism; its political system was based on the bedrock of a broad consensus shared by all

From *Current Sweden*, September 1995, pp. 1-5. Reprinted by permission of *Current Sweden*, a publication of the Swedish Institute.

the major political parties but orchestrated by a dominant Social Democratic Party. In short order the Swedes created a complex system which rested on a large and powerful public sector, a high level of civic trust, a closed circle of private interest groups involved in public decision-making, a belief in social engineering, egalitarian distribution of the national income, voluntary labor peace (the so-called spirit of Saltsjöbaden), and low unemployment—altogether a heady mixture of democracy, prosperity, and social security.

The decline of the Swedish Model

By the early 1990's, it was becoming clear that the Swedish Model no longer accurately described a country plagued with high unemployment, strikes, declining consensus, ethnic tensions, persistent problems of public finance, uncertain about its place in the wider world or the future direction of public policy at home. A number of analysts, professional and amateur, foreign and domestic, responded with a flourish of attempts to explain what had caused the deterioration in the Swedish Model. The safe, sure, and predictable Sweden that one had come to expect with almost boring regularity had vanished in a cloud of malaise and a crisis of confidence.

Actually the changes had begun much earlier, probably in the early 1970's. The successful operation of the Swedish Model had depended on a number of factors, some domestic, others international, and when these began to change, it was inevitable that the Model would have to respond.

It should be emphasized that while the Swedish Model is widely associated with the Social Democrats and their trade-union allies, it was ultimately a creation of the non-socialist parties as well. One major condition on which the entire accomplishment rested was the presence of a highly stable party system in which the Social Democrats were the only party large enough to set and realize such an ambitious agenda. Following on the heels of a succession of weak governments in the 1920's and early 1930's, the Social Democrats were in power, alone or in coalition with a much weaker partner, for the entire period between 1932 and 1976, a world record for democratically sustained continuity. The first minor challenges to their pre-eminence came in the 1960's from amorphous New Left movements. Later, in the 1970's, their ideological hegemony was weakened somewhat by the rise of the Center Party, and later by the Greens, over the issues of nuclear power and other ecological concerns.

The more serious challenge to Social Democratic hegemony came, however, from the Right. In the parliamentary elections of 1976, the non-socialist parties—Center, Liberals and Moderates—wrested power from its long accustomed holders, and despite problems in holding together their uneasy coalition, won re-election in 1979. The Social Democrats regained office in 1982, and remained there until 1991. However, during the 1980's the Moderate Party and its private-sector supporters introduced a vigorous infusion of neo-liberal ideology into the Swedish public debate, challenging the near monopoly of democratic socialist and social-liberal ideas that had provided the context of public debate throughout most of the post WW II era.

By the 90's, even when the Social Democrats recaptured power in 1994, things were clearly not the same. No longer did they enjoy the commanding heights of their hey-day, and this made it difficult for them to provide an agenda for a renewal of the Swedish Model, even if they had possessed one. The Social Democrats ended up victims of their own success. During their long tenure in power, the very class distinctions on which their movement had been founded had all but disappeared. Sweden had become a predominantly middle-class country; the Social Democrats had become more and more a white-collar party, and the earlier close association with the trade unions had become increasingly strained.

Some foundations of the Swedish Model

The Swedish Model, furthermore, was dependent on a spirit of compromise and mutual restraint prevailing between the labor movement (unions and Social Democrats) on the one hand and the large corporations and interest groups of Swedish industry on the other. This harmonious spirit was based on the awareness by all sides that a small Sweden could survive in a large and competitive world only if all could pull together. Swedish industry, whose role in producing the national wealth available to be distributed by the welfare state has been persistently underestimated by social scientists, perceived itself from the early 1970's in an increasingly disadvantageous position within the Swedish policy-making process. By the 1980's it had begun to fear for its very existence; high taxation, the enormous growth of the public sector, and fears of creeping nationalization prompted by the wage-earner funds and other new departures proposed by Labor caused it to launch a vigorous neo-liberal counterattack on the fundamental assumptions of continued governmental growth.

The Swedish Model, at least in its idealized form, presumed the existence of a society with an unusual degree of ethnic and religious homogeneity, its highly organized system of interest groups led by elites—political, economic, and social—and a rather docile citizenry disposed to follow its leaders. Today, the population is much less homogeneous. The heavy postwar immigration of workers, mostly from Europe, followed by a later influx of asylum-seekers, frequently of non-European origin, has created problems of assimilation and brought to the surface a latent xenophobia in Swedish society.

The loss of elite control was a serious one in a system based on peak-level corporative bargaining between the leaders of the government, political parties, trade unions, business organizations and the other major players in national policy-making. It is obviously easier to maintain control over events if the circle of decision-makers is a limited one. Some slippage could have been detected by an astute observer as early as the late 1960's, with demands originating among the young New Left for less bureaucracy and more grass-roots democracy. Although these pressures were contained and co-opted, a wave of labor unrest, most notably the LKAB strike in the iron mines of Kiruna at the decade's end, provided eloquent testimony to a serious decline in the ability of the Swedish Model to contain and channel social conflict.

There were other signs of similar decay, including the appearance of issues, i.e. nuclear power, and later EU membership, which from their inception could not be comfortably accommodated within the existing party system, but required the unusual expedient of referendums to reconcile the electoral contradictions.

The success of the Greens in obtaining seats in the Riksdag (Parliament) in the 1988 election (the first new party to do so in 70 years), and the rise of an openly populist party, New Democracy, in 1991, however fleeting its electoral success, are further signs of electoral decomposition.

Finally, and perhaps most importantly, the Swedish Model

presumed the existence of a domestic arena within which Swedish decision-makers, while obviously not totally impervious to world movements and trends, nevertheless were in a position to control the main outlines of Swedish domestic policy.

This situation has been utterly transformed in the past two or three decades. The gobalization of the economy, the arrival of larger European groupings such as the EU, and the global communications revolution have forever ended the illusion that the so-called sovereign State—much less one the size of Sweden—was any longer in complete control over its own political destinies. The cruel reality is that the room for internal political maneuver has been drastically reduced by global influences such as currency fluctuations, international business cycles, capital flows, the fax machine and the Internet, the Eurocrats in Brussels, and even by those semi-sovereign companies which evaluate the credit-worthiness of entire countries.

Sic transit gloria Sueciae?

When the awareness of Swedish difficulties began to sink in, journalists and social scientists alike struggled to find explanations for this change in national fortunes. The more perceptive scholars, alert to the nuances of what seemed to have been a stable and permanent system, were understandably bewildered. Critics of the Swedish Welfare State rushed in like scavengers at a long-deferred feast to explain all the Trouble in Paradise. The weakness in this analysis was, however, that Sweden had never been a paradise in the first place. Much of the popular publicity about Sweden had described, not a Model of reality but a romantic image, one which in fact obscured many of the real accomplishments of the Swedes.

Without in any way detracting from the efficacy of conscious efforts to attain the extraordinary combination of prosperity and security that were the hallmarks of the Swedish Model at its height, one is nevertheless compelled to conclude that much of that success was a happy accident. Neutral Sweden emerged from WW II with its industrial plant intact, its exports in demand, equipped with a skilled work force, a highly organized and homogeneous society, and a political system dominated by one large party which combined pragmatic good sense with fiscal responsibility, and strong government with a highly developed social conscience. Under these favorable conditions, including a period of vigorous economic growth of between 3 and 5% annually from the the late 40's through the 60's, the private sector could grow, welfare could expand, and there seemed to be no ceiling to the success of the Swedish Model.

Actually, the Swedish Model might better have been called the Swedish Image, one which served not only the needs of model-builders but also promoted the interests of Swedes and their foreign admirers alike. Liberals, would-be Social Democrats, and reformers of all persuasions in countries like America, could from Marquis Childs on, point to Sweden as a confirming case for the cause of democratic social reform. For Swedes it provided a powerful image, even a kind of marketing device with which to maximize their country's political and economic influence throughout the world. It is in fact illuminating to read today the descriptions of Sweden commonly encountered during the period of the Model's ascendancy. One is struck by the degree to which these accounts are not only congruent, but practically identical, whether they originated with politicians, business interests, civil servants, or scholars.

Swedes were also able, to a considerable extent, to view their foreign and domestic situation in idealistic, non-cynical terms. There is in Swedish history (as in American) a long tradition of exceptionalism, the incorporation into the national ethos of an unshakeable conviction that the country, unlike most others, has been blessed by Providence with a special mission. Having renounced Great Power ambitions in the 18th century (and it should be remembered that 17th century Sweden was in fact a genuine major power), the Swedes were able in the 20th century to transform their smallness into goodness, and replace the more conventional forms of national chauvinism with a kind of "Welfare Patriotism" or "moral imperialism."

Once the Swedish Model began to show signs of wear and tear, the government made efforts at repair. Most of the attempts were temporizing improvisations, aimed at keeping the wolf as far from the national door as long as possible. Devaluations of the krona, expansion of public-sector employment, and crisis packages negotiated by the politicians did not, however, really reduce the budget deficits, the growing national debt, and the rising unemployment. It is in fact a tribute to the strength of the Swedish system that it could be maintained for so long before it became apparent that the problems were profound, structural, and to some extent shared by most European countries. Neither the socialists nor the non-socialists had any sure-fire solutions.

Half-good may not be half-bad

In spite of the bewilderment, occasioned by these near-tectonic shifts in the Swedish political landscape, there is a bright positive side to all this change. Much of the malaise which observers began to detect during the 80's and 90's was nothing more than the harvest of the exaggerated expectations which had long grown around the Swedish Model; as a general rule, the greater the expectations, the deeper the disillusionment.

One reason why Sweden was becoming a more confusing place to interpret, for Swedes and foreign observers alike, is that it was—like most advanced industrial countries—rapidly becoming a much more heterogeneous pluralistic society. In its ethnic composition, the media, public debate, cuisine, religion (only a few years ago, who would have believed that by 1995 there would be in Sweden an estimated quarter of a million ethnic Moslems?) Sweden has become a country of greater, and admirable, variety. Small wonder it was that politics inevitably became less predictable as the society became less uniform and conformist. New political parties formed and re-formed, new political journals, such as *Moderna Tider* (Modern Times), provided a more cosmopolitan tone to public debate and even television was utterly transformed, for better or worse, with the advent of advertising and cable/satellite transmission.

It is especially apparent to the outside observer that Sweden has become less inward-looking, more vital, complex, politically nuanced, less Manichaean in the way the choices are posed—in short, the country has become more like other countries that long ago lost perfectionist ambitions. Sweden has become less perfect, but at the same time more human and more interesting. The ambivalent and changeable Swedish attitudes towards EU membership are illustrative. Having approved membership by only a 5% margin in the November 1994 referendum, the electorate was almost immediately seized by doubts, and only one half-year later, the opinion polls revealed a large majority against membership.

The Swedish Model was grounded philosophically in the paramount ideals of the 18th century Enlightenment: rationality, progress, social ameliorism, secularism—ultimately in the belief that one could attain social perfection through the wise use of concentrated political resources. It is not, however, totally unhealthy to learn that there are limits to perfection, that total control and predictability are impossible, and that even enlightened government can become overloaded. In short, what Sweden has been discovering is the contingent, fallible, unscientific, irrational, downright messy side of social and political life.

Even if the Swedish Model is clearly no longer what it once was, this does not mean that important components of it have not survived the buffeting of recent years. There is still a core of agreement on ethical and aesthetic matters, a remarkably durable set of attitudes towards Nature and Society, notions of order and propriety, an abhorrence of extremes, and a widely shared sense of social compassion. Even in the political realm there is agreement on fundamental principles of human rights, respect for law, democracy, parliamentary government, constitutionalism, honesty in government, and there is still immense support in Sweden for the main lines of a welfare state. There is a Civil Service of uncommonly high competence ready to implement the products of the policy-makers.

Confusion, maybe; paralysis, no

Confusion caused by the unexpected setbacks of the Swedish Model has not resulted in paralysis. While the government has yet to develop a new vision of how State and Society should relate to each other, there has begun a tentative, cautious step-by-step down-sizing of the public sector. Some cuts have already been made in areas like unemployment compensation, day care, parental leave and health care. These reductions have predictably been criticized by some as too small, and by others as too great, depending on whose ox is being gored. But the public as well as the politicians have gradually become aware that serious change is unavoidable, even if there is no sizeable body of opinion in favor of dismantling the welfare state.

Swedes have by necessity been a resourceful people. From earliest times, their beautiful but demanding natural environment has compelled them to develop coping skills. More than most peoples they are well situated to deal with the new kind of internationalized and pluralized world that is emerging. They have strong ties with other Nordic countries, the Baltic, Western Europe, the United States, and the Third World. They have shown a remarkable penchant for invention, a capacity for social and industrial organization, and—like the Japanese—a supple willingness to borrow and transform to their own purposes the discoveries of other nations. The increased prominence of women in the Riksdag and the Cabinet, the already global mindset of Swedish industry, the renewed public debate over the place of government at all levels, from neighborhood to globe, are only a few of the hopeful signs of adaptation.

Swedish skills will be severely tested in the immediate years ahead, in a world of constantly evolving challenges, where it will be extraordinarily difficult for any country to maintain strong governments which can make long-term policies and provide stable expectations for their citizens. The swollen Swedish public sector, the largest in a democratic industrial country, as well as the monumental national debt and budget deficits are the products of a country that lived for a long time beyond its means, and they will not disappear without painful adjustments.

The Golden Age in perspective

Actually the period from the 1930's to the 1970's—the Golden Age of the Swedish Model—may have constituted an exception in modern Sweden. The weak and changing governments that characterized the earlier decades of the 20th century may well be the most likely types encountered in the forseeable future, an unenviable series of holding actions complicated by the public's lack of confidence in politicians and political solutions. It is a time of difficult choices, rendered more complicated by the natural inclination of a public to have it both ways—egalitarian social programs and fiscal discipline, low taxes and extensive benefits. It is one thing to distribute the benefits of growth another to distribute the burdens of a contracting economy.

Even if the celebrated Golden Age was part accident,

and only partly the intentional result of policy, the story of what the Swedes did with their windfall after the Depression and WW II is in the main a good one, a tale of cooperation between Capital, Labor, and Government to care for the disadvantaged, all within a democratic framework. It was certainly not an opportunity disfigured by greed, narrow selfishness, or pettiness. There is scant prospect for a return to the Golden Age, or to the unbridled Capitalism that preceded it, and the choices confronting any Swedish government, whether of the Left or Right, will be difficult. There remains a lot of hard bargaining over the proper balance between the public and private sectors before the Swedes are out of the woods, but this is what politics is all about, and for the enterprise ahead Sweden—for all its present burdens—has a better point of departure than most.

The author alone is responsible for the opinions expressed in this article.

DIAGNOSIS: HEALTHIER IN EUROPE

By most standards, Western Europeans are in better medical shape than Americans. And costs are sharply lower. But bureaucracies and under-the-table payments mar the system.

Joel Havemann

Times Staff Writer

BRUSSELS—For someone with a potentially fatal disease, Regine Delvaux is exceptionally healthy. A diabetic for 26 of her 37 years, Delvaux holds down a part-time office job in Brussels and, in the past four years, has been able to adopt two young children.

She owes her active life to the Belgian national health system, which, like those of other Western European governments, guarantees that virtually all Belgians are insured and pays the lion's share of the costs. That means Delvaux receives virtually free care, including the regular insulin she needs to fend off kidney failure, blindness and the other scourges that diabetes can bring.

The contrast with the United States is striking. Europeans have better access to health care than Americans, an estimated 35 million of whom are uninsured. By most objective measures, they are healthier.

And what is most extraordinary, Europe actually spends less for health care—about one-third to one-half less in most countries—than the United States. The U.S. health bill, growing far faster than overall inflation, will reach something like $800 billion this year, or about 13.5% of the nation's entire economic output.

No wonder President-elect Bill Clinton is looking at Europe as he seeks to redeem his campaign promise to overhaul the U.S. health care system. Clinton has promised to require employers to provide insurance to all workers, to guar-antee public insurance for those who do not work and to set a national limit on overall health-care spending.

Most Western European countries already do all this.

Clinton and his health-care planners will not want to copy everything they find across the Atlantic. European-style health care is hardly trouble-free.

Inflexible bureaucracies sometimes interfere with the delivery of care. Some doctors, unwilling to settle for government-prescribed fee schedules, take part of their payments under the table. For a minor operation to correct nearsighted-ness, a Brussels clinic charges not only the official rate of about $300 but also another $900 in unreported cash.

Medical services are rationed, especially in countries that spend relatively little on health care. In Britain, which spends less than all but the poorest Western European nations, the elderly frequently wait two years for hip replacements and cataract operations.

Even in the Netherlands, which spends 30% more per person than Britain for health care, a recent survey found that one-third of all hospital admissions came only after excessive waits. At the same

Who Pays the Freight?

Here is the share of health care spending paid by governments and by private individuals and insurers, 1989:

	Governments	Private
France	75%	25%
Germany	72	28
Britain	87	13
Italy	79	21
Netherlands	73	27
Sweden	90	10
United States	**42**	**58**

HOW DOCTORS ARE DOING

The average after-tax income of general practitioners in 1985, the latest year with available data:

France	$24,700
Germany	48,200
Britain	27,900
Netherlands	32,400
Sweden	22,200
United States	**77,900**

Reliable figures for salaries of Italian doctors were not available.
Sources: American Medical Assn., Organization for Economic Cooperation and Development

time, under pressure from health care providers and patients, the Dutch government pays for such dubious treatments as herbal medicine and psychic healing.

In a range of European countries, rising costs have triggered reform movements that have a distinctly American flavor. The Netherlands, for example, is edging toward competition between insurance companies in an effort to introduce incentives to control costs.

Yet for all the flaws, analysts on both sides of the Atlantic rank European health care miles ahead of America's. "What can Europeans learn from Americans about the financing and organization of medical care?" asked Alain C. Enthoven, a health-care financing specialist at Stanford University. "The obvious answer is, 'Not much.' "

The reasons that America spends more and gets less are legion: uncontrolled use of sophisticated medical technology, massive administrative costs, expensive malpractice insurance and higher-paid doctors, to name a few.

All this is rooted in the uniquely American pioneer experience and distrust of big government. The legacy is an every-man-for-himself approach to health care. Except for the elderly and the very poor who are enrolled in Medicare and Medicaid, those on the receiving end of the health care system get what they—or their employers—can pay for.

"In America, part of your population is accustomed to getting every available medical technology," said Henk ten Have, a professor of medical ethics at Catholic University in Nijmegen, the Netherlands. "But another large part gets no care at all."

COLLECTIVE CARE

Health care in Europe, by contrast, is grounded in collective responsibility. European governments either directly provide most health care, as in Britain, or require that everyone be insured, while paying for most of their citizens' insurance, as in Germany.

Either way, European countries operate on the same principle that governs public education in the United States: All of society benefits from a healthy citizenry, and all of society should shoulder the costs.

It is an attitude that Abram de Swaan, a University of Amsterdam sociologist,

---

Health Care: America vs. Europe

For all the flaws, analysts on both sides of the Atlantic rank European health care far ahead of what the U.S. offers.

Americans Spend More . . .

(health expenditures per capita, 1990)

United States	**$2,566**
France	1,543
Germany	1,487
Sweden	1,479
Netherlands	1,266
Italy	1,234
Britain	974

. . . but Are Less Satisfied . . .

(share of persons who believe the health care system works pretty well and only minor changes are needed)

United States	**10%**
Netherlands	47
France	41
Germany	41
Sweden	32
Britain	27
Italy	12

. . . and Achieve Poorer Results

(infant mortality rates per 1,000 births, 1990)

United States	**9.2%**
Italy	8.5
Britain	7.9
Germany	7.5
France	7.2
Netherlands	6.9
Sweden	5.9

Sources: Organization for Economic Cooperation and Development; Robert J. Blendon, Harvard School of Public Health

---

traces back 150 years to cholera epidemics that broke out in urban slums throughout Europe and claimed the lives of the rich as well as the poor. Out of self-protection more than charity, Europe developed modern sewage systems. Now cholera is largely under control, but the principle of collective responsibility remains intact.

"The social welfare systems in West European countries promote the dignity and well-being of all persons and the welfare of society as a whole," said

---

Reinhard Priester of the Center for Biomedical Ethics at the University of Minnesota. "In contrast, the United States embraces individualism, sees provider autonomy as the preeminent value and neglects community-oriented values."

In only two of the 24 industrial nations that make up the Organization for Economic Cooperation and Development does the government pay for less than half of the health care. Those two are the United States and Turkey.

In Western Europe, by contrast, all governments pick up at least two-thirds of health care costs. Each country has its own approach.

In Britain and Sweden, the government owns and operates most of the health care system, with the money coming largely from income tax revenue. Most other countries offer a mix of public insurance and compulsory, government-subsidized private insurance, with the government's contribution coming from a Social Security-like tax on employers and workers.

The Netherlands relies relatively heavily on private insurance. But even there, the 70% of the population at the bottom of the income scale is covered mostly by public insurance; for the rest, a combination of public and private insurers pays most of the bills.

No matter what the system, patients may generally choose their doctors, and they can buy supplementary insurance to cover what their government-financed insurance does not. Most governments dictate what doctors may charge, and some play a role in determining what procedures are appropriate to diagnose and treat particular conditions.

PATIENT SATISFACTION

To Americans, the European approach might seem heavily centralized, bureaucratic and rigid. But Europeans are happier with their approach than Americans are with theirs.

A 1990 study by the Harvard School of Public Health found that only 10% of Americans said their "health care system works pretty well." That put the U.S. system squarely at the bottom of the 10 nations included in the survey.

Of the six European countries surveyed, satisfaction levels ranged from 47% in the Netherlands to 12% in Italy. Canadians, whose national health insurance system is much more European than

American, were the most satisfied of all, with a 56% rating.

These ratings square with the few objective ways of measuring national health. Although America's diverse population, with its many minority groups, makes comparisons with more homogeneous Europe somewhat uncertain, it is nevertheless true that the United States falls consistently below Western European nations in infant mortality rates and life expectancy.

Europe achieves these results even though it spends substantially less for health care than the United States—typically 7% to 9% of national economic output, compared with America's 13.5%. Central to Europe's approach is a technique that seems unthinkable in the United States: Governments set strict health-care budgets, and local health authorities must live within their allowances.

"The strict planning systems for hospital care in Switzerland and the Netherlands, the two European systems most similar to those of the United States, are the major reason why expenditures are constrained in these countries," said Bengt Jonsson, a health specialist at the Stockholm School of Economics.

With strict health-care budgets, Europe has escaped America's uncontrolled growth in the purchase of medical technology. Two nearby European hospitals may not both buy the same piece of sophisticated machinery unless they can show a clear need; instead, one gets the equipment, and the patients at both hospitals use it.

Dr. Niek Klazinga, an official with the Dutch National Organization for Quality Assurance in Hospitals, said a single hospital in Houston three years ago had 13 sophisticated and expensive magnetic resonance imaging machines, more than all of the Netherlands.

American hospitals, armed with the latest medical gadgetry, are compelled to use it to recoup the cost. "When a patient with a headache is told that he needs a brain scan to make sure he doesn't have a tumor, his natural reaction is, 'Where do I lie down?' " said Arthur L. Caplan, director of biomedical ethics at the University of Minnesota.

In most of Europe, by contrast, the expensive brain scan may be used as a last resort—or not at all. In the Netherlands, every neighborhood has a general practitioner who serves as the gatekeeper to medical technology.

"General practitioners know that 70% of all headaches are emotional," Klazinga said. Before they permit brain scans to check for tumors, he said, they test all other possible causes.

Joseph Newhouse, a professor of health policy at Harvard, estimates that "technological change, or what might loosely be called the march of science and the increased capabilities of medicine," accounts for at least half the explosive growth of U.S. medical costs in the last half-century.

Robert Brook, senior health services researcher at the RAND Corp. in Santa Monica, said the use of costly technology often does not help and sometimes is downright dangerous to patients' health.

"Perhaps one-third of the financial resources devoted to health care today are being spent on ineffective or unproductive care," Brook and Kathleen Lohr of RAND's Washington office wrote recently.

FOOTING THE BILL

Technology aside, Europe is more willing to pay for preventive care than is the United States, where the uninsured generally benefit from no such care at all and even those with insurance sometimes find reimbursement unavailable.

Americans, and especially the poor, must typically get sicker than Europeans before they can get the care they need, said Jean-Pierre Poullier, a health policy analyst with the Paris-based Organization for Economic Cooperation and Development. That has the perverse effect, he said, of jacking up the cost of their treatment when they finally get it.

Diabetes provides a stark example. Dr. Ann Owen, an American who was born and trained as a physician in the United States but has specialized in treating diabetics in Belgium since 1983, said uninsured or underinsured diabetics in the United States often have no access to the insulin they need to control their blood sugar. Nor can they afford to care for the non-life-threatening complications of their disease.

"That means many people have to go into a coma before they can get treatment," Owen said. "By then, they need intensive care at a hospital, and in a few days you're up to $50,000."

"In Belgium," she added, "insulin is considered so essential to life that it's available for free."

Delvaux, the long-term diabetic, is glad it is. Since 1989, when the Belgian government set up a special program for diabetics, Delvaux has also been reimbursed for most of the costs of her regular doctor visits and blood sugar tests. "I have hardly had to pay more than a couple of hundred francs [about $7] a month," she said.

Thanks to her regular treatment, which includes a steady supply of insulin that is administered by a pump permanently implanted in an underarm, she has not been hospitalized for about 20 years.

In Los Angeles, Felipe Perez shows what might have happened to Delvaux. Perez, 39, has a less serious form of diabetes. Although he does not require regular insulin, he would benefit from other forms of routine treatment.

But as one of America's 35 million uninsured persons, he does not receive it. Two years ago, Perez lost his paid health insurance when he was laid off from his city job. Once last year he went to a community health clinic in Lincoln Heights and was prescribed medication for his diabetes. But he couldn't afford to buy it.

Earlier this year, he landed a part-time job with Los Angeles County as a home health-care worker for the elderly, but he gets no health benefits himself.

As a consequence, he found himself at L.A. County-USC Medical Center for the better part of a week recently so that doctors could treat an infection in his underarm that, because of his diabetes, had grown to the size of a walnut. The cost, most of which will be absorbed by the hospital: about $5,500.

DOCTORS' PAY

Medical salaries are another part of the cost-quality equation. General practitioners in the United States earned an average income of $77,900 in 1985 after covering their expenses but before paying taxes, according to the American Medical Assn.'s most recent data. That compares with $48,200 in Germany, $32,400 in the Netherlands, $24,700 in France and $19,700 in Belgium.

The United States has fewer doctors for its population than most European countries, with the notable exception of

Britain, and its supply of registered nurses falls at about the European average.

Yet its health care system employs more people than Europe's—especially those who sell health insurance and administer claims. "Behind every hospital bed in the United States is a clerk filling out forms," said Poullier of the OECD.

Jack A. Meyer, an analyst with New Directions for Policy, a Washington research group, said administrative costs soak up 22% of U.S. health-care spending. The American urban landscape, said Caplan of the University of Minnesota, is dotted with insurance company towers (Prudential, John Hancock) and even an entire city (Hartford, Conn.).

"We have a huge administrative bureaucracy to keep the rich from having to share costs with the poor, the healthy from having to share costs with the sick and the able-bodied from having to share costs with the disabled," Caplan said.

European nations avoid a substantial share of these administrative costs because they do not make such distinctions. At least in this respect, their decision to make health a collective rather than an individual responsibility actually saves money. **Times staff writer Somini Sengupta in Los Angeles contributed to this story.**

EUROPE AND THE UNDERCLASS

The slippery slope

ROTTERDAM

As yet, Western Europe does not have an urban underclass to compare with that of the United States. But the growth of long-term unemployment seems to be dragging it inexorably in that direction

IN ROTTERDAM'S vast harbour, a million containers a year are loaded and unloaded. Giant cranes poke towards the sky. Dry docks and oil refineries stretch to the horizon. But for all the gigantism of the harbour—the big ships, big machines, big statistics—there is something missing. People. The modernisation that began in the 1970s has meant that the burly types who used to do the heavy work have been mechanised out of their jobs. It is possible to cruise around Europe's busiest port on an average day and see only a handful of workers.

The decline of port employment, combined with a collapse of the Dutch textile industry, means that Rotterdam, a hardworking city where, it is said, shirts are sold with the sleeves already rolled up, has an unemployment rate of more than 20%. Of the 50,000 jobless, 32,000 have been unemployed for more than a year, and many for more than three years. Even this has come against a background of economic recovery. The finance and retail industries expanded in Rotterdam in the 1980s, yet unemployment still tripled. Few longshoremen were ready to become financial analysts.

In poor parts of the city where unemployment has become almost the norm, crime, drug abuse and one-parent families are increasingly common. The uneven concentration of unemployment—35% of Turks and 42% of Moroccans in Holland are unemployed, compared with 7% of ethnic Dutch—has provided fertile ground for political extremism. "People feel rejected. They don't participate in the social process. It's kind of a time bomb," says Jaap Timmer, a Dutch social scientist.

Lumped together

Such conditions are far from unique to Rotterdam. In cities across Western Europe—such as Frankfurt and Berlin, Lyons and Paris, Amsterdam and Utrecht, Naples and Dublin, Liverpool and Manchester—the shadowed lives of the urban poor are getting darker. Does Europe have an underclass to compare with that of America? Not yet. But the situation is deteriorating in ways that cause the question to be posed more often and more plausibly. And there are no ready solutions in view.

In America, the term "underclass" entered common usage in the 1970s and was a cliché, albeit a controversial one, by the end of the 1980s. It came to connote ghetto populations that were overwhelmingly black, isolated, unemployed, welfare-dependent, poorly educated and with disrupted family patterns. The origins of the underclass lay somewhere in a mix of racial inequality, middle-class black flight from the cities, public-housing policy and the loss of industrial jobs. As the underclass grew more entrenched, so too did a perception that those who peopled it were fundamentally different from other Americans—a universe of teenage moms, crack addicts, drop-outs and criminals.

When America was discerning the early outlines of its underclass in the 1970s, Europe had no poverty debate to speak of. There were some poor people in Europe's cities, certainly, but it was assumed they would not stay that way for very long; the welfare state, that most generous of European inventions, would help them to help themselves. Two decades on, that confidence seems tragically misplaced. Even the richest European countries are seeing new, intractable and growing problems among troubled urban populations. Hamburg, Europe's richest city measured by income per head, had by 1990 Germany's highest proportion of millionaires—and its highest proportion of people on social welfare. Unemployment was 40% higher than the national average. A third of industrial jobs had disappeared in the past 15 years.

"You could use the old Marxist concept of a *lumpenproletariat*", says Pierre Bourdieu, a professor at the Collège de France in Paris. "That describes more exactly the kind of people below the level they need to be at in order to behave rationally, to be able to master the future. The main thing is, there are many, many poor people. When you have many, you have a sort of destruction of solidarity. Nobody can help the others."

Unlike in America, where the fundamental urban tension is that of race, the fundamental tension pulling at the social fabric of Europe's cities is that caused by long-term unemployment. But the effect, in both cases, is one of polarisation and marginalisation. The question is whether Europe's cities are now in the process of producing their distinctive brand of "underclass", different in its origins from that of America but equally damning to those that it claims.

For every new job of aerobics instructor or government clerk created in Europe in the past few decades, at least one older job, probably an industrial one, has disappeared. Blue-collar workers have suffered the most. People who are unskilled, uneducated or merely thick have little chance of finding even a toehold in the workforce. Job shifts are a natural part of economic progress: no surprise that there are far fewer blacksmiths and chimney sweeps, for example, than a century ago. The disappearance of some kinds of jobs would not be an issue if new jobs were springing up to absorb those affected. The problem is they are not. More than 40% of the 17m unemployed in the European Union have been out of work for at least a year; a third have never worked at all. In the United States, which creates and destroys jobs with a verve Europe gawps at, only 11% of the unemployed have been looking for work for more than a year.

But if Europe's unemployment is not fundamentally a racial issue—the majority of poor or unemployed people in any European country are indigenous whites—minorities and first- and second-generation migrants often have a particularly tough time. Large numbers of North Africans came to France, Turks to Germany, Surinamese to Holland, Cape Verdeans to Portugal and West Indians to Britain 20 or 30 years ago to do dirty work that Europeans spurned. When those jobs disappeared in the 1980s and 1990s, they and their children were often ill-equipped to adapt.

Coming to no good

Historically, immigration has been a positive economic force around the world. America absorbed large immigrant surges in the late 19th century and in the 1980s; its wide-open economy put to good use the commitment and hard work of those who made the effort to get in. But Europe does not have the same tradition of openness and individual enterprise, and new arrivals can find these more structured societies tough to crack. Generous social benefits may also blunt the sense of urgency that drives many immigrants in America.

Over time, these later immigrants to Europe, or their children, or their children's children, will probably make themselves at home as other immigrants have done before them. But the shorter-term outlook is so troubling because economic conditions are so straitened. In the former West Berlin, the number of unemployed foreigners nearly doubled between 1989 and 1993, while the unemployment rate for ethnic Germans rose by less than a third.

Unemployment exacerbates geographical divides as easily as it does racial ones. Mr Bourdieu evokes a street in the town of St Marcellin, central France: on one side are nice little single-family dwellings where working families live, on the other are big ugly buildings into which the poorest are stuffed. He speaks of a "translation of economic division into spatial division." People on the wrong side of the line start to cut themselves off from society, sometimes in minor but telling ways. In Holland, disproportionate numbers of the long-term unem-

ployed opt for unlisted telephone numbers; in Ireland they attend church less often.

In Europe as in America, when middle-class people start deserting a district and leaving it to the poor, the process feeds on its own momentum. The only people willing to move in become those with nowhere else to go. Private commerce shrinks or retreats. Long-term unemployment and economic segregation become mutually aggravating. Theft and violence rise as frustrated youths turn to crime and drugs. Because non-working men are less marriageable, illegitimacy rates rise (see chart, next page); the proliferation of one-parent families creates a new hard core of dependency. Public order can easily become fragile. Examples of such places can be found across Europe. Many Frankfurters will name Gallusviertel and Gutleutviertel as areas to avoid; residents of Griesheim, says Michael Wegener of the University of Dortmund in a report to the European Commission, "view their neighbourhood as a ghetto—the Bronx in Frankfurt." Some taxi drivers in Manchester refuse to take fares to Moss Side, an area of high unemployment notorious nationally for its incidence of violent crime.

Overlapping concentrations of urban decay and immigrant communities also provide an easy target for racists and political extremists. In Dreux, near Paris, five youths recently fired shots at a group of North Africans. Racist political parties have struck a chord in distressed neighbourhoods in France, Belgium, Germany, Hol-

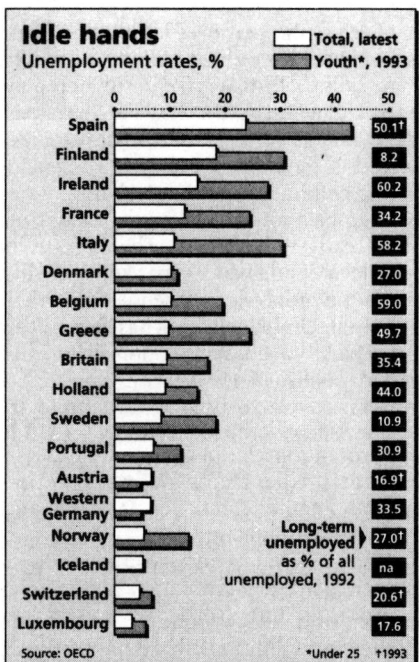

Idle hands
Unemployment rates, %

□ Total, latest
▨ Youth*, 1993

Spain	50.1†
Finland	8.2
Ireland	60.2
France	34.2
Italy	58.2
Denmark	27.0
Belgium	59.0
Greece	49.7
Britain	35.4
Holland	44.0
Sweden	10.9
Portugal	30.9
Austria	16.9†
Western Germany	33.5
Norway	27.0†
Iceland	na
Switzerland	20.6†
Luxembourg	17.6

Long-term unemployed as % of all unemployed, 1992

Source: OECD

*Under 25 †1993

land, Italy and Britain. The technique is simple: blame foreigners (preferably non-white ones) for economic problems, call for them to be kicked out, and collect the votes. In Sossenheim in western Frankfurt, ex-

tremist parties won 20% of the vote, the highest in the city. They have made similar breakthroughs in Rotterdam's Nieuwe Westen and in the East End of London.

A theory of relativity

Still, in important ways, Europe's poor are better off than America's. In the American perception, the underclass is threatening because those who compose it are believed to be different—a perception often reinforced by racial prejudice. Europe has managed to avoid this extreme degree of marginalisation, although there are hints of it in some British political attitudes and in the way some of France's wilder banlieusards are regarded. The continuing willingness of the mainstream of society to go on identifying with its poorest members (and vice-versa), and the preservation of a generally superior physical environment, is still sufficient to deny Europe anything classifiable as a full-blown underclass.

Europe's poor are less segregated than America's; their streets are cleaner and safer; and they are more likely to have access to medical care. Schools do not have gun detectors. In Wilhelmsburg, one of the poorest parts of Hamburg, there are boutiques, banks and grocery shops, even a travel agency and a Mormon church—the sort of institutions that have trouble keeping a foothold in America's ghettos. Public telephones work, and the modest three-storey brick council flats are in good shape. Even the dodgier bits of Manchester, London or Brussels look positively serene compared with America's urban war zones.

In another contrast with America, the living standards of Europe's poor have risen in absolute terms over the past couple of decades, even if differentials with those of Europe's rich have widened. The Policy Studies Institute, an independent British think-tank, found that infant mortality rates declined throughout Britain between 1977 and 1990 because people were generally better off, better fed and better cared-for*. Older Germans can remember being rationed to 700 calories a day after the war. Today, 96% of German households dependent on social-welfare benefits have a colour television, 89% have a washing machine and 52% have a car.

The reassurance communicated by such statistics may be misleading, however. Colour televisions cannot make people feel useful, or feel that they matter to the community in which they live; and these are the fault-lines along which Europe's social foundation is cracking. "I now hear constantly the question: Are we going to become like Los Angeles?" says Michael Parkinson of the European Institute for Urban Affairs at John Moores University in Liver-

....
* "Urban Trends 1". Edited by Peter Wilmott and Robert Hutchison. Policy Studies Institute, London, 1992

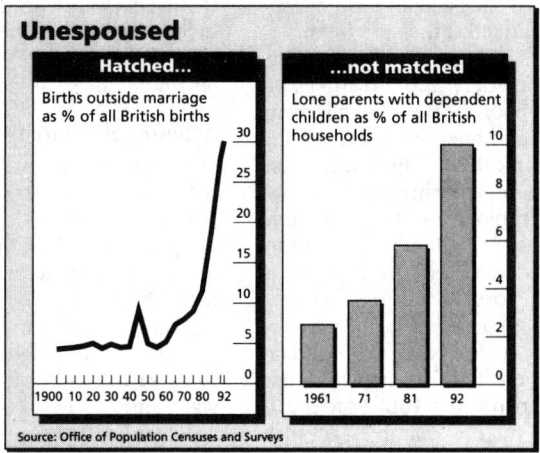

Unespoused

Hatched...

Births outside marriage
as % of all British births

1900 10 20 30 40 50 60 70 80 92

...not matched

Lone parents with dependent
children as % of all British
households

1961 71 81 92

Source: Office of Population Censuses and Surveys

pool. "Crime, drugs, poverty, unemployment, social exclusion, segregation ... People are beginning to raise the spectre of the ghetto in the [American] sense."

Many of Europe's young adults may never work, or work only occasionally, and are going to pass their frustration and isolation on to their children. Even when Europe's economies are doing as well as most were in the late 1980s, they have ceased to create the kinds of jobs needed to absorb the long-term unemployed. "Roughly, until the 1970s, the expansion of the economy translated into improvements at the bottom of the class structure," says Loïc Wacquant, a scholar at the Russell Sage Foundation, a New York think-tank, who has compared urban poverty in the United States and Europe. "Now when the economy goes into a downward spiral, neighbourhoods of exclusion get worse. But when it goes into an upward progression, they don't join in."

A system stalled

An absence of work promotes a growth in dependency among those who lose the energy to keep plugging away for an opening or for a chance to upgrade their skills. But there is, too, a kind of considered, calculated dependency practised by those who devote their energies to "working the system" as an end in itself. When four Dutch sociologists interviewed hundreds of people in three Dutch cities, they found that about 55% of the long-term unemployed in their sample had stopped looking for work[†]. More than half of this group had quit because they had found "other activities to give meaning to their lives: hobbies, volun-

[†] "Cultures of Unemployment: A Comparative Look at Long-Term Unemployment and Urban Poverty". By Godfried Engbersen, Kees Schuyt, Jaap Timmer and Frans Van Waarden, foreword by William Julius Wilson. Westview Press, Boulder, Colorado, and Oxford, England, 1993

tary work, studying, or working in the informal economy." Such findings seem to bear out the contention of an American sociologist, Charles Murray, that some people will, given the chance, make a rational economic choice to live on social welfare. The Dutch researchers concluded that Holland, with its generous, multifarious benefits, had produced "a group of enterprising and calculating unemployed people . . . the strategically operating welfare client." Across Europe, this kind of willful semi-poverty can be seen evolving into something entrenched, even socially acceptable. The mayor of Roubaix in northern France, for example, has complained publicly that too many residents prefer to collect their basic welfare payments rather than to seek work.

Such is the perverse destiny of a European model of a welfare state, devised in the expectation of universal full-time employment for men. The idea was that lots of people would pay into the system and far fewer would take money out of it. Most benefits would be administered through the payroll. But the balance has swung far away from those early expectations. The number of people receiving benefits has kept growing, while the proportion of people in work in European Union countries has been falling since 1960. The European Commission, in a report published last year, estimated Europe's needy at 52m poor, 17m unemployed, 3m homeless. Holland has only four full-time workers for every three people on full-time benefits. In western Germany, the number of recipients of social benefits doubled in the 1980s. "The worst scenario is people not feeling responsible for each other," says Radboud Engbersen, a social worker who lives in one of Rotterdam's poorer areas. "And yes, this is happening."

Yet, for all the evidence accumulating around them, many of Europe's academics

and politicians have still to drop the presumption that poverty and unemployment can best be addressed by, in effect, subsidising the poor and unemployed. The French prime minister, Edouard Balladur, gave a warning earlier this year of the risks of "social explosion" if France's 1.4m hard-core poor stayed that way. But the French poverty debate centres on purported solutions such as work-sharing, guaranteed incomes, liberation from employment and enhanced social benefits: ideas that are at best illusory, at worst dangerous. Europe cannot afford to spend any more than it does on welfare and other social programmes. In many instances, it cannot afford what it is spending already. In headier days Frankfurt spent 11% of its budget on culture; now it is DM8.5 billion ($5.4 billion) in debt and fighting off bankruptcy.

If Europe is to reverse the drift towards an underclass of American finality, the answer must lie in creating more jobs rather than in helping people to get by without them. Unfortunately, job-creation is something for which Europe seems to have lost the knack. The public sector, provider of millions of jobs over the past 30 years, is stretched to the limit; and the private sector seems incapable of filling the gap. As the European Commission's 1994 white paper on employment acknowledged, European industrial policy has concentrated "too much on the rents and positions established in traditional industries."

In effect, Europe has priced much of its labour force out of employment, compensating it with welfare payments. Only a thoroughgoing reversal of that strategy can do much to get Europe's unemployed off the park bench and back into work. Encouraging the kind of dynamic economy in which lots of jobs are created will mean hacking away at policies that have long operated in favour of rigid work rules, high social costs, subsidies and protectionism; and that may mean things getting worse for the poor before they can get better.

For years, Europeans sniffed at America's frisky but cruel economy. The New World opted for high risk and high reward, and left its losers to be pushed far from the economic and social mainstream. The Old World favoured a stabler, more secure economic order in which the losers would be looked after. Seen in those terms, the trade-off was a defensible one. But the terms were not what they seemed. As even prosperous cities like Hamburg, Rotterdam and Paris can testify, the European model has proved insecure and unsustainable. In Europe, too, there are millions in danger of slipping beyond the point of no return.

Inequalities in Europe: Affirmative Laissez Faire

Richard W. Stevenson

LONDON, Nov. 25—As a Nigerian-born chef working in Britain, Richard Olufeko has encountered plenty of workplace discrimination, including being demoted and then dismissed two years ago from a London restaurant in what a Government equal-opportunity board later ruled was an act of blatant racism.

But when it comes to redressing discrimination, Mr. Olufeko is wary of American-style affirmative action plans, where jobs can be seen to go to people because of their race or sex. Although he has some reservations, he broadly supports Britain's system, which outlaws employment discrimination generally, but bars the use of quotas or any preference programs to help end bias in hiring and promotion.

"It's important to have a certain number of black people in a workplace to provide representation and encouragement," Mr. Olufeko said. "But we have to be careful here. When you try to force people to do something, it often backfires."

Affirmative action is not yet as hotly debated in Europe as it is in the United States. But as their populations become more racially and ethnically diverse, and as women demand greater economic opportunities, many European countries are being forced to deal more directly with employment discrimination.

And while they are still grappling with how to address the issue, there is a growing consensus among governments, employers, unions and groups representing minorities and women that the American model of aggressive affirmative action creates more problems than it solves.

The European approach, which has generally involved governments' financing training programs, encouraging employers to step up recruitment and taking legal action in discrimination cases, has yielded some successes. The successes have come mostly in increasing the proportion of women hired by national and local governments. But progress in changing employment patterns in corporate Europe has been much slower, and little effort has been directed at increasing minority opportunities in either the public or private sector.

"The mentality is such that if you want to make progress toward equality you have to adopt means that are acceptable to people," said Catherine Comtet-Simpson, a lawyer with the International Labor Organization in Geneva. "If you engage in discrimination to find remedies to discrimination, it would not be accepted. In the U.S. it was accepted, and perhaps it went too far."

People who study employment discrimination say that women in Europe are badly underrepresented outside of traditional female jobs like those of cashier, nurse and teacher, and that the underrepresentation is particularly acute in the upper ranks of big corporations.

Women in Europe are also paid substantially less on the average than men for the same work. The International Labor Organization said the disparity ranges from 20 percent to 50 percent depending on job category and country. In France the average differential is 30 percent, the group said.

About 85 percent of the 53,000 employees of Marks & Spencer, the British retailer, are women. But none of the company's top 17 executives and only two of its 32 divisional directors are women. The company said the proportion of women in its senior executive ranks is increasing.

In Britain, men and women from racial and ethnic minorities are twice as likely as white people to be unemployed, although officials said job discrimination is just one reason for the disparity. In London, where members of minority groups constitute roughly 20 percent of the population, the Metropolitan Police force is 97.3 percent white, although the department said applications from nonwhites are increasing as it steps up recruitment efforts.

Even where Europe does have programs that give preference to women and minorities, they are coming under intense legal scrutiny.

In October the European Court of Justice, which applies the legal directives adopted by the European

Union to cases in the member nations, struck down a program in the German city of Bremen that required municipal agencies to give preference to women over men in job categories where women were underrepresented, assuming the women had at least equal qualifications.

Even the victims of discrimination are reluctant to adopt American policies.

The court held that the program violated a 1976 European Union directive that requires equal treatment for men and women in employment, even though the directive provided for exceptions in cases where a measure was intended to remove existing inequalities.

In its ruling, the court said, "Rules which guarantee women absolute and unconditional priority for appointment or promotion go beyond promoting equal opportunities and overstep the limits of the exception."

Lawyers and government officials said it was still unclear how broad a precedent the ruling set.

But people who study employment discrimination in Europe said the ruling fits into what has become the predominant approach to the issue.

European labor experts said there are many differences between discrimination problems in Europe and those in the United States. For one thing, affirmative action programs in the United States were developed largely in response to longstanding patterns of discrimination against a large black population. In European nations other than Britain, the issue has so far been framed primarily in terms of sex, in part because minority populations are relatively small.

Most European countries have outlawed employment discrimination on the basis of sex, but only Britain has a statute extending equal opportunity to race. Even in Britain, however, employers are not required to monitor the racial composition of their work forces. Most employers believe that asking job applicants or employees their race could be construed as discriminatory.

For the most part, efforts in Europe to bring equal opportunity to private industry center on providing education and training programs to women and minorities to help them compete for jobs. In many countries, government has taken more of an advocacy role when it comes to filling jobs in the public sector, often through programs intended to recruit more women.

In the Netherlands, Ms. Comtet-Simpson said, a government program raised the number of women in certain categories of civil service positions to more than 25 percent in 1994, from about 1.3 percent in 1990, although there was little change in the higher-ranking positions.

The European systems generally allow a job-seeker to bring legal action against employers when he or she feels that a job or promotion has been denied because of discrimination. In the last several years the penalties that can be levied on employers who are found to have discriminated have been increased, giving the laws some financial bite for the first time.

In Germany, a 1980 anti-discrimination law limited financial compensation so strictly that it became known as the stamp law, because the biggest awards available to women barely covered the cost of mailing the necessary documents.

The legislation was changed in 1985 to allow maximum compensation of one month's pay. Last year the limit was increased to three months' pay, said Peter Hanau, director of the Research Institute for Social Law at the University of Cologne.

Even with the increased compensation, relatively few women take legal action because it is so hard to prove discrimination, Mr. Hanau said.

Indeed, even while they shy away from quotas, strict monitoring and other features of American affirmative action programs, Europeans involved in the field acknowledge that their less aggressive and less confrontational approach is working much more slowly.

"The evidence indicates slow progress, but it has to be seen in the context of what is happening overall in society," said Herman Ouseley, the chairman of Britain's Commission for Racial Equality.

"While it is painfully slow and allows discrimination to continue, we are able to move race relations in a more productive way than in the States," he said.

Experts said that in the current climate in Western Europe it would be hard to generate additional support for programs to promote the hiring of more women and minorities—much less to impose job quotas or other preference programs. Unemployment is stubbornly high. And immigration is on the rise in France and Germany, among other countries, bringing growing support for right-wing nationalist political parties.

Poland: back to the future.

Ex-coms

Anne Applebaum

ANNE APPLEBAUM's book, *Between East and West: Across the Borderlands of Europe* (Pantheon), was published in 1994.

The last time I saw Alexander Kwasniewski, it was late in the summer of 1989, and he was hanging around the press gallery of the Polish Parliament. It was an auspicious day: Tadeusz Mazowiecki, Poland's first modern, non-communist prime minister, was due to make his inaugural speech. There were lots of foreign reporters about and lots of Polish journalists, too, along with lots and lots of television cameras. But not one of the latter was pointed in Kwasniewski's direction.

"Morose" is not exactly the right word to describe the mood of the man who was, at the time, Minister of Youth and Sport in the last Communist government; "remorseful" doesn't exactly capture it, either. It was more a combination of the two, with a soupçon of self-pity thrown in the mix. Alexander Kwasniewski had always prided himself on being the most reform-minded of communists; he counted among his friends many leading dissidents, including Adam Michnik, the polemicist and publisher. Now, however, all of those hours wasted at leaden Politburo meetings, all of that time spent buttering up boring Central Committee members and all of those years of hacking in the communist student unions (Kwasniewski never actually graduated from university; he lied about this on his electoral application forms) seemed to have been wasted. Mazowiecki had not asked him to join the new Solidarity-led government, and a gloomy Kwasniewski thought that his carefully cultivated political career had finally come to an end.

Only six years have passed since that day—but they have been six good years for Alexander Kwasniewski. In what must count as one of the great political comebacks in recent Polish history, Kwasniewski was elected president of Poland last weekend, defeating the incumbent, Lech Walesa—Solidarity hero, Nobel Prize winner, household name—by a narrow, but decisive, 4 percent margin.

No doubt many will now describe Kwasniewski's victory purely as a rejection of "harsh" economic reform: at least two news broadcasts that I heard within a few hours of the election used that expression. And certainly it is true that some of his supporters are among the approximately one-quarter to one-third of Poles who have not managed to succeed in what is now, in fact, the fastest-growing economy in Europe. A few are probably pensioners, and others feel nostalgic. Some of the unemployed long for the certainties of the past and believe that Kwasniewski will bring them back.

It is equally worth noting that Kwasniewski's victory resulted, in large part, from the failure of his opponents. Lech Walesa, who surrounded himself with an absurd collection of fools, flattering courtiers and former chauffeurs, proved an unpredictable and ineffective president; the former dissident intellectuals, who should have become the core members of the new democratic political system, have spent the past six years squabbling with one another. They can also be blamed for failing to remove the privileges and perks of the former communists when they could have done so. Girding themselves up to fight a "nationalist" right-wing threat that never emerged, many failed to perceive the resurgence of the left-wing threat happening under their noses.

But what is more important about Kwasniewski's victory—and what many in the West still don't seem to understand about former communists—is that in most countries they no longer represent the past. They represent the capitalist future; in fact, they *are* the capitalist future, however corrupt, kleptocratic and unfair that future may be. For the most part, in fact, I believe that

Poles voted for Kwasniewski because since 1989, he, like other former communists in Central Europe, has come to represent success: he has become prosperous, his friends are prosperous, he promises to make other people prosperous, too.

There is no mystery about how this transformation in image was effected. In the past six years, Alexander Kwasniewski has lost weight, stopped drinking, taught himself to speak good English. He has familiarized himself with the concepts of "NATO" and "European Community." He has even dutifully toured Western capitals, making appearances at the offices of *The Wall Street Journal* and the Royal Institute for International Affairs in London, impressing audiences in a way that Walesa, who is rumored never to have read a book, could not.

Since 1989, Kwasniewski has also managed, one way or another, to enrich himself. During the election campaign, for example, it emerged that his wife owns, among other things, about $65,000 (quite a lot in Polish terms) worth of shares in an insurance company, which had been "privatized" a few years earlier. Although most of the company's shares are publicly traded, it seems that a few people were given the privilege of buying them privately, at an unknown rate. According to one Polish newspaper, another $100,000 worth are owned by the wife of the Polish prime minister; either shareholders include two former communist deputy prime ministers, as well as a former communist finance minister and a former Communist Party first secretary. Curiously, the new Polish president failed to declare his wife's interest in the company in his parliamentary register of holdings, not that that prevented him from winning.

In doing all of these things, however, Kwasniewski has behaved no differently from other former communists in Poland; indeed, he has behaved no differently from other former communists anywhere in Eastern Europe. Marxist-Leninism is dead, but the social structure it created is not. Far from being eliminated by the onset of democracy and capitalism in 1989, former communists have been by far the biggest beneficiaries. One Polish sociologist tracked the careers of several hundred top nomenklatura—officials in the government and the bureaucracy—from 1988 to 1993. He discovered that over half of the Poles had become top executives in the private sector, and in Hungary the number was about 60 percent. As heads of factories, banks and government bureaucracies, they were in the best position to take advantage of privatization. As owners of houses and cars and secret bank accounts—again, those privileges and perks which remained in place—they were in a better position to find jobs when they lost their old ones.

Most of all, former communists have been the primary beneficiaries of what Poles call the "concessionary capitalist" economy: that part of the private sector, enormous in Central Europe (as it is in some Western European countries) which still, in one way or another, lives off state subsidies, state contracts, state largess. Former communists who bought shares through corrupt deals—and Mrs. Kwasniewski is not the only one—are concessionary capitalists. Friends of the old regime who can start companies with soft loans guaranteed by the government are also concessionary capitalists. Those who have quicker and easier access to licenses because of their friends in the mayor's office are concessionary capitalists, too.

It is fair to say, in fact, that most concessionary capitalists came legally into their riches through so-called "nomenklatura privatization," a process which gave, or sold for a nominal sum, state property to its current managers. While this can be a legitimate process—management buyouts happen in the West, too—in the former Eastern bloc, where there is very little public accountability, they are not always ideal. I once came across an astonishing example of this process in Lviv, in western Ukraine, where an electronics company—really a conglomerate including thirty-nine subsidiaries, twenty-two daughter companies and nine joint ventures—called Elektron was being privatized by "selling shares." Just like the West—except that the company was valued according to the cost of its buildings (under $18 million at the exchange rates of the time) and managers were using company profits to "buy" their own shares. Even after privatization, one of them told me, Elektron would still have the same privileged access to raw materials—subsidized by the government—as other state companies.

All of this meant that, while the Communist Party might have dissolved, the old boys' network attached to it remained in place. Most party members never mattered much and don't now, but the inner core—perhaps 100,000 people—still have, as they have always had, a strong sense of identity, not unlike the class identity of, say, the British aristocracy. They have been to the same schools, the same universities, the same higher institutes of Marxist-Leninism; they recognize one another, as does any ruling class in any country, through dress, accent, mutual friends and manner of speech. They help one another to find jobs, obtain state subsidies and get bank loans. In most countries, former communist politicians have better contacts with the media, especially the regional media. They know what party organizations are for; most of all, they have supporters who will pour money into their party coffers.

Hardly surprising, then, that they seem wealthier, better organized and more experienced than their opponents. Hardly surprising that Kwasniewski's advertising was sleeker, his campaign better financed, his wife better dressed. Kwasniewski had the funds to spend last summer traveling around the country, visiting small towns and cities, making speeches everywhere he went; no other political candidate, with the exception of Walesa, who was presumably too arrogant, could possibly have afforded to do that.

And, again not surprisingly, Kwasniewski seemed the candidate more likely to build upon Poland's substantial economic achievements. When the former Communist Party came back to power in Hungary last year, it turned out that over 60 percent of people who described their occupation as "businessman" had voted for it—not what one would expect if one still thought that the words "former communist" and "capitalist" were somehow contradictory. The numbers are no doubt similar in Poland; the statistics show that Kwasniewski's electorate is certainly younger and wealthier than Walesa's in any case. One can call him a sleazy opportunist, but it doesn't matter: Kwasniewski succeeded in post-communist Poland in the way that many people would like to succeed in post-communist Poland. This is not an American economy, where anybody, at least in theory, can succeed if they work hard: sleaze and opportunism are the paths to Polish success.

What this election really proves, in fact, is not that Poland has rejected the legacy of Solidarity, or that Poles long for bread queues and censorship, but that Poland is finally—at last—becoming a normal country. As in a normal country, the more telegenic candidate won. As in a normal country, the candidate with the most money won. As in a normal country, the candidate who kept talking about the past emerged the loser; Walesa's attacks on Kwasniewski, mostly focused on his communist career, were not powerful enough to sway even an essentially anti-communist country like Poland. As in a normal country, the winning candidate is a super-professional political operator, with a handful of shady friends and the odd hidden business deal kicking around in the background. Perhaps we should not have expected any less.

The Return of the Habsburgs

The countries of Central Europe, unavoidably detained a while, are clamouring to join the European Union. When they do, it will be a homecoming, says David Lawday.

The Economist

The railway stations, you soon notice, are invariably yellow. The opera houses are all built by the same pair of architects. In cafes, the day's papers from far and wide hang on the wall with wooden slats up their middle. If you are lucky enough to receive flowers, count them and you are likely to find 11 or 13, not a round dozen. Central Europe has a certain harmony that goes deeper than the dilapidation bequeathed by communist times; deeper even than anguish over what Russia will get up to next. Yet it derives from something that Central Europeans seem curiously reluctant to recognize: theirs are the lands of the old Habsburg empire. Now those Central Europeans stand at the head of a queue of former eastern block nations that want to join the European Union. To be sure they owe this front place to their own brave efforts at economic renewal. They also owe it to pedigree.

They are the Hungarians, the Czechs, the Slovaks, the Slovenes and, particularly, the Poles, more numerous than the others put together. Grant generous historical license in the Poles' case. Only a quarter or so of modern Poland was part of the Habsburg monarchy's Austro-Hungarian realm that disappeared from the map in 1918. With that proviso, the Central European nations hold common credentials for entering the EU: they will be not so much joining Western Europe as coming home to it.

Bronislaw Geremek, an early hero of Poland's Solidarity movement, traces their western roots 100 years back—to a time when medieval German Kings launched the Holy Roman Empire (headed, in due course, by the Habsburgs) and set about Christianising nearby Slavs by the sword. Those Slavs and the Hungarians went into the Roman Catholic church; Slavs to the east of them landed in the Orthodox church. This is the line between the western traditions of Rome and the eastern traditions of Byzantium.

Today's Central Europeans are very precise about where the boundaries lie. They object to the title "East Europeans," which they bore through the Cold War. Eastern Europe, they say, lies to their east. It is Russia, Ukraine, Romania, and Bulgaria that look to the Black Sea. The Central Europeans look to the Mediterranean or to northern waters, at a pinch to the Atlantic. Some talk, rather less precisely, of the "vodka line," separating beer and wine drinkers in Central Europe from those who prefer harder stuff further east; or of the "secret police line," separating those who fully dismantled their old security services when communism collapsed in 1990 from those who did rather less.

Through Renaissance, Enlightenment, and balance-of-power wars, Central Europeans have undergone the western experience. The administrative and education systems they have today are rooted in Habsburg tradition. That is what still strikes Otto von Habsburg, heir to a vanished realm to which he has given up all claim. Mr. von Habsburg, a German member of the European Parliament, instead works hard pressing the Central Europeans' claim to membership of the EU. His family's aura still has some of its glow. He spends a lot of time in Central Europe these days, having been banned under communism, and there is not a taxi driver who will not wave aside his money when he tries to pay his fare.

Joze Mencinger, who was economics minister of Slovenia when it broke free from chaotic Yugoslavia, is convinced that if Central Europe is now in better shape than its neighbours to the east, it is because it was helped through the communist period by whatever remained of Habsburg method, whereas East Europeans were left to their own devices. "That is the sole reason I can find for the difference," Mr. Mencinger concludes.

As Central Europe turns west again, it is already beginning to look the part it wants to play. Its great cities, starting with Prague and Budapest, feel western once more. But stop for a moment. The Habsburg spirit was as quarrelsome as it was liberal; and quarrelsomeness is the trait most common to Central Europeans as they elbow their way to their western destination. Instead of co-operating with each other, they compete. Harmony is not helped by mutual distrust left behind by Comecon, the former Soviet trading block. They squabble as they chase exports to the EU to earn hard currency, and as they compete for foreign investment.

The Czech Republic, top of the economic class, can hardly resist showing off. Unlike its rivals, it has so far made a point of not formally requesting membership of the EU (a conceit it plans to drop before the year is out). It irritates its neighbors by frequently pointing out that its capital, Prague, lies west of Vienna. Hungary, the best performer in the years immediately following the fall of communism, and still the strongest magnet for foreign investors, wants the EU to admit candidates on individual merits, not as a group. Quirky Slovakia, anxious to assert its identity, annoys the Czech Republic by reinterpreting customs

Austro-Hungarian empire in 1914
00.0 Population, million, 1993
0   Km   200
Source: World Bank

IMPERIAL HANDFUL

THE man who gave the Habsburg empire its identity in its later stages was Emperor Franz Joseph, who reigned from 1848 to 1916. Patriarchal yet liberal, this monarch managed to retain the affections of Central Europeans beyond the grave and to this day. He did not live to see his empire expire, predeceasing it by a couple of years. At the time it all came to an end in 1918, his successor, Charles I, bore the following string of titles:

"Emperor of Austria and King of Hungary; King of Bohemia, Dalmatia, Croatia, Slavonia, Galicia, Lodomeria and Illyria; King of Jerusalem, Grand Duke of Tuscany and Cracow; Duke of Lorraine, of Salzburg, Steyr, Carinthia, Krain and Bukovina; Grand Prince of Siebenburgen; Margrave of Moravia; Duke of Upper and Lower Silesia, of Modena, Parma, Piacenza, of Auschwitz and Zator, of Friuli, Ragusa and Zara; Count of Habsburg and Tyrol, of Kyburg, Gorizia and Gradisca; Prince of Trento and Bressanone; Margrave of Upper and Lower Lusatia, and of Istria; Count of Bregenz; Lord of Trieste; Grand Voivod of the Voivodinate of Serbia etc., etc."

(from "Requiem Pour Un Empire Defunt", by Francois Fejto) ❑

agreements they made when separating in 1993. Little Slovenia, having divorced itself from its erratic Balkan neighbors, is now involved in a spat with Italy going straight back to Habsburg times. Giant Poland, facing one of the largest tasks of economic renewal, thinks all the applicants should enter Europe at the same time. Yet the co-operation it favors seems to go no further than freer trade among Central Europeans. Since their mutual trade is dwarfed by their vastly increased trade with Europe, that adds up to very little.

ALL INDIVIDUALISTS NOW

Central Europeans simply do not want to be regarded as a block any more. They have quietly dropped the name "Visegrad group," the title that stuck to four of them after their leaders got together in 1991 in Visegrad, Hungary, to consider life after communism. Membership of Comecon and of the Warsaw Pact, its military counterpart, has made them sick of working in political harness. Besides, they now fear that if they were to show up in Brussels as a political team, Europe might tell them that they had no pressing need to join the union. So they will not publicly admit to aiming for simultaneous entry (although privately they will admit that this is the likely outcome).

Helmut Kohl, the German chancellor, has promised Poland that it will be in the EU—and, for that matter, NATO, too, before the decade is out. Mr. Kohl has strong German reasons for promoting Polish membership, but he would not expose himself to charges of favoritism by backing Poland alone. His promise can be taken to extend to Central Europe as a whole. Just bluster? After all, no westerner would seriously propose extending the EU eastwards purely for economic benefit. With almost 70 million people, ex-communist Central Europe is an inviting new market, but a poor one: living standards are a third of the EU's average.

Granted, no one who has recently been to lively Budapest would give credence to statistics suggesting that life in Hungary is five times humbler than life in Austria, a boat ride up the Danube. But the statistics cannot be ignored. Central Europe is strapped for cash; few of the various, sometimes ingenious, schemes used to privatize its economies have been accomplished with real money. And bureaucratic torpor, a chronic ailment left over from communist times, contrives to put off would-be investors. As in Russia, from which most of Central Europe is desperate to dissociate itself, red tape puts a brake on almost everything.

COUNT TO THREE

Bringing Central Europe into the EU is essentially a political decision. Put aside miserly debate about the cost; consider the political imperatives. The European club requires members to meet three basic conditions: they must be European; they must be market-oriented; and they must be democratic. Thanks to geography, the new Central Europe has always met the first condition; it now meets the second; and, for the moment, its problems with the third are confined to a few areas of doubt. On the other hand the region is congenitally jittery, and during this century in particular its genius has been spent on sheer survival. The last thing the EU needs is an unhinged neighbor at its side. The stability and peace of mind which Central Europe hopes to secure by rejoining Western Europe surely promises as much benefit to those opening the door as to those coming through it.

There are those in Brussels who claim that all the countries formerly under Soviet sway in Europe are in the same boat; and certainly the EU has no business discouraging easterners or indulging in favoritism.

But enlargement to the east has to start somewhere, and to maintain that there are no differences is hypocritical. The Baltic states, for all the economic progress they have made, still carry heavy baggage from their spell within the Soviet Union, including large Russian minorities. Romania and Bulgaria remain economically backward, as does Ukraine. Their time may come, but this survey will argue that for now the EU should concentrate on admitting the five states of Central Europe. They have a coherence which qualifies them for speedy integration. Since the decision to let them in is essentially political, not economic, there is no merit in delay: they should be in by the end of the decade.

The growing temptation in Brussels to seek an accountant's solution and send them off with partial membership at the lowest possible cost should be resisted. The Central Europeans will put up with all manner of transitional arrangements as long as it does not water down membership to the point where they feel it is no longer the real thing. Their simultaneous quest for membership of NATO, this survey will also argue, stands to create deeper insecurity even than the kind they suffer from now. Their priority must be integration with Western Europe to provide them with a better way of life and higher living standards. Membership of the EU is the basis of the kind of society they are already turning into.

◆—◆—◆—◆—◆—◆—◆

Rich Man, Poor Men

All Central European roads lead to Germany

The shadow over Central Europe is not only Russia's. Germany casts a bigger one, and for once the region is happy to see it there. Austria, the Habsburg power of old, is curiously shy about championing its kin, perhaps because it is small and itself new to the European Union. The role of sponsor falls to Germany; or rather, it is assumed by Germany as a duty. However, since worries about German domination are never far from the surface in this region, Germany tactfully refers to itself as the Central Europeans' "tutor" or "advocate." In the same vein, Germans refrain from talking about *Mitteleuropa,* a handy term but one fraught with history. It harks back to a time when the German Reich made precious little distinction between its economic and its military ambitions there. It is better for Germany not to overplay its new hand. After all, everyone knows that Berlin, its reinstated capital, is part of what one might call greater Central Europe—of which Berlin will in all probability emerge as the metropolis.

There are limits to Germany's leverage today. It still has its own eastern half to

How the West was won Trade figures as % of total, 1994

Imports from: Germany / other EU — Exports to: Germany / other EU

Poland
Slovenia
Hungary
Czech Republic
Slovakia

Source: IMF

lick into capitalist shape. The former East Germany, which under communism was regarded as the most affluent in Eastern Europe, continues to have DM200 billion ($140 billion) a year of west German taxpayers' money poured into it—four times the likely annual cost to the EU of extending membership to the Central Europeans.

Clearly the new Germany has no spare cash to lavish on its eastern neighbors; nor would it ever contemplate providing support for them on anywhere near the scale it has done for eastern Germany. Just think: it has installed more new telephones in the east in three years than were plugged in there in the century from the

invention of the telephone to the demise of East Germany. No one can stop Central Europeans dreaming that EU membership will bring them living standards like Germany's and Austria's. If ownership of consumer durables and cars is any guide, some of them are already better off than the poorest EU countries. But if they want to do better still, the help they must count on, Germany tells them, is the help they can give themselves.

Yet Germany is genuinely concerned about Poland and the others, and for good reasons. Integration of the Central Europeans meets a dual need: for stability on Germany's eastern border, and for new business opportunities. These two things matter to the whole of Europe, but to Germany more than others. Chancellor Kohl is not comfortable with the idea that Germany's eastern frontiers are also the EU's eastern frontiers. The government in Bonn shrinks from talking about a buffer, but that is what Poland-in-the-EU will be for Germany.

There may, however, be more to it than that. Poles think that Mr. Kohl's willingness to bat for them reflects a deep desire to atone for the Nazi period. Germany made a point of asking for Polish "forgiveness," and got it. An agreement to fix the Oder-Neisse line as the immutable boundary between the two countries, belatedly signed in 1991, allayed the distrust between the two countries. The Poles are convinced that a united Europe has changed Germany for the better. The Czechs, who have an even longer border with Germany than does Poland, are of the same mind. To them, belonging to the same club as Germany is the best safeguard against German domination.

Germany's role as sponsor for Central Europe also arises naturally from its economic magnetism. This part of the world used to do the bulk of its trade with the communist east. In the space of five years the flow has been dramatically redirected. Well over half the region's trade is now done with Western Europe, and invariably Germany is the leading partner. Russia often comes lowish on the list, although it remains an important provider of energy. In foreign investment, too, it is most often the Germans who lead, with America and Italy in pursuit. Central European hotels can count on German businessmen to keep up their occupancy rate. At least informally, the D-mark zone has already expanded to embrace Central Europe. From Poland to Slovenia, ask

anyone what their car is worth, and the answer is likely to come in D-marks.

It may seem odd, then, that the Poles, in particular, are not opening their arms wider towards German investors. At heart they fret that, as they privatize, German capital might buy them out. German industry complains about resistance to German buyers. Not so, says the government in Warsaw: it must be red tape regrettably holding things up. "It is the same for Americans and Japanese," says Andrzej Wroblewski, editor of *Nowa Europe*, a Warsaw business newspaper, "except that there may be some patriotic Polish bureaucrats who apply more red tape to Germans than to others."

Yet at the same time Poland bemoans a disappointingly slow rate of foreign investment, in Warsaw you will be told that the $4 billion or so of foreign capital invested in Poland since it turned democratic is roughly what the Germans are spending on doing up a single street in east Berlin, Friedrichstrasse. Hungary and the Czech Republic have indeed proved more attractive to German capital than Poland, mainly because they have been politically more stable.

ENDURING MEMORIES

One relic from the past that complicates Germany's role as Central Europe's sponsor is the issue of stranded and expelled Germans: the Silesians left in Poland when that country was awarded a chunk of Hitler's Reich at the end of the Second World War, and those pushed out of the Sudetenland when the Czechs regained sovereignty after the war. Hungary, Slovakia, and Slovenia have no borders with Germany, so mercifully they have no such problems. But even though the German government would prefer to leave well alone, sensitivities in the other

two countries remain acute. In Poland, president Lech Walesa and the government are doubtful about the loyalty of more than 500,000 Poles of German extraction to whom Bonn, bound by Germany's federal constitution, will award German nationality on request. These folk live mainly in Upper Silesia near Poland's border with the Czech Republic. The idea of their having access to dual nationality does not go down well in Warsaw, despite the large sums in educational and social support that Germany pays to encourage Silesian Germans to stay in Poland.

The Sudeten Germans pose an even more difficult dilemma. At the end of the Second World War an estimated 2.5 million ethnic Germans were expelled from Czech lands. Most of them went to Bavaria, where they and their descendants continue to make loud claims on their former property. They are a pillar of support for Bavaria's ruling conservative party, which in turn is a pillar of Mr. Kohl's government, which finds itself in a fix: it cannot ignore the Sudeten Germans, but nor can it seriously demand restitution from the Czechs. The Bonn government now hopes that early EU entry for Central Europe, with the freedom of movement that eventually brings for its people, might just sort out both the Sudeten Germans and the Silesians.

Despite these problems, and despite Germany's (and everyone else's) reservations about Slovakia's fitness to enter the EU under its unpredictable prime minister, Vladimir Meciar, it is hard to avoid the impression that Germany has never enjoyed quite such good relations with all its neighbors—to east and west, to north and south—at the same time. If ever there was a time to hope that Germany will champion Europe's underdogs in a manner all Europeans can support, this is it.

A Cold-War Reality Check: Didn't Communism Die?

Dictatorship is passé in old Soviet bloc, but communist parties see resurgence

George Moffett

Staff writer of The Christian Science Monitor

WASHINGTON

Two things have been amply demonstrated in the six years that have elapsed since the collapse of the Berlin Wall: that communism is dead—and that it isn't.

It is a measure of the halting nature of the revolution that swept communist regimes from the face of Europe that, to a degree, both conclusions are valid.

"If you define communism as dictatorship, censorship, and sealed borders, then communism is dead as a door-nail," says John Micgiel, director of the Institute on East Central Europe at Columbia University, in New York. "But if you're talking about a closed system in which an economic oligarchy dominates in an undemocratic fashion, then communism is not dead."

The ambiguities were underscored most recently in Polish elections, held last month. The balloting ended the presidency of Lech Walesa, who, as head of the Solidarity trade-union movement, led the rebellion that ended communist rule in Poland six years ago.

But diplomatic analysts say the return to power of old communists—like Mr. Walesa's rival and now president-elect Alexander Kwasniewski—does not presage the return of the old communism epitomized by Lenin and Stalin.

"Even if communism comes back there will never be the same type of dictatorial rule," says Veljko Vujacic, of Harvard University's Center for International Affairs. "What is possible is not totalitarianism but other types of authoritarianism, with at least limited freedom of press and elements of democracy."

Freedom House, which annually ranks nations according to their polity, listed only five nations as "communist one-party states" at the beginning of the year: China,

North Korea, Laos, Vietnam, and Cuba. There were 18 just before the Berlin Wall fell.

Except for Yugoslavia and Belarus, all the former Soviet bloc and newly independent states of Central Europe are ranked as "formal democracies" by the New York-based human rights group, even though several—including Poland, Lithuania, and Hungary—have elected parliamentary majorities of former communists.

Experts say the communist legacy in Europe is a political culture that is hostile to the excesses that have come with sudden market reforms and that is generally supportive of strong central government that redistributes national wealth.

"There are ingrained ways of thinking that survive," says Adrian Karatnycky, president of Freedom House. In practice, communism in its post-cold-war incarnation varies widely.

In countries like Hungary, Poland, and Slovenia, neo-communists who favor a welfare state, private property, and democracy are barely distinguishable from the social democrats of Western Europe or from the so-called "new democrats" in their own countries. Leaders like Poland's Mr. Kwasniewski, who was once a Cabinet minister in a communist government, are even eager to join the NATO military alliance—an alliance conceived half a century ago to contain communism and the armies of Soviet bloc nations including Poland.

In Russia and Serbia, on the other hand, communist politicians have acquired a mixed ideology that reminds some experts of the fascism of Germany and Italy during the 1930s: a belief in continued state ownership of some industries, a cartellized bureaucratic system, and a messianic strain of nationalism.

Mr. Karatnycky notes another coincidence that dramatically distinguishes the new communists from the old: In Russia and Serbia, the nationalism of communist politicians is linked to alliance with religious groups.

One example: Russia's resurgent Communist Party, headed by Gennadi Zyuganov, stresses a kinship with Ukraine and Belarus, some of whose Orthodox churches are under the Moscow patriarchate.

"In both countries, there is a desire to recapture lost territory that frequently coincides with the reach of parishes of Russian and Serbian Orthodoxy," says Mr. Karatnycky. "Communist leaders pay homage to religious beliefs as a means of exploiting religious fervor."

Paradoxically, the return of an ex-communist in Poland will mean the opposite: looser ties between church and state. Kwasniewski has called for strict separation of church and state in the new constitution and favors liberalizing restrictions on abortion that were advocated by the Roman Catholic church and enacted after communist rule in Poland ended in 1989.

One reason communism has survived in any form is that in most of the former Soviet-bloc nations there was no formal process of de-communization comparable to the de-Nazification of Germany that took place after World War II. One consequence is that many institutions with roots in the communist system, like trade unions and sports associations, have survived.

Many former communist leaders have also survived, largely because they retained control over industries, now semiprivatized, that were once bastions of party power. They have used durable political networks to maintain positions of power.

In the Russian context, communism has retained a degree of legitimacy because it is associated with two national achievements: the Soviet Union's emergence as a world power and its resistance to fascism during World War II, which has become a central part of the nation's mythology.

Russia's thriving Communist Party has also tapped successfully into a widespread distrust of the outside world—especially the Western world—which is blamed for Russia's halting progress since the collapse of the Soviet Union.

"In Ziuganov's opinion, the current plight of Russia cannot be considered an accident, but rather the logical consequence of a long-term plan concocted by Western intelligence services to destroy the Soviet state, and carried out with the intentional or unintentional support of their Russian collaborators," notes Mr. Vujacic. Neo-communism has also been nourished by the turmoil of transition. With market reforms have come economic disruption, crime, corruption, and uncertainty that, especially among older people and pensioners, have created a longing for the stability and predictability of life under communism.

"It's the longing for security that communism brought: that you could work and expect not to have to work very hard; that at the end of two weeks you would have a paycheck; that every year you would have a vacation," says Mr. Micgiel. "Those perks are an attraction for those who have not made the adjustment" to a market economy.

"Life under communism was unpleasant but it was safe and predictable," adds Charles Fairbanks Jr., a research professor at the Johns Hopkins Foreign Policy Institute. "Now, nobody knows what will happen to them."

Even so, few who lived under communism have any illusion that the economic and political system that grew out of the Russian revolution was anything other than a failure. A Marxist-Leninist party at the top of a one-party state is now the dream only of fringe groups. More typical is Russia's Zyuganov, who is eager to renationalize some but not all of Russian industries and is a reluctant advocate of multiparty democracy, private property, and freedom of religion.

"I don't think the pendulum can swing back to communism as the sole force in Russian society," says Karatnycky. "But it may veer in a different direction, toward an ultranationalism bordering on fascism."

Seeing Red, Then and Now

Communist Countries in 1988		Communist Countries in 1995
Afghanistan	Hungary	China
Albania	Laos	Cuba
Bulgaria	Mongolia	Laos
Cambodia	North Korea	North Korea
China	Poland	Vietnam
Cuba	Romania	
Czechoslovakia	'Soviet Union	
East Germany	Vietnam	
Ethiopia	Yugoslavia	

Source: Freedom House

The Reform of Russia: For Worse, for Better

John Lloyd, the FT's Moscow correspondent for five years, reported the collapse of the Soviet era and the start of reforms which left the Russian people freer but poorer. Now, with Chechnya in flames, the economy stumbling, corruption rife and fears of a communist victory in June's presidential election, he assesses the former superpower's prospects as it struggles to escape its past.

Thirteen months have passed since President Boris Yeltsin sent the Russian army to crush a three-year rebellion in the southern republic of Chechnya, a rebellion by a gangster regime which no civilised state could tolerate. Now, the uncivilised methods used in the effort to suppress it, and a mixture of incompetence and division over policy in Moscow, have turned the Chechen crisis into a crisis for Russia.

It is a tragedy for the Chechens. And it is a tragedy for the Russians, and it may yet be a crisis for the remaining hopes for reform. The confrontation has driven to the right a government and president already forced to bend before the voters' harsh judgment last month.

Now, poised between the swing to communists and nationalists in the December parliamentary elections and the very large stakes looming in the June presidential elections, it is urgent that we clarify what we think of the state of Russia. And that can only start with the recognition that so much has changed for the better in the past decade.

A simple test: is it now likely that Russian authorities would jail a man who calls for democratic reforms? That they would punish nations which gave sanctuary to one of their critics?

These expressions fit authoritarian states such as China, Saudi Arabia and Nigeria. Russia is not of their number—though it *was* within the past ten years, and gave succour and a political and moral rationale to many who acted likewise. If its rulers do not wholly trust their citizens, at least they have been

constrained, or have persuaded themselves, to treat them as citizens, as people with a potential stake in a potential society.

More than 40 parties sought, last month, to win seats in a 450-member parliament. Too many for sensible political choice? Yes, for those who are used to choosing between two or three leviathans slugging it out for the centre ground. But a democrat cannot much object a choice covering a spectrum from anarchist and Stalinist left, to authoritarian and liberal right. Dozens of newspapers and magazines propagandise and exhort every day—too many for rational analysis of the issues? Yes, for those accustomed to a judicious and commercially constrained press, but a pluralist can see little wrong in such a marketplace of views and voices. Neither the party system, nor the press, lacks problems and failings; but neither is under threat of extinction, or even of substantial curtailment.

Talking and writing are no longer dangerous pursuits. Travel is limited by the purse, not by the police. The transmission of information is limited by habit, not (usually) by decree. A host of taboo issues have been opened to public debate: the death penalty, the treatment of women, rights of homosexuals, care of the mentally sick, the need for national service and the persistence of racism. By liberal standards, the situation in all of these is worse than in the rich states. But that is more often because Russia is relatively poor than because it is politically totalitarian.

The economy will, this year, probably grow. It has a long way to grow before it recovers the losses of the horrible years from

1989, when it began (officially) to go into rapid fall. In 1992, the economy contracted by 19 per cent and by another 12 per cent in 1993, according to the OECD. The fall has not been as devastating as the figures suggest, nor the decline of living standards as catastrophic. But there is no doubt that there has been shock and a prolonged sense of misery. Yet, from this year, barring political adventurism or unforeseeable disasters, there should be a little, then an accelerating, sense of betterment. The government has not relaxed its rigorous monetary policy in order to tempt the voters to elect the liberals. Inflation, 3.2 per cent last month, remains lower than it has been since serious reforms began four years ago. Trade remains comfortably in surplus. The central bank is no longer pursuing a course opposite to that of the finance and economic ministries. All's well with the world? Of course not. But it is no longer all wrong.

Four years of a liberal, if erratic, economic policy have allowed a class of business people—already visible in the Gorbachev years, and encouraged even then—to become part of the landscape. They are mostly unlovely: grasping, conspicuous, surrounded by muscle and weaponry, their business practices unethical by the most lax of standards and their relationships with government officials necessarily corrupt. But they are increasingly obliged to come to grips with both the domestic and international market, in which demand and choice play larger parts of their daily calculations and strategies. The era of primitive acquisition is not yet over, but it begins to give

---

Russia's citizens have the problem of finding a place in a state which no longer pays them the supreme compliment of fearing and suppressing them when they try to tell the truth.

---

way to a period in which corporate governance, the need to invest and the development of stable institutions and regulations are recognised as the next challenges.

The great motors of mass consumption and the mass media, which churn over a widening range of the world's societies, fragmenting and reassembling them ceaselessly and feverishly, are beginning to work in Russia. It is neither a consumer society nor a society overwhelmed by media hype, but these germs have entered the social body, and will not be easily countered. Such societies do not resolve all tensions. On the contrary, they create new fields of conflict which shape their politics and economic character. But they tend, over time, to be hostile to wars and the mobilisation of aggression.

It is true that those who scorn the new Russia—including the communists and nationalists who did well at the polls last month—have many good tunes to play. Russia is a very reduced power, as the agony of its engagement in Chechnya makes clear. But in being confined to cramped borders, cut off from large stretches of the Baltic and the Black Seas, unbuffered by allies in

central Europe, it has been required to come to terms with its own and others' national identities in ways it never bothered to do before. It is one thing to claim, as many Russians do, that it is absurd that Ukraine and Belarus are separate nations, and that the 25m Russians living outside of the new Russia's borders should still be citizens. It is another to think of something to do about it which is not self-defeating. The members of the Commonwealth of Independent States are artificial nations, say the Russian nationalists: but which nation is not an artifice, with some merely more time-hallowed than others?

Living within its borders, defining itself, is the task before Russia. The great stream of Russia's culture was partly destroyed (especially its religion), partly co-opted, by the communists. Where co-opted, the communists successfully remoulded the institutions and traditions to conform with their ideological preferences. They preserved and even enhanced the arts, so that ballet and musical performance in particular remained pre-eminent; they encouraged the natural sciences, and created world class nuclear physicists and mathematicians; they promoted and funded sport so that Russians were always among the fastest, or most graceful, or most competitive in the world. The vigour and longevity of totalitarian rule produced responses of outstanding courage and clarity: the suffering beauty of poet Anna Akhmatova, for instance, the stubborn bearing of witness of Alexander Solzhenitsyn, the patient and engaged humanism of Andrei Sakharov—and the bravery and fidelity of millions less famed, whose memory these three and others, in their different ways, preserved as moral examples to all.

Of course, the stakes seem less heroic now, both in the old, building-of-socialism sense and in the opposition to it. They are humanized. No place any more for the prophet, secular or holy, whose example and faith are required to lighten the darkness. New generations see no sense in such heroics: those in their teens, even in their twenties, have dimmed memories of a totalitarian state, much dimmer than their sharp desire for an Italian bedroom suite or a CD-ROM. Artists, writers and artists of the older generations regret the good old days when there was a common warm feeling of being opposed to and superior to the System: they now feel lost without it. But their successors have the task of engaging with a society not of stereotypes (either communist or anti-communist) but of human and social fragments. They have in common with their counterparts abroad the problem of finding a place in a state which no longer pays them the supreme compliment of fearing and suppressing them when they try to tell the truth. No longer obliged to support the myth if obedient, or to oppose it if dissident, they must simply come to terms with what they understand to be reality.

But the question must be: is reality too much for Russia? It is so much better now by western standards, and by those of a minority of the Russian population. The advances in human rights and freedoms; the development of democratic and market institutions; the freedom of speech. All of these are either reviled as shams by the resurgent political forces and parties, or held on an increasingly tight leash by a presidential administration more ambiguous about its aims and purposes than it has been since 1991.

The old Russia did live by myths, much more so than most nations. The gap between the myth and reality became too wide for the weakening forces of repression to close—and the system collapsed. But the reality which has resulted is terribly harsh. Harsh in a physical sense, but also in a psychological one. It is, apparently, the psychological hardship of coping with a disorienting post-Soviet universe which has reduced the average male mortality age to 59 (compared to 74 in Britain).

Much of the past four years of economic change had been preparation for large tasks just begun. Though unemployment is rising, rapidly in some areas, it is still below west European levels, but won't be for long. Huge plants have yet to shed workers, though they have shed work. Whole cities in the far north, sustained as in the past by large subsidies, have little work for their citizens and are populated only because their inhabitants have nowhere else to go. Management, many with virtual title to the plants through privatisation programmes, have done little to change their practices and products. And the institutional investors, mainly the banks, have yet to face up to the challenge of forcing them to change. The trade balance is healthy because oil and gas still make up the bulk (41 percent) of exports and little of the capital equipment which would be required for a sustained recovery is being imported. But oil production continues to fall, while investment in that sector is still far too small to reverse the trend. Foreign investors would like to be part of that, but continue to be rebuffed. The paltry amounts they have put into a giant economy show they are preoccupied by the uncertainties in the law, taxes and government.

Even the largest achievement is a danger. The reformers still in government point to the macroeconomic successes. Reformers out of government agonise that the cuts they have made to public spending to bring down the budget deficit to International Monetary Fund-approved levels will degrade the health and education services and the public infrastructure to levels from which it will be very hard to recover. One of the largest drains of public money is agriculture. Despite four years of radical reform, the land is still farmed in the same wasteful, slovenly way it has been for decades, while pioneering private farmers, those who have survived, find it harder to preserve their smallholdings from the surrounding hostility of collectivised peasants.

The Russian working class voted last month for the Soviet Union they had lost. It may be they know they have lost it for ever, and merely wish to punish the authorities while recognising there is no other option. However, it may also be that they think nothing of the sort, and believe the country should be set to rights by a strong hand and will vote communist again in the much more important election, for the presidency, in June. To counter that, the benefits of an improving economy had better come through good and strong. That is not likely, with the ruinous Chechen war still to pay for.

Russia is indeed limited, constrained and cramped; by the new states all about it, which include the three small Baltic countries whose rhetoric and sometimes actions are at best cold; by its former allies in central Europe who are vociferously suspicious of it; by the rich states of the west and the east which are weary of trying to help and are no longer inclined to be over-helpful; and especially by the US, now the undisputed single superpower and hurtful to national pride because of that.

However well Russia's rulers might strive to govern (and sometimes they do not strive all that well), they are faced with a large absence where a national consensus should be.

No surprise that the battered westerniser Andrei Kozyrev was replaced as foreign minister by the wily foreign intelligence chief and Gorbachev-era survivor Yevgeny Primakov: well enough known in and not over-feared by Washington, he has nevertheless been put in the Stalinesque tower which houses the foreign ministry (still with the hammer and sickle embedded into its facade). He will make growling noises at those states which irritate Russia's frayed nerves—and woo or chivvy back into the Russian fold those in the CIS amenable to persuasion or bullying.

General Pavel Grachev, the defence minister, went to Ukraine this month to do some growling of his own about the iniquity of the Start I and Start II nuclear disarmament agreements which Russia has signed. US officials say that all real progress on disarmament has stalled. Should this go beyond growling, the uneasy joviality which still surrounds the US-Russian relationship would freeze over. The language of confrontation, with which many on both sides still feel comfortable, would be back. And there would be the heart-wrenching threats of a cold war less stable than the old one.

Imagine, say those Russians who still wish to have a dialogue with the west, what *you* (a US citizen) would feel if the central American states acquired strongly anti-US governments. If Canada began disenfranchising all on its territory who had US ancestry, your gross domestic product was dropping through the floor, your allies were joining the Warsaw Pact, and the native Americans had claimed the oil wells and were paying no tax on their output? And if the presidents of Chase Manhattan and Bank-America were assassinated (possibly by each other's bodyguards), Arkansas had declared independence and was paying for it by drug-running and arms dealing . . . and so on. Uneasy, perhaps?

The parallel may be overdrawn, but it expresses something of the dilemma which unites the Russian people and rulers. It is that, however well the latter might strive to govern (and sometimes they do not strive all that well), they are faced with a large absence where a national consensus should be. There is no agreement as to the ground rules of its economy, no agreement as to who should be its friends, and who its enemies.

In this vacuum, the features of a constitutional, democratic liberal state float above, rather than are embedded within, the nation. The constitution is long and full of many good things, but it is most bitterly attacked by those parties which did best in the December elections. It is hardly seen by the citizens as their shield against an authority which, if less arbitrary than the communist one, is more overtly corrupt. The parties are free to organise and to be elected, but their hold on the national life of the country is weak. The very meaning of Russia itself, which had always had some overarching mission, has disappeared, to be replaced with no agreed concept. Orthodox Christianity, suppressed and corrupted by communism, has revived more in form than in content. Spiritual hunger is filled by charlatanism and obscurantism.

Half a decade ago, we interpreted the events in the Soviet Union as a triumph and a liberation. We have all kinds of vested interests in clinging to that interpretation, even as a growing chorus dismisses such a posture as wishful thinking and naive. Should another reality—which recognises that reaction is already present, that repression already operates, that hostilities have already begun, take its place?

No. Russia is no more doomed to reduplicate for ever an authoritarian past than is Chile or Japan. Mikhail Gorbachev and Boris Yeltsin, though neither would wish to see himself so coupled, have unwittingly conspired to throw open their country in a way none of its rulers had before—in explicit freedom and in friendship. The world all about Russia has broken into it, and Russia has broken out into the world which surrounds it with a vigour and an appetite hitherto limited to the aristocratic elite. The pains of each adjusting to the other are very large, most of all in Russia, the more because they have been so suddenly and so unexpectedly felt. But we cannot now "lose Russia" any more than Russia can lose us. It has become, already, part of us and we of it.

The Splintering of Russia's Reformers

The gains by Communists and nationalists bode ill for the June vote

Lee Hockstader

Washington Post Foreign Service

MOSCOW

The triumph of Russian Communists and ultra-nationalists, who together beat reformers by more than a 3 to 2 ratio in the Dec. 17 parliamentary races, means that the forces most hostile to a free market and democratic values are now in a much stronger position to capture the presidency in June.

The importance of the vote was not in any basic electoral shift. Despite two years of social upheaval and economic crisis, various Communist and nationalist parties combined fared no better than in the 1993 parliamentary elections. The party of Vladimir Zhirinovsky, the country's best-known ultra-nationalist, did just half as well as it did two years ago.

Rather, Boris Yeltsin and the democrats are now in trouble not because of their rivals' strength, but because of their own disunity. The one-two finish by Communists and nationalists was made possible in large part by Russia's squabbling reformers. Their mutual distrust and ceaseless feuding did as much to boost extremists of the left and right as the nation's economic upheaval.

Together, the three main reformist parties—those broadly in favor of continuing Yeltsin's free-market economic reforms and his commitment to democracy—received about 23 percent of the vote, enough to have beaten the Communists. But the pro-reform vote was badly split.

In next June's presidential balloting, if no candidate wins a majority, the top two go on to compete in a runoff. Unless the democratic parties are able to unite behind Yeltsin—an ailing, unpopular incumbent—or another reformer, anti-progressive candidates could finish first and second, analysts said. That means the runoff could be between such contenders as Communist leader Gennady Zyuganox and Zhirinovsky.

"Do you really seriously think that [the various democratic parties] will join President Yeltsin if he runs? I don't think so," says Vyacheslav Nikonov, a democratic member of the current parliament who was not reelected. "The situation as I regard it is very, very bad. I'm sure the democrats will not come up with a united candidate" for the presidential election next June.

Russia's splintered reformist camp is filled with towering political egos—Yelsin, pro-reform economist Grigory Yavlinsky, former prime minister Yegor Gaidar, former finance minister Boris Fyodorov.

Yavlinsky, whose Yabloko party received about 8.4 percent of the Dec. 17 vote, has refused to join forces with Gaidar. Gaidar, whose Russia's Choice party did less well, broke with Yeltsin over the war in Chechnya. Fyudorov also formed his own party, which bombed in the balloting.

"They're playing with fire, I think," Michael McFaul of Stanford University, an expert on Russian politics, says of the reformers. "It would be nice if they could agree who's going to be the candidate before the first ballot—it'd be strategically wise, let's put it that way."

McFaul says Yeltsin is more likely than ever to run for reelection in June, painting himself as a bulwark for reform against Communist and nationalist extremists who want to turn back the clock and recreate the Soviet Union.

"With him [at the head] of a large coalition of united democratic parties, he'll do well," McFaul says. "He'll get to the second ballot and run off against a nationalist or Communist, and I think he can beat either of them. The scary thing is if there are 15 candidates in the first round again. In a race like that, the Communists will get the same percentage as [they did Dec. 17], which gets them on the second ballot. And it's a real Russian roulette kind of thing as to who's number two."

Yet there are a few factors working in the reformers' favor. One is the nature of the Communist Party, which unlike most other parties in Russia is held together by ideology rather than a charismatic leader. Zyuganov, the party chief, is in fact utterly lacking in charisma and would have problems broadening his appeal beyond the party faithful in a presidential race. Some who voted for the Communists may have second thoughts about this former mid-level party functionary actually running the country.

Moreover, despite their strong showing, the Communists have disunity problems of their own. In addition to Zyuganov's Communist Party of the Russian Federation, a handful of other, smaller Communist parties split the leftist vote.

Mindful of the divisions, Zyuganov has promised to consult "all [our] allies and fellow travelers" in the new parliament. He has even made a friendly overture toward Zhirinovsky.

Zhirinovsky, the leading nationalist, is by far the best campaigner in Russia and has a gift for inflaming a dispirited electorate with acid rhetoric. His showing—about 11 percent of the vote—was well below the 22.8 percent he collected in 1993 but enough to finish second after the Communists. But despite his political savvy and mysteriously strong financial backing, he would not necessarily fare as well in a presidential race. Many

TALLY

Communist Surge in Russia

Final results of the Dec. 17 election to the lower house of the Russian Parliament, according to the Central Electoral Commission. Each voter cast two votes: one for a single candidate and one for a party. Half of the 450 members were elected in single-seat constituencies; the other 225 were elected according to party lists.

Party	Percentage of party-list votes	Party-list seats	Single-candidate seats	Total seats	Seats won in 1993
Communist Party	22.30%	99	58	**157**	45
Liberal Democratic Party	11.18	50	1	**51**	63
Our Home Is Russia	10.13	45	10	**55**	—
Yabloko	6.89	31	14	**45**	25

Parties needed a minimum of 5 percent of the vote to win party-list seats.

Women of Russia	4.61	0	3	**3**	23
Working Russia	4.53	0	1	**1**	0
Congress of Russian Communities	4.31	0	5	**5**	—
Party of Svyatoslav Fyodorov	3.98	0	1	**1**	—
Democratic Choice of Russia	3.86	0	9	**9**	76
Agrarian Party	3.78	0	20	**20**	55
Power to the People	1.61	0	9	**9**	—
Other parties	Unavailable	0	17	**17**	—
Independents	—	0	77	**77**	—

Source: Reuters

Russians regard him as a raving lunatic. Female voters tend to despise him. In interviews with Zhirinovsky's supporters, many say they find him entertaining as a lawmaker but would not support him for the presidency.

But if Yeltsin is a candidate, he will have his own problems of image and appeal. A large number of Russians who supported such reformers as Yavlinsky or Prime Minister Viktor Chernomyrdin say they would not vote for Yeltsin.

Yeltsin has been a political fixture for so many years that he has given practically everyone in Russia a reason to be angry at him. His rumored drinking, poor health and sometimes slurred speech do not inspire confidence in many Russians, especially younger ones.

Moreover, he has practiced divide-and-rule politics for so long that a sudden stab at coalition-building may be difficult for him at this stage. He fired Gaidar as prime minister in 1992, brought him back as a deputy prime minister 1993, then fired him again in 1994. He fired Fyodorov as finance minister, and

he passed over Yavlinsky for a top job in his administration.

Georgy Satarov, a top aide to Yeltsin, predicted optimistically that the outcome of the Dec. 17 election would lead reformers to unite behind the president. "The threat of a Communist majority in parliament will make the democrats both consolidate and unite around President Boris Yeltsin, a stalwart supporter of economic and political reforms in the country," he told the Interfax news agency.

But Yavlinsky blames Yeltsin's policies for the Communist-nationalist victory. He mentions nothing of his own refusal to join forces with other pro-reform parties.

Sergei Kovalyov, a reformist member of parliament and Russia's human rights commissioner, has lectured democrats on the consequences of their infighting. "In refusing to cooperate . . . and in putting personal ambitions first, you retreat from the very idea of democracy," he told the newspaper Izvestia in its Dec. 19 issue. "Common people, your electorate, do not see any radical difference in your programs, because no radical difference exists."

Post-Soviet Politics

Does the Communists' Rise Augur a 'Weimar' Russia?

Gregory Freidin

Gregory Freidin, chairman of the Slavic department at Stanford University, is co-author of "Russia at the Barricades: Eyewitness Accounts of the August, 1991, Coup" (M. E. Sharp Publishers).

BERKELEY, CALIF.
Once again, the specter of Weimar Germany haunts Russia. If the outcome of last month's parliamentary elections is taken as a straw poll for the presidential race in June, one can easily imagine a nightmare choice between Communist Gennady A. Zyuganov and ultranationalist Vladimir V. Zhirinovsky, or between Zyuganov and a weak reform candidate like Grigory A. Yavlinsky. A less nightmarish choice would pit Zyuganov against an ailing Boris N. Yeltsin or Viktor S. Chernomyrdin, a prime minister fatally damaged by his loyalty to an unpopular president. In short, a new authoritarian or even totalitarian regime may enter Russia, not through a coup, as in 1917, but through the ballot box and according to all the rules of Russia's democratic, presidency-oriented constitution.

Like Weimar Germany, Russia has experienced, by losing its superpower status, a national humiliation; like Weimar Germany, it has been gripped by an economic crisis, compounded by a rupture in its social fabric, and like Weimar Germany, Russia has sustained bloody political upheavals, most notably the dissolution of the Soviets, in the fall of 1993, and the seemingly interminable war in Chechnya.

The Communists' success at the polls, raising their representation in the Duma to 35% from 10%, practically closes the Weimar analogy. Like Adolf Hitler's party comrades, Russia's Communists showed plenty of political savvy, running a miserly campaign in the face of lavish spending by opponents and relying on grassroots support instead of garish advertising. They demonstrated, where their constituency was concerned, that promises of bread have greater voter appeal than the political circus served up to the people for their amusement by their heavyweight rivals.

But was it a "victory of the Communists," or a "victory for communism"?

After all the bad press the Communists endured during *perestroika* and, especially, after the collapse of Soviet communism Zyuganov's party is, indeed, a comeback kid. The Communist Party of Russia will be the largest single party faction in the new Duma. But a closer look reveals a less sanguine picture:

- That 35% is "padded," enlarged by the peculiarity of Russia's electoral law. Had the seats been distributed according to the votes cast, the Communist bloc would not have exceeded 25%.
- More than one-third of the Communist deputies were elected from single-mandate districts—meaning they owe their victories not so much to their party as to their local constituencies, a significant factor, given the growing autonomy of the regions.
- Even if the Duma deputies from the other "left parties"—the barely breathing Agrarians and the microscopic old *nomenklatura* party, Power to the People—are counted in, the total comes to 41%.
- Zyuganov is consummately dull. His dogged, unassuming manner and lack of charisma served him well in the parliamentary campaign by taking the edge off the harsh revanchist radicalism of his party's program. But a presidential campaign is made for candidates who have a fire in their belly.
- Gen. Alexander I. Lebed's recent offer to lend the Communists his charismatic appeal in exchange for the presidential prize is a bad deal for the Commu-

nists and is bound to be rejected. The Russian presidency is powerful enough to enable the president to forget who made his victory possible, and Lebed, the hero of the war in Afghanistan, is unlikely to be obliging.

• Zhirinovsky will continue to draw the less-structured protest vote from the opposition to reform. Indeed, unless he undergoes a personality change, submits to Zyuganov's questionable charm (he recently rejected such an alliance), and manages, at the same time, to bring with him his volatile constituency, the results of the Duma elections do not translate into a Communist victory in the presidential sweepstakes.

The Communists' presidential prospects dim further when the reform faction identifying with Chernomyrdin's Our Home is Russia – Yavlinsky's "yabloko," Yegor T. Gaidar's Russia's Democratic Choice and Sviatoslav Fyodorov's Party of Free Labor – is factored in. This bloc, more than a quarter of the Duma, held its own or even gained, if marginally, compared to the results of the 1993 elections. More important, the government's party, now strongly represented in the Duma, is in a position to attract independent deputies. If, as some important indicators suggest, Russia has entered a period of economic recovery, Chernomyrdin's party may increase its ranks substantially, stealing momentum from the Communists in the six months leading up to the presidential vote.

Chernomyrdin's own story holds a key to understanding Russia's political dynamic in the post-communist era. The collapse of Soviet communism was a structural phenomenon. Both the ideological and natural resources that sustained Russia's superpower status were exhausted by the 1980s. Mikhail S. Gorbachev's resistance to radical economic reform had, in effect, bankrupted the country by the time Yeltsin took over in 1991. Reform was the only option, and Chernomyrdin's ascendancy in Yeltsin's government and his ever-growing commitment to reform demonstrate that the transformation of Russia's economy stems not from a politician's will, but from a structural need for change that cannot be avoided, not even by a Zyuganov.

Russia's major urban centers are most cognizant of the need not to return to the past. Indeed, Moscow and St. Petersburg voted overwhelmingly in favor of the reform politicians, while Zyuganov's supporters were older and retired and clustered in the woefully inefficient coal-mining regions, the primarily agricultural belt in Southern Russian and in areas like the northern Caucasus republic of Daghestan, which are chronically dependent on the central government. These constituencies represent Russia's past, a nostalgia for the simplicity and ignorance of the Soviet era, not Russia's future – not even its present with its multiethnic composition; weak central state; increasing autonomy of the regions; dependency on raw-material exports and economic integration with the West; emergence of private economic conglomerates linked to the state in the center and the regions, and the utter unwillingness of the population to shed blood for one imperial dream or another.

Even Zyuganov, the spokesman for a sentimental National Bolshevism, understands this, eagerly offering his assurances of forward economic movement to foreign investors, articulating the fear of every major Russian politician that capital flight from Russia may precipitate the country's collapse and disintegration. If even Zyuganov understands the severe limitations on national sovereignty in the post-Cold War world, there is little place in Russian politics for a grandiose utopia and self-hypnosis that once led Russia, Italy, Germany and so recently Serbia to the brink of national suicide. The budget fright in Washington between Bill Clinton and Republicans in Congress, or the stand-off between the unions and the Alain Jupe's government in France – all of this unglamorous mess of a democracy – offer a far better analogy to contemporary Russian politics than the twilight of the Weimar Republic.

For Russia's Reformers, A Time of Despair

Communist gains at the polls spotlight the gulf between the intelligentsia and the workers

Lee Hockstader

Washington Post Foreign Service

ST. PETERSBURG, Russia
When Russia elected a parliament heavily weighted toward anti-Western Communists and nationalists in mid-December, progressives across the country threw up their hands and despaired.

Concentrated in Moscow and St. Petersburg, they had voted overwhelmingly for candidates who stood squarely for continued political and economic reform—and who were soundly defeated. If they had always seen themselves as distinct from the rest of Russia—and a little above it—now it seemed they were living almost on a different continent.

"Secede! That's the slogan of the day," proclaims Alexander Kan, a jazz critic and journalist here who writes a column for the Moscow Times. "We need to encase ourselves within an artificial border, create a new state out of our city and pursue liberal democratic reforms without worrying about the vast country to the south and east." An extreme view, maybe. But one that accurately catches the post-election mood of the Russian intelligentsia—the Western-leaning, reform-minded elite that over the years has set itself against czars and Communist Party secretaries alike and embodies the conscience of the nation.

The results of the Dec. 17 parliamentary elections show a Russian electorate sharply divided between haves and have-nots, between the two biggest cities and the rest of the country—and most of all, between the intelligentsia and everyone else.

Liberals who have hoped Russia would gradually evolve into a Western-style democracy are now losing heart. Many are blaming the Russian people, suggesting that the weight of czarist history and Soviet power has created an ignorant, brutish rabble ill-suited to democracy.

"There are many people in Russia who don't analyze or think, and this is to be expected," says Mikhail Berg, a novelist and editor here.

Some are convinced that because the Soviet state's fall four years ago was relatively bloodless, the country may still be ripe for a violent reckoning before it can finally be rid of its Communist past. Others, slightly less apocalyptic, are predicting a return of Communist power in presidential elections this June, followed by a period of political turmoil.

Nearly all agree that the gulf between Russia's intelligentsia and working people is enormous.

"No matter how strange it seems, Moscow and St. Petersburg are among the places most unhappy and dissatisfied with the political situation that has come about in Russia," Berg says. "But unlike the rest of the country, which is opting for communism or socialism, people here are still clinging to the same old dream of liberalism that has never really materialized.

"The Russian intelligentsia are more liberal than the government. They think reforms haven't gone far enough. And the rest of the country has despaired in its hopes and thinks they have gone too far. The divide between the two has become much more distinct."

Many Russian intellectuals say they do not know anyone who voted for the Communists or for Vladimir Zhirinovsky's ultra-nationalist party. Yet between them, the Communists and Zhirinovsky's party attracted a third of the vote.

Nationwide, the main pro-reform parties were swamped, totaling barely 20 percent of the vote. But in Moscow and St. Petersburg, nearly half the voters pulled the lever for moderate and radical reformers.

The Communists, who received 22 percent of the vote nationwide, were considerably weaker in Moscow and St. Petersburg. Zhirinovsky, who received 11 percent of the national party-list vote, barely cleared 2 percent in the two big cities.

"Who voted for Zhirinovsky? Probably, like Zhirinovsky himself, they have some sort of inferiority complex," says Yuri Kleiner, a linguist at St. Petersburg State University. "I don't know. Many of them are cases for psychoanalysis."

The figure who most dramatically symbolizes the intelligentsia's break with the rest of Russia is Yegor Gaidar, the young economist who lasted less than a year as Yeltsin's first prime minister in 1992.

Vilified by retirees who blame him for lifting price controls, unleashing inflation and wiping out their personal savings, Gaidar is one of Russia's most unpopular figures. Yet to the intelligentsia, he remains the standard-bearer of liberal reforms, pro-Western values and the free market.

"Gaidar's guilt is no worse than that of a radio announcer who says it's minus 20 degrees outside," says Yuri Vdovin, a St. Petersburg television executive and an advocate of openness in government. "He was just the bearer of bad news. But people don't like him because he's too much of the intelligentsia, he's too tolerant, he speaks Russian too well. Russia is used to having thugs in power."

Nationwide, Gaidar's Democratic Choice of Russia managed just 4 percent of the party-list vote—below the 5 percent minimum required to win seats; the party did win nine seats in individual races. In Moscow and St. Petersburg, Gaidar's group polled three times better in the party-list vote than it did nationwide.

No part of Russian society has a greater emotional stake in the collapse of Soviet power and the embrace of liberal values than the intelligentsia. For years they had chipped away at the Soviet monolith, passing around banned manuscripts, listening to news from the West on short-wave radios, living by choice or circumstance at the margins of a society defined by its intolerance.

When the Communist regime folded in 1991, liberals rejoiced. For a brief moment, the intelligentsia felt something like unity with the coal miners, factory workers and urban office workers who were rallying in the streets for Boris Yeltsin and faster reforms. The union proved short-lived. In parliamentary elections in 1993, most liberals stuck with Gaidar. But millions of factory workers and farmers, squeezed by Russia's economic crisis and angry at the upheaval all around them, voted for Zhirinovsky.

Among liberals who had been cheerleaders for the reforms of Yeltsin and Soviet leader Mikhail Gorbachev, the disillusionment and disgust are intense. There is a strong sense that, having lost its enemy—a powerful, totalitarian government—the intelligentsia has slipped in status and influence. Russian voters are disdained as an uncouth mob.

"People were subjected to such primitive propaganda for so long that they were driven to total political blindness," says Vdovin. "They accept and comprehend only the old demagoguery that is familiar to them. . . . [The Soviet Union] was a paternalistic state, and many people still want their decisions made for them. They lack any feeling of responsibility and self-reliance."

Amid the growing alarm, the intelligentsia are running out of political options. Gaidar clearly is not a viable candidate for the presidential elections in June. If Yeltsin runs, many liberals will not be able to support the man who launched the bloody assault on the separatist region of Chechnya in December 1994. Economist Grigory Yavlinsky is seen as an acceptable if opportunistic alternative, but his Yabloko party garnered just 7 percent of the parliamentary vote and he is given little chance in presidential elections.

Disillusioned and depressed, many intellectuals see themselves with neither a role nor a voice at the very moment the country may be edging toward a new Communist regime.

"Liberating ourselves finally from communism is possible only through a major disaster," Berg says. "A lot of blood will have to be shed. . . . A velvet revolution is not for Russia."

Political Diversity in the Developing World

- **Politics of Development (Articles 50 and 51)**
- **Latin America: Mexico (Articles 52 and 53)**
- **Africa (Articles 54–56)**
- **China and India (Articles 57 and 58)**
- **Newly Industrialized Countries (Articles 59 and 60)**

Until recently, the so-called Third World was a widely used umbrella term for a disparate group of states that are now more frequently called the developing countries. Their most important shared characteristic may well be what these countries have *not* become—namely relatively modern, industrial societies. Otherwise they differ vastly from one another, both in terms of their past and present situations as well as their future prospects. The Third World designation has been used so variously and loosely that it is now dismissed by many critical observers as a category that produces more confusion than analytical precision or political insight. Such objections should at least make one cautious when speaking about these developing countries. Perhaps the time has come to let go of this vague and slippery concept, as the first essay of this unit suggests. But even this report acknowledges that there are some commonalities among these countries that need conceptual recognition of some kind. Moreover, as Barbara Crossette explains in her article, the lingering "spirit" of this now-incoherent Third World oratory still retains some of its power.

Originally the term referred to countries—many of them recently freed former colonies—that chose to remain nonaligned in the cold war confrontation between the so-called First World (Western bloc) and the Second World (Communist bloc). It was common to speak of "three worlds," but the categories of first world and second world themselves never gained wide usage. They make even less sense today in view of the collapse of communist rule in Central and Eastern Europe, including Russia and the other former Soviet republics.

Even so, the Third World category continues to be a handy, if imprecise and misleading, term of reference. It sometimes still carries the residual connotation of not-Western and not-Communist. Increasingly, however, this label is used to cover all largely nonindustrialized countries and connotes the image of predominantly nonmodern economic and social infrastructures. In that sense, the remaining communist-ruled countries would belong to the Third World category, with China and a few of its Asian neighbors as prime examples. Also in the same sense, Cuba is one of many Third World countries in Latin America, although it differs from the others by being Communist-ruled.

Most of the Third World nations also share the problems of poverty and, though now less frequently, rapid population growth. Their comparative economic situations and potential for development can vary enormously, however, as a simple alphabetical juxtaposition of countries such as Angola and the Argentines, Bangladesh and Brazil, or Chad and China illustrates. An additional term, Fourth World, has therefore been proposed to designate countries that are so desperately short of resources that they appear to have little or no prospect for self-sustained economic improvement. Adding to the terminological inflation and confusion, the Third World countries are now often referred to collectively as the "South" and contrasted with the largely industrialized "North." Most of them in fact are located in the southern latitudes of the planet—in Latin America, Africa, Asia, and the Middle East. But Greenland would also qualify for Third World status, along with much of Russia

and Siberia, while Australia and New Zealand clearly would not. South Africa would be a case of "uneven" or "combined" development, as would some Latin American countries where significant enclaves of advanced modernity are located within a larger context of premodern social and economic conditions.

It is very important to remember that the countries of the developing world vary tremendously in their sociocultural and political characteristics. Some of them have representative systems of government, and a few of these even have an impressive record of stability, such as India. Many more are governed by authoritarian, often military-based regimes that advocate an ideologically adorned strategy of rapid economic development. Closer examination will sometimes reveal that the avowed determination of leaders to improve their societies carries less substance than their determination to maintain and expand their own power and privilege. In any case, the strategies and politics of development and modernization in these countries vary greatly.

In recent years, market-oriented development has gained in favor in many countries that previously subscribed to some version of heavy state regulation or socialist planning of the economy. The renewed interest in markets resembles a strategic policy shift that has also occurred in former communist-ruled nations and the more advanced industrialized countries. It usually represents a pragmatic acceptance of a "mixed economy" rather than a doctrinaire espousal of laissez-faire capitalism. In other words, targeted state intervention continues to play a role in economic development, but it is no longer as pervasive and heavy-handed as in the past; the belief in some form of centralized state planning has long since withered away.

In studying the attempts by developing world countries to create institutions and policies that will promote their socioeconomic development, it is important not to leave out the international context. The political and intellectual leaders of these countries have often drawn upon some version of what is called *dependency theory* to explain their plight, often combining it with demands for special treatment or compensation from the industrialized world for having initiated this dependency. The theory is itself an outgrowth of the Marxist/Leninist ideology of imperialism, according to which advanced capitalist countries have established exploitative relationships with the weaker economic systems of the Third World. The focus of such theories has been on finding external reasons for a country's failure to generate self-sustained growth. They totally exclude any explanations that would give greater emphasis to a country's internal obstacles to development (whether sociocultural, political, environmental, or a combination of these). Such theoretical disagreements are not only of academic interest. These theories themselves are likely to provide the framework for strikingly different policy conclusions and strategies for development. In other words, theory has consequences.

The debate has had some tangible consequences in recent years. It now appears that dependency theory in its simplest form has lost intellectual and political support. Instead of serving as an explanatory paradigm, it is now more frequently encountered as a more pluralist explanation of lagging development, which recognizes the diversity of internal and external factors that are likely to affect economic development. There is much to be said for middle-range theory, which pays greater attention to the contextual and situational aspects of each case of development. On the whole, multivariable explanations seem preferable to monocausal ones. Strategies of development that may work in one setting may come to naught in a different environment.

Sometimes called the Group of 77 but eventually consisting of some 120 countries, the Third World states linked themselves together in the United Nations to promote whatever interests they may have had in common. In their demand for a New International Economic Order, they focused on promoting changes designed to improve their relative commercial position vis-à-vis the affluent industrialized nations of the North. This common front, however, has turned out to be more rhetorical than real. It would be a mistake to assume that there is a necessary identity of national interest among these countries or that they pursue complementary foreign policies.

Outside the United Nations, some of these same countries have tried to increase and control the price of industrially important primary exports through the building of cartel agreements among themselves. The result has sometimes been detrimental to other Third World nations. The most successful of these cartels, the Organization of Petroleum Exporting Countries (OPEC), was established in 1960 and held sway for almost a decade. Its cohesion has since eroded, resulting in drastic reductions in oil prices. While this latter occurrence was welcomed by the oil-importing countries as well as many developing countries, it left some oil-producing nations such as Mexico in economic disarray for a while. Moreover, the need to find outlets for the huge amounts of petrodollars, which had been deposited by some oil producers in Western banks during the period of cartel-induced high prices, led the financial institutions to make huge and often ill-considered loans to many Third World nations. Their frantic and often unsuccessful efforts to repay on schedule created new economic, social, and political dislocations that hit particularly hard in Latin America during the 1980s. The memory of these recent misadventures is likely to have some prudential influence on policy makers in the future.

The problems of poverty, hunger, and malnutrition in much of the developing world are socially and politically explosive. In their fear of revolution and their opposition to meaningful reform, the privileged classes often resort to brutal repression as a means to preserve a status quo favorable to themselves. In Latin America, this led to a politicalization of many lay persons and clergy of the Roman Catholic Church, who demanded social reform in the name of what was called *liberation theology*. For them, some variant of dependency theory filled a very practical ideological function by providing a relatively simple analytical and moral explanation of a complex reality. It also gave some strategic guidance for political activists who were determined to change this state of affairs. Their views on the inevitability of class struggle, and the need to take an active part in it, often clashed with the Vatican's outlook.

The collapse of communist rule in Europe has had a profound impact on the ideological explanation of the developing world's poverty and on the resulting strategies to overcome it. The Soviet model of modernization, which until recently fascinated many developing countries' leaders, now appears to have very little practical value. The fact that even the communists who remain in power in China have been willing to experiment with market reforms, including the private profit motive, has added to the general discredit of the centrally planned economy concept. Perhaps even more important is

the positive example of certain countries in Africa and Latin America that have pursued more market-oriented strategies of development; on the whole, they appear to have performed much better than some of their more statist neighbors. That may help explain the intellectual journey of such decision makers as Michael Manley, the former prime minister of Jamaica, who broke away from the combination of dependency theory and socialist strategies that he had once defended vigorously. During the 1980s, Manley made an intellectual U-turn as he gained a new respect for market-oriented economic strategies without abandoning his interest in using reform politics to promote the interests of the poor. More recently, Jorge G. Castañeda has called upon the Left in Latin America to abandon utopian goals and instead seek realistic social reforms within "mixed" market economies.

Latin America illustrates the difficulty of establishing stable pluralist democracies in many parts of the developing world. Some analysts have argued that its dominant political tradition is basically authoritarian-corporatist rather than competitively pluralist. They see the region's long tradition of centralized authoritarian governments, whether of the Left or Right, as being the result of an authoritarian "unitary" bias in the political culture. From this perspective, there is little hope for a lasting pluralist development, and the current trend toward democratization in much of Latin America is unlikely to last. Today, however, the cultural explanation for the prevalence of authoritarian governments in Latin America appears to meet with more skepticism than it did a few years ago. One simple reason is the fact that dictatorships in the region have serially been replaced by elected governments. The exemplary progress of democratic governments in Spain and Portugal may also have been important for the Latin American countries. Finally, the negative social, economic, and political experiences with authoritarian rulers may well be one of the strongest cards held by their democratic successors. But unless they also meet the pragmatic test—Does it work?—by providing evidence of social and economic progress, the new democracies in Latin America could also be in trouble shortly. Developments there may yet turn out to have been merely short interludes between authoritarian regimes that achieve at least a modicum of political and social order through repression.

In much of Latin America there has been a turn toward a greater emphasis on market economics, replacing the traditional commitment to strategies that favored statist interventions. An important example is the attempt by former president Carlos Salinas of Mexico to move his country toward a more competitive form of market enterprise. His modernization strategy included Mexico's entry into a North American Free Trade Agreement (NAFTA) with the United States and Canada. In a time of enormous socioeconomic dislocation, however, Salinas showed considerable reluctance to move on from economic to political reform. Such a shift would have undermined the long-time hegemony of his own Institutional Revolutionary Party (PRI) and given new outlets for protest. Critics of Salinas argued that his approach was too technocratic in its assumption that economic modernization can be accomplished without a basic change of the political system. During his last year in office, Salinas was confronted by an armed peasant rebellion in the southern province of Chiapas, which gave voice to the demand for land reform and economic redistribution. Mexican criticism of Salinas intensified after he left office in December 1994 and three months later sought political exile in the United States. Since then, some top Mexican officials and their associates have been accused of having links to major drug traffickers with a sordid record of corruption and political assassination.

The successor to Salinas was elected in August 1994 in a competitive contest that was reported as not seriously distorted by fraud. The ruling party won with 51 percent of the vote. The PRI's first presidential candidate, Luis Donaldo Colosio, had been assassinated in the early part of the campaign. His place was taken by Ernesto Zedillo, an economist and former banker who fits the technocratic mold of recent Mexican leaders. He was expected to continue the basic economic policies of Salinas, but he appeared ready to listen to demands for meaningful political reform as well. He had hardly taken office at the beginning of December 1994, however, when the Mexican peso collapsed and brought the economy to ruins. A major factor was the country's huge trade deficit and the resultant loss of confidence in the peso. It remains to be seen whether Mexico's political institutions will be more resilient than its economic ones have proven to be.

Africa: South Africa faces the monumental task of introducing democracy in a multiracial society where the ruling white minority had never shared political or economic power with black Africans or Asian immigrants. A new transitional constitution was adopted in late 1993, followed by the first multiracial national elections in April 1994. Former president Frederik de Klerk will go into history as an important reformer, but his political work could not possibly have pleased a broad cross section of South African society. His reforms were judged to have gone much too far and too fast by members of the privileged white minority; they did not go far and quickly enough for many more people who demanded measures that went well beyond formal racial equality.

Nelson Mandela, who succeeded de Klerk, has an even more difficult historical task. He has some strong political cards in addition to his undisputed leadership qualities. He clearly represents the aspirations of a long-repressed majority, but he has managed to retain the respect of a sizable number of the white minority. It will be important that he continues to bridge the racial cleavages that otherwise threaten to ravage South African society. The reformers have sought political accommodation through an institutional form of power sharing. The task of keeping such a coalition government together will be only one of Mandela's many problems. In order for the democratic changes to have much meaning for the long-suppressed majority, it will be necessary to find policies that reduce the social and economic chasm separating the races. The politics of redistribution will be no simple or short-term task, and one may expect many conflicts in the future. Nevertheless, for the first time since the beginning of colonization, South Africa now offers some hope for a major improvement in interracial relations, and some sober optimists believe that a firm foundation has been laid that should ensure political stability also in the post-Mandela era.

China is the homeland of over a billion people, or more than one-fifth of the world's population. Here the reform communists who took power after Mao Zedong's death in 1976 began much earlier than their Soviet counterparts to steer the country toward a relatively decontrolled market economy. They also introduced some political relaxation by ending Mao's recurrent ideological campaigns to mobilize the masses. In their place came a domestic tranquillity such as China had not known for over half a century. But the regime encountered a basic dilemma: It wished to maintain tight controls over politics and society while reforming the economy. When a new openness developed in Chinese society that was comparable to the pluralism encouraged, albeit more actively, by Gorbachev's glasnost in the Soviet Union, it ran into determined opposition among hard-line communist leaders. The aging reform leader Deng Xiaoping presided over a bloody crackdown on student demonstrations in Beijing's Tiananmen Square in May 1989. The regime still refuses to let up on its tight political controls of society, but it has continued to loosen the economic controls. In recent years, China has experienced a remarkable economic surge with growth rates that appear unmatched elsewhere in the world. One unanswered question, however, is whether their emerging industrialized society can long coexist with its repressive political system. It would be surprising if the succession in political leadership does not produce tensions and conflicts at the elite level. In early 1996, Beijing ordered large-scale military exercises in the coastal waters between the mainland and Taiwan. There was good reason to believe that these maneuvers were intended to direct national and international attention away from the succession crisis and toward the continuing Chinese claim to the island.

India is often referred to as a subcontinent. With its almost 900 million people, this country ranks second only to China in population and ahead of the continents of Latin America and Africa combined. India is deeply divided by ethnic, religious, and regional differences. In recent years, Hindu extremists have become politicized and now constitute a threat to the Muslim minority as well as the secular foundation of the state. For the vast majority of the huge population, a life of material deprivation seems inescapable. Some policy critics, however, point to the possibility of relief if the country's struggling economy were freed from its long tradition of heavyhanded state interference. Although there have been some promising steps in that direction, the potential for political crisis nevertheless looms over the country. In 1992 the national elections were marred by the assassination of Rajiv Gandhi, the former prime minister and leader of the Congress party. Prime Minister P. V. Narasimha Rao, the political veteran who took charge of a tenuous minority government after the election, has followed in the steps of other reform governments in the developing world by adopting more market-oriented policies. This attempt to bring India, with its long tradition of heavy state regulation and protectionism, into the world economy bears careful watching.

The *Newly Industrialized Countries (NICs)* have received much attention as nations that are breaking out of the cycle of chronic poverty and low productivity. It is not fully clear what lessons we can draw from the impressive records of these "tigers" and "dragons"—Singapore, Hong Kong, South Korea, Taiwan, and potentially Thailand and Malaysia. Some observers have suggested that their combination of authoritarian politics and market economics has provided a successful blend of discipline and incentives that have made the economic take-off possible. Others point to the presence of special cultural factors in these countries (such as strong family units and values that emphasize hard work, postponement of self-gratification, and respect for education) that apparently encourage rational forms of economic behavior. It would also be possible

to cite some geopolitical and historical advantages that helped the NICs accumulate investment capital at a critical phase. This subject is of great importance and seems bound to become one of the main topics in the field of study that we call the politics of development. These countries are clearly of interest as possible role models for economic development elsewhere. They can also serve as examples of how authoritarian political and social traditions can be reformed in tandem with the development of a more affluent consumer society. The articles in this section give a detailed perspective on these newly industrialized countries by carefully reviewing the contributory effects of market forces, state intervention, and cultural and social factors on their remarkable economic development.

Looking Ahead: Challenge Questions

Why is the Third World label now of little analytical value? What have these countries in common, and how are they diverse? Is there any value in keeping the concept, or should we scrap it? Why did some observers promote usage of another term, the Fourth World?

Regarding explanations for their poverty and slow development, which conditions can be assigned to external (foreign) and which to internal (domestic) factors? Why can theories of

development be important factors in shaping strategies of modernization?

What is dependency theory, and why has it had so much appeal especially in Latin America? How do you explain the current wave of market-oriented reforms? How did the widespread optimism about Mexico's economic development arise, and why did it come to such an abrupt end?

Why do economic development and representative government run into such difficulties in most of Latin America and much of Africa? What are some of the major political, economic, and social problems that South Africa still has to face in overcoming the legacy of apartheid?

How do you explain China's relative success in turning toward market reforms for their economy as compared to attempts by the Soviet Union? Why can we expect future political tension at both the elite and mass levels of Chinese society?

How has India managed to maintain itself as a parliamentary democracy, given the many cleavages that divide this multiethnic society?

What can the newly industrialized countries of Asia teach us about the possibility of economic modernization and democratic reform?

LET'S ABOLISH THE THIRD WORLD

It never made much sense, and it doesn't exist in practice.
So why not get rid of it in theory?

Sometimes language lags history. Take the Third World. Did we ever have another name for the poor, unstable nations of the south? In fact, the Third World is a 1950s coinage, invented in Paris by French intellectuals looking for a way to lump together the newly independent former European colonies in Asia and Africa. They defined *le tiers monde* by what it wasn't: neither the First World (the West) nor the Second (the Soviet bloc). But now the cold war is over, and we are learning a new political lexicon, free of old standbys like "Soviet Union" that no longer refer to anything. It's a good time to get rid of the Third World, too.

The Third World should have been abolished long ago. From the very beginning, the concept swept vast differences of culture, religion and ethnicity under the rug. How much did El Salvador and Senegal really have in common? And what did either share with Bangladesh? One of the bloodiest wars since Vietnam took place between two Third World brothers, Iran and Iraq. Many former colonies remained closer to erstwhile European metropoles than to their fellow "new nations."

Nevertheless, the Third World grew. Intellectuals and politicians added a socioeconomic connotation to its original geopolitical meaning. It came to include all those exploited countries that could meet the unhappy standard set by Prime Minister Lee Kuan Yew of Singapore in 1969: "poor, strife-ridden, chaotic." (That was how Latin America got into the club.) There's a tendency now to repackage the Third World as the "South" in a global North-South, rich-poor division. To be

sure, in this sense the Third World does refer to something real: vast social problems—disease, hunger, bad housing—matched by a chronic inability to solve them. And relative deprivation does give poor nations some common interests: freer access to Western markets, for example.

But there are moral hazards in defining people by what they cannot do or what they do not have. If being Third World meant being poor, and if being poor meant being a perennial victim of the First and Second Worlds, why take responsibility for your own fate? From Cuba to Burma, Third Worldism became the refuge of scoundrels, the "progressive" finery in which despots draped their repression and economic mismanagement. Remember "African socialism" in Julius Nyerere's Tanzania? It left the country's economy a shambles. A good many Western intellectuals hailed it as a "homegrown" Third World ideology.

Paternalism is one characteristic Western response to a "victimized" Third World. Racism is another. To nativists such as France's Jean-Marie Le Pen or Patrick Buchanan, "Third World" is a code phrase for what they see as the inherent inferiority of tropical societies made up of dark-skinned people. Either way, the phrase Third World, so suggestive of some alien plant, abets stereotyping. "The Third World is a form of bloodless universality that robs individuals and societies of their particularity," wrote the late Trinidad-born novelist Shiva Naipaul. "To blandly subsume, say, Ethiopia, India, and Brazil under the one banner of Third Worldhood is as

absurd and as denigrating as the old assertion that all Chinese look alike."

Today, two new forces are finishing off the tattered Third World idea. The first is the West's victory in the cold war. There are no longer two competing "worlds" with which to contrast a "third." Leaders can't play one superpower off the other, or advertise their misguided policies as alternative to "equally inappropriate" communism and capitalism. The second is rapid growth in many once poor countries. The World Bank says developing countries will grow twice as fast in the '90s as the industrialized G-7. So much for the alleged immutability of "Third World" poverty—and for the notion that development must await a massive transfer of resources from north to south. No one would call the Singapore of Lee Kuan Yew poor, strife-ridden or chaotic: per capita GNP is more than $10,000, and its 1990 growth rate was 8 percent. South Korea, Taiwan and Hong Kong also have robust economies, and Thailand and Malaysia are moving up fast.

American steelmakers have recently lodged "dumping" complaints against half a dozen Asian and Latin American countries. Cheap wages explains much of these foreign steelmakers' success, but the U.S. industry's cry is still a backhanded compliment. "A nation without a manufacturing base is a nation heading toward Third World status," wrote presidential candidate Paul Tsongas. But Tsongas was using obsolete imagery to make his point: soon, bustling basic industries may be the *hallmark* of a "Third World" nation.

Patina of modernity: Nor can the Third World idea withstand revelations about what life was really like in the former "Second World." It was assumed that, whatever the U.S.S.R.'s political deformities, that country was at least modern enough to give the West a run for its money in science and technology. In fact, below a patina of modernity lay gross industrial inefficiency, environmental decay and ethnic strife. Nowadays, it's more common to hear conditions in the former Soviet Union itself described as "Third World," and Russia seeks aid from South Korea. Elsewhere in Europe, Yugoslavia's inter-ethnic war is as bad as anything in Asia or Africa. The United States itself is pocked with "Third World" enclaves: groups with Bangladeshi life expectancies and Latin American infant-mortality rates.

A concept invoked to explain so many things probably can't explain very much at all. The ills that have come to be associated with the Third World are not confined to the southern half of this planet. Nor are democracy and prosperity the exclusive prerogatives of the North. Unfair as international relations may be, over time, economic development and political stability come to countries that work, save and organize to achieve them. Decline and political disorder come to those who neglect education, public health—and freedom. The rules apply regardless of race, ethnicity, religion or climate. There's only one world.   CHARLES LANE

The 'Third World' Is Dead, but Spirits Linger

Indonesia saw a movement born, and now hosts its wake.

Barbara Crossette

Not more than 60 miles down the highway from the Indonesian hill town of Bogor, where President Clinton will take part this week in an economic summit of Asian-Pacific nations, is a genteel city that once symbolized everything the third world believed in and hoped for when it was young. The city is Bandung. There, another generation of world leaders—Nehru, Nasser, Nkrumah, Sukarno, Zhou Enlai—met at another summit, the 1955 Afro-Asian Conference, a gathering full of post-colonial promise, with dreams of self-sufficiency, solidarity among newly independent nations and commitment to an anti-super-power international policy that became known as nonalignment.

"Sisters and brothers!" President Sukarno of Indonesia told the delegates. "How terrifically dynamic is our time!"

The fraternal third world these founders envisioned is dead. The agenda for Bogor, where the heirs of the Bandung generation plan to talk mostly about economic liberalization, competition for foreign investment and free trade, is its obituary. The hollowness of the dream of Afro-Asian commonality is never so starkly evident as when Pacific Rim countries get together, a number of them boasting higher living standards than some European nations.

Nehru's India is barely on the horizon of this world; Nkrumah's Africa isn't even in the picture.

The "third world," a phrase first used by French journalists in the 1950's, was meant to describe those who were not part of the industrial world or the Communist bloc. The distinction has no more relevance now than the idea that developing nations automatically have much in common with each other. People speak of the "tigers" who form a class of their own, or a "fourth world" of the poorest countries. A "fifth world" might be found among proliferating populations of rootless refugees. And so on.

"We no longer have a coherent image of the third world," says Jean-Bernard Mérimée, France's chief delegate to the United Nations and a former Ambassador to India. "It is now composed of totally different elements. What do nations like Burkina Faso and Singapore have in common? Nothing, except a sort of lingering perception that they belong to something that had the tradition of opposing the West and the developed world." All that is left, the envoy said, are "remnants of the Bandung attitude" and memories of the fight against colonialism that once bonded emerging nations.

Bandung's oratory lives on, however, resurfacing regularly in the frustration of poor countries looking for easy explanations for develop-ment shortcomings. The new "imperialists" now tend to be lending organizations like the World Bank and International Monetary Fund, which have tried to impose stringent fiscal regimes. The "neocolonial" tag has also been attached to donor nations asking questions about rights abuses, child labor, religious or sex discrimination and population policy. At the recent United Nations population conference in Cairo, some of the hottest buttons and bumper stickers proclaimed angrily, "No to Contraceptive Imperialism."

The days of Bandung were heady days of shared underdevelopment, before yawning material gaps between the richest and poorest of these nations began to widen. In Asia, Pakistani business leaders say ruefully that a few decades ago their nation was roughly on a par with South Korea and both had military governments. Both are now democracies, at least on paper, but South Koreans live a decade longer, earn 10 times as much and send 10 times as many children to college with less than half Pakistan's population. In Egypt, intellectuals recall how their country once exported skilled labor to other Arabic-speaking nations that now import a more educated work force, even for menial jobs, from Southeast Asia. In decades of building organizations—the Non-aligned Movement, the Group of 77—third world nations never de-

 From the *New York Times*, November 13, 1994, pp. 1, 16. © 1994 by The New York Times Company. Reprinted by permission.

vised effective mechanisms to help one another.

Ideologies, economic policies, cultural differences and the creation of superpower clienteles all played a part in widening fissures among developing countries. Different growth rates were not always predictable. Singapore's lack of natural resources did not prevent it from growing into an economic powerhouse. A sea of oil has not turned Nigeria into Texas or Mexico. Authoritarian policies contributed to the boom in some nations. Repression and corruption drained the life of others, or drove the dispossessed into violence.

Dirt Poor, With Tanks

What happened to the shared dreams of the third world is documented in the United Nations' Human Development Index. Looking at daily lives rather than macroeconomic figures, the index has for the last five years ranked more than 100 developing nations in education, access to basic services and conditions of women, among other topics. "What emerges is an arresting picture of unprece-dented human progress and unspeakable human misery, of humanity's advances on several fronts mixed with humanity's retreat on several others, of a breath-taking globalization of prosperity side by side with a depressing globalization of poverty," the 1994 report says.

This year, the index focuses on big military spenders. "Many nations have sacrificed human security in the search for more sophisticated arms," it says. "For example, India ordered 20 advanced MIG-29 fighters that could have provided basic education to all the 15 million girls now out of school. Nigeria bought 80 battle tanks from the United Kingdom at a cost that would have immunized all two million unimmunized children in that country while also providing family-planning services to nearly 17 million couples."

While the third world had divided itself into unequal streams of development well before the end of the cold war, developing nations hoped there would be peace dividends for them after the collapse of communism. They have been disappointed. Not only have sources of aid from the former Soviet bloc withered, as Cuba has discovered most painfully, but also the European nations reborn as democracies—now labeled "economies in transition"—have moved in to claim a lot of attention and scarce development funds.

What to do? Development experts say doing nothing about the Global South—the new term—will lead only to more ethnic wars, migrations from overpopulated regions and rapid depletion of natural resources. On the other hand, those "remnants of the Bandung attitude" that the French envoy identified do not want the industrialized world to get an opportunity to intervene in national policies as a condition of granting more aid.

"You get a certain feeling that on many issues—social policies, environmental policies, human rights—the developing countries get a feeling of interference," said Austria's United Nations delegate, Ernst Sucharipa. "We would not say this is true, though I can see why some countries would feel that way. We have to have an open discussion on issues of global consequence." The need for universal sisterhood and brotherhood is now no longer confined to the world of Bandung.

Common Sense over Charisma

Forget the flamboyant populists of old. Across Latin America, today's presidents are winning the vote with tough austerity plans. Voters embrace pain for gain—long-desired stability.

William R. Long

Times Staff Writer

BUENOS AIRES—Election day, time to vote. El Presidente has raised taxes, slashed popular subsidies, let unemployment soar to record rates. *Adios* and out he goes? Not in the new Latin America.

After inflicting just that kind of painful austerity, Presidents Carlos Menem of Argentina and Alberto Fujimori of Peru wangled constitutional amendments allowing them to run for reelection and then won by landslides.

Along with the pain, of course, Menem and Fujimori gave voters something they apparently craved: economic and political stability.

As democracy matures across Latin America, the region's latest crop of leaders reflects an increasingly sober and practical approach to politics. Voters have learned what stability costs, and they are willing to pay the price. Politicians have learned that rhetoric, paternalism and populism are no substitute for competence and results.

Gone is the heady excitement sparked by many Latin American leaders of the past. Rationality reigns.

"The enthusiasm and magic aren't there . . . that colored earlier leaders," said Rosendo Fraga, an Argentine political analyst. "This was very clear to whoever was here for the elections of May 14. Menem won 50% of the votes, but there was no great popular fervor. It was a rational vote."

Today's Latin American presidents vary as widely in their styles and backgrounds as the geographies they govern, from the cactus fields of the Sonora Desert to the icy forests of Tierra del Fuego. But with few exceptions, they are part of a regional trend toward pragmatic leadership.

Old-style *caudillos*—strongmen—depended heavily on macho personality, florid oratory or costly patronage to win mass support. One famous master at this was Gen. Juan D. Peron, who captivated Argentina's working masses with grand speeches, pro-labor policies and generous spending.

During two presidential terms, from 1946 to 1955, Peron created jobs, raised wages and subsidized social programs on a huge scale. Economists now agree that such lavish ways helped set the stage for later super-inflation and an economic debacle not only in Argentina but also in many other Latin American countries.

Because economic and political instability often go together, many an old-style administration got into terminal trouble of both kinds. And like Peron, many a *caudillo* lost his job by military coup.

Today's "*caudillos* of stability," as Fraga calls them, put far greater stock in realistic economic programs and prudent management. "The predominant option today is a kind of popular conservatism, which is what Menem and Fujimori represent," Fraga said in an interview.

Partly, they are riding the neo-liberal wave that is sweeping most of the world, following the example of Asia's rapidly developing tigers and sticking to the dictates of the International Monetary Fund. But Latin Americans and their leaders have learned valuable lessons from hard experience.

They're fed up with guerrilla war, terrorism and harsh military rule. They've had it with leftist economic experiments and irresponsible public spending that fuels inflation and fiscal crises. Those things, they've found, can end up hurting more than government austerity.

In countries such as Argentina, where monthly inflation once raged in triple digits, voters are especially keen on leaders—no matter how uncharismatic—who know how to keep prices in line.

"Inflation has made a major change in Latin American political culture," Fraga said. "I think the key to this is the suffering of people . . . from inflation. This, to a large extent, is what has produced political, social and economic maturation."

The political culture is now marked by widespread awareness that economic and political stability reinforce each other and that, in fact, it is not possible to have one without the other.

Citizens and leaders alike are gaining skill in the orderly give-and-take of democracy. As people learn to participate, leaders are forced to keep them in mind. Peter Cleaves, director of the Institute for Latin American Studies at the University of Texas, said political power has become more broadly distributed: New parties, more powerful interest groups and more aggressive news media help electorates keep politicians on their toes.

"Citizens are more skeptical about leaving decisions up to a *jefe supremo* [supreme leader]," Cleaves said. "They're a lot more critical and evaluative of leadership than they have been in the past."

BIG HATS AND BRASS BUTTONS

The end of the Cold War has also contributed to the rise of the "*caudillos* of stability." Since the collapse of the Soviet Union and the economic failure of communism in Cuba, leftist politicians have little clout in Latin America and rightists no longer have a formidable foe. As a result, leadership based on ideology, and disruptive left-right strife, has faded from the scene.

And because of the Cold War's end, the military option has waned as well. Fears of Communist subversion no longer serve as justification for a takeover by the military. Almost everyone agrees now that elections are the best way to change government and ensure stability. Powerful elites and common people are less willing than ever to call in the men with big hats and brass buttons.

During most of this century, Latin America was a kaleidoscope of dictatorial and democratic governments with civilian and military leaders of varying ideological colors. Military strongmen often seized power to straighten out political and economic messes created under populist civilian leadership.

The majority of the region's population was under military rule during much of the 1960s and 1970s. But during the 1980s, civilian government returned to one nation after another. Now, elected leaders govern every country except Cuba.

In elections over the past 18 months, voters in seven countries that account for more than three-quarters of the region's 450 million people chose presidents to lead until 1999 or 2000. In each of those countries, the winner is at least the second straight civilian president to be elected.

SEVEN POLITICAL INSIDERS

All seven are political insiders, associated with incumbent or previous administrations. All are closely identified with economic stability, and none could be called a classical populist.

Chilean President Eduardo Frei, elected in December, 1993, is a somber, soft-spoken engineer who has little of the crowd appeal that made his father a popular president in the 1970s. But the younger Frei was a candidate of the incumbent coalition that took power in 1990 after 16 years of repressive military rule and kept the country on a successful economic course.

Frei's Christian Democrats are united with socialists and other leftists behind a pragmatic program of free-market policies. Few Chileans now would think of voting for a populist leader like Salvador Allende, whose socialist administration ended in chaos and a coup in 1973.

Ernesto Samper won Colombian elections in May, 1994, mostly because he was a faithful member of the dominant Liberal Party. Samper, an economist and former government minister, stood for continuing free-market reforms, but at a more cautious pace.

Mexico's Ernesto Zedillo, who won the presidency in August, 1994, also is a technocrat, with a doctorate in economics from Yale. His personality might best be described as neutral, but that was just fine when he was picked by the long-ruling Institutional Revolutionary Party to replace assassinated candidate Luis Donaldo Colosio.

Although Mexicans voted for continuity and stability, they were slapped with a peso devaluation and a deep financial crisis soon after Zedillo took office Dec. 1. In working to bring back the economy, he is sticking to a pragmatic, hard-slogging approach.

Brazil's Fernando Henrique Cardoso won the presidency in October, 1994, largely on the strength of an economic stabilization plan that he had launched as finance minister. Cardoso, a former sociology professor, has a calm and reasoned style of discourse that sometimes is called blase.

Voters rejected populist labor leader Luis Inacio (Lula) da Silva, a populist outsider with a leftist platform. Earlier in his career, Cardoso was a leftists. His shift to free-market pragmatism reflects the prevailing political mood in Brazil—despite its bad experience with former President Fernando Collor de Mello, a free-marketeer who was impeached on corruption charges in 1992.

In Uruguay, former President Julio Sanguinetti defeated the party in power when he won election in November, 1994. His policies are chiefly aimed at economic and social stability, which were trademarks of his previous presidency.

Although Sanguinetti has promised to address the social costs of free-market policies, he has been careful not to question the need for government austerity and business expansion. Uruguayans are still fond of their country's traditional welfare programs. But economic crises and hardships have taught them to appreciate spending restraints and private-sector growth.

Peru's Fujimori won reelection in April, followed by Menem in Argentina. Both has rescued their countries from economic debacles of hyper-inflation and disinvestment. In both countries, market policies and anti-inflation austerity brought increased unemployment, but most voters seemed willing to pay those costs.

Fujimori's first term not only achieved economic stability but the near-defeat of the once-fearsome Sendero Luminoso (Shining Path) terrorist and guerrilla movement. Fujimori has shown populist tendencies, touring the countryside to hand over tractors and schoolhouses, but his popularity is not based chiefly on that, analysts say.

NOT POPULAR, BUT THEY GET RESULTS

"People didn't vote for him because they like him, they voted for him because he has produced results," said Peruvian political analyst Enrique Obando. It is telling that one of Fujimori's most popular acts was to close Congress in 1992, breaking up what was widely perceived as a nest of traditional populists and demagogues.

Menem, a former provincial governor, won his first presidential election in 1989 as the candidate of a party founded by Peron. In those days, Menem had the reputation of a populist pol in the old Peronist style. But changing with the times, he has toned down his flamboyant style and stuck to a program of hard-nosed, free-market reforms.

A few days before the May elections in Argentina, opposition candidate Jose Octavio Bordon promised to increase retirement pensions. Menem said no, there wasn't enough money. People voted for Menem at a moment when the Argentine economy was shaken by regional shock waves from Mexico's crisis.

The longer the current trend of democracy lasts, the more the political winds shift in democratic directions. Just a couple of decades ago, much of the region was dominated by traditional business and political elites. Democratic traditions and institutions were weak, and there were relatively few strong interest groups.

"Now you've got a much richer political tapestry, one that calls for a different kind of leadership," said Paul H. Boeker, who heads the San Diego-based Institute of the Americas. There are exceptions, Boeker said, in countries such as Guatemala and Nicaragua, where politics remains relatively primitive. But he said that in most of Latin America, leaders are learning to make government work through negotiated compromises between conflicting demands from different quarters.

"I think you have more and more Latin American politicians looking more like U.S. or European politicians," Boeker said.

"It's pragmatism, but . . . there is a certain steadiness of vision too," he said. "Their pragmatism takes place within a set of strategic goals."

One exception, Boeker said, is Venezuelan President Rafael Caldera, a "decent man" and simpatico politician who has been trying to solve Venezuela's staggering economic problems with price controls, exchange controls and other measures that have failed in the past. "He's winging it, and winging it on the basis of instincts from the past," Boeker said. "I don't see a strategic vision."

According to a recent Gallup poll, Caldera's public disapproval rating has risen to 52%—one more sign that today's Latin Americans don't support politicians just for being congenial. But Eduardo Gamarra, acting director of the Latin America and Caribbean Center at Florida International University, argued that the traditional hunger for strong, personalist leaders is not dead.

LEADERS COULD USE *SOME* CHARISMA

"We do need those old-style *caudillos* dressed in modern garb," Gamarra said. For example, he said, Zedillo could use some charisma to lead Mexicans through their problems. And Bolivian President Gonzalo Sanchez de Lozada could use some to push through his ambitious program of economic and political reforms, which are meeting widespread resistance.

In Bolivia and many Latin American countries, economic reforms have brought job losses, an end to government subsidies and stagnant wages. The painful squeeze has evoked groans that prevailing neo-liberal policies benefit business oligarchies at the expense of poor masses. Many leaders are acknowledging such complaints and giving at least lip service to "social programs" they say will ease the pain of reform and reduce poverty.

Argentine analyst Fraga predicted that the pressure will increase on leaders with more social-democratic tendencies: "If stability is consolidated and there is a growth phenomenon, there will be more social demands."

MEXICO

The long haul

The PRI has ruled Mexico for 66 years. It is the most tenacious political party in the world. Has the country's present economic crisis loosened its grip?

MEXICO CITY

THE minister was unavailable, visitors were told. He could not be reached and nobody knew where he was. Getting to his office, had he tried, would have posed a problem. Hundreds of strikers, protesting at wage cuts and job losses in the public sector, clogged the street outside the building, and the front doors were barred. The demonstrators leaned on their banners and munched their tortillas. Here and there, disappointed supplicants spoke into mobile phones, summoning their cars and adjusting their schedules for the day.

In other words, it was business as usual in Mexico city. Strikes and demonstrations are an almost daily event, and the government is frequently the object of complaint. Since Mexico's current economic crisis began last December, the number of marchers has swollen, and tempers are sometimes lost. Even so, these demos remain mostly placid and good-natured, and are easily put up with. This is partly because they are well organised. Mexico's trade unions take some care over this. Nearly all of them are affiliated to the PRI—the Institutional Revolutionary Party— whose rule in Mexico has been unbroken since 1929.

Mexico's current crisis is putting new strains on this old, if not grand, institution. As a result, the PRI has got a new party president, Santiago Onate, previously labour secretary in Ernesto Zedillo's cabinet. This shuffling does not, in itself, change things very much. The PRI is not, as such, a source of power or doctrine (always a flexible matter in Mexico); it is the mechanism through which the country's rulers give themselves legitimacy, a mechanism for encompassing or otherwise tolerating dissent and thus allowing the entrenched bureaucracy to continue its rule.

The PRI outlived the Communist Party of the Soviet Union for many reasons, but one was that the communists, their foundations sunk deep into ideology, never learned to cope with, as opposed to stamp on, critics. Opponents had to be silenced. As soon as they were allowed to speak, the regime began to crack. To be sure, the hard men of Mexico's regime have brutal—indeed lethal—ways of dealing with some opponents. But so effectively does the system accommodate well-behaved dissent that, except in the most difficult times, only moderate and selective repression has been needed to keep things under control.

The potential challengers to this carefully maintained status quo are the rightwing PAN and the left-wing PRD, a party which split off from the PRI in the 1980s. Both appear to have entered into tacit accommodations with the PRI to a greater—in the case of the PAN—or lesser—in the case of the PRD—extent. Mexico has elections. Its vote-counters, supervised mainly by PRI officials, allow the opposition parties to win some. As support for these parties has grown, they have been allowed to win more. As domestic and international scrutiny of Mexican elections has increased, the PRI's old hands have relied less on ballot-stuffing and misplaced polling stations, and more on bribes and computer breakdowns.

The terms of the bargain are shifting in the opposition's direction, but the basic formula holds. The PAN and the PRD are granted seats in parliament, the odd state governorship and their say—provided they and their supporters keep their attacks on the PRI within bounds. By such means, Mexico has remained the world's only multi-party dictatorship.

This moderation in repression, these democratic appearances, have served the PRI's purpose in another way. They have been essential in maintaining something that the regime, at certain points, might have collapsed without: the backing of the United States. That backing was sorely needed this year. As in 1982, Mexico came within a hair's breadth of defaulting on its debts. The Clinton administration bent the rules, lending Mexico $20 billion from coffers over which Congress has no direct control. And the White House urged similar flexibility on the IMF— which quickly promised Mexico $8 billion, by far the biggest credit it has ever granted, with as much as $10 billion more to follow.

America's motives, of course, were selfish: among other things, its government fears a huge influx of immigrants should Mexico fall into chaos. Nonetheless, the help arrived at least partly because the PRI is a regime that, for all its failings, the United States feels able to support.

The rulers' dilemma

For years, people have been asking how much longer the PRI can continue to balance the interests that keep it in power. Certainly its task is becoming more difficult. One way to sum up its dilemma is this. To survive, it must deliver growth. This requires it to liberalise the economy (nothing else works). But that denies office-holders the perquisites of economic control—and in Mexico, as in many other countries, corruption is the glue that holds the ruling party together. So the prognosis must be gloomy. Yet earlier reports of the PRI's impending demise, and there have been many, all proved premature.

The immediate challenge facing the PRI is at least as formidable as that of 1988. Then, thanks to the split in the party which produced the PRD, the PRI had to use all the electoral chicanery at its disposal to avoid losing control of both the national congress and the presidency itself. The incoming president, Carlos Salinas, had to rebuild the party's support. Some of his methods are being used again now, and for the moment the PRI can say: so far, so good. The path out of the current financial mess can be discerned. For now, the centre holds.

In 1995 the government's immediate difficulties are economic. So were many of the problems at election-time in 1988—they underlay the split in the party. The PRI's popularity had slumped after nearly a decade of economic failure. The country was weary of high inflation, falling living standards and mounting unemployment. But it was time to choose a new leader: Mexico's presidents serve a single term of six years, and Miguel de la Madrid's time was up. The party's nominee, Mr Salinas, was narrowly elected in a poll that was blatantly rigged. He set about legitimising himself in the tried and tested manner.

First came the traditional crackdown on corruption. Mr Salinas began by locking up a union boss who, as it happened, had failed to deliver his workers' votes in the election. He also promised, as tradition further requires, a radical shift in economic policy—denouncing, in so many words, the previous government and its works. In conveying this message, it helps that in Mexico a new president brings with him not only a new cabinet but also a substantially new administration: despite the uninterrupted rule of the PRI, the turnover of senior jobs in Mexico's government is faster than in most industrial democracies. In short, Mexico was going to make a new start.

And so it did—though not in quite the way Mr Salinas claimed. His new economic reforms were bold, but they did not overturn the policies of Mr de la Madrid. They took those earlier changes further. It would have been easy, and more accurate, to emphasise continuity between the two administrations, but Mexico wanted a break with the past, not more of the same. Mr Salinas presented his programme accordingly. Gradually, the economy improved. Gradually, the PRI repaired some of the political damage it had suffered in the 1980s.

Seven years later the PRI is deeply unpopular again. The country's hopes of faster economic growth, which had seemed to be coming true under Mr Salinas, have been shattered. The currency's devaluation at the end of 1994 has caused inflation to soar: in July prices rose by 2.04% (27% at an annual rate); last November the rise was just 0.5% (equivalent to 6% a year). Worse, despite the generous help from the United States and the IMF, Mexico has had to curb its overall foreign borrowing very sharply. In 1994 it borrowed from abroad an amount equivalent to 8% of its GDP; this year its external deficit will be close to zero.

This switch is putting the economy under great strain. It requires a correspondingly large cut in consumption and investment. This, in turn, is being brought about by a ferocious programme of higher taxes, higher interest rates and lower public spending. An exceptionally severe recession is already apparent in the cities, where public-sector jobs and services are concentrated. The contraction in output—10% in the year to the second quarter—is already greater than the slump of the 1980s (though it should prove of far shorter duration).

Mr Salinas's successor, Mr Zedillo, was elected in August last year and took office shortly before the new economic crisis broke. Unsurprisingly, like Mr Salinas before him, Mr Zedillo talks of a break with the past. Again, the new economic policies (some promised, some already in place) extend and accelerate the policies of the previous administration. Just as before, the electorate is desperate to believe that things will

be different from now on—and that is what it is told.

Happily for Mr Zedillo, Mr Salinas has done much to discredit himself. Unlike Mr de la Madrid, he declined to fade away, as Mexico's political etiquette requires. Compromised by the investigation of his brother's alleged involvement in a political assassination, and by other revelations and allegations, he sought farcically to restore his reputation by going on hunger strike. The new leadership issued a soothing statement. Mr Salinas duly vanished, heading north. This comedy served to emphasise that a discredited administration had come to a definitive end.

Mr Salinas's distress was understandable. His fall from domestic and international acclaim (especially international: no president of Mexico has been so lauded by foreigners) to pariah at home and joke abroad was extraordinarily abrupt. But some of that turnabout was only to be expected, just as Mr Zedillo must expect some of the same in due course. It is the destiny of most Mexican presidents to be disdained by their successors—even though their successors not only belong to the same party but are, moreover, picked by the outgoing president. Liberal democracy meets the electorate's desire to punish bad governments or simply have a change. Mexico's regime is neither liberal nor democratic—but knows nonetheless how to satisfy that desire.

The Salinas factor

Similarities between the early days of the Salinas and Zedillo administrations reveal a lot about the resilience of the PRI. However, a crucial difference must not be overlooked. Mr Zedillo's inheritance, bleak as it seems right now, is far more promising than was that of Mr Salinas.

The Mexican economy was indeed transformed between 1988 and 1994. In the United States, politicians such as Alfonse D'Amato opposed American help for the Mexican economy this year. They argued that Mexico had only been pretending to change, and that its relapse into economic crisis last year exposed the fraud. This is wrong. The economic reforms of the Salinas years were both real and sweeping, among the most radical the developing world has ever seen.

Mr Salinas began by putting the Mexican government's books in order, trimming government spending and turning enormous fiscal deficits into surpluses. At the same time, in a remarkably ambitious programme of privatisation, he sold a raft of state-owned assets—banks, utilities, steel mills, you name it—and raised over $20 billion in the process. Through efforts to deregulate and decentralise the economy, he also began to attack the oligopolies that had long dominated the privately owned parts of Mexican business.

If Mexico's economy had changed so much for the better, why did it plunge once more into financial crisis? Were the reforms a confidence trick? Not at all. The government's difficulties began precisely because the reforms were genuine. Such was the enthusiasm of foreign investors for what they saw in Mexico, that capital flooded into the country. This presented the Salinas administration with a difficult problem of macroeconomic control. Out of incompetence and bad luck, it botched the job—but the trouble started because Mexico was a victim of its own success.

During 1994 investors at home and abroad began to worry that the peso—which had been pegged to the dollar as part of the government's anti-inflation plan—was overvalued. This anxiety was worsened by a dreadful run of bad news: the uprising in Chiapas in January; a series of political assassinations, including that of a presidential candidate; growing uncertainty over the outcome of the elections due in August. The markets became jittery, and the inflow of capital began to dry up.

Mr Salinas and his deputies—notably, his finance minister, Pedro Aspe—would not hear of devaluing the currency. They argued partly that the peso was not overvalued at all (exports were still booming) and partly that the interruption to capital flows was temporary. The right policy was therefore to finance the shortfall of capital by running down the country's ample reserves. Long before they were run too low, the private flow of capital would resume.

At the time, this calculation was not self-evidently wrong (though the subsequent outcry from economists wise after the event would lead you to think otherwise). Nonetheless, wrong it proved—and how. By the end of the year, the reserves had all but gone. The crisis broke; the peso collapsed; Mexico's stockmarket plunged.

For weeks Mr Zedillo's new government was paralysed. But its response, when it finally came, could hardly be faulted for lack of resolve. New privatisations of ports, airports and railways were announced, and are already under way. The value-added tax was raised from 10% to 15%. The prices of petrol and electricity were sharply increased in real terms. Deep spending cuts, amounting to 1.6% of GDP, were imposed. The minimum wage was raised, but by much less than the rate of inflation.

The price, in falling living standards and mounting unemployment, is already high and will rise further. The sharpness of the recession poses further economic dangers. Greatest among these is the perilous condition of the banking system. If the recession endures into next year, if big banks begin to go under, and if Mr Zedillo's commendable attempts to restructure them (for instance, by attracting new foreign owners) do not succeed, then a further downward spiral may ensue.

The financial crisis of the 1980s cost Mexico more than five years of lost development. This time, there are reasons to hope for a faster recovery. In 1994, the economy was fundamentally much stronger than in the early 1980s. With one or two exceptions, Mr Zedillo's new policies amount to an intensification of the liberalising changes. That speaks volumes about the new Mexico: far from being driven off course, the reforms are speeding faster along it. And the financial markets have noticed. Already Mexico is finding buyers for its bonds.

Bad luck helped to bring Mexico's economy to its present unhappy state. A measure of good luck will be needed to deliver it quickly back to health. Without a speedy recovery, however, Mexico's politics could turn bad. The PRI's delicate balance might be disturbed. The government might then have to choose between stepping aside and stepping more firmly on its opponents.

A Yeltsin for Mexico

Mr Salinas famously remarked that he would never make Mikhail Gorbachev's mistake: he would not free Mexico politically until he had completed the task of freeing it economically. If his policies so far are any guide, Mr Zedillo agrees that Mexico's economic changes must be extended and entrenched. On politics, however, the signs are that he thinks Mr Salinas was wrong.

The new president has made "the rule of law" the mantra of his administration. His first act as president, forced through as the financial markets collapsed about him, was to start a reform of the country's notoriously crooked system of justice. He has opened negotiations with the opposition parties on new political changes, and has won some support in that quarter. He has appointed a member of the PAN as attorney-general. He is also trying to democratise the PRI itself, by changing the way candidates are selected. He has promised that, unlike his predecessors, he will not choose the PRI's next president—sorry, presidential candidate.

Is this the PRI up to old tricks—another cynical attempt to appease popular anger at the mess the previous lot left behind? Possibly. But Mr Zedillo, an austere and impressive man, is unlike most of his predecessors: nobody expected him to become president, so he comes to the job with fewer debts to PRI grandees than is usual. Remember too the PRI's dilemma. In many ways—ways that the party's members do not, for the most part, recognise—Mr Zedillo's avowed aim of further economic reform combined with faster political change may make better sense, from the party's point of view, than the economic radicalism and political complacency of Mr Salinas.

If the economy continues to modernise, the advantages that can be got through regulation and monopoly—the PRI's lifeblood—will slowly drain away. They need not vanish altogether; even in a rich democracy, politics can remain an illicitly profitable profession, as many a well-appointed apartment in Rome can testify.

Nonetheless, there will be less to go round, and the PRI will be forced to adapt. In doing so, there is just a chance that it could start to become an orthodox political party rather than an all-encompassing system of graft wrapped around a bureaucracy.

If such a transition is ever to be peacefully accomplished, however, the party had better be steered towards it. That is Mr Zedillo's challenge. If he fails, and the PRI's fate comes to be decided, the results could be messy. The party's *dinosaurios* would prefer to go down fighting, and will resist. But the conservatives can be beaten; the Salinas reforms, bitterly resented by many of the old guard, showed that.

There are growing signs that Mexicans want more of both sorts of freedom—political and economic. For now, at least, it is enough that the country's economic pain has not discredited the goal of economic liberalisation among Mexicans at large, as it might have. Mexico's economic reforms appear to have put down roots, strong enough with luck to withstand this year's gales.

On the day of the demonstration outside the finance ministry, there was another protest in Mexico city. Scores of battered old cars with American licence plates paraded through the town, their Mexican importer-owners demanding that regulations intended to discourage such personal initiative be abolished. In the past few years, Mexico has acquired a taste for such ideas. If the PRI can see where they lead, it might yet learn to live with democracy.

"As a result of its economic marginalization and relatively feeble attempted [economic] reform, Africa is in many respects lost between state and market. It wanders between ineffective states and weak markets, both domestic and international, and the latter are increasingly indifferent."

Africa: Falling Off the Map?

THOMAS M. CALLAGHY

THOMAS M. CALLAGHY *is an associate professor of political science at the University of Pennsylvania; he is coeditor, with John Ravenhill, of* Hemmed In: Responses to Africa's Economic Decline *(New York: Columbia University Press, 1993).*

In the mid-nineteenth century, after the end of the slave trade and before the imposition of direct colonial domination, Africa found itself both marginalized from the world economy and highly dependent on it. A leading historian of Africa has pointed out this paradox, and noted that it operated in the opposite direction as well: the world's "increasing involvement in the African economy...[was] at odds with the decreasing economic importance of Africa" for the world economy.[1] At the end of the twentieth century, this paradox still holds; in fact, it is truer now than it was in the pre-colonial period.

Africa's increased marginalization has been both economic and political-strategic, but the former is most significant. Africa is no longer very important to the international division of labor or to the major actors in the world economy—multinational corporations, international banks, the economies of the major Western countries or those of the newly industrializing countries such as South Korea, Taiwan, Brazil, and Mexico. Africa generates a declining share of world output. The main commodities it produces are becoming less sought after or are more effectively produced by other third world countries. Trade is declining, nobody wants to lend, and few want to invest except in selected parts of the mineral sector.

Africa's per capita income levels and growth rates have declined since the first oil crisis in 1973, while its percentage of worldwide official development assistance rose from 17 percent in 1970 to about 38 percent in 1991. Since 1970, nominal gross domestic product has risen more slowly than in other developing countries, while real GDP growth rates have dropped dramatically since 1965.

Other developing countries performed better in spite of the poor world economic climate, especially in the 1980s. For the period 1982–1992, average annual GDP growth for Africa was 2 percent; for South Asia, the most comparable region, it was a little over 5 percent, while the East Asian rate was 8 percent. The rate for all developing countries was 2.7 percent. The per capita GDP rates are even more revealing: Africa, 1 percent; South Asia, 3 percent; and East Asia, 6.4 percent. The World Bank's baseline projections for the decade beginning in 1992 are more optimistic, projecting annual GDP growth of 3.7 percent for Africa, but the bank's estimates for Africa have often proved overly hopeful, and the assumptions of the current forecast are startling. They assume less unfavorable external conditions, including a break in falling commodity prices; more liberalized world trade regimes; and no real decline in the growth of industrial countries; less civil strife; improvement in economic policies and implementation; a higher percentage of foreign investment; the continuation of current foreign aid; and no major adverse weather! The forecast does, however, anticipate a 50 percent rise in the number of poor people, from 200 million to 300 million, making Africa the only region in the world with an overall increase in poverty.

In addition, African export levels have stayed relatively flat or have actually declined since 1970, while

---

[1] Ralph Austen, *African Economic History* (London: James Currey, 1987), pp. 102, 109. In this article, Africa means sub-Saharan Africa minus South Africa.

From *Current History* magazine, 80th Anniversary Issue, January 1994, pp. 31-36. Original version of this revised article first appeared in *Africa in World Politics, 2/e,* edited by John Harbeson and Donald Rothchild. © 1995 by Westview Press, Boulder, CO. Reprinted by permission.

those of other developing countries have risen significantly. For example, the continent's share of developing-country agricultural exports slumped from 17 percent to 8 percent between 1970 and 1990, with South and East Asian exports expanding rapidly. Africa's marginalization becomes more startling when its performance is compared with that of other low income regions, particularly South Asia. The difference between the two is striking for per capita GDP growth; Africa's has slipped markedly while that of South Asia has climbed slowly but steadily as the African population growth rate continues to rise while that of South Asia has begun to decline.

The most important differences, however, relate to the level and quality of investment. Africa's investment as a percentage of GDP declined in the 1980s, while that of South Asia continued to increase despite the difficult economic conditions of the decade. South Asia followed better economic policies, and above all provided a much more propitious socioeconomic and political environment for investment. This is most vividly manifested in the rate of return on investment: in Africa, the rate fell from almost 31 percent in the 1960s to just 2.5 percent in the 1980s, while in South Asia it inched steadily upward, from 21.3 percent to 22.4 percent.

Given this dismal economic performance, both substantively and comparatively, it is not surprising that world business leaders take an increasingly jaundiced view of Africa. As one business executive said to this author, "Who cares about Africa; it is not important to us; leave it to the IMF [International Monetary Fund] and the World Bank." Some observers have referred to this phenomenon as "postneocolonialism." For the most dynamic actors in a rapidly changing world economy, even a neocolonial Africa is not of much interest anymore, especially after the amazing changes wrought in Eastern Europe and elsewhere beginning in 1989. According to this viewpoint, the African crisis really should be left to the international financial institutions, and if their salvage effort works, fine; if not, so be it, the world economy will hardly notice.

Thus, whatever one thinks about the role of foreign business and capital, it is important to remember that Africa increasingly imposes enormous difficulties for them, such as political arbitrariness and administrative, infrastructural, and economic inefficiency. Because foreign capital has the considerable ability to select the type of state with which it cooperates, it is very doubtful that Africa will play any significant role in current shifts in the patterns of production in the international division of labor. For most businesspeople from abroad Africa has become a sinkhole that swallows their money with little or no return. Two arresting facts further underscore Africa's marginalization: the amount of external financing through bonds for East

Asia in 1991 was $2.4 billion, and for South Asia $1.9 billion, while it was zero for Africa; and flight capital as a percentage of GDP at the end of 1990 was 15 for South Asia, 19 for East Asia, and 28 for developing Europe and for Central Asia, while it was 80 for Africa.

Disinvestment, in fact, has emerged as a trend. During the 1980s, for example, 43 of 139 British firms with industrial investments in Africa withdrew. Ironically, the retrenchment has in part been due to economic reforms that have done away with overvalued exchange rates and import tariff protection. The British firms were unwilling to inject new capital to make their investments efficient by world standards of competitiveness. While Japan is now the major donor, it is not likely to be a major investor in Africa; in the 1980s, for example, the number of Japanese commercial companies operating in Kenya dwindled from 15 to 2.

The second aspect of Africa's marginalization is at the strategic level, which has also had negative economic consequences. Africa has become of much less interest to the major world powers with the dramatic changes in the international arena, especially the end of the cold war. As one senior African diplomat put it, "Eastern Europe is the most sexy beautiful girl, and we are an old tattered lady. People are tired of Africa. So many countries, so many wars." The rise of warlords in regional and civil wars similar to those in nineteenth-century Africa has challenged the very notion of the nation-state borrowed at independence in the 1960s. Eritrea's independence from Ethiopia, made official last year, and the potential breakup of countries such as Zaire, raise the potentially inflammatory issue of redrawing old colonial boundaries sacrosanct for 30 years. External intervention on the scale seen in Somalia recently is not likely to be repeated; the malign neglect applied to the greater Liberian, Angolan, and Sudanese civil wars is likely to be the more common reaction to such conflicts.

THE NEW NEOCOLONIALISM

Yet in other ways Africa has become more tightly linked to the world economy. This increased involvement has two aspects: an extreme dependence on public actors from outside Africa, particularly the IMF and the World Bank, in the determination of African economic policy; and the liberal or neoclassical thrust of the policy so developed, which pushes the continent toward more intense reliance on and integration with the world economy. Both these aspects are directly linked to Africa's debt crisis.

In 1974 total African debt was about $14.8 billion; by 1992 it had reached an estimated $183.4 billion, or about 109 percent of Africa's total GNP. (In comparison, in South Asia it was 36 percent, and in East Asia 28 percent.) Much of the recent rise has come through borrowing from international financial institutions, especially the IMF and the World Bank, that has been associated with economic reform programs sponsored from outside, usually referred to as structural adjustment. In 1980 debt through international financial institutions constituted 19 percent of the total, whereas by 1992 it accounted for 28 percent. This cannot be rescheduled and significant arrears are accumulating, with the result that IMF and World Bank assistance to some countries has been cut off. Much of the rest of Africa's debt is bilateral or government-guaranteed private medium- and long-term debt and thus is rescheduled by leading Western governments through the Paris Club, and not by the private banks as in Latin America. Countries cannot obtain Paris Club rescheduling relief without being in the good graces of the IMF and the World Bank.

Despite its relative smallness by world standards, the enormous buildup of African debt puts terrible strains on fragile economies. By the end of the 1980s the debt was the equivalent of 350 percent of exports. Africa's debt service ratio (debt service owed as a percentage of export earnings) averaged a little less than 30 percent by the mid-1980s. By 1992 it still averaged more than 25 percent, with some African countries showing much higher rates; Uganda's, for example, was 80 percent. The debt service ratios would be significantly lower, however, if African export growth had kept pace with the performance of other less developed countries. Only about half of debt service owed is paid in any given year, which tends to dampen foreign direct investment.

Given such debt, African countries have benefited from rescheduling concessions such as longer terms and grace periods, lower interest rates, and the rescheduling of previously rescheduled debt. Between 1989 and 1991, about $10 billion in concessional debt, especially that incurred by the continent's low-income nations, was written off by Western countries, including the initially unwilling United States. Despite strong pressure from the IMF, the World Bank, various UN agencies, and private organizations such as Oxfam, most of the major donor countries are still resisting significant debt cancellation.

As in other areas of the third world, this external debt burden and the consequent desperate need for foreign exchange have left African countries highly dependent on a variety of actors from outside the continent, all of which have used their leverage to "encourage" economic liberalization. This process, which some have referred to as "the new neocolonialism," means intense dependence on international financial institutions and major Western countries for the design of economic reform packages and for the resources needed to implement them. Specific economic policy changes are requested in return for the lending of resources. The primary intent of these economic reform efforts is to more fully integrate African economies into the world economy by resurrecting the primary-product export economies that existed at independence and making them work better this time by creating a more "liberal" political economy.

The track record of IMF and World Bank economic reform in Africa since the early 1980s has been quite modest. Ghana under the authoritarian military government of Jerry Rawlings has been about the only case of sustained economic transformation, and it is still fragile. Even African countries that traditionally did relatively well economically in the postcolonial period are now in considerable trouble—Nigeria, Kenya, Ivory Coast, Cameroon, and Senegal have grave economic problems and weak or failed economic reform efforts.

As a result of its economic marginalization and relatively feeble reform efforts, Africa is in many respects lost between state and market. It wanders between ineffective states and weak markets, both domestic and international, and the latter are increasingly indifferent. Many African officials fail to realize just how unimportant Africa is becoming to the world economy. Many are still looking for a quick fix, while the last decade of world history shows that one does not exist. If African countries are to survive, changes must be made. If not, changes in the world political economy will continue to pass Africa by, with very serious long-term consequences for the people of the continent.

DEBATING WHAT TO DO

By the end of the 1980s, with obstacles to reform on all sides, the key question remained: what should Africa do to cope with its devastating economic crisis? The answer from outside, led by the World Bank, was to persevere with the thrust of reforms while making modifications to make them work more effectively. Many Africans remained unconvinced. This fundamental disagreement had simmered quietly throughout the decade behind what appeared to many as a growing consensus around a modified neo-orthodox position.

This disagreement erupted with surprising vigor in what could be called "the bloody spring of 1989." A major battle ensued between the World Bank and the UN's Economic Commission for Africa (ECA) as the former tried to defend structural adjustment and the latter attack it and present its own alternative strategy. Both sides made inappropriate claims. The record of structural adjustment was not nearly as strong as the World Bank tried to make it appear. On the African side, the ECA's "alternative framework" was a warmed-over version of earlier statist and "self-reliant" policies that were vague, often contradictory, and could not be implemented under the best of conditions—all linked to staggering demands for money and other resources. Many Africans were still running from the world economy while looking for a shortcut to development.

By late 1989 the visceral emotions of the bloody spring had been substantially tamed, though without resolution of many of the underlying disagreements. One of the main pacifying factors was the World Bank's release of its long-awaited "long-term perspective study," *Sub-Saharan Africa: From Crisis to Sustainable Growth,* which had been drafted following extensive consultation with Africans—from government officials and entrepreneurs in both the formal and informal economies to the heads of African private volunteer organizations. The report demonstrated that the World Bank had learned many lessons from the attempts at structural adjustment in the 1980s, especially the desperate need for institutional change and for a slower, more sequenced transition that recognized the sociopolitical obstacles to change. Its major themes were that Africa requires an enabling environment—above all, technical and administrative capacity (both state and private) and better political governance.

The report sought a second-generation development strategy in which the state listens carefully to the market even if it does not precisely follow it. Although not put in these terms, this strategy would attempt a move away from the predatory and inefficient mercantilism of the first 30 years of independence and back toward a more productive and efficient, though limited, version of what some have called "benign mercantilism"—that is, toward a more productive tension between state and market.

From the African point of view, this second-generation strategy is clearly a second-best one. But critics of structural adjustment, both inside and outside Africa, do not have a viable alternative to this modified version of neo-orthodoxy. The current African state does not have the capabilities for the more interventionist versions of benign mercantilism represented by South Korea and Taiwan. Governments can, and should, work in that direction, but the transition will be slow and uneven.

Creative tinkering with the neo-orthodox strategy by both African governments and the IMF and World Bank could begin to move the continent in useful directions. The long-term perspective study seemed to represent a step down that road. Ultimately it is not just a question of finding the "precarious balance" between state and market or state and society, but rather of searching for the balance between state, market, and the international arena.

This author would argue that the debate was reignited because many of the nice-sounding "lessons" of *From Crisis to Sustainable Growth,* which were meant to placate a variety of critics, have either been very difficult to implement or the IMF and the World Bank have simply not tried to do so seriously. Largely this is because structural adjustment requires difficult tradeoffs that most opponents refuse to face squarely. Structural adjustment cannot be all things to all people; if it could, there would be no crisis.

DEMOCRACY AND ECONOMY

The three-way balance between state, market, and the international arena has proved hard to achieve. In part this is because the international arena has a habit of presenting new and unexpected challenges for African rulers. While *From Crisis to Sustainable Growth* was initially well received by many Africans, it contained a time bomb called governance—the issue of how African states are ruled—which has brought considerable new tension and uncertainty to relations between Africans and influential groups from outside, and to economic policy.

With the shifts in the world since 1989, especially in Eastern Europe but also in Central America and South Africa, and the search for a new direction in foreign policy to replace containment—what the Clinton administration has recently called "enlargement" of the world's free community of market democracies—governance has been transformed by the major Western industrial democracies into a strategy for the promotion of democracy. The convergence of these two policy thrusts—one largely technocratic from the World Bank, the other distinctly political from the major powers—has posed a real dilemma for Africa.

Political conditionality, or making bilateral assistance and loans from international financial institutions conditional on domestic political changes, greatly increases African dependence on outside actors. Many African leaders fear this, including a few who are committed to economic reform. Guinea's finance minister, Soriba Kaba, for example, recently complained about the proliferation of conditions that African regimes have to face, "especially relating to governance and performance," saying that "application of these criteria, without agreed parameters and precise definitions, may be used as a pretext to reduce the volume of resource flows to our continent."[2] Some leaders resist energetically, such as Zaire's Mobutu Sese Seko; others, such as Kenya's Daniel arap Moi and Cameroon's Paul Biya, stall while playing charades with critics both inside and outside their countries.

However, a major contradiction may indeed exist between economic and political conditionality, one that Western governments either do not see or ignore. The primary assumptions appear to be that economic structural adjustment and political liberalization are mutually reinforcing processes, and that since authoritarian politics in large part caused the economic malaise, democratic politics can help lift it. Yet evidence from the second and third worlds over the last decade does not support such optimism. This is not to

---

[2]Cited in "The IMF and the World Bank: Arguing about Africa," *Africa Confidential,* vol. 34, no. 20 (October 8, 1993), p. 3.

say that authoritarian regimes can guarantee economic reform or even produce it very often. Nor is it to say that economic reform under democratic conditions is impossible; it is just very difficult.

Presumptions about the mutually reinforcing nature of political and economic reform in Africa rely on an extension of neoclassical economic logic: economic liberalization creates sustained growth, growth produces winners as well as losers, winners will organize to defend their newfound welfare and create sociopolitical coalitions to support continued economic reform. This logic, however, does not appear to hold for Africa, even under authoritarian conditions, much less under democratic ones.

The winners of economic reform in Africa are few, appear only slowly over time, and are hard to organize politically. The neoclassical political logic of reform is too mechanistic for Africa; there are real "transaction costs" to organizing winners, and not just infrastructural ones. Other organizational bases of political solidarity exist—ethnic, regional, religious, linguistic, and patron-client—that make mobilization around policy-specific economic interests difficult in much of Africa.

Some have argued that Africa does not have a democratic tradition, but in fact it has a vivid one, although its day was brief and ended in failure, and the reasons for its demise have not disappeared. The periodic reemergence of democratic regimes in Ghana and Nigeria over the last two decades indicates that old patterns of politics reappear with amazing vigor; political liberalization is not likely to guarantee the appearance of new political alignments that favor sustained economic reform.

The progress of democratization in Africa has been very uneven. Outside actors tried political conditionality in Kenya only to have it undermined by the maneuvering of the Moi government and the inability of the opposition to come up with a single presidential candidate and slate of legislators. In Zambia, where a full transition did take place in late 1992, the new government of Frederick Chiluba has been confronted with political factionalism, renewed corruption, ethnic and regional tension, and uneven economic performance, despite good intentions and help from abroad.

Is this version of the "thesis of the perverse effect"—that political liberalization might have a negative impact on the chances for sustained economic reform—likely to hold across the board for Africa? No, it is not. It is important to assess particular countries. But if not handled properly, political conditionality might well impede rather than facilitate Africa's relinking to the world economy in more productive ways. The widespread emergence of what UCLA professor Richard Sklar has called "developmental democracies" is not likely in Africa any time soon.

Finally, the actions of Western governments in other areas of the world will be important. Many Africans, for example, are likely to see recent support for Russian President Boris Yeltsin's accumulation of executive power and manipulation of constitutional and electoral practices, largely in the hope of getting more coherent economic reform, as highly hypocritical: one standard for strategically important Russia and another for marginal and dependent Africa.

ENDING AS THEY BEGAN

With or without political conditionality, what are the prospects that African countries will engage successfully in economic reform and establish more a productive relationship with the world economy? The answer appears to be that simultaneous marginalization and dependence are likely to continue, and probably increase, for most countries. A few, with hard work, propitious circumstances, and luck, may begin to improve their situation. Differentiation among African states, long evident, may well increase; a few countries will stay in the third world and do relatively better economically, while most will continue to descend. The countries likely to do better are those that are already more advantaged, partly because of better performance over the last 30 years: Kenya, Ivory Coast, Cameroon, Nigeria, Zimbabwe, and possibly Senegal. As noted above, however, even these cases are now fragile, largely for political reasons. A handful of countries in serious decline, such as Ghana, may be able to reverse course, but chances for this are even more tenuous.

A quiet debate is under way among Western officials and business executives about what to do with Africa. Should they provide some resources to all countries to create a sort of international social safety net for declining countries, which then become de facto wards of the world community, or should they "pick a few and work with them," as one Western official has put it? With the first option, it is not at all clear how effective such an international safety net would be, as the recent intervention in Somalia has shown. With the second option, resources would be concentrated in countries that have some good prospects for sustained economic performance, and possibly some strategic importance—Nigeria and Zimbabwe, for example. This is a delicate political task, however, and the recent performance of both of these countries might give one considerable pause.

The trajectory of individual countries will be affected by both internal and external factors. On the internal side, the degree of effective "stateness"—the technical and administrative capabilities to formulate and implement rational economic policies—will be crucial. On average, Africa has the lowest level of state capabilities of any region in the world. As the IMF and the World Bank have begun to realize, it takes a relatively capable state to implement their neo-orthodox economic reform consistently over time. To sustain a solid base in the international political economy, a country needs a high degree of "stateness," including the crucial ability to bargain with all types—private business groups, states, and the international financial institutions. Whether "stateness" will emerge or increase in many places, however, is questionable; certainly political dynamics will play a vital role in arriving at a productive balanced tension between state and market and between state and society. Some African leaders, such as Jerry Rawlings in Ghana, have begun to understand this.

Although it is largely a self-help world, external factors are also very important. They revolve around two central issues. First is the degree of openness of the world political economy. Second is the degree to which both sides fulfill their part of the "implicit bargain" between international financial institutions and the major Western countries and Africans: if African countries successfully reform their economies with the help and direction of the IMF and the World Bank, then new international private bank lending and direct foreign investment will be made available.

John Ruggie has characterized the current international political economy as one of "embedded liberalism," in which the major Western countries intervene in their domestic economies to buffer the costs of adjusting to shifts in the world economy. A precarious openness, based on liberal economic norms, is maintained, despite increasing tensions. Others, such as Robert Gilpin, see the world moving toward an increasingly conflictual and closed international political economy, which might be characterized as "malign mercantilism." Africa's prospects would not be very bright under a shift from embedded liberalism to malign mercantilism by the major Western powers. Despite its marginalization and dependence, Africa desperately needs openness in the world economy; in fact, the neo-orthodox adjustment strategy is predicated on it. Whether some form of benign mercantilism would benefit Africa is also open to question.

Chances for fulfillment of the "implicit bargain" may not be much better, however. Because private actors in the world economy increasingly pass Africa by, Western countries and the international financial institutions will continue to play central roles. If African countries are to have any hope of making economic progress, these actors must help to fulfill this bargain, primarily through increased aid levels and substantial debt relief. Given the domestic politics of Western industrial democracies, debt relief might be the easier route to take, since it is more politically malleable. But major debt relief has not occurred, and there are signs that aid levels may decline as these Western countries become increasingly preoccupied with domestic problems and those of more important regions.

Because resources are scarce, aid and debt relief should be given only to those actually undertaking difficult economic reforms and without being tied automatically to political change. The Jerry Rawlingses of Africa should be supported; nonreforming leaders should not. It is not clear, however, how many leaders like Rawlings actors outside Africa can actually support at the level required for sustained economic change. Since such reform is difficult, stop-and-go cycles are a fact of life, and external actors need to learn to adjust to them more effectively. The primary obstacle is how to cope with a huge debt and substantial arrears to the IMF and the World Bank without setting precedents with worldwide implications.

Finally, given the enormous obstacles confronting African countries, undue optimism and inflated expectations about what is possible in Africa can be dangerous. Slow, steady, consistent progress is preferable. Neither international nor African policymakers can unduly hasten, control, or speed up social processes such as institution and capacity building. Change is incremental, uneven, often contradictory, and dependent on the outcome of unpredictable socioeconomic and political struggles. Policymakers must try to bring about important changes, but they need to retain a sense of the historical complexity involved. Today's policy fads can easily become tomorrow's failed initiatives.

Africa really is caught between a rock and a hard place when it comes to the world economy and the international state system, and all will have to work extremely hard to alter this fact. Although pessimism about Africa is appropriate analytically, try they must, for not trying to keep Africa from falling off the map could have even worse consequences for its long-suffering peoples.

Why Is Africa Eating Asia's Dust?

While one scrambles toward development, the other slips into despair

Keith B. Richburg

Washington Post Foreign Service

NAIROBI—Ugandan President Yoweri Museveni is a thoughtful, analytical man who often takes on a professorial tone when discussing Africa's myriad problems. So he seemed uncharacteristically at a loss when asked at a recent news conference: Why has African development lagged so far behind that of East Asia, a region that suffered from a somewhat similar set of obstacles?

After offering several well-explored explanations, he paused and admitted some hesitancy to go further. Finally, he said what seemed most on his mind: "The discipline of Asians compared to Africans." People from East Asian countries with scarce resources and large populations "may tend to be more disciplined than people who take life for granted," he said. Some Africans, he intoned, "have so much land that they don't know what to do with it."

It is an explanation heard time and again to a question that fascinates and perplexes anyone who has spent time in both Africa and East Asia. Why has East Asia over the past two decades become a model of economic success, while Africa, since independence, has seen largely failure—increasing poverty, hunger and economies propped up by foreign aid? Is it largely a matter of discipline, as Museveni suggests, or are other factors at work?

There was nothing innate in the peoples of East Asia and Africa that made this outcome inevitable. In 1957, Ghana—one of the bright hopes of black Africa—had a higher gross national product than South Korea, then emerging from a devastating war. Now South Korea is a newly industrialized country—one of the "four dragons" of Southeast Asia. Ghana, meanwhile, has actually slid backwards; its gross national product is lower than it was at independence. It is fair to ask, what happened?

For four years, from 1986 until late 1990, I traveled throughout Southeast Asia as a Washington Post correspondent, seeing firsthand the economic dynamism of a region that has been largely defined by its successful growth and development. Some countries—Singapore, Malaysia and Indonesia—emerged just as Africa did from under colonial tutelage. Singapore became independent as a tiny city-state, with no natural resources. Indonesia and Malaysia at independence were as divided, along ethnic, religious and linguistic lines, as many African countries are today. Thailand, which was never colonized, was a front-line state for the Indochina wars of the late 1960s and was beset by its own Communist insurgency.

Yet from these uncertain beginnings, Southeast Asian nations have prospered. Their average growth rates for the 1980s measured between 8 percent and 10 percent. They avoided the pitfall of heavy external debt through deft management of their economies. And they have successfully diversified away from reliance on single commodity exports, making them less vulnerable to world market price shocks.

There are, of course, examples in East Asia of nonprospering countries, such as Cambodia, Vietnam and Laos—all of which opted for a Communist path and were wracked by lengthy wars. And the Philippines—once the most prosperous country in East Asia—was ravaged by 20 years of authoritarian rule by Ferdinand Marcos.

Moving last year to sub-Saharan Africa, I found a continent in a dismal state of disrepair. From the statistics and the background briefings, one expects to find Africa underdeveloped; the surprise is discovering just how underdeveloped it is. Africa has most of the world's poorest nations. Its children are most likely to die before the age of 5. Its adults are least likely to live beyond the age 50. Africans are, on the whole, more malnourished, less educated and more likely to be afflicted by fatal diseases than any other people on earth.

Any Asia-Africa comparison must allow for many important differences. Although the two continents became independent at roughly the same time, they didn't begin the economic race at the same starting point. East Asian

From *The Washington Post National Weekly Edition*, July 20–26, 1992, pp. 11-12. © 1992 by The Washington Post Company. Reprinted by permission.

ECONOMIC DISPARITY

A generation ago, Nigeria's gross national product and exports topped those of South Korea, Malaysia and Thailand. Today, however, Nigeria lags behind its Asian counterparts.

Nigeria is not atypical. In Ghana, Kenya, Tanzania and Zaire as well, per capita gross national product has declined over the past decade even as it has increased steadily in Asia's Little Dragons.

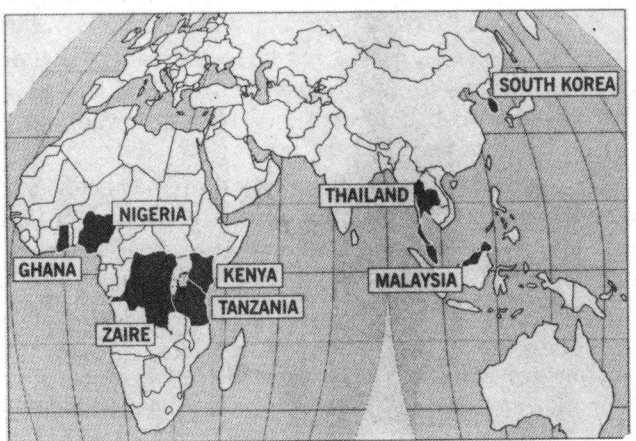

PER CAPITA GROSS NATIONAL PRODUCT
IN THOUSANDS OF U.S. DOLLARS

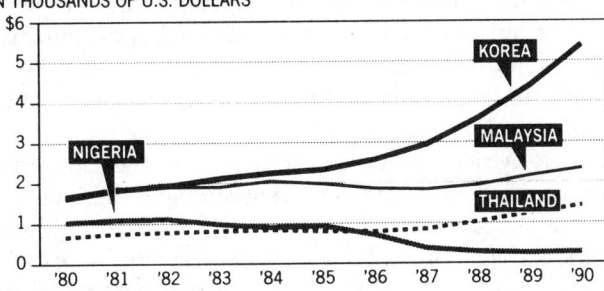

GROSS NATIONAL PRODUCT
IN BILLIONS OF U.S. DOLLARS

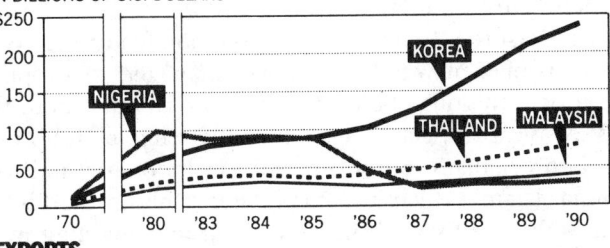

EXPORTS
IN BILLIONS OF U.S. DOLLARS

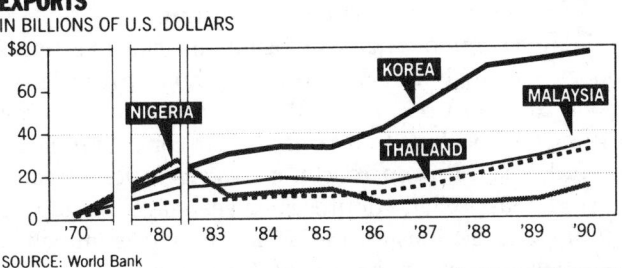

SOURCE: World Bank

economies had a substantial head start; they had developed elaborate patterns of trade and development long before the European colonists arrived. The East Asians, in addition to starting out ahead, also have had a stronger push from the West. In the years since independence, they have received far more Western and Japanese investment. And East Asia, unlike Africa, did not have to spend its early post-colonial years recovering from the physical and psychological trauma associated with three centuries of slavery.

What follows is not a detailed statistical comparison; it is rather a set of interviews and impressions gathered by a reporter who has lived in both places. For the past seven months, I have lived in Kenya and traveled to seven other countries of this troubled continent. One, Somalia, has in fact ceased to be a functioning country, divided as it is between armed warring clans and now in a state of anarchy. Zaire and Malawi are reeling under repressive dictatorships—and in Zaire, years of corruption and neglect have brought the official economy to collapse. Ethiopia and Uganda are struggling to emerge from the shadow of decades of ethnic conflict and dictatorial repression that have driven the economies of both those countries into the ground.

Tanzania in many ways is the saddest, because it has enjoyed 30 years of peace and considerable foreign assistance, but its economy has been ravaged by years of socialist mismanagement. Dar es Salaam, its capital, is in a worse state of disrepair than Hanoi; the road system has collapsed, telephones do not work, electricity is sporadic, its store shelves are bare. Tanzania remains, by many estimates, the third-poorest place on earth.

Kenya and Nigeria, along with Ghana, represented hope in sub-Saharan Africa. But neither has realized its potential. Both have seen their economic advances canceled out by debilitating corruption. Nigeria has often been compared to Indonesia—big, diverse and oil-rich. But where Indonesia managed the oil boom of the 1970s successfully, and has begun to diversify away from its dependence on oil, Nigeria used the boom years to borrow heavily, creating a debt burden that today constrains government action. And Nigeria, unlike Indonesia, remains dependent on oil for 95 percent of its export earnings and 80 percent of its budget receipts.

These resource-rich African countries need not have emerged as basket cases. And Tanzania and Malawi have had ample opportunities to develop through foreign assistance.

Foreign reporters often are criticized for not reporting more "good news" from Africa. There seems a simple reason for that: So much of what happens here is so bad. In East Asia, the stories are largely about economic growth. But in Africa, the issues are more basic. Thirty years after independence, Africans are still trying to learn how to live together in civil societies and how to forge a sense of national identity inside the artificial boundaries of their nation-states.

The continent today is on the economic sidelines. It accounts for a mere pittance of the world's trade. Its share of world markets has fallen by half since the 1970s.

African trade accounts for less than 0.1 percent of North American imports.

How did Africa reach this current predicament? And what lessons, if any, does the East Asian success hold for this troubled region?

Africans themselves, when asked the questions, often point to a familiar list of reasons: the legacy of colonialism; the problem of having diverse ethnic groups within national boundaries; the long-running East–West conflict that constrained Africa's independent decision-making; small countries with fragmented markets; widespread corruption of Africa's ruling elite; and now, more recently, the lack of popular participation in governance. "There is absolutely no way you can achieve economic development without democracy," said Museveni.

Yet many of the East Asian nations also have had to contend with these problems. East Asia, more than Africa, became a playing field for the East–West rivalry. Some of East Asia's most economically successful countries—Thailand, Malaysia and Indonesia, for example—are notoriously corrupt. And precious few East Asian countries can be called democratic, as evidenced by the recent protests in Thailand against the military's continued domination of politics.

An answer, then, would seem to lie deeper. It may be found in the respective patterns of colonialism, in the economic choices pursued and in the differences in the post-independence leadership that emerged in East Asia and Africa. And, as Museveni suggests, it may also be a question of differing cultural traditions.

At a restaurant in Washington last year, a diplomat from the Embassy of Cameroon was explaining to a reporter the problem of Africa's black elite. Go to the cafes and the bistros, he said. See them in their European suits, reading the latest editions of European newspapers. The problem of African development, he said, is that the educated elite have never developed indigenous models, but instead have tried to transplant Europe to Africa.

It doesn't take long in Africa to see what the diplomat was talking about. Basil Davidson, a renowned British scholar on Africa, writes in his new book "The Black Man's Burden" how European colonialism in Africa set out to deny and eventually eliminate the continent's precolonial history. And in that, the Europeans found willing accomplices among Africa's European-oriented elite, the "modernizers," who were in constant conflict with Africa's "traditionalists," including the acknowledged tribal chiefs.

These modernizing Africans clung to the notion that anything traditional was by definition primitive. And it was this elite that came to the forefront of the independence movements and proceeded to impose European models on their new African states. Rather than seek to build on tradition, as the Confucianist societies of East Asia tried to do even in their revolutionary phases, the new Africans often sought to purge what was deepest and most authentic in their cultures.

That influence can still be seen today. Judges in Kenyan courts wear white wigs and speak in a flowery, archaic English that might be considered "quaint." Governmental institutions in the former British colonies—from parliaments to the "special branch" internal security forces—are near-duplicates of their counterparts at Westminster and Whitehall. Colonial governments in Africa were dictatorships backed up by a top-heavy bureaucracy. Independence seems to have substituted black autocrats for the old white colonial governors, with little thought of Africa's traditions.

The suppression of indigenous culture has been especially pronounced in the former French colonies of West Africa, which were treated as an overseas department of France, notes Pauline Baker, an Africa specialist with the Aspen Institute. "The French tried to have black Frenchmen," she says.

After traveling through East Africa, the late Shiva Naipaul concluded in his book "North of South" that the black man's contact with the European had only succeeded in destroying African culture. "Black Africa, with its gimcrack tyrannies, its field marshals and emperors, its false philosophies, its fabricated statehoods, returns to Europe its own features," he wrote, "but grotesquely caricatured—as they might be seen in one of those distorting funhouse mirrors."

Black African leaders also point to the deleterious effects on their continent's development, heritage and traditions caused by slavery. They note that slavery robbed the continent of its brightest and most able-bodied men and women for more than 300 years, and some leaders today are going so far as to demand "reparations" from the West.

Contrast that to East Asia. A common feature of Western colonialism was that it never managed to supplant historic traditions—be it the emphasis on education, the hierarchical respect for elders, or the religious traditions of Confucianism, Buddhism and, in Indonesia and Malaysia, Islam, which had come later. Only in the Philippines did the Spanish friars succeed in converting most of the population to Roman Catholicism.

Today, a common theme of East Asian leaders is how to modernize without Westernizing, how to pick and choose the most relevant of Western technology without losing sight of their traditions. A fear commonly voiced around Asia is that encroaching Westernization threatens to erode East Asian culture. Four years ago, Singapore's deputy prime minister, Lee Hsien Loong, summed up the challenge in an interview. "If we reach the point where we all become Americanized," he said, "then that's the end of Singapore."

After independence, many of the African countries became swayed by socialism, the ideology in vogue throughout Europe at the time. Theirs became an African variety, whether dubbed "humanism" as in Zambia, or *ujamaa* in Tanzania. But even in avowedly capitalist countries such as Kenya, the result became the same: government ownership of most enterprises, and a distrust of private-sector initiative and foreign investment.

Asia found another way. Theirs was a brand of state-centered capitalism that was neither completely free enterprise nor dogmatically Marxist. The state intervened in the economy, but in a positive way, supporting "winning" corporations and settling wage disputes. East Asia also had three wars fought on its soil—World War II, Korea and Vietnam—leading the United States to offer benign trading relations to secure stable partners in its fight against Communist expansion.

In a paper examining East Asian and African responses to the global debt crisis, World Bank economist Ishrat Husain detailed how from the mid-1970s, East Asian countries adopted "outward" development policies—meaning liberal trade with low tariff barriers to imports, and realistic exchange rates that enhanced exports. This outward orientation allowed the East Asians to diversify their imports while the international competition improved the efficiency of its producers.

Africa, on the other hand, pursued "inward" economic policies, throwing up trade restrictions and maintaining overvalued currencies.

Herman Cohen, the U.S. assistant secretary for African affairs, sees another reason East Asia has largely prospered. "They did all the right things—plus land reform," he says. By privatizing land holdings, East Asian countries saw agricultural production increase, Cohen says. In Africa, land was communally owned in traditional society and expropriated by the state after independence; prices for farm products typically have been set by state marketing boards.

In comparing East Asia and Africa, it has become fashionable among those who know both regions to say the key difference is that Africa has not produced a Lee Kuan Yew. As long-time prime minister of tiny Singapore, Lee has come to personify the idea of benevolent authoritarianism, a paternalistic ruler who brooked no dissent but nonetheless guided his city-state into the ranks of East Asia's "little dragons."

Africa has had its share of towering figures. But by contrast, some of the best known—such as Tanzania's Julius Nyerere and Zambia's Kenneth Kaunda—ran their countries' economies into the ground. Africa also has produced more than its share of dictators, tyrants and buffoons—such as Uganda's Idi Amin and Jean Bedel Bokassa, who declared himself emperor and his impoverished country the Central African Empire. Zaire's Mobutu Sese Seko and Malawi's H. Kamuzu Banda cling to power through repression. In between are a host of corrupt dictators and military men who seem more intent on padding their European bank accounts than improving the lot of their impoverished peoples.

To be sure, Asia is not without its corruption. In Thailand, corrupt military officers and unscrupulous politicians are involved in a host of illegal activities. But there is a difference between corruption Asian-style and its African equivalent. In Asia, the corruption has not been as debilitating to economic growth. In fact, corruption and growth seem to run parallel.

A Western economist in Nigeria, who lived previously in Indonesia, puts it this way: "In Indonesia, the president's daughter might get the contract to build the toll roads, but the roads do get built and they do facilitate traffic flow. . . . That sort of corruption is productive corruption as opposed to malignant corruption."

In Addis Ababa, an official of the Organization of African Unity, Mamadon Bah, was explaining to a visiting reporter the problem of bringing more democracy to the continent. "What we need in Africa these days is mainly discipline," he said, "but discipline from the top."

Any discussion of cultural differences between Asians and Africans by definition treads on explosive ground, since it feeds on past racist stereotypes of Asians as hard-working and Africans as lazy.

"People work like dogs in Kenya," says Makau wa Mutua, a Kenyan exile at the Harvard University law school's human rights program. "Nobody sits around waiting for mangos to drop from trees." Referring to Museveni's comments about discipline, Mutua recalls how Kenyan President Daniel arap Moi once visited Asia and similarly came back urging Kenyans to emulate the Asian example. "As a leader, one has to talk about discipline to get people to work harder," Mutua says. "That is the stereotype of the Asian machine, that people work so hard. But I think that's pure garbage."

Still, many other Africans agree with Museveni and the OAU official that cultural factors do play a role in development. They argue that lack of discipline among African leaders is a particular problem. For even the hardest-working African has difficulty building a solid life if his country's political leadership is corrupt and undisciplined.

Pauline Baker speaks of the "five bads" that she says help explain Africa's poor record of economic development: "bad luck, bad environment, bad policy, bad government and bad faith [by Western governments that failed to deliver on expected aid and investment]." Baker says that although cultural analysis has gone out of fashion among academics, it may be appropriate to add a sixth factor—"bad outlook."

As examples of the cultural factors that enrich African life but may limit economic development, Baker cites "the role of the extended family" and "the role of tradition." In Africa, she notes, "the real obligations are blood ties to the family or tribe, rather than national ties." The extended family provides a private welfare system that helps take care of people, but it also limits the development of a middle class. The lucky entrepreneur who makes a little money finds he is expected to house, feed

193

and educate his cousins, nieces and nephews. He is pulled back, toward family and village. It is typical, says Baker, that the first thing a newly wealthy city dweller will do with his money is build a big house back in his village.

In most of the Southeast Asian countries, discipline has been imposed from the top. Singapore's People's Action Party under Lee Kuan Yew has been highly authoritarian, micro-managing people's lives to the point of prohibiting chewing gum, using financial incentives to encourage better-educated couples to have more children and launching nationwide campaigns to encourage people to smile more. Governments in Malaysia and Indonesia, trying to forge cohesion out of diverse populations, have force-fed their people a common language policy. In all the Southeast Asian countries except the Philippines, civil liberties are sacrificed as a necessary price of stability—something Asians call the "social contract" between rulers and the ruled.

These Asian regimes draw support from cultural traditions that foster order, hierarchy and stability. The Confucian tradition, for example, is widespread throughout East Asia. It encourages a disciplined work ethic and a stable, stratified political system; it also reinforces the Asian emphasis on education, which is prized in disciplined, authoritarian societies such as Korea and China almost as a secular religion.

Africa has had its share of authoritarian regimes. But far from fostering discipline, most of them have led to chaos. Dictators who tried to enforce unity and discipline—Ethiopia's Mengistu Haile Mariam and Somalia's Mohamed Siad Barre are just two examples—were overthrown last year in bloody revolutions; other African autocrats are teetering. The single feature of African autocracies seems to be their inability to impose their will on their populations.

Even when the military tries to impose political discipline from the top down, as in Nigeria, moral discipline remains lax among the top leaders—and corruption is widespread.

On the individual level, the question of discipline is more difficult to address. No one, for example, would say that the average farmer in Tanzania or Malawi works less than his Asian counterpart. People in hard-pressed Kinshasa, Zaire, survive only by their endurance—working several jobs, selling goods on the streets. In Uganda, government offices are largely empty during the daytime, because low-paid bureaucrats are out running private businesses. In Kenya, even when no milk was available on store shelves because of government price controls, farmers with cows were busy building their own networks of urban buyers. Together, this private sector activity accounts for a disciplined economic sector often overlooked in official statistics.

Lawrence Harrison, a retired Foreign Service officer who has written two books exploring cultural values in the developing world, says he has found Confucianism to be the key ingredient in East Asian development.

"Confucius imparts to his followers a strong sense of future, the importance of education, the importance of merit, the importance of saving for future generations," he says. "All of those things in an economic sense are things that you don't associate with the African culture."

But some African leaders are beginning to express similar themes in their own terms. As Museveni put it recently in Kampala, Uganda, this is the time "for the people of Africa to take their destiny in their own hands."

Post-Mandela South Africa: Slow but Steady Progress

Michael Clough

Michael Clough, a senior fellow at the Council on Foreign Affairs, just returned from a trip to South Africa.

JOHANNESBURG, SOUTH AFRICA Last week, as I listened to South Africans describe the challenges their country faces, I sensed that something big had changed: The Nelson Mandela phase of the post-apartheid era is drawing to a close.

It began when Mandela walked out of prison in February, 1990, and continued on through his successful negotiations to end three centuries of white domination. High drama and miracles marked this phase. At times, the country was held together only by the sheer force of Mandela's personality.

But South Africa is now on more secure footing. Immense problems remain, but they are unlikely to derail the country's transition to democracy—and, for better or worse, they are not the kinds of problems that can be resolved by one man, even one as remarkable as Mandela.

During the past five years, South Africa's leaders have successfully met two major challenges. The first was to persuade both the white minority and the black majority to accept a gradual, negotiated transition. Mandela's reassuring presence and unceasing efforts to promote reconciliation gave white voters the confidence they needed to gamble and entrust their future to a black-led government. At the same time, Mandela's commanding role in the liberation struggle enabled him to keep in check black demands for an immediate seizure of power and swift retribution against the old regime.

The second challenge was to prevent a civil war between supporters of the African National Congress and Chief Mangosuthu Buthelezi's Inkatha Freedom Party. Here, too, Mandela's moral stature and ability to stand above the partisan fray was crucial both in forcing Buthelezi to abandon his threat to boycott national elections and in preventing ANC supporters from launching a war of retribution against Inkatha.

Today, white South Africans appear to have completed their psychological trek from domination to multiracial democracy. The National Party, which created the apartheid system, is busy reinventing itself. In talks with foreign visitors, Frederik W. de Klerk now emphasizes the party's growing non-white constituency, which includes a majority of the country's Afrikaans-speaking colored population and Indians. In government and Parliament, the "government of national unity," which began as an uneasy and often awkward alliance between the national party and the ANC, has become a close working partnership. Disagreements between the leaders of the two parties now seem to be minimal, even on sensitive issues such as the investigation of past human rights abuses.

The once widely feared threat from far-right whites seems to have vanished. Small pockets of militant white racism still exist, but the danger of a white counterrevolution is past. South Africa's most prominent white conservative is Gen. Constand Viljoen, an easy-going former head of the South African Defense Forces who mixes easily with Mandela and the ANC leadership. Viljoen's party, the Freedom Front, remains committed to the idea of a "boerstaat"—a territory within South Africa in which whites would be in a majority and Afrikaner culture would predominate. But there is no longer any talk of creating such a territory through armed violence.

Within the black community, there is discontent with the pace of change. Too few jobs have been created. Too few houses have been built. For most of the population, living conditions have not dramatically changed. But this dissatisfaction is no longer directed against whites; nor is it likely to lead to an outbreak of violence or calls to abandon the new constitutional framework.

The danger of a civil war pitting the government of national unity against Chief Buthelezi and his supporters in Natal has also diminished. While the petulant Zulu leader continues to try to thwart efforts to hammer out the details of a permanent constitution that would greatly diminish his personal power, his support, both internally and internationally, is eroding. His call for international mediation on the issue of the powers of provincial government in the future South Africa is not supported by any of the other parties. And, within Inkatha itself, there are signs of a growing division between those who support Buthelezi's attempts to separate KwaZulu-Natal from the rest of the country and those who favor working within the existing framework.

A dramatic indication of the extent to which the South African agenda has shifted was provided by one leading National Party member who told a visiting delegation that he did not consider the drafting of a permanent constitution to be a major priority. Far more important, he contended, were efforts to promote economic growth, control crime and institute effective local governments.

The long-term peace and stability of South Africa depends, first and foremost, on the ability of its government and its private sector to open up the economy and promote growth with jobs in an increasingly competitive global environment. This is not an easy task. Unemployment in many parts of South Africa is running at 40% to 50%. The legacy of apartheid schooling and township unrest has left a large, undereducated and poorly skilled black labor pool. Ownership of South African industry, which had been highly protected and often subsidized, is concentrated in the hands of a small number of traditionally minded conglomerates. Exchange controls have created a large pool of captive capital that is likely to flow abroad as soon as restrictions are lifted. The country's tax base is small. Demands for public services are immense and growing.

But the government's economic team, which includes an unlikely mix of erstwhile communists, former National Party technocrats and others, is extremely capable. Talk of nationalization of industry has evaporated. Instead, priority is being given to creating "a stable macroeconomic environment" for sustained growth. In practice, that has meant a remarkable degree of fiscal restraint.

For the South African economy to grow, two things must happen: Foreign investment will have to flow into the country, and ways must be found to promote the emergence of small- and intermediate-sized businesses. Neither is going to happen overnight, but there are signs of progress. Almost all the foreign businesses that left South Africa in the 1980s have returned, and they are being joined by a host of new investors. Increasingly, the biggest complaint of potential investors is that existing South African businesses are trying to block their entry. This should change once the big South African conglomerates are free to shift their own capital out of the country and the government begins to privatize some of the large parastatals that were created during the apartheid era.

Black business is also beginning to prosper. In one of the great ironies of South Africa, a number of the leading figures in the anti-apartheid struggle are quickly becoming scions of industry. Zwelakhe Sisulu, the son of Mandela's fellow prisoner on Robben Island, Walter Sisulu, and a prominent opposition leader throughout the 1980s, is head of the South African Broadcasting Corporation. The Kagiso Trust, run by Eric Molobi, was created to help funnel foreign funds to anti-apartheid organizations. Today, it is an investment fund.

The most visible negative development in South Africa is the spread of crime. In fact, there are two different crime problems. Ordinary crime, especially muggings and carjackings, has become a major problem, particularly in Johannesburg, the country's economic capital. This part of the problem is directly linked to the state of the economy—and exacerbated by the large number of illegal immigrants who have come to South Africa. Organized crime is also becoming more of a problem due to the growing international air traffic in and out of the country. The government's ability to combat crime has been hampered by problems in reorganizing the police, which had previously devoted most of its resources to enforcing apartheid laws and combatting the liberation struggle. As serious as the crime problem is, however, it is not significantly worse than in many other parts of the world, including America.

Another pressing challenge—and the one foremost in the minds of most South African officials—is the need to create effective local governments. On Nov. 1, the country will hold elections across the country to put in place new local authorities. These authorities will be expected to assume much of the burden of delivering essential services to South African citizens, especially housing, electricity and water. The fact that so much importance is being attached to them is a sign that national leaders clearly recognize the limits of the central government's ability to satisfy popular expectations.

The next phase in South Africa's evolution toward a multiracial democracy will not be dominated by one man. Rather, thousands of yet-to-be-elected men and women will try to make real the grand designs hatched at the top. The challenges ahead—economic growth, crime control and creation of local government—are beyond the powers of even a Mandela. They can only be met by a whole country committed to overcoming its past.

■ TWILIGHT OF THE TITAN

China—the End of an Era

Orville Schell

Orville Schell's last book was Mandate of Heaven *(Simon and Schuster). A longtime China observer, he [is] a Freedom Forum senior fellow at Columbia University.*

If he does not die in the next few weeks, Deng Xiaoping will turn 91 this August. While he is reported to be so infirm that he can hardly move on his own, the country over which he has presided since returning to power in the late 1970s is very much alive. In fact, winging toward China these days, one has the feeling of approaching a nuclear reactor that is operating over capacity and approaching meltdown. Indeed, flying over Beijing or Shanghai, all that one can usually see is an ominous penumbra of smog emanating from the industrial boom that has gripped this mutant People's Republic since 1992, when Deng gave his people permission to forget politics and focus on getting rich.

I.

Once one is on the ground, the feeling of being in a field of uncontained energy is only heightened. Driving in from the Shanghai airport is like being in one of those American children's workbooks in the thirties that boastfully limned futuristic landscapes filled with belching smokestacks, trains barreling down tracks toward distant horizons, planes zooming overhead and freeways coursing through thickets of skyscrapers. For anyone who knew time-warped China before its bizarre post-Mao metamorphosis began, the country today is an endless series of jolting surprises. Streets are clogged with traffic. There is construction everywhere. Indoor malls with glittering new department stores surge with customers for whom shopping is rapidly becoming the recreational pastime of choice. At night, restaurants are packed with China's new urban middle class raucously eating, drinking and chain-smoking until the air inside turns gray. Outside, the lights from all these restaurants, *karaoke* bars, discos, nightclubs, dance halls and flashing billboards irradiate the polluted darkness with glowing neon until well past midnight.

Nowhere has more money been made than in real estate, a supreme irony given the fact that after "liberation" in 1949 almost all the property now being sold was expropriated by the state from private owners. Now, however, local officials are selling it back again and in the process creating a new class of socialist millionaires and even billionaires, a wealth through which they themselves find nefarious ways to enrich themselves as deals come down. During the past three years Shanghai officials alone have put the land rights of some 600 parcels of land (each approximately the size of a New York City block) on the market. The 520-square-kilometer Pudong Special Zone, which is rising on the east side of the Huangpu River, is an urban development project whose scale is unmatched in world history. As far as the eye can see, there are nothing but crane-topped highrise office and apartment buildings under construction. Already Shanghai boasts Asia's tallest TV tower, one of its biggest and most modern department stores and its newest stock market. In the planning stage is its largest airport. Along the Bund on the west side of the river things are also moving at breathtaking speed. Where the headquarters of Western banks and multinational corporations clustered during the first half of this century, thirty-seven of the city's grandest deco buildings have now been put up for commercial auction. Among those bidding tens of millions of dollars are some of the very foreign firms from which these buildings were originally confiscated. Usually, however, developers simply wreck old edifices and use the land for new and more cost-effective highrise construction. People returning to the city after even a short absence find that houses of friends and relatives, indeed whole neighborhoods, have vanished.

M*ao's 'put politics in command' has given way to money-making and hedonism.*

Shanghai's People's Square was a Stalinist Platz built in the fifties on the site of what had been the British-run Shanghai Race Club's horse track. The reviewing stands, from which party bigwigs once watched parades of goose-stepping P.L.A. soldiers and phalanxes of marching youths producing totemic images of the revolution like socialist pompom girls at a football stadium, have disappeared. In their stead, a modern office building for the city government has arisen. On the opposite side of the square stands another new construction, which looks something like an ultramodern washing machine, the Museum of Art and History. But it is the parade ground in between where one really feels how China has changed. Its vast emptiness has been torn up and redone—transformed into a neo-Italianate piazza decorated with four enormous metal urns that look as if they have been expropriated from the stage set of an old Victor Mature epic. Courtesy of the party, each afternoon pop music begins to pour out of speakers hidden in these giant urns. As if none of them had been locked up during the Cultural Revolution for their bourgeois habits, flocks of senior citizens materialize and, dressed in long underwear and baggy Mao suits, begin rumba-ing, jitterbugging, tangoing and twisting away as crowds of intrigued gawkers, even some policemen, stare in wonder. One old man was even giving lessons (for a fee, to be sure) to dance-crazed middle-agers whose revolutionarily blighted lives had deprived them of a chance to learn how to shake, rattle and roll.

A walk down Beijing's new "miracle mile" from Tiananmen Square to Jianguomenwai is no less disorienting. Although Mao's famous portrait still hangs on Tiananmen Gate, and the Monument to the Martyrs of the People still stands in front of his mausoleum, things have radically changed. In fact, Mao's most dire fears of revolutionary sellout have come to pass. As he told Edgar Snow in 1965, Mao worried that future generations might "negate the revolution . . . ; make peace with imperialism; bring the remnants of the Chiang Kai-shek clique back to the Mainland and take a stand beside the small percentage of counterrevolutionaries still in the country." Indeed, just behind Mao's mausoleum, as well as on top of Tiananmen Gate, there are now a number of tacky souvenir stands filled with Mao pocket watches, Mao chopsticks, Mao sun-visors, Mao thermometers, Mao pendants and other Mao kitsch.

At the five-star Grand Hotel Beijing, just down the Avenue of Eternal Peace, there is a completely different new ambience. A chamber-music group plays Mozart divertimenti and Strauss waltzes in a swank upstairs restaurant where entrepreneurs in double-breasted suits make deals over cellular flip-phones. A little farther along the avenue the unmistakably American aroma of burgers and fries wafts from the world's highest-volume McDonald's outlet, which sits astride an intersection where protesters were gunned down by the P.L.A. on June 4, 1989.

One could not have guessed from the size of the crowds inside this spanking-new McDonald's that it and the surrounding neighborhood are both slated to be turned into a new commercial and residential development, the $2.1 billion Oriental Plaza, funded by Hong Kong mega-magnate Li Ka-shing along with Goldman Sachs. So lucrative was the new deal on this prime piece of real estate that Beijing officials insouciantly ripped up the fast-food giant's twenty-year lease, forced thousands of residents from their homes and then approved the plaza's building permit even though it violated height restrictions just passed by the National People's Congress. (In the words of Liang Congjie, a preservationist critic fighting to stop the colossal project, "The plaza will make the Forbidden City look like a toy town in comparison.") The cavalier way in which the McDonald's contract was abrogated provided stark evidence to overseas investors eager to break into the country's market of how poorly rooted the rule of law still is in China.

Nowhere is the change gripping this city more obvious than in the half-square-mile area between the Beijing train station and the old imperial observatory. For centuries, this district was part of a maze of *hutong* (alleys) that veined Beijing. Sequestered from the outside world behind high walls and closed gates, the traditional-style *siheyuan* (courtyard houses) that honeycombed these alleys helped give the city much of its distinctive feel. Even after the houses fell into ruin during the Mao era, there was still something about leaving the hurly-burly of the city and entering their labyrinthine universe that was unlike any other urban experience in the world. When walking nearby, in the past I frequently found myself taking detours through these *hutong* just to enjoy the refuge they afforded from the noise and car exhaust of Beijing's charmless boulevards. It is indicative of Deng's own traditionalism that instead of living in the grandeur of the Zhongnanhai leadership compound next to the Forbidden City he too chose to live in a *hutong*. However, on a recent walk from the train station, I was stunned to find not only that this neighborhood had been obliterated but that colossal new office buildings and shopping malls have already erupted out of the rubble.

In this erstwhile Maoist redoubt where once all good comrades "put politics in command," they now wave off mention of anything political as if it were an offensive odor, the better to get back to making money and enjoying themselves. Even government officials and state-employed professionals are looking for ways to *xiahai* (jump into the ocean of commerce). China's reawakening to the profit motive has all the madcap energy of adolescents discovering their sexuality. In the past year, the number of private businesses in China has increased by more than a third. Doctors at state-run hospitals moonlight in private clinics doing everything from treating venereal diseases to performing cosmetic surgery (including sex-change operations). Low-paid teachers are defecting to new private schools. State-run research institutes are clamoring to set up labs, commercial think tanks and consulting services. Even the bureaus of Culture and Religious Affairs are busy *xiahai*-ing, converting their real estate—even parts of museums and churches—into money-making furniture showrooms, video parlors, cabarets and pool halls. In Shanghai, officials from the Bureau of Religious Affairs have even rented out the Mission Russian Orthodox Church to a stock-brokerage firm and a disco.

Everyone is looking for a way to get rich lest this bubble of opportunity suddenly burst. Nowhere is the obsession with private wealth and materialism more vividly illustrated than in China's new, officially sanctioned love affair with the automobile. Since 1949, autos have been reserved for high-ranking party cadres and official business. Last year, however, the government designated automobile manufacturing a "pillar industry" and approved plans not only to create a low-cost "family mini-car" but to develop ways to make bank loans and installment-payment plans available so that more Chinese can become car owners. Such grand plans have created a sense of urgency approaching panic among foreign car manufacturers hungrily eyeing China as the next century's great untapped market. Never mind the fact that there are few roads and less parking, and that China's cities are already suffocating in exhaust from gasoline that is still leaded.

'Seek Enjoyment'

China, which for so many years sternly commanded its people under penalty of persecution to sacrifice for the future, has now been reborn as an epicenter of a new Asian hedonism. Nowhere is this hedonistic urge to *zhaole* (seek enjoyment) more starkly manifest than in the fixation of Chinese on pop culture, particularly music and dancing. Not only are senior citizens dancing away their golden years in public plazas but China's youth have become slavishly devoted to disco and Karaoke Kultur. New York, one of Shanghai's newest and most luxurious nightspots, ensconced in an old 1930s theater, features svelte young female ticket-takers in garbage-bag plastic dresses or miniskirts. Most of its habitués are dressed to kill. Young men favor double-breasted suits accessorized with beepers and flip-phones holstered at their sides, and young women are coiffed, made up and turned out in clothing that puts most American youths to shame. Once such a fixation on the self would have guaranteed a one-way ticket to the gulag; now narcissism is flaunted with ostentatious abandon as the hallmark of success. No one bats an eye when film star Chen Chong, known as Joan Chen in Hollywood, "launches" a new perfume line called "Little Flower" after her very first screen role. In fact, "on assignment" at her press conference at the Shanghai Mansions were reporters from none other than the *People's Daily* (the Communist Party's main propaganda organ) and *Liberation Daily* (mouthpiece of the Shanghai Municipal Communist Party).

From the inside of other famous Shanghai nightspots such as the Casablanca, J.J.'s and the Shanghai Moon Club, which have financial backing from the Chinese military and public security establishments, one feels as if one is back in the twenties and thirties, when taxi girls and prostitutes made Shanghai "an adventurer's paradise." Once again, young women sashay each night into the city's clubs to dance and feed their expensive habits in clothes, cosmetics and consumer goods by selling their bodies to wealthy local millionaires and overseas businessmen. Many of the latter no longer troll nightclubs for sex, but keep a "second wife" in an apartment or hotel room for the sake of convenience.

The dizzying succession of contrary "correct lines" that has presaged these changes has made it almost impossible for Chinese to imbue their past with any coherence. The result has been a tendency to want to escape from history. So resistant are most people to recalling where they as a society have been and where they are going that it often seems as if their present fever to produce and consume is as much a quest for an anesthetic to numb the reflective impulse as an urge to make up for lost time. Finding themselves caught between the catastrophe of Mao's revolution and the uncertainty of Deng's ongoing "counterrevolution" (as some wags call it), they have responded not with an effort to understand how they have arrived at this state of precarious ambiguity but with a wave of national amnesia. Ever fearful of interpretations that might undermine its infallibility and authority, the party has, of course, aided this mass forgetting by putting much of the past out of bounds. At the same time, uncertainty about what tomorrow holds and a widely held feeling of powerlessness to affect the political course of events has caused most Chinese to avoid thinking about the future, much less doing anything to try to influence it. Despite the fact that Deng has been grandly dubbed the "general architect" of China's evolving society, even his own conception of China's future has been strikingly vague. "We are crossing the river by feeling our way over the stones," he has proclaimed with some bravado.

Such ahistoricism is, of course, a great paradox for a people who have been traditionally so enamored of their past and the way their millennia of uninterrupted culture have conferred both a sense of gravity to the present and continuity to the future. For the moment, the excitement of the marketplace and of being able to indulge in purely recreational activities has created a Chinese version of *carpe diem*. The haze that envelops and blurs so much of the urban landscape is an all too apt metaphor for the reluctance of this society and its government to reflect lucidly on where it has come from, much less where it is headed.

II.

One does not have to be in China long to become aware that beneath the surface of this frenzy of commerce and self-indulgence another drama is being played out. This involves a shadowy power struggle by party rivals who know they do not have much time now before 90-year-old Deng "goes to meet Marx" [see Jonathan Mirsky, "It's Purge Time in Beijing," June 19]. The recognition that soon China will no longer have a "big leader" at the helm to steady its often erratic course creates a dissonant background hum behind the economic miracle that is unsettling to anyone who allows himself to hear it. As dissident astrophysicist Fang Lizhi recently warned, "We must remember that the most typical source of chaos in a monolithic, totalitarian state is the power struggle among top leaders for succession. It is a dangerous game without regulation." It is the virtual inevitability that such a struggle will take place sometime after Deng dies that makes efforts to ignore the future so futile.

'Although Mao unified China, history will hold Deng up to be every bit as great.'

"He's just like a candle burned down to the last little stub so that any small breeze can snuff him out," a friend in Beijing who is an intimate of one of Deng's doctors recently told me. "There's no telling how long they can keep those old guys going on Chinese herbs and breathing machines. What's important is to be able to say that a leader is technically still alive to avoid a scramble for power."

Gossip about Deng's health and rumors of his imminent demise have been sweeping the capital for months and causing manic fears for China's stability. The last time he was seen in public was during the 1994 Chinese New Year, when Central Chinese Television (CCTV) showed him on tape for a few minutes. Chinese political spin doctors probably hoped that by simply producing Deng's live remains they would allay fears that his reign was nearing an end. What appeared on the screen, however, was not so reassuring. Viewers saw a palsied old man staring blankly off into space, doddering forward between two supporting aides. Of course, when he failed to make even a cameo appearance this past New Year, people took it as an even worse sign. Last fall, just as the *People's Daily* was trumpeting that "our Party has already victoriously completed the transfer of power to the current President and Party chief Jiang Zemin," more hearsay about Deng's poor health sent the Shanghai Securities Exchange plummeting some 40 percent. When a Foreign Ministry spokesman insisted that Deng was fine, the volatile exchange shot up 36 percent. But then, when Hong Kong papers reported Deng in a coma this January, the Hang Seng Index took a similar dive.

After surviving almost a century of Chinese history, Deng is now very deaf and variously said to be suffering from Parkinson's disease, kidney failure, the effects of several strokes and/or prostate, pancreatic and testicular cancer. He is currently believed to be lying barely conscious in Military Hospital 301. By using his enormous personal prestige as a leader, Deng has been able to balance different interests and factions against one another and thus avoid major breakdown at the top. So important has Deng's role been in maintaining the status quo that many would welcome almost any subterfuge delaying the day when the leadership has to reconfigure itself. There have even been rumors that if he dies at a particularly sensitive political moment, "relevant authorities" might withhold news of his death until a more propitious time. When Deng's main rival, the 90-year-old Chen Yun, died this April, it took authorities almost two days to make an announcement.

The Mystique of Power

Deng's success as a "big leader" has grown out of his long tenure as a veteran revolutionary, which included a stint in the Shanghai underground during the twenties, the Long March in the thirties and his role as a military commander in the Civil War against Chiang Kai-shek in the forties. More recently, his mass appeal was reinforced by his practical bent. When in 1978 he proclaimed, "Our motto is 'Less talk, more action,' " he summed up the essence of his pragmatism. But even in the early sixties he was dropping such adages as, "Black cat, white cat, it's a good cat as long as it catches mice." After twice being deposed by Mao for such heretical sentiments, he finally returned to power in 1978. "Not only did he start the reform process in 1979, [he] restarted it in 1992, thereby irrevocably changing the whole direction of China," reminds Larry Lau, a Stanford economist. "Although Mao unified China, I think history will hold Deng up to be every bit as great."

Deng's effectiveness has also borrowed heavily from the tradition of bygone emperors who relied on detachment and seclusion to spin a mystique of power around their rule. Like Dostoyevsky's Grand Inquisitor in *The Brothers Karamazov*,

Deng has ruled by the three powers of miracle, mystery and authority. When a Foreign Ministry spokesman was recently asked at a press briefing how and where Deng was, the answer was characteristically enigmatic: "Mr. Deng Xiaoping is wherever he is."

Unlike Mao, Deng has steadfastly eschewed the titles of premier, president, or party general secretary. When he visited the United States in 1979 to normalize relations, he was just a lowly vice premier. In fact, since 1993, when he gave up his position as chairman of the powerful Central Military Commission, Deng's only title has been president of the All-China Bridge Association. "Shunning grandiose titles only lent him a greater air of mystery and invincibility," writes M.I.T. political scientist Lucien Pye. "People were thus free to imagine him as being truly omnipotent, far more in command than if his powers were only those assigned to a particular position or job." Since Deng's authority had such an insubstantial institutional basis, foreign journalists were left scratching their heads for a shorthand way to convey the eminence of this man who ran China's politics from behind the scenes. They finally settled on the suitably vague but evocative "China's paramount leader."

If ruling ex officio has served Deng admirably, it has served his country less well. By allowing so much authority to reside in the hands of an uncrowned and unelected patriarch, institutional and legal structures were never able to come into their own. But what Deng wanted for China was not political democracy but the dream of nineteenth-century reformers: *fuqiang* (wealth and power). By holding the reform of China's political system hostage to his own whim even as he spurred the country to new heights of economic development, Deng has kept his country in a state of arrested political development. Moreover, with him alive, other party leaders have remained fearful of making major decisions that might prove a liability to them in the post-Deng scramble for power.

Struggling to Succeed

Deng's current anointed successor is Jiang Zemin, a 69-year-old electrical engineer who was sent to the Soviet Union as a student in the fifties and became the mayor and party chief of Shanghai in the eighties. Jiang's problem is not that he is actively disliked but that ordinary people don't really care about him. Viewing him as belonging to the "wind faction," which blows without conviction according to the prevailing political breezes, they treated his enthronement the way employees of a family-owned company might acquiesce in the appointment of the boss's lackluster son as C.E.O. To compensate for his deficit of political magnetism, Deng got Jiang appointed to an embarrassing abundance of official posts. Currently, he is party general secretary, president, Politburo member, member of the Standing Committee of the Politburo, chairman of the Central Military Commission, head of the Central Financial and Economic Group and head of the Central Taiwan Work Group, just to name a few. As the "core" of the party's central leadership, allies have also tried to fan to flame a mini-cult of personality by, among other things, releasing a painted poster bearing the inscription "Glad and at Ease" that shows an avuncular Jiang standing solicitously behind Deng.

Such efforts, however, are dubiously effective. In China, what is important for a leader is not simply his position and titles but how others assess the clout of his *guanxi* (network of personal relationships) through which political business is really transacted. While it is true that Jiang's "Shanghai clique" has become increasingly powerful on the Politburo, what he lacks are the strong ties to the military that Deng forged over half a century of soldiering. So it came as no surprise when Jiang recently launched his "Thousand Generals Program" and began pinning medals on a newly promoted crop of young Army officers and installing loyalists in the upper ranks of the 800,000-strong People's Armed Police, the national police force that was hastily beefed up after 1989. As Mao learned after the Cultural Revolution and Deng learned in 1989, the military is the last line of defense for a politically besieged party leader. With the central party's discipline failing and regionalization of the country advancing due to the power of booming local economies, the military is one of the last national institutions that remains intact, and it could end up as the key arbiter in any post-Deng power struggle.

Even in the military, however, the situation is in flux. Although Jiang tirelessly emphasizes the need to "uphold the party's absolute leadership over the army," with military units also becoming ever more deeply involved in commerce (through investments in commercial projects such as hotels, nightclubs, arms trading and even in companies pirating foreign CDs and computer programs), it is harder than ever to predict whether, despite the frequency with which they are rotated, regional commanders will be loyal to the party if political push once again comes to shove.

While the party likes to speak of its central leadership as if it were a coherent structure with Jiang Zemin at its core, it is actually composed of a nebulous welter of rival factions that serve as a chaotic substitute for political parties. Each faction has its putative leaders whose political differences tend to center around their differing views on the pace of reform and the degree to which the party should relax ideological and social controls. Those who view further opening up to the outside world and continued economic liberalization as essential to China's development are generally referred to as "reformers," while leaders who are more ideological and unwilling to see China drift too far from its revolutionary moorings are referred to as "hard-liners." The hard-liners, who tend to view many of Deng's economic reforms as a betrayal of Mao's revolution, have lost influence over the past decade and a half. Nonetheless, they continue to exert real power within the party and the army, especially during times of uncertainty or incipient crisis, when they are not averse to exploiting patriotic sentiment, even to inciting xenophobia, to gain mass support.

Every tea-leaf reader in China is, of course, trying to figure out who will inherit the mantle of leadership after Deng's death. It is a measure of how uncertain things are that "China experts" have no consensus about how the cards of leadership will ultimately get reshuffled. If Jiang Zemin fails to hang on, the enigmatic National People's Congress president, Qiao Shi—who is being touted by some observers as a closet liberal, although his elusive political predilections make him seem more a Chinese Colin Powell than anything else—could pick up the reins. Then again, if there is an economic crisis, the heirs of Chen Yun's hard-line legacy may be able to regain substantial influence, as they did after the Tiananmen uprising. Or if the political jousting really begins to threaten the status quo, the military will perhaps be provoked into staging a countercoup under 88-year-old former general, president and Deng ally Yang Shangkun. If the whole situation really begins to unravel and if pressure to reverse the verdict on the 1989 protest movement mounts, it is even possible that Zhao Ziyang, the 77-year-old former premier and party chief (still under modified house arrest for his pro-student position in 1989) could be summoned back to head a caretaker government.

Not to be forgotten in any post-Deng power struggle are the so-called *taizidang* (prince faction), who have parlayed their privileged positions as children of high-ranking party leaders into fortunes stashed in foreign bank accounts and into behind-the-scenes political power. Some are even said to have lofted rumors about Deng's poor health just to send the stock market into a tailspin so they could capitalize by buying low and then selling high when, a few days later, their rumors were officially denied and the market rebounded. The backbone of a new crypto-capitalist authoritarianism, the *taizidang* are united only by their unwillingness to see the status quo and their privileged positions disturbed. Deng's own daughter Deng Rong, who came to New York this past March to promote her book *Deng Xiaoping: My Father* and attend a series of international coming-out parties in her honor hosted by the likes of Alexander Haig and Rupert Murdoch, is perhaps the most internationally visible representative of this wealthy and powerful group.

Nothing illustrates the politically unpredictable nature of things better than two recent votes in the National People's Congress, which has usually acted as a rubber stamp for decisions already handed down by key leaders. First, over a third of the delegates refused to vote for Jiang Chunyun, a newly designated vice premier who was supported by Jiang Zemin despite evidence of massive corruption in Shandong Province when he was governor there. Several days later, the Congress again reasserted itself when 661 delegates defiantly refused to vote for a new education law and almost a third of them failed to support a new banking law. These were such unexpected signs of life in the Congress that the *Beijing Youth Daily* facetiously compared them to a Chinese scientist's recent discovery of DNA traces in a 65-million-year-old dinosaur egg.

To cap off the unprecedented week, N.P.C. vice chairman Tian Jiyun proclaimed to delegates from Guangdong Province that "comrades serving the N.P.C. have not been courageous enough. They have been afraid of offending other people." Then, president Qiao Shi seemed to expand the boundaries of permissible political dialogue with a closing speech that attacked "lawless government cadres" and insisted that China could only consider itself truly modernized when it was ruled by law rather than by personality. In another telling statement, he also declared that the N.P.C., because its power derived from the 1982 Constitution, should be viewed as a "primary" rather than "secondary" government institution.

Industrial Dinosaurs

Whether this trend toward greater parliamentarian independence continues or not, the terms of the political leadership game in China could radically change when the last titans of the revolution die. At the very least, it is doubtful that any successor will be able to write his will so grandly on China's history. Instead of shaping history, Mao and Deng's successors seem destined to be shaped by it and by the grave problems that have been ineluctably arising as a result of economic reform.

Perhaps the most refractory problem China faces is the more than 100,000 state-owned enterprises (S.O.E.s), two-thirds of which fail to turn a profit. Despite the fact that their losses amount to between 2.4 and 5.3 percent of the gross domestic product and necessitate huge government subsidies (draining around 70 percent of state investment funds), that the output value of S.O.E.s has recently fallen below 50 percent of the country's total and that the World Bank has called them the country's "underlying structural problem," the Communist Party continues to cling to the notion of state ownership of "the means of production," especially of heavy industry. After all, if party leaders cannot claim to be implementing some kind of socialism—Deng's term of choice is "socialism with Chinese characteristics"—what rationalization do they have for continuing their authoritarian rule?

The most hopeful strategy for resolving the problem is for the state to find foreign joint-venture partners for money-losing factories. But few foreign C.E.O.s want to make matches with Chinese enterprises that are badly managed, burdened with outmoded technology, overstaffed with unproductive workers who cannot be fired for incompetence and weighed down by large rolls of retirees on pension. The alternative is to activate the bankruptcy law that has been on the books, although largely unused, since 1986. However, party officials are loath to strip members of the proletariat of their jobs, housing, health care benefits and pensions not simply because such actions would appear brazenly un-Communist but because they fear what is known as the "Polish disease": the convergence of labor unrest with growing dissatisfaction among dissident intellectuals that could lead to a Solidarity-type protest movement. Last June the official *Market News* admitted that in 1993 alone there had been 12,358 significant labor disputes between factories and workers, many of whom have been fired or *xiagang*ed (put on partial salary).

So desperate have some Chinese officials become to relieve their ministries of the burden of failing S.O.E.s that they have sometimes ignored the niceties of the party's ideological commitment to state ownership. Last September, for example, the vice minister of the State Economic and Trade Commission went so far as to urge some local cadres to simply cut off supplies of power and raw materials to S.O.E.s that did not shape up and become self-reliant.

Masses and Classes

As a result of all the economic changes, China's once relatively stable social structure is rapidly changing. While some people are getting fabulously wealthy and creating a whole new myth of prosperity, others, especially those living on state pensions and fixed incomes, are having trouble even keeping up with an inflation rate that has been hovering around 20 percent. Party leaders vividly remember the unrest that resulted after the inflation rate rose to 19 percent in 1988. The way the country's once largely classless society has been delaminating is deeply disturbing, particularly to old revolutionaries who still remember Marx's warning in *The Communist Manifesto* about "society splitting into two great hostile camps." As early as 1993, some 4.3 million people saw their incomes skyrocket to twelve times the urban average and thirty-two times the rural average, while at the same time another 400 million people suffered a decline.

Beneath the official version of China's miracle lies a darker subtext of corruption.

Nowhere has the income gap widened more rapidly than between the urban and backward rural areas. In 1994, annual urban income was 3,150 yuan ($373) per capita, while rural income was only 1,200Y ($142). And with the government keeping the price at which it purchases agricultural commodities artificially low, with venal local officials imposing more and more arbitrary taxes and levies, and with inflation driving up the cost of farm implements, fertilizers and insecticides, the temptation for peasants to leave for the city and become part of the *liudong renkou* (floating population) has steadily increased. Some 100 million people (almost 10 percent of the country's population) are now officially estimated to have moved from the countryside to the city in what has quietly become the largest mass migration in recent human history. As China's overall population is increasing by some 12 million a year, the amount of arable land continues to shrink because of all the new factories, industrial parks, golf courses, housing developments and highways. Experts predict that another 100-200 million peasants could easily become surplus rural laborers in the near future.

Nowadays railroads are so crowded with "floaters" that lavatories and luggage racks are often occupied by passengers. The neighborhoods surrounding train and bus stations often look like urban refugee centers as thousands of new arrivals are forced to camp out there because they have nowhere else to go. At best, they end up in shantytowns and find jobs doing piecework in factories, toiling as day laborers on construction sites, serving as domestics or, if they're young and female, working in China's burgeoning sex industry, which many still find better than rural life.

While these migrants do deliver a virtually unlimited supply of cheap labor to China's dynamic coastal economy and send significant funds back home to poor rural areas, floaters have not only strained municipal services to the limit but are seriously undermining the government's ability to carry out such crucial national programs as its "one family, one child" policy. Even more worrisome to China's leaders is the rising crime rate caused by this migration. The papers are filled with crime statistics, but every now and again one comes across something that hammers home how things have broken down. A poll recently conducted by a Beijing radio station revealed that 80 percent of respondents claimed that someone in their family had had a bicycle stolen over the past year, a major crime in a society in which ordinary people are dependent on bikes for basic transportation. In large cities, floaters now account for between 40 and 80 percent of all convicted criminals.

Crime à la Mode

Lawlessness is not, of course, limited to floaters. There has been a tenfold rise in overall criminal activity since Deng's reforms began shaking up Chinese society in 1979. Hardly a day goes by that one does not read in the papers about such things as counterfeiters printing fake currency and securities; con men setting up phony banks with forged documents; syndicates kidnapping young women to sell as wives, concubines or prostitutes; pornographers with computerized production and distribution networks becoming millionaires; drug traffickers supplying domestic and world markets with heroin; weapons merchants peddling guns to gangsters; and criminal rings making fortunes selling everything from fake medicine to the blood of children, who are rounded up in the countryside and then "milked" like dairy cows. Thieves have even stolen thousands of manhole covers from the streets of Beijing for resale as scrap iron!

To make matters worse, it is increasingly difficult to distinguish police from criminals dressed up as police to fool their victims. During a recent crackdown in Henan Province, out of thirty-eight uniformed officers checked in the street, only seven turned out to be legitimate officers of the law. Moreover, many real police have become more dedicated to graft, collecting bribes and racketeering than to the suppression of crime. Officers in local bureaus of the Ministry of Public Security (China's secret police), for instance, are renowned for demanding bribes from ordinary citizens before issuing such crucial documents as passports or releasing inmates from prison. They are also widely rumored to be raking in huge payoffs from protection schemes for *karaoke* bars, nightclubs, massage parlors and brothels in cities like Shenzhen and Shanghai. They are even reported to be taking payoffs in return for giving hospitals access to organs extracted from executed prisoners for transplants [see Aryeh Neier, "Watching Rights," June 12].

Rot at the Top

Without a free press, most major instances of high-level government corruption are never exposed. Sometimes, however, an instance of official corruption on a staggering scale reveals itself. Take the case of Li Min, deputy chief of Beijing's municipal State Security Bureau, China's C.I.A. He was recently arrested for the role he and his bureau played in the bogus Xinxing Industrial Company, which, before it got busted, bilked some 3.2 billionY ($380 million) from government and private investors by promising them annual returns as high as 50 percent.

Beneath the official storybook version of China as an economic miracle lies a darker subtext of corruption permeating all levels of government and life. The situation is so bad that in 1993 Deng himself was quoted in the *People's Daily* as decrying the way China has become "dominated by corruption, embezzlement and bribery." Although the party has sponsored numerous "anti-corruption campaigns," they have focused almost exclusively on making examples of low-level officials—what the Chinese refer to as "scaring the monkey by killing the chicken." However, after a February Cabinet meeting at which Premier Li Peng warned that corruption was "a life and death" struggle in which the party could "lose the trust of the people," something unprecedented began to happen. Suddenly the anti-corruption effort began to topple some very high-ranking figures. Their fall suggested that the post-Deng power struggle had begun to break out into the open, albeit in a somewhat oblique and mysterious form.

First to fall was Zhou Beifang, who was arrested for "serious economic crimes." Zhou was chairman of Shougang Concord Holdings in Hong Kong and son of Deng's old comrade-in-arms Zhou Guanwu, who was himself chairman of the state-owned behemoth Capital Iron & Steel Works. One of Zhou the Younger's business cohorts in Hong Kong was none other than Deng's son, Deng Zhifang. Moreover, one of his main investors was Li Ka-shing, the billionaire who was also constructing the mammoth $2.1 billion Oriental Plaza in Beijing, which was slated to devour McDonald's.

It wasn't long before a secretary of Beijing Vice Mayor Zhang Baifa became enmeshed in the investigation as well, suggesting that whatever tectonic political orogeny was taking place, the shock waves were spreading. Then in early April, another Beijing Deputy Mayor, Wang Baosen, who headed the municipal planning commission, had his chauffeur drive him out toward the Great Wall to the outskirts of town, where he unceremoniously blew his brains out. Although his death received only the most cursory announcement in the New China News Agency, word quickly spread over the *xiaodao xiaoxi* (back-alley news), filling the city with rumors of shady real estate deals, including the official permission given to the Oriental Plaza despite the fact that it violated recently passed height limitations on new buildings. Soon, there was even speculation that Wang might have been murdered to protect higher-ups who were implicated in a far larger web of corrupt deals.

What all this meant and whether further accusations would follow was not completely clear. However, such unusual public manifestations of high-level intrigue suggested big maneuverings beneath the surface. In the recent past, anti-corruption drives have come and gone without disturbing the veneer of high-level unity. But this spring, Jiang, who had been building up files on his rivals' involvement in corruption, started using this information both as a political weapon and as a way to gain public support for his leadership. When hard-line Beijing party chief Chen Xitong, who had been a militant supporter of suppressing student protesters in 1989 and whose personal secretary was already under arrest, was forced to resign and was put under house arrest in late April, it began to look as if Jiang, who as mayor had avoided violence in Shanghai, was trying to project himself as being more self-assured by taking such resolute, independent and, as it turned out, popular action because it seemed to attack corruption. Some even suggested that by arresting Chen, Jiang was also trying to distance himself from the 1989 massacre in anticipation of the "verdict" on it as a "counterrevolutionary rebellion" being reversed, a hypothesis that seemed all the more plausible after he also visited the grave of Hu Yaobang, the former party leader whose death presaged the protest movement and whose career has since become a symbol of unsullied public service.

"Sure, something's happening," one Chinese friend laughingly told me. "If they arrested every corrupt official, there would be no government left." But still, something had to be done. As Fang Lizhi recently observed, "For anyone who knows China's long history of collapsed dynasties and upheavals triggered by corruption, there can be little comfort in the belief that the most pervasive corruption in our history will somehow, this time, result in enduring stability."

Marx Meets Confucius

Corruption is just the most obvious expression of a deeper malady that now grips Chinese society. Changes have come so precipitately and suddenly that few people have a sense any longer of what they believe in, whether traditional Confucian values, revolutionary Maoist values or some sort of East-West amalgam. The result is a normative vacuum in which no one seems to know what it means to be "Chinese." As the rock star Cui Jian sings on his recent album *Eggs Under the Red Flag*, "Money is fluttering in the wind. We have no ideals." A Chinese writer friend put it even more bluntly: "All that is left uniting us is greed."

To fill this void, the party Central Committee launched a propaganda campaign last October calling for a mind-numbing "great new undertaking to build a political party of Marxism which is armed with the theory of building socialism with Chinese characteristics; serves the people wholeheartedly; is fully consolidated ideologically, politically, and organizationally; can stand the test of all hazards; and which always advances ahead of the times." As part of this campaign, cadres from government organizations were required to spend a week at a party school studying *The Selected Works of Deng Xiaoping*. "You don't have to listen, but you can't go to sleep either," commented a friend who works for a state trading company. "We even had to write papers, but it doesn't matter what you write because even the teachers don't bother to read them!"

At the same time the party launched a crusade to revive Confucianism. On the occasion of the sage's 2,545th birthday, last October, a conference of some 300 scholars from twenty countries was dutifully convened. For the Communist Party to rehabilitate Confucius, whom it had formerly reviled as a degenerate apostle of China's exploitative feudal society, was an act of unsurpassed opportunism. After all, Confucius was a political philosopher who stressed the traditional virtues of rank, obedience and harmony rather than the Maoist virtues of equality, revolution and class struggle. Moreover, while Deng had proclaimed that "to get rich is glorious," Confucius had held commerce and merchants in distinctly low esteem.

Laissez-faire economics coexist with the old Leninist political system.

"It is shameful," he said, "to make gain your sole object, irrespective of whether the *dao* prevails in the state or not." This was hardly a testimonial for the kind of rapacious capitalism that Deng has unleashed. And if initiators of this revival thought the Confucian emphasis on orthodoxy, authority and social harmony might help them thwart China's dissident movement, they were ignoring another seminal tenet of this traditional doctrine, which teaches that only when leaders are benevolent and just should the people submit to their rule.

Coming at a time when most people were yearning to indulge their basic capitalist urges, the attempt to raise Confucius from the dead did little more than add to the sense of cognitive dissonance. That sense was further heightened by a larger party effort to dredge up other symbols that might appeal to nationalist sentiment. This past National Day, leaders deluged the public with syrupy appeals to love the country and love the party, as if they were one and the same. At the same time the propaganda department of the Central Committee issued a document titled "Implementation Program for Patriotic Education," which ordered all schools to revise their curriculums to "make patriotic thought the principal melody of society" so that the "masses" could be bombarded at "any time, anywhere, in every aspect of their daily social life" with "the spiritual infection and uplifting influence of patriotism."

Not only have old socialist values and ideology been seriously eroded but the party and the central government, though still autocratic, have suffered a substantial loss of power due to the growing economic independence of outlying regions such as Guangdong Province (adjacent to Hong Kong), Fujian Province (across the straits from Taiwan) and the Shanghai/Yangtze River Valley area (in south-central China). Because of the strength of local industry and direct trade with the outside world, these regions have gained a new and independent spirit that was plain to see in the recent N.P.C. votes. Their independence has also tempted them to try to dodge central regulations on everything from environmental quality and management of state property to birth control and the payment of taxes. Even though centralized power is a crucial element in assuring economic stability—without it there will be no force able to exercise the macroeconomic control needed to lower inflation and cool off growth of the economy as a whole—for now the trend toward greater regionalization seems unstoppable.

Let a Thousand Flowers Die

One thing Deng has taken pains to impart to Jiang and his "core leadership" is that while economic reform may be essential to fulfilling people's rising expectations and maintaining party power, political reform, especially freedom of expression, is dangerous because it allows critical voices to challenge the party's stranglehold on government. This strategy of egging China's economic system on to become more laissez-faire while tenaciously maintaining its old Leninist political system has helped create the appearance that intellectual and political dissent have vanished. It is true that most Chinese are now preoccupied with business and making money. After all, when presented with a choice between business and the possibility of freedom and wealth, or opposition politics and the likelihood of imprisonment and certainty of penury, most people choose the former. However, there remains a small group of determined intellectuals and labor activists who continue to speak out and to insist that it is deceptive and self-defeating to imagine that politics can be so completely separated from economics. As Wei Jingsheng, China's most celebrated dissident, put it during the 1978-79 Democracy Wall movement, "To accomplish modernization, the Chinese people must first practice democracy and modernize China's social system. . . . Without this condition, society will become stagnant and economic growth will encounter insurmountable obstacles." For such heretical views, Wei was given a fifteen-year jail sentence at Deng's behest.

After being released in September 1993, Wei immediately and unrepentantly resumed decrying China's backward state of democracy. The party perceived his solitary voice as such a threat that in April 1994 he was mysteriously spirited away again, this time without any charges being brought or any notification given to his family. More than a year later, he remains "disappeared," and his secretary, Tong Yi, who was administratively detained, is reported to have been seriously beaten in a "re-education-through-labor" camp for her role in keeping Wei in touch with members of the foreign press.

Tellingly, last July the N.P.C.'s Standing Committee passed a law that makes anyone who "maintains connections with or accepts financial support from groups abroad" subject to arrest for "carrying out activities which endanger state security." Fearful that such dissident voices might become the sparks that light the next prairie fire of political dissent and wary that any sign of political tolerance might appear as weakness, Deng and his minions have taken a line on free speech that is harsher than at any time during the past decade and a half. Sentences of up to twenty years continue to be meted out to those who commit crimes of "counterrevolutionary propaganda and incitement" by speaking out. Last November, for instance, a journalist named Gao Yu was arrested as she prepared to leave China to study at Columbia University and was accused of hav-

ing leaked state secrets. Her crime, it turned out, was quoting a Beijing source in a Hong Kong paper as having said that Jiang Zemin had advised the Central Committee at a closed meeting that certain personnel assignments were decided "after consultation with senior comrades, especially after hearing the opinion of Deng Xiaoping." For this lèse-majesté Gao was sentenced to six years in prison, and the State Council official who had leaked the news to her was given thirteen years.

As the sixth anniversary of the June 4, 1989, massacre approached, democratic activists began distributing a new flurry of manifestoes and petitions calling on the government to allow greater political tolerance. In February, before the N.P.C. convened, four such petitions were signed and then in May five more surfaced in what has been the biggest recrudescence of public protest since 1989. A petition released on May 15 and signed by forty-five prominent intellectuals commemorated the U.N.'s "Year of Tolerance." Calling tolerance "a mark of human civilization," it urged the government "to promote and encourage respect for human rights" as stipulated in the U.N. Charter. Another petition signed by fifty-two intellectuals called for reversing the official verdict on the 1989 demonstrations as "counterrevolutionary" and warned that China faced another "blood-soaked tragedy" if it did not implement political reforms and begin to respect human rights. The party's response was to round up, interrogate and detain dozens of activists and intellectuals for "disturbing the social order." Such a reaction made it clear that far from feeling a new confidence in its right to rule because of China's economic successes, the party continues to feel very vulnerable to the critique of dissidents.

Deng's policies have succeeded in maintaining an uneasy stability for the past fifteen years. But whether such a strategy will continue to be successful after his death is another question. Unreleased political pressure has a way of building up, especially when economic problems arise, and unless relieved, creating massive ruptures. "It must be said that as the contradictions in society accumulate and sharpen, the use of such repressive measures is not only unreasonable but harmful," writes 26-year-old Wang Dan, a Tiananmen Square student leader who served three and a half years in prison and has been under almost continuous police surveillance since being released. "When all the channels for expression of political opposition in an open, legal fashion are closed, such political forces as already exist will merely be forced to participate politically in secret and illegal ways. In terms of social stability and progress, the disadvantages of this greatly outweigh any possible benefits."

And the Future . . . ?

Whereas with most other great nations it is possible to look ahead and know that certain fundamental ideas, institutions and values will endure for years to come, in today's China there is almost nothing that is fixed or certain. What makes reading the future so difficult is that there is a range of sharply conflicting scenarios, each of which has almost equal plausibility.

It may be that China will be able to muddle through after Deng and become the first socialist-bloc country to successfully reform itself under the aegis of a Communist Party. However, it is also plausible that the Beijing government will continue to lose control until China finds itself back in some state of quasi-feudal fragmentation, even anarchy exacerbated by feuding party factions. Whatever happens, all that is certain is that because of China's long history of authoritarianism, political reform and a more democratic society will not come as easily as this last rush of economic development. What causes apprehension in China is not just the obvious recognition of Deng's mortality but the unspoken recognition that China's old system of "great leader" governance will die with him. However brutal party rule has been, leaders like Mao and Deng at least created the illusion that someone was leading history. Ordinary Chinese still yearn for an effective leader or emperor, but now all they see on the horizon in post-Deng China is a collection of unconvincing understudies waiting in the wings. As the writer-in-exile Liu Binyan recently pointed out, "The government Deng Xiaoping leaves behind will be the weakest in China since Communist rule began in 1949. . . . At the same time, the populace has become more difficult to rule than any other in Chinese history."

In his *Theses on Feuerbach*, Marx wrote that "philosophers have only interpreted the world, in various ways; the point, however, is to change it." From Sun Yat-sen and Chiang Kai-shek to Mao Zedong and Deng Xiaoping, throughout the twentieth century there has been a mythic big leader to serve as figurehead and give China the appearance of coherence and greatness. Now, as the last leader of truly mythic proportions runs out of life, it is perhaps understandable that ordinary Chinese should turn away from politics and grab at whatever material advantages they can. After all, they know better than anyone the problems the next generation of party leaders will have to confront; how hastily and unsystematically Deng's economic miracle has been thrown together; how murky China's sense of direction is; and how unstable the edifice of the party's political leadership has always been in China—especially when it comes to passing the baton from one ruler to another.

India's Juggernaut of Change

Political scandals add uncertainty to April's elections but are providing impetus for reform, say Mark Nicholson and Peter Montagnon

On a salary of just Rs5,000 (£88) a month, Mr Salman Kurshid, India's minister of state for external affairs and a member of parliament for Uttar Pradesh, finds it difficult to afford some of the demands of his constituents and party workers.

One worker recently asked him for a colour television for his daughter's wedding, costing the equivalent of two months' ministerial salary. The assumption was that if the minister himself could not afford it, he would have the contacts to conjure up the gift from somewhere else.

That, says Mr Kurshid, is the feudal style of traditional Indian politics. It is also "totally unacceptable" in the type of modern industrial economy which India is seeking to become after four years of reform.

The latest Indian political scandal, which erupted in January and involves accusations of illegal payments to numerous politicians, illustrates the upheaval caused by this painful transition to modernity. It has added a note of uncertainty to the country's politics ahead of an election in April.

But younger and more open politicians such as Mr Kurshid believe that the scandal may also provide an impetus for further modernisation of a system based as much on patronage as on democracy.

Since the scandal broke last month, 10 leading politicians, including three ministers and the leader of the largest opposition party, have been charged with taking bribes. Dozens more politi-

cians are being investigated, including several ministers, after their names were found in diaries belonging to the Jains, a Madhya Pradesh family under investigation for alleged illegal foreign exchange dealing.

The incriminating notebooks were first discovered in 1991, but the investigation was low-key until two journalists took the matter to the Supreme Court, which insisted last year that inquiries should lead to prosecutions.

The timing of the charges—three months before a general election—were widely seen as a ploy by Mr P. V. Narasimha Rao, the prime minister whose ruling Congress party has been dogged by opposition accusations of Corruption. He was seen as using the scandal as an opportunity to spread allegations across the political spectrum in an effort to defuse corruption as a decisive election issue.

But Mr Rao has opened up a Pandora's box, creating a scandal of unprecedented proportions. Among other developments, opposition parties allege there is evidence implicating Mr Rao himself in the scandal—although his officials have denied any involvement.

Unlike the Bofors weapons procurement scandal of the late 1980s, the Jain scandal has already resulted in criminal charges against politicians. For the first time, supervision by the Central Bureau of Investigation has been wrested from the politicians by an increasingly activist Supreme Court.

The extensive media coverage, the Supreme Court's determination to ensure that the inquiry is completed without hindrance, and the suggestions of Mr Rao's involvement have all lent the affair a momentum which many believe will extend beyond the elections.

"Something has started which cannot be stopped," says Mr Prem Shankar Jha, a newspaper columnist. "The political class is in a panic."

In India's volatile political climate it is difficult to judge the impact of the scandal on April's elections. Congress supporters argue that most voters, especially those in rural areas, are interested primarily in local issues. Corruption among political leaders has long ceased to surprise them.

Moreover, rural Indian voters appear to enjoy the spectacle of larger-than-life politicians who exude power and plenty: witness the phenomenon of filmstar politicians such as the late N. T. Rama Rao, former chief minister of Andhra Pradesh, who commanded fanatical popular support from voters even while pursuing policies that undermined the financial stability of his state.

But voters are unlikely to ignore the scandal altogether. The involvement of other parties will not necessarily free Congress from its reputation for corruption. The allegations against Mr L. K. Advani, leader of the main opposition Hindu nationalist Bharatiya Janata Party, look weak. And support has been growing for the leftwing parties, including India's two communist parties, the leaders of which have been largely untainted.

The implications of the scandal for economic reforms, which have sought to liberalise trade and industry after 40 years of protection and state control, could be as significant as the impact on politics. Some Indians argue that the country's politicians are so discredited that they no longer have the moral authority to deliver the good government and politically sensitive economic reforms on which the country's future prosperity depends.

But others, such as Mr Kurshid, believe the scandal may represent a milestone on India's road to modernity. Economic reforms, including privatisation and deregulation of industry, have reduced the role of government in the economy.

And national politicians no longer matter so much with power in India devolving to the states and away from central government as centralised licensing procedures have been swept away.

"There's a change in the way business looks at politicians these days," says Mr Tarun Das, director-general of the Confederation of Indian Industries. "They don't need to pay them. They're no longer so powerful."

As India modernises, business executives and others say there is a need for a class of politicians dedicated to economic management rather than old-fashioned patronage. "We have good managers both in politics and in the corporate sector, and in administration," says Mr Kurshid. "But they are working with tools that are not adequate. We need to focus also on a system of governance which is compatible with economic restructuring."

Since the scandal broke the confederation and other business groups have intensified lobbying for increases in the salaries of ministers and MPs to attract better quality people into politics. They also advocate direct state funding of political parties, along with a review of the 26-year-old ban on corporate donations to political parties. India's political parties at present survive largely on undeclared backhanders from powerful business leaders to individual politicians.

Mr Jairam Ramesh, a former state planner turned business journalist, says state funding of political parties would cost only about Rs10bn a year, tiny in comparison with total budget outlays exceeding Rs1,600bn.

He believes such a system will probably be introduced by whoever comes out ahead in the next election. But there is scepticism about how fast it will come, and about whether more transparent political funding would eliminate corruption.

One advantage of the state funding, adds Mr Shankar Jha, is that it would allow party leaders to control more directly which candidates run for office. The present system of patronage places too much power in the hands of individual politicians able to procure the greatest resources, whatever their formal position in the party hierarchy.

Such changes could help transform standards in Indian politics, Mr Kurshid believes. But there must also be changes in the expectations of voters, who expect favours in return for their support and, because they rarely pay taxes, have no incentive to fight against the cost of inefficiency created by corruption. The attitudes of politicians and bureaucrats, some of whom see their jobs as a source of wealth that could not possibly be provided by their salaries, also need to change.

"The problem will go away only with a change in social behaviour. It will not happen overnight," says Mr Kurshid. "But you would get a working system and some incentive for decent people to come in and remain decent and honest."

Whether Mr Rao has any such political evolution in mind is questionable. The prime minister appears as ambivalent towards political reform as he has been towards the economy. He has never argued from an ideological standpoint for the economic reforms, which were hatched as a result of the balance of payments crisis in 1991. It is thus unclear how vigorously he would pursue constitutional reform if re-elected in April.

However, some analysts believe that pursuing reform may be popular among India's more affluent urban voters, who hold the swing vote in Indian polls. This is also arguably the class most interested in economic reform, which could be helped by a restructuring of the political system.

With a government less dependent on patronage, for instance, it would prove easier to liberalise activities such as land sales and the sugar and fertiliser industries. These are still controlled, and thus still lucrative sources of revenue for politicians, says Mr Ramesh.

Other economists say political reform would also make it easier to cut India's yawning budget deficit, set to exceed 6 per cent of gross domestic product this year. Tax claims could be enforced against wealthy individuals and businesses which have routinely paid bribes to evade them in the past.

Other countries such as Japan and Korea are cleaning up the relationship between their politicians and business. The scandal may help India make its break with the corruption of the past.

"Somebody's got to begin the change. This will give us the impetus," says Mr Kurshid.

Miracles beyond the free market

Michael Prowse

The biggest challenge for economists today is understanding the extraordinary success of east Asia. The region has nearly quadrupled per capita incomes in the past quarter of a century—a record unparalleled in economic history. On present trends it may begin to overtake much of the industrialised west early in the 21st century.

If its startling success could be replicated elsewhere, billions of people in developing and formerly communist countries could look forward to improved living standards. And the hope, eventually, of eliminating the scourge of grinding poverty would seem less quixotic.

Yet the region is as puzzling as three-dimensional chess. It has done far better than conventional theories predict, even allowing for such quantifiable pluses as macroeconomic stability, high rates of investment and a focus on exports. There is just no generally accepted explanation for its main distinguishing feature—supercharged rates of productivity growth.

The puzzle is deepened by the region's lack of homogeneity. The high-fliers are far from being carbon copies. At one extreme, Hong Kong has pursued a broadly free market approach; at the other, South Korea has intervened in just about every way conceivable. And the magic formula for growth has entirely eluded some countries in the region, such as the Philippines.

At the World Bank in Washington, an exhaustive analysis of the "Asia miracle" is nearing completion. Bank staff are distilling lessons from Japan, the four "tigers"—South Korea, Taiwan, Hong Kong and Singapore—and the so-called "cubs"—Malaysia, Thailand and Indonesia. They have also taken a look at the recent explosive growth in parts of southern China.

The study was undertaken partly at the instigation of Japan, the bank's second-largest shareholder, which has long wanted to play a bigger role in policy design. Japan has been critical of aspects of conventional World Bank/International Monetary Fund prescriptions and, justifiably, believes more attention should be paid to its own outstandingly successful development strategies—which formed a model for much of east Asia.

In 1991, Japan's Overseas Economic Co-operation Fund told the bank it was putting too much emphasis on deregulation and privatisation and made a case for selective import protection in developing countries and for the use of subsidised credits as a tool in industrial policy.

Mr John Page, a senior member of the bank's Asia miracle team, says the Japanese criticism struck a chord because the results of market-oriented reforms had often proved disappointing in developing economies. By cutting budget deficits, eliminating market distortions and shrinking government, client countries had stabilised their economies. But too often they had not achieved a virtuous cycle of rapid growth; they still lay "at the bottom of the league table relative to east Asia". The question became: "What now?"

The bank's benchmark for judging Asian policies is not an extreme free market philosophy, which would have the public sector shun responsibility for just about everything bar national defence. It is rather the less controversial "market friendly" strategy set out at length in the bank's 1991 World Development Report.

This clearly delineates the role of markets and the state. Development would be fastest, it claimed, when government concentrated on two jobs: maintaining macroeconomic stability through conservative fiscal and monetary policies; and investing in people through public education, training and healthcare programmes.

Beyond this, developing countries should rely on market forces. They should create as competitive as possible a regime in industry, commerce and the financial sector. And they should eliminate all barriers to trade and foreign investment. The core idea is that governments should focus on the things only they can do and leave everything else to markets.

It turns out that most of the Asian high-fliers have adopted a more permissive attitude to the role of government. Indeed, Mr Page argues that the success of the region can best be understood in terms of a "strategic growth" model that focuses more on what has to be done to achieve rapid growth than on who should do what.

On the strategic theory, development will be rapid provided countries find a way of: accumulating capital rapidly; allocating resources efficiently; and catching up technologically.

But there is no presumption that any of these functions should be reserved exclusively for the private sector. The miracle economies appear to have used a mixture of market incentives and state intervention in each of these areas:

• Accumulation. Gross domestic investment averages a startling 37 per cent of GDP in east Asia against an average of 26 per cent in developing countries as a whole. Yet this advantage was not won purely by adhering to the market-friendly approach.

The region has admittedly created a positive climate for business investment by pursuing conservative fiscal and monetary policies—inflation has averaged 9 per cent over the past 30 years, less than half the rate in other developing countries. The public sector has also invested effectively in people (enrollment in primary education far exceeds levels elsewhere, as does attention to vocational education), although it has not spent an atypical proportion of national income on social services.

But most of the Asian high-fliers have also interfered with market mechanisms.

They have limited the personal sector's ability to consume and heavily regulated the financial sector so as to ensure a predictable supply of low-cost capital for industry. Mechanisms for forcibly shifting resources from consumption to investment vary—Japan, South Korea and Taiwan, for example have maintained stringent controls on consumption and housing. The net effect, however, is the same everywhere: an abnormally high rate of savings.

• Efficient allocation of resources. Governments have striven to ensure that the most important market of all—that for labour—is flexible, if not fully competitive. Wages have largely reflected market supply and demand, partly because trade unions have been suppressed. Focusing hard on success in export markets has also imposed crucial competitive discipline and prevented domestic prices for industrial inputs moving far out of line with world markets.

Yet bank research indicates governments have also intervened vigorously. While less protectionist than the third world as a whole, few accepted western free-trade principles. Many have used import controls to protect strategic sectors (for example, quotas in South Korea, high tariffs in Thailand) and showered offsetting subsidies on export industries. At one time or another state-owned industries have played an important role in many of the economies, including South Korea, Taiwan, Indonesia, Singapore and Thailand. Many have not hesitated to direct the supply of credit to particular sectors. Both South Korea and Taiwan provided automatic credit for exporters in the early stages of development.

• Technological catch-up. The lesson again is that remarkable productivity growth only partly reflects market-oriented policies. Singapore, Malaysia, Thailand and, to some degree, Taiwan, have welcomed foreign investment. Early developers such as Japan and South Korea used other devices, such as licences letting them copy foreign technology. But unlike many other developing countries none tried to rely on home-grown technology.

However, all high-fliers intervened selectively to promote particular industries, with varying intensity and success. The process of trying to shift industrial output towards high-valued-added sectors is described by enthusiasts as "getting prices wrong in order to create dynamic comparative advantage".

South Korea provides a wealth of examples of aggressive and successful intervention. The government's most audacious move was perhaps to create from scratch a domestic steel industry despite foreign donor opposition and lack of private-sector enthusiasm. The state-run business went on to become the world's most efficient steel producer.

An internal bank memo sums up South Korea's record: "From the early 1960s, the government carefully planned and orchestrated the country's development. . . . [It] used the financial sector to steer credits to preferred sectors and promoted individual firms to achieve national objectives. . . . [It] socialised risk, created large conglomerates (chaebols), created state enterprises when necessary, and moulded a public-private partnership that rivalled Japan's."

Singapore provides another classic example of directed growth. When private sector companies failed to respond to opportunities identified by bureaucrats, state-owned or controlled groups were often pushed to the fore, the memo says. The bank has documented selective interventions throughout the region, even in supposedly free market Hong Kong.

The Asian example poses a dilemma for bodies such as the IMF and the World Bank, especially in former communist countries. Does it still make sense to advocate a form of "shock therapy"—the doctrine that deregulating and privatising everything as fast as possible is the optimum policy? Or should they recommend east Asia's slower, more interventionist path to economic maturity? It all depends on whether east Asia's deviations from orthodoxy can be replicated.

There are some grounds for caution. Mr Vinod Thomas, the bank's chief economist for east Asia and an architect of the market-friendly strategy, points out that government activism outside east Asia has produced dismal results. A distinction should also be drawn between the earlier "northern tier" of Asian highfliers—Japan, South Korea and Taiwan—and the later "southern tier" of Malaysia, Thailand and Indonesia.

Until the 1980s, countries such as South Korea were able to promote exports and protect imports without provoking much criticism. But pressure for a more level playing field has since grown intense. Broadly speaking, the southern tier of later developers has pursued more market-oriented policies than the first wave of Asian stars. Indus-trial interventions have also tended to be less successful. A bank memo describes Malaysia's efforts as "by and large a costly failure" and Thailand's as "largely ineffective".

Less tangible political and cultural factors may also be crucial. Most Asian highfliers benefited from long periods of stable (if authoritarian) political rule. This encouraged long-term horizons. Public-sector bureaucracies have also tended to be more able and less corrupt than in most other third world countries. Governments were thus unusually well placed to implement development strategies.

Policymakers were also remarkably pragmatic; if a policy did not work it was rapidly dropped. South Korea, for example, went through several phases. It was relatively market-oriented in the early 1960s, became highly interventionist during the "heavy and chemical industries" drive of the 1970s, and then reverted to greater reliance on market forces in the mid-1980s. No region, it seems, has been less weighed down by ideology or more willing to seek advice from abroad.

The bank has only just begun the politically charged process of drawing conclusions from mountains of research papers. But senior officials believe the study may lead to a new paradigm for development in the 1990s. The evidence confirms that the miracle economies did indeed "do things differently". In many instances, "government played a big role, trade was not open and financial markets were repressed", concedes Mr Thomas.

"If we're right," says Mr Page, "the economic policy arsenal has many more weapons than we suspected." Mr Thomas agrees: the lesson from east Asia is that "you need a government guiding hand; you cannot just abdicate development to the private sector". He predicts that the bank will pay more attention to the role of institutions and to the potential for partnerships between the public and private sectors.

The most encouraging aspect of the Asian story, officials say, is that habits and institutions crucial for economic success were created rather than inherited. To raise the social standing of entrepreneurs, for example, South Korea had to overcome its Confucian traditions, which had glorified the scholar-bureaucrat. Singapore raised its savings rate from 1 per cent in 1965 to more than 40 per cent today. The implication is that sufficiently determined governments can work similar miracles in other places.

Confucius Says: Go East, Young Man

Many Asians now think their lives and values are superior to 'the American Way'

T. R. Reid

T. R. Reid, who just completed a five-year tour as The Washington Post's Tokyo bureau chief, is on leave from the paper while writing a book, "Confucius Lives Next Door."

The Asian leaders who gathered in Osaka for the annual Asian-Pacific Economic Cooperation (APEC) summit expressed pious regrets that Bill Clinton had to cancel his attendance at the last minute. At some level, though, they were probably delighted. The image of a U.S. president trapped in Washington by political chaos surrounding a red-ink budget can only strengthen the Asians' growing superiority complex toward the once-revered U.S.A.

Many Asian politicians, scholars and business leaders are proudly proclaiming these days that there is an ocean of difference in basic social values across the Pacific. They have decided that the Western, democratic, Judeo-Christian value structure, with its emphasis on the primacy of the individual—in short, "The American Way"—is fundamentally different from the Eastern, group-oriented, vaguely Confucian cultural pattern that is now proudly labeled "The Asian Way."

And it's not just that the values are different. Rather, these Asian Neo-Confucianists insist that their cultural values are better than ours.

"Many Western societies—including the United States—are doing some major things fundamentally wrong today, while a great number of East Asian societies are doing the same things right," argues Kishore Mahbubani, a Singaporean scholar and diplomat who has emerged as the Max Weber of this new "Confucian Ethic."

In an endless series of articles and lectures bearing titles like "The Dangers of Decadence" and "Go East, Young Man," the engaging and articulate Mahbubani tells his fellow Asians that "the American boat is sinking" and that a strong dose of Confucian values is needed to set things right. "If Americans were to try to begin learning from Asians, their nation would become a better place."

Even in Japan, most Westernized of the Asian nations, there is a movement to turn back East. "By following the insights of Confucianism," insists the Japanese academician Kichitaro Katsuta, "we can avoid the social catastrophe befalling the West, the result of centuries of individualism and egotism."

Americans, still patting themselves on the back for winning the Cold War, may not be ready just yet for another global ideological struggle over first principles. But an increasingly wealthy and confident East Asia is eager to engage us in a debate that raises direct challenges to cherished Western ideals.

Fueling the notion of "Asia Good, America Bad" is the palpable sense of social and economic well-being sweeping over East Asia. Overall, the Asian members of APEC have much higher economic growth rates than the Western democracies—coupled with much lower rates of unemployment, violent crime, drug use, broken homes, welfare dependency and other detritus of Euro-American society.

From Kuala Lumpur to Kawasaki, people cite the 1994 World Bank report that sought to predict which countries would be the richest on earth a quarter-century from now. In that ranking, four of the five wealthiest nations, and seven of the top 10, are Asian. The United States, the world's richest nation today, is projected in second place in the year 2020, between China and Japan.

Economic statistics can go up and down, of course—just ask Japan, yesterday's Asian Superman, now wallowing in extended recession. But Asia's current crop of Neo-Confucians look more at social indicators than economic statistics. "You Americans have this mantra about your high standard of living," Mahbubani told me once, soft-spoken and amiable even as he plunged the rhetorical dagger.

"And yes, if standard of living means the number of square feet in your home, or the number of channels on your TV,

America leads the world. But if standard of living means not being afraid to go outside that home after dark, or not worrying about what filth your children will see on all those TV channels, then our Asian societies have the higher standard."

That gets to the core of the Neo-Confucian case against Western democracy. The free nations of Europe and America are simply too free, the argument runs; they have gone too far to indulge individual freedom at the expense of society as a whole. When Asian leaders talk about American democracy, the names that come up are not Washington or Jefferson, but rather Tonya Harding, Howard Stern, the Menendez brothers and the Michigan Militia. "Democracies are only beginning to learn that too much freedom is dangerous," argues Mahathir Mohamad, prime minister of Malaysia, who is perhaps the most caustic critic of Western values among Asia's current political leadership.

"Whether the West admits it or not, David Koresh and the [Jim] Jones cult were the products of the Western form of democracy," Mahathir told an applauding audience in Tokyo this spring. "So also is the recent bombing in Oklahoma. The Michigan Militia corps has as yet done no real harm. But you can bet that sooner or later they will be using those guns which they democratically own."

There's an arrogant flavor to this kind of attack—not terribly surprising for people who have decided they are winners. "The growing realization among East Asians," Mahbubani says, "that they can do anything as well as, if not better than, other cultures has led to an explosion of confidence."

Most of today's Neo-Confucianists grew up in an Asia where Westerners were the colonial governors, the preachers, the teachers, the founders of great colleges and giant business enterprises. Now the Asian Way folks want to reverse the cultural flow.

Naturally, the Neo-Confucianists are encouraged to see Americans agreeing with them on some points.

When Mahathir complains that "Abolition of religious instruction in [public] schools . . . has resulted in a loss of direction," he is singing a chorus right out of Pat Robertson's hymn book. His criticism of the freedom to own guns resonates with a whole different group of Americans. Singapore strongman Lee Kuan Yew likes to point out that when his island state subjected teenager Michael Fay to a whipping for the crime of vandalizing cars, opinion polls showed that most Americans supported the sentence.

One of the nicer ironies of the Neo-Confucian boom is that this whole "pan-Asian" movement borrows its most basic concept from Western thought. The very existence of a "Far East," a place called "Asia," is a modern Western invention, dreamed up by European geographers and traders.

If the geography underpinning the Neo-Confucian boom is a tad ambiguous, the same can be said for the basic philosophy. As with the ancient prophets of other cultures, Confucius and his ideas are open to a wide range of interpretations.

The great sage K'ung Fu-tzu (that Latinate name "Confucius" is another Western concoction) was appalled by the vice and corruption all about him in Chou dynasty China of the 5th century B.C. He taught that the remedy for broad social ills lay in individual dedication to basic virtues.

The Confucian virtues, as they are generally described nowadays, include thrift, hard work, honoring the family unit and obeying the law. There is also a deep commitment to education, to pass along these virtues and other necessary skills.

None of this sounds particularly alien to anybody who grew up in a Judeo-Christian Western society. As Michael Armacost, the president of the Brookings Institution, used to say during his tenure as ambassador to Japan, "Americans can't criticize people for working hard, saving a lot, investing in the future, educating rigorously. Those are things we've always prided ourselves on."

At at least two points in the Confucian Cannon, the master declares that the most important single guide to life can be found in the term shu. Confucius defines it this way: "Do not impose on others what you do not want done to yourself." To any veteran of Sunday school, of course, this is simply The Golden Rule.

In their contempt for Western ways, however, the Neo-Confucianists insist that the teachings of their ancient Chinese ancestor involve a unique set of values. Even that Confucian statement of The Golden Rule is "different in a subtle way," argues Katsuta, the Japanese academician. The Confucian Golden Rule is stated in the negative, he notes. "Confucius thus advocated tolerance, " Katsuta maintains. "The Christian rule encourages well-intentioned activism. But sometimes well-meaning people are importunate and self-righteous. . . . Western individualism leads to a clash of egos that will destroy tolerance."

Katsuta has Westerners in mind when he denounces intolerance and self-righteousness. In fact, though, the world capital of self-righteousness at the moment may well be the tidy, industrious and thoroughly intolerant city-state of Singapore, a place tightly controlled by Lee Kuan Yew's personal clique of self-styled Neo-Confucians.

Lee charges that Americans "have abandoned an ethical basis for society"—and he's not about to let the same thing happen on his island. Thus police keep watch from the rooftops of Singapore to catch people committing such crimes as littering or chewing gum. Parents of school children deemed to be overweight receive letters ordering them to change the family menus. The government tells people how much of their money to save.

And almost nobody complains about this—at least, not publicly. Quick to attack the problems they see in the West, the thin-skinned Singapore Confucianists go ballistic the minute anyone criticizes them. No media outlet circulating in Singapore would dare reproduce this article, for example; the sentence a few paragraphs up describing Lee as the nation's "strongman" would likely draw libel fines in the tens of thousands of dollars.

If this is The Asian Way, most people would probably be happy to do without it. But many Neo-Confucianists say Lee's Singapore is a gross perversion of the sage's teaching. These critics say that autocrats like Lee and Malaysia's Mahathir have appropriated Confucius as a high-minded rationale for maintaining personal power.

Confucianism need not necessarily involve the spic-and-span authoritarianism of Singapore. South Korea, a bulwark of Confucian learning to this day, is a noisy, dirty, rambunctious nation where people not only chew gum on the streets but do many more offensive things there as well. But Koreans furiously deny that they are less Asian than Lee Kuan Yew.

"Lee's view of Asian culture is not only unsupportable but also self-serving," charges Kim Dae Jung, the veteran South Korean politician who risked his life repeatedly opposing military dictators in his own country. Kim insists that dissent and democracy are cherished Confucian ideals, and that the master's teaching was a key element in South Korea's dramatic switch to democracy in 1987. In short, proponents of The Asian Way are hazy about which direction their Way is headed. In Asia, though, the most important point is that it is not The American Way. The Neo-Confucianists are convinced that their cultural pattern is preferable, and they want the whole world to know it.

"For the past several hundred years, the world has been dominated by Greek and Judeo-Christian ideas," Kim Dae Jung wrote recently. "Now it is time for the world to turn to . . . Asia for another revolution in ideas."

Comparative Politics: Some Major Trends, Issues, and Prospects

- **The Democratic Trend: How Strong, Thorough, and Lasting? (Articles 61 and 62)**
- **The Turn toward the Market: What Role for the State? (Articles 63–66)**
- **Ethnic and Cultural Conflict: The Political Assertion of Group Identities (Articles 67–69)**

The articles in this unit deal with three major political trends and patterns of development that can be observed in much of the contemporary world. It is important at the outset to stress that, with the possible exception of Benjamin Barber, none of the authors predict some form of global convergence in which all political systems would become alike in major respects. On closer examination, even Professor Barber turns out to argue that a strong tendency toward global homogenization is offset by a concurrent tendency toward intensified group differentiation and fragmentation.

Thus the trends discussed here are neither unidirectional nor universal. They are situationally defined and therefore come in a great variety of combinations. They may well turn out to be temporary and partly reversible. Moreover, they do not always reinforce one another but instead show considerable mutual tension. Indeed, their different forms of development are the very stuff of comparative politics, which seeks an informed understanding of the political dimension of social life by making careful comparisons across time and space.

After such cautionary preliminaries, we can proceed to identify three recent developments that singly and together have had a major role in changing the political world in which we live. One is *the democratic revolution,* which has been sweeping much of the world. This refers to a widespread trend toward some form of popular government that often, but not always, takes the form of a search for representative, pluralist democracy in countries that were previously ruled by some form of authoritarian oligarchy or dictatorship.

Another trend, sometimes labeled *the capitalist revolution,* is the even more widespread shift toward some form of market economy. It includes a greater reliance on private enterprise and the profit motive and involves a concurrent move away from heavy regulation, central planning, and state ownership. But this need not mean laissez-faire capitalism. The social market economy, found in much of Western Europe, allows a considerable role for the state in providing services, redistributing income, and setting overall societal goals. In some of the Asian communist-ruled countries, above all China, we have become used to seeing self-proclaimed revolutionary socialists introduce a considerable degree of capitalist practices into their formerly planned economies. Some have suggested that it is now time to speak of "Market-Leninists."

The third major trend could be called the *revival of ethnic* or *cultural politics.* This refers to a growing emphasis on some form of an exclusive group identity as the primary basis for political expression. In modern times, it has been common for a group to identify itself by its special ethnic, religious, linguistic, or other cultural traits and to make this identity the primary basis for a claim to rule. The principle of national self-determination received the blessing of Woodrow Wilson, and it continues to have a democratic appeal, even though some critics warn against the potential dangers that often stem from a fractious politics of ethnocracy. They detect a collectivist or anti-

pluralist potential in this form of political expression and point out that it can contribute to intolerance and conflicts among groups as well as between the group and the individual.

The articles in the first section cover democratization as the first of these trends, that is, the startling growth in the number of representative governments in recent years. Even if this development is likely to be reversed in some countries, we need to remember how remarkable it has been in the first place. Using very different criteria and data, skeptics on both the Right and the Left have for a long time doubted whether representative government was sufficiently stable, efficient, accountable, attractive or, ultimately, legitimate to survive and flourish in the modern world. It would be instructive to review their more recent discussion of the 1970s and early 1980s, not in order to refute the pessimists but to learn from their insights as well as their oversights.

Samuel Huntington is one of the best-known observers of democratization; in the past he has emphasized the cultural, social, economic, and political obstacles to representative government in most of the world. In the aftermath of the collapse of communist regimes in Eastern and Central Europe, he has further identified a broad pattern of democratization that began in the mid-1970s, when three dictatorships in Southern Europe came to an end (in Greece, Portugal, and Spain). In the following decade, democratization spread to most of Latin America. Central and Eastern Europe followed, and the trend also reached some states in Eastern and Southern Asia as well as some parts of Africa, above all, South Africa.

In a widely adopted phrase, Huntington identifies this trend as the "third wave" of democratization in modern history. The first wave was both slow and long in its reach. It began in the 1820s and lasted about one century, until 1926, a period during which first the United States and subsequently 28 other countries established governments based on a wide and eventually universal suffrage. In 1922, however, Benito Mussolini's capture of power in Italy began a period of reversal that lasted until the early 1940s. During these two decades, the number of democracies fell from 29 to 12 as many became victims of dictatorial takeovers or military conquests.

A second wave of democratization started with the Allied victory in World War II and continued during the early postwar years of decolonization. This wave lasted until about 1962 and resulted in the conversion of about two dozen authoritarian systems into various forms of democracies, sometimes of very short duration. There followed a second reverse wave, lasting from 1962 to 1973. During this period, the number of democracies fell from 36 to 30 and the number of nondemocracies increased from 75 to 95 as various postcolonial infant democracies fell under revived authoritarian or dictatorial rule. In the mid-1970s, then, the "third wave" of democratization got its start.

At the beginning of the 1990s, Huntington counted about 60 democracies in the world, which roughly amounts to a doubling of their number in less than two decades. It is an impressive change, but he points out that the process is likely to be reversed once again in a number of the new democracies. His discussion supports the conclusion that democracy's advance has always been a "two steps forward, one step back" kind of process. The expectations associated with the coming of democracy are so high in some countries so high that disappointments are bound to follow. Already, the third wave of democratic advances in such countries as the Sudan, Nigeria, Algeria, and Peru have been followed by authoritarian reversals. Haiti has gone through its own double wave. The prospects for democracy on that poverty-stricken Caribbean island do not seem bright, but there has been some positive news to report. In 1994 Jean-Bertrand Aristide could return to the presidential office for which he had been elected in 1991 and overthrown by a military coup in the same year. He stepped down at the end of his regular term in 1996, and Haiti has just experienced its first democratic succession in office. There are ominous signs of authoritarian revivals elsewhere in the world, including some parts of the former Soviet Union.

What are the general conditions that inhibit or encourage the spread and stabilization of democracy? Huntington and other scholars have identified some specific historical factors that appear to have contributed to the third wave. One important factor is the loss of legitimacy by both right- and left-wing authoritarian regimes as they become discredited by failures. Another factor is the expansion in some developing countries of an urban middle class that has a strong interest in representative government and constitutional rule. In Latin America, especially, the influence of a more liberal Catholic Church has been important. There have also been various forms of external influence by the United States and the European Union as they strive to promote a human rights agenda. A different but crucial instance of external influence took the form of Mikhail Gorbachev's shift toward nonintervention by the Soviet Union in the late 1980s, when he abandoned the Brezhnev Doctrine's commitment to defend established communist rulers in Eastern Europe and elsewhere against counterrevolution. Finally, there is the snowballing effect in such countries as Spain and Poland of a successful early transition to democracy, which has served as models for other countries in similar circumstances. This has also been very important in Latin America.

Huntington's rule of thumb is that a democratic form of government can be considered to have become stable when a country has had at least two successive peaceful turnovers of power. Such a development may take a generation or longer to complete, even under fortunate circumstances. Many of the new democracies have little historical experience with a democratic way of life. Where there has been such an experience, it may have been spotty and not very positive. There also may be important cultural and socioeconomic obstacles to democratization. Huntington, like most other observers, sees extreme poverty as a principal obstacle to successful democratization.

Both old and new democracies face dangers, as Philipe Schmitter points out in his article. He gives a very systematic analysis of the many internal standards against which democracies are measured by their citizenries. Popular dissatisfaction normally focuses on the government in the established political systems, but where representative government itself is a new development, there is a danger that democracy itself may become the target of criticism.

Germany provides a valuable case study for testing some of these interpretations of democracy. After World War I, antidemocratic critics identified its Weimar Republic with international disaster, socioeconomic ruin, and political weakness and instability. After World War II, by contrast, the Federal Republic became increasingly credited with stability and prosperity. At first accepted passively, the fledgling West German state soon generated an increasing measure of pragmatic support from its citizenry, based on its widely perceived effectiveness. In time, the new republic also appeared to gain a deeper, more affective support from much of the population. A major question is how national reunification, with its accompanying wrenching changes and inevitable disappointments, will influence German attitudes toward representative government. In the new Eastern European states, in particular, reunification was linked to unrealistic expectations of almost immediate socioeconomic alignment with the prosperous West. How will east Germans react if the new polity fails to deliver promptly and bountifully? Comparatively speaking, Germany is fortunate in having a stable set of institutions, a well-developed democratic culture in the well-established Western states of the Federal Republic, and a solid economic structure. Unfortunately, many of the new democracies face dislocations that make them more comparable to the conditions of the Weimar Republic rather than the successful West German state after World War II.

The second section of this unit covers the trend toward capitalism, specifically, market economics. Here Gabriel Almond explores the connections between capitalism and democracy in an article that draws upon both theory and empirical studies. His systematic discussion shows that there are ways in which capitalism and democracy support each other and ways in which they tend to undermine each other. Is it possible to have the best of both? Almond answers at length that there is a nonutopian manner in which capitalism and democracy can be reconciled, namely in democratic welfare capitalism.

Almond's discussion can be linked to a theme emphasized by some contemporary political economists. They point out that, in its communist form of state ownership and centralized planning, the economic competition between capitalism and socialism has become a largely closed chapter in world history. The central question now is, Which form of capitalism/market economy will be more successful? A similar argument has been made by the French theorist Michel Albert, who also distinguishes between the British-American and the continental "Rhineland" models of capitalism. The former is more individualistic and antigovernmental and is characterized by such traits as high employee turnover and short-term profit-maximizing. It differs considerably from what the Germans themselves like to call their "social market economy." The latter is more team-oriented, emphasizes cooperation between management and organized labor, and leaves a considerable role for government in promoting general economic strategy, the training of an educated labor force, and the provision of social welfare services. William Pfaff's article in unit one addresses various pitfalls in the evolution of social capitalism and the conflicting "politico-economic" ideologies that societies have historically adopted in pursuit of the good life.

Both Great Britain and the United States experienced a head start in their industrial revolutions and felt no need for deliberate government efforts to encourage growth. By contrast, Germany and Japan both played the role of latecomers, who looked to government intervention and protection in their attempts to catch up. To be sure, governments were also swayed by military considerations to promote German and Japanese industrialization. But the emergence of social capitalism in other continental countries of Europe suggests that cultural rather than military factors played a major role in this development.

A crucial question is whether or not the relative prosperity and social security associated with this kind of mixed economy can be maintained in a time of technological breakthroughs and global trade competition. Ralf Dahrendorf addresses these questions in his article and provides a combination of thoughtful analysis and assessment.

The third section deals with the revival of the ethnic and cultural dimension in politics. Until recently, relatively few analysts foresaw that this element would play such a divisive role in the contemporary world. There were forewarnings, such as the ethnonationalist stirrings in the late 1960s and early 1970s in peripheral areas of such countries as Britain, Canada, and Spain. It also fueled many of the conflicts in the newly independent countries of the developing world. But most Western observers seem to have been poorly prepared for the task of anticipating and understanding the resurgence of politicized religious, ethnic, and other cultural forces. Many non-Westerners were taken by surprise as well. Mikhail Gorbachev, for example, grossly underestimated the centrifugal force of the nationality question in his own country.

The politicization of religion in many parts of the world falls into this development of a "politics of identity." In recent years, religious groups in parts of Latin America, Asia, the Middle East, sub-Saharan Africa, Asia, and Southern Europe have variously set out on the political road in the name of their faith. As Max Weber warned in a classic lecture shortly before his death, it can be dangerous to seek "the salvation of souls" along the path of politics. The coexistence of people of divergent faiths is possible only because religious conviction need not fully determine or direct a person's or a group's politics. Where absolutist and fervent convictions take over, they make it difficult to compromise pragmatically and live harmoniously with people who believe differently. Pluralist democracy requires an element of tolerance, which for many takes the form of a casual "live and let live" attitude rather than a well-intentioned but always ultimately futile determination to make others conform to one's central beliefs.

There is an important debate among political scientists concerning the sources and scope of politics based on ethnic, religious, and cultural differences. Samuel Huntington argues forcefully that our most important and dangerous future conflicts will be based on clashes of civilizations. In his view, they will be far more difficult to resolve than those rooted in socioeconomic or even ideological differences. His critics, including the German Josef Joffe, argue that Huntington distorts the differences *among* civilizations and trivializes the differences *within* civilizations as sources of political conflict. Chandra Muzaffar, a Malaysian commentator, goes much further by contending that Huntington's "clash of civilizations" thesis provides a rationalization for a Western policy goal of continued covert domination of the developing world.

In the final article, Benjamin Barber brings a broad perspective to the discussion of identity politics in the contemporary world. He sees two major tendencies that threaten democracy. One is the force of globalism, brought about by modern technology, communications, and commerce. Its logical end point is what he calls a "McWorld," in which human diversity, individuality, and meaningful identity are erased. The second tendency works in the opposite direction. It is the force of tribalism, which drives human beings to exacerbate their group differences, become intolerant of "others," and thereby engage in purify holy wars against each other. Barber argues that globalism is at best indifferent to democracy and that militant tribalism is deeply antithetical to it. He argues in favor of seeking a confederal solution, based on democratic civil societies, which could provide human beings with a nonmilitant, parochial communitarianism as well as a framework that more appropriately suits the global market economy.

Looking Ahead: Challenge Questions

What is meant by the first, second, and third waves of democratization? Describe the reversals that followed the first two.

Where are most of the countries affected by the third wave located? What factors appear to have contributed to their democratization?

What are some main problems and dilemmas of both old and new democracies?

In what ways can market capitalism and liberal democracy be said to be mutually supportive? How can they undermine each other?

Why is it so difficult to resolve political conflicts that arise from the political assertion of an exclusive religious or ethnic identity?

What factors demonstrate that democracy is threatened by globalism and tribalism?

A NEW ERA IN DEMOCRACY
DEMOCRACY'S THIRD WAVE

SAMUEL P. HUNTINGTON

Mr. Huntington is professor of government at Harvard University.

Between 1974 and 1990, at least 30 countries made transitions to democracy, just about doubling the number of democratic governments in the world. Were these democratizations part of a continuing and ever-expanding "global democratic revolution" that will reach virtually every country in the world? Or did they represent a limited expansion of democracy, involving for the most part its reintroduction into countries that had experienced it in the past?

The current era of democratic transitions constitutes the third wave of democratization in the history of the modern world. The first "long" wave of democratization began in the 1820s, with the widening of the suffrage to a large proportion of the male population in the United States, and continued for almost a century until 1926, bringing into being some 29 democracies. In 1922, however, the coming to power of Mussolini in Italy marked the beginning of a first "reverse wave" that by 1942 had reduced the number of democratic states in the world to 12. The triumph of the Allies in World War II initiated a second wave of democratization that reached its zenith in 1962 with 36 countries governed democratically, only to be followed by a second reverse wave (1960–1975) that brought the number of democracies back down to 30.

At what stage are we within the third wave? Early in a long wave, or at or near the end of a short one? And if the third wave comes to a halt, will it be followed by a significant third reverse wave eliminating many of democracy's gains in the 1970s and 1980s? Social science cannot provide reliable answers to these questions, nor can any social scientist. It may be possible, however, to identify some of the factors that will affect the future expansion or contraction of democracy in the world and to pose the questions that seem most relevant for the future of democratization.

One way to begin is to inquire whether the causes that gave rise to the third wave are likely to continue operating, to gain in strength, to weaken, or to be supplemented or replaced by new forces promoting democratization. Five major factors have contributed significantly to the occurrence and the timing of the third-wave transitions to democracy:

1. The deepening legitimacy problems of authoritarian regimes in a world where democratic values were widely accepted, the consequent dependence of these regimes on successful performance, and their inability to maintain "performance legitimacy" due to economic (and sometimes military) failure.

2. The unprecedented global economic growth of the 1960s, which raised living standards, increased education, and greatly expanded the urban middle class in many countries.

3. A striking shift in the doctrine and activities of the Catholic Church, manifested in the Second Vatican Council of 1963–65 and the transformation of national Catholic churches from defenders of the status quo to opponents of authoritarianism.

4. Changes in the policies of external actors, most notably the European Community, the United States, and the Soviet Union.

5. "Snowballing," or the demonstration effect of transitions earlier in the third wave in stimulating and providing models for subsequent efforts at democratization.

I will begin by addressing the latter three factors, returning to the first two later in this article.

Historically, there has been a strong correlation between Western Christianity and democracy. By the early 1970s, most of the Protestant countries in the world had already become democratic. The third wave of the 1970s and 1980s was overwhelmingly a Catholic wave. Beginning in Portugal and Spain, it swept through six South American and three

From *Current*, September 1991, pp. 27-39. Originally "Democracy's Third Wave" from *Journal of Democracy*, Spring 1991, pp. 12-34. © 1991 by the National Endowment for Democracy and the Johns Hopkins University Press. Reprinted by permission.

Central American countries, moved on to the Philippines, doubled back to Mexico and Chile, and then burst through in the two Catholic countries of Eastern Europe, Poland and Hungary. Roughly three-quarters of the countries that transited to democracy between 1974 and 1989 were predominantly Catholic.

By 1990, however, the Catholic impetus to democratization had largely exhausted itself. Most Catholic countries had already democratized or, as in the case of Mexico, liberalized. The ability of Catholicism to promote further expansion of democracy (without expanding its own ranks) is limited to Paraguay, Cuba, and a few Francophone African countries. By 1990, sub-Saharan Africa was the only region of the world where substantial numbers of Catholics and Protestants lived under authoritarian regimes in a large number of countries.

THE ROLE OF EXTERNAL FORCES

During the third wave, the European Community (EC) played a key role in consolidating democracy in southern Europe. In Greece, Spain, and Portugal, the establishment of democracy was seen as necessary to secure the economic benefits of EC membership, while Community membership was in turn seen as a guarantee of the stability of democracy. In 1981, Greece became a full member of the Community, and five years later Spain and Portugal did as well.

In April 1987, Turkey applied for full EC membership. One incentive was the desire of Turkish leaders to reinforce modernizing and democratic tendencies in Turkey and to contain and isolate the forces in Turkey supporting Islamic fundamentalism. Within the Community, however, the prospect of Turkish membership met with little enthusiasm and even some hostility (mostly from Greece). In 1990, the liberation of Eastern Europe also raised the possibility of membership for Hungary, Czechoslovakia, and Poland. The Community thus faced two issues. First, should it give priority to broadening its membership or to "deepening" the existing Community by moving toward further economic and political union? Second, if it did decide to expand its membership, should priority go to European Free Trade Association members like Austria, Norway, and Sweden, to the East Europeans, or to Turkey? Presumably the Community can only absorb a limited number of countries in a given period of time. The answers to these questions will have significant implications for the stability of democracy in Turkey and in the East European countries.

The withdrawal of Soviet power made possible democratization in Eastern Europe. If the Soviet Union were to end or drastically curtail its support for Castro's regime, movement to-ward democracy might occur in Cuba. Apart from that, there seems little more the Soviet Union can do or is likely to do to promote democracy outside its borders. The key issue is what will happen within the Soviet Union itself. If Soviet control loosens, it seems likely that democracy could be reestablished in the Baltic states. Movements toward democracy also exist in other republics. Most important, of course, is Russia itself. The inauguration and consolidation of democracy in the Russian republic, if it occurs, would be the single most dramatic gain for democracy since the immediate post-World War II years. Democratic development in most of the Soviet republics, however, is greatly complicated by their ethnic heterogeneity and the unwillingness of the dominant nationality to allow equal rights to ethnic minorities. As Sir Ivor Jennings remarked years ago, "the people cannot decide until somebody decides who are the people." It may take years if not decades to resolve the latter issue in much of the Soviet Union.

During the 1970s and 1980s the United States was a major promoter of democratization. Whether the United States continues to play this role depends on its will, its capability, and its attractiveness as a model to other countries. Before the mid-1970s the promotion of democracy had not always been a high priority of American foreign policy. It could again subside in importance. The end of the Cold War and of the ideological competition with the Soviet Union could remove one rationale for propping up anti-communist dictators, but it could also reduce the incentives for any substantial American involvement in the Third World.

American will to promote democracy may or may not be sustained. American ability to do so, on the other hand, is limited. The trade and budget deficits impose new limits on the resources that the United States can use to influence events in foreign countries. More important, the ability of the United States to promote democracy has in some measure run its course. The countries in Latin America, the Caribbean, Europe, and East Asia that were most susceptible to American influence have, with a few exceptions, already become democratic. The one major country where the United States can still exercise significant influence on behalf of democratization is Mexico. The undemocratic countries in Africa, the Middle East, and mainland Asia are less susceptible to American influence.

Apart from Central America and the Caribbean, the major area of the Third World where the United States has continued to have vitally important interests is the Persian Gulf. The Gulf War and the dispatch of 500,000 American troops to the region have stimulated demands for movement toward democracy in

PROMOTION OF DEMOCRACY

Kuwait and Saudi Arabia and delegitimized Saddam Hussein's regime in Iraq. A large American military deployment in the Gulf, if sustained over time, would provide an external impetus toward liberalization if not democratization, and a large American military deployment probably could not be sustained over time unless some movement toward democracy occurred.

The U.S. contribution to democratization in the 1980s involved more than the conscious and direct exercise of American power and influence. Democratic movements around the world have been inspired by and have borrowed from the American example. What might happen, however, if the American model ceases to embody strength and success, no longer seems to be the winning model? At the end of the 1980s, many were arguing that "American decline" was the true reality. If people around the world come to see the United States as a fading power beset by political stagnation, economic inefficiency, and social chaos, its perceived failures will inevitably be seen as the failures of democracy, and the worldwide appeal of democracy will diminish.

SNOWBALLING

The impact of snowballing on democratization was clearly evident in 1990 in Bulgaria, Romania, Yugoslavia, Mongolia, Nepal, and Albania. It also affected movements toward liberalization in some Arab and African countries. In 1990, for instance, it was reported that the "upheaval in Eastern Europe" had "fueled demands for change in the Arab world" and prompted leaders in Egypt, Jordan, Tunisia, and Algeria to open up more political space for the expression of discontent.

The East European example had its principal effect on the leaders of authoritarian regimes, not on the people they ruled. President Mobutu Sese Seko of Zaire, for instance reacted with shocked horror to televised pictures of the execution by firing squad of his friend Romanian dictator Nicolae Ceaușescu. A few months later, commenting that "You know what's happening across the world," he announced that he would allow two parties besides his own to compete in elections in 1993. In Tanzania, Julius Nyerere observed that "If changes take place in Eastern Europe then other countries with one-party systems and which profess socialism will also be affected." His country, he added, could learn a "lesson or two" from Eastern Europe. In Nepal in April 1990, the government announced that King Birendra was lifting the ban on political parties as a result of "the international situation" and "the rising expectations of the people."

If a country lacks favorable internal conditions, however, snowballing alone is unlikely to bring about democratization. The democratization of countries A and B is not a reason for democratization in country C, unless the conditions that favored it in the former also exist in the latter. Although the legitimacy of democratic government came to be accepted throughout the world in the 1980s, economic and social conditions favorable to democracy were not everywhere present. The "worldwide democratic revolution" may create an external environment conducive to democratization, but it cannot produce the conditions necessary for democratization within a particular country.

WORLDWIDE DEMOCRATIC REVOLUTION

In Eastern Europe the major obstacle to democratization was Soviet control; once it was removed, the movement to democracy spread rapidly. There is no comparable external obstacle to democratization in the Middle East, Africa, and Asia. If rulers in these areas chose authoritarianism before December 1989, why can they not continue to choose it thereafter? The snowballing effect would be real only to the extent that it led them to believe in the desirability or necessity of democratization. The events of 1989 in Eastern Europe undoubtedly encouraged democratic opposition groups and frightened authoritarian leaders elsewhere. Yet given the previous weakness of the former and the long-term repression imposed by the latter, it seems doubtful that the East European example will actually produce significant progress toward democracy in most other authoritarian countries.

By 1990, many of the original causes of the third wave had become significantly weaker, even exhausted. Neither the White House, the Kremlin, the European Community, nor the Vatican was in a strong position to promote democracy in places where it did not already exist (primarily in Asia, Africa, and the Middle East). It remains possible, however, for new forces favoring democratization to emerge. After all, who in 1985 could have foreseen that Mikhail Gorbachev would facilitate democratization in Eastern Europe?

In the 1990s the International Monetary Fund (IMF) and the World Bank could conceivably become much more forceful than they have heretofore been in making political democratization as well as economic liberalization a precondition for economic assistance. France might become more active in promoting democracy among its former African colonies, where its influence remains substantial. The Orthodox churches could emerge as a powerful influence for democracy in southeastern Europe and the Soviet Union. A Chinese proponent of *glasnost* could come to power in Beijing, or a new Jeffersonian-style Nasser could spread a democratic version of Pan-Arabism in the Middle East. Japan could use its growing economic clout to encourage human rights and democracy in the poor countries to which it makes loans and grants. In 1990, none of these possibilities seemed very likely, but after the surprises of 1989 it would be rash to rule anything out.

A THIRD REVERSE WAVE?

By 1990 at least two third-wave democracies, Sudan and Nigeria, had reverted to authoritarian rule; the difficulties of consolidation could lead to further reversions in countries with unfavorable conditions for sustaining democracy. The first and second democratic waves, however, were followed not merely by some backsliding but by major reverse waves during which most regime changes throughout the world were from democracy to authoritarianism. If the third wave of democratization slows down or comes to a halt, what factors might produce a third reverse wave?

Among the factors contributing to transitions away from democracy during the first and second reverse waves were:

1. the weakness of democratic values among key elite groups and the general public;

2. severe economic setbacks, which intensified social conflict and enhanced the popularity of remedies that could be imposed only by authoritarian governments;

3. social and political polarization, often produced by leftist governments seeking the rapid introduction of major social and economic reforms;

4. the determination of conservative middle-class and upper-class groups to exclude populist and leftist movements and lower-class groups from political power;

5. the breakdown of law and order resulting from terrorism or insurgency;

6. intervention or conquest by a nondemocratic foreign power;

7. "reverse snowballing" triggered by the collapse or overthrow of democratic systems in other countries.

Transitions from democracy to authoritarianism, apart from those produced by foreign actors, have almost always been produced by those in power or close to power in the democratic system. With only one or two possible exceptions, democratic systems have not been ended by popular vote or popular revolt. In Germany and Italy in the first reverse wave, antidemocratic movements with considerable popular backing came to power and established fascist dictatorships. In Spain in the first reverse wave and in Lebanon in the second, democracy ended in civil war.

The overwhelming majority of transitions from democracy, however, took the form either of military coups that ousted democratically elected leaders, or executive coups in which democratically chosen chief executives effectively ended democracy by concentrating power

in their own hands, usually by declaring a state of emergency or martial law. In the first reverse wave, military coups ended democratic systems in the new countries of Eastern Europe and in Greece, Portugal, Argentina, and Japan. In the second reverse wave, military coups occurred in Indonesia, Pakistan, Greece, Nigeria, Turkey, and many Latin American countries. Executive coups occurred in the second reverse wave in Korea, India, and the Philippines. In Uruguay, the civilian and military leadership cooperated to end democracy through a mixed executive-military coup.

In both the first and second reverse waves, democratic systems were replaced in many cases by historically new forms of authoritarian rule. Fascism was distinguished from earlier forms of authoritarianism by its mass base, ideology, party organization, and efforts to penetrate and control most of society. Bureaucratic authoritarianism differed from earlier forms of military rule in Latin America with respect to its institutional character, its presumption of indefinite duration, and its economic policies. Italy and Germany in the 1920s and 1930s and Brazil and Argentina in the 1960s and 1970s were the lead countries in introducing these new forms of nondemocratic rule and furnished the examples that antidemocratic groups in other countries sought to emulate. Both these new forms of authoritarianism were, in effect, responses to social and economic development: the expansion of social mobilization and political participation in Europe, and the exhaustion of the import-substitution phase of economic development in Latin America.

POTENTIAL CAUSES

Although the causes and forms of the first two reverse waves cannot generate reliable predictions concerning the causes and forms of a possible third reverse wave, prior experiences do suggest some potential causes of a new reverse wave.

First, systemic failures of democratic regimes to operate effectively could undermine their legitimacy. In the late twentieth century, the major nondemocratic ideological sources of legitimacy, most notably Marxism-Leninism, were discredited. The general acceptance of democratic norms meant that democratic governments were even less dependent on performance legitimacy than they had been in the past. Yet sustained inability to provide welfare, prosperity, equity, justice, domestic order, or external security could over time undermine the legitimacy even of democratic governments. As the memories of authoritarian failures fade, irritation with democratic failures is likely to increase. More specifically, a general international economic collapse on the 1929–30 model could undermine the legitimacy of democracy in many countries. Most democracies did survive the Great Depression of the 1930s; yet some succumbed, and presumably some would be likely to succumb in response to a comparable economic disaster in the future.

SHIFT TO AUTHORITAR-IANISM

Second, a shift to authoritarianism by any democratic or democratizing great power could trigger reverse snowballing. The reinvigoration of authoritarianism in Russia or the Soviet Union would have unsettling effects on democratization in other Soviet republics, Bulgaria, Romania, Yugoslavia, and Mongolia and possibly in Poland, Hungary, and Czechoslovakia as well. It could send the message to would-be despots elsewhere: "You too can go back into business." Similarly, the establishment of an authoritarian regime in India could have a significant demonstration effect on other Third World countries. Moreover, even if a major country does not revert to authoritarianism, a shift to dictatorship by several smaller newly democratic countries that lack many of the usual preconditions for democracy could have ramifying effects even on other countries where those preconditions are strong.

If a nondemocratic state greatly increased its power and began to expand beyond its borders, this too could stimulate authoritarian movements in other countries. This stimulus would be particularly strong if the expanding authoritarian state militarily defeated one or more democratic countries. In the past, all major powers that have developed economically have also tended to expand territorially. If China develops economically under authoritarian rule in the coming decades and expands its influence and control in East Asia, democratic regimes in the region will be significantly weakened.

Finally, as in the 1920s and the 1960s, various old and new forms of authoritarianism that seem appropriate to the needs of the times could emerge. Authoritarian nationalism could take hold in some Third World countries and also in Eastern Europe. Religious fundamentalism, which has been most dramatically prevalent in Iran, could come to power in other countries, especially in the Islamic world. Oligarchic authoritarianism could develop in both wealthy and poorer countries as a reaction to the leveling tendencies of democracy. Populist dictatorships could emerge in the future, as they have in the past, in response to democracy's protection of various forms of economic privilege, particularly in those countries where land tenancy is still an issue. Finally, communal dictatorships could be imposed in democracies with two or more distinct ethnic, racial, or religious groups, with one group trying to establish control over the entire society.

All of these forms of authoritarianism have existed in the past. It is not beyond the wit of humans to devise new ones in the future. One possibility might be a technocratic "electronic dictatorship," in which authoritarian rule is made possible and legitimated by the regime's ability to manipulate information, the media, and sophisticated means of communication. None of these old or new forms of authoritarianism is highly probable, but it is also hard to say that any one of them is totally impossible.

OBSTACLES TO DEMOCRATIZATION

Another approach to assessing democracy's prospects is to examine the obstacles to and opportunities for democratization where it has not yet taken hold. As of 1990, more than one hundred countries lacked democratic regimes. Most of these countries fell into four sometimes overlapping geocultural categories:

1. Home-grown Marxist-Leninist regimes, including the Soviet Union, where major liberalization occurred in the 1980s and democratic movements existed in many republics;

2. Sub-Saharan African countries, which, with a few exceptions, remained personal dictatorships, military regimes, one-party systems, or some combination of these three;

3. Islamic countries stretching from Morocco to Indonesia, which except for Turkey and perhaps Pakistan had nondemocratic regimes;

4. East Asian countries, from Burma through Southeast Asia to China and North Korea, which included communist systems, military regimes, personal dictatorships, and two semi-democracies (Thailand and Malaysia).

The obstacles to democratization in these groups of countries are political, cultural, and economic. One potentially significant political obstacle to future democratization is the virtual absence of experience with democracy in most countries that remained authoritarian in 1990. Twenty-three of 30 countries that democratized between 1974 and 1990 had had some history of democracy, while only a few countries that were nondemocratic in 1990 could claim such experience. These included a few third-wave backsliders (Sudan, Nigeria, Suriname, and possibly Pakistan), four second-wave backsliders that had not redemocratized in the third wave (Lebanon, Sri Lanka, Burma, Fiji), and three first-wave democratizers that had been prevented by Soviet occupation from redemocratizing at the end of World War II (Estonia, Latvia, and Lithuania). Virtually all the 90 or more other nondemocratic countries in 1990 lacked significant past experience with democratic rule. This obviously is not a decisive impediment to democratization—if it were, no countries would now be democratic—but it does make it more difficult.

Another obstacle to democratization is likely to disappear in a number of countries in the 1990s. Leaders who found authoritarian regimes or rule them for a long period tend to be-

LEADERSHIP CHANGE

come particularly staunch opponents of democratization. Hence some form of leadership change within the authoritarian system usually precedes movement toward democracy. Human mortality is likely to ensure such changes in the 1990s in some authoritarian regimes. In 1990, the long-term rulers in China, Côte d'Ivoire, and Malawi were in their eighties; those in Burma, Indonesia, North Korea, Lesotho, and Vietnam were in their seventies; and the leaders of Cuba, Morocco, Singapore, Somalia, Syria, Tanzania, Zaire, and Zambia were sixty or older. The death or departure from office of these leaders would remove one obstacle to democratization in their countries, but would not make it inevitable.

Between 1974 and 1990, democratization occurred in personal dictatorships, military regimes, and one-party systems. Full-scale democratization has not yet occurred, however, in communist one-party states that were the products of domestic revolution. Liberalization has taken place in the Soviet Union, which may or may not lead to full-scale democratization in Russia. In Yugoslavia, movements toward democracy are underway in Slovenia and Croatia. The Yugoslav communist revolution, however, was largely a Serbian revolution, and the prospects for democracy in Serbia appear dubious. In Cambodia, an extraordinarily brutal revolutionary communist regime was replaced by a less brutal communist regime imposed by outside force. In 1990, Albania appeared to be opening up, but in China, Vietnam, Laos, Cuba and Ethiopia, Marxist-Leninist regimes produced by home-grown revolutions seemed determined to remain in power. The revolutions in these countries had been nationalist as well as communist, and hence nationalism reinforced communism in a way that obviously was not true of Soviet-occupied Eastern Europe.

One serious impediment of democratization is the absence or weakness of real commitment to democratic values among political leaders in Asia, Africa, and the Middle East. When they are out of power, political leaders have good reason to advocate democracy. The test of their democratic commitment comes once they are in office. In Latin America, democratic regimes have generally been overthrown by military coups d'état. This has happened in Asia and the Middle East as well, but in these regions elected leaders themselves have also been responsible for ending democracy: Syngman Rhee and Park Chung Hee in Korea, Adnan Menderes in Turkey, Ferdinand Marcos in the Philippines, Lee Kwan Yew in Singapore, Indira Gandhi in India, and Sukarno in Indonesia. Having won power through the electoral system, these leaders then proceeded to undermine that system. They had little commitment to democratic values and practices.

Even when Asian, African, and Middle Eastern leaders have more or less abided by the rules of democracy, they often seemed to do so grudgingly. Many European, North American, and Latin American political leaders in the last half of the twentieth century were ardent and articulate advocates of democracy. Asian and African countries, in contrast, did not produce many heads of government who were also apostles of democracy. Who were the Asian, Arab, or African equivalents of Rómulo Betancourt, Alberto Llera Camargo, José Figueres, Eduardo Frei, Fernando Belaúnde Terry, Juan Bosch, José Napoleón Duarte, and Raúl Alfonsin? Jawaharlal Nehru and Corazon Aquino were, and there may have been others, but they were few in number. No Arab leader comes to mind, and it is hard to identify any Islamic leader who made a reputation as an advocate and supporter of democracy while in office. Why is this? This question inevitably leads to the issue of culture.

CULTURE

It has been argued that the world's great historic cultural traditions vary significantly in the extent to which their attitudes, values, beliefs, and related behavior patterns are conducive to the development of democracy. A profoundly antidemocratic culture would impede the spread of democratic norms in the society, deny legitimacy to democratic institutions, and thus greatly complicate if not prevent the emergence and effective functioning of those institutions. The cultural thesis comes in two forms. The more restrictive version states that only Western culture provides a suitable base for the development of democratic institutions and, consequently, that democracy is largely inappropriate for non-Western societies. In the early years of the third wave, this argument was explicitly set forth by George Kennan. Democracy, he said, was a form of government "which evolved in the eighteenth and nineteenth centuries in northwestern Europe, primarily among those countries that border on the English Channel and the North Sea (but with a certain extension into Central Europe), and which was then carried into other parts of the world, including North America, where peoples from that northwestern European area appeared as original settlers, or as colonialists, and laid down the prevailing patterns of civil government." Hence democracy has "a relatively narrow base both in time and in space; and the evidence has yet to be produced that it is the natural form of rule for peoples outside those narrow perimeters." The achievements of Mao, Salazar, and Castro demonstrated, according to Kennan, that authoritarian regimes "have been able to introduce reforms and to improve the lot of masses of people, where more diffuse forms of political authority had failed."

Democracy, in short, is appropriate only for northwestern and perhaps central European countries and their settler-colony offshoots.

The Western-culture thesis has immediate implications for democratization in the Balkans and the Soviet Union. Historically these areas were part of the Czarist and Ottoman empires; their prevailing religions were Orthodoxy and Islam, not Western Christianity. These areas did not have the same experiences as Western Europe with feudalism, the Renaissance, the Reformation, the Enlightenment, the French Revolution, and liberalism. As William Wallace has suggested, the end of the Cold War and the disappearance of the Iron Curtain may have shifted the critical political dividing line eastward to the centuries-old boundary between Eastern and Western Christendom. Beginning in the north, this line runs south roughly along the borders dividing Finland and the Baltic republics from Russia; through Byelorussia and the Ukraine, separating western Catholic Ukraine from eastern Orthodox Ukraine; south and then west in Romania, cutting off Transylvania from the rest of the country; and then through Yugoslavia roughly along the line separating Slovenia and Croatia from the other republics. This line may now separate those areas where democracy will take root from those where it will not.

WESTERN CULTURE THESIS

A less restrictive version of the cultural obstacle argument holds that certain non-Western cultures are peculiarly hostile to democracy. The two cultures most often cited in this regard are Confucianism and Islam. Three questions are relevant to determining whether these cultures now pose serious obstacles to democratization. First, to what extent are traditional Confucian and Islamic values and beliefs hostile to democracy? Second, if they are, to what extent have these cultures in fact hampered progress toward democracy? Third, if they have significantly retarded democratic progress in the past, to what extent are they likely to continue to do so in the future?

CONFUCIANISM

Almost no scholarly disagreement exists regarding the proposition that traditional Confucianism was either undemocratic or antidemocratic. The only mitigating factor was the extent to which the examination system in the classic Chinese polity opened careers to the talented without regard to social background. Even if this were the case, however, a merit system of promotion does not make a democracy. No one would describe a modern army as democratic because officers are promoted on the basis of their abilities. Classic Chinese Confucianism and its derivatives in Korea, Vietnam, Singapore, Taiwan, and (in diluted fashion) Japan emphasized the group over the individual, authority over liberty, and responsibilities over rights. Confucian societies lacked a tradition of rights against the state; to the extent that individual rights did exist, they were created by the state. Harmony and cooperation were preferred over disagreement and competition. The maintenance of order and respect for hierarchy were central values. The conflict of ideas, groups, and parties was viewed as dangerous and illegitimate. Most important, Confucianism merged society and the state and provided no legitimacy for autonomous social institutions at the national level.

In practice Confucian or Confucian-influenced societies have been inhospitable to democracy. In East Asia only two countries, Japan and the Philippines, had sustained experience with democratic government prior to 1990. In both cases, democracy was the product of an American presence. The Philippines, moreover, is overwhelmingly a Catholic country. In Japan, Confucian values were reinterpreted and merged with autochthonous cultural traditions.

Mainland China has had no experience with democratic government, and democracy of the Western variety has been supported over the years only by relatively small groups of radical dissidents. "Mainstream" democratic critics have not broken with the key elements of the Confucian tradition. The modernizers of China have been (in Lucian Pye's phrase) the "Confucian Leninists" of the Nationalist and Communist parties. In the late 1980s, when rapid economic growth in China produced a new series of demands for political reform and democracy on the part of students, intellectuals, and urban middle-class groups, the Communist leadership responded in two ways. First, it articulated a theory of "new authoritarianism," based on the experience of Taiwan, Singapore, and Korea, which claimed that a country at China's stage of economic development needed authoritarian rule to achieve balanced economic growth and contain the unsettling consequences of development. Second, the leadership violently suppressed the democratic movement in Beijing and elsewhere in June of 1989.

In China, economics reinforced culture in holding back democracy. In Singapore, Taiwan, and Korea, on the other hand, spectacular growth created the economic basis for democracy by the late 1980s. In these countries, economics clashed with culture in shaping political development. In 1990, Singapore was the only non-oil-exporting "high-income" country (as defined by the World Bank) that did not have a democratic political system, and Singapore's leader was an articulate exponent of Confucian values as opposed to those of Western democracy. In the 1980s, Premier Lee Kwan Yew made the teaching and promulgation of Confucian values a high priority for his city-state and took vigorous measures to limit and suppress dissent and to prevent media criticism of the government and its policies. Singapore was thus an authoritarian Confucian anomaly among the wealthy countries of the world. The interesting question is whether it will remain so now that Lee, who created the state, appears to be partially withdrawing from the political scene.

TAIWAN AND KOREA

In the late 1980s, both Taiwan and Korea moved in a democratic direction. Historically, Taiwan had always been a peripheral part of China. It was occupied by the Japanese for 50 years, and its inhabitants rebelled in 1947 against the imposition of Chinese control. The Nationalist government arrived in 1949 humiliated by its defeat by the Communists, a defeat that made it impossible "for most Nationalist leaders to uphold the posture of arrogance associated with traditional Confucian notions of authority." Rapid economic and social development further weakened the influence of traditional Confucianism. The emergence of a substantial entrepreneurial class, composed largely of native Taiwanese, created (in very un-Confucian fashion) a source of power and wealth independent of the mainlander-dominated state. This produced in Taiwan a "fundamental change in Chinese political culture, which has not occurred in China itself or in Korea or Vietnam—and never really existed in Japan." Taiwan's spectacular economic development thus overwhelmed a relatively weak Confucian legacy, and in the late 1980s Chiang Ching-kuo and Lee Teng-hui responded to the pressures produced by economic and social change and gradually moved to open up politics in their society.

In Korea, the classical culture included elements of mobility and egalitarianism along with Confucian components uncongenial to democracy, including a tradition of authoritarianism and strongman rule. As one Korean scholar put it, "people did not think of themselves as citizens with rights to exercise and responsibilities to perform, but they tended to look up to the top for direction and for favors in order to survive." In the late 1980s, urbanization, education, the development of a substantial middle class, and the impressive spread of Christianity all weakened Confucianism as an obstacle to democracy in Korea. Yet it remained unclear whether the struggle between the old culture and the new prosperity had been definitively resolved in favor of the latter.

THE EAST ASIAN MODEL

The interaction of economic progress and Asian culture appears to have generated a distinctly East Asian variety of democratic institutions. As of 1990, no East Asian country except the Philippines (which is, in many respects, more Latin American than East Asian in culture) had experienced a turnover from a popularly elected government of one party to a popularly elected government of a different party. The prototype was Japan, unquestionably a democracy, but one in which the ruling party has never been voted out of power. The Japanese model of dominant-party democracy, as Pye has pointed out, has spread elsewhere in East Asia. In 1990, two of the three opposition parties in Korea merged with the government party to form a political bloc that would effectively exclude the remaining opposition party, led by Kim Dae Jung and based on the Cholla region, from ever gaining power. In the late 1980s, democratic development in Taiwan seemed to be moving toward an electoral system in which the Kuomintang (KMT) was likely to remain the dominant party, with the Democratic Progressive Party confined to a permanent opposition role. In Malaysia, the coalition of the three leading parties from the Malay, Chinese, and Indian communities (first in the Alliance Party and then in the National Front) has controlled power in unbroken fashion against all competitors from the 1950s through the 1980s. In the mid-1980s, Lee Kwan Yew's deputy and successor Goh Chok Tong endorsed a similar type of party system for Singapore:

> I think a stable system is one where there is a mainstream political party representing a broad range of the population. Then you can have a few other parties on the periphery, very serious-minded parties. They are unable to have wider views but they nevertheless represent sectional interests. And the mainstream is returned all the time. I think that's good. And I would not apologize if we ended up in that situation in Singapore.

A primary criterion for democracy is equitable and open competition for votes between political parties without government harassment or restriction of opposition groups. Japan has clearly met this test for decades with its freedoms of speech, press, and assembly, and reasonably equitable conditions of electoral competition. In the other Asian dominant-party systems, the playing field has been tilted in favor of the government for many years. By the late 1980s, however, conditions were becoming more equal in some countries. In Korea, the government party was unable to win control of the legislature in 1989, and this failure presumably was a major factor in its subsequent merger with two of its opponents. In Taiwan, restrictions on the opposition were gradually lifted. It is thus conceivable that other East Asian countries could join Japan in providing a level playing field for a game that the government party always wins. In 1990 the East Asian dominant-party systems thus spanned a continuum between democracy and authoritarianism, with Japan at one extreme, Indonesia at the other, and Korea, Taiwan, Malaysia, and Singapore (more or less in that order) in between.

Such a system may meet the formal requisites of democracy, but it differs significantly from the democratic systems prevalent in the West, where it is assumed not only that political parties and coalitions will freely and equally compete for power but also that they are likely to *alternate* in power. By contrast, the East Asian dominant-party systems seem to involve competition for power but not alternation in power, and participation in elections for all, but participation in office only for those in the "mainstream" party. This type of political system offers democracy without turnover. It represents an adaptation of Western democratic practices to serve not Western values of competition and change, but Asian values of consensus and stability.

Western democratic systems are less dependent on performance legitimacy than authoritarian systems because failure is blamed on the incumbents instead of the system, and the ouster and replacement of the incumbents help to renew the system. The East Asian societies that have adopted or appear to be adopting the dominant-party model had unequalled records of economic success from the 1960s to the 1980s. What happens, however, if and when their 8-percent growth rates plummet; unemployment, inflation, and other forms of economic distress escalate; or social and economic conflicts intensify? In a Western democracy the response would be to turn the incumbents out. In a dominant-party democracy, however, that would represent a revolutionary change. If the structure of political competition does not allow that to happen, unhappiness with the government could well lead to demonstrations, protests, riots, and efforts to mobilize popular support to overthrow the government. The government then would be tempted to respond by suppressing dissent and imposing authoritarian controls. The key question, then, is to what extent the East Asian dominant-party system presupposes uninterrupted and substantial economic growth. Can this system survive prolonged economic downturn or stagnation?

ISLAM

"Confucian democracy" is clearly a contradiction in terms. It is unclear whether "Islamic democracy" also is. Egalitarianism and voluntarism are central themes in Islam. The "high culture form of Islam," Ernest Gellner has argued, is "endowed with a number of features—unitarianism, a rule-ethic, individualism, scripturalism, puritanism, an egalitarian aversion to mediation and hierarchy, a fairly small load of magic—that are congruent, presumably, with requirements of modernity or modernization." They are also generally congruent with the requirements of democracy. Islam, however, also rejects any distinction between the religious community and the political community. Hence there is no equipoise between Caesar and God, and political participation is linked to religious affiliation. Fundamentalist Islam demands that in a Muslim country the political rulers should be practicing Muslims, *shari'a* should be the basic law, and *ulema* should have a "decisive vote in articulating, or at least reviewing and ratifying, all governmental policy." To the extent that governmental legitimacy and policy flow from religious doctrine and religious expertise, Islamic concepts of politics differ from and contradict the premises of democratic politics.

Islamic doctrine thus contains elements that may be both congenial and uncongenial to democracy. In practice, however, the only Islamic country that has sustained a fully democratic political system for any length of time is Turkey, where Mustafa Kemal Ataturk explicitly rejected Islamic concepts of society and politics and vigorously attempted to create a secular, modern, Western nation-state. And Turkey's experience with democracy has not been an unmitigated success. Elsewhere in the Islamic world, Pakistan has made three attempts at democracy, none of which lasted long. While Turkey has had democracy interrupted by occasional military interventions, Pakistan has had bureaucratic and military rule interrupted by occasional elections.

The only Arab country to sustain a form of democracy (albeit of the consociational variety) for a significant period of time was Lebanon. Its democracy, however, really amounted to consociational oligarchy, and 40 to 50 percent of its population was Christian. Once Muslims became a majority in Lebanon and began to assert themselves, Lebanese democracy collapsed. Between 1981 and 1990, only two of 37 countries in the world with Muslim majorities were ever rated "Free" by Freedom House in its annual surveys: the Gambia for two years and the Turkish Republic of Northern Cyprus for four. Whatever the compatibility of Islam and democracy in theory, in practice they have rarely gone together.

Opposition movements to authoritarian regimes in southern and eastern Europe, in Latin America, and in East Asia almost universally have espoused Western democratic values and proclaimed their desire to establish democracy. This does not mean that they invariably would introduce democratic institutions if they had the opportunity to do so, but at least they articulated the rhetoric of democracy. In authoritarian Islamic societies, by contrast, movements explicitly campaigning for democratic politics have been relatively weak, and the most powerful opposition has come from Islamic fundamentalists.

ECONOMIC PROBLEMS   In the late 1980s, domestic economic problems combined with the snowballing effects of democratization elsewhere led the governments of several Islamic countries to relax their controls on the opposition and to attempt to renew their legitimacy through elections. The principal initial beneficiaries of these openings were Islamic fundamentalist groups. In Algeria, the Islamic Salvation Front swept the June 1990 local elections, the first free elections since the country became independent in 1962. In the 1989 Jordanian elections, Islamic fundamentalists won 36 of 80 seats in parliament. In Egypt, many candidates associated with the Muslim Brotherhood were elected to parliament in 1987. In several countries, Islamic fundamentalist groups were reportedly plotting insurrections. The strong electoral showings of the Islamic groups partly reflected the absence of other opposition parties, some because they were under government proscription, others because they were boycotting the elections. Nonetheless, fundamentalism seemed to be gaining strength in Middle Eastern countries, particularly among younger people. The strength of this tendency induced secular heads of government in Tunisia, Turkey, and elsewhere to adopt policies advocated by the fundamentalists and to make political gestures demonstrating their own commitment to Islam.

Liberalization in Islamic countries thus enhanced the power of important social and political movements whose commitment to democracy was uncertain. In some respects, the position of fundamentalist parties in Islamic societies in the early 1990s raised questions analogous to those posed by communist parties in Western Europe in the 1940s and again in the 1970s. Would the existing governments continue to open up their politics and hold elections in which Islamic groups could compete freely and equally? Would the Islamic groups gain majority support in those elections? If they did win the elections, would the military, which in many Islamic societies (e.g., Algeria, Turkey, Pakistan, and Indonesia) is strongly secular, allow them to form a government? If they did form a government, would it pursue radical Islamic policies that would undermine democracy and alienate the modern and Western-oriented elements in society?

THE LIMITS OF CULTURAL OBSTACLES

Strong cultural obstacles to democratization thus appear to exist in Confucian and Islamic societies. There are, nonetheless, reasons to doubt whether these must necessarily prevent democratic development. First, similar cultural arguments have not held up in the past. At one

point many scholars argued that Catholicism was an obstacle to democracy. Others, in the Weberian tradition, contended that Catholic countries were unlikely to develop economically in the same manner as Protestant countries. Yet in the 1960s, 1970s, and 1980s Catholic countries became democratic and, on average, had higher rates of economic growth than Protestant countries. Similarly, at one point Weber and others argued that countries with Confucian cultures would not achieve successful capitalist development. By the 1980s, however, a new generation of scholars saw Confucianism as a major cause of the spectacular economic growth of East Asian societies. In the longer run, will the thesis that Confucianism prevents democratic development be any more viable than the thesis that Confucianism prevents economic development? Arguments that particular cultures are permanent obstacles to change should be viewed with a certain skepticism.

Second, great cultural traditions like Islam and Confucianism are highly complex bodies of ideas, beliefs, doctrines, assumptions, and behavior patterns. Any major culture, including Confucianism, has some elements that are compatible with democracy, just as both Protestantism and Catholicism have elements that are clearly undemocratic. Confucian democracy may be a contradiction in terms, but democracy in a Confucian society need not be. The real question is which elements in Islam and Confucianism are favorable to democracy, and how and under what circumstances these can supersede the undemocratic aspects of those cultural traditions.

Third, cultures historically are dynamic, not stagnant. The dominant beliefs and attitudes in a society change. While maintaining elements of continuity, the prevailing culture of a society in one generation may differ significantly from what it was one or two generations earlier. In the 1950s, Spanish culture was typically described as traditional, authoritarian, hierarchical, deeply religious, and honor-and-status oriented. By the 1970s and 1980s, these words had little place in a description of Spanish attitudes and values. Cultures evolve and, as in Spain, the most important force bringing about cultural changes is often economic development itself.

ECONOMICS

Few relationships between social, economic, and political phenomena are stronger than that between the level of economic development and the existence of democratic politics. Most wealthy countries are democratic, and most democratic countries—India is the most dramatic exception—are wealthy. The correlation between wealth and democracy implies that transitions to democracy should occur primarily in countries at the mid-level of economic development. In poor countries democratization is unlikely; in rich countries it usually has already occurred. In between there is a "political transition zone": countries in this middle economic stratum are those most likely to transit to democracy, and most countries that transit to democracy will be in this stratum. As countries develop economically and move into the transition zone, they become good prospects for democratization.

In fact, shifts from authoritarianism to democracy during the third wave were heavily concentrated in this transition zone, especially at its upper reaches. The conclusion seems clear. Poverty is a principal—probably *the* principal—obstacle to democratic development. The future of democracy depends on the future of economic development. Obstacles to economic development are obstacles to the expansion of democracy.

The third wave of democratization was propelled forward by the extraordinary global economic growth of the 1950s and 1960s. That era of growth came to an end with the oil price increases of 1973–74. Between 1974 and 1990, democratization accelerated around the world, but global economic growth slowed down. There were, however, substantial differences in growth rates among regions. East Asian rates remained high throughout the 1970s and 1980s, and overall rates of growth in South Asia increased. On the other hand, growth rates in the Middle East, North Africa, Latin America, and the Caribbean declined sharply from the 1970s to the 1980s. Those in sub-Saharan Africa plummeted. Per capita GNP in Africa was stagnant during the late 1970s and declined at an annual rate of 2.2 percent during the 1980s. The economic obstacles to democratization in Africa thus clearly grew during the 1980s. The prospects for the 1990s are not encouraging. Even if economic reforms, debt relief, and economic assistance materialize, the World Bank has predicted an average annual rate of growth in per capita GDP for Africa of only 0.5 percent for the remainder of the century. If this prediction is accurate, the economic obstacles to democratization in sub-Saharan Africa will remain overwhelming well into the twenty-first century.

The World Bank was more optimistic in its predictions of economic growth for China and the nondemocratic countries of South Asia. The current low levels of wealth in those countries, however, generally mean that even with annual per capita growth rates of 3 to 5 percent, the economic conditions favorable to democratization would still be long in coming.

In the 1990s, the majority of countries where the economic conditions for democratization are already present or rapidly emerging are in the Middle East and North Africa (see Table 1). The economies of many of these countries (United Arab Emirates, Kuwait, Saudi Arabia, Iraq, Iran, Libya, Oman) depend heavily on oil exports, which enhances the control of the state bureaucracy. This does not, however, make democratization impossible. The state bureaucracies of Eastern Europe had far more power than do those of the oil exporters. Thus at some point that power could collapse among the latter as dramatically as it did among the former.

In 1988 among the other states of the Middle East and North Africa, Algeria had already reached a level conducive to democratization; Syria was approaching it; and Jordan, Tunisia, Morocco, Egypt, and North Yemen were well below the transition zone, but had grown rapidly during the 1980s. Middle Eastern economies and societies are approaching the point where they will become too wealthy and too complex for their various traditional, military, and one-party systems of authoritarian rule to sustain themselves. The wave of democratization that swept the world in the 1970s and 1980s could become a dominant feature of Middle Eastern and North African politics in the 1990s. The issue of economics versus culture would then be joined: What forms of politics might emerge in these countries when economic prosperity begins to interact with Islamic values and traditions?

In China, the obstacles to democratization are political, economic, and cultural; in Africa they are overwhelmingly economic; and in the rapidly developing countries of East Asia and in many Islamic countries, they are primarily cultural.

ECONOMICS VERSUS CULTURE

ECONOMIC DEVELOPMENT AND POLITICAL LEADERSHIP

History has proved both optimists and pessimists wrong about democracy. Future events will probably do the same. Formidable obstacles to the expansion of democracy exist in many societies. The third wave, the "global democratic revolution" of the late twentieth century, will not last forever. It may be followed by a new surge of authoritarianism sustained enough to constitute a third reverse wave. That, however, would not preclude a fourth wave of democratization developing some time in the twenty-first century. Judging by the record of the past, the two most decisive factors affecting the future consolidation and expansion of democracy will be economic development and political leadership.

Most poor societies will remain undemocratic so long as they remain poor. Poverty, however, is not inevitable. In the past, nations such as South Korea, which were assumed to be mired in economic backwardness, have as-

TABLE 1. *Upper and Middle Income Nondemocratic Countries—GNP Per Capita (1988)*

Income level	Arab-Middle East	Southeast Asia	Africa	Other
Upper income (>$6,000)	UAE[a] Kuwait[a] Saudi Arabia[a]	Singapore		
Upper middle income ($2,000–5,500)	Iraq[a] Iran[a] Libya[a] Oman[a,b] Algeria[b]		(Gabon)	Yugoslavia
Lower middle income ($500–2,200)	Syria Jordan[b] Tunisia[b]	Malaysia[b] Thailand[b]	Cameroon[b]	Paraguay
$1,000	Morocco[b] Egypt[b] Yemen[b] Lebanon[b]		Congo[b] Côte d'Ivoire Zimbabwe Senegal[b] Angola	

Source: World Bank, *World Bank Development Report 1990* (New York: Oxford University Press, 1990), 178–181.

[a]Major oil exporter.
[b]Average annual GDP growth rate 1980–1988 > 3.0%.

tonished the world by rapidly attaining prosperity. In the 1980s, a new consensus emerged among developmental economists on the ways to promote economic growth. The consensus of the 1980s may or may not prove more lasting and productive than the very different consensus among economists that prevailed in the 1950s and 1960s. The new orthodoxy of neoorthodoxy, however, already seems to have produced significant results in many countries.

Yet there are two reasons to temper our hopes with caution. First, economic development for the late, late, late developing countries—meaning largely Africa—may well be more difficult than it was for earlier developers because the advantages of backwardness come to be outweighed by the widening and historically unprecedented gap between rich and poor countries. Second, new forms of authoritarianism could emerge in wealthy, information-dominated, technology-based societies. If unhappy possibilities such as these do not materialize, economic development should create the conditions for the progressive replacement of authoritarian political systems by democratic ones. Time is on the side of democracy.

Economic development makes democracy possible; political leadership makes it real. For democracies to come into being, future political elites will have to believe, at a minimum, that democracy is the least bad form of government for their societies and for themselves. They will also need the skills to bring about the transition to democracy while facing both radical oppositionists and authoritarian hard-liners who inevitably will attempt to undermine their efforts. Democracy will spread to the extent that those who exercise power in the world and in individual countries want it to spread. For a century and a half after Tocqueville observed the emergence of modern democracy in America, successive waves of democratization have washed over the shore of dictatorship. Buoyed by a rising tide of economic progress, each wave advanced further—and receded less—than its predecessor. History, to shift the metaphor, does not sail ahead in a straight line, but when skilled and determined leaders are at the helm, it does move forward.

Dangers and Dilemmas
of Democracy

Philippe C. Schmitter

Philippe C. Schmitter is professor of political science at Stanford University. He has previously taught at the University of Chicago and the European University Institute in Florence. This is an abbreviated version of a longer essay written at the request and with the financial support of UNESCO. It is published here with the permission of UNESCO's Division on Human Rights and Peace.

The celebrations that have accompanied shifts from autocracy to democracy since 1974 have tended to obscure some serious dangers and dilemmas. Together, these presage a political future that, instead of embodying "the end of history," promises to be tumultuous, uncertain, and very eventful. Far from being secure in its foundations and practices, modern democracy will have to face unprecedented challenges in the 1990s and beyond.

For the world's established liberal democracies, the very absence in the present context of a credible "systemic" alternative is bound to generate new strains. Defenders of these regimes have long argued—and their citizens have generally agreed—that whatever its faults, this mode of political rule was clearly preferable to any of several forms of autocracy. Now, these external models for comparison have (mostly) disappeared, or in any case are no longer supported by the propaganda and military might of a great power. All that remains are internal standards for evaluation enshrined in a vast body of normative democratic theory and in the expectations of millions of ordinary citizens. What will happen when well-entrenched elite practices in such countries are measured against these long-subordinated ideals of equality, participation, accountability, responsiveness, and self-realization?

Second, the widespread desire of fledgling neo-democracies to imitate the basic norms and institutions of established liberal democracies is by no means a guarantee of success. There is no proof that democracy is inevitable, irrevocable, or a historical necessity. It neither fills some indispensable functional requisite of capitalism, nor corresponds to some ineluctable ethical imperative in

social evolution. There is every reason to believe that its consolidation demands an extraordinary and continuous effort—one that many countries are unlikely to be able to make.

My focus here will be limited to the dangers and dilemmas inherent in the difficult and uncertain task of consolidating democracy in the aftermath of the recent collapse, overthrow, or self-transformation of autocracy. I will set aside the many problems involved in reforming and religitimating "real existing" liberal democracies, although I know that the two challenges are linked in the longer run. To the extent that citizens in established democracies, who have long been accustomed to limited participation and accountability, begin to question these practices and to express their disenchantment openly, they are bound to have some impact on their counterparts in new democracies, who are just aspiring to acquire these same practices. Conversely, the failure of many of these young regimes to consolidate themselves will certainly shake the confidence of liberal democrats in the West and increase pressures for more substantial institutional and policy reforms.

AN EXPLORATION OF DANGERS

"Democracy," in some form or another, may well be the only legitimate and stable form of government in the contemporary world—if one sets aside those entrenched autocracies where monarchs, dictators, technocrats, fundamentalists, or nativists have thus far been able to sell the notion that competitive elections, freedom of association, civil liberties, and executive accountability are merely instruments of Western imperialism or manifestations of cultural alienation. It is striking how few contemporary parties or movements openly advocate a nondemocratic mode of rule. Even the above-mentioned *régimes d'exception* sometimes hold (rigged) elections, tolerate (limited) contestation, and usually claim that their (authoritarian) tutelage will eventually lead to some culturally appropriate kind of democracy.

If democracy has become "the only game in town" in so many polities, why bother to explore its dangers? Is

From *Journal of Democracy*, April 1994, pp. 57-74. © 1994 by the National Endowment for Democracy and the Johns Hopkins University Press. Reprinted by permission.

not the absence of a plausible alternative enough to ensure the success of its consolidation in most if not all neodemocracies? The answer is no, for two reasons:

1) Democracy's current ideological hegemony could well fade as disillusionment with the actual performance of neodemocracies mounts and as disaffected actors revive old authoritarian themes or invent new ones.

2) Even if autocracy fails to experience a revival, democracies may stumble on without satisfying the aspirations of their citizens and without consolidating an acceptable and predictable set of rules for political competition and cooperation.[1]

The first scenario implies a "sudden death," usually by coup d'état; the second involves a "lingering demise," whereby democracy gradually gives way to a different form of rule.[2]

So far, the first scenario has occurred with astonishing rarity. One of the most striking things about the more than 40 transitions that have transpired since the demise of the Salazar-Caetano regime in Portugal on 25 April 1974 is how few of these experiments have failed outright. Soon after each of the previous periods of widespread democratization (in 1848–52, 1914–20, and 1945–56, respectively), many, if not most, of the affected polities regressed to the *status quo ante* or worse. Recent neodemocracies, however, have so far avoided this most serious danger. Moreover, even the few apparent exceptions—Burma, Burundi, Haiti, Togo, Gabon, the Congo, Algeria, Suriname—suggest that the most vulnerable moment usually comes with the attempt to hold a "founding election." If the autocrats tolerate such a vote and allow the rise of a government accountable to parliament, then the odds against outright regression improve dramatically. Thailand and Nigeria seem to be rather special cases of persistent oscillation in regime type. The former has shown signs recently of swinging back toward greater democracy, whereas the latter has yet to break the cycle. Haiti is a particularly telling example. Its initial experiment with free and contested elections of uncertain outcome resulted in a reassertion of military power. The democratic trajectory resumed after a short interlude, but again met with a violent overthrow by the armed forces. The outcome has long hung in the balance. In mid-1993, it seemed to be moving toward an internationally mediated solution with President Jean-Bertrand Aristide resuming office, but this subsequently met with the intransigence of the Haitian military. As the recent case of Guatemala demonstrates, massive external intervention, when combined with internal fragmentation, can quickly turn back an authoritarian challenge and even leave the polity more dramatic than before.

Which is not to say that, having survived the founding experience, these polities are surely on the road to consolidation. There is no simple choice between *regression* to autocracy and *progression* to democracy, for at least two other alternatives are available: 1) a hybrid regime that combines elements of autocracy and democracy; and 2) persistent but unconsolidated democracy.

Especially when the transition is initiated and imposed from above, the previous rulers attempt to protect their interests by "embedding" authoritarian practices within the emergent regime. Where they liberalize without democratizing (i.e., where they concede certain individual rights but do not render themselves accountable to the citizenry), the hybrid has been labeled *dictablanda*. For those cases where they appear to democratize but do not liberalize (i.e., where elections are held, but under conditions that guarantee the victory of the governing party, that exclude specific sociopolitical groups from participating, or that deprive those elected of the effective capacity to govern), the neologism *democradura* has been proposed. Neither outcome in itself deserves to be called democratic, although both could lead eventually to competitive and accountable rule. *Dictablandas* may not last long, since liberalization can lead to a resurgent civil society that winds up gaining more rights than the autocrats ever meant to concede. Elections in *democraduras* have a habit of producing unexpected winners who, in turn, may use the authority of civilian government to reduce the prerogatives of authoritarian enclaves like the military. But let us not exaggerate. These hybrid arrangements can also serve as facades for enduring autocracy. Once external pressures diminish or internal foes lose resolve, the rulers may quickly revert to the *status quo ante* or worse.

Dictablandas and *democraduras* have become increasingly common, especially in Central America and Africa, as authoritarian rulers seek to introduce democratic mechanisms into their polities in order to placate international forces demanding democratization. Guatemala was one such *democradura* in which elections have been held regularly since 1984–85, but where civilian officials have found their actions restricted by the military. El Salvador, where elections since 1982 have been accompanied by the systematic violation of political and human rights, is another such case, although it may cross the threshold to democracy if UN-negotiated peace accords manage to guarantee a different context for the 1994 elections. Kenya, Togo, Gabon, Zaire. Côte d'Ivoire, and many other African cases seem more like *dictablandas*—increased contestation and even multiparty activities are tolerated, but elections (if held at all) are manipulated to favor the governing clique. In neither region do hybrid regimes seem capable of providing a stable solution to the problems of transition. In central America, one can hope that their likely demise will give rise to genuine experiments with democracy. In Africa, they may be more usefully viewed as improvisations by rulers who are buying time, waiting for the international climate to change so they can engineer a regression to autocracy.[3]

In South America, Eastern Europe, and Asia the specter haunting the transition is not hybridization but nonconsolidation. Many polities in these regions may fail to establish a form of stable self-governance that is appropriate to their respective social structures or accepted by their respective citizenries. Democracy in its most generic sense persists after the demise of autocracy, but never gels into a specific, reliable, and generally accepted set of rules. These countries are "doomed" to remain democratic almost by default. No serious alternative to democracy seems available. Elections are held; associations are tolerated; rights may be respected; arbitrary treatment by authorities may decline—in other words, the procedural minima are met with some degree of regularity—but regular, acceptable, and predictable democratic patterns never quite crystallize. "Democracy" is not replaced, it just persists by acting in *ad hoc* and *ad hominem* ways as successive problems arise. Under these circumstances, there is no underlying consensus defining relations among parties, organized interests, and ethnic or religious groups.

Argentina is often cited as an exemplar of persistently unconsolidated democracy punctuated by periodic returns to dictatorship. Virtually no two successive elections proceed by the same rules; each party fears the hegemonic pretensions of its opponents; voter preferences swing dramatically from one party to another; constitutional rules are no guarantee against intervention by the central government; executive power is concentrated and exercised in a personalistic fashion; and segments of the military remain involved in a permanent conspiracy against elected officials. Brazil, Peru, and the Philippines also seem more or less to fit this description.[4] It is a bit too early to tell, but "Argentinization" may be the most likely prospect for several new democracies in Eastern Europe and the successor republics of the former Soviet Union.

A TAXONOMY OF DILEMMAS

One way in which analysts have tried to introduce greater precision into this discussion of the dangers of democratization is through the notion of "dilemmas."[5] All new democracies, if they are to consolidate a viable set of institutions, must make difficult choices. Unlike the decisions of the transition, which are usually made in a hurry and under the influence of an overriding agreement on the need to get rid of autocracy, the choices involved in consolidation usually require protracted and explicit negotiations among actors who not only have much greater information about one another's intentions and resources, but are fully aware that the outcome will have a lasting impact on how they cooperate and compete in the future. There are no illusions that everyone or nearly everyone can benefit equally, but only the unavoidable realization that preferences with regard to rules and institutions are incompatible and that any alternatives chosen will hurt some and help others. It is by resolving these dilemmas, by making disagreeable procedural choices, that a given polity chooses "its" type of democracy. If these choices somehow do not get made, then the danger of regression, hybridization, or nonconsolidation increases greatly.

Given the high initial expectations of the people at large, it may come as a shock to realize that the fall of tyrants fails to spell the rise of endless harmony and good feelings: that the popular uprising or the resurrection of civil society is powerless to produce an actionable "general will"; that "honest democrats" can bicker incessantly over seemingly minor details; that the mere advent of democracy does not also bring freedom and equality, growth and equity, security and opportunity, efficiency and responsiveness, autonomy and accountability, *la pluie et le beau temps*. Is it any wonder, then, that disenchantment sets in and that more and more people begin to question whether democracy is really worth so much anxiety and uncertainty?

What is needed is some generic idea of what these dilemmas are. Obviously, each new democracy will have perplexing and painful choices to make that are peculiar to its own history, geostrategic situation, and natural and human resources, but there will surely be common threads. If we could specify these shared dilemmas, we would be better able to assess the probable dangers—although to predict the outcome in any given case, we would still have to incorporate an understanding of all the relevant particulars.

Let us begin by distinguishing two overall categories of dilemmas: 1) those that are *intrinsic* to modern democracy, no matter where it exists or when it came into existence; and 2) those that are *extrinsic,* in the sense that they call into question the compatibility of emerging democratic rules and practices with existing social, cultural, and economic circumstances.

INTRINSIC DILEMMAS

It may come as another shock to discover that democracy, even if stable and well-entrenched, does not always work well. These intrinsic difficulties will occupy us only briefly in this essay, partly because scholars have already extensively treated them, and also because it is the extrinsic class of dilemmas that most preoccupies new democracies. Still, it seems likely that the intrinsic dilemmas that I am about to list will interact with the difficulties of coming up with rules and practices compatible with prevailing social, cultural, or economic institutions.

1) *Oligarchy:* Roberto Michels was the first to observe that even in the most democratic institutions, professional leaders and staff tend to possess certain advantages of incumbency that insulate them from the threat of being deposed by challengers. His "Iron Law" implies that parties, associations, and movements—to say nothing of legislatures—all become increasingly oligarchic and therefore less accountable to their members or the public at large.[6]

2) *"Free-riding"*: Mancur Olson may not have been the first, but he has been the most systematic in demonstrating that much of what sustains and is produced by democracy consists of public goods to which individuals have no rational incentive to contribute voluntarily. In the absence of private selective payoffs, citizens in a democracy should "learn" that it is not worth their while to vote, to join associations or movements, or even to participate in public affairs since their various discrete contributions will normally have little or no impact upon the outcome. Increasingly, they will leave most of this activity to professional "political entrepreneurs" acting more or less independently of their followers, constituents, or clients.[7]

3) *"Policy-cycling"*: All modern democracies have to make decisions involving the uneven distribution of costs and benefits among groups and individuals. Whenever this is done by majority vote, rather than by unanimity, the possibility arises of "cycling," i.e., of unstable majorities formed by shifting coalitions composed of groups with incompatible preferences on other issues. If choices are presented pairwise, no stable majority emerges, and there may ensue a vacillating series of policy measures that pass in sequence, but have the net effect of alienating everyone.[8]

4) *Functional autonomy:* All democracies must depend for their survival on specialized institutions that cannot themselves be democratic—the armed forces and the central bank are the most obvious examples. For these to perform their respective functions efficiently, they must be insulated from popular pressures and partisan competition. To the extent that the role of such institutions increases in a more turbulent, competitive, and (as we shall see below) internationally interdependent environment, the power of the experts who run these institutions will increase at the expense of congressional and executive leaders accountable to the citizenry.

5) *Interdependence:* All contemporary democracies, even the largest and most powerful of them, are entangled in complex webs of interdependence with other democracies and some autocracies. In principle, elected national leaders are sovereign (i.e., accountable to no authority higher than their own countries' constitutions). In practice, however, they are quite limited in their ability to control the decisions of transnational firms, the movement of ideas and persons across their borders, and the impact of their neighbors' policies. Their authority confined to nation-states, these leaders find themselves decreasingly capable of ensuring the welfare and security of their own citizens.

EXTRINSIC DILEMMAS

Such are the major generic dilemmas that are plaguing established democracies. They will have to be faced eventually by fledgling democracies. But before the institu-

tions of the latter can become oligarchic, before the diminishing enthusiasm of their citizens teaches them to free-ride, before policy-cycling can settle in, maybe even before their armed forces and central banks can establish their functional autonomy, and before they can come to terms with their de facto restricted national sovereignty, politicians in new democracies are going to have to settle on rules and practices for resolving even more pressing extrinsic dilemmas.

The core of the problem with regard to these extrinsic dilemmas is well-captured by the Spanish verb *adecuar,* which means to come up with solutions that are at least adequate, if less than optimal. The trick is to make binding and collective choices (or, as we shall see, nonchoices) between alternative institutional arrangements that are compatible with existing socioeconomic structures and cultural identities. In the longer run, it may become possible for consolidated democracies to change these "confining conditions."[9] In the shorter run, those polities that have democratized and *simultaneously* sought to produce rapid changes in the rights of property owners, the distribution of wealth, the balance of public-private power, and so forth have usually failed and, in so doing, rendered the consolidation of democracy much more difficult. The Portuguese learned this the hard way in 1974–75. The Spaniards next door took the lesson to heart and resolved their major extrinsic dilemmas one after another. The Chileans, faced with more deliberately placed "confining conditions" than any other recently democratizing nation, have moved very carefully and gradually to remove them. Alas, in Eastern Europe and the successor republics of the old Soviet Union, the gradualist option is unavailable. These countries face a knotty tangle of dilemmas that simultaneously demand urgent attention and force crucial decisions affecting virtually all realms of political, social, economic, and cultural life.[10]

The response to these extrinsic dilemmas may involve varying degrees of "reflection and choice." The "classic" model (best exemplified by the Philadelphia Convention of 1787) is that of a constituent assembly, composed of delegates deliberating (perhaps secretly) about the country's rules and institutions. Spain is the best recent example of how that founding moment can be seized to great effect.[11] In some countries, by contrast, the key players have agreed on a "nonchoice" by simply reviving some previously employed institutional format, either because the ensuing authoritarian period was short and relatively inconsequential (as in Greece in the late 1970s), or because some ancient founding document was thought still to be adequate (as in Argentina and Lithuania more recently). In the Philippines, the metaprocedural choices were made not by deliberation among elected representatives or by resuscitation of the past, but by a committee of experts. Chile continues to operate under a document imposed on it by onetime dictator Augusto Pinochet. Brazil and some East European countries have taken a long time before formally attempting to "adequate" their institutions. Russia stands out as an extreme case of incapacity to choose any set of self-limiting institutions.

Few democratizing countries face their extrinsic dilemmas in a purely reflective and logical manner. Most have historical experience to draw upon, even if they may be compelled to modify their choices in the light of subsequent economic, demographic, generational, and cultural changes. Sentiment and habit also play a role. This does not always ensure an adequate institutional fit, much less an optimal one, but at least the comforts of familiarity are secured.

The last 20 years of democratization have included an unusual number of polities that either have had virtually no previous experience with democracy (Paraguay, Mongolia, Albania, Bulgaria, Ethiopia, Angola, all the Central Asian republics, Taiwan, and Russia), or whose previous experiences with it have been notoriously short and unsuccessful (Hungary, Poland, Romania, Estonia, Latvia, Lithuania, Mali, the Congo, Benin, Togo, Thailand, and South Korea). In principle, this should place them in a more favorable position to select adequate institutions; in practice, one suspects that most will end up relying extensively (if clandestinely) upon outside advisors and foreign models. As we shall see below, political science may have little to say about what are the most adequate institutions for resolving specific dilemmas.

It should also be kept in mind that those who make the metachoices governing long-term democratic consolidation must also pay attention to banal near-term considerations like staying in office. This is especially significant today, when most democratizers are career politicians. They may have no other vocation and source of income than politics and, therefore, are even less likely to put general interests ahead of their own immediate interests in pursuing their political careers.

The single most important influence on these choices—beyond that of habit and precedent—is the mode of transition.[12] Differences in the level of mass mobilization (as opposed to elite domination) and in the extent of violence (as opposed to negotiation) produce variations in constraints and opportunities. The most favorable context for an eventual consolidation is a "pacted transition" in which elites from the previous autocracy and its opposition reach a stalemate and find themselves compelled to respect each other's interests. The least favorable is a revolution, with mobilized masses using force to topple the *ancien régime*. Falling somewhere in between are: imposed transitions, in which elements of the autocracy dictate the conditions and pace of the changeover; and reform transitions, in which mass mobilization plays a vital role but incumbents are not violently removed from power.

As we briefly describe the major extrinsic dilemmas, let us remember that only by knowing the habits instilled by a given country's experience with democracy, and only by situating the actors within their respective modes of transition, does it become possible to estimate the most adequate institutional response.

1) *Boundaries and identities:* If there is one overriding political requisite for democracy, it is the prior existence of a legitimate political unit. Before actors can expect to settle into a routine of competition and cooperation, they must have some reliable idea of who the other players are and what will be the physical limits of their playing field. The predominant principle in establishing these boundaries and identities is that of "nationality." Unfortunately, it is not always clear what constitutes a nation—before, during, or even after democratization. Common ancestry, language, symbols, and historical memories may all play a role, but there always remain residual elements of opportunistic choice and collective enthusiasm. All one can say for sure is that the sentiment of national identity and boundaries is the outcome of arcane and complex historical processes that are, nevertheless, subject to manipulation. Democratization itself may encourage actors to attempt such manipulations in order to create constituencies favorable to their respective purposes, but it does not and cannot resolve the issue. *There is simply no democratic way of deciding what a nation and its corresponding political unit should be.* Slogans such as the self-determination of peoples and devices such as plebiscites or referenda simply beg the question of who is eligible to vote within which constituencies, and whether the winning majority can legitimately impose its will on eventual minorities.

2) *Capitalist production, accumulation, and distribution:* All of the established democracies are located in countries in which economic production and accumulation are largely in the hands of privately owned firms and in which distribution is mainly effected through market mechanisms. In all of these polities, however, the outcome of these processes is affected—admittedly in different ways and to different degrees—by public intervention that has been decided by democratic governments and generally supported by most of the citizenry. The paradoxical conclusion is inescapable that 1) capitalism must be a necessary (though not sufficient) condition for democracy; and 2) that capitalism must be modified significantly to make it compatible with democracy.

The dilemma is not merely the static one of deciding on what mix of public-private ownership, income redistribution, monetary intervention, welfare expenditure, health-and-safety regulation, consumer protection, credit subsidization, industrial promotion, tariff protection, and so on will best satisfy citizens' expectations of justice or fairness without stifling economic growth (and impeding the incumbents' chances for reelection). It also involves a dynamic set of choices concerning the development of capitalism at different stages and in different locations within the world system. Playing "catch-up" seems to require greater reliance on state intervention by peripheral economies; overcoming critical thresholds in capital accumulation may even require recourse to authoritarian methods, if not to outright bureaucratic-authoritarian rule.[13]

In the best of circumstances, the preceding autocracy may have already concentrated profits, encouraged private accumulation, increased the state's fiscal capacity, developed the country's physical infrastructure, and improved its international competitiveness, thereby doing much to resolve this dilemma. New democracies that have inherited this sort of legacy—Spain, Chile, and to a much lesser extent Turkey, Greece, Uruguay, and Brazil—have found the task of consolidation easier.

In the worst of circumstances, the *ancien régime* leaves a legacy of corruption, protectionism, price distortions, foreign indebtedness, inefficient public enterprises, trade imbalances, and fiscal instability. The Argentinean and Peruvian cases demonstrate how costly it is to put off dealing with these issues. The experience of Bolivia and, in a different way, Portugal suggest that it may be possible to tackle such problems and still make progress toward consolidation. The countries of Eastern Europe and the former Soviet Union find themselves in a dramatically more difficult situation. Not only must many of the institutions of pricing, credit, monetary policy, collective bargaining, consumer protection, and the like, be created *ex nihilo*, but this must be done at the same time that key political arrangements are being chosen. The first project often implies an exaggerated dependence on foreign models and advice; the latter will likely involve serious unexpected coincidences and unforeseen interaction effects.

It is important to stress that the problematic relationship between capitalism and democracy—"necessary, but necessarily modified"—is structural. It stems from the root difference between a polity that distributes power and status relatively equally and an economy that distributes property and income relatively unequally. This poses a dilemma no matter how well the economic system is performing at a given moment.[14]

Not surprisingly, however, most observers assume that crises in growth, employment, foreign-exchange earnings, and debt repayment bode ill for the consolidation of democratic rule, and few would question the long-run value of growth for political stability. But austerity may have some perverse advantages, at least for initial survivability. In the context of the difficult economic conditions of the late 1980s and early 1990s, the exhaustion of utopian ideologies and even of rival policy prescriptions has become painfully evident. Neither the extreme right nor the extreme left has a plausible alternative to offer. Populism, driven by the disappointment of rising expectations and disenchantment with the travails of democracy, is always a possibility, but unlike in the past, it can deliver no immediate rewards to the masses.

To the extent that this situation diminishes the rewards expected from engaging in antisystem activity, the likelihood is enhanced that some form of democracy will persist. This suggests that the conditions for bargaining over rules and institutions may be as favorable in times of austerity as in time of plenty. Such conditions are likely to worsen, however, when the economy is fitful, going through stop-and-go cycles or experiencing sudden gluts or shortages.

3) Overload and ungovernability: Democracies are not anarchies. They must be capable of governing, of using public authority to modify the behavior of individual citizens, and of regulating the performance of firms and markets. One of the enduring mysteries of established democracies is their source of political obligation. Why do citizens generally obey the law and pursue their demands through regular institutional channels, even when there might seem to be a greater payoff and little fear of punishment from doing otherwise? The usual answers of political scientists rest on such abstract notions as "tradition," "trust in institutions," "socialization" and, of course, "legitimacy." Unfortunately, they are rarely very explicit about where these things come from in the first place—often noting only the gradual accumulation of custom and the explicit inculcation of norms through the educational system. These lessons are not likely to give much comfort to those concerned with the consolidation of democracy in a relatively short period of time.

Moreover, there is growing evidence from the older democracies that traditional partisan identifications, habits of self-restraint, trust in institutions, and belief in the legitimacy of rulers have all been persistently and markedly declining, whether measured by attitudes in surveys or behavior in polling booths or in the streets. The reasons for such declines have been extensively (if inconclusively) discussed: greater physical mobility, higher levels of education, more leisure time, decline in the quality of public education, increasing intellectual disaffection, and so forth.[15]

The problem for so many new democracies is that their own respective populations are often subject to the same trends and are therefore more mobile, educated, disaffected and, certainly, skeptical than were the citizens of older democracies when those countries went through their early phases of political development. Most importantly, modern mass communications have made citizens vastly more aware of events taking place elsewhere in the world and of alternative means for pursuing their interests and passions. Hence the shift away from political parties as the exclusive intermediaries for citizens and the primary source of legitimacy for rulers. Interest associations (and more recently, various kinds of social movements) have moved into this space. They are particularly important in expressing the demands of classes, professions, generations, religions, ethnic groups, and other segments of the population whose numbers preclude them from creating or dominating parties, but whose interests and passions motivate them to participate with special intensity.[16]

New democracies thus need legitimacy in order to build institutions, and institutions in order to establish legitimacy. Success will depend on many factors, especially the mode of transition and prior experience with democracy. Even though most new democracies today contain relatively sophisticated, well-informed groups whose interests are diverse and whose organizational skills are formidable, political parties will probably still provide the principal linkage between citizens and government, and it is likely that the choice of rules and institutions will involve bargaining between party leaders. Hence the nature of the emerging party system will be a major determinant of governability. But it will not be the only one. Today's fledgling democracies will not repeat the trajectory of their older cousins. They will have to cope with (and govern with) the full range of associations and movements that have accumulated in the meantime—all the exotic flora and fauna of a media-saturated, urbanized, postindustrial society.

4) Corruption and decay: At first glance, especially given recent headlines in Western Europe and the United States, this would seem an intrinsic dilemma. All democracies, old as well as new, are subject to the abuse of power and the appropriation of public goods for private benefit—evils ultimately held in check by the periodic opportunity citizens have to go to the polls and "throw the rascals out." The criteria of malfeasance may shift a bit from one culture to another; the magnitude seems to vary inversely with the extent to which capitalism offers alternative sources of self-enrichment. Democracies as a group are still far behind autocracies when it comes to either corruption or decay.

The element which makes the dilemma extrinsic is the professionalization of politics. When democratic politicians were usually well-to-do male amateurs, positions of representation were usually unremunerated. Upon losing them, officeholders would return to private life, often at a profit to their fortunes. This began to change with the rise of socialist parties in the early twentieth century, and has continued unabated. Today, not only do those who hold elected office expect to be well-paid for their services, but many have no other source of income. Add to this the spiralling costs of getting elected and servicing one's constituents, and the problem of extracting sufficient revenues to pay for democratic politics becomes even more acute.

How do the citizens pay for democracy? At what point does its peculiar "political economy" become a serious impediment to its legitimacy, even its perpetuation? Some more senior democracies—Japan, France, Italy, and Spain—are currently facing this issue; others have had to deal with recurrent scandals in the past. New democracies are usually born in a burst of civic enthusiasm and moral outrage against the corrupt decadence of the *ancien régime,* so that the dilemma only emerges later. When it does, the effect can be particularly devastating, for politicians have less secure alternative sources of income, while citizens are less convinced of the need to pay their representatives generously.

What tends to compound the problem in fledgling democracies is that regime transition is often accompanied by the simultaneous need to make major transformations in other socioeconomic domains: property rights, industrial subsidies, price controls, privatization, deregulation, licensing of services and media, and the like. Even where the thrust of change is toward "unleashing market forces," the process of accomplishing this offers very attractive opportunities for illicit enrichment on the part of the politicians who set the norms, sell off the enterprises, and award the contracts. Ironically, while the long-term intent is precisely to reduce the rent seeking intrinsic to public ownership and regulation, the short-term effect is to increase the potential payoffs to be had from the exploitation of public authority.

The crux of the matter is that modern democratic practice, especially given its professionalization and the expansion of its policy tasks, has never come to terms with its own political economy. Understandably, democratic citizens find the financing of parties, the remunerating of deputies, the extracting of fees-for-service, and the profiting from government contracts to be murky and often repugnant. It should therefore come as no surprise to discover that they are reluctant to pay—even for the type of regime that they manifestly prefer.

5) External security and internal insecurity: The advent of democracy does not guarantee national security. Depending on a country's size, resources, strategic location, and neighbors, it may even make the problem worse. Fledgling democracies can present an attractive "target of opportunity" to aggressors as the case of Bosnia tragically testifies. They may also, however be able to count upon greater regional and global solidarity—consider Macedonia, where 1,100 foreign troops are now stationed to guard its territorial integrity.

Furthermore, almost every country undergoing the changeover to democracy has suffered from greater domestic insecurity: higher crime rates, increases in political violence, and more frequent disruptions of basic services. In a few cases, dissidents have even resorted to terrorism in their efforts to redefine the identity of the political unit (e.g., the Basque-based ETA in Spain); to bring about a rupture with capitalism (e.g., Sendero Luminoso in Peru); or simply to return the country to autocracy (e.g., the *carapintada* officer clique in Argentina).

At the center of the security dilemma lies the very delicate issue of civil-military and civil-police relations—a dilemma made all the more acute if the previous regime was a military dictatorship. Not only will the transition have to face the issues of extricating the armed forces from power and meting out justice for crimes committed during their tenure, but the consolidation will have to give the soldiers a satisfactory and credible role under democratic auspices. In the past, this was not too difficult since the communist threat could provide reason (or rationale) enough for retaining an autonomous national defense capability. Communism's collapse, plus that of most domestic armed insurrections, has left a "functional vacuum" in several areas of the world. membership in NATO was sufficient in the 1970s to provide a *raison d'être* (and substantial military assistance) to the armed forces of Southern Europe's neodemocracies. Two of these Greece and Turkey, even had plausible enemies in each other! Elsewhere, especially in Latin America, it will take more imagination to find the armies a plausible role.

Moreover, civilian governments in new democracies that lack border conflicts or internal insurrections find themselves assailed with competing demands from myriad newly enfranchised groups. To the extent that these governments are simultaneously following neoliberal strictures to cut budget imbalances, implement austerity measures, and privatize public (and often military-run) enterprises, the military must seem like the most likely place for cuts. One can hardly blame citizens for thinking that military expenditures were swollen under the preceding dictatorship and should be slashed drastically—just when the shift to a new mission might temporarily require additional expenditures. And these potential new missions—such as combatting drug traffic, policing common crime, repressing social unrest, building infrastructure, providing health and relief services to stricken areas, and participating in UN and regional peacekeeping forces—all have their risks. Some virtually invite officers to intervene in policy making outside their traditional domain; others are profoundly repugnant to their usual sense of mission; none of them would provide a sufficient excuse for maintaining existing levels of expenditure and personnel for very long.

Establishing control over the police can also pose some delicate choices—especially where it has previously been under the control of the military or the intelligence services. On the one hand, there is the enhanced need for policing due to the likely increase in crime. On the other, there is the enhanced expectation that the police will respect due process of law and basic human rights. Few things can be more subversive of trust in institutions and the legitimacy of the government than the popular perception that "nothing has changed" at the level of face-to-face contacts between police authorities and the population. Here is an area where a modest but firm investment in civilian control can yield high symbolic benefits (as happened in Spain), and where its absence can undermine not only the regime's legitimacy but the authority of the state itself.

As with all of these extrinsic dilemmas, the long-run prospects are favorable—provided that the neodemocracies cope with the nearer-term consequences of the choices that they have made (or not made) during the transition. Eventually, civil-police relations will become institutionalized, and guarantees for human rights will be made to stick. Internal security should stabilize, if not increase, once consolidation is accomplished. The proliferation of popularly accountable governments within a given region or across the entire globe should be good for

external security. One of the few "invariant laws" of international relations is that democracies do not go to war with other democracies. Autocracies have frequently fought each other as well as democracies, but a world or a region populated by democracies is definitely likely to be less insecure and less violent. Its member states will still have their quarrels but are much more likely to resort to negotiation, mediation, or adjudication to settle them. Barring the regression of any of its members to autocracy, such a democratized region should be able to organize itself into a "security community" wherein the resort to arms would be unimaginable.[17] This, in turn, should facilitate a firm assertion of civilian supremacy and perhaps even a gradual reduction in military expenditures and personnel.

FORBEARANCE AND DISENCHANTMENT

This essay has suggested that there are some good reasons to be less than triumphal about the longer-term prospects for contemporary democratization. Historically, very few countries have ever consolidated democracy on their first try. All previous waves of regime change eventually receded—and it may be too early to tell how many polities will be swept back to autocracy this time. Certainly, those that have not yet resolved the dilemma of defining their national identity and territorial boundaries are unlikely to make much progress in other domains. Moreover, with most neodemocracies facing declining economic performance, accelerating inflation, heavy loads of foreign debt, severe budgetary and fiscal imbalances, and the pressure of international competition and capital flight in the new global economy, resolving the fundamental structural dilemmas concerning capitalist institutions is not getting any easier.

What is most striking so far is that citizens have responded to these dilemmas of choice and strains of adjustment by focusing their discontent on governments rather than on democracy as such. They have frequently voted transitional leaders and parties out of office, but they have rarely demanded or supported a return to authoritarianism in any guise. Despite this rather remarkable display of forbearance, there are growing signs of what the Spaniards have called *desencanto* (disenchantment) with democracy itself. The perception is widespread that corruption has increased and that decay has set in even *before* consolidation has been assured. With astonishing regularity, one hears complaints that professional politicians have arranged disproportionate salaries and perquisites for themselves; that political parties are clandestinely enriching themselves; that privileged groups are evading the law; that entrenched powers such as the military have protected and even increased their share of the budget; that crime has increased; that violations of human rights by police forces persist; that taxes are unfairly distributed or collected; and that unsavory nationals or even foreigners are reaping too many of the benefits from privatization and deregulation. Complaints like these suggest that one or more extrinsic dilemmas are not being addressed.

But these problems of economic suffering and political disappointment pale when compared to those generated by cultural conflict. Autocracies commonly suppress or manipulate ethnolinguistic minorities; nascent democracies then inherit the resulting resentments while providing an environment in which they can be freely aired. In Southern Europe and Latin America, where national borders and identities have long been secure, the demands of subnational groups proved to be relatively easy to accommodate through policies of territorial devolution, although in the case of the Spanish Basques this was accomplished only after a lengthy and bloody armed struggle. In Eastern Europe and Africa, where historical resentments run much deeper and existing political frontiers often run through rather than around nations, ethnolinguistic divisions can become explosive and easily overwhelm the usual social cleavages—of class, status, profession, generation, and the like—that underlie stable party and interest-group systems.

The suggestion that the current wave of regime changes is likely to be followed by fewer regressions to autocracy than in the past may prove of scant comfort to those presently attempting to consolidate new democracies. They still must face some formidable dilemmas and make some arduous choices before settling into the routinized patterns of political cooperation and competition that will ensure the perpetuation of democratic rule.

NOTES

1. See Juan Linz, *The Breakdown of Democratic Regimes: Crisis, Breakdown and Reequilibration* (Baltimore: Johns Hopkins University Press, 1978). Linz observed that, on many occasions in the interwar period, the worst enemies of democracy were themselves genuine democrats who believed that by taking certain extraordinary measures they were protecting democracy. The breakdown came, not because the alternative was so popular or overwhelming, but because the existing regime had transformed itself into a quasiautocracy.

2. Cf. Guillermo O'Donnell, "Transitions, Continuities and Paradoxes," in Scott Mainwaring et al., eds., *Issues in Democratic Consolidation: The New South American Democracies in Comparative Perspective* (Notre Dame: University of Notre Dame Press, 1992), 17–56.

3. For a detailed account of this tendency in Africa, with some references to Latin America, see Max Liniger-Goumax, *La démocrature: Dictature camouflée; démocratie truquée* (Paris: Editions L'Harmattan, 1992).

4. Guillermo O'Donnell has drawn attention to other aspects of this subset of countries, which he calls "delegative democracies." See his "Delegative Democracy," *Journal of Democracy* 5 (January 1994): 55–69.

5. The first to have done so (to my knowledge) was Terry Karl in her "Dilemmas of Democratization in Latin America," *Comparative Politics* 23 (October 1990): 1–23. Much of my

thinking on this subject has been influenced by this article and subsequent conversations with her.

6. Roberto Michels, *Political Parties: A Sociological Study of the Oligarchic Tendencies of Modern Europe* (New York and London: The Free Press, 1962).

7. Mancur Olson, *The Logic of Collective Action: Public Goals and the Theory of Groups* (Cambridge: Harvard University Press, 1965).

8. The classic statement of this problem is Kenneth J. Arrow, *Social Choice and Individual Values* (New York: John Wiley, 1951). For a more recent restatement, along with other logical dilemmas of collective choice, see Dennis C. Mueller, *Public Choice II* (Cambridge: Cambridge University Press, 1989), 63ff.

9. Cf. Otto Kirchheimer, "Confining Conditions and Revolutionary Breakthroughs," *American Political Science Review* 59 (1965): 964–74.

10. Several authors have stressed this issue of simultaneity: Claus Offe, "Capitalism by Democratic Design? Democratic Theory Facing the Triple Transition in East Central Europe," *Social Research* 58 (Winter 1991): 865–92; Jon Elster, "Constitution-Making in Eastern Europe," *Public Administration* (forthcoming, 1994); Philippe C. Schmitter and Terry Karl. "The Types of Democracy Emerging in Southern and Eastern Europe and South and Central America." in Peter Volten, ed., *Bound to Change: Consolidating Democracy in Central Europe* (New York: IEWSS, 1992), 42–68.

11. A. Bonimé-Blanc, *Spain's Transition to Democracy: The Politics of Constitution-Making* (Boulder and London: Westview Press, 1987). For general remarks on the desirability of seizing this moment early, see Bruce Ackerman, *The Future of Liberal Revolution* (New Haven: Yale University Press, 1992).

12. Terry Lynn Karl and Philippe C. Schmitter, "Modes of Transition in Latin America, Southern and Eastern Europe." *International Social Science Journal* 128 (1991)l 269–84; also Donald Share, "Transitions to Democracy and Transition through Transaction," *Comparative Political Studies* 19 (1987): 545.

13. See Alexander Gerschenkron, *Economic Backwardness in Historical perspective* (Cambridge: Harvard University Press, 1962); and Guillermo O'Donnell, *Modernization and Bureaucratic Authoritarianism: Studies in South American Politics* (Berkeley: University of California, Institute of International Studies, 1973).

14. No one has pursued this theme more exhaustively than Adam Przeworski. For his latest exploration, see *Democracy and the Market* (New York: Cambridge University Press, 1992).

15. The *locus classicus* of this discussion is Michel Crozier, Samuel P. Huntington, and Joji Watanuki, *The Crisis of Democracy* (New York: New York University Press, 1975). For Huntington's revised thoughts on the prospects for democracy, see his "Will More Countries Become Democratic?" *Political Science Quarterly* 99 (Spring 1984): 193–218.

16. This theme is further developed in Philippe C. Schmitter, "The Consolidation of Democracy and Representation of Social Groups," *American Behavioral Scientist* 35 (March–June 1992): 422–49.

17. See Michael W. Doyle, "Liberalism and World Politics," *American Political Science Review* 80 (December 1986): 1151–70; and Bruce Russett, "Political and Alternative Security: Towards a More Democratic and Therefore More Peaceful World," in Burns H. Weston, ed., *Alternative Security: Living Without Nuclear Deterrence* (Boulder, Colo.: Westview Press, 1990). For a case study of the impact of democratization upon foreign relations in the Southern Cone of Latin America, see Philippe C. Schmitter, "Change in Regime Type and Progress in International Relations," in Emanuel Adler and Beverly Crawford, eds., *Progress in Postwar International Relations* (New York: Columbia University Press, 1991), 89–127.

DEMOCRACY AND GROWTH

Why voting is good for you

Believers in the "Asian Way" argue that democracy undermines economic development. They are wrong. Democracy entrenches economic freedoms, and in doing so underpins growth

IN 1992 Lee Kuan Yew, Singapore's leader for many years and one of the world's most successful economic policy-makers, told an audience in the Philippines: "I do not believe that democracy necessarily leads to development. I believe that what a country needs to develop is discipline more than democracy. The exuberance of democracy leads to indiscipline and disorderly conduct which are inimical to development."

Several other Asian leaders have echoed those thoughts. The unelected ones may reasonably be suspected of bias. More telling, in a way, is that some elected leaders have said the same for much longer, without meaning to commend authoritarian rule. For years Indian politicians excused their country's slow growth as the price of democracy, albeit one worth paying. Having to justify policies to an electorate, they said, made it harder to get things done. (In 1991, nonetheless, India launched bold economic reforms; let that pass.) Lately, the theme has been taken up by many in the West who recognise the success of the East Asian tigers—South Korea, Taiwan, Singapore and Hong Kong—as one of the great human achievements of modern times. What did these places have in common? One answer: in varying degree, undemocratic government.

There are plausible economic reasons why "strong government" should be associated with economic success. A much-cited study of Taiwan, by Robert Wade of Sussex University's Institute of Development Studies, argues that Taiwan's government was able to intervene intelligently in economic management partly because it was spared popular pressure to intervene unintelligently* (for footnotes, see final page). Instead of saving jobs in doomed industries it could concentrate on policies likely to create new jobs and new wealth.

Then, compare East Asia with Eastern Europe and the former Soviet Union, where democracy arrived before economic reform—making it much more difficult, you might argue, for governments to introduce the policies that were needed to promote rapid economic growth. It has become a cliché to hold that the Soviet Union got its political and economic reforms the wrong way round—unlike China, with its repressive politics and booming economy.

The grip that these ideas and examples have taken on many shades of western opinion is in one way unsurprising. Authoritarianism has a strong populist appeal. No free speech, perhaps, but the trains run on time. The more politically sophisticated find subtler arguments for agreeing that democracy and economic efficiency are at odds. The left, loosely speaking, thinks markets are unjust; democracy is a good thing precisely because it can subordinate efficiency to fairness. The right, again loosely speaking, sees the same trade-off in a different way: democracy sometimes entails things, such as levying punitive taxes, which cause economic harm and which infringe freedoms more basic than the right to vote. But there is broad agreement on the proposition that democracy and economic growth are in conflict: a consensus which ought to be surprising indeed, since, according to the most obvious evidence, the proposition is false.

A map on the next page shows a three-way classification of the world's political systems. It counts countries as free, partly free, or not free, according to whether they have free and fair elections, protection of civil liberties, multi-party legislatures, an uncontrolled press and so forth. The distribution has changed a lot in recent years. Democracy has spread across much of Latin America and the former Soviet block; sev-

eral of the tigers have become less authoritarian; many other countries have become less free. But it remains true that nearly all of the world's richest countries are free (meaning, among other things, democratic) and nearly all of the poorest countries are not. A map that classified the world into rich, middle-income and poor, according to income per head, would not look very different from this political map. Across the world, in other words, the correlation between political freedom and prosperity is a close one.

The democratic rich

This correlation may not, on further examination, mean much—but on one point the map brooks no argument. It is absurd to conclude from East Asia's success, and from that fact alone, that non-democratic government is best for development. To account for East Asia's growth, factors common to that region but not to others need to be identified. East Asia's governments were not unusual in being non-democratic. This was, and is, something common to much of the third world. If dictators made countries rich, Africa would be an economic colossus.

The correlation between wealth and democracy must not be pressed too far. It does not prove that democracy promotes growth, for instance. Arguably, as people grow richer, democracy is one of the things they want, and it becomes ever more difficult for governments to deny them. So it may be that growth promotes democracy, rather than the other way round. Despite the correlation, therefore, non-democratic government may still be conducive to (though plainly not sufficient for) radical change, such as a successful shift from agriculture to industry, say, or from communist central planning to market economics. And, more generally, it could still be true that democracy, once in place, inhibits growth.

But other evidence suggests that these ideas are wrong, too. First, consider the demands of radical economic change. Such change usually makes some groups—and often, for a time, the population at large—worse off. It poses a great challenge to democratic governments. But it poses just as great a challenge to authoritarian governments. These, too, need to retain the support of certain constituencies (trade unions, say, or the army) in order to hang on to power. It is unclear in principle, therefore, which form of government should cope best with the pressures of economic change. A strong authoritarian government may be more secure, and thus a more effective reformer, than a weak democratic government—just as a strong democracy may be more secure than a weak dictator. But one-off comparisons are unhelpful. It is better to consider a range of cases, and look for some general lessons.

Studies that do this have given democratic governments high marks for effectiveness in economic reform. A recent one edited by John Williamson, of the Institute for International Economics, looked at 13 cases of bold reform (typically, radical trade liberalisation and/or drastic changes in taxes and public spending)**. The sample included rich and poor countries, democratic and non-democratic regimes.

In four cases, the governments "would generally be classified as authoritarian" when the reforms began: Chile in 1983, Indonesia in 1982, Mexico in 1987 and South Korea in 1979. The study judged all these programmes to have worked—the changes were successfully introduced and consolidated. The case of Turkey (1980), is more complicated: a democratic government began the reforms but was overthrown by the army, which gave way to another democratic government that continued them. This programme was a success too.

Six of the governments were "unambiguously democratic": Australia in 1983, Colombia in 1989, New Zealand in 1984, Poland in 1990, Portugal in 1985 and Spain in 1982. The reforms in Poland and Spain were exceptionally far-reaching. All these programmes succeeded. In two cases, Brazil (1987) and Peru (1980), democratic governments failed to stay the course of reform, but in both countries democracy had been newly restored in difficult circumstances.

A crunchy result

There is little in that to support the view that democratic governments are worse than non-democratic ones at carrying out re-

form. It is worth noting, too, that in every case bar that of Chile, successful authoritarian reformers were dealing with problems that they or their authoritarian predecessors had helped to create; and that the most radical of the successful democratic reformers, Poland and Spain, were coping with problems inherited from non-democratic days.

So much for the view that democracy and radical economic change do not mix. What of the idea that democracy, once in place, inhibits growth? This question has been much analysed by political scientists, less so (surprisingly) by economists. On the whole, their research has been inconclusive. In some studies democracy appears to promote growth, in others to retard it; and as a rule the results are statistically insecure.

However, a recent paper by Surjit Bhalla, formerly of the World Bank, improves on the methodology of earlier work[†]. It uses an econometric technique to test the direction of causation—ie, it asks explicitly whether democracy affects growth or vice versa. It examines 90 countries for the period 1973-90, looking not just at growth, which it measures in three different ways, but also at two other measures of economic progress: falls in infant mortality, and increases in secondary-school enrolment. And it is careful

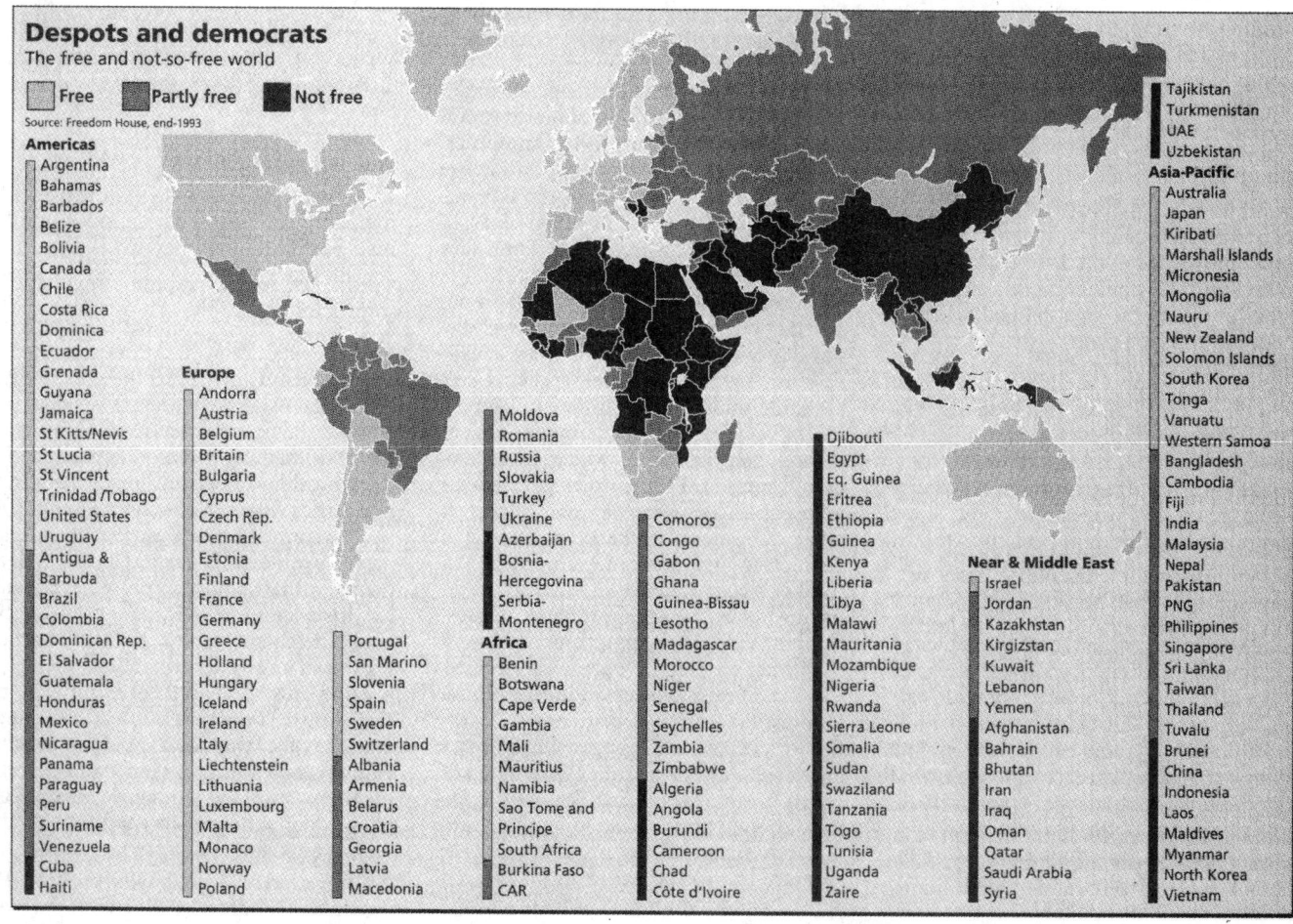

Despots and democrats
The free and not-so-free world

☐ Free   ▨ Partly free   ■ Not free

Source: Freedom House, end-1993

Americas
Argentina
Bahamas
Barbados
Belize
Bolivia
Canada
Chile
Costa Rica
Dominica
Ecuador
Grenada
Guyana
Jamaica
St Kitts/Nevis
St Lucia
St Vincent
Trinidad /Tobago
United States
Uruguay
Antigua &
Barbuda
Brazil
Colombia
Dominican Rep.
El Salvador
Guatemala
Honduras
Mexico
Nicaragua
Panama
Paraguay
Peru
Suriname
Venezuela
Cuba
Haiti

Europe
Andorra
Austria
Belgium
Britain
Bulgaria
Cyprus
Czech Rep.
Denmark
Estonia
Finland
France
Germany
Greece
Holland
Hungary
Iceland
Ireland
Italy
Liechtenstein
Lithuania
Luxembourg
Malta
Monaco
Norway
Poland

Portugal
San Marino
Slovenia
Spain
Sweden
Switzerland
Albania
Armenia
Belarus
Croatia
Georgia
Latvia
Macedonia

Moldova
Romania
Russia
Slovakia
Turkey
Ukraine
Azerbaijan
Bosnia-
Hercegovina
Serbia-
Montenegro

Africa
Benin
Botswana
Cape Verde
Gambia
Mali
Mauritius
Namibia
Sao Tome and
Principe
South Africa
Burkina Faso
CAR

Comoros
Congo
Ethiopia
Gabon
Ghana
Guinea-Bissau
Lesotho
Madagascar
Morocco
Niger
Senegal
Seychelles
Zambia
Zimbabwe
Algeria
Angola
Burundi
Cameroon
Chad
Côte d'Ivoire

Djibouti
Egypt
Eq. Guinea
Eritrea
Guinea
Kenya
Liberia
Libya
Malawi
Mauritania
Mozambique
Nigeria
Rwanda
Sierra Leone
Somalia
Sudan
Swaziland
Tanzania
Togo
Tunisia
Uganda
Zaire

Near & Middle East
Israel
Jordan
Kazakhstan
Kirgizstan
Kuwait
Lebanon
Yemen
Afghanistan
Bahrain
Bhutan
Iran
Iraq
Oman
Qatar
Saudi Arabia
Syria

Tajikistan
Turkmenistan
UAE
Uzbekistan

Asia-Pacific
Australia
Japan
Kiribati
Marshall Islands
Micronesia
Mongolia
Nauru
New Zealand
Solomon Islands
South Korea
Tonga
Vanuatu
Western Samoa
Bangladesh
Cambodia
Fiji
India
Malaysia
Nepal
Pakistan
PNG
Philippines
Singapore
Sri Lanka
Taiwan
Thailand
Tuvalu
Brunei
China
Indonesia
Laos
Maldives
Myanmar
North Korea
Vietnam

to distinguish between different sorts of freedom—an especially important point.

India, for example, has real democracy, which is one sort of political freedom. But it is much less impressive on civil rights; and, at least until recently, it imposed repressive controls on economic activity. Most firms needed government licences to start up, close down, change prices or products, sell to new customers or shift suppliers. Previous research tended to see in India an association between slow growth and freedom—even though, in important ways, India was not free. Similarly, successful East Asian economies which scored high on economic freedom but low on political freedom tended to be pigeon-holed as places where fast growth was associated with authoritarian rule. Mr Bhalla separates economic freedoms from civil and political freedoms, and measures the effect of each in turn.

First comes a finding that is no surprise: economic freedom, as measured by the extent of various price distortions, promotes growth. The next is more interesting: civil and political freedoms do the same. Ranking countries on a seven-mark scale ranging from free (America is 1) to not free (Iraq is 7), the implication is this: other things being equal, an improvement of one mark in civil and political freedom raises annual growth per head by roughly a full percentage point. On this scale, admittedly, one mark is quite a big change. Still, the effect on growth is extremely strong. It persists in many different versions of the model used by Mr Bhalla, and survives batteries of statistical tests.

How is this result to be explained? Democracies are notoriously susceptible to interest-group pressure: they favour policies, such as trade protection, that benefit the few at the expense of the many and that reduce incomes in the aggregate. Democracies also arouse, and try to meet, demands for relief from poverty and for other forms of social insurance—policies that call for taxes on the non-poor. Such arrangements, however desirable, blunt incentives for rich and poor alike to work. Democracy might thus be expected to curb output. Evidently, however, it does the opposite.

It is easy to see why economic freedom encourages growth. The clearest lesson from the collapse of communism is that, to prosper, an economy must be allowed to order itself spontaneously in the main, according to the principles of competition and voluntary exchange. The invisible hand, in other words, works better than the visible boot. The question is why political freedom adds to the economic benefits already secured by economic freedom. The answer may be that it encourages firms and people to behave as if those freedoms will endure.

For centuries it has been argued that security of property (protection from theft, legal or otherwise) is the foundation for material progress. In effect, the concept of economic freedom looks at security of property in the present, by asking whether taxes are non-confiscatory, contracts are enforced, trade is free and so on. But people also need to know that these freedoms, where they exist, will not soon disappear. Here lies the decisive advantage conferred by political freedom—meaning democracy, and the dispersion of political power that goes with it.

A benevolent dictator may do everything right in economic policy; and if he does, his economy will grow faster. But he cannot promise credibly that freedoms created by these policies will last: partly because he can suspend them at a moment's notice, and partly because when he dies or steps down he may be replaced by a non-benevolent dictator. Not, of course, that democracy offers cast-iron guarantees. Democratic governments can be overthrown, constitutions torn up. But it is plausible to believe that, over time, democracy entrenches economic freedoms, making them more stable and more credible. In this way, political freedom makes a contribution in its own right to economic growth.

Rulers and ranchers

Mancur Olson, of the University of Maryland, is a leading analyst of the economic weaknesses of democratic government. His is the definitive account of the economics of rent-seeking, free-riding, lobbying and the destructiveness of interest-group politics. Yet he also argues forcefully that democracy is far more conducive to long-term economic growth than dictatorship, even of an apparently benevolent kind[††].

Mr Olson agrees that security of property is more firmly anchored under democracy than under autocratic rule. He argues that regard for individual rights is necessary for lasting democracy, and that regard for exactly the same rights is also needed if there is to be any lasting commitment to security of property and enforcement of contracts. That is why countries tend to have democracy and security of property together, or not at all. Mr Olson then takes the argument further. Throughout history, despots have tended to take the most income possible from their subjects. Note, that did not mean taking everything, for the subjects would then have had no reason to work, leaving the ruler with nothing. A revenue-maximising autocrat taxes at a rate that is punitive rather than self-defeating. He even invests in some public goods, such as protection from outlaws, in order to encourage production and thereby improve his own income.

Such a government, therefore, is not really a "predatory state" (a term often used to describe some modern third-world dictatorships). A predator kills and moves on. Rather, a despot is a rancher. The sensible autocrat takes care of his cattle in order to maximise his yield. That is why, for all his faults, he is a lot better than no government at all.

Taking an equally unsentimental view of democracy, Mr Olson asks how far a vote-buying democratic leader would raise taxes on the whole economy in order to reward the constituencies that put him in power. The answer is: maybe a lot, but most likely less than the revenue-maximising despot would do. The reason is simple. The despot does not care about the income left over for his subjects, only about his own slice. The democratic majority cares about both—the slice taken in taxes from everybody and redistributed in its direction, and its own post-tax income. On this account, democracy is superior economically in two ways: tax proceeds are shared with at least some of the citizenry, and the incentive to grab as much as possible is muted.

Accordingly, Mr Olson and others see the centuries-long pattern of economic growth in Europe and its former colonies as intimately linked to the earlier development of democracy. After the Glorious Revolution of 1688, rights to property were more secure in Britain, with a limited monarchy and an independent judiciary, than anywhere else. Britain, not long after, was where the industrial revolution began. In the same spirit, other work has discovered a strong correlation between absolutist rule and economic stagnation in Europe's cities over the seven centuries to 1800.

All this may seem remote from the issues of political and economic reform that now confront developing countries. It is not. The claim that authoritarian government works best for development is a claim about history—but it draws mainly on evidence from one region, East Asia, over a comparatively short period. This evidence is anyway unpersuasive: East Asia may well be special, but not because it has had authoritarian rulers. Broaden the evidence, chronologically and geographically, and the claim looks weaker still. Dictatorships with wise economic policies can achieve rapid economic growth; but they are rare, and, being dictatorships, will lack the economic strengths of stable democracy. Far from inhibiting growth, democracy promotes it.

....

* "Governing the Market: Economic Theory and the Role of Government in East Asian Industrialisation". Princeton University Press, 1990

** "The Political Economy of Policy Reform". Institute for International Economics, Washington, DC, 1994

† "Free Societies, Free Markets and Social Welfare". Unpublished paper to be presented at this month's Nobel symposium on democracy, Uppsala University

†† See, eg, "Dictatorship, Democracy and Development". *American Political Science Review*, September 1993

Capitalism and Democracy*

Gabriel A. Almond

Gabriel A. Almond, professor of political science emeritus at Stanford University, is a former president of the American Political Science Association.

Joseph Schumpeter, a great economist and social scientist of the last generation, whose career was almost equally divided between Central European and American universities, and who lived close to the crises of the 1930s and '40s, published a book in 1942 under the title, *Capitalism, Socialism, and Democracy.* The book has had great influence, and can be read today with profit. It was written in the aftergloom of the great depression, during the early triumphs of Fascism and Nazism in 1940 and 1941, when the future of capitalism, socialism, and democracy all were in doubt. Schumpeter projected a future of declining capitalism, and rising socialism. He thought that democracy under socialism might be no more impaired and problematic than it was under capitalism.

He wrote a concluding chapter in

*Lecture presented at Seminar on the Market, sponsored by The Ford Foundation and the Research Institute on International Change of Columbia University, Moscow, October 29–November 2.

the second edition which appeared in 1946, and which took into account the political-economic situation at the end of the war, with the Soviet Union then astride a devastated Europe. In this last chapter he argues that we should not identify the future of socialism with that of the Soviet Union, that what we had observed and were observing in the first three decades of Soviet existence was not a necessary expression of socialism. There was a lot of Czarist Russia in the mix. If Schumpeter were writing today, I don't believe he would argue that socialism has a brighter future than capitalism. The relationship between the two has turned out to be a good deal more complex and intertwined than Schumpeter anticipated. But I am sure that he would still urge us to separate the future of socialism from that of Soviet and Eastern European Communism.

Unlike Schumpeter I do not include Socialism in my title, since its future as a distinct ideology and program of action is unclear at best. Western Marxism and the moderate socialist movements seem to have settled for social democratic solutions, for adaptations of both capitalism and democracy producing acceptable mixes of market competition, political pluralism, participation, and welfare. I deal with these modifications

of capitalism, as a consequence of the impact of democracy on capitalism in the last half century.

At the time that Adam Smith wrote *The Wealth of Nations,* the world of government, politics and the state that he knew—pre-Reform Act England, the French government of Louis XV and XVI—was riddled with special privileges, monopolies, interferences with trade. With my tongue only half way in my cheek I believe the discipline of economics may have been traumatized by this condition of political life at its birth. Typically, economists speak of the state and government instrumentally, as a kind of secondary service mechanism.

I do not believe that politics can be treated in this purely instrumental and reductive way without losing our analytic grip on the social and historical process. The economy and the polity are the main problem solving mechanisms of human society. They each have their distinctive means, and they each have their "goods" or ends. They necessarily interact with each other, and transform each other in the process. Democracy in particular generates goals and programs. You cannot give people the suffrage, and let them form organizations, run for office, and the like, without their developing all kinds of ideas as to

From *PS: Political Science and Politics,* September 1991, pp. 467-474. © 1991 by The American Political Science Association. Reprinted by permission.

how to improve things. And sometimes some of these ideas are adopted, implemented and are productive, and improve our lives, although many economists are reluctant to concede this much to the state.

My lecture deals with this interaction of politics and economics in the Western World in the course of the last couple of centuries, in the era during which capitalism and democracy emerged as the dominant problem solving institutions of modern civilization. I am going to discuss some of the theoretical and empirical literature dealing with the themes of the positive and negative interaction between capitalism and democracy. There are those who say that capitalism supports democracy, and those who say that capitalism subverts democracy. And there are those who say that democracy subverts capitalism, and those who say that it supports it.

The relation between capitalism and democracy dominates the political theory of the last two centuries. All the logically possible points of view are represented in a rich literature. It is this ambivalence and dialectic, this tension between the two major problem solving sectors of modern society—the political and the economic—that is the topic of my lecture.

Capitalism Supports Democracy

Let me begin with the argument that capitalism is positively linked with democracy, shares its values and culture, and facilitates its development. This case has been made in historical, logical, and statistical terms.

Albert Hirschman in his *Rival Views of Market Society* (1986) examines the values, manners and morals of capitalism, and their effects on the larger society and culture as these have been described by the philosophers of the 17th, 18th, and 19th centuries. He shows how the interpretation of the impact of capitalism has changed from the enlightenment view of Montesquieu, Condorcet, Adam Smith and others, who stressed the *douceur* of commerce, its "gentling," civilizing effect

on behavior and interpersonal relations, to that of the 19th and 20th century conservative and radical writers who described the culture of capitalism as crassly materialistic, destructively competitive, corrosive of morality, and hence self-destructive. This sharp almost 180-degree shift in point of view among political theorists is partly explained by the transformation from the commerce and small-scale industry of early capitalism, to the smoke blackened industrial districts, the demonic and exploitive entrepreneurs, and exploited laboring classes of the second half of the nineteenth century. Unfortunately for our purposes, Hirschman doesn't deal explicitly with the capitalism–democracy connection, but rather with culture and with manners. His argument, however, implies an early positive connection and a later negative one.

Joseph Schumpeter in *Capitalism, Socialism, and Democracy* (1942) states flatly, "History clearly confirms . . . [that] . . . modern democracy rose along with capitalism, and in causal connection with it . . . modern democracy is a product of the capitalist process." He has a whole chapter entitled "The Civilization of Capitalism," democracy being a part of that civilization. Schumpeter also makes the point that democracy was historically supportive of capitalism. He states, ". . . the bourgeoisie reshaped, and from its own point of view rationalized, the social and political structure that preceded its ascendancy. . ." (that is to say, feudalism). "The democratic method was the political tool of that reconstruction." According to Schumpeter capitalism and democracy were mutually causal historically, mutually supportive parts of a rising modern civilization, although as we shall show below, he also recognized their antagonisms.

Barrington Moore's historical investigation (1966) with its long title, *The Social Origins of Dictatorship and Democracy; Lord and Peasant in the Making of the Modern World,* argues that there have been three historical routes to industrial modernization. The first of these followed by Britain, France, and the United States, involved the subordination and transformation of the

agricultural sector by the rising commercial bourgeoisie, producing the democratic capitalism of the 19th and 20th centuries. The second route followed by Germany and Japan, where the landed aristocracy was able

---

The relation between capitalism and democracy dominates the political theory of the last two centuries.

---

to contain and dominate the rising commercial classes, produced an authoritarian and fascist version of industrial modernization, a system of capitalism encased in a feudal authoritarian framework, dominated by a military aristocracy, and an authoritarian monarchy. The third route, followed in Russia where the commercial bourgeoisie was too weak to give content and direction to the modernizing process, took the form of a revolutionary process drawing on the frustration and resources of the peasantry, and created a mobilized authoritarian Communist regime along with a state-controlled industrialized economy. Successful capitalism dominating and transforming the rural agricultural sector, according to Barrington Moore, is the creator and sustainer of the emerging democracies of the nineteenth century.

Robert A. Dahl, the leading American democratic theorist, in the new edition of his book (1990) *After the Revolution? Authority in a Good Society,* has included a new chapter entitled "Democracy and Markets." In the opening paragraph of that chapter, he says:

It is an historical fact that modern democratic institutions . . . have existed only in countries with predominantly privately owned, market-oriented economies, or capitalism if you prefer that name. It is also a fact that all "socialist" countries with predominantly state-owned centrally directed economic orders—command economies—have not enjoyed democratic governments, but have in fact been ruled by authoritarian dictatorships. It is also an historical fact that some "capitalist" countries have also been, and are, ruled by authoritarian dictatorships.

To put it more formally, it looks to be the case that market-oriented economies are necessary (in the logical sense) to democratic institutions, though they are certainly not sufficient. And it looks to be the case that state-owned centrally directed economic orders are strictly associated with authoritarian regimes, though authoritarianism definitely does not require them. We have something very much like an historical experiment, so it would appear, that leaves these conclusions in no great doubt. (Dahl 1990)

Peter Berger in his book *The Capitalist Revolution* (1986) presents four propositions on the relations between capitalism and democracy:

Capitalism is a necessary but not sufficient condition of democracy under modern conditions.

If a capitalist economy is subjected to increasing degrees of state control, a point (not precisely specifiable at this time) will be reached at which democratic governance becomes impossible.

If a socialist economy is opened up to increasing degrees of market forces, a point (not precisely specifiable at this time) will be reached at which democratic governance becomes a possibility.

If capitalist development is successful in generating economic growth from which a sizable proportion of the population benefits, pressures toward democracy are likely to appear.

This positive relationship between capitalism and democracy has also been sustained by statistical studies. The "Social Mobilization" theorists of the 1950s and 1960s which included Daniel Lerner (1958), Karl Deutsch (1961), S. M. Lipset (1959) among others, demonstrated a strong statistical association between GNP per capita and democratic political institutions. This is more than simple statistical association. There is a logic in the relation between level of economic development and democratic institutions. Level of economic development has been shown to be associated with education and literacy, exposure to mass media, and democratic psychological propensities such as subjective efficacy, participatory

aspirations and skills. In a major investigation of the social psychology of industrialization and modernization, a research team led by the sociologist Alex Inkeles (1974) interviewed several thousand workers in the modern industrial and the traditional economic sectors of six countries of differing culture. Inkeles found empathetic, efficacious, participatory and activist propensities much more frequently among the modern industrial workers, and to a much lesser extent in the traditional sector in each one of these countries regardless of cultural differences.

The historical, the logical, and the statistical evidence for this positive relation between capitalism and democracy is quite persuasive.

Capitalism Subverts Democracy

But the opposite case is also made, that capitalism subverts or undermines democracy. Already in John Stuart Mill (1848) we encounter a view of existing systems of private property as unjust, and of the free market as destructively competitive—aesthetically and morally repugnant. The case he was making was a normative rather than a political one. He wanted a less competitive society, ultimately socialist, which would still respect individuality. He advocated limitations on the inheritance of property and the improvement of the property system so that everyone shared in its benefits, the limitation of population growth, and the improvement of the quality of the labor force through the provision of high quality education for all by the state. On the eve of the emergence of the modern democratic capitalist order John Stuart Mill wanted to control the excesses of both the market economy and the majoritarian polity, by the education of consumers and producers, citizens and politicians, in the interest of producing morally improved free market and democratic orders. But in contrast to Marx, he did not thoroughly discount the possibilities of improving the capitalist and democratic order.

Marx argued that as long as capitalism and private property existed there could be no genuine democracy, that democracy under capitalism was bourgeois democracy,

which is to say not democracy at all. While it would be in the interest of the working classes to enter a coalition with the bourgeoisie in supporting this form of democracy in order

---

There is a logic in the relation between level of economic development and democratic institutions.

---

to eliminate feudalism, this would be a tactical maneuver. Capitalist democracy could only result in the increasing exploitation of the working classes. Only the elimination of capitalism and private property could result in the emancipation of the working classes and the attainment of true democracy. Once socialism was attained the basic political problems of humanity would have been solved through the elimination of classes. Under socialism there would be no distinctive democratic organization, no need for institutions to resolve conflicts, since there would be no conflicts. There is not much democratic or political theory to be found in Marx's writings. The basic reality is the mode of economic production and the consequent class structure from which other institutions follow.

For the followers of Marx up to the present day there continues to be a negative tension between capitalism, however reformed, and democracy. But the integral Marxist and Leninist rejection of the possibility of an autonomous, bourgeois democratic state has been left behind for most Western Marxists. In the thinking of Poulantzas, Offe, Bobbio, Habermas and others, the bourgeois democratic state is now viewed as a class struggle state, rather than an unambiguously bourgeois state. The working class has access to it; it can struggle for its interests, and can attain partial benefits from it. The state is now viewed as autonomous, or as relatively autonomous, and it can be reformed in a progressive direction by working class and other popular movements. The bourgeois democratic state can be moved in the direction of a socialist state by political action short of violence and institutional destruction.

Schumpeter (1942) appreciated the tension between capitalism and democracy. While he saw a causal connection between competition in the economic and the political order, he points out ". . . that there are some deviations from the principle of democracy which link up with the presence of organized capitalist interests. . . . [T]he statement is true both from the standpoint of the classical and from the standpoint of our own theory of democracy. From the first standpoint, the result reads that the means at the disposal of private interests are often used in order to thwart the will of the people. From the second standpoint, the result reads that those private means are often used in order to interfere with the working of the mechanism of competitive leadership." He refers to some countries and situations in which ". . . political life all but resolved itself into a struggle of pressure groups and in many cases practices that failed to conform to the spirit of the democratic method." But he rejects the notion that there cannot be political democracy in a capitalist society. For Schumpeter full democracy in the sense of the informed participation of all adults in the selection of political leaders and consequently the making of public policy, was an impossibility because of the number and complexity of the issues confronting modern electorates. The democracy which was realistically possible was one in which people could choose among competing leaders, and consequently exercise some direction over political decisions. This kind of democracy was possible in a capitalist society, though some of its propensities impaired its performance. Writing in the early years of World War II, when the future of democracy and of capitalism were uncertain, he leaves unresolved the questions of ". . . Whether or not democracy is one of those products of capitalism which are to die out with it. . ." or ". . . how well or ill capitalist society qualifies for the task of working the democratic method it evolved."

Non-Marxist political theorists

have contributed to this questioning of the reconcilability of capitalism and democracy. Robert A. Dahl, who makes the point that capitalism historically has been a necessary precondition of democracy, views contemporary democracy in the United States as seriously compromised, impaired by the inequality in resources among the citizens. But Dahl stresses the variety in distributive patterns, and in politico-economic relations among contemporary democracies. "The category of capitalist democracies" he writes, "includes an extraordinary variety . . . from nineteenth century, laissez faire, early industrial systems to twentieth century, highly regulated, social welfare, late or postindustrial systems. Even late twentieth century 'welfare state' orders vary all the way from the Scandinavian systems, which are redistributive, heavily taxed, comprehensive in their social security, and neocorporatist in their collective bargaining arrangements to the faintly redistributive, moderately taxed, limited social security, weak collective bargaining systems of the United States and Japan" (1989).

In *Democracy and Its Critics* (1989) Dahl argues that the normative growth of democracy to what he calls its "third transformation" (the first being the direct city-state democracy of classic times, and the second, the indirect, representative inegalitarian democracy of the contemporary world) will require democratization of the economic order. In other words, modern corporate capitalism needs to be transformed. Since government control and/or ownership of the economy would be destructive of the pluralism which is an essential requirement of democracy, his preferred solution to the problem of the mega-corporation is employee control of corporate industry. An economy so organized, according to Dahl, would improve the distribution of political resources without at the same time destroying the pluralism which democratic competition requires. To those who question the realism of Dahl's solution to the problem of inequality, he replies that history is full of surprises.

Charles E. Lindblom in his book, *Politics and Markets* (1977), concludes his comparative analysis of the

political economy of modern capitalism and socialism, with an essentially pessimistic conclusion about contemporary market-oriented democracy. He says

> We therefore come back to the corporation. It is possible that the rise of the corporation has offset or more than offset the decline of class as an instrument of indoctrination. . . . That it creates a new core of wealth and power for a newly constructed upper class, as well as an overpowering loud voice, is also reasonably clear. The executive of the large corporation is, on many counts, the contemporary counterpart to the landed gentry of an earlier era, his voice amplified by the technology of mass communication. . . . [T]he major institutional barrier to fuller democracy may therefore be the autonomy of the private corporation.

Lindblom concludes, "The large private corporation fits oddly into democratic theory and vision. Indeed it does not fit."

There is then a widely shared agreement, from the Marxists and neo-Marxists, to Schumpeter, Dahl, Lindblom, and other liberal political theorists, that modern capitalism with the dominance of the large corporation, produces a defective or an impaired form of democracy.

Democracy Subverts Capitalism

If we change our perspective now and look at the way democracy is said to affect capitalism, one of the dominant traditions of economics from Adam Smith until the present day stresses the importance for productivity and welfare of an economy that is relatively free of intervention by the state. In this doctrine of minimal government there is still a place for a framework of rules and services essential to the productive and efficient performance of the economy. In part the government has to protect the market from itself. Left to their own devices, according to Smith, businessmen were prone to corner the market in order to exact the highest possible price. And according to Smith businessmen were prone to bribe public officials in order to gain special privileges, and legal monopolies. For Smith good capitalism was competitive capitalism, and good government provided just those goods and services which the market needed to flourish, could not itself provide, or would not provide. A good government according to Adam Smith was a minimal government, providing for the national defense, and domestic order. Particularly important for the economy were the rules pertaining to commercial life such as the regulation of weights and measures, setting and enforcing building standards, providing for the protection of persons and property, and the like.

For Milton Friedman (1961, 1981), the leading contemporary advocate of the free market and free government, and of the interdependence of the two, the principal threat to the survival of capitalism and democracy is the assumption of the responsibility for welfare on the part of the modern democratic state. He lays down a set of functions appropriate to government in the positive inter-

---

. . . one of the dominant traditions of economics from Adam Smith until the present day stresses the importance for productivity and welfare of an economy that is relatively free of intervention by the state.

---

play between economy and polity, and then enumerates many of the ways in which the modern welfare, regulatory state has deviated from these criteria.

A good Friedmanesque, democratic government would be one ". . . which maintained law and order, defended property rights, served as a means whereby we could modify property rights and other rules of the economic game, adjudicated disputes about the interpretation of the rules, enforced contracts, promoted competition, provided a monetary framework, engaged in activities to counter technical monopolies and to overcome neighborhood

effects widely regarded as sufficiently important to justify government intervention, and which supplemented private charity and the private family in protecting the irresponsible, whether madman or child. . . ." Against this list of proper activities for a free government, Friedman pinpointed more than a dozen activities of contemporary democratic governments which might better be performed through the private sector, or not at all. These included setting and maintaining price supports, tariffs, import and export quotas and controls, rents, interest rates, wage rates, and the like, regulating industries and banking, radio and television, licensing professions and occupations, providing social security and medical care programs, providing public housing, national parks, guaranteeing mortgages, and much else.

Friedman concludes that this steady encroachment on the private sector has been slowly but surely converting our free government and market system into a collective monster, compromising both freedom and productivity in the outcome. The tax and expenditure revolts and regulatory rebellions of the 1980s have temporarily stemmed this trend, but the threat continues. "It is the internal threat coming from men of good intentions and good will who wish to reform us. Impatient with the slowness of persuasion and example to achieve the great social changes they envision, they are anxious to use the power of the state to achieve their ends, and confident of their own ability to do so." The threat to political and economic freedom, according to Milton Friedman and others who argue the same position, arises out of democratic politics. It may only be defeated by political action.

In the last decades a school, or rather several schools, of economists and political scientists have turned the theoretical models of economics to use in analyzing political processes. Variously called public choice theorists, rational choice theorists, or positive political theorists, and employing such models as market exchange and bargaining, rational self interest, game theory, and the like, these theorists have produced a substantial literature throwing new and often controversial light on dem-

ocratic political phenomena such as elections, decisions of political party leaders, interest group behavior, legislative and committee decisions, bureaucratic, and judicial behavior, lobbying activity, and substantive public policy areas such as constitutional arrangements, health and environment policy, regulatory policy, national security and foreign policy, and the like. Hardly a field of politics and public policy has been left untouched by this inventive and productive group of scholars.

The institutions and names with which this movement is associated in the United States include Virginia State University, the University of Virginia, the George Mason University, the University of Rochester, the University of Chicago, the California Institute of Technology, the Carnegie Mellon University, among others. And the most prominent names are those of the leaders of the two principal schools: James Buchanan, the Nobel Laureate leader of the Virginia "Public Choice" school, and William Riker, the leader of the Rochester "Positive Theory" school. Other prominent scholars associated with this work are Gary Becker of the University of Chicago, Kenneth Shepsle and Morris Fiorina of Harvard, John Ferejohn of Stanford, Charles Plott of the California Institute of Technology, and many others.

One writer summarizing the ideological bent of much of this work, but by no means all of it (William Mitchell of the University of Washington), describes it as fiscally conservative, sharing a conviction that the ". . . private economy is far more robust, efficient, and perhaps, equitable than other economies, and much more successful than political processes in efficiently allocating resources. . . ." Much of what has been produced ". . . by James Buchanan and the leaders of this school can best be described as contributions to a theory of the failure of political processes." These failures of political performance are said to be inherent properties of the democratic political process. "Inequity, inefficiency, and coercion are the most general results of democratic policy formation." In a democracy the demand for publicly provided services seems to be insatiable. It ultimately turns into a special interest, "rent seeking" society. Their remedies take the form of proposed constitutional limits on spending power and checks and balances to limit legislative majorities.

One of the most visible products of this pessimistic economic analysis of democratic politics is the book by Mancur Olson, *The Rise and Decline of Nations* (1982). He makes a strong argument for the negative democracy–capitalism connection. His thesis is that the behavior of individuals and firms in stable societies inevitably leads to the formation of dense networks of collusive, cartelistic, and lobbying organizations that make economies less efficient and dynamic and polities less governable. "The longer a society goes without an upheaval, the more powerful such organizations become and the more they slow down economic expansion. Societies in which these narrow interest groups have been destroyed, by war or revolution, for example, enjoy the greatest gains in growth." His prize cases are Britain on the one hand and Germany and Japan on the other.

> The logic of the argument implies that countries that have had democratic freedom of organization without upheaval or invasion the longest will suffer the most from growth-repressing organizations and combinations. This helps explain why Great Britain, the major nation with the longest immunity from dictatorship, invasion, and revolution, has had in this century a lower rate of growth than other large, developed democracies. Britain has precisely the powerful network of special interest organization that the argument developed here would lead us to expect in a country with its record of military security and democratic stability. The number and power of its trade unions need no description. The venerability and power of its professional associations is also striking. . . . In short, with age British society has acquired so many strong organizations and collusions that it suffers from an institutional sclerosis that slows its adaptation to changing circumstances and technologies. (Olson 1982)

By contrast, post-World War II Germany and Japan started organizationally from scratch. The organizations that led them to defeat were all

dissolved, and under the occupation inclusive organizations like the general trade union movement and general organizations of the industrial and commercial community were first formed. These inclusive organizations had more regard for the general national interest and exercised some discipline on the narrower interest organizations. And both countries in the post-war decades experienced "miracles" of economic growth under democratic conditions.

The Olson theory of the subversion of capitalism through the propensities of democratic societies to foster special interest groups has not gone without challenge. There can be little question that there is logic in his argument. But empirical research testing this pressure group hypothesis thus far has produced mixed findings. Olson has hopes that a public educated to the harmful consequences of special interests to economic growth, full employment, coherent government, equal opportunity, and social mobility will resist special interest behavior, and enact legislation imposing anti-trust, and anti-monopoly controls to mitigate and contain these threats. It is somewhat of an irony that the solution to this special interest disease of democracy, according to Olson, is a democratic state with sufficient regulatory authority to control the growth of special interest organizations.

Democracy Fosters Capitalism

My fourth theme, democracy as fostering and sustaining capitalism, is not as straightforward as the first three. Historically there can be little doubt that as the suffrage was extended in the last century, and as mass political parties developed, democratic development impinged significantly on capitalist institutions and practices. Since successful capitalism requires risk-taking entrepreneurs with access to investment capital, the democratic propensity for redistributive and regulative policy tends to reduce the incentives and the resources available for risk-taking and creativity. Thus it can be argued that propensities inevitably resulting from democratic politics, as Friedman, Olson and many others argue, tend to reduce productivity, and hence welfare.

But precisely the opposite argument can be made on the basis of the historical experience of literally all of the advanced capitalist democracies in existence. All of them without exception are now welfare states with some form and degree of social insurance, health and welfare nets, and regulatory frameworks designed to mitigate the harmful impacts and shortfalls of capitalism. Indeed, the welfare state is accepted all across the political spectrum. Controversy takes place around the edges. One might make the argument that had capitalism not been modified in this welfare direction, it is doubtful that it would have survived.

This history of the interplay between democracy and capitalism is clearly laid out in a major study involving European and American scholars, entitled *The Development of Welfare States in Western Europe and America* (Flora and Heidenheimer 1981). The book lays out the relationship between the development and spread of capitalist industry, democratization in the sense of an expanding suffrage and the emergence of trade unions and left-wing political parties, and the gradual introduction of the institutions and practices of the welfare state. The early adoption of the institutions of the welfare state in Bismarck Germany, Sweden, and Great Britain were all associated with the rise of trade unions and socialist parties in those countries. The decisions made by the upper and middle class leaders and political movements to introduce welfare measures such as accident, old age, and unemployment insurance, were strategic decisions. They were increasingly confronted by trade union movements with the capacity of bringing industrial production to a halt, and by political parties with growing parliamentary representation favoring fundamental modifications in, or the abolition of capitalism. As the calculations of the upper and middle class leaders led them to conclude that the costs of suppression exceeded the costs of concession, the various parts of the welfare state began to be put in place—accident, sickness, unemployment insurance, old age insurance, and the like. The problem of maintaining the loyalty of the working classes through two world wars resulted in additional concessions to working class demands: the filling out of the social security system, free public education to higher levels, family allowances, housing benefits, and the like.

Social conditions, historical factors, political processes and decisions produced different versions of the welfare state. In the United States, manhood suffrage came quite early, the later bargaining process emphasized free land and free education to the secondary level, an equality of opportunity version of the welfare state. The Disraeli bargain in Britain resulted in relatively early manhood suffrage and the full attainment of parliamentary government, while the Lloyd George bargain on the eve of World War I brought the beginnings of a welfare system to Britain. The Bismarck bargain in Germany produced an early welfare state, a postponement of electoral equality and parliamentary government. While there were all of these differences in historical encounters with democratization and "welfarization," the important outcome was that little more than a century after the process began all of the advanced capitalist democracies had similar versions of the welfare state, smaller in scale in the case of the United States and Japan, more substantial in Britain and the continental European countries.

We can consequently make out a strong case for the argument that democracy has been supportive of capitalism in this strategic sense. Without this welfare adaptation it is doubtful that capitalism would have survived, or rather, its survival, "unwelfarized," would have required a substantial repressive apparatus. The choice then would seem to have been between democratic welfare capitalism, and repressive undemocratic capitalism. I am inclined to believe that capitalism as such thrives more with the democratic welfare adaptation than with the repressive one. It is in that sense that we can argue that there is a clear positive impact of democracy on capitalism.

* * *

We have to recognize, in conclusion, that democracy and capitalism are both positively and negatively related, that they both support and subvert each other. My colleague, Moses Abramovitz, described this dialectic more surely than most in his presidential address to the American Economic Association in 1980, on the eve of the "Reagan Revolution." Noting the decline in productivity in the American economy during the latter 1960s and '70s, and recognizing that this decline might in part be attributable to the "tax, transfer, and regulatory" tendencies of the welfare state, he observes,

> The rationale supporting the development of our mixed economy sees it as a pragmatic compromise between the competing virtues and defects of decentralized market capitalism and encompassing socialism. Its goal is to obtain a measure of distributive justice, security, and social guidance of economic life without losing too much of the allocative efficiency and dynamism of private enterprise and market organization. And it is a pragmatic compromise in another sense. It seeks to retain for most people that measure of personal protection from the state which private property and a private job market confer, while obtaining for the disadvantaged minority of people through the state that measure of support without which their lack of property or personal endowment would amount to a denial of individual freedom and capacity to function as full members of the community. (Abramovitz, 1981)

Democratic welfare capitalism produces that reconciliation of opposing and complementary elements which makes possible the survival, even enhancement of both of these sets of institutions. It is not a static accommodation, but rather one which fluctuates over time, with capitalism being compromised by the tax-transfer-regulatory action of the state at one point, and then correcting in the direction of the reduction of the intervention of the state at another point, and with a learning process over time that may reduce the amplitude of the curves.

The case for this resolution of the capitalism-democracy quandary is made quite movingly by Jacob Viner who is quoted in the concluding paragraph of Abramovitz's paper, ". . . If . . . I nevertheless conclude that I believe that the welfare state, like old Siwash, is really worth fighting for and even dying for as compared to any rival system, it is because, despite its imperfection in theory and practice, in the aggregate it provides more promise of preserving and enlarging human freedoms, temporal prosperity, the extinction of mass misery, and the dignity of man and his moral improvement than any other social system which has previously prevailed, which prevails elsewhere today or which outside Utopia, the mind of man has been able to provide a blueprint for" (Abramovitz, 1981).

References

Abramovitz, Moses. 1981. "Welfare Quandaries and Productivity Concerns." *American Economic Review,* March.

Berger, Peter. 1986. *The Capitalist Revolution.* New York: Basic Books.

Dahl, Robert A. 1989. *Democracy and Its Critics.* New Haven: Yale University Press.

_____. 1990. *After the Revolution: Authority in a Good Society.* New Haven: Yale University Press.

Deutsch, Karl. 1961. "Social Mobilization and Political Development." *American Political Science Review,* 55 (Sept.).

Flora, Peter, and Arnold Heidenheimer. 1981. *The Development of Welfare States in Western Europe and America.* New Brunswick, NJ: Transaction Press.

Friedman, Milton. 1981. *Capitalism and Freedom.* Chicago: University of Chicago Press.

Hirschman, Albert. 1986. *Rival Views of Market Society.* New York: Viking.

Inkeles, Alex, and David Smith. 1974. *Becoming Modern: Individual Change in Six Developing Countries.* Cambridge, MA: Harvard University Press.

Lerner, Daniel. *The Passing of Traditional Society.* New York: Free Press.

Lindblom, Charles E. 1977. *Politics and Markets.* New York: Basic Books.

Lipset, Seymour M. 1959. "Some Social Requisites of Democracy." *American Political Science Review,* 53 (September).

Mill, John Stuart. 1848, 1965. *Principles of Political Economy,* 2 vols. Toronto: University of Toronto Press.

Mitchell, William. 1988. "Virginia, Rochester, and Bloomington: Twenty-Five Years of Public Choice and Political Science." *Public Choice,* 56: 101-119.

Moore, Barrington. 1966. *The Social Origins of Dictatorship and Democracy.* New York: Beacon Press.

Olson, Mancur. 1982. *The Rise and Decline of Nations.* New Haven: Yale University Press.

Schumpeter, Joseph. 1946. *Capitalism, Socialism, and Democracy.* New York: Harper.

Preserving prosperity

How can the affluent societies of the world retain their wealth, freedom and social cohesion in the face of the destructive pressures of economic globalisation? **Ralf Dahrendorf** examines the problems and suggests some tentative solutions

At its best, the first world was not a bad place in which to live and to thrive. Its member countries—the United States from Roosevelt to Kennedy, the United Kingdom for long periods of this century, those parts of the former British Empire that made up the "temperate Commonwealth", most of western Europe in the decades after the second world war—combined three virtues:

• economies that offered a decent life to many and opened up opportunities to those not yet prosperous;

• societies that had taken the step from status to contract, from unquestioned dependence to questioning individualism, without destroying the communities in which people lived;

• polities that combined respect for the rule of law with those chances of political participation, of dismissing as well as choosing governments, that we have come to call democracy.

Of course, the first world in its heyday was flawed. All of its members excluded some of their people from the benefits of their achievements, and even from opportunities. Economic inequality meant for many that the promise of citizenship remained unreal. It took decades of internal struggles—class struggles as they were correctly called at the time—and the socially levelling effects of two modern wars to assert the basic equality of all human beings in these societies.

The first world also excluded people internationally. As long as some were condemned to remain poor because they lived outside the world market altogether, prosperity everywhere remained an unjust advantage. The only answer to this, the universalisation of the benefits

of the first world—in other words, development—was, and remains, incomplete. Several large countries, notably in Asia but also in Latin America, have embarked so successfully on the road of economic development that the old first world regards them as a threat. When people speak of the third world these days, they mean, very largely, Africa; and by Africa they do not mean Tunisia or the liberated South Africa.

But development is a long and precarious process. Although it is likely that economic development, coupled with political democracy and a civil society, generates both an internal sense of tolerance and peaceful international relations, the road leading to such a state is full of dangers. Military aggression; militant *integrisme*, the French term that is preferable to "fundamentalism" because it emphasises the non-differentiation of religion and secular concerns such as the rule of law; protectionism with regard to goods as well as to people—these and other evils are all possible, and all too often real, by-products of the early phases of development, and they will be with us for generations to come.

And yet the process is necessary, not because of any hidden hand of history, but because the very values of an enlightened and civilised society demand that privilege be replaced by generalised entitlements—if not ultimately by world citizenship, then by citizenship rights for all human beings in the world.

The most important point about the first world's blessings of prosperity, civil society and democracy, however, is that, increasingly, they seem to belong to the past—or at least to be under threat.

Put at its crudest, the countries of the

first world (roughly speaking, those in the Organisation for Economic Cooperation and Development) have reached a point at which the economic opportunities of their citizens are leading to perverse choices. In order to remain competitive in growing world markets, they have to take measures that damage the cohesion of civil societies beyond repair. If they are unprepared to take such measures, they have to resort to restrictions on civil liberties and political participation that amount to a new authoritarianism, no less.

At least, this appears to be the quandary. The overriding task of the first world in the decade ahead is to square the circle of wealth creation, social cohesion and political freedom.

It would be possible to consider economy, society and polity separately; in fact, this has often been done. Economic growth is uppermost on government agendas in the OECD world, and government advisers help their employers focus on the issue to the exclusion of all others. Extreme proponents of "economism"—economics as a political ideology—not only ignore but decry social factors.

But there is a strong case for saying that in the OECD world, economic, social and political well-being are intertwined in a new and vexing manner. The reason, in one word, is globalisation. All economies are interrelated in one competitive marketplace, and everywhere the entire economy is engaged in the cruel games played on that stage.

Of course, globalisation is, so far, by no means total. Whole economies, including that of China, are more national than

5. COMPARATIVE POLITICS: The Turn Toward the Market

global. Economic regions are forming to provide common markets or free trade areas. Within countries, important activities, like the provision of health services or of nursery and primary education (if not education in general), seem removed from global competition. But none of this is to deny the force of globalisation. There is no getting away from it: the effect of globalisation is felt in all areas of social life.

Why should globalisation have happened at all, and why now? The obvious answers are probably the best. Whether the end of the cold war is cause or effect may be a moot question; certainly the Soviet bloc countries were economically no longer viable. One reason was that the concept of country, or nation, lost a good part of its economic meaning. This, in turn, was a result of the emergence of transnational entities that found it surprisingly easy to combine a degree of adjustment to local needs with the advancement of worldwide strategic planning, direction and profit-making.

Add to this the two related "revolutions" of information technology and financial markets, and an economic scene emerges the likes of which the world has never seen before. Not only in terms of movements of money, but also in terms of services (like booking airplane tickets), and in the end even in terms of production, conventional physical boundaries begin to lose all meaning.

Globalisation does not mean a homogenisation of economic cultures. There has never been just one economic culture, even among the market economies. We have long sensed that Japan is different from America, and Germany from the UK. The differences are quite profound, even if they are badly understood. The rest of the world keeps on pressing Japan to open up its markets when one cause of their inaccessibility is people's ingrained tastes and the Japanese language. Germany and the UK speak much the same language of economic policy, yet the textbook capitalism of the UK and Germany's textbook corporatism create very different attitudes.

Such cultural differences will not disappear. To what extent they will in future be national may be an open question. There is a certain cultural plausibility, after all, to the regions that are beginning to form, those of Europe, of the Americas, and of east and south-east Asia.

This said, the global marketplace requires some of the same virtues from all. To use the fashionable word, economic actors need, above all, flexibility. Flexibility means, in the first instance, the removal of rigidities. Deregulation and less government interference gener-

ally help create flexibility; many would add a lighter burden of taxation on companies and individuals. Flexibility has increasingly come to signify the loosening of the constraints of the labour market. Hiring and firing become easier; wages can move downwards as well as upwards; there is more and more part-time and limited-term employment; workers must be expected to change jobs, change employers, change locations of employment. Flexibility also means the readiness of all to accept technological changes and respond to them quickly. In marketing terms, flexibility is the ability to move in wherever an opportunity offers itself, and also to move out when opportunities close. The story is familiar enough, as is its accompanying language of structural adjustment, efficiency gains, competitiveness and seemingly unending increases in productivity.

Yet choices remain. One is that between a low-pay and a high-skill economy. Low-pay economies find their place on the world market by undercutting others. Their products are cheaper, though their workers are also poorer. Some say that this is the only road to success, but the evidence is that high skills can also create a competitive advantage. This is not just the case because by high skills, and only by high skills, the frontiers of technology are advanced, but also because, despite computerisation, certain quality products and product qualities require a skill input. Indeed, there even comes a point at which one highly skilled person is cheaper than five low-paid ones who produce the same effect. It seems to be the case that the US moves in the direction of low pay, whereas Japan opts for high skill; the UK prefers low pay and Germany high skill.

Another choice, related to the first, is harder to describe precisely. This is the choice between a low-tax/high-profit economy and a high-tax/low-profit economy. Crucially, the difference can be investment-neutral in the sense that the funds in question are distributed differently between, say, shareholders and workers, with investment held constant. In practice, the signs are that the low-profit route makes long-term investment more probable than the low-taxation route. However, modes of investment will vary; the low-profit route is likely to involve a greater role for banks and a lesser one for the stock market, and vice versa. In practice, the Anglo-American economies are on the side of low taxes and high distributed profits, and Japan and continental Europe on the other.

Still on choices, one other point needs to be reiterated in connection with incomplete globalisation. Despite the

enormous force of the global marketplace, there is and always will be privileged access to markets. Even without explicit protectionism, the Japan phenomenon exists everywhere to a greater or lesser extent. People will "buy American" in the US, "buy German" in Germany, and even "buy British" in the UK. Regional trade arrangements are about extending these privileged markets.

None of this should detract from the main point at issue, however. The options alluded to here are minor variations on the major theme of globalisation. By choosing one or the other variant, companies and countries can take the edge off certain effects or give additional edge to others; but they cannot opt out of the global marketplace.

Globalisation threatens civil society in a variety of consequential ways. Civil society describes the associations in which we conduct our lives, and which owe their existence to our needs and initiatives rather than to the state. Some of these associations are highly deliberate and sometimes short-lived, like sports clubs or political parties. Others have a very long life, like churches or universities. Still others are the places in which we work and live—enterprises, local communities. The family is an element of civil society. The criss-crossing network of such associations makes up the reality of civil society. It is a precious reality, far from universal, itself the result of a long civilising process; yet it is often threatened, by authoritarian rulers or by the forces of globalisation.

The social effects of economic responses to the challenges of globalisation have become the subject of public and scholarly attention, especially in the US. This is no accident. North America is the home of modern civil society, where threats to its strength are most acutely felt. It is little consolation that America is not alone in this predicament. The following sketchy catalogue of pressures on civil society draws from European as much as American experience, and is at least in part applicable to other OECD countries as well.

Economic globalisation appears to be associated with new kinds of social exclusion. For one thing, income inequalities have grown. Some regard all inequalities as incompatible with a decent civil society: this is not my view. Inequality can be a source of hope and progress in an environment that is sufficiently open to enable people to make good and improve their life chances by their own efforts. The new inequality, however, is of a different kind; it would be better described as inequalisation, the opposite of levelling, building paths to the top for some and digging holes for others, creating cleavages, splitting. The income of the top 20 per cent is rising significantly, whereas the bottom 40 per cent see their earnings decline. Such a divergence of the life chances of large social groups is incompatible with civil society.

The process is aggravated by the fact that a smaller but significant set seems to have fallen through the net of citizenship altogether. The concept and the phenomenon of the underclass is much discussed. Not everybody likes the term, which is clearly misleading if one considers it in terms of class theory. The socially excluded are not a class; they are at most a category of people who have many different life stories. Though some of them manage to get out of the predicament, many are in a position in which they have lost touch with the "official" world, with the labour market, the political community, the wider society. Five per cent? Ten per cent? Figures vary, but most OECD countries now have in their midst would-be citizens who are non-citizens.

Many of them are not just economically excluded; they are also excluded on other grounds, as "strangers" by virtue of race, nationality, religion, or whatever distinguishing marks are chosen to provide excuses for discrimination, xenophobia, often violence. Declining social groups are the breeding ground for such sentiments. Borders, including social boundaries, are always particularly noticeable for those closest to them. A wave of "ethnic cleansing" threatens to engulf us all.

The new inequality—the increasing divergence of those near the top and those near the bottom—takes us back to the low pay-high skill option. Those whose skills are needed are paid a good salary, but many who had a reasonable wage or salary in the past have now sunk to a miserable and often irregular real income. Nor is there any evident route back to the upward slope. Indeed, some are simply not needed. The economy can grow without their contribution. Whichever way you look at them, they are a cost to the rest, not a benefit.

Milder, though if anything more acutely felt, versions of the experience have now hit the middle classes. The latest wave of efficiency gains has meant, especially for large companies, making office workers redundant even in middle management. Such trends are part of a fundamental change in the world of work. No one would argue that there is not enough work to be done, but work at decent rates of pay is increasingly hard to come by. It is a privilege, not a realistic aspiration for all. Manufacturing and

many services are following agriculture into a productivity revolution in which half or fewer of those employed in the past can produce twice as much output or more. What remains is a strange assortment of ill-paid personal-service jobs, numerous forms of hidden unemployment—some called "education", others "self-employment"—and, in Europe, long-term unemployment for at least 5, and probably before long 10, per cent of the population of working age.

Poverty and unemployment threaten the very fabric of civil societies. Civil society requires opportunities of participation which in the OECD societies (if not universally) are provided by work and a decent minimum standard of living. Once these are lost by a growing number, civil society goes with them.

Let me move on to another set of social issues associated with economic globalisation. Flexibility may be the other side of rigidity, but it is the reverse of stability and security as well. One may fairly debate the extent to which stability and security are preconditions of civil society. Both geographical immobility and welfare state security may have gone too far in parts of Europe in the 1960s and 1970s. The American experience of the past shows that effective communities can be created despite high mobility and low welfare provision. But the economic response to globalisation is intrinsically inimical to both stability and security. Uprooting people becomes a condition of efficiency and competitiveness; the "get on your bike and look for work" mentality rules. In addition, the dismantling of the welfare state is on the agenda everywhere.

The dual effect of all this is the destruction of important features of community life and a growing sense of personal insecurity for many. Inner cities tell a shocking part of the story, aggravated by the tendency to erect green-field shopping centres at the expense of high streets and market squares. Limited-term contracts—like part-time work—are fine for a while, notably for the young and the able-bodied and perhaps for child-bearing women; but discovering at the age of 55 and sometimes earlier that you are no longer needed is enough to turn many into "grey panthers".

Add to such phenomena the return of social Darwinism under the pressures of globalisation, and the concoction becomes even more lethal. At times one detects strange similarities, at least in Europe, between the end of the 19th and the end of the 20th centuries. Then, as now, people had been through a period of rampant individualism. Individuals were

set against each other in fierce competition and the strongest prevailed, or rather those who prevailed were described as the strongest, whatever qualities had led them to their success. Then, as now, there was a reaction. Around 1900, it was called collectivism. Today, the new vogue is called communitarianism.

Perhaps the most serious effect of the values that go with flexibility, efficiency and productivity, with competitiveness and profitability, is the destruction of public services. The prevailing carrot-and-stick philosophy has overlooked and then attacked those other motives that lead people to do things because they are right, or even because people have a sense of duty, a commitment. Introducing pseudo-economic motives into public spaces robs them of their essential quality. A national health service, universal public education, basic income guarantees under whatever name become victims of an economism running amok. Small wonder that commuter transport, or environmental protection, or public safety suffer in the process.

Why is there no massive movement to defend civil society? Where is the 20th-century equivalent of the labour movement of the late 19th century? It does not, and it will not, exist. For reasons that antedate the challenges of globalisation, individualisation has transformed not just civil society, but social conflicts too. Many people may suffer the same fate, but there is no unified and unifying explanation of their suffering, no enemy that can be fought and forced to give way. More importantly, and worse still, the truly disadvantaged and those who fear to slide into their condition do not represent a new productive force, nor even a force to be reckoned with at present. The rich can get richer without them; governments can even get re-elected without their votes; and GNP can rise and rise and rise.

Individualisation means that people have no sense of belonging, no sense of commitment, and therefore no reason to observe the law of the values behind it. If there are no jobs, why not smoke pot, steal cars to go on joy rides, mug old women, beat up rival gangs and, if need be, kill? It is hard to dispute the observation that social disintegration has become associated with a degree of active disorder. Young men, increasingly young women too, and many who are not so young, see no reason to abide by allegedly prevailing rules that for them are the rules of others. They opt out of a society that has pushed them to the margin already. They become a threat. Those who can afford it pay for their protection. Those who cannot afford protection become victims. A sense that something has gone badly wrong is spreading, a sense of anomie or lawless and deep insecurity.

The condition of global competitiveness coupled with social disintegration is not favourable to the constitution of liberty. Freedom and confidence go well together—confidence in oneself, in the opportunities offered by one's environment, and in the ability of the community in which one lives to guarantee certain basic rules, the rule of law. When confidence crumbles, freedom soon turns into a more primordial condition, the war of all against all. People do not like the prospect, especially if they once were citizens. They look for a way out, for authority.

Again, it is important to turn dramatic and metaphorical language into precise analysis. One obvious aspect of globalisation is that the OECD countries are no longer alone in the world. There are new players, which are not yet and perhaps never will be OECD members, notably in Asia. From little more than 5 per cent of world exports even in 1980, the Asian tigers and China moved up to nearly 15 per cent by 1994; since the mid-1980s the GNP of these countries has been growing at almost three times the rate of the OECD countries.

More importantly, the new Asian economies, or at least their political spokesmen, show no sign of emulating European ways. *The Asia That Can Say No* is the title of a book by Malaysian prime minister Mahathir Mohammed, which sets out a "policy to combat Europe and America". His thesis is simple—that Asia can compete with anyone in world markets without abandoning its values. Social cohesion will remain the moral basis of life, and will not interfere with economic growth. Indeed, such values may contribute to growth. And how are the dreaded western values supposed to be kept out? By strong government, is the answer. Law-abiding citizens who assiduously attend to their own affairs and otherwise live inoffensive private lives need not fear the wrath of their leaders. But those who criticise government for its unaccountable power, those who use their freedom of speech to expose nepotism, those who dare put up alternative candidates at elections, are in trouble. The limits of civic freedom are tightly drawn.

Is this, then, the alternative with which modern societies are faced: economic growth and political freedom without social cohesion—or economic growth and social cohesion without political freedom? Is there, after all, an alternative to the western model, equally viable, and more attractive to some, though unac-

ceptable to others? More and more people in the OECD world think so. Many businessmen like the Asian model, and conservative politicians from Margaret Thatcher to Silvio Berlusconi follow suit. Asian values have become the new temptation, and political authoritarianism with them. Economic progress can be combined with social stability and conservative values, the argument goes.

The story is not as new as it sounds. Under different names it has accompanied economic development for over a century. After all, was not imperial Germany a case of the combination of the industrial revolution with an authoritarian regime? For countries that embrace modern economic ways before their societies have become civil and their polities democratic, the temptation of authoritarianism is great indeed. In the early stages, the creation of a market economy invariably requires sacrifices from the people subjected to it. It requires what is called deferred gratification, or in economic terms savings—that is, investment before consumption. People have to work hard for low wages and tolerate miserable working and living conditions before their countries turn the corner and join the developed world.

Such sacrifices are rarely, if ever, made voluntarily. It is hard to think of an example from western history where ascetic values were not reinforced by strong secular powers. But for the most part, the combination did not last. Capitalism itself changed, to be sure, from saving to spending and on to borrowing. As it progressed, however, society and politics also changed. Increasingly, people demanded a share of the wealth they produced; they also wanted to be masters of their own lives. They wanted to travel and watch television and choose their own neighbours. They wanted to have a say in their affairs, a vote, the right to form associations, the possibility to tell a government to go away. Civil society and political liberty followed economic development if they did not precede it.

But do they now? There are signs that Japan will go down the western route, which is one reason Asian leaders criticise it so much. But once again there is no inexorable march of history. It is possible that a new Asian—essentially Chinese—balance will be found that combines world competitiveness in economic terms with a social cohesion that is traditional rather than civil, and with authoritarian political regimes. It is also possible that the example will affect European leaders and voters, and that a growing number will wish to take a similar route.

The temptations of such authoritarianism are considerable. They are likely to arise in many policy areas. For a start,

integrating the young into society is no longer easy. Many young people begin to drift and to embrace unsocial behaviour. People want to see them disciplined. Some kind of national service is only a beginning. Someone should be able to tell them what to do, people say, and to punish them if they do not obey. Punishment is also the main demand of those who speak incessantly about law and order. The police should be given greater powers. Life in prisons should be really hard. The death penalty needs to be reintroduced.

The welfare state needs to be reformed, which cannot be done without hardship. But such hardship, people think, should hit first the scroungers who live on other people's money without contributing themselves. If people do not want to work, they must be made to do so, or not get anything. Parents who do not look after their children must, if necessary, be forced to do so. Then there is the invasion of foreigners. Somehow this mess has to be sorted out again, and England returned to the English, Germany to the Germans, France to the French...

It would be only too easy to go on. Nor are these the most extreme demands for change. One could probably quote a respectable academic author to give reasons for every one of them. They all add up to the demand for a regime that is less tolerant, one that enforces values at the risk of violating civil rights, and one that cannot simply be removed by an electoral misfortune.

It is not easy to assess the strength of authoritarian sentiments of this kind in the OECD world. Not everything said by a businessman or a taxi driver in a moment of exasperation amounts to demands for a regime change. Some suspect that law and order will dominate the political agenda to such an extent that perpetrators are bound to face harsher treatment. It would not be surprising to see the death penalty reintroduced in countries that abolished it for good reasons. Certainly, in the context of a widespread lack of confidence in traditional political parties and leaders, adjustment to global competitiveness, with its economic cost for many and the pains attendant on social disintegration, tests the ability of democracies to promote change without violence and without violation of the rule of law.

While we wonder about risks, we must not forget to think about solutions. The point of this argument is now clear. We want prosperity for all, and that means acceptance of the needs of competitiveness in global markets. We want civil societies that hold together and provide the basis of an active and civilised life for all citizens. We want the rule of law and political institutions that allow change as well as critical discourse and the exploration of new horizons. The three desires are not automatically compatible. So what can be done to preserve a civilised balance of wealth creation, social cohesion and political freedom?

Whoever claims to have the answer to every question answers none: viable answers are bound to look woefully inadequate. The six suggestions below all fall into this category. They are a beginning, no more.

First, we have to change the language of public economics. It is remarkable how unquestioningly we have all adopted economism in public discourse while leading economists have moved away from it. For governments, to say nothing of international organisations, GNP growth is still the fetish—although they are sometimes surprised when such growth is not accompanied by jobs or a "feel-good factor". Yet welfare has long been a concept used by economists; and it is clear that wealth and well-being are more than *per capita* GNP. Governments and international organisations should be encouraged to add certain other information every time they produce GNP figures, information about trends in inequality, about measurable opportunities for people, and about human rights and liberties. A proper wealth audit should take the place of a single simple and often misleading figure.

Second, the nature of work is changing. A career for life will be the exception rather than the model. Over a lifetime, people will be in and out of work, employed full-time and part-time, in training and retraining. But this can work only if everyone has, at an early stage, gained some experience of the labour market. The new world of work makes it imperative that proper provision be made for young people to pass through a phase of vocational training, closely related to real jobs, that ends up in a period of regular employment. Education linked to employment at the critical age provides a basis of experience and of motivation that can sustain people through a lifetime of changes. Conversely, if the early opportunity to encounter the uses of education and the constraints of the labour market is missed, much if not all is lost.

Third, the truly disadvantaged—the underclass—present an almost unmanageable problem. Clearly, just offering opportunities to those who have fallen through the net is not enough. People will not take such chances without much more inducement. It is unpopular to speak of motivation as an obstacle to the return of some of the truly disadvantaged to the labour market; yet it is a fact that

many have become indolent and accustomed to a life at the margin. Everything that can be done to include the excluded must be done. Yet the more critical task is to cut the supply routes to tomorrow's underclass. We may not be able to do enough for those already excluded, but we must do enough to prevent another generation from having the same dismal experience. In part, vocational training for all may do the trick. Possibly some form of generalised social service would aid the integration of all into the values of a changing society. Community building through housing and the creation of public spaces might be useful. Simply turning public attention from the remedial to the prospective, from helping today's underclass to preventing the emergence of tomorrow's, would itself help.

Fourth, globalisation means centralisation. It individualises and centralises at the same time. Intermediate agencies and instances—indeed civil society—are to some extent obstacles to straight globalisation. There is a sense in which competitiveness in world markets helps destroy communities. But this does not have to be the case. It is possible to counteract the simultaneous pressures towards individualisation and centralisation by a new emphasis on local power. The word "local" is deliberately chosen. Nations within nations—like Wales, or Quebec, or Catalonia—do not have the same effect. They may contribute to a general sense of belonging, but as a principle of social and political organisation they divide and produce unhelpful rigidities. Local communities, on the other hand, can provide a practical basis for vocational training, for small and medium-sized businesses, for personal involvement and participation, for strengthening the public domain—in short, for civil society—without detracting from economic imperatives. As always, there is no general blueprint for sustaining local communities, but some form of political identity, from revenue-raising powers to elected mayors, undoubtedly helps.

Fifth, local power is but one factor in the wider concept of stakeholder economy. Some economists, notably in the US, do not like the concept. They think that shareholders are the only stakeholders and that the actions of shareholders keep businesses on the straight and narrow. But the point about stakeholders is that (contrary to shareholders) they cannot put their interest in companies up for sale. The workforce, the local community and also banks and even suppliers and buyers are, as it were, stuck with the companies to which they are committed. This can be regarded as an undesirable rigidity only in an inhuman world in which it

does not matter whether firms are bought or sold, taken over, merged, extended, reduced, or closed as long as the shareholders get a maximum yield for their investment. In truth, it does matter. What is more, competitiveness is not increased by lack of commitment, especially if companies choose to go down the high-skill rather than the low-pay route. Reliability and predictability have their own value in business relations across the globe. Recognition and involvement of stakeholders is the practical answer. This can be brought about in many ways, from works councils for employees to the involvement of banks in investment decisions, from business participation in school boards to the activity of local chambers of commerce.

Sixth, there is the role of governments. Acceptance of the fact that in the global marketplace the actors are transnational companies, and a preference for the creative chaos of civil society, seem to leave governments out. Yet they clearly are not out of the picture. Nor are they simply the guardians of the rules of the game, as some liberal theorists want it. At the very least, governments set the tone for the economy and for society more generally.

Beyond that, governments have a special responsibility for the public domain. Public services require by definition government involvement in funding and administration. Much depends on how such involvement is expressed, both in terms of the value placed on service as a human activity and in terms of the organisation of public services. It is quite possible that some OECD countries have gone further in using the public service model than they can afford, or even than is good for the quality of service. It is also possible that, in reacting to the experience, some have introduced so-called business values into the public sphere to a point at which both the intended service and the general readiness for commitment suffer. A new balance needs to be found. Health care is quite likely to provide the main example, given its importance for individuals, its cost, and its location on the borderline of global constraints and local or even national opportunities.

This list leaves out many matters that need consideration. Above all, it leaves undecided the critical question of the institutional—one might almost say geopolitical—response to the challenges of globalisation. Regional blocs of some sort may well be where the world is heading. But if we are talking about prosperity for all, civil society everywhere, and political freedom wherever people live, in the end we are not concerned with privileged regions but with one world and its appropriate institutions.

Cyberspace: Why Nations Could Fear the Internet

Michael Clough

Michael Clough is a senior fellow at the Council on Foreign Relations.

NEW YORK

The first shots in what could prove to be the most significant battle of the new global era are being fired: Who controls the emerging international information highway? The struggle pits government officials intent on preserving national authority against "netizens" of an emerging cyber/civil society that refuses to recognize international boundaries. One of the first major battlegrounds is almost certain to be China.

Earlier this month, the Chinese State Council authorized the Xinhua News Agency, the government's mouthpiece, to supervise the activities of all foreign news agencies selling economic information in China. Shortly thereafter, one senior Chinese official warned that outside information services would be more tightly regulated to protect Chinese secrets, privacy and property rights. It was also reported that the State Council was restricting the number of Internet providers and ordering existing providers to stop processing new-user registrations.

Beijing's actions should not be surprising. Despite dramatic economic reforms that have enlarged its playing field for Chinese entrepreneurs and international investors, China is the world's most stubborn defender of state control over civil society—at a time when the Internet is fast becoming global civil society's chief weapon.

Global civil society consists of two sectors: the private economic, which is dominated by large and increasingly stateless corporations and worldwide investors, and the independent, which is composed of non-governmental organizations, polit-ical movements and transnational ethnic groups. In the old world order, both sectors were heavily dependent on the whims and will of national governments.

During the last decade, global civil society has grown exponentially. Two developments—the end of the Cold War and a general crisis of confidence in national governments around the world—created an opportunity for both the corporate and independent sectors to expand. But neither would have grown as rapidly without the communications revolution. For example, the international investment funds and global corporate management and production structures that now exist would have been inconceivable without the advent of computers, faxes and high-speed data transmission. These same technologies enabled human rights activists, women groups and other independent groups to form alliances across national borders.

Both the private and independent sectors have quickly found ways to use the Internet to advance their global interests—and some national governments are beginning to feel threatened by their success. For China, the immediate causes of concern are twofold. The first, and probably foremost, fear in the minds of senior Chinese Communist Party members is that the Internet will weaken their political authority at home and help their opponents attract international support. They are not being paranoid about this. Many experts believe that the fax machine was integral to successful efforts to mobilize international opposition to Beijing following the Tian An Men massacre in 1989. The Internet, which didn't arrive in China until 1994, is a much more effective means of communication.

Predictably, human rights groups have begun to use the Internet to campaign for more freedom in China.

- The Human Rights Web (www.traveller.com/hrweb) organized e-mail to free dissident Harry Wu from Chinese detention and to protest the imprisonment of democratic activist Wei Jingsheng.
- The Swedish branch of Save the Children recently created a Web page (childhouse.uio.no) to encourage protests against conditions in Chinese orphanages.
- The Free Tibet Home Page (www.many-media.com/tibet) provides support for Tibet's struggle for independence from China.

Chinese students and other emigres have established an impressive presence on the Web outside China, including a volunteer-run news electronic service, the China News Digest, that now has its own Web page (www.cnd.org) and more than 35,000 e-mail subscribers. As Chinese access to the Internet grows, the ability of individuals and groups in China to read alternative news sources and develop connections with counterparts overseas will inevitably expand. As Beijing well understands, in the new global era, information and connections (power) grow out of the barrel of a modem.

The Chinese government is anxious about the private sector's use of the information highway for different reasons. In today's world, where capital can move from one locale to another in a key stroke, daily events can affect national economic prospects. Bad news can ravage a currency or dry up financing for a major development project. Censoring such news is a means to exert national control over the economy.

The problem China's rulers face, however, is that the country's economic future largely depends upon its ability to attract foreign capital and compete in global markets, both of which will require a rapid upgrade of its national informa-

 From the *Los Angeles Times,* February 4, 1996, pp. M1, M6.

tion infrastructure. But, once that infrastructure is in place, it will be difficult to prevent civil society from making use of it. Moreover, if the government were to attempt to impede the spread of computers and telecommunications, it would create tremendous resentment in a population eager to enter the computer age.

The challenge, then, for Chinese officials is to find ways to move into cyberfuture without losing their ability to control society. Their strategy, so far, is to develop their own Internet service provider—a sort of nationalized America Online. Toward this end, the China Internet Corp., based in Hong Kong, was established last fall. Billed as a "no-sex, no sedition" provider, it would act as a gatekeeper to outside information and enable the government (represented by Xinhua) to capture a hefty share of the profits that would be made by providing online services to China's potentially enormous market. By monopolizing control over Internet service in China, the bureaucrats in Beijing would also acquire a valuable bargaining chip in their dealings with other major international news and Internet providers. They could ask outside services to restrict their news about China in return for access to the Chinese market.

But can China really control its slice of cyberspace? Most analysts doubt it. The government lacks the technical know-how or manpower necessary to defeat determined cyberdemocrats. Moreover, in China, as in other parts of the world, control over economic development is devolving into the hands of local and provincial leaders—and they are likely to resist attempts by Beijing to cut them out of the potentially lucrative Internet game.

While China's efforts to control the information highway are heavy-handed, other governments are moving in similar directions. Speaking at the launch of a Malaysian online service, prime Minister Mahathir Mohamad warned that unlimited access to the Internet could have a negative impact on society unless people were a "moral fortress" to withstand undesirable information. Efforts by the German government and the U.S. Congress to keep pornography off the Internet are much more targeted, but the basic clash of principles—freedom of information versus state authority—are the same.

If governments augment their efforts to regulate the Internet, the "netizens" of the independent sector are likely to respond by launching a series of cyber insurrections. The practice of "spamming," punishing users who violate the norms of cybersociety by swamping their Internet service provider with e-mail, is just one example of how electronic guerrilla war could be waged.

The outcome of this struggle may ultimately depend on which side is able to gain the support of the private sector.

While the corporate community is intellectually hostile to government, many businesses will come under pressure to align themselves with governments. For example, most of the emerging information giants, including AT&T, Microsoft and Oracle, have signed commercial agreements with China. Over time, it is likely that Beijing and other governments with an interest in filtering cyberspace will make such agreements contingent on a company's willingness to help curb the independent sector. In addition, some transnational companies such as Shell Oil, now a major target of Internet activists because of its failure to prevent the execution of Nigerian writer and activist Ken Daro-Wiya, have their own reasons to want to limit cyberactivism.

Still, the private sector, especially the growing international financial community, has a major stake in ensuring the free flow of information. Many analysts believe that the peso crisis, which cost global investors billions of dollars, was partly caused by the Mexican government's manipulation of information about the state of the Mexican economy. Over the long run, moreover, as China's decision to focus on financial news indicates, the private sector is likely to be as much of a target as the independent sector.

In short, despite their differences, both sectors of civil society have a shared interest in preserving the freedom of cyberspace.

Communal Conflicts
and Global Security

"Progress toward the objective of a more pluralist world system requires that the international community accept a common obligation to protect collective rights within such an emergent system... The counterpart...is the obligation not to impose cultural standards or political agendas on other peoples. This applies with special force to situations in which the international community supports the establishment of new states as a way of resolving conflicts within multiethnic societies, as in the former Yugoslavia."

TED ROBERT GURR

TED ROBERT GURR *is Distinguished University Professor of government and politics at the University of Maryland and distinguished scholar at the university's Center for International Development and Conflict Management. He has written or edited more than a dozen books, including the award-winning* Why Men Rebel *(Princeton: Princeton University Press, 1970).*

Since the end of the cold war, conflicts between communal groups and states have been recognized as the major challenges to domestic and international security in most parts of the world. Minority peoples also are now the principal victims of gross human rights violations. In 1993 more than 25 million refugees were fleeing from communal conflicts, including 3 percent of the population of sub-Saharan Africa. Communal conflict has devastated the former Yugoslavia and East-Central Africa, and threatens the stability of most of the former republics of the Soviet Union. This century's longest conflicts are still being fought over ethnonational issues in the Middle East and Southeast Asia. Communal conflict is also ascen-

dant in the West: ethnic tensions and inequalities drive the most divisive conflicts in the United States in the 1990s, and Quebec is edging toward secession from Canada. Virtually every country in western Europe is beset by growing public antagonism toward immigrant groups of third world origin.

Before now, there was no firm basis for generalizing about the nature of communal conflicts beyond the groups or region examined in specific case studies. However, the Minorities at Risk project, an ongoing study of the status, demands, and conflicts of virtually all politically active communal groups throughout the world during the 1980s and 1990s, has found that some generalizations can be made.[1]

The 292 communal groups that this study examines differ widely in their defining traits, political status, and aspirations. Many of the comparisons that follow distinguish between national peoples and minority peoples. National peoples are regionally concentrated groups that have lost their autonomy to expansionist states but still preserve culturally distinct features and desire some degree of political separation. Minority peoples, by contrast, have a defined socioeconomic or political status within a larger society—based on some combination of their ethnicity, immigrant origin, economic roles, and religion—and are concerned about protecting or improving that status. The table on page 257 makes distinctions between these two general types.

Global analysis suggests answers to 11 general questions about politically active communal groups.

[1]This article is a revision of chapter 11 in Ted Robert Gurr, with Barbara Harff, Monty G. Marshall, and James R. Scarritt, *Minorities at Risk: A Global View of Ethnopolitical Conflicts* (Washington, D.C.: United States Institute of Peace Press, 1993). It incorporates updated information from the 1990s phase of the Minorities at Risk project, funded by the National Science Foundation, the United States Institute of Peace, and the Korea Foundation.

Types of Politically Active Communal Groups

National Peoples:

Ethnonationalists — Large, regionally concentrated peoples with a history of organized political autonomy who have pursued separatist objectives at some time during the last 50 years.

Indigenous peoples — Conquered descendants of the original inhabitants of a region who typically live in peripheral regions, practice subsistence agriculture or herding, and have cultures sharply distinct from dominant groups.

Minority Peoples:

Ethnoclasses — Ethnically or culturally distinct peoples, usually descended from slaves or immigrants, with special economic roles, usually of low status.

Militant sects — Communal groups whose political status and activities are centered on the defense of their religious beliefs.

Communal contenders — Culturally distinct peoples, tribes, or clans in heterogeneous societies who hold or seek a share in state power.

---

1. What proportion of the world's population identifies with politically assertive communal groups? Where are they most numerous?

In 1994 about one-sixth the global population (989 million people) belonged to 292 groups whose members either have experienced systematic discrimination or have taken political action to assert their collective interests against the states that claim to govern them. Not everyone in each group agrees about their common identities and interests; most minorities are divided by crosscutting loyalties to different clans, localities, classes, or political movements. Therefore the aggregate numbers represent the outer bounds of the populations that might be mobilized for collective action on behalf of communal interests. Shared adversity and conflict with dominant groups almost invariably sharpen the sense of common interest and build support for political action.

Of the world's 190 countries, 120 have politically significant minorities.[2] The table on page 258 shows that sub-Saharan Africa has the greatest concentration of minorities at risk—81 groups whose people constitute more than 50 percent of the regional population. Before the breakup of the Soviet Union and Yugoslavia, eastern Europe had the second largest percentage of minorities at 35 percent. However, while the number of politically salient minorities in the region has nearly

doubled, from 32 to 59, they comprise only 14 percent of the region's total population. Asia, Latin America, and the Western democracies have had the smallest proportions, between 11 percent and 13 percent each.

2. Which communal minorities in which world regions are most seriously disadvantaged?

Ethnoclasses, such as Maghrebins in France, people of color in the Americas, and immigrant Chinese communities in Asian countries, experience on average greater political and economic inequalities and discrimination than other groups. Indigenous peoples face disadvantages nearly as great, and are threatened by severe ecological pressures on their traditional lands and resources as well. Ethnonationalists and communal contenders are less likely to be economically disadvantaged than other types of groups, but they usually face substantial political restrictions, often because their political aspirations are seen as a threat by state elites.

At the end of the 1980s, inequalities and discriminatory barriers overall were markedly lower in eastern Europe, the Soviet Union, and the industrial democracies than in other world regions. But in the 1990s most Soviet successor states have imposed discriminatory restrictions on nontitular nationalities, erasing most of the Soviet regime's socially engineered equality of status and opportunity for national minorities. The rump Yugoslavia, Croatia, and Romania also pursue discriminatory policies toward national minorities; most other eastern and central European states have followed the Western democratic precedent.

In Africa and Asia, inequalities and discrimination against communal minorities have remained relatively high, though the new Asian democracies have been notably successful in reducing historical patterns of discrimination.[3] Indigenous and Afro-American minorities in Latin America, though proportionally small in numbers, experienced the greatest economic differen-

---

[2]The study excludes countries with 1994 populations of less than 500,000. A handful also have politically salient minorities, so our count is slightly understated. Also excluded are immigrant workers and refugees, unless and until they become permanent residents in the host country, as has happened with Palestinians in Lebanon and Turks in Germany.

[3]Ted Robert Gurr, ''Democracy and the Rights of Ethnic and Regional Minorities in Asia'' (Paper presented to the thirteenth International Conference of the Korean Association of International Studies, Seoul, October 1994).

Minorities at Risk in 1994, by Region

World Region	Number of Countries with Minorities at Risk	Number of Minorities at Risk	Population of Minorities (1994 Estimates)	
			Total	Percent of Regional Population
Western democracies and Japan (28 countries)	15	31	94,291,000	12
Eastern Europe and Soviet successor states (27 countries)	25	59	59,671,000	14
East, Southeast and South Asia (34 countries)	21	62	397,474,000	13
North Africa and the Middle East (19 countries)	11	27	89,840,000	26
Africa south of the Sahara (48 countries)	30	81	294,460,000	51
Latin America and the Caribbean (34 countries)	18	32	52,965,000	11
Total (190 countries)	120	292	988,701,000	18

tials and most severe economic discrimination observed in any world region. Communal minorities in the Middle East and North Africa have been subject to the most severe political restrictions.

3. Are ethnopolitical grievances and demands mainly the result of inequalities and discrimination?

Two different dynamics underlie the demands and strategies of activist communal groups. First, contemporary movements for secession or regional autonomy are strongly motivated by a desire to protect and assert group identity. These autonomy demands are concentrated among ethnonationalists and indigenous peoples with a tradition of political independence and sharp cultural differences from dominant groups. The second dynamic is that ethnoclasses, communal contenders, and militant sects usually have more tangible concerns. Their strongest demands are for greater rights within societies, not a desire to exit from them. Discrimination motivates demands for greater political and economic rights, while cultural differences prompt demands for protection of the group's social and cultural rights.

4. How much has ethnopolitical conflict increased?

Every form of ethnopolitical conflict increased sharply from the 1950s through the early 1990s. Nonviolent

political action by communal groups more than doubled between 1950 and 1990, and both violent protest and rebellion quadrupled. Trends differ widely among regions and types of groups, however. In the democracies communal conflict peaked in the early 1970s and declined through the end of the 1980s. In contrast, ethnic protest and rebellion in eastern Europe and the Soviet Union were low for most of the postwar period but began to escalate in the early 1980s, even before perestroika and glasnost. Nonviolent protest and rebellion steadily increased in Asia and the Middle East from the 1950s onward. The decline of some communal conflicts in these regions since 1990—for example by the Kurds and non-Burmese nationalists in Myanmar—have been offset by intensified communal conflicts in India, Afghanistan, and Pakistan. Communal conflict in Africa was shaped by decolonization and its consequences. Protest reached a peak in the decade before 1960, when most African countries gained independence, but since then a pronounced shift from protest to rebellion has occurred. Africa now has the most intense ethnopolitical conflicts of any world region.[4] Latin America has the lowest levels of communal conflict. Disputes there are mainly nonviolent protest by indigenous activists that reached a climacteric in the late 1970s and early 1980s; since 1990, however, there has been a fresh upsurge of activism among indigenous Latin Americans.

Worldwide comparisons show that indigenous groups have seen the greatest proportional increase in conflict, a testimony to the influence of the global indigenous rights movement that was established in the 1970s. The long-term global increase in rebellion is

[4]Detailed regional comparisons of ethnopolitical rebellions are summarized in Ted Robert Gurr, "Peoples Against States: Ethnopolitical Conflict and the Changing World System," *International Studies Quarterly*, September 1994.

mainly attributable to autonomy movements by ethnonationalists, whose magnitudes of rebellion increased fivefold between the early 1950s and the 1980s. Communal contenders, a group type found mainly in sub-Saharan Africa, have shifted from nonviolent protest to rebellion. Ethnoclasses, most of whom live in Western democracies and Latin America, have mainly relied on nonviolent protest; this escalated into sporadic episodes of rioting and terrorism from the late 1960s to the early 1980s.

5. How serious is religiously based communal conflict?

Religious cleavages are usually a contributing factor in communal conflict but seldom the root cause. Only 8 of the 49 militant sects in the study are defined solely or mainly by their religious beliefs. An example of these are the politically mobilized Shiite communities in Iraq and Lebanon, whose goals are political rights and recognition, not the propagation of their faith. Other sectarian minorities also have class identifications, such as the Catholics of Northern Ireland and Turkish immigrants in Germany, or nationalist objectives, such as the Palestinians in Israel's occupied territories and the Moros in the Philippines. The driving force behind the most serious and protracted communal conflicts in the Middle East is not militant Islam but the unsatisfied nationalist aspirations of the Kurds and Palestinians.

Religiously inspired political conflict was uncommon anywhere in the world until the 1960s. It doubled in magnitude from then through the end of the 1980s, but its rate of increase was outpaced by rebellion by other kinds of groups, especially ethnonationalists. Overall, groups defined wholly or partly by sectarian differences from dominant groups accounted for one-quarter of rebellions in the 1980s.

6. Is the trend in ethnopolitical activism moving toward protest or rebellion?

Since 1945, nonviolent political action has been far more common among minorities in Western societies, including Latin America, than violent ethnopolitical protest and rebellion. This was also the case in eastern Europe and the Soviet Union until 1990. Deadly communal conflicts in the former Yugoslavia and the Caucasus distract attention from a significantly larger phenomenon: the breakup of the Soviet Union into 15 independent countries was accomplished without protracted civil wars or communal rebellions. Ethnic relations in most of the new countries are thus far fractious but seldom deadly; the exceptions have been Moldova, Georgia, Azerbaijan, and Tajikistan. Communal conflicts in the first three were in remission in early 1995; Tajikistan's civil war is a consequence of political rivalries, not communal ones.

The protagonists in the most persistent communal rebellions of the last 50 years have been ethnonationalists such as the Tibetans, the Eritreans, southern Sudanese, the Palestinians, the Kurds, the Basques, the Karen and Kachin in Burma, and the Nagas and Tripuras in India. Eighty guerrilla and civil wars were fought by these and other communal rebels between 1945 and 1989: 26 were in Asia, 25 in sub-Saharan Africa, 22 in the Middle East and North Africa, 4 in Eastern Europe and the Soviet Union, and 2 in Latin America. A look at 33 ethnopolitical wars and militarized conflicts in 1993–1994 shows proportional increases in sub-Saharan Africa and the former Soviet sphere, but declines elsewhere. Twelve of the 33 were in sub-Saharan Africa, 7 in eastern Europe and the Soviet successor states, 9 in Asia, 3 in the Middle East and North Africa, and 2 in Latin America.

7. Do reformist responses to ethnic demands lead toward accommodation or escalation of communal conflict?

Most communal conflicts begin with acts of protest that escalate into violent conflict. In authoritarian, third world regimes the escalation usually happens very quickly, in part because official responses are more likely to be repressive than reformist. In democracies, however, escalation to violence is usually limited and based on the actions of small, militant factions. All 24 minorities in the Western democracies and Japan used nonviolent political tactics at some time between 1945 and 1989; half resorted to violent protest, and half had militant factions that engaged in terrorism. Setting aside two movements that used violence from the onset (the Irish Republican Army and Puerto Rican nationalist groups), an average of 13 years elapsed between the establishment of political movements representing communal interests in the Western democracies and the first occurrence of violence. This gave societies ample time to respond to communal grievances while conflict was muted. Moreover, the fact that most democratic regimes have attempted reforms helps explain why communal violence in Western societies, once it did occur, is usually limited.

8. Does regional autonomy lead to escalating wars of independence?

Ethnonationalist civil wars have been the most protracted and deadly conflicts of the late twentieth century. They are fought with great intensity because communal demands for independence imply the breakup of existing states. Until the Soviet Union's dissolution, the only ethnonationalists since 1945 who had won independence from existing states were the Bangladeshis, whose independence was bought at the price of political mass murder and India's intervention. Since then a revolutionary coalition has overthrown the Ethiopian regime, which paved the way for Eritrean independence.

Many political leaders on both sides of such struggles have been willing to consider autonomy arrangements that do not grant total independence. When the outcomes of 28 civil wars fought since 1950 in which one of the protagonists sought independence or autonomy are compared, the ledger is almost evenly balanced between winners and losers. On the positive side are four groups in Ethiopia that have won effective autonomy and seven national peoples elsewhere that secured autonomy agreements largely ending open conflict. Outcomes in four cases are under negotiation. On the negative side are nine national movements that were suppressed without significant gains; in four cases serious conflict continues.

Autonomy agreements have helped dampen rebellions by the Basques, the Moros, the Miskitos in Nicaragua, the Nagas and Tripuras, the people of Bangladesh's Chittagong Hill Tracts, and the Afars of Ethiopia. They failed to do so in Sudan and Sri Lanka, and have been aborted elsewhere. The success of autonomy arrangements in ending or preempting civil wars lies in the details and implementation of the arrangements. The details concern the division of powers and responsibilities between the contending parties; successful agreements have required a delicate balancing of communal and state interests, arrived at through protracted negotiations. The challenge for implementation is that both parties must honor the agreements and not defect—even in the face of political challenges and the continuation of violence by militant factions.

9. What approaches work to balance the interests of contending groups within states?

Most politically assertive minorities want access to political and economic opportunities, and protection of their rights in existing societies and states. Can any general lessons be drawn about how to accommodate their demands and deflect violent conflict? The answers depend on the cultural and political context.

Western democracies: Public policy toward minorities in Western democracies has evolved during the past half century from segregation to assimilation to pluralism and, in some countries, powersharing. Pluralism (multiculturalism, as it is known in North America) means arrangements that guarantee communal groups equal individual and collective rights, including the right to separate and coexisting identities. A shift toward pluralism, coupled with the devolution of power to peripheral regions and indigenous peoples, was mainly responsible for the decrease in communal conflicts in France, the United States, and other Western societies in the 1970s and 1980s. The liability is that pluralism and powersharing, if vigorously promoted, can trigger a backlash from dominant groups. Whether pluralist approaches to the growing concentrations of third world immigrants and refugees in Western countries can overcome the political and cultural resistance of dominant majorities, is an especially important question.

Africa South of the Sahara: At the other end of the spectrum of development, most African societies are heterogeneous, poor, and ruled by weak governments composed of unstable multiethnic coalitions. With a few exceptions—Nigeria and Zambia for example—they lack the capacity to suppress or fully incorporate all their diverse peoples. There are two keys to managing communal conflict in these societies. One is to strengthen and stabilize political parties to ensure that all communal groups have a fair chance at joining governing coalitions—if not now, then in the future. The second is to devolve power to local governments to ensure citizen participation and to protect the local power base of those who lose their place in national coalitions. Both steps are consistent with the trends toward democratization that are evident in much of Africa. In a general way, they also resemble the policies of pluralism and devolution that have dampened communal conflicts in Western societies.

Middle East and North Africa: Communal conflicts in the Middle East are more intractable, especially civil wars centered on Palestinian and Kurdish claims for statehood. Inequalities between dominant groups and minorities in the Middle East are greater than in Western societies or Africa; sectarian cleavages have deeper historical roots, and ethnoconflict has been more intense and protracted. There are several examples of the accommodation of contending communal interests in the region: governments in the Maghreb have made significant concessions to Berber culture, and the Egyptian government has sustained largely successful efforts to protect the Coptic minority against discrimination and attacks by Islamic militants.

Elsewhere, however, the role of outside powers is vital for the management of communal conflicts. Progress toward settlement of the Palestinian-Israeli conflict hinges on continued United States involvement in the peace process as well as on internal politics in Israel. The Lebanese civil war ended only after the establishment of Syrian hegemony in central and northern Lebanon and Israel's withdrawal from the south. The outcome of the Persian Gulf War and allied protection of Iraqi Kurds provided the Kurds a rare opportunity to establish a fragile autonomy—one that is not likely to survive the eventual lifting of international sanctions against the Iraqi government. And the Iranian government's desire to rebuild the economy and reestablish Iran's leading role in the region has made Iran susceptible to international pressures to moderate its repressive policies toward the Bahais.

Eastern Europe and the Soviet Successor States: The collapse of the Soviet Union and its hegemony in Eastern Europe has transformed communal conflict in the region. Half the Soviet Union's population before the breakup was non-Russian and 40 percent of the total was at risk. Now the sources of communal demands are the new minorities of the Soviet successor states who constitute as many as 60 percent (in Kazakhstan) of the population. In the aggregate, the new minorities are 25 percent of the former republics' populations, and many are pressing their own claims against new regimes. But thus far most are doing so with the strategies found in democratic societies (that is, mass mobilization and civil protest), not the classic forms of armed rebellion.

Most of the new regimes of eastern Europe are also responding democratically: the Czechoslovakian government negotiated Slovakia's independence; the Bulgarian government aims at the pluralistic incorporation of its Muslim and Turkish minority. Only the authoritarian communist regime of Serbia continues to play by Stalinist rules. Its policies of hegemonical nationalism and repression are unlikely to be restrained without international sanctions and military intervention, or reversed except by a democratic revolution from within.

10. Where are ethnopolitical conflicts most likely to escalate in the 1990s?

The potential for escalating ethnopolitical conflict remains high in the Soviet successor states. However, in the Slavic states most conflicts will be settled democratically. The prospects for rebellion, civil war, and deadly intercommunal conflict are considerably greater in the Caucasian and Central Asian regions. The botched Russian effort to end Chechnya's secession by force conveys two lessons: to the Russians that they must resume their reliance on compromise in such disputes; and to restive national minorities that they must choose cautious political strategies. Nonetheless, if Russian democracy survives, civil and multicultural societies are likely to prevail in most of the region by the year 2000.

The western European and North American democracies will see a resurgence of ethnic conflict. Some conflicts will be based on regional claims by people like the Quebecois and the Scots, but most will be a consequence of class and communal tensions between dominant groups and minorities of third world origin. The virtues of democratic politics are that they allow the expression of minority interests and encourage accommodation. The vice is that they are susceptible to the politics of ethnocentric reaction. The norms of democratic accommodation will likely prevail and by 2000 various kinds of pluralist arrangements will be in place in the Western societies that do not have them now.

Indigenous activism is also likely to escalate throughout the Americas, especially in the Latin American societies that have been most resistant to the claims of native peoples. Positive responses will be seen in democratic societies in the region, but within limits: indigenous demands for control of land and resources are not likely to be met if they constrain the economic development Latin American leaders regard as essential to political stability. Eight Central and South American societies also have significant Afro-American minorities, most of whom are seriously disadvantaged; except in Brazil, they probably will remain politically quiescent.

In the third world, South Asia will suffer the most severe escalation of communal conflicts in the 1990s. Long-standing regional conflicts in India—in Assam, Punjab, and Kashmir—have intensified in the early 1990s, prompting communal demands by other peoples. Religiopolitical tensions are increasing between Muslim and Hindu communities in most countries in the region. Settlers from Bangladesh's densely crowded lowlands continue to push into the uplands, where they are embroiled in violent communal conflict with tribal peoples. Pakistani politics is rent by communal divisions among Pashtuns, Sindhis, Baluchis, and smaller minorities. In the aftermath of Afghanistan's failed communist revolution, communal rivalries have intensified among the once-dominant Pashtuns and Tajiks, Uzbeks, Hazaris, and others. The only de-escalating communal conflict in the subcontinent is between Tamils and the Sinhalese-dominated state in Sri Lanka, and its decline is the result of repression more than accommodation.

Forecasting the future of communal conflict elsewhere in the third world is even more speculative. Most of the Middle East's conflicts are already under way, but few are likely to be settled decisively in the near future. Some ethnopolitical wars in Southeast Asia are winding down but others may intensify. In Africa the bitter communal conflicts in Ethiopia and South Africa are being worked out in the political arena, but others continue in Sudan and Somalia. In 1993–1994 stunning violence erupted in Burundi and Rwanda and is very likely to flare again in Burundi. The potential for communal warfare in Nigeria and Zaire is equally threatening.

11. What is the functional place of communal groups in the global system of states?

The most radical proposal for resolving conflicts between states and peoples is to reconstruct the state system so that territorial boundaries correspond more closely to the social and cultural boundaries among peoples. But such a strategy would leave unsatisfied the aspirations of many nonterritorial communal groups. For most others it would create as many problems as it resolved. The most likely means taken toward achieving such an objective are destructive civil wars, such as those in the former Yugoslavia, Ethiopia, Chechnya and Georgia. Even if political reconstruction is achieved peacefully, it is likely to create or intensify new communal conflicts. Few ethnonationalist regions are homogeneous, and the leaders of new states are at risk of being trapped in new communal dilemmas.

A more constructive and open-ended answer is to

recognize and strengthen communal groups within the existing state system. Elise Boulding contends that devolving authority to communal groups will help resolve the fundamental structural problems of modern states: most are too large in scale and too far removed from many of their citizens to understand or deal with local concerns.[5]

Progress toward the objective of a more pluralist world system requires that the international commu-

nity accept a common obligation to protect collective rights within such an emergent system. Communal groups should have protected rights to individual and collective existence and to cultural self-expression without fear of political repression. The counterpart of such rights is the obligation not to impose cultural standards or political agendas on other peoples. This applies with special force to situations in which the international community supports the establishment of new states as a way of resolving conflicts within multiethnic societies, as in the former Yugoslavia. No new claims to statehood or autonomy ought to be recognized internationally unless the claimants assume the obligation, under pain of sanctions, to respect the rights of minorities within their borders.

---

[5]Elise Boulding, "Ethnicity and New Constitutive Orders: An Approach to Peace in the Twenty-First Century" (Paper prepared for a Festschrift for Kinhide Mushakoji, n.d. [1990]).

A Debate on Cultural Conflicts

The Coming Clash of Civilizations—Or, the West Against the Rest

Samuel P. Huntington

Samuel P. Huntington is professor of government and director of the Olin Institute for Strategic Studies at Harvard. This article is adapted from the lead essay in the summer issue of Foreign Affairs.

World politics is entering a new phase in which the fundamental source of conflict will be neither ideological or economic. The great divisions among mankind and the dominating source of conflict will be cultural. The principal conflicts of global politics will occur between nations and groups of different civilizations. The clash of civilizations will dominate global politics.

During the cold war, the world was divided into the first, second and third worlds. Those divisions are no longer relevant. It is far more meaningful to group countries not in terms of their political or economic systems or their level of economic development but in terms of their culture and civilization.

A civilization is the highest cultural grouping of people and the broadest level of cultural identity people have short of that which distinguishes humans from other species.

Civilizations obviously blend and overlap and may include sub-civilizations. Western civilization has two major variants, European and North American, and Islam has its Arab, Turkic and Malay subdivisions. But while the lines between them are seldom sharp, civilizations are real. They rise and fall; they divide and merge. And as any student of history knows, civilizations disappear.

Westerners tend to think of nation-states as the principal actors in global affairs. They have been that for only a few centuries. The broader reaches of history have been the history of civilizations. It is to this pattern that the world returns.

Global conflict will be cultural.

Civilization identity will be increasingly important and the world will be shaped in large measure by the interactions among seven or eight major civilizations. These include the Western, Confucian, Japanese, Islamic, Hindu, Slavic-Orthodox, Latin American and possibly African civilizations.

The most important and bloody conflicts will occur along the borders separating these cultures. The fault lines between civilizations will be the battle lines of the future.

Why? First, differences among civilizations are basic, involving history, language, culture, tradition and, most importantly, religion. Different civilizations have different views on the relations between God and man, the citizen and the state, parents and children, liberty and authority, equality and hierarchy. These differences are the product of centuries. They will not soon disappear.

Second, the world is becoming smaller. The interactions between peoples of different civilizations are increasing. These interactions intensify civilization consciousness: awareness of differences between civilizations and commonalities within civilizations. For example, Americans react far more negatively to Japanese investment than to larger investments from Canada and European countries.

Third, economic and social changes are separating people from long-standing local identities. In much of the world, religion has moved in to fill this gap, often in the form of movements labeled fundamentalist.

Such movements are found in Western Christianity, Judaism, Buddhism, Hinduism and Islam. The "unsecularization of the world," . . . George Weigel has remarked, "is one of the dominant social facts of life in the late 20th century."

Fourth, the growth of civilization consciousness is enhanced by the fact that at the moment that the West is at the peak of its power a return-to-the-roots phenomenon is occurring among non-Western civilizations—the "Asianization" in Japan, the end of the Nehru legacy and the "Hinduization" of India, the failure of Western ideas of socialism and nationalism and, hence, the "re-Islamization" of the Middle East, and now a debate over Westernization versus Russianization in Boris Yeltsin's country.

More importantly, the efforts of the West to promote its values of democracy and liberalism as universal values, to maintain its military predominance and to advance its economic interests engender countering responses from other civilizations.

The central axis of world politics is likely to be the conflict between "the West and the rest" and the responses of non-Western civilizations to Western power and values. The most prominent example of anti-Western cooperation is the connection between Confucian and Islamic states that are challenging Western values and power.

Fifth, cultural characteristics and differences are less mutable and hence less easily compromised and resolved than political and economic ones. In the former Soviet Union, Communists can become democrats, the rich can become poor and the poor rich, but Russians cannot become Estonians. A person can be half-French and half-Arab and even a citizen of two countries. It is more difficult to be half Catholic and half Muslim.

Finally, economic regionalism is increasing. Successful economic regionalism will reinforce civilization consciousness. On the other hand, economic regionalism may succeed only when it is rooted in common civilization. The European Community rests on the shared foundation of European culture and Western Christianity. Japan, in contrast, faces difficulties in creating a comparable economic entity in East Asia because it is a society and civilization unique to itself.

As the ideological division of Europe has disappeared, the cultural division of Europe between Western Christianity and Orthodox Christianity and Islam has re-emerged. Conflict along the fault line between Western and Islamic civilizations has been going on for 1,300 years. This centuries-old military interaction is unlikely to decline. Historically, the other great antagonistic interaction of Arab Islamic civilization has been with the pagan, animist and now, increasingly, Christian black peoples to the south. On the northern border of Islam, conflict has increasingly erupted between Orthodox and Muslim peoples, including the carnage of Bosnia and Sarajevo, the simmering violence between Serbs and Albanians, the tenuous relations between Bulgarians and their Turkish minority, the violence between Ossetians and Ingush, the unremitting slaughter of each other by Armenians and Azeris and the tense relations between Russians and Muslims in Central Asia.

The historic clash between Muslims and Hindus in the Subcontinent manifests itself not only in the rivalry between Pakistan and India but also in intensifying religious strife in India between increasingly militant Hindu groups and the substantial Muslim minority.

Groups or states belonging to one civilization that become involved in war with people from a different civilization naturally try to rally support from other members of their own civilization. Decreasingly able to mobilize support and form coalitions on the basis of ideology, governments and groups will increasingly attempt to mobilize support by appealing to common religion and civilization identity. As the conflicts in the Persian Gulf, the Caucasus and Bosnia continued, the positions of nations and the cleavages between them increasingly were along civilizational lines. Populist politicians, religious leaders and the media have found it a potent means of arousing mass support and of pressuring hesitant governments. In the coming years, the local conflicts most likely to escalate into major wars will be those, as in Bosnia and the Caucasus, along the fault lines between civilizations. The next world war, if there is one, will be a war between civilizations.

Only Japan is non-Western and modern.

If these hypotheses are plausible, it is necessary to consider their implications for Western policy. These implications should be divided between short-term advantage and long-term accommodation. In the short term, it is clearly in the interest of the West to promote greater cooperation and unity in its own civilization, particularly between its European and North American components; to incorporate into the West those societies in Eastern Europe and Latin America whose cultures are close to those of the West; to maintain close relations with Russia and Japan; to support in other civilizations groups sympathetic to Western values and interests; and to strengthen international institutions that reflect and legitimate Western interests and values. The West must also limit the expansion of the military strength of potentially hostile civilizations, principally Confucian and Islamic civilizations, and exploit differences and conflicts among Confucian and Islamic states. This will require a moderation in the reduction of Western military capabilities, and, in particular, the maintenance of American military superiority in East and Southwest Asia.

In the longer term, other measures would be called for. Western civilization is modern. Non-Western civilizations have attempted to become modern without becoming Western. To date, only Japan has fully succeeded in this quest. Non-Western civilizations will continue to attempt to acquire the wealth, technology, skills, machines and weapons that are part of being modern. They will attempt to reconcile this modernity with their traditional culture and values. Their economic and military strength relative to the West will increase.

Hence, the West will increasingly have to accommodate to these non-Western modern civilizations, whose power approaches that of the West but whose values and interests differ significantly from those of the West. This will require the West to develop a much more profound understanding of the basic religious and philosophical assumptions underlying other civilizations and the ways in which people in those civilizations see their interests. It will require an effort to identify elements of commonality among Western and other civilizations. For the relevant future, there will be no universal civilization but instead a world of different civilizations, each of which will have to learn to co-exist with others.

Global debate on a controversial thesis

A Clash Between Civilizations —or Within Them?

Süddeutsche Zeitung

■ *A recent essay by Harvard professor Samuel P. Huntington in "Foreign Affairs" magazine—"The Clash of Civilizations?"—has attracted a good deal of attention not only in the U.S. but abroad, as well. Huntington is attempting to establish a new model for examining the post-cold-war world, a central theme around which events will turn, as the ideological clash of the cold war governed the past 40 years. He finds it in cultures. "Faith and family, blood and belief," he has written, "are what people identify with and what they will fight and die for." But in the following article, Josef Joffe, foreign-affairs specialist at the independent "Süddeutsche Zeitung" of Munich, argues that "kulturkampf"—cultural warfare—is not a primary threat to world security. And in a more radical view, Malaysian political scientist Chandra Muzaffar writes for the Third World Network Features agency of Penang, Malaysia, that Western dominance—economic and otherwise—continues to be the overriding factor in world politics.*

A ghost is walking in the West: cultural warfare, total and international. Scarcely had we banished the 40-year-long cold war to history's shelves, scarcely had we begun to deal with the seductive phrase "the end of history," when violence broke out on all sides. But this time it was not nations that were behind the savagery but peoples and ethnic groups, religions and races—from the Serbs and Bosnians in the Balkans to the Tiv and Jukun in Nigeria.

Working from such observations, one of the best brains in America, Harvard professor Samuel Huntington, produced a prophecy, perhaps even a philosophy of history. His essay "The Clash of Civilizations?" has caused a furor. For centuries, it was the nations that made history; then, in the 20th century, it was the totalitarian ideologies. Today, at the threshold of the 21st century, "the clash of civilizations will dominate global politics." No longer will "Which side are you on?" be the fateful question but "What are you?" Identity will no longer be defined by passport or party membership card but by faith and history, language and customs—culture, in short. Huntington argues that "conflicts between cultures" will push the old disputes between nations and

Reprinted with permission from *World Press Review*, February 1994, pp. 24-26. Originally from *Süddeutsche Zeitung*.

265

ideologies off center stage. Or put more apocalyptically: "The next world war, if there is one, will be a war between civilizations."

Between which? Huntington has made a list of more than half a dozen civilizations, including the West (the U.S. plus Europe), the Slavic-Orthodox, the Islamic, the Confucian (China), the Japanese, and the Hindu. At first glance, he seems to be right. Are not Catholic Croats fighting Orthodox Serbs—and both of them opposing Muslim Bosnians? And recently, the ruthless struggle between the Hindus and Muslims of India has re-erupted. Even such a darling of the West as King Hussein of Jordan announced during the Persian Gulf war: "This is a war against all Arabs and all Muslims and not against Iraq alone." The long trade conflict pitting Japan against the United States (and against Europe) has been called a "war"—and not only by the chauvinists. Russian Orthodox nationalists see themselves in a two-front struggle: against the Islamic Turkic peoples in the south and the soulless modernists of the West. And even worse: The future could mean "the West against the rest."

But this first look is deceptive; after a closer look, the apocalypse dissolves, to be replaced by a more complex tableau. This second look shows us a world that is neither new nor simple. First of all, conflicts between civilizations are as old as history itself. Look at the struggle of the Jews against Rome in the first century, or the revolt of the Greeks against the Turks in the 19th century. The Occident and Orient have been in conflict, off and on, for the last 1,300 years. Second, the disputes with China, Japan, or North Korea are not really nourished by conflicts among civilizations. They are the results of palpable national interests at work. Third, if we look only at the conflicts between cultures, we will miss the more important truth: Within each camp, divisions and rivalries are far more significant than unifying forces.

The idea of cultural war seems to work best when we examine Islam. The demonization of the West is a part of the standard rhetoric of Islamic fundamentalists. The Arab-Islamic world is one of the major sources of terrorism, and most armed conflicts since World War II have involved Western states against Muslim countries. But if we look more closely, the Islamic monolith fractures into many pieces that cannot be reassembled. There is the history of internecine conflicts, coups, and rebellions: a 15-year-long civil war of each against all in Lebanon (not simply Muslims against Maronite Christians), the Palestine Liberation Organization against Jordan, and Syria against the PLO. Then consider the wars among states in the Arab world: Egypt versus Yemen, Syria against Jordan, Egypt versus Libya, and finally Iraq versus Kuwait. Then the wars of ideologies and finally, the religiously tinted struggles for dominance within the faith—between Sunnis and Shiites, Iraq and Iran.

But most important: What does the term "Islam" really mean? What does a Malay Muslim have in common with a Bosnian? Or an Indonesian with a Saudi? And what are we to understand by "fundamentalism"? The Saudi variety is passive and inward-looking, while the expansive Iranian variety arouses fear. It is true that, from Gaza to Giza, fundamentalists are shedding innocent blood. But most of the Arab world sided with the West during the Gulf war. And, beyond this, only 10 percent of the trade of the Middle East takes place within the region; most of it flows westward. Economic interdependence, a good index of a common civilization, is virtually nonexistent in the Islamic world.

The real issue is not a cultural war but actually another twofold problem. Several Islamic nations are importing too many weapons, and some are exporting too many people. The first demands containment and denial, calling for continued military strength and readiness in the West. And what of the "human exports"? They are not just a product of the Islamic world but of the entire poor and overpopulated world—no matter what culture they are part of. Along with the spread of nuclear weapons and missiles, this is the major challenge of the coming century, because massive migrations of people will inevitably bring cultural, territorial, and political struggles in their wake. No one has an answer to this. But a narrow vision produced by the "West-against-the-rest" notion is surely the worst way to look for answers.

—*Josef Joffe*

The West's Hidden Agenda

Third World Network
FEATURES

Like Francis Fukuyama's essay "The End of History?" published in 1989, Samuel Huntington's "The Clash of Civilizations?" has received a lot of publicity in the mainstream Western media. The reason is not difficult to fathom. Both articles serve U.S. and Western foreign-policy goals. Huntington's thesis is simple enough: "The clash of civilizations will dominate global politics. The fault lines between civilizations will be the battle lines of the future."

The truth, however, is that cultural, religious, or other civilizational differences are only some of the many factors responsible for conflict. Territory and resources, wealth and property, power and status, and individual personalities and group interests are others. Indeed, religion, culture, and other elements and symbols of what Huntington would regard as "civilization identity" are sometimes manipulated to camouflage the naked pursuit of wealth or power—the real source of many conflicts.

 Reprinted with permission from *World Press Review*, February 1994, pp. 25-26. Originally from *Third World Network Features*.

But the problem is even more serious. By overplaying the "clash of civilizations" dimension, Huntington has ignored the creative, constructive interaction and engagement between civilizations. This is a much more constant feature of civilization than conflict per se. Islam, for instance, through centuries of exchange with the West, laid the foundation for the growth of mathematics, science, medicine, agriculture, industry, and architecture in medieval Europe. Today, some of the leading ideas and institutions that have gained currency within the Muslim world, whether in politics or in economics, are imports from the West.

That different civilizations are not inherently prone to conflict is borne out by another salient feature that Huntington fails to highlight. Civilizations embody many similar values and ideals. At the philosophical level at least, Buddhism, Christianity, Hinduism, Islam, Judaism, Sikhism, and Taoism, among other world religions, share certain common perspectives on the relationship between the human being and his environment, the integrity of the community, the importance of the family, the significance of moral leadership, and, indeed, the meaning and purpose of life. Civilizations, however different in certain respects, are quite capable of forging common interests and aspirations. For example, the Association of Southeast Asian Nations encompasses at least four "civilization identities," to use Huntington's term—Buddhist (Thailand), Confucian (Singapore), Christian (the Philippines), and Muslim (Brunei, Indonesia, and Malaysia). Yet it has been able to evolve an identity of its own through 25 years of trials.

It is U.S. and Western dominance, not the clash of civilizations, that is at the root of global conflict. By magnifying the so-called clash of civilizations, Huntington tries to divert attention from Western dominance and control even as he strives to preserve, protect, and perpetuate that dominance. He sees a compelling reason for embarking on this mission. Western dominance is under threat from a "Confucian-Islamic connection that has emerged to challenge Western interests, values, and power," he writes. This is the most mischievous—and most dangerous—implication of his "clash of civilizations."

By evoking this fear of a Confucian-Islamic connection, he hopes to persuade the Western public, buffeted by unemployment and recession, to acquiesce to huge military budgets in the post-cold-war era. He argues that China and some Islamic nations are acquiring weapons on a massive scale. Generally, it is the Islamic states that are buying weapons from China, which in turn "is rapidly increasing its military spending." Huntington observes that "a Confucian-Islamic military connection has thus come into being, designed to promote acquisition by its members of the weapons and weapons technologies needed to counter the military power of the West." This is why the West, and the U.S. in particular, should not, in Huntington's view, be "reducing its own military capabilities."

There are serious flaws in this argument. One, it is not true that the U.S. has reduced its military capability; in fact, it has enhanced its range of sophisticated weaponry. Two, though China is an important producer and exporter of arms, it is the only major power whose military expenditures consistently declined throughout the 1980s. Three, most Muslim countries buy their weapons not from China but from the U.S. Four, China has failed to endorse the Muslim position on many global issues. Therefore, the Confucian-Islamic connection is a myth propagated to justify increased U.S. military spending.

It is conceivable that Huntington has chosen to target the Confucian and Islamic civilizations for reasons that are not explicitly stated in his article. Like many other Western academics, commentators, and policy analysts, Huntington, it appears, is also concerned about the economic ascendancy of so-called Confucian communities such as China, Hong Kong, Taiwan, Singapore, and overseas Chinese communities in other Asian countries. He is of the view that "if cultural commonality is a prerequisite for economic integration, the principal East Asian economic bloc of the future is likely to be centered on China." The dynamism and future potential of these "Confucian" economies have already set alarm bells ringing in various Western capitals. Huntington's warning to the West about the threat that China poses should be seen in that context—as yet another attempt to curb the rise of yet another non-Western economic competitor.

> "U.S. and Western dominance is at the root of global conflict."

As far as the "Islamic threat" is concerned, it is something that Huntington and his kind have no difficulty selling in the West. Antagonism toward Islam and Muslims is deeply embedded in the psyche of mainstream Western society. The rise of Islamic movements has provoked a new, powerful wave of negative emotions against the religion and its practitioners. Most Western academics and journalists, in concert with Western policy makers, grant no legitimacy to the Muslim resistance to Western domination and control. When Huntington says, "Islam has bloody borders," the implication is that Islam and Muslims are responsible for the spilling of blood. Yet anyone who has an elementary knowledge of many current conflicts will readily admit that, more often than not, it is the Muslims who have been bullied, bludgeoned, and butchered.

The truth, however, means very little to Huntington. The title of his article "The Clash of Civilizations?" is quoted from [British educator] Bernard Lewis's "The Roots of Muslim Rage," an essay that depicts the Islamic resurgence as an irrational threat to Western heritage. Both Huntington and Lewis are "Islam baiters" whose role is to camouflage the suffering of and the injustice done to the victims of U.S. and Western domination by concocting theories about the conflict of cultures and the clash of civilizations. Huntington's "The Clash of Civilizations?" will not conceal the real nature of the conflict: The victims—or at least some of them—know the truth.

—*Chandra Muzaffar*

Jihad vs. McWorld

*The two axial principles of our age—tribalism and globalism—clash at every point
except one: they may both be threatening to democracy*

Benjamin R. Barber

*Benjamin R. Barber is the Whitman Professor of Political Science at Rutgers
University. Barber's most recent books
are* Strong Democracy *(1984),* The Conquest of Politics *(1988), and* An Aristocracy of Everyone.

Just beyond the horizon of current
events lie two possible political figures—both bleak, neither democratic.
The first is a retribalization of large
swaths of humankind by war and bloodshed: a threatened Lebanonization of national states in which culture is pitted
against culture, people against people,
tribe against tribe—a Jihad in the name of
a hundred narrowly conceived faiths
against every kind of interdependence,
every kind of artificial social cooperation and civic mutuality. The second is
being borne in on us by the onrush of
economic and ecological forces that demand integration and uniformity and that
mesmerize the world with fast music, fast
computers, and fast food—with MTV,
Macintosh, and McDonald's, pressing
nations into one commercially homogenous global network: one McWorld tied
together by technology, ecology, communications, and commerce. The planet
is falling precipitantly apart and coming
reluctantly together at the very same
moment.

These two tendencies are sometimes
visible in the same countries at the same
instant: thus Yugoslavia, clamoring just
recently to join the New Europe, is exploding into fragments; India is trying to
live up to its reputation as the world's
largest integral democracy while powerful new fundamentalist parties like the
Hindu nationalist Bharatiya Janata Party,
along with nationalist assassins, are im-
periling its hard-won unity. States are
breaking up or joining up: the Soviet
Union has disappeared almost overnight,
its parts forming new unions with one
another or with like-minded nationalities
in neighboring states. The old interwar
national state based on territory and political sovereignty looks to be a mere
transitional development.

The tendencies of what I am here
calling the forces of Jihad and the forces
of McWorld operate with equal strength
in opposite directions, the one driven by
parochial hatreds, the other by universalizing markets, the one re-creating ancient subnational and ethnic borders
from within, the other making national
borders porous from without. They have
one thing in common: neither offers
much hope to citizens looking for practical ways to govern themselves democratically. If the global future is to put
Jihad's centrifugal whirlwind against
McWorld's centripetal black hole, the
outcome is unlikely to be democratic—or
so I will argue.

MCWORLD, OR THE GLOBALIZATION OF POLITICS

Four imperatives make up the dynamic
of McWorld: a market imperative, a resource imperative, an information-technology imperative, and an ecological
imperative. By shrinking the world and
diminishing the salience of national borders, these imperatives have in combination achieved a considerable victory over
factiousness and particularism, and not
least of all over their most virulent traditional form—nationalism. It is the realists who are now Europeans, the utopians
who dream nostalgically of a resurgent
England or Germany, perhaps even a
resurgent Wales or Saxony. Yesterday's
wishful cry for one world has yielded to
the reality of McWorld.

The market imperative. Marxist and
Leninist theories of imperialism assumed
that the quest for ever-expanding markets
would in time compel nation-based capitalist economies to push against national
boundaries in search of an international
economic imperium. Whatever else has
happened to the scientist predictions of
Marxism, in this domain they have proved
farsighted. All national economies are
now vulnerable to the inroads of larger,
transnational markets within which trade
is free, currencies are convertible, access
to banking is open, and contracts are
enforceable under law. In Europe, Asia,
Africa, the South Pacific, and the Americas such markets are eroding national
sovereignty and giving rise to entities—
international banks, trade associations,
transnational lobbies like OPEC and
Greenpeace, world news services like
CNN and the BBC, and multinational
corporations that increasingly lack a
meaningful national identity—that neither reflect nor respect nationhood as an
organizing or regulative principle.

The market imperative has also reinforced the quest for international peace
and stability, requisites of an efficient
international economy. Markets are enemies of parochialism, isolation, fractiousness, war. Market psychology attenuates
the psychology of ideological and religious cleavages and assumes a concord
among producers and consumers—categories that ill fit narrowly conceived
national or religious cultures. Shopping
has little tolerance for blue laws, whether
dictated by pub-closing British paternalism, Sabbath-observing Jewish Orthodox
fundamentalism, or no-Sunday-liquor-sales
Massachusetts puritanism. In the context
of common markets, international law
ceases to be a vision of justice and be-

comes a workaday framework for getting things done—enforcing contracts, ensuring that governments abide by deals, regulating trade and currency relations, and so forth.

Common markets demand a common language, as well as a common currency, and they produce common behaviors of the kind bred by cosmopolitan city life everywhere. Commercial pilots, computer programmers, international bankers, media specialists, oil riggers, entertainment celebrities, ecology experts, demographers, accountants, professors, athletes—these compose a new breed of men and women for whom religion, culture, and nationality can seem only marginal elements in a working identity. Although sociologists of everyday life will no doubt continue to distinguish a Japanese from an American mode, shopping has a common signature throughout the world. Cynics might even say that some of the recent revolutions in Eastern Europe have had as their true goal not liberty and the right to vote but well-paying jobs and the right to shop (although the vote is proving easier to acquire than consumer goods). The market imperative is, then, plenty powerful; but, notwithstanding some of the claims made for "democratic capitalism," it is not identical with the democratic imperative.

The resource imperative. Democrats once dreamed of societies whose political autonomy rested firmly on economic independence. The Athenians idealized what they called autarky, and tried for a while to create a way of life simple and austere enough to make the polis genuinely self-sufficient. To be free meant to be independent of any other community or polis. Not even the Athenians were able to achieve autarky, however: human nature, it turns out, is dependency. By the time of Pericles, Athenian politics was inextricably bound up with a flowering empire held together by naval power and commerce—an empire that, even as it appeared to enhance Athenian might, ate away at Athenian independence and autarky. Master and slave, it turned out, were bound together by mutual insufficiency.

The dream of autarky briefly engrossed nineteenth-century America as well, for the underpopulated, endlessly bountiful land, the cornucopia of natural resources, and the natural barriers of a continent walled in by two great seas led many to believe that America could be a world unto itself. Given this past, it has been harder for Americans than for most to accept the inevitability of interdependence. But the rapid depletion of resources even in a country like ours, where they once seemed inexhaustible, and the maldistribution of arable soil and mineral resources on the planet, leave even the wealthiest societies ever more resource-dependent and many other nations in permanently desperate straits.

Every nation, it turns out, needs something another nation has; some nations have almost nothing they need.

The information-technology imperative. Enlightenment science and the technologies derived from it are inherently universalizing. They entail a quest for descriptive principles of general application, a search for universal solutions to particular problems, and an unswerving embrace of objectivity and impartiality.

Scientific progress embodies and depends on open communication, a common discourse rooted in rationality, collaboration, and an easy and regular flow and exchange of information. Such ideals can be hypocritical covers for power-mongering by elites, and they may be shown to be wanting in many other ways, but they are entailed by the very idea of science and they make science and globalization practical allies.

Business, banking, and commerce all depend on information flow and are facilitated by new communication technologies. The hardware of these technologies tends to be systemic and integrated—computer, television, cable, satellite, laser, fiber-optic, and microchip technologies combining to create a vast interactive communications and information network that can potentially give every person on earth access to every other person, and make every datum, every byte, available to every set of eyes. If the automobile was, as George Ball once said (when he gave his blessing to a Fiat factory in the Soviet Union during the Cold War), "an ideology on four wheels," then electronic telecommunication and information systems are an ideology at 186,000 miles per second—which makes for a very small planet in a very big hurry. Individual cultures speak particular languages; commerce and science increasingly speak English; the whole world speaks logarithms and binary mathematics.

Moreover, the pursuit of science and technology asks for, even compels, open societies. Satellite footprints do not respect national borders; telephone wires penetrate the most closed societies. With photocopying and then fax machines having infiltrated Soviet universities and *samizdat* literary circles in the eighties, and computer modems having multiplied like rabbits in communism's bureaucratic warrens thereafter, *glasnost* could not be far behind. In their social requisites, secrecy and science are enemies.

The new technology's software is perhaps even more globalizing than its hardware. The information arm of international commerce's sprawling body reaches out and touches distinct nations and parochial cultures, and gives them a common face chiseled in Hollywood, on Madison Avenue, and in Silicon Valley. Throughout the 1980s one of the most-watched television programs in South Africa was *The Cosby Show.* The demise of apartheid was already in production. Exhibitors at the 1991 Cannes film festival expressed growing anxiety over the "homogenization" and "Americanization" of the global film industry when, for the third year running, American films dominated the awards ceremonies. America has dominated the world's popular culture for much longer, and much more decisively. In November of 1991 Switzerland's once insular culture boasted best-seller lists featuring *Terminator 2* as the No. 1 movie, *Scarlett* as the No. 1 book, and Prince's *Diamonds and Pearls* as the No. 1 record album. No wonder the Japanese are buying Hollywood film studios even faster than Americans are buying Japanese television sets. This kind of software supremacy may in the long term be far more important than hardware superiority, because culture has become more potent than armaments. What is the power of the Pentagon compared with Disneyland? Can the Sixth Fleet keep up with CNN? McDonald's in Moscow and Coke in China will do more to create a global culture than military colonization ever could. It is less the goods than the brand names that do the work, for they convey life-style images that alter perception and challenge behavior. They make up the seductive software of McWorld's common (at times much too common) soul.

Yet in all this high-tech commercial world there is nothing that looks particularly democratic. It lends itself to surveillance as well as liberty, to new forms of manipulation and covert control as well as new kinds of participation, to skewed, unjust market outcomes as well as greater productivity. The consumer society and the open society are not quite synonymous. Capitalism and democracy have a relationship, but it is something less than a marriage. An efficient free market after all requires that consumers be free to vote their dollars on competing goods, not that citizens be free to vote their values and beliefs on competing political candidates and programs. The free market flourished in junta-run Chile, in military-governed Taiwan and Korea, and, earlier, in a variety of autocratic European empires as well as their colonial possessions.

The ecological imperative. The impact of globalization on ecology is a cliché even to world leaders who ignore it. We know well enough that the German forests can be destroyed by Swiss and Italians driving gas-guzzlers fueled by leaded gas. We also know that the planet can be asphyxiated by greenhouse gases because Brazilian farmers want to be part of the twentieth century and are burning down tropical rain forests to clear a little land to plough, and because Indonesians make a living out of converting their lush jungle into toothpicks for fastidious Japanese diners, upsetting the delicate oxygen balance and in effect puncturing our global lungs. Yet this ecological consciousness has meant not only greater awareness but also greater inequality, as modernized nations try to slam the door behind them, saying to developing nations, "The world cannot afford *your* modernization; ours has wrung it dry!"

Each of the four imperatives just cited is transnational, transideological, and transcultural. Each applies impartially to Catholics, Jews, Muslims, Hindus, and Buddhists; to democrats and totalitarians; to capitalists and socialists. The Enlightenment dream of a universal rational society has to a remarkable degree been realized—but in a form that is commercialized, homogenized, depoliticized, bureaucratized, and, of course, radically incomplete, for the movement toward McWorld is in competition with forces of global breakdown, national dissolution, and centrifugal corruption. These forces, working in the opposite direction, are the essence of what I call Jihad.

JIHAD, OR THE LEBANONIZATION OF THE WORLD

OPEC, the World Bank, the United Nations, the International Red Cross, the multinational corporation . . . there are scores of institutions that reflect globalization. But they often appear as ineffective reactors to the world's real actors: national states and, to an ever greater degree, subnational factions in permanent rebellion against uniformity and integration—even the kind represented by universal law and justice. The headlines feature these players regularly: they are cultures, not countries; parts, not wholes; sects, not religions; rebellious factions and dissenting minorities at war not just with globalism but with the traditional nation-state. Kurds, Basques, Puerto Ricans, Ossetians, East Timoreans, Quebecois, the Catholics of Northern Ireland, Abkhasians, Kurile Islander Japanese, the Zulus of Inkatha, Catalonians, Tamils, and, of course, Palestinians—people without countries, inhabiting nations not their own, seeking smaller worlds within borders that will seal them off from modernity.

A powerful irony is at work here. Nationalism was once a force of integration and unification, a movement aimed at bringing together disparate clans, tribes, and cultural fragments under new, assimilationist flags. But as Ortega y Gasset noted more than sixty years ago, having won its victories, nationalism changed its strategy. In the 1920s, and again today, it is more often a reactionary and divisive force, pulverizing the very nations it once helped cement together. The force that creates nations is "inclusive," Ortega wrote in *The Revolt of the Masses.* "In periods of consolidation, nationalism has a positive value, and is a lofty standard. But in Europe everything is more than consolidated, and nationalism is nothing but a mania. . . ."

This mania has left the post-Cold War world smoldering with hot wars; the international scene is little more unified than it was at the end of the Great War, in Ortega's own time. There were more than thirty wars in progress last year, most of them ethnic, racial, tribal, or religious in character, and the list of unsafe regions doesn't seem to be getting any shorter. Some new world order!

The aim of many of these small-scale wars is to redraw boundaries, to implode states and resecure parochial identities: to escape McWorld's dully insistent imperatives. The mood is that of Jihad: war not as an instrument of policy but as an emblem of identity, an expression of community, an end in itself. Even where there is no shooting war, there is fractiousness, secession, and the quest for ever smaller communities. Add to the list

of dangerous countries those at risk: In Switzerland and Spain, Jurassian and Basque separatists still argue the virtues of ancient identities, sometimes in the language of bombs. Hyperdisintegration in the former Soviet Union may well continue unabated—not just a Ukraine independent from the Soviet Union but a Bessarabian Ukraine independent from the Ukrainian republic; not just Russia severed from the defunct union but Tatarstan severed from Russia. Yugoslavia makes even the disunited, ex-Soviet, nonsocialist republics that were once the Soviet Union look integrated, its sectarian fatherlands springing up within factional motherlands like weeds within weeds within weeds. Kurdish independence would threaten the territorial integrity of four Middle Eastern nations. Well before the current cataclysm Soviet Georgia made a claim for autonomy from the Soviet Union, only to be faced with its Ossetians (164,000 in a republic of 5.5 million) demanding their own self-determination within Georgia. The Abkhasian minority in Georgia has followed suit. Even the good will established by Canada's once promising Meech Lake protocols is in danger, with Francophone Quebec again threatening the dissolution of the federation. In South Africa the emergence from apartheid was hardly achieved when friction between Inkatha's Zulus and the African National Congress's tribally identified members threatened to replace Europeans' racism with an indigenous tribal war after thirty years of attempted integration using the colonial language (English) as a unifier, Nigeria is now playing with the idea of linguistic multiculturalism—which could mean the cultural breakup of the nation into hundreds of tribal fragments. Even Saddam Hussein has benefited from the threat of internal Jihad, having used renewed tribal and religious warfare to turn last season's mortal enemies into reluctant allies of an Iraqi nationhood that he nearly destroyed.

The passing of communism has torn away the thin veneer of internationalism (workers of the world unite!) to reveal ethnic prejudices that are not only ugly and deep-seated but increasingly murderous. Europe's old scourge, anti-Semitism, is back with a vengeance, but it is only one of many antagonisms. It appears all too easy to throw the historical gears into reverse and pass from a Communist dictatorship back into a tribal state.

Among the tribes, religion is also a battlefield. ("Jihad" is a rich word whose generic meaning is "struggle"—usually the struggle of the soul to avert evil. Strictly applied to religious war, it is used only in reference to battles where the faith is under assault, or battles against a government that denies the practice of Islam. My use here is rhetorical, but does follow both journalistic practice and history.) Remember the Thirty Years War? Whatever forms of Enlightenment universalism might once have come to grace such historically related forms of monotheism as Judaism, Christianity, and Islam, in many of their modern incarnations they are parochial rather than cosmopolitan, angry rather than loving, proselytizing rather than ecumenical, zealous rather than rationalist, sectarian rather than deistic, ethnocentric rather than universalizing. As a result, like the new forms of hypernationalism, the new expressions of religious fundamentalism are fractious and pulverizing, never integrating. This is religion as the Crusaders knew it: a battle to the death for souls that if not saved will be forever lost.

The atmospherics of Jihad have resulted in a breakdown of civility in the name of identity, of comity in the name of community. International relations have sometimes taken on the aspect of gang war—cultural turf battles featuring tribal factions that were supposed to be sublimated as integral parts of large national, economic, postcolonial, and constitutional entities.

THE DARKENING FUTURE OF DEMOCRACY

These rather melodramatic tableaux vivants do not tell the whole story, however. For all their defects, Jihad and McWorld have their attractions. Yet, to repeat and insist, the attractions are unrelated to democracy. Neither McWorld nor Jihad is remotely democratic in impulse. Neither needs democracy; neither promotes democracy.

McWorld does manage to look pretty seductive in a world obsessed with Jihad. It delivers peace, prosperity, and relative unity—if at the cost of independence, community, and identity (which is generally based on difference). The primary political values required by the global market are order and tranquillity, and freedom—as in the phrases "free trade," "free press," and "free love." Human rights are needed to a degree, but not citizenship or participation—and no more social justice and equality than are necessary to promote efficient economic production and consumption. Multinational corporations sometimes seem to prefer doing business with local oligarchs, inasmuch as they can take confidence from dealing with the boss on all crucial matters. Despots who slaughter their own populations are no problem, so long as they leave markets in place and refrain from making war on their neighbors (Saddam Hussein's fatal mistake). In trading partners, predictability is of more value than justice.

The Eastern European revolutions that seemed to arise out of concern for global democratic values quickly deteriorated into a stampede in the general direction of free markets and their ubiquitous, television-promoted shopping malls. East Germany's Neues Forum, that courageous gathering of intellectuals, students, and workers which overturned the Stalinist regime in Berlin in 1989, lasted only six months in Germany's mini-version of McWorld. Then it gave way to money and markets and monopolies from the West. By the time of the first all-German elections, it could scarcely manage to secure three percent of the vote. Elsewhere there is growing evidence that *glasnost* will go and *perestroika*—defined as privatization and an opening of markets to Western bidders—will stay. So understandably anxious are the new rulers of Eastern Europe and whatever entities are forged from the residues of the Soviet Union to gain access to credit and markets and technology—McWorld's flourishing new currencies—that they have shown themselves willing to trade away democratic prospects in pursuit of them: not just old totalitarian ideologies and command-economy production models but some possible indigenous experiments with a third way between capitalism and socialism, such as economic cooperatives and employee stock-ownership plans, both of which have their ardent supporters in the East.

Jihad delivers a different set of virtues: a vibrant local identity, a sense of community, solidarity among kinsmen, neighbors, and countrymen, narrowly conceived. But it also guarantees parochialism and is grounded in exclusion. Solidarity is secured through war against outsiders. And solidarity often means obedience to a hierarchy in governance, fanaticism in beliefs, and the obliteration of individual selves in the name of the group. Deference to leaders and intolerance toward outsiders (and toward "enemies within") are hallmarks of tribalism—hardly the attitudes required for the cultivation of new democratic women and men capable of governing themselves. Where new democratic experiments have been conducted in retribalizing societies, in both Europe and the Third World, the result has often been anarchy, repression, persecution, and the coming of new, noncommunist forms of very old kinds of despotism. During the past year, Havel's velvet revolution in Czechoslovakia was imperiled by partisans of "Czechland" and of Slovakia as independent entities. India seemed little less rent by Sikh, Hindu, Muslim, and Tamil infighting than it was immediately after the British pulled out, more than forty years ago.

To the extent that either McWorld or Jihad has a *natural* politics, it has turned out to be more of an antipolitics. For McWorld, it is the antipolitics of globalism: bureaucratic, technocratic, and meritocratic, focused (as Marx predicted it would be) on the administration of things—with people, however, among the chief things to be administered. In its politico-economic imperatives McWorld has been guided by laissez-faire market principles that privilege efficiency, productivity, and beneficence at the expense of civic liberty and self-government.

For Jihad, the antipolitics of tribalization has been explicitly antidemocratic: one-party dictatorship, government by military junta, theocratic fundamentalism—often associated with a version of the *Führerprinzip* that empowers an individual to rule on behalf of a people. Even the government of India, struggling for decades to model democracy for a people who will soon number a billion, longs for great leaders; and for every Mahatma Gandhi, Indira Gandhi, or Rajiv Gandhi taken from them by zealous assassins, the Indians appear to seek a replacement who will deliver them from the lengthy travail of their freedom.

THE CONFEDERAL OPTION

How can democracy be secured and spread in a world whose primary tendencies are at best indifferent to it (McWorld) and at worst deeply antithetical to it (Jihad)? My guess is that globalization will eventually vanquish retribalization.

The ethos of material "civilization" has not yet encountered an obstacle it has been unable to thrust aside. Ortega may have grasped in the 1920s a clue to our own future in the coming millennium.

Everyone sees the need of a new principle of life. But as always happens in similar crises—some people attempt to save the situation by an artificial intensification of the very principle which has led to decay. This is the meaning of the "nationalist" outburst of recent years . . . things have always gone that way. The last flare, the longest; the last sigh, the deepest. On the very eve of their disappearance there is an intensification of frontiers—military and economic.

Jihad may be a last deep sigh before the eternal yawn of McWorld. On the other hand, Ortega was not exactly prescient; his prophecy of peace and internationalism came just before blitzkrieg, world war, and the Holocaust tore the old order to bits. Yet democracy is how we remonstrate with reality, the rebuke our aspirations offer to history. And if retribalization is inhospitable to democracy, there is nonetheless a form of democratic government that can accommodate parochialism and communitarianism, one that can even save them from their defects and make them more tolerant and participatory: decentralized participatory democracy. And if McWorld is indifferent to democracy, there is nonetheless a form of democratic government that suits global markets passably well—representative government in its federal or, better still, confederal variation.

With its concern for accountability, the protection of minorities, and the universal rule of law, a confederalized representative system would serve the political needs of McWorld as well as oligarchic bureaucratism or meritocratic elitism is currently doing. As we are already beginning to see, many nations may survive in the long term only as confederations that afford local regions smaller than "nations" extensive jurisdiction. Recommended reading for democrats of the twenty-first century is not the U.S. Constitution or the French Declaration of Rights of Man and Citizen but the Articles of Confederation, that suddenly pertinent document that stitched together the thirteen American colonies into what then seemed a too loose confederation of independent states but now appears a new form of political realism, as veterans of Yeltsin's new Russia and the new Europe created at Maastricht will attest.

By the same token, the participatory and direct form of democracy that engages citizens in civic activity and civic judgment and goes well beyond just voting and accountability—the system I have called "strong democracy"—suits the political needs of decentralized communities as well as theocratic and nationalist party dictatorships have done. Local neighborhoods need not be democratic, but they can be. Real democracy has flourished in diminutive settings: the spirit of liberty, Tocqueville said, is local. Participatory democracy, if not naturally apposite to tribalism, has an undeniable attractiveness under conditions of parochialism.

Democracy in any of these variations will, however, continue to be obstructed by the undemocratic and antidemocratic trends toward uniformitarian globalism and intolerant retribalization which I have portrayed here. For democracy to persist in our brave new McWorld, we will have to commit acts of conscious political will—a possibility, but hardly a probability, under these conditions. Political will requires much more than the quick fix of the transfer of institutions. Like technology transfer, institution transfer rests on foolish assumptions about a uniform world of the kind that once fired the imagination of colonial administrators. Spread English justice to the colonies by exporting wigs. Let an East Indian trading company act as the vanguard to Britain's free parliamentary institutions. Today's well-intentioned quick-fixers in the National Endowment for Democracy and the Kennedy School of Government, in the unions and foundations and universities zealously nurturing contacts in Eastern Europe and the Third World, are hoping to democratize by long distance. Post Bulgaria a parliament by first-class mail. Fed Ex the Bill of Rights to Sri Lanka. Cable Cambodia some common law.

Yet Eastern Europe has already demonstrated that importing free political parties, parliaments, and presses cannot establish a democratic civil society; imposing a free market may even have the opposite effect. Democracy grows from the bottom up and cannot be imposed from the top down. Civil society has to be built from the inside out. The institutional superstructure comes last. Poland may become democratic, but then again it may heed the Pope, and prefer to found its politics on its Catholicism, with uncertain consequences for democracy. Bulgaria may become democratic, but it may prefer tribal war. The former Soviet Union may become a democratic confederation, or it may just grow into an anarchic and weak conglomeration of markets for other nations' goods and services.

Democrats need to seek out indigenous democratic impulses. There is always a desire for self-government, always some expression of participation, accountability, consent, and representation, even in traditional hierarchical societies. These need to be identified, tapped, modified, and incorporated into new democratic practices with an indigenous flavor. The tortoises among the democratizers may ultimately outlive or outpace the hares, for they will have the time and patience to explore conditions along the way, and to adapt their gait to changing circumstances. Tragically, democracy in a hurry often looks something like France in 1794 or China in 1989.

It certainly seems possible that the most attractive democratic ideal in the face of the brutal realities of Jihad and the dull realities of McWorld will be a confederal union of semi-autonomous communities smaller than nation-states, tied together into regional economic associations and markets larger than nation-states—participatory and self-determining in local matters at the bottom, representative and accountable at the top. The nation-state would play a diminished role, and sovereignty would lose some of its political potency. The Green movement adage "Think globally, act locally" would actually come to describe the conduct of politics.

This vision reflects only an ideal, however—one that is not terribly likely to be realized. Freedom, Jean-Jacques Rousseau once wrote, is a food easy to eat but hard to digest. Still, democracy has always played itself out against the odds. And democracy remains both a form of coherence as binding as McWorld and a secular faith potentially as inspiriting as Jihad.

Credits/ Acknowledgments

Cover design by Charles Vitelli

1. Pluralist Democracies: Country Studies
Facing overview—British Information Service photo.

2. Modern Pluralist Democracies: Factors in the Political Process
Facing overview—AP/Wide World photo by Michel Euler.

3. Europe—West, Center, and East
Facing overview—AP/Wide World photo.

4. Political Diversity in the Developing World
Facing overview—United Nations photo by M. Guthrie.

5. Comparative Politics
Facing overview—United Nations photo.

PHOTOCOPY THIS PAGE!!!*

ANNUAL EDITIONS ARTICLE REVIEW FORM

■ NAME: _____ DATE: _____

■ TITLE AND NUMBER OF ARTICLE: _____

■ BRIEFLY STATE THE MAIN IDEA OF THIS ARTICLE: _____

_____

■ LIST THREE IMPORTANT FACTS THAT THE AUTHOR USES TO SUPPORT THE MAIN IDEA:

_____

_____

_____

_____

_____

■ WHAT INFORMATION OR IDEAS DISCUSSED IN THIS ARTICLE ARE ALSO DISCUSSED IN YOUR
TEXTBOOK OR OTHER READING YOU HAVE DONE? LIST THE TEXTBOOK CHAPTERS AND PAGE
NUMBERS:

_____

_____

_____

_____

_____

_____

■ LIST ANY EXAMPLES OF BIAS OR FAULTY REASONING THAT YOU FOUND IN THE ARTICLE:

_____

_____

_____

_____

■ LIST ANY NEW TERMS/CONCEPTS THAT WERE DISCUSSED IN THE ARTICLE AND WRITE A SHORT
DEFINITION:

_____

_____

_____

_____

_____

*Your instructor may require you to use this Annual Editions Article Review Form in any number of
ways: for articles that are assigned, for extra credit, as a tool to assist in developing assigned papers, or
simply for your own reference. Even if it is not required, we encourage you to photocopy and use this
page; you'll find that reflecting on the articles will greatly enhance the information from your text.

ANNUAL EDITIONS: COMPARATIVE POLITICS 96/97

Article Rating Form

Here is an opportunity for you to have direct input into the next revision of this volume. We would like you to rate each of the 69 articles listed below, using the following scale:

1. **Excellent: should definitely be retained**
2. **Above average: should probably be retained**
3. **Below average: should probably be deleted**
4. **Poor: should definitely be deleted**

Your ratings will play a vital part in the next revision. So please mail this prepaid form to us just as soon as you complete it.
Thanks for your help!

We Want Your Advice

Annual Editions revisions depend on two major opinion sources: one is our Advisory Board, listed in the front of this volume, which works with us in scanning the thousands of articles published in the public press each year; the other is you—the person actually using the book. Please help us and the users of the next edition by completing the prepaid article rating form on this page and returning it to us. Thank you.

Rating	Article	Rating	Article
	1. The Next Prime Minister		35. Presidents and Prime Ministers
	2. Newts Across the Pond Rework the British Right		36. Citizens Immune to Euro-Fever
	3. British Third Party Bids for Role as Kingmaker		37. Europe's Parliament on the Move
	4. Revamping Britain's Constitution		38. The Challenge to EMU: Europe Learns Its Alphabet
	5. What Is Scotland's Future?		39. Sweden: A Model Crisis
	6. After the Talking Stopped		40. Diagnosis: Healthier in Europe
	7. Outstripping Adenauer		41. Europe and the Underclass: The Slippery Slope
	8. A New Leader for the Social Democrats. A New Orientation as Well?		42. Inequalities in Europe: Affirmative Laissez Faire
	9. Man Who Put Cheer Back in German Greens		43. Ex-Coms
	10. Eastern Germany: The Eagle's Embrace		44. The Return of the Habsburgs
	11. Germany's Reckoning		45. A Cold-War Reality Check: Didn't Communism Die?
	12. The Fifth President of the Fifth Republic		46. The Reform of Russia: For Worse, for Better
	13. Will the Real France Stand Up?		47. The Splintering of Russia's Reformers
	14. Political Strikes and Demonstrations: Two Views		48. Post-Soviet Politics: Does the Communists' Rise Augur a 'Weimar' Russia?
	15. The Bulldozer Hits a Roadblock		49. For Russia's Reformers, a Time of Despair
	16. Tocqueville in Italy		50. Let's Abolish the Third World
	17. Italy's Dirty Linen		51. The 'Third World' Is Dead, but Spirits Linger
	18. Unhappy Italy		52. Common Sense over Charisma
	19. Mess Continues		53. Mexico: The Long Haul
	20. Reforming Japan, The Third Opening		54. Africa: Falling off the Map?
	21. Japan's New Prime Minister		55. Why Is Africa Eating Asia's Dust?
	22. Intellectual Warfare		56. Post-Mandela South Africa: Slow but Steady Progress
	23. The Left's New Start		57. China—the End of an Era
	24. Guide to the West European Left		58. India's Juggernaut of Change
	25. Europe's Far Right: Something Nasty in the Woodshed		59. Miracles beyond the Free Market
	26. The Migration Challenge: Europe's Crisis in Historical Perspective		60. Confucius Says: Go East, Young Man
	27. Europeans Redefine What Makes a Citizen		61. A New Era in Democracy: Democracy's Third Wave
	28. Women, Power, and Politics: The Norwegian Experience		62. Dangers and Dilemmas of Democracy
	29. Political Power Is Only Half the Battle		63. Democracy and Growth: Why Voting Is Good for You
	30. Despite Global Gains, Women's Status Still Suffers		64. Capitalism and Democracy
	31. What Democracy Is . . . and Is Not		65. Preserving Prosperity
	32. Parliament and Congress: Is the Grass Greener on the Other Side?		66. Cyberspace: Why Nations Could Fear the Internet
	33. Campaign and Party Finance: What Americans Might Learn from Abroad		67. Communal Conflicts and Global Security
	34. Electoral Reform: Good Government? Fairness? Or Vice Versa. Or Both		68. A Debate on Cultural Conflicts
			69. Jihad vs. McWorld

(Continued on next page)

ABOUT YOU

Name _____ Date _____

Are you a teacher? ❑   Or student? ❑

Your School Name _____

Department _____

Address _____

City _____ State _____ Zip _____

School Telephone # _____

YOUR COMMENTS ARE IMPORTANT TO US!

Please fill in the following information:

For which course did you use this book? _____

Did you use a text with this Annual Edition?   ❑ yes   ❑ no

The title of the text? _____

What are your general reactions to the Annual Editions concept?

Have you read any particular articles recently that you think should be included in the next edition?

Are there any articles you feel should be replaced in the next edition? Why?

Are there other areas that you feel would utilize an Annual Edition?

May we contact you for editorial input?

May we quote you from above?
